Starting and Running a Business

A Pearson Custom Publication

Starting and Running a Business

Compiled from:

Operations Management
Sixth Edition
by Nigel Slack, Stuart Chambers and Robert Johnston

Operations Management
Tenth Edition
by Jay Heizer and Barry Render

Operations Management
Ninth Edition
by Lee J. Krajewski, Larry P. Ritzman and Manoj K. Malhotra

Accounting and Finance for Non-Specialists
Sixth Edition
by Peter Atrill and Eddie McLaney

PEARSON
Custom
Publishing

Pearson Education Limited
Edinburgh Gate
Harlow
Essex CM20 2JE

And associated companies throughout the world

Visit us on the World Wide Web at:
www.pearsoned.co.uk

First published 2011

This Custom Book Edition © 2011 Published by Pearson Education Limited

Taken from:

Operations Management Sixth Edition
by Nigel Slack, Stuart Chambers and Robert Johnston
ISBN 978 0 273 73046 0
Copyright © Nigel Slack, Stuart Chambers, Christine Harland, Alan Harrison,
Robert Johnston 1995, 1998
Copyright © Nigel Slack, Stuart Chambers, and Robert Johnston 2001, 2004, 2007, 2010

Operations Management Tenth Edition
by Jay Heizer and Barry Render
ISBN 978 0 13 611941 8
Copyright © 2011, 2008, 2006, 2004, 2001 Pearson Education, Inc., publishing as
Prentice Hall, One Lake Street, Upper Saddle River, New Jersey.

Operations Management Ninth Edition
by Lee J. Krajewski, Larry P. Ritzman and Manoj K. Malhotra
ISBN 978 0 13 606576 0
Copyright © 2010, 2007, 2005, 2002 by Pearson Education, Inc., Upper Saddle River,
New Jersey, 07458.

Accounting and Finance for Non-Specialists Sixth Edition
by Peter Atrill and Eddie McLaney
ISBN 978 0 273 71694 5
Copyright © Pearson Education Limited 2008

ISBN 978 1 84959 852 1

Printed and bound by in Great Britain by Henry Ling Limited at the Dorset Press,
Dorchester, DT1 1HD.

Contents

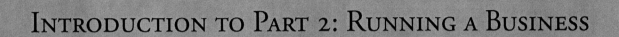

INTRODUCTION TO PART 2: RUNNING A BUSINESS

Chapter 1

Operations management

Key questions

➤ What is operations management?

➤ Why is operations management important in all types of organization?

➤ What is the input–transformation–output process?

➤ What is the process hierarchy?

➤ How do operations processes have different characteristics?

➤ What are the activities of operations management?

Introduction

Operations management is about how organizations produce goods and services. Everything you wear, eat, sit on, use, read or knock about on the sports field comes to you courtesy of the operations managers who organized its production. Every book you borrow from the library, every treatment you receive at the hospital, every service you expect in the shops and every lecture you attend at university – all have been produced. While the people who supervised their 'production' may not always be called operations managers that is what they really are. And that is what this book is concerned with – the tasks, issues and decisions of those operations managers who have made the services and products on which we all depend. This is an introductory chapter, so we will examine what we mean by 'operations management', how operations processes can be found everywhere, how they are all similar yet different, and what it is that operations managers do.

Operations in practice IKEA[1]

(All chapters start with an 'Operations in practice' example that illustrates some of the issues that will be covered in the chapter.)

Source: Alamy Images

Love it or hate it, IKEA is the most successful furniture retailer ever. With 276 stores in 36 countries, it has managed to develop its own special way of selling furniture. The stores' layout means customers often spend two hours in the store – far longer than in rival furniture retailers. IKEA's philosophy goes back to the original business, started in the 1950s in Sweden by Ingvar Kamprad. He built a showroom on the outskirts of Stockholm where land was cheap and simply displayed suppliers' furniture as it would be in a domestic setting. Increasing sales soon allowed IKEA to start ordering its own self-designed products from local manufacturers. But it was innovation in its operations that dramatically reduced its selling costs. These included the idea of selling furniture as self-assembly flat packs (which reduced production and transport costs) and its 'showroom–warehouse' concept which required customers to pick the furniture up themselves from the warehouse (which reduced retailing costs). Both of these operating principles are still the basis of IKEA's retail operations process today.

Stores are designed to facilitate the smooth flow of customers, from parking, moving through the store itself, to ordering and picking up goods. At the entrance to each store large notice-boards provide advice to shoppers. For young children, there is a supervised children's play area, a small cinema, and a parent and baby room so parents can leave their children in the supervised play area for a time. Parents are recalled via the loudspeaker system if the child has any problems. IKEA 'allow customers to make up their minds in their own time' but 'information points' have staff who can help. All furniture carries a ticket with a code number which indicates its location in the warehouse. (For larger items customers go to the information desks for assistance.) There is also an area where smaller items are displayed, and can be picked directly. Customers then pass through the warehouse where they pick up the items viewed in the showroom. Finally, customers pay at the checkouts, where a ramped conveyor belt moves purchases up to the checkout staff. The exit area has service points and a loading area that allows customers to bring their cars from the car park and load their purchases.

Behind the public face of IKEA's huge stores is a complex worldwide network of suppliers, 1,300 direct suppliers, about 10,000 sub-suppliers, wholesale and transport operations include 26 Distribution Centres. This supply network is vitally important to IKEA. From purchasing raw materials, right through to finished products arriving in its customers' homes, IKEA relies on close partnerships with its suppliers to achieve both ongoing supply efficiency and new product development. However, IKEA closely controls all supply and development activities from IKEA's home town of Älmhult in Sweden.

But success brings its own problems and some customers became increasingly frustrated with overcrowding and long waiting times. In response IKEA in the UK launched a £150 m programme to 'design out' the bottlenecks. The changes included:

- Clearly marked in-store short cuts allowing customers who just want to visit one area, to avoid having to go through all the preceding areas.
- Express checkout tills for customers with a bag only rather than a trolley.
- Extra 'help staff' at key points to help customers.
- Redesign of the car parks, making them easier to navigate.
- Dropping the ban on taking trolleys out to the car parks for loading (originally implemented to stop vehicles being damaged).
- A new warehouse system to stop popular product lines running out during the day.
- More children's play areas.

IKEA spokeswoman Nicki Craddock said: *'We know people love our products but hate our shopping experience. We are being told that by customers every day, so we can't afford not to make changes. We realized a lot of people took offence at being herded like sheep on the long route around stores. Now if you know what you are looking for and just want to get in, grab it and get out, you can.'*

→

Operations management is a vital part of IKEA's success

IKEA shows how important operations management is for its own success and the success of any type of organization. Of course, IKEA understands its market and its customers. But, just as important, it knows that the way it manages the network of operations that design, produce and deliver its products and services must be right for its market. No organization can survive in the long term if it cannot supply its customers effectively. And this is essentially what operations management is about – designing, producing and delivering products and services that satisfy market requirements. For any business, it is a vitally important activity. Consider just some of the activities that IKEA's operations managers are involved in.

- Arranging the store's layout to gives smooth and effective flow of customers (called process design)
- Designing stylish products that can be flat-packed efficiently (called product design)
- Making sure that all staff can contribute to the company's success (called job design)
- Locating stores of an appropriate size in the most effective place (called supply network design)
- Arranging for the delivery of products to stores (called supply chain management)

- Coping with fluctuations in demand (called capacity management)
- Maintaining cleanliness and safety of storage area (called failure prevention)
- Avoiding running out of products for sale (called inventory management)
- Monitoring and enhancing quality of service to customers (called quality management)
- Continually examining and improving operations practice (called operations improvement).

And these activities are only a small part of IKEA's total operations management effort. But they do give an indication, first of how operations management should contribute to the businesses success, and second, what would happen if IKEA's operations managers failed to be effective in carrying out any of its activities. Badly designed processes, inappropriate products, poor locations, disaffected staff, empty shelves, or forgetting the importance of continually improving quality, could all turn a previously successful organization into a failing one. Yet, although the relative importance of these activities will vary between different organizations, operations managers in all organizations will be making the same *type* of decision (even if *what* they actually decide is different).

What is operations management?

Operations management
Operations function

Operations management is the activity of managing the resources which produce and deliver products and services. The **operations function** is the part of the organization that is responsible for this activity. Every organization has an operations function because every organization produces some type of products and/or services. However, not all types of organization will necessarily call the operations function by this name. (Note that we also use the shorter terms 'the operation' and 'operations' interchangeably with the 'operations function'). **Operations managers** are the people who have particular responsibility for managing some, or all, of the resources which compose the operations function. Again, in some organizations the operations manager could be called by some other name. For example, he or she might be called the 'fleet manager' in a distribution company, the 'administrative manager' in a hospital, or the 'store manager' in a supermarket.

Operations managers

Operations in the organization

The operations function is central to the organization because it produces the goods and services which are its reason for existing, but it is not the only function. It is, however, one of the **three core functions** of any organization. These are:

Three core functions

- the marketing (including sales) function – which is responsible for *communicating* the organization's products and services to its markets in order to generate customer requests for service;

- the product/service development function – which is responsible for *creating* new and modified products and services in order to generate future customer requests for service;
- the operations function – which is responsible for *fulfilling* customer requests for service through the production and delivery of products and services.

Support functions

In addition, there are the **support functions** which enable the core functions to operate effectively. These include, for example:

- the accounting and finance function – which provides the information to help economic decision-making and manages the financial resources of the organization;
- the human resources function – which recruits and develops the organization's staff as well as looking after their welfare.

Remember that different organizations will call their various functions by different names and will have a different set of support functions. Almost all organizations, however, will have the three core functions, because all organizations have a fundamental need to sell their services, satisfy their customers and create the means to satisfy customers in the future. Table 1.1 shows the activities of the three core functions for a sample of organizations.

Broad definition of operations

In practice, there is not always a clear division between the three core functions or between core and support functions. This leads to some confusion over where the boundaries of the operations function should be drawn. In this book we use a relatively **broad definition of operations**. We treat much of the product/service development, technical and information systems activities and some of the human resource, marketing, and accounting and finance activities as coming within the sphere of operations management. We view the operations function as comprising all the activities necessary for the day-to-day fulfilment of customer requests. This includes sourcing products and services from suppliers and transporting products and services to customers.

Working effectively with the other parts of the organization is one of the most important responsibilities of operations management. It is a fundamental of modern management that functional boundaries should not hinder efficient internal processes. Figure 1.1 illustrates some of the relationships between operations and some other functions in terms of the flow of information between them. Although it is not comprehensive, it gives an idea of the nature of each relationship. However, note that the support functions have a different relationship with operations than operations has with the other core functions. Operations management's responsibility to support functions is primarily to make sure that they understand operations' needs and help them to satisfy these needs. The relationship with the other two core functions is more equal – less of *'this is what we want'* and more *'this is what we can do currently – how do we reconcile this with broader business needs?'*

Table 1.1 The activities of core functions in some organizations

Core functional activities	Internet service provider (ISP)	Fast food chain	International aid charity	Furniture manufacturer
Marketing and sales	Promote services to users and get registrations Sell advertising space	Advertise on TV Devise promotional materials	Develop funding contracts Mail out appeals for donations	Advertise in magazines Determine pricing policy Sell to stores
Product/service development	Devise new services and commission new information content	Design hamburgers, pizzas, etc. Design décor for restaurants	Develop new appeals campaigns Design new assistance programmes	Design new furniture Coordinate with fashionable colours
Operations	Maintain hardware, software and content Implement new links and services	Make burgers, pizzas etc. Serve customers Clear away Maintain equipment	Give service to the beneficiaries of the charity	Make components Assemble furniture

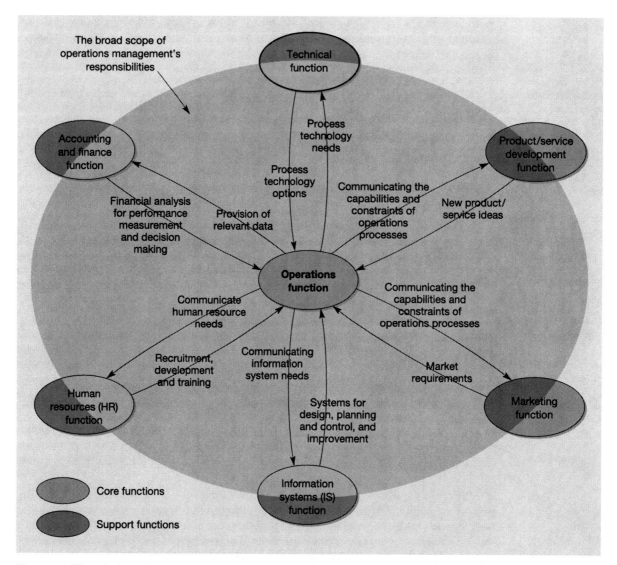

The broad scope of operations management's responsibilities

Technical function

Process technology needs

Process technology options

Accounting and finance function

Product/service development function

Financial analysis for performance measurement and decision making

Provision of relevant data

Communicating the capabilities and constraints of operations processes

New product/ service ideas

Operations function

Communicate human resource needs

Communicating the capabilities and constraints of operations processes

Recruitment, development and training

Communicating information system needs

Market requirements

Human resources (HR) function

Marketing function

Systems for design, planning and control, and improvement

Information systems (IS) function

Core functions

Support functions

Figure 1.1 The relationship between the operations function and other core and support functions of the organization

Operations management is important in all types of organization

In some types of organization it is relatively easy to visualize the operations function and what it does, even if we have never seen it. For example, most people have seen images of automobile assembly. But what about an advertising agency? We know vaguely what they do – they produce the advertisements that we see in magazines and on television – but what is their operations function? The clue lies in the word 'produce'. Any business that produces something, whether tangible or not, must use resources to do so, and so must have an operations activity. Also the automobile plant and the advertising agency do have one important element in common: both have a higher objective – to make a profit from producing their products or services. Yet not-for-profit organizations also use their resources to produce services, not to make a profit, but to serve society in some way. Look at the following examples of what operations management does in five very different organizations and some common themes emerge.

Automobile assembly factory – *Operations management uses machines to efficiently assemble products that satisfy current customer demands*

Physician (general practitioner) – *Operations management uses knowledge to effectively diagnose conditions in order to treat real and perceived patient concerns*

Management consultant – *Operations management uses people to effectively create the services that will address current and potential client needs*

Disaster relief charity – *Operations management uses our and our partners' resources to speedily provide the supplies and services that relieve community suffering*

Advertising agency – *Operations management uses our staff's knowledge and experience to creatively present ideas that delight clients and address their real needs*

Start with the statement from the 'easy to visualize' automobile plant. Its summary of what operations management did was that . . . *'Operations management uses machines to efficiently assemble products that satisfy current customer demands.'* The statements from the other organizations were similar, but used slightly different language. Operations management used, not just machines but also . . . *'knowledge, people, "our and our partners' resources"'* and *'our staff's experience and knowledge'*, to *efficiently* (or *effectively*, or *creatively*) *assemble* (or *produce, change, sell, move, cure, shape*, etc.) *products* (or *services* or *ideas*) that *satisfy* (or *match* or *exceed* or *delight*) *customers'* (or *clients'* or *citizens'* or *society's*) *demands* (or *needs* or *concerns* or even *dreams*). So whatever terminology is used there is a common theme and a common purpose to how we can visualize the operations activity in any type of organization: small or large, manufacturing or service, public or private, profit or not-for-profit. Operations management uses *resources* to *appropriately create outputs* that *fulfil defined market requirements*. *See* Figure 1.2. However, although the essential nature and purpose of operations management is the same in every type of organization, there are some special issues to consider, particularly in smaller organizations and those whose purpose is to maximize something other than profit.

Operations management uses . . .

resources	appropriately	create	outputs		fulfil	defined	market	requirements
		produce						
experience		change				potential	citizens'	
people	effectively	sell	ideas		match	perceived	client	dreams
machines	efficiently	assemble	products	that	satisfy	current	customer	demands
knowledge	creatively	move	services		exceed	emerging	society	needs
partners	etc.	cure	etc.		delight	real	etc.	concerns
etc.		shape			etc.	etc.		etc.
		etc.						

(In the "machines" row, "to" appears between "machines" and "effectively")

Figure 1.2 Operations management uses resources to appropriately create outputs that fulfil defined market requirements

Operations management in the smaller organization

Operations management is just as important in small organizations as it is in large ones. Irrespective of their size, all companies need to produce and deliver their products and services efficiently and effectively. However, in practice, managing operations in a small or medium-size organization has its own set of problems. Large companies may have the resources to dedicate individuals to specialized tasks but smaller companies often cannot, so people may have to do different jobs as the need arises. Such an informal structure can allow the company to respond quickly as opportunities or problems present themselves. But decision making can also become confused as individuals' roles overlap. Small companies may have exactly the same operations management issues as large ones but they can be more difficult to separate from the mass of other issues in the organization. However, small operations can also have significant advantages; the short case on Acme Whistles illustrates this.

The role of operations management in smaller organizations often overlaps significantly with other functions

Short case
Acme Whistles[2]

Acme Whistles can trace its history back to 1870 when Joseph Hudson decided he had the answer to the London Metropolitan Police's request for something to replace the wooden rattles that were used to sound the alarm. So the world's first police whistle was born. Soon Acme grew to be the premier supplier of whistles for police forces around the world. *'In many ways'*, says Simon Topman, owner and Managing Director of the company, *'the company is very much the same as it was in Joseph's day. The machinery is more modern, of course, and we have a wider variety of products, but many of our products are similar to their predecessors. For example, football referees seem to prefer the traditional snail-shaped whistle. So, although we have dramatically improved the performance of the product, our customers want it to look the same. We have also*

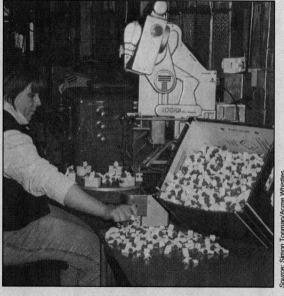

Source: Simon Topman/Acme Whistles

maintained the same manufacturing tradition from those early days. The original owner insisted on personally blowing every single whistle before it left the factory. We still do the same, not by personally blowing them, but by using an air line, so the same tradition of quality has endured.'

The company's range of whistles has expanded to include sports whistles (they provide the whistles for the soccer World Cup), distress whistles, (silent) dog whistles, novelty whistles, instrumental whistles (used by all of the world's top orchestras), and many more types. *'We are always trying to improve our products'*, says Simon, *'it's a business of constant innovation. Sometimes I think that after 130 years surely there is nothing more to do, but we always find some new feature to incorporate. Of course, managing the operations in a small company is very different to working in a large one. Everyone has much broader jobs; we cannot afford the overheads of having*

specialist people in specialized roles. But this relative informality has a lot of advantages. It means that we can maintain our philosophy of quality amongst everybody in the company, and it means that we can react very quickly when the market demands it.' Nor is the company's small size any barrier to its ability to innovate. *'On the contrary'*, says Simon, *'there is something about the culture of the company that is extremely important in fostering innovation. Because we are small we all know each other and we all want to contribute something to the company. It is not uncommon for employees to figure out new ideas for different types of whistle. If an idea looks promising, we will put a small and informal team together to look at it further. It is not unusual for people who have been with us only a few months to start wanting to make innovations. It's as though something happens to them when they walk through the door of the factory that encourages their natural inventiveness.'*

Operations management in not-for-profit organizations

Operations decisions are the same in commercial and not-for-profit organizations

Terms such as *competitive advantage*, *markets* and *business*, which are used in this book, are usually associated with companies in the for-profit sector. Yet operations management is also relevant to organizations whose purpose is not primarily to earn profits. Managing the operations in an animal welfare charity, hospital, research organization or government department is essentially the same as in commercial organizations. **Operations have to take the same decisions** – how to produce products and services, invest in technology, contract out some of their activities, devise performance measures, and improve their operations performance and so on. However, the strategic objectives of not-for-profit organizations may be more complex and involve a mixture of political, economic, social and environmental objectives. Because of this there may be a greater chance of operations decisions being made under conditions of conflicting objectives. So, for example, it is the operations staff in a children's welfare department who have to face the conflict between the cost of providing extra social workers and the risk of a child not receiving adequate protection. Nevertheless the vast majority of the topics covered in this book have relevance to all types of organization, including non-profit, even if the context is different and some terms may have to be adapted.

Short case
Oxfam International[3]

Oxfam International is a confederation of 13 like-minded organizations based around the world that, together with partners and allies, work directly with communities seeking to ensure that poor people can improve their lives and livelihoods and have a say in decisions that affect them. With an annual expenditure that exceeds US$700 million, Oxfam International focuses its efforts in several areas, including development work, long-term programmes to eradicate poverty and

Source: Rex Features

→

combat injustice, emergency relief delivering immediate life-saving assistance to people affected by natural disasters or conflict, helping to build their resilience to future disasters, campaigning and raising public awareness of the causes of poverty, encouraging ordinary people to take action for a fairer world, and advocacy and research that pressures decision-makers to change policies and practices that reinforce poverty and injustice.

All of Oxfam International's activities depend on effective and professional operations management. For example, Oxfam's network of charity shops, run by volunteers, is a key source of income. The shops sell donated items and handcrafts from around the world giving small-scale producers fair prices, training, advice and funding. Supply chain management and development is just as central to the running of these shops as it is to the biggest commercial chain of stores. The operations challenges involved in Oxfam's ongoing 'Clean Water' exercise are different but certainly no less important. Around 80 per cent of diseases and over one-third of deaths in the developing world are caused by contaminated water and Oxfam has a particular expertise in providing clean water and sanitation facilities. The better their coordinated efforts of identifying potential projects, working with local communities, providing help and education, and helping to providing civil engineering expertise, the more effective Oxfam is at fulfilling its objectives.

More dramatically, Oxfam International's response to emergency situations, providing humanitarian aid where it is needed, must be fast, appropriate and efficient. Whether the disasters are natural or political, they become emergencies when the people involved can no longer cope. In such situations, Oxfam, through its network of staff in local offices, is able to advise on what and where help is needed. Indeed, local teams are often able to provide warnings of impending

disasters, giving more time to assess needs and coordinate a multi-agency response. The organization's headquarters in Oxford in the UK provides advice, materials and staff, often deploying emergency support staff on short-term assignments. Shelters, blankets and clothing can be flown out at short notice from the Emergencies Warehouse. Engineers and sanitation equipment can also be provided, including water tanks, latrines, hygiene kits and containers. When an emergency is over, Oxfam continues to work with the affected communities through their local offices to help people rebuild their lives and livelihoods. In an effort to improve the timeliness, effectiveness and appropriateness of its response to emergencies, Oxfam recently adopted a more systematic approach to evaluating the successes and failures of its humanitarian work. Real-time evaluations, which seek to assess and influence emergency response programmes in their early stages, were implemented during the response to floods in Mozambique and South Asia, the earthquake in Peru, Hurricane Felix in Nicaragua and the conflicts in Uganda. These exercises provided Oxfam's humanitarian teams with the opportunity to gauge the effectiveness of their response, and make crucial adjustments at an early stage if necessary. The evaluations highlighted several potential improvements. For example, it became evident that there was a need to improve preparation ahead of emergencies, as well as the need to develop more effective coordination planning tools. It was also decided that adopting a common working approach with shared standards would improve the effectiveness of their response to emergencies. Oxfam also emphasizes the importance of the role played by local partners in emergencies. They are often closer to, and more in tune with, affected communities, but may require additional support and empowerment to scale up their response and comply with the international humanitarian standards.

The new operations agenda

Modern business pressures have changed the operations agenda

The business environment has a significant impact on what is expected from operations management. In recent years there have been new pressures for which the operations function has needed to develop responses. Table 1.2 lists some of these **business pressures** and the operations responses to them. These operations responses form a major part of a *new agenda* for operations. Parts of this agenda are trends which have always existed but have accelerated, such as globalization and increased cost pressures. Part of the agenda involves seeking ways to exploit new technologies, most notably the Internet. Of course, the list in Table 1.2 is not comprehensive, nor is it universal. But very few businesses will be unaffected by at least some of these concerns. When businesses have to cope with a more challenging environment, they look to their operations function to help them respond.

Table 1.2 Changes in the business environment are shaping a new operations agenda

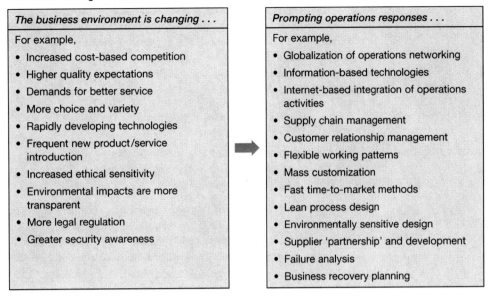

The business environment is changing . . .	*Prompting operations responses . . .*
For example, • Increased cost-based competition • Higher quality expectations • Demands for better service • More choice and variety • Rapidly developing technologies • Frequent new product/service introduction • Increased ethical sensitivity • Environmental impacts are more transparent • More legal regulation • Greater security awareness	For example, • Globalization of operations networking • Information-based technologies • Internet-based integration of operations activities • Supply chain management • Customer relationship management • Flexible working patterns • Mass customization • Fast time-to-market methods • Lean process design • Environmentally sensitive design • Supplier 'partnership' and development • Failure analysis • Business recovery planning

The input–transformation–output process

Transformation process model

Input resources

Outputs of goods and services

All operations produce products and services by changing *inputs* into *outputs* using an 'input-transformation-output' process. Figure 1.3 shows this general **transformation process model**. Put simply, operations are processes that take in a set of **input resources** which are used to transform something, or are transformed themselves, into **outputs of products and services**. And although all operations conform to this general input–transformation–output model, they differ in the nature of their specific inputs and outputs. For example, if you stand far enough away from a hospital or a car plant, they might look very similar, but move closer and clear differences do start to emerge. One is a manufacturing operation producing 'products', and the other is a service operation producing 'services' that change the physiological or psychological condition of patients. What is inside each operation will also be

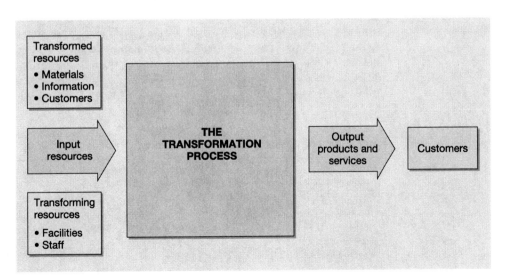

Figure 1.3 All operations are input–transformation–output processes

different. The motor vehicle plant contains metal-forming machinery and assembly processes, whereas the hospital contains diagnostic, care and therapeutic processes. Perhaps the most important difference between the two operations, however, is the nature of their inputs. The vehicle plant transforms steel, plastic, cloth, tyres and other materials into vehicles. The hospital transforms the customers themselves. The patients form part of the input to, and the output from, the operation. This has important implications for how the operation needs to be managed.

Inputs to the process

Transformed resources

One set of inputs to any operation's processes are **transformed resources**. These are the resources that are treated, transformed or converted in the process. They are usually a mixture of the following:

- **Materials** – operations which process materials could do so to transform their *physical properties* (shape or composition, for example). Most manufacturing operations are like this. Other operations process materials to change their *location* (parcel delivery companies, for example). Some, like retail operations, do so to change the *possession* of the materials. Finally, some operations *store* materials, such as in warehouses.
- **Information** – operations which process information could do so to transform their *informational properties* (that is the purpose or form of the information); accountants do this. Some change the *possession* of the information, for example market research companies sell information. Some *store* the information, for example archives and libraries. Finally, some operations, such as telecommunication companies, change the *location* of the information.
- **Customers** – operations which process customers might change their *physical properties* in a similar way to materials processors: for example, hairdressers or cosmetic surgeons. Some *store* (or more politely *accommodate*) customers: hotels, for example. Airlines, mass rapid transport systems and bus companies transform the *location* of their customers, while hospitals transform their *physiological state*. Some are concerned with transforming their *psychological state*, for example most entertainment services such as music, theatre, television, radio and theme parks.

Material inputs
Customer inputs

Information inputs

Often one of these is dominant in an operation. For example, a bank devotes part of its energies to producing printed statements of accounts for its customers. In doing so, it is processing **inputs of material** but no one would claim that a bank is a printer. The bank is also concerned with processing **inputs of customers**. It gives them advice regarding their financial affairs, cashes their cheques, deposits their cash, and has direct contact with them. However, most of the bank's activities are concerned with processing **inputs of information** about its customers' financial affairs. As customers, we may be unhappy with badly printed statements and we may be unhappy if we are not treated appropriately in the bank. But if the bank makes errors in our financial transactions, we suffer in a far more fundamental way. Table 1.3 gives examples of operations with their dominant transformed resources.

Table 1.3 Dominant transformed resource inputs of various operations

Predominantly processing inputs of materials	*Predominantly processing inputs of information*	*Predominantly processing inputs of customers*
All manufacturing operations	Accountants	Hairdressers
Mining companies	Bank headquarters	Hotels
Retail operations	Market research company	Hospitals
Warehouses	Financial analysts	Mass rapid transport
Postal services	News service	Theatres
Container shipping line	University research unit	Theme parks
Trucking companies	Telecoms company	Dentists

Transforming resources

The other set of inputs to any operations process are **transforming resources**. These are the resources which act upon the transformed resources. There are two types which form the 'building blocks' of all operations:

Facilities
Staff

- **facilities** – the buildings, equipment, plant and process technology of the operation;
- **staff** – the people who operate, maintain, plan and manage the operation. (Note that we use the term 'staff' to describe all the people in the operation, at any level.)

The exact nature of both facilities and staff will differ between operations. To a five-star hotel, its facilities consist mainly of 'low-tech' buildings, furniture and fittings. To a nuclear-powered aircraft carrier, its facilities are 'high-tech' nuclear generators and sophisticated electronic equipment. Staff will also differ between operations. Most staff employed in a factory assembling domestic refrigerators may not need a very high level of technical skill. In contrast, most staff employed by an accounting company are, hopefully, highly skilled in their own particular 'technical' skill (accounting). Yet although skills vary, all staff can make a contribution. An assembly worker who consistently misassembles refrigerators will dissatisfy customers and increase costs just as surely as an accountant who cannot add up. The balance between facilities and staff also varies. A computer chip manufacturing company, such as Intel, will have significant investment in physical facilities. A single chip fabrication plant can cost in excess of $4 billion, so operations managers will spend a lot of their time managing their facilities. Conversely, a management consultancy firm depends largely on the quality of its staff. Here operations management is largely concerned with the development and deployment of consultant skills and knowledge.

Outputs from the process

Tangibility

Although products and services are different, the distinction can be subtle. Perhaps the most obvious difference is in their respective **tangibility**. Products are usually tangible. You can physically touch a television set or a newspaper. Services are usually intangible. You cannot touch consultancy advice or a haircut (although you can often see or feel the results of these services). Also, services may have a shorter stored life. Products can usually be stored, at least for a time. The life of a service is often much shorter. For example, the service of 'accommodation in a hotel room for tonight' will perish if it is not sold before tonight – accommodation in the same room tomorrow is a different service.

Most operations produce both products and services

'Pure' products
'Pure' service

Facilitating services

Facilitating products

Some operations produce just products and others just services, but most operations produce a mixture of the two. Figure 1.4 shows a number of operations (including some described as examples in this chapter) positioned in a spectrum from **'pure' product** producers to **'pure' service** producers. Crude oil producers are concerned almost exclusively with the product which comes from their oil wells. So are aluminium smelters, but they might also produce some services such as technical advice. Services produced in these circumstances are called **facilitating services**. To an even greater extent, machine tool manufacturers produce facilitating services such as technical advice and applications engineering. The services produced by a restaurant are an essential part of what the customer is paying for. It is both a manufacturing operation which produces meals and a provider of service in the advice, ambience and service of the food. An information systems provider may produce software 'products', but primarily it is providing a service to its customers, with **facilitating products**. Certainly, a management consultancy, although it produces reports and documents, would see itself primarily as a service provider. Finally, pure services produce no products, a psychotherapy clinic, for example. Of the short cases and examples in this chapter, Acme Whistles is primarily a product producer, although it can give advice or it can even design products for individual customers. Pret A Manger both manufactures and serves its sandwiches to customers. IKEA subcontracts the manufacturing of its products before selling them, and also offers some design services. It therefore has an even higher service content.

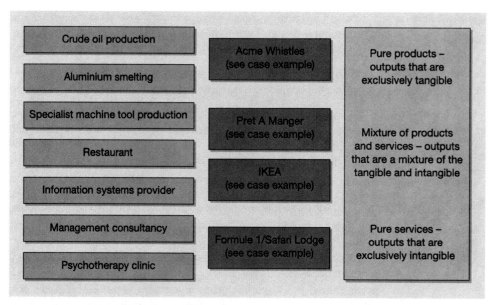

Figure 1.4 The output from most types of operation is a mixture of goods and services

Formule 1 and the safari park (see later) are close to being pure services, although they both have some tangible elements such as food.

Services and products are merging

Increasingly the distinction between services and products is both difficult to define and not particularly useful. Information and communications technologies are even overcoming some of the consequences of the intangibility of services. Internet-based retailers, for example, are increasingly 'transporting' a larger proportion of their services into customers' homes. Even the official statistics compiled by governments have difficulty in separating products and services. Software sold on a disc is classified as a product. The same software sold over the Internet is a service. Some authorities see the essential purpose of all businesses, and therefore operations processes, as being to 'service customers'. Therefore, they argue, **all operations are service providers** which may produce products as a part of serving their customers. Our approach in this book is close to this. We treat operations management as being important for all organizations. Whether they see themselves as manufacturers or service providers is very much a secondary issue.

All operations are service providers

Short case
Pret A Manger[4]

Described by the press as having *'revolutionized the concept of sandwich making and eating'*, Pret A Manger opened their first shop in the mid-1980s, in London. Now they have over 130 shops in UK, New York, Hong Kong and Tokyo. They say that their secret is to focus continually on quality – not just of their food, but in every aspect of their operations practice. They go to extraordinary lengths to avoid the chemicals and preservatives common in most 'fast' food, say the company. *'Many food retailers focus on extending the shelf life of their food, but that's of no interest to us. We maintain our edge by selling food that simply can't be beaten for freshness. At the end of the day, we give whatever we haven't sold to charity to help feed those who would otherwise go hungry. When we were just starting out, a big supplier tried to sell us coleslaw that lasted sixteen days. Can you imagine! Salad that lasts sixteen days? There and then we decided Pret would stick to wholesome fresh food – natural stuff. We have not changed that policy.'*

The first Pret A Manger shop had its own kitchen where fresh ingredients were delivered first thing every morning, and food was prepared throughout the day. Every Pret shop since has followed this model. The team members serving on the tills at lunchtime will have been making sandwiches in the kitchen that morning. The company rejected the idea of a huge centralized sandwich factory even though it could significantly reduce costs. Pret also own and manage all their shops directly so that they can ensure consistently high standards in all their shops. *'We are determined never to forget that our hard-working people make all the difference. They are our heart and soul. When they care, our business is sound. If they cease to care, our business goes down the drain. In a retail sector where high staff turnover is normal, we're pleased to say our people are much more likely to stay around! We work hard at building great teams. We take our reward schemes and career opportunities very seriously. We don't work nights (generally), we wear jeans, we party!'* Customer feedback is regarded as being particularly important at Pret. Examining customers' comments for improvement ideas is a key part of weekly management meetings, and of the daily team briefs in each shop.

The processes hierarchy

So far we have discussed operations management, and the input–transformation–output model, at the level of 'the operation'. For example, we have described 'the whistle factory', 'the sandwich shop', 'the disaster relief operation', and so on. But look inside any of these operations. One will see that all operations consist of a collection of processes (though these processes may be called 'units' or 'departments') interconnecting with each other to form a network. Each process acts as a smaller version of the whole operation of which it forms a part, and transformed resources flow between them. In fact within any operation, the

Processes

mechanisms that actually transform inputs into outputs are these **processes**. A process is 'an arrangement of resources that produce some mixture of products and services'. They are the 'building blocks' of all operations, and they form an 'internal network' within an operation.

Internal supplier
Internal customer

Each process is, at the same time, an **internal supplier** and an **internal customer** for other processes. This 'internal customer' concept provides a model to analyse the internal activities of an operation. It is also a useful reminder that, by treating internal customers with the same degree of care as external customers, the effectiveness of the whole operation can be improved. Table 1.4 illustrates how a wide range of operations can be described in this way.

Within each of these processes is another network of individual units of resource such as individual people and individual items of process technology (machines, computers, storage facilities, etc.). Again, transformed resources flow between each unit of transforming resource. So any business, or operation, is made up of a network of processes and any process is made up of a network of resources. But also any business or operation can itself be viewed as part of a greater network of businesses or operations. It will have operations that supply it with the products and services it needs and unless it deals directly with the end-consumer, it will supply customers who themselves may go on to supply their own customers. Moreover, any operation could have several suppliers and several customers and may be in competition with other operations producing similar services to those it produces itself. This network

Supply network

of operations is called the **supply network**. In this way the input–transformation–output model can be used at a number of different 'levels of analysis'. Here we have used the idea

Operations can be analysed at three levels

to **analyse businesses at three levels**, the process, the operation and the supply network. But one could define many different 'levels of analysis', moving upwards from small to larger processes, right up to the huge supply network that describes a whole industry.

Table 1.4 Some operations described in terms of their processes

Operation	Some of the operation's inputs	Some of the operation's processes	Some of the operation's outputs
Airline	Aircraft Pilots and air crew Ground crew Passengers and freight	Check passengers in Board passengers Fly passengers and freight around the world Care for passengers	Transported passengers and freight
Department store	Goods for sale Sales staff Information systems Customers	Source and store goods Display goods Give sales advice Sell goods	Customers and goods 'assembled' together
Police	Police officers Computer systems Information systems Public (law-abiding and criminals)	Crime prevention Crime detection Information gathering Detaining suspects	Lawful society, public with a feeling of security
Frozen food manufacturer	Fresh food Operators Processing technology Cold storage facilities	Source raw materials Prepare food Freeze food Pack and freeze food	Frozen food

Hierarchy of operations

This idea is called the **hierarchy of operations** and is illustrated for a business that makes television programmes and videos in Figure 1.5. It will have inputs of production, technical and administrative staff, cameras, lighting, sound and recording equipment, and so on. It transforms these into finished programmes, music, videos, etc. At a more macro level, the business itself is part of a whole supply network, acquiring services from creative agencies, casting agencies and studios, liaising with promotion agencies, and serving its broadcasting company customers. At a more micro level within this overall operation there are many individual processes: workshops manufacturing the sets; marketing processes that liaise with potential customers; maintenance and repair processes that care for, modify and design technical equipment; production units that shoot the programmes and videos; and so on. Each of these individual processes can be represented as a network of yet smaller processes, or even individual units of resource. So, for example, the set manufacturing process could consist of four smaller processes: one that designs the sets, one that constructs them, one that acquires the props, and one that finishes (paints) the set.

Critical commentary

The idea of the internal network of processes is seen by some as being over-simplistic. In reality the relationship between groups and individuals is significantly more complex than that between commercial entities. One cannot treat internal customers and suppliers exactly as we do external customers and suppliers. External customers and suppliers usually operate in a free market. If an organization believes that in the long run it can get a better deal by purchasing goods and services from another supplier, it will do so. But internal customers and suppliers are not in a 'free market'. They cannot usually look outside either to purchase input resources or to sell their output goods and services (although some organizations are moving this way). Rather than take the 'economic' perspective of external commercial relationships, models from organizational behaviour, it is argued, are more appropriate.

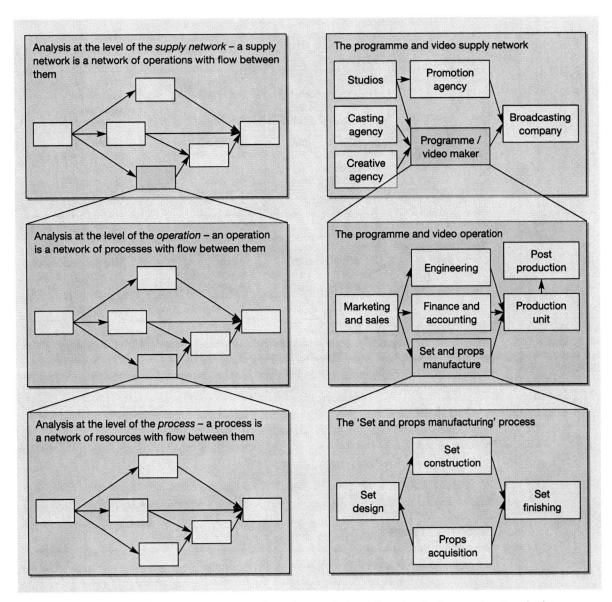

Figure 1.5 Operations and process management requires analysis at three levels: the supply network, the operation, and the process

Operations management is relevant to all parts of the business

All functions manage processes

The example in Figure 1.5 demonstrates that it is not just the operations function that manages processes; **all functions manage processes**. For example, the marketing function will have processes that produce demand forecasts, processes that produce advertising campaigns and processes that produce marketing plans. These processes in the other functions also need managing using similar principles to those within the operations function. Each function will have its 'technical' knowledge. In marketing, this is the expertise in designing and shaping marketing plans; in finance, it is the technical knowledge of financial reporting. Yet each will also have a 'process management' role of producing plans, policies, reports and services. The implications of this are very important. Because all managers have some responsibility for managing processes, they are, to some extent, operations managers. They all should want to give good service to their (often internal) customers, and they all will

Table 1.5 Some examples of processes in non-operations functions

Organizational function	Some of its processes	Outputs from its process	Customer(s) for its outputs
Marketing and sales	Planning process Forecasting process Order taking process	Marketing plans Sales forecasts Confirmed orders	Senior management Sales staff, planners, operations Operations, finance
Finance and accounting	Budgeting process Capital approval processes Invoicing processes	Budgets Capital request evaluations Invoices	Everyone Senior management, requesters External customers
Human resources management	Payroll processes Recruitment processes Training processes	Salary statements New hires Trained employees	Employees All other processes All other processes
Information technology	Systems review process Help desk process System implementation project processes	System evaluation Advice Implemented working systems and aftercare	All other processes All other processes All other processes

All managers, not just operations managers, manage processes

want to do this efficiently. So, **operations management is relevant for all functions**, and all managers should have something to learn from the principles, concepts, approaches and techniques of operations management. It also means that we must distinguish between two meanings of 'operations':

Operations as a function

- **'Operations' as a function**, meaning the part of the organization which produces the products and services for the organization's external customers;

Operations as an activity

- **'Operations' as an activity**, meaning the management of the processes within any of the organization's functions.

Table 1.5 illustrates just some of the processes that are contained within some of the more common non-operations functions, the outputs from these processes and their 'customers'.

Business processes

Whenever a business attempts to satisfy its customers' needs it will use many processes, in both its operations and its other functions. Each of these processes will contribute some part to fulfilling customer needs. For example, the television programme and video production company, described previously, produces two types of 'product'. Both of these products involve a slightly different mix of processes within the company. The company decides to re-organize its operations so that each product is produced from start to finish by a dedicated process that contains all the elements necessary for its production, as in Figure 1.6. So customer needs

'End-to-end' business processes

for each product are entirely fulfilled from within what is called an **'end-to-end' business process**. These often cut across conventional organizational boundaries. Reorganizing (or 're-engineering') process boundaries and organizational responsibilities around these business

Business process re-engineering

processes is the philosophy behind **business process re-engineering** (BPR) which is discussed further in Chapter 18.

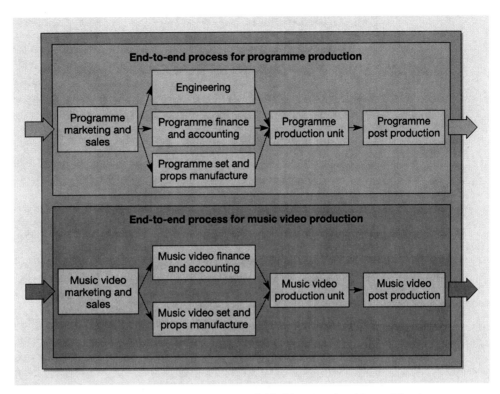

Figure 1.6 The television and video company divided into two 'end-to-end' business processes, one dedicated to producing programmes and the other dedicated to producing music videos

Operations processes have different characteristics

Although all operations processes are similar in that they all transform inputs, they do differ in a number of ways, four of which, known as the four Vs, are particularly important:

Volume
Variety
Variation
Visibility

- The **volume** of their output;
- The **variety** of their output;
- The **variation** in the demand for their output;
- The degree of **visibility** which customers have of the production of their output.

The volume dimension

Repeatability
Systematization

Let us take a familiar example. The epitome of high-volume hamburger production is McDonald's, which serves millions of burgers around the world every day. Volume has important implications for the way McDonald's operations are organized. The first thing you notice is the **repeatability** of the tasks people are doing and the **systematization** of the work where standard procedures are set down specifying how each part of the job should be carried out. Also, because tasks are systematized and repeated, it is worthwhile developing specialized fryers and ovens. All this gives *low unit costs*. Now consider a small local cafeteria serving a few 'short-order' dishes. The range of items on the menu may be similar to the larger operation, but the volume will be far lower, so the repetition will also be far lower and the number of staff will be lower (possibly only one person) and therefore individual staff are likely to perform a wider range of tasks. This may be more rewarding for the staff, but less open to systematization. Also it is less feasible to invest in specialized equipment. So the cost per burger served is likely to be higher (even if the price is comparable).

The variety dimension

A taxi company offers a high-variety service. It is prepared to pick you up from almost anywhere and drop you off almost anywhere. To offer this variety it must be relatively *flexible*. Drivers must have a good knowledge of the area, and communication between the base and the taxis must be effective. However, the cost per kilometre travelled will be higher for a taxi than for a less customized form of transport such as a bus service. Although both provide the same basic service (transportation), the taxi service has a high variety of routes and times to offer its customers, while the bus service has a few well-defined routes, with a set schedule. If all goes to schedule, little, if any, flexibility is required from the operation. All is **standardized** and regular, which results in relatively low costs compared with using a taxi for the same journey.

Standardized

The variation dimension

Consider the demand pattern for a successful summer holiday resort hotel. Not surprisingly, more customers want to stay in summer vacation times than in the middle of winter. At the height of 'the season' the hotel could be full to its capacity. Off-season demand, however, could be a small fraction of its capacity. Such a marked variation in demand means that the operation must change its capacity in some way, for example, by hiring extra staff for the summer. The hotel must try to predict the likely level of demand. If it gets this wrong, it could result in too much or too little capacity. Also, recruitment costs, overtime costs and under-utilization of its rooms all have the effect of increasing the hotel's costs operation compared with a hotel of a similar standard with level demand. A hotel which has relatively level demand can plan its activities well in advance. Staff can be scheduled, food can be bought and rooms can be cleaned in a *routine* and *predictable* manner. This results in a high utilization of resources and unit costs which are likely to be lower than those in hotels with a highly variable demand pattern.

The visibility dimension

Visibility means process exposure

Visibility is a slightly more difficult dimension of operations to envisage. It refers to how much of the operation's activities its customers experience, or how much the operation is **exposed** to its customers. Generally, customer-processing operations are more exposed to their customers than material- or information-processing operations. But even customer-processing operations have some choice as to how visible they wish their operations to be. For example, a retailer could operate as a high-visibility 'bricks and mortar', or a lower-visibility web-based operation. In the 'bricks and mortar', high-visibility operation, customers will directly experience most of its 'value-adding' activities. Customers will have a relatively *short waiting tolerance*, and may walk out if not served in a reasonable time. Customers' perceptions, rather than objective criteria, will also be important. If they perceive that a member of the operation's staff is discourteous to them, they are likely to be dissatisfied (even if the staff member meant no discourtesy), so high-visibility operations require staff with good customer contact skills. Customers could also request goods which clearly would not be sold in such a shop, but because the customers are actually in the operation they can ask what they like! This is called **high received variety**. This makes it difficult for high-visibility operations to achieve high productivity of resources, so they tend to be relatively high-cost operations. Conversely, a web-based retailer, while not a pure low-contact operation, has far lower visibility. Behind its web site it can be more 'factory-like'. The *time lag* between the order being placed and the items ordered by the customer being retrieved and dispatched does not have to be minutes as in the shop, but can be hours or even days. This allows the tasks of finding the items, packing and dispatching them to be *standardized* by staff who need few **customer contact skills**. Also, there can be relatively *high staff utilization*. The web-based organization can also centralize its operation

High received variety

Customer contact skills

Two very different hotels

Formule 1

Hotels are high-contact operations – they are staff-intensive and have to cope with a range of customers, each with a variety of needs and expectations. So, how can a highly successful chain of affordable hotels avoid the crippling costs of high customer contact? Formule 1, a subsidiary of the French Accor group, manages to offer outstanding value by adopting two principles not always associated with hotel operations – standardization and an innovative use of technology. Formule 1 hotels are usually located close to the roads, junctions and cities which make them visible and accessible to prospective customers. The hotels themselves are made from state-of-the-art volumetric prefabrications. The prefabricated units are arranged in various configurations to suit the characteristics of each individual site. All rooms are nine square metres in area, and are designed to be attractive, functional, comfortable and soundproof. Most important, they are designed to be easy to clean and maintain. All have the same fittings, including a double bed, an additional bunk-type bed, a wash basin, a storage area, a working table with seat, a wardrobe and a television set. The reception of a Formule 1 hotel is staffed only from 6.30 am to 10.00 am and from 5.00 pm to 10.00 pm. Outside these times an automatic machine sells rooms to credit card users, provides access to the hotel, dispenses a security code for the room and even prints a receipt. Technology is also evident in the washrooms. Showers and toilets are automatically cleaned after each use by using nozzles and heating elements to spray the room with a disinfectant solution and dry it before it is used again. To keep things even simpler, Formule 1 hotels do not include a restaurant as they are usually located near existing restaurants. However, a continental breakfast is available, usually between 6.30 am and 10.00 am, and of course on a 'self-service' basis!

Mwagusi Safari Lodge

The Mwagusi Safari Lodge lies within Tanzania's Ruaha National Park, a huge undeveloped wilderness, whose beautiful open landscape is especially good for seeing elephant, buffalo and lion. Nestled into a bank of the Mwagusi Sand River, this small exclusive tented camp overlooks a watering hole in the riverbed. Its ten tents are within thatched bandas (accommodation), each furnished comfortably in the traditional style of the camp. Each banda has an en-suite bathroom with flush toilet and a hot shower. Game viewing can be experienced even from the seclusion of the veranda. The sight of thousands of buffalo flooding the riverbed below the tents and dining room banda is not uncommon, and elephants, giraffes, and wild dogs are frequent uninvited guests to the site. There are two staff for each customer, allowing individual needs and preferences to be met quickly at all times. Guest numbers vary throughout the year, occupancy being low in the rainy season from January to April, and full in the best game viewing period from September to November. There are game drives and walks throughout the area, each selected for individual customers' individual preferences. Drives are taken in specially adapted open-sided four-wheel-drive vehicles, equipped with reference books, photography equipment, medical kits and all the necessities for a day in the bush. Walking safaris, accompanied by an experienced guide can be customized for every visitor's requirements and abilities. Lunch can be taken communally, so that visitors can discuss their interests with other guides and managers. Dinner is often served under the stars in a secluded corner of the dry riverbed.

on one (physical) site, whereas the 'bricks and mortar' shop needs many shops close to centres of demand. Therefore, the low-visibility web-based operation will have lower costs than the shop.

Mixed high- and low-visibility processes

Some operations have both high- and low-visibility processes within the same operation. In an airport, for example: some activities are totally 'visible' to its customers such as information desks answering people's queries. These staff operate in what is termed a **front-office** environment. Other parts of the airport have little, if any, customer 'visibility', such as the baggage handlers. These rarely-seen staff perform the vital but low-contact tasks, in the **back-office** part of the operation.

Front office

Back office

The implications of the four Vs of operations processes

All four dimensions have implications for the cost of creating the products or services. Put simply, high volume, low variety, low variation and low customer contact all help to keep processing costs down. Conversely, low volume, high variety, high variation and high customer contact generally carry some kind of cost penalty for the operation. This is why the volume dimension is drawn with its 'low' end at the left, unlike the other dimensions, to keep all the 'low cost' implications on the right. To some extent the position of an operation in the **four dimensions** is determined by the demand of the market it is serving. However, most operations have some discretion in moving themselves on the dimensions. Figure 1.7 summarizes the implications of such positioning.

'Four Vs' analysis of processes

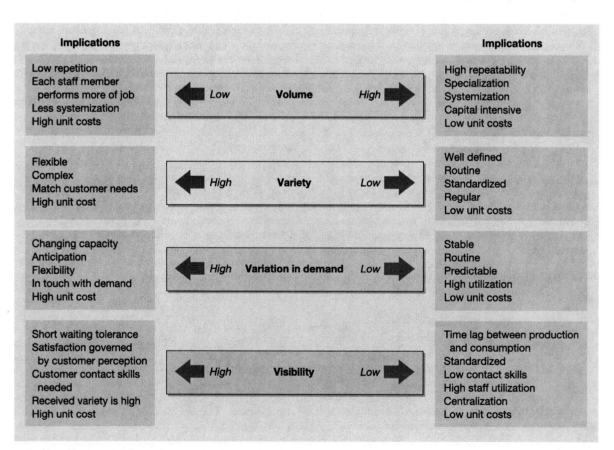

Figure 1.7 A typology of operations

Worked example

Figure 1.8 illustrates the different positions on the dimensions of the Formule 1 hotel chain and the Mwagusi Safari Lodge (*see* the short case on 'Two very different hotels'). Both provide the same basic service as any other hotel. However, one is of a small, intimate nature with relatively few customers. Its variety of services is almost infinite in the sense that customers can make individual requests in terms of food and entertainment. Variation is high and customer contact, and therefore visibility, is also very high (in order to ascertain customers' requirements and provide for them). All of this is very different from Formule 1, where volume is high (although not as high as in a large city-centre hotel), variety of service is strictly limited, and business and holiday customers use the hotel at different times, which limits variation. Most notably, though, customer contact is kept to a minimum. The Mwagusi Safari Lodge hotel has very high levels of service but provides them at a high cost (and therefore a high price). Conversely, Formule 1 has arranged its operation in such a way as to minimize its costs.

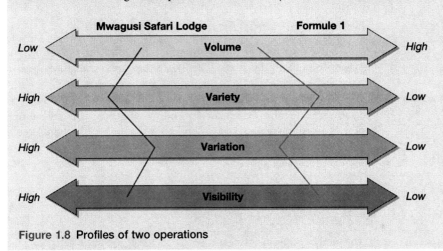

Figure 1.8 Profiles of two operations

The activities of operations management

Operations managers have some responsibility for all the activities in the organization which contribute to the effective production of products and services. And while the exact nature of the operations function's responsibilities will, to some extent, depend on the way the organization has chosen to define the boundaries of the function, there are some general classes of activities that apply to all types of operation.

- **Understanding the operation's strategic performance objectives.** The first responsibility of any operations management team is to understand what it is trying to achieve. This means understanding how to judge the performance of the operation at different levels, from broad and strategic to more operational performance objectives. This is discussed in Chapter 2.
- **Developing an operations strategy for the organization.** Operations management involves hundreds of minute-by-minute decisions, so it is vital that there is a set of general principles which can guide decision-making towards the organization's longer-term goals. This is an operations strategy and is discussed in Chapter 3.

- **Designing the operation's products, services and processes.** Design is the activity of determining the physical form, shape and composition of products, services and processes. It is a crucial part of operations managers' activities and is discussed in Chapters 4 to 9.
- **Planning and controlling the operation.** Planning and control is the activity of deciding what the operations resources should be doing, then making sure that they really are doing it. Chapters 10 to 17 explain various planning and control activities.
- **Improving the performance of the operation.** The continuing responsibility of all operations managers is to improve the performance of their operation. Chapters 18 to 20 describes improvement activities.
- **The social responsibilities of operations management.** It is increasingly recognized by many businesses that operations managers have a set of broad societal responsibilities and concerns beyond their direct activities. The general term for these aspects of business responsibility is 'corporate social responsibility' or CSR. It should be of particular interest to operations managers, because their activities can have a direct and significant effect on society. This is discussed in Chapter 21.

The model of operations management

Operations activities define operations management and operations strategy

We can now combine two ideas to develop the model of operations management which will be used throughout this book. The first is the input–transformation–output model and the second is the categorization of operations management's activity areas. Figure 1.9 shows how these two ideas go together. The model now shows two interconnected loops of **activities**. The bottom one more or less corresponds to what is usually seen as operations management, and the top one to what is seen as operations strategy. This book concentrates on the former but tries to cover enough of the latter to allow the reader to make strategic sense of the operations manager's job.

Critical commentary

The central idea in this introductory chapter is that all organizations have operations processes which produce products and services and all these processes are essentially similar. However, some believe that by even trying to characterize processes in this way (perhaps even by calling them 'processes') one loses or distorts their nature, depersonalizes or takes the 'humanity' out of the way in which we think of the organization. This point is often raised in not-for-profit organizations, especially by 'professional' staff. For example the head of one European 'Medical Association' (a doctors' trade union) criticized hospital authorities for expecting a *'sausage factory service based on productivity targets'.*[5] No matter how similar they appear on paper, it is argued, a hospital can never be viewed in the same was a factory. Even in commercial businesses, professionals, such as creative staff, often express discomfort at their expertise being described as a 'process'.

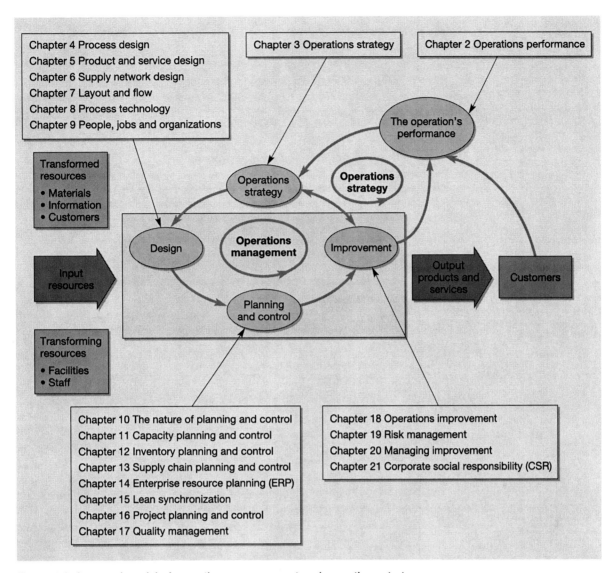

Figure 1.9 A general model of operations management and operations strategy

Summary answers to key questions

Check and improve your understanding of this chapter using self assessment questions and a personalised study plan, audio and video downloads, and an eBook – all at www.myomlab.com.

➤ What is operations management?

■ Operations management is the activity of managing the resources which are devoted to the production and delivery of products and services. It is one of the core functions of any business, although it may not be called operations management in some industries.

■ Operations management is concerned with managing processes. And all processes have internal customers and suppliers. But all management functions also have processes. Therefore, operations management has relevance for all managers.

➔

➤ Why is operations management important in all types of organization?

■ Operations management uses the organization's resources to create outputs that fulfil defined market requirements. This is the fundamental activity of any type of enterprise.

■ Operations management is increasingly important because today's business environment requires new thinking from operations managers.

➤ What is the input–transformation–output process?

■ All operations can be modelled as input–transformation–output processes. They all have inputs of transforming resources, which are usually divided into 'facilities' and 'staff', and transformed resources, which are some mixture of materials, information and customers.

■ Few operations produce only products or only services. Most produce some mixture of tangible goods or products and less tangible services.

➤ What is the process hierarchy?

■ All operations are part of a larger supply network which, through the individual contributions of each operation, satisfies end-customer requirements.

■ All operations are made up of processes that form a network of internal customer–supplier relationships within the operation.

■ End-to-end business processes that satisfy customer needs often cut across functionally based processes.

➤ How do operations processes have different characteristics?

■ Operations differ in terms of the volume of their outputs, the variety of outputs, the variation in demand for their outputs, and the degree of 'visibility' they have.

■ High volume, low variety, low variation and low customer 'visibility' are usually associated with low cost.

➤ What are the activities of operations management?

■ Responsibilities include understanding relevant performance objectives, setting an operations strategy, the design of the operation (products, services and processes), planning and controlling the operation, and the improvement of the operation over time.

■ Operations managers also have a set of broad societal responsibilities. These are generally called 'corporate social responsibility' or CSR objectives.

Case study
Design house partnerships at Concept Design Services[6]

'I can't believe how much we have changed in a relatively short time. From being an inward-looking manufacturer, we became a customer-focused "design and make" operation. Now we are an integrated service provider. Most of our new business comes from the partnerships we have formed with design houses. In effect, we design products jointly with specialist design houses that have a well-known brand, and offer them a complete service of manufacturing and distribution. In many ways we are now a "business-to-business" company rather than a "business-to-consumer" company.' (Jim Thompson, CEO, Concept Design Services (CDS))

CDS had become one of Europe's most profitable homeware businesses. Originally founded in the 1960s, the company had moved from making industrial mouldings, mainly in the aerospace sector, and some cheap 'homeware' items such as buckets and dustpans, sold under the 'Focus' brand name, to making very high-quality (expensive) stylish homewares with a high 'design value'.

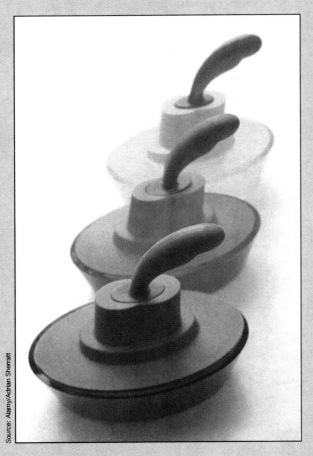

Source: Alamy/Adrian Sherratt

The move into 'Concept' products
The move into higher-margin homeware had been master-minded by Linda Fleet, CDS's Marketing Director, who had previously worked for a large retail chain of paint and wallpaper retailers. *'Experience in the decorative products industry had taught me the importance of fashion and product development, even in mundane products such as paint. Premium-priced colours and new textures would become popular for one or two years, supported by appropriate promotion and features in lifestyle magazines. The manufacturers and retailers who created and supported these products were dramatically more profitable than those who simply provided standard ranges. Instinctively, I felt that this must also apply to homeware. We decided to develop a whole coordinated range of such items, and to open up a new distribution network for them to serve up-market stores, kitchen equipment and speciality retailers. Within a year of launching our first new range of kitchen homeware under the "Concept" brand name, we had over 3000 retail outlets signed up, provided with point-of-sale display facilities. Press coverage generated an enormous interest which was reinforced by the product placement on several TV cookery and "lifestyle" programmes. We soon developed an entirely new market and within two years "Concept" products were providing over 75 per cent of our revenue and 90 per cent of our profits. The price realization of Concept products is many times higher than for the Focus range. To keep ahead we launched new ranges at regular intervals.'*

The move to the design house partnerships
'Over the last four years, we have been designing, manufacturing and distributing products for some of the more prestigious design houses. This sort of business is likely to grow, especially in Europe where the design houses appreciate our ability to offer a full service. We can design products in conjunction with their own design staff and offer them a level of manufacturing expertise they can't get elsewhere. More significantly, we can offer a distribution service which is tailored to their needs. From the customer's point of view the distribution arrangements appear to belong to the design house itself. In fact they are based exclusively on our own call centre, warehouse and distribution resources.'

The most successful collaboration was with Villessi, the Italian designers. Generally it was CDS's design expertise which was attractive to 'design house' partners. Not only did CDS employ professionally respected designers, they had also acquired a reputation for being able to translate difficult technical designs into manufacturable and saleable →

products. Design house partnerships usually involved relatively long lead times but produced unique products with very high margins, nearly always carrying the design house's brand. *'This type of relationship plays to our strengths. Our design expertise gains us entry to the partnership but we are soon valued equally for our marketing, distribution and manufacturing competence.'* (Linda Fleet, Marketing Director)

Manufacturing operations

All manufacturing was carried out in a facility located 20 km from head office. Its moulding area housed large injection-moulding machines, most with robotic material handling capabilities. Products and components passed to the packing hall, where they were assembled and inspected. The newer more complex products often had to move from moulding to assembly and then back again for further moulding. All products followed the same broad process route but with more products needing several progressive moulding and assembly stages, there was an increase in 'process flow recycling' which was adding complexity. One idea was to devote a separate cell to the newer and more complex products until they had 'bedded in'. This cell could also be used for testing new moulds. However, it would need investment in extra capacity that would not always be fully utilized. After manufacture, products were packed and stored in the adjacent distribution centre.

'When we moved into making the higher-margin Concept products, we disposed of most of our older, small injection-moulding machines. Having all larger machines allowed us to use large multi-cavity moulds. This increased productivity by allowing us to produce several products, or components, each machine cycle. It also allowed us to use high-quality and complex moulds which, although cumbersome and more difficult to change over, gave a very high-quality product. For example, with the same labour we could make three items per minute on the old machines, and 18 items per minute on the modern ones using multi-moulds. That's a 600 per cent increase in productivity. We also achieved high-dimensional accuracy, excellent surface finish, and extreme consistency of colour. We could do this because of our expertise derived from years making aerospace products. Also, by standardizing on single large machines, any mould could fit any machine. This was an ideal situation from a planning perspective, as we were often asked to make small runs of Concept products at short notice.' (Grant Williams, CDS Operations Manager)

Increasing volume and a desire to reduce cost had resulted in CDS subcontracting much of its Focus products to other (usually smaller) moulding companies. *'We would never do it with any complex or design house partner products, but it should allow us to reduce the cost of making basic products while releasing capacity for higher-margin ones. However, there have been quite a few 'teething problems'. Coordinating the production schedules is currently a problem, as is agreeing quality standards. To some extent it's our own fault. We didn't realize that subcontracting was a skill in its own right. And although we have got over some of the problems, we still do not have a satisfactory relationship with all of our subcontractors.'* (Grant Williams, CDS Operations Manager)

Planning and distribution services

The distribution services department of the company was regarded as being at the heart of the company's customer service drive. Its purpose was to integrate the efforts of design, manufacturing and sales by planning the flow of products from production, through the distribution centre, to the customer. Sandra White, the Planning Manager, reported to Linda Fleet and was responsible for the scheduling of all manufacturing and distribution, and for maintaining inventory levels for all the warehoused items. *'We try to stick to a preferred production sequence for each machine and mould so as to minimize set-up times by starting on a light colour, and progressing through a sequence to the darkest. We can change colours in 15 minutes, but because our moulds are large and technically complex, mould changes can take up to three hours. Good scheduling is important to maintain high plant utilization. With a higher variety of complex products, batch sizes have reduced and it has brought down average utilization. Often we can't stick to schedules. Short-term changes are inevitable in a fashion market. Certainly better forecasts would help ... but even our own promotions are sometimes organized at such short notice that we often get caught with stockouts. New products in particular are difficult to forecast, especially when they are "fashion" items and/or seasonal. Also, I have to schedule production time for new product mould trials; we normally allow 24 hours for the testing of each new mould received, and this has to be done on production machines. Even if we have urgent orders, the needs of the designers always have priority.'* (Sandra White)

Customer orders for Concept and design house partnership products were taken by the company's sales call centre located next to the warehouse. The individual orders would then be dispatched using the company's own fleet of medium and small distribution vehicles for UK orders, but using carriers for the Continental European market. A standard delivery timetable was used and an 'express delivery' service was offered for those customers prepared to pay a small delivery premium. However, a recent study had shown that almost 40 per cent of express deliveries were initiated by the company rather than customers. Typically this would be to fulfil deliveries of orders containing products out of stock at the time of ordering. The express delivery service was not required for Focus products because almost all deliveries were to five large customers. The size of each order was usually very large, with deliveries to customers' own distribution depots. However, although the organization of Focus delivery was relatively straightforward, the consequences of failure were large. Missing a delivery meant upsetting a large customer.

Challenges for CDS

Although the company was financially successful and very well regarded in the homeware industry, there were a number of issues and challenges that it knew it would have to address. The first was the role of the design department and its influence over new product development.

New product development had become particularly important to CDS, especially since they had formed alliances with design houses. This had led to substantial growth in both the size and the influence of the design department, which reported to Linda Fleet. 'Building up and retaining design expertise will be the key to our future. Most of our growth is going to come from the business which will be bought in through the creativity and flair of our designers. Those who can combine creativity with an understanding of our partners' business and design needs can now bring in substantial contracts. The existing business is important of course, but growth will come directly from these people's capabilities.' (Linda Fleet)

But not everyone was so sanguine about the rise of the design department. 'It is undeniable that relationships between the designers and other parts of the company have been under strain recently. I suppose it is, to some extent, inevitable. After all, they really do need the freedom to design as they wish. I can understand it when they get frustrated at some of the constraints which we have to work under in the manufacturing or distribution parts of the business. They also should be able to expect a professional level of service from us. Yet the truth is that they make most of the problems themselves. They sometimes don't seem to understand the consequences or implications of their design decisions or the promises they make to the design houses. More seriously they don't really understand that we could actually help them do their job better if they cooperated a bit more. In fact, I now see some of our design house partners' designers more than I do our own designers. The Villessi designers are always in my factory and we have developed some really good relationships.' (Grant Williams)

The second major issue concerned sales forecasting, and again there were two different views. Grant Williams was convinced that forecasts should be improved. 'Every Friday morning we devise a schedule of production and distribution for the following week. Yet, usually before Tuesday morning, it has had to be significantly changed because of unexpected orders coming in from our customers' weekend sales. This causes tremendous disruption to both manufacturing and distribution operations. If sales could be forecast more accurately we would achieve far high utilization, better customer service, and I believe, significant cost savings.'

However, Linda Fleet saw things differently. 'Look, I do understand Grant's frustration, but after all, this is a fashion business. By definition it is impossible to forecast accurately. In terms of month-by-month sales volumes we are in fact pretty accurate, but trying to make a forecast for every week end every product is almost impossible to do accurately. Sorry, that's just the nature of the business we're in. In fact, although Grant complains about our lack of forecast accuracy, he always does a great job in responding to unexpected customer demand.'

Jim Thompson, the Managing Director, summed up his view of the current situation. 'Particularly significant has been our alliances with the Italian and German design houses. In effect we are positioning ourselves as a complete service partner to the designers. We have a world-class design capability together with manufacturing, order processing, order-taking and distribution services. These abilities allow us to develop genuinely equal partnerships which integrate us into the whole industry's activities.'

Linda Fleet also saw an increasing role for collaborative arrangements. 'It may be that we are seeing a fundamental change in how we do business within our industry. We have always seen ourselves as primarily a company that satisfies consumer desires through the medium of providing good service to retailers. The new partnership arrangements put us more into the "business-to-business" sector. I don't have any problem with this in principle, but I'm a little anxious as to how much it gets us into areas of business beyond our core expertise.'

The final issue which was being debated within the company was longer-term, and particularly important. 'The two big changes we have made in this company have both happened because we exploited a strength we already had within the company. Moving into Concept products was only possible because we brought our high-tech precision expertise that we had developed in the aerospace sector into the homeware sector where none of our new competitors could match our manufacturing excellence. Then, when we moved into design house partnerships we did so because we had a set of designers who could command respect from the world-class design houses with whom we formed partnerships. So what is the next move for us? Do we expand globally? We are strong in Europe but nowhere else in the world. Do we extend our design scope into other markets, such as furniture? If so, that would take us into areas where we have no manufacturing expertise. We are great at plastic injection moulding, but if we tried any other manufacturing processes, we would be no better than, and probably worse than, other firms with more experience. So what's the future for us?' (Jim Thompson, CEO CDS).

Questions

1 Why is operations management important in CDS?

2 Draw a 4 Vs profile for the company's products and services.

3 What would you recommend to the company if they asked you to advise them in improving their operations?

Problems and applications

These problems and applications will help to improve your analysis of operations. You can find more practice problems as well as worked examples and guided solutions on MyOMLab at www.myomlab.com.

1 Read the short case on Pret A Manger and **(a)** identify the processes in a typical Pret A Manger shop together with their inputs and outputs, **(b)** Pret A Manger also supplies business lunches (of sandwiches and other take-away food). What are the implications for how it manages its processes within the shop? **(c)** What would be the advantages and disadvantages if Pret A Manger introduced 'central kitchens' that made the sandwiches for a number of shops in an area? (As far as we know, they have no plans to do so.)

2 Compare and contrast Acme Whistles and Pret A Manger in terms of the way that they will need to manage their operations.

3 Visit a furniture store (other than IKEA) and a sandwich or snack shop (other than Pret A Manger). Observe how each shop operates, for example, where customers go, how staff interact with them, how big it is, how the shop has chosen to use its space, what variety of products it offers, and so on. Talk with the staff and managers if you can. Think about how the shops you have visited are similar to IKEA and Pret A Manger, and how they differ. Then consider the question, *'What implications do the differences between the shops you visited and the two described in Chapter 1 have for their operations management?'*

4 Visit and observe three restaurants, cafés or somewhere that food is served. Compare them in terms of the Volume of demand that they have to cope with, the Variety of menu items they service, the Variation in demand during the day, week and year, and the Visibility you have of the preparation of the food. Think about and discuss the impact of volume, variety, variation and visibility on the day-to-day management of each of the operations and consider how each operation attempts to cope with its volume, variety, variation and visibility.

5 (Advanced) Find a copy of a financial newspaper (*Financial Times, Wall Street Journal, Economist*, etc.) and identify one company which is described in the paper that day. Using the list of issues identified in Table 1.1, what do you think would be the *new operations agenda* for that company?

Selected further reading

Chase, R.B., Jacobs, F.R. and Aquilano, N.J. (2004) *Operations Management for Competitive Advantage* (10th edn), McGraw-Hill/Irwin, Boston. There are many good general textbooks on operations management. This was one of the first and is still one of the best, though written very much for an American audience.

Chopra, S., Deshmukh, S., Van Mieghem, J., Zemel, E. and Anupindi, R. (2005) *Managing Business Process Flows: Principles of Operations Management*, Prentice-Hall, NJ. Takes a 'process' view of operations. Mathematical but rewarding.

Hammer, M. and Stanton, S. (1999) How process enterprises really work, *Harvard Business Review*, Nov–Dec. Hammer is one of the gurus of process design. This paper is typical of his approach.

Heizer, J. and Render, B. (2006) *Operations Management* (8th edn), Prentice Hall, New Jersey. Another good US authored general text on the subject.

Johnston, R. and Clark, G. (2008) *Service Operations Management* (3rd edn), Financial Times-Prentice Hall, Harlow. What can we say! A great treatment of service operations from the same stable as this textbook.

Slack, N. and Lewis, M.A. (eds) (2005) *The Blackwell Encyclopedic Dictionary of Operations Management* (2nd edn), Blackwell Business, Oxford. For those who like technical descriptions and definitions.

Useful web sites

www.opsman.org Useful materials and resources.

www.iomnet.org The Institute of Operations Management site. One of the main professional bodies for the subject.

www.poms.org A US academic society for production and operations management. Academic, but some useful material, including a link to an encyclopaedia of operations management terms.

www.sussex.ac.uk/users/dt31/TOMI/ One of the longest-established portals for the subject. Useful for academics and students alike.

www.ft.com Useful for researching topics and companies.

www.journaloperationsmanagement.org The home site for the best known operations management journal. A bit academic, but some pages are useful.

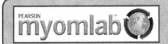

Now that you have finished reading this chapter, why not visit MyOMLab at www.myomlab.com where you'll find more learning resources to help you make the most of your studies and get a better grade?

WINNING CONTRACTS IN A B2B ENVIRONMENT

11

Managing the Supply Chain

10

OM Strategy Decisions

► Design of Goods and Services
► Managing Quality
► Process Strategy
► Location Strategies
► Layout Strategies
► Human Resources
► Supply-Chain Management
► Inventory Management
► Scheduling
► Maintenance

GLOBAL COMPANY PROFILE: DARDEN RESTAURANTS

DARDEN'S SUPPLY CHAIN YIELDS A COMPETITIVE EDGE

Darden Restaurants, Inc., is the largest publicly traded casual dining restaurant company in the world. It serves over 400 million meals annually from more than 1,700 restaurants in the U.S. and Canada. Each of its well-known flagship brands—Olive Garden and Red Lobster—generates sales of $2 billion annually. Darden's other brands include Bahama Breeze, Seasons 52, Capital Grille, and LongHorn Steakhouse. The firm employs more than 150,000 people and is the 29th largest employer in the U.S.

"Operations is typically thought of as an execution of strategy. For us it is the strategy," Darden's former chairman, Joe R. Lee, stated.

In the restaurant business, a winning strategy requires a winning supply chain. Nothing is more important than sourcing and delivering healthy, high-quality food; and there are very few other industries where supplier performance is so closely tied to the customer.

Darden sources its food from five continents and thousands of suppliers. To meet Darden's needs for fresh ingredients, the company has developed four distinct supply chains: one for seafood; one for dairy/produce/other refrigerated foods; a third for other food items, like baked goods; and a fourth for restaurant supplies (everything from dishes to ovens to uniforms). Over $1.5 billion is spent in these supply chains annually. (See the *Video Case Study* at the end of this chapter for details.)

Darden's four supply channels have some common characteristics. They all require *supplier qualification*, have *product tracking*, are subject to *independent audits*, and employ *just-in-time delivery*. With best-in-class techniques and processes, Darden creates worldwide supply-chain partnerships and alliances that are rapid, transparent, and efficient. Darden achieves competitive advantage through its superior supply chain.

▲ **Qualifying Worldwide Sources:** Part of Darden's supply chain begins with a crab harvest in the frigid waters off the coast of Alaska. But long before a supplier is qualified to sell to Darden, a total quality team is appointed. The team provides guidance, assistance, support, and training to the suppliers to ensure that overall objectives are understood and desired results accomplished.

▲ **Aquaculture Certification:** Shrimp in this Asian plant are certified to ensure traceability. The focus is on quality control certified by the Aquaculture Certification Council, of which Darden is a member. Farming and inspection practices yield safe and wholesome shrimp.

▲ **Independent audits of suppliers:** To provide fair and accurate assessment, Darden's Total Quality Supplier Program includes an independent verification program. Each supplier is evaluated regularly by independent auditors on a risk-based schedule to determine the supplier's effectiveness.

▲ **Product tracking:** Darden's seafood inspection team developed an integral system that uses a lot ID to track seafood from its origin through shipping and receipt. Darden uses a modified atmosphere packaging (MAP) process to extend the shelf life and preserve the quality of its fresh fish. The tracking includes time temperature monitoring.

▲ **JIT Delivery:** For many products, temperature monitoring begins immediately and is tracked through the entire supply chain, to the kitchen at each of Darden's 1,700 restaurants and ultimately to the guest.

Chapter 11 **Learning Objectives**

LO1: Explain the strategic importance of the supply chain

LO2: Identify six supply-chain strategies

LO3: Explain issues and opportunities in the supply chain

LO4: Describe the steps in vendor selection

LO5: Explain major issues in logistics management

LO6: Compute the percentage of assets committed to inventory and inventory turnover

THE SUPPLY CHAIN'S STRATEGIC IMPORTANCE

Most firms, like Darden, spend a huge portion of their sales dollars on purchases. Because an increasing percentage of an organization's costs are determined by purchasing, relationships with suppliers are increasingly integrated and long term. Joint efforts that improve innovation, speed design, and reduce costs are common. Such efforts, when part of a corporate-wide strategy, can dramatically improve both partners' competitiveness. This integrated focus places added emphasis on managing supplier relationships.

Supply-chain management is the integration of the activities that procure materials and services, transform them into intermediate goods and final products, and deliver them to customers. These activities include purchasing and outsourcing activities, plus many other functions that are important to the relationship with suppliers and distributors. As Figure 11.1 suggests, supply-chain management includes determining (1) transportation vendors, (2) credit and cash transfers, (3) suppliers, (4) distributors, (5) accounts payable and receivable, (6) warehousing and

Supply-chain management

Management of activities that procure materials and services, transform them into intermediate goods and final products, and deliver them through a distribution system.

▼ **FIGURE 11.1** **A Supply Chain for Beer**

The supply chain includes all the interactions among suppliers, manufacturers, distributors, and customers. The chain includes transportation, scheduling information, cash and credit transfers, as well as ideas, designs, and material transfers. Even can and bottle manufacturers have their own tiers of suppliers providing components such as lids, labels, packing containers, etc. (Costs are approximate and include substantial taxes.)

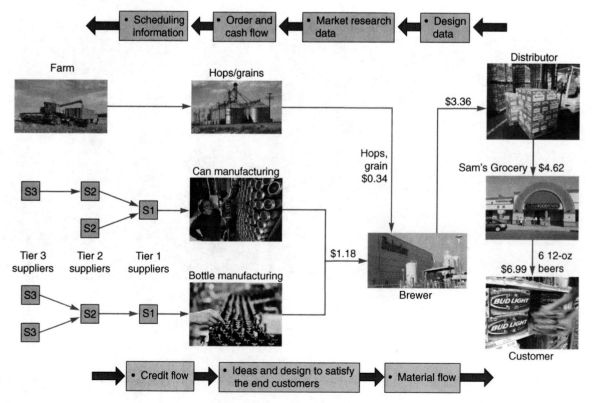

▼ **TABLE 11.1** How Supply-Chain Decisions Affect Strategy*

	Low-Cost Strategy	Response Strategy	Differentiation Strategy
Supplier's goal	Supply demand at lowest possible cost (e.g., Emerson Electric, Taco Bell)	Respond quickly to changing requirements and demand to minimize stockouts (e.g., Dell Computer)	Share market research; jointly develop products and options (e.g., Benetton)
Primary selection criteria	Select primarily for cost	Select primarily for capacity, speed, and flexibility	Select primarily for product development skills
Process characteristics	Maintain high average utilization	Invest in excess capacity and flexible processes	Use modular processes that lend themselves to mass customization
Inventory characteristics	Minimize inventory throughout the chain to hold down costs	Develop responsive system, with buffer stocks positioned to ensure supply	Minimize inventory in the chain to avoid obsolescence
Lead-time characteristics	Shorten lead time as long as it does not increase costs	Invest aggressively to reduce production lead time	Invest aggressively to reduce development lead time
Product-design characteristics	Maximize performance and minimize cost	Use product designs that lead to low setup time and rapid production ramp-up	Use modular design to postpone product differentiation for as long as possible

*See related table and discussion in Marshall L. Fisher, "What Is the Right Supply Chain for Your Product?" *Harvard Business Review* (March–April 1997): 105.

inventory, (7) order fulfillment, and (8) sharing customer, forecasting, and production information. The *objective is to build a chain of suppliers that focuses on maximizing value to the ultimate customer.*

As firms strive to increase their competitiveness via product customization, high quality, cost reductions, and speed to market, added emphasis is placed on the supply chain. Effective supply chain management makes suppliers "partners" in the firm's strategy to satisfy an ever-changing marketplace. A competitive advantage may depend on a close long-term strategic relationship with a few suppliers.

To ensure that the supply chain supports the firm's strategy, managers need to consider the supply chain issues shown in Table 11.1. Activities of supply chain managers cut across accounting, finance, marketing, and the operations discipline. Just as the OM function supports the firm's overall strategy, the supply chain must support the OM strategy. Strategies of low cost or rapid response demand different things from a supply chain than a strategy of differentiation. For instance, a low-cost strategy, as Table 11.1 indicates, requires suppliers be selected based primarily on cost. Such suppliers should have the ability to design low-cost products that meet the functional requirements, minimize inventory, and drive down lead times. However, if you want roses that are fresh, build a supply chain that focuses on response (see the *OM in Action* box "A Rose Is a Rose, but Only if It Is Fresh").

Firms must achieve integration of strategy up and down the supply chain, and must expect that strategy to be different for different products and to change as products move through their life cycle. Darden Restaurants, as noted in the opening *Global Company Profile*, has mastered worldwide product and service complexity by segmenting its supply chain and at the same time integrating four unique supply chains into its overall strategy.

LO1: Explain the strategic importance of the supply chain

VIDEO 11.1
Darden's Global Supply Chain

Supply-Chain Risk

AUTHOR COMMENT
The environment, controls, and process performance all affect supply-chain risk.

In this age of increasing specialization, low communication cost, and fast transportation, companies are making less and buying more. This means more reliance on supply chains and more risk. Managing the new integrated supply chain is a strategic challenge. Having fewer suppliers makes the supplier and customer more dependent on each other, increasing risk for both. This risk is compounded by globalization and logistical complexity. In any supply chain, vendor reliability and quality may be challenging, but the new paradigm of a tight, fast, low-inventory supply chain, operating across political and cultural boundaries, adds a new dimension to risk. As organizations go global, shipping time may increase, logistics may be less reliable, and tariffs

OM in Action ▶ A Rose Is a Rose, but Only if It Is Fresh

Supply chains for food and flowers must be fast, and they must be good. When the food supply chain has a problem, the best that can happen is the customer does not get fed on time; the worst that happens is the customer gets food poisoning and dies. In the floral industry, the timing and temperature are also critical. Indeed, flowers are the most perishable agricultural item—even more so than fish. Flowers not only need to move fast, but they must also be kept cool, at a constant temperature of 33 to 37 degrees. And they must be provided preservative-treated water while in transit. Roses are especially delicate, fragile, and perishable.

Seventy percent of the roses sold in the U.S. market arrive by air from rural Colombia and Ecuador. Roses move through this supply chain via an intricate but fast transportation network. This network stretches from growers who cut, grade, bundle, pack and ship, to importers who make the deal, to the U.S. Department of Agriculture personnel who quarantine and inspect for insects, diseases, and parasites, to U.S. Customs agents who inspect and approve, to facilitators who provide

clearance and labeling, to wholesalers who distribute, to retailers who arrange and sell, and finally to the customer. Each and every minute the product is deteriorating. The time and temperature sensitivity of perishables like roses requires sophistication and refined standards in the supply chain.

Success yields quality and low losses. After all, when it's Valentine's Day, what good is a shipment of roses that arrives wilted or late? This is a difficult supply chain; only an excellent one will get the job done.

Sources: IIE Solutions (February 2002): 26–32; and *World Trade* (June 2004): 22–25.

and quotas may block companies from doing business. In addition, international supply chains complicate information flows and increase political and currency risks.

Thus, the development of a successful strategic plan for supply-chain management requires careful research, an understanding of the risk involved, and innovative planning. Reducing risk in this increasingly global environment suggests that management must be able to mitigate and react to disruptions in:

1. *Processes* (raw material and component availability, quality, and logistics)
2. *Controls* (management metrics and reliable secure communication for financial transactions, product designs, and logistics scheduling)
3. *Environment* (customs duties, tariffs, security screening, natural disaster, currency fluctuations, terrorist attacks, and political issues)

Let's look at how several organizations address these risks in their supply chains:

- To reduce *process risk*, McDonald's planned its supply chain 6 years in advance of its opening in Russia. Creating a $60 million "food town," it developed independently owned supply plants in Moscow to keep its transportation costs and handling times low and its quality and customer-service levels high. Every component in this food chain—meat plant, chicken plant, bakery, fish plant, and lettuce plant—is closely monitored to make sure that all the system's links are strong.
- Ford's *process risk* reduction strategy is to develop a global network of *few but exceptional* suppliers who will provide the lowest cost and highest quality. This has driven one division's supplier base down to only 227 suppliers worldwide, compared with 700 previously.
- Darden Restaurants has placed extensive *controls*, including third-party audits, on supplier processes and logistics to ensure constant monitoring and reduction of risk.
- Boeing is reducing *control* risk through its state-of-the-art international communication system that transmits engineering, scheduling, and logistics data not only to Boeing facilities but to the suppliers of the 75% to 80% of the 787 Dreamliner that is built by non-Boeing companies.
- Hard Rock Cafe is reducing *environmental* (political) risk by franchising and licensing, rather than owning, when the political and cultural barriers seem significant.
- Toyota, after its experience with both fire and earthquakes, has moved to reduce *environmental* (natural disaster) risk with a policy of having at least two suppliers for each component.

Tight integration of the supply chain can have significant benefits, but the risks can and must be managed.

ETHICS AND SUSTAINABILITY

AUTHOR COMMENT
Because so much money passes through the supply chain, the opportunity for ethical lapses is significant.

Let's look at three aspects of ethics in the supply chain: personal ethics, ethics within the supply chain, and ethical behavior regarding the environment.

Personal Ethics   Ethical decisions are critical to the long-term success of any organization. However, the supply chain is particularly susceptible to ethical lapses, as the opportunities for unethical behavior are enormous. With sales personnel anxious to sell and purchasing agents spending huge sums, temptations abound. Many salespeople become friends with customers, do favors for them, take them to lunch, or present small (or large) gifts. Determining when tokens of friendship become bribes can be challenging. Many companies have strict rules and codes of conduct that limit what is acceptable. Recognizing these issues, the Institute for Supply Management has developed principles and standards to be used as guidelines for ethical behavior (as shown in Table 11.2). As the supply chain becomes international, operations managers need to expect an additional set of ethical issues to manifest themselves as they deal with new cultural values.

Ethics within the Supply Chain   In this age of hyper-specialization, much of any organization's resources are purchased, putting great stress on ethics in the supply chain. Managers may be tempted to ignore ethical lapses by suppliers or offload pollution to suppliers. But firms must establish standards for their suppliers, just as they have established standards for themselves. Society expects ethical performance throughout the supply chain. For instance, Gap Inc. reported that of its 3,000-plus factories worldwide, about 90% failed their initial evaluation.[1] The report indicated that 10% to 25% of its Chinese factories engaged in psychological or verbal abuse, and more than 50% of the factories visited in sub-Saharan Africa operate without proper safety devices. The challenge of enforcing ethical standards is significant, but responsible firms such as Gap are finding ways to deal with this difficult issue.

Ethical Behavior Regarding the Environment   While ethics on both a personal basis and in the supply chain are important, so is ethical behavior in regard to the environment. Good ethics extends to doing business in a way that supports conservation and renewal of resources. This requires evaluation of the entire environmental impact, from raw material, to manufacture, through use, and final disposal. For instance, Darden and Walmart require their shrimp and fish suppliers in Southeast Asia to abide by the standards of the Global Aquaculture Alliance. These standards must be met if suppliers want to maintain the business relationship. Operations

▼ **TABLE 11.2   Principles and Standards of Ethical Supply Management Conduct**

INTEGRITY IN YOUR DECISIONS AND ACTIONS; VALUE FOR YOUR EMPLOYER; LOYALTY TO YOUR PROFESSION

1. **PERCEIVED IMPROPRIETY** Prevent the intent and appearance of unethical or compromising conduct in relationships, actions and communications.
2. **CONFLICTS OF INTEREST** Ensure that any personal, business or other activity does not conflict with the lawful interests of your employer.
3. **ISSUES OF INFLUENCE** Avoid behaviors or actions that may negatively influence, or appear to influence, supply management decisions.
4. **RESPONSIBILITIES TO YOUR EMPLOYER** Uphold fiduciary and other responsibilities using reasonable care and granted authority to deliver value to your employer.
5. **SUPPLIER AND CUSTOMER RELATIONSHIPS** Promote positive supplier and customer relationships.
6. **SUSTAINABILITY AND SOCIAL RESPONSIBILITY** Champion social responsibility and sustainability practices in supply management.
7. **CONFIDENTIAL AND PROPRIETARY INFORMATION** Protect confidential and proprietary information.
8. **RECIPROCITY** Avoid improper reciprocal agreements.
9. **APPLICABLE LAWS, REGULATIONS AND TRADE AGREEMENTS** Know and obey the letter and spirit of laws, regulations and trade agreements applicable to supply management.
10. **PROFESSIONAL COMPETENCE** Develop skills, expand knowledge and conduct business that demonstrates competence and promotes the supply management profession.

Source: www.ism.ws

---

[1]Amy Merrick, "Gap Offers Unusual Look at Factory Conditions," *The Wall Street Journal* (May 12, 2004): A1, A12.

managers also ensure that sustainability is reflected in the performance of second- and third-tier suppliers. Enforcement can be done by in-house inspectors, third-party auditors, governmental agencies, or nongovernmental watchdog organizations. All four approaches are used.

The incoming supply chain garners most of the attention, but it is only part of the ethical challenge of sustainability. The "return" supply chain is also significant. Returned products can only be burned, buried, or reused. And the first two options have adverse consequences. Once viewed in this manner, the need for operations managers to evaluate the entire product life cycle is apparent.

While 84% of an automobile and 90% of an airplane are recycled, these levels are not easily achieved. Recycling efforts began at product and process design. Then special end-of-product-life processes were developed. Oil, lead, gasoline, explosives in air bags, acid in batteries, and the many components (axles, differentials, jet engines, hydraulic valves) that still have many years of service all demand their own unique recovery, remanufacturing, or recycling process. This complexity places significant demands on the producer as well as return and reuse supply chains in the quest for sustainability. But pursuing this quest is the ethical thing to do. Saving the earth is a challenging task.

SUPPLY-CHAIN ECONOMICS

The supply chain receives such attention because it is an integral part of a firm's strategy and the most costly activity in most firms. For both goods and services, supply chain costs as a percent of sales are often substantial (see Table 11.3). Because such a huge portion of revenue is devoted to the supply chain, an effective strategy is vital. The supply chain provides a major opportunity to reduce costs and increase contribution margins.

Table 11.4 and Example 1 illustrate the amount of leverage available to the operations manager through the supply chain.

These numbers indicate the strong role that supply chains play in profitability.

AUTHOR COMMENT
A huge part of a firm's revenue is typically spent on purchases, so this is a good place to look for savings.

▼ **TABLE 11.3**
Supply-Chain Costs as a Percentage of Sales

Industry	% Purchased
Automobile	67
Beverages	52
Chemical	62
Food	60
Lumber	61
Metals	65
Paper	55
Petroleum	79
Transportation	62

EXAMPLE 1 ▶

Profit potential in the supply chain

Hau Lee Furniture Inc. spends 50% of its sales dollar in the supply chain and has a net profit of 4%. Hau wants to know how many dollars of sales is equivalent to supply-chain savings of $1.

APPROACH ▶   Table 11.4 (given Hau's assumptions) can be used to make the analysis.

SOLUTION ▶   Table 11.4 indicates that every $1 Hau can save in the supply chain results in the same profit that would be generated by $3.70 in sales.

▶ **TABLE 11.4**
Dollars of Additional Sales Needed to Equal $1 Saved through the Supply Chain[a]

Percentage Net Profit of Firm	Percentage of Sales Spent in the Supply Chain						
	30%	40%	50%	60%	70%	80%	90%
2	$2.78	$3.23	$3.85	$4.76	$6.25	$9.09	$16.67
4	$2.70	$3.13	$3.70	$4.55	$5.88	$8.33	$14.29
6	$2.63	$3.03	$3.57	$4.35	$5.56	$7.69	$12.50
8	$2.56	$2.94	$3.45	$4.17	$5.26	$7.14	$11.11
10	$2.50	$2.86	$3.33	$4.00	$5.00	$6.67	$10.00

[a]The required increase in sales assumes that 50% of the costs other than purchases are variable and that half the remaining costs (less profit) are fixed. Therefore, at sales of $100 (50% purchases and 2% margin), $50 are purchases, $24 are other variable costs, $24 are fixed costs, and $2 profit. Increasing sales by $3.85 yields the following:

Purchases at 50%	$ 51.93 (50% of $103.85)
Other Variable Costs	24.92 (24% of $103.85)
Fixed Cost	24.00 (fixed)
Profit	3.00 (from $2 to $3 profit)
	$103.85

Through $3.85 of additional sales, we have increased profit by $1, from $2 to $3. The same increase in margin could have been obtained by reducing supply-chain costs by $1.

INSIGHT ▶   Effective management of the supply chain can generate substantial benefits.

LEARNING EXERCISE ▶   If Hau increases his profit to 6%, how much of an increase in sales is necessary to equal $1 savings? [Answer: $3.57.]

RELATED PROBLEMS ▶   11.6, 11.7

Make-or-Buy Decisions

A wholesaler or retailer buys everything that it sells; a manufacturing operation hardly ever does. Manufacturers, restaurants, and assemblers of products buy components and subassemblies that go into final products. As we saw in Chapter 5, choosing products and services that can be advantageously obtained *externally* as opposed to produced *internally* is known as the **make-or-buy decision**. Supply-chain personnel evaluate alternative suppliers and provide current, accurate, and complete data relevant to the buy alternative. Increasingly, firms focus not on an analytical make-or-buy decision but on identifying their core competencies.

Outsourcing

Outsourcing transfers some of what are traditional internal activities and resources of a firm to outside vendors, making it slightly different from the traditional make-or-buy decision. Outsourcing is part of the continuing trend toward utilizing the efficiency that comes with specialization. The vendor performing the outsourced service is an expert in that particular specialty. This leaves the outsourcing firm to focus on its critical success factors, that is, its core competencies that yield a competitive advantage. Outsourcing is the focus of the supplement to this chapter.

SUPPLY-CHAIN STRATEGIES

For goods and services to be obtained from outside sources, the firm must decide on a supply chain strategy. One such strategy is the approach of *negotiating with many suppliers* and playing one supplier against another. A second strategy is to develop *long-term "partnering"* relationships with a few suppliers to satisfy the end customer. A third strategy is *vertical integration*, in which a firm decides to use vertical backward integration by actually buying the supplier. A fourth approach is some type of collaboration that allows two or more firms to combine resources—typically in what is called a *joint venture*—to produce a component. A fifth variation is a combination of few suppliers and vertical integration, known as a *keiretsu*. In a *keiretsu, suppliers become part of a company coalition.* Finally, a sixth strategy is to develop *virtual companies that use suppliers on an as-needed basis.* We will now discuss each of these strategies.

Many Suppliers

With the many-suppliers strategy, a supplier responds to the demands and specifications of a "request for quotation," with the order usually going to the low bidder. This is a common strategy when products are commodities. This strategy plays one supplier against another and places the burden of meeting the buyer's demands on the supplier. Suppliers aggressively compete with one another. Although many approaches to negotiations can be used with this strategy, long-term "partnering" relationships are not the goal. This approach holds the supplier responsible for maintaining the necessary technology, expertise, and forecasting abilities, as well as cost, quality, and delivery competencies.

Few Suppliers

A strategy of few suppliers implies that rather than looking for short-term attributes, such as low cost, a buyer is better off forming a long-term relationship with a few dedicated suppliers. Long-term suppliers are more likely to understand the broad objectives of the procuring firm and the end customer. Using few suppliers can create value by allowing suppliers to have economies of scale and a learning curve that yields both lower transaction costs and lower production costs.

Few suppliers, each with a large commitment to the buyer, may also be more willing to participate in JIT systems as well as provide design innovations and technological expertise. Many firms have moved aggressively to incorporate suppliers into their supply systems. Ford, for one, now seeks to choose suppliers even before parts are designed. Motorola also evaluates suppliers on rigorous criteria, but in many instances has eliminated traditional supplier bidding, placing added emphasis on quality and reliability. On occasion these relationships yield contracts that extend through the product's life cycle. The expectation is that both the purchaser and

Make-or-buy decision

A choice between producing a component or service in-house or purchasing it from an outside source.

Outsourcing

Transferring a firm's activities that have traditionally been internal to external suppliers.

> **AUTHOR COMMENT**
> Supply-chain strategies come in many varieties; choosing the correct one is the trick.

LO2: Identify six supply-chain strategies

VIDEO 11.2
Supply-Chain Management at Regal Marine

supplier collaborate, becoming more efficient and reducing prices over time. The natural outcome of such relationships is fewer suppliers, but those that remain have long-term relationships.

Service companies like Marks & Spencer, a British retailer, have also demonstrated that cooperation with suppliers can yield cost savings for customers and suppliers alike. This strategy has resulted in suppliers that develop new products, winning customers for Marks & Spencer and the supplier. The move toward tight integration of the suppliers and purchasers is occurring in both manufacturing and services.

Like all strategies, a downside exists. With few suppliers, the cost of changing partners is huge, so both buyer and supplier run the risk of becoming captives of the other. Poor supplier performance is only one risk the purchaser faces. The purchaser must also be concerned about trade secrets and suppliers that make other alliances or venture out on their own. This happened when the U.S. Schwinn Bicycle Co., needing additional capacity, taught Taiwan's Giant Manufacturing Company to make and sell bicycles. Giant Manufacturing is now the largest bicycle manufacturer in the world, and Schwinn was acquired out of bankruptcy by Pacific Cycle LLC.

Vertical Integration

Vertical integration

Developing the ability to produce goods or services previously purchased or actually buying a supplier or a distributor.

Purchasing can be extended to take the form of vertical integration. By **vertical integration**, we mean developing the ability to produce goods or services previously purchased or to actually buy a supplier or a distributor. As shown in Figure 11.2, vertical integration can take the form of *forward* or *backward integration*.

Backward integration suggests a firm purchase its suppliers, as in the case of Ford Motor Company deciding to manufacture its own car radios. Forward integration, on the other hand, suggests that a manufacturer of components make the finished product. An example is Texas Instruments, a manufacturer of integrated circuits that also makes calculators and flat-screens containing integrated circuits for TVs.

Vertical integration can offer a strategic opportunity for the operations manager. For firms with the capital, managerial talent, and required demand, vertical integration may provide substantial opportunities for cost reduction, quality adherence, and timely delivery. Other advantages, such as inventory reduction and scheduling, can accrue to the company that effectively manages vertical integration or close, mutually beneficial relationships with suppliers.

Because purchased items represent such a large part of the costs of sales, it is obvious why so many organizations find interest in vertical integration. Vertical integration appears to work best when the organization has large market share and the management talent to operate an acquired vendor successfully.

The relentless march of specialization continues, meaning that a model of "doing everything" or "vertical integration" is increasingly difficult. Backward integration may be particularly dangerous for firms in industries undergoing technological change if management cannot keep abreast of those changes or invest the financial resources necessary for the next wave of technology. The alternative, particularly in high-tech industries, is to establish close-relationship suppliers. This allows partners to focus on their specific contribution. Research and development costs are too high and technology changes too rapid for one company to sustain leadership in every component. Most organizations are better served concentrating on their specialty and leveraging

► **FIGURE 11.2**
Vertical Integration Can Be Forward or Backward

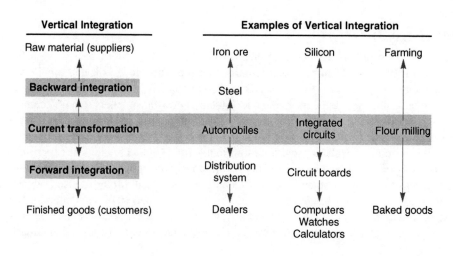

the partners' contributions. Exceptions do exist. Where capital, management talent, and technology are available and the components are also highly integrated, vertical integration may make sense. On the other hand, it made no sense for Jaguar to make commodity components for its autos as it did until recently.

Joint Ventures

Because vertical integration is so dangerous, firms may opt for some form of formal collaboration. As we noted in Chapter 5, firms may engage in collaboration to enhance their new product prowess or technological skills. But firms also engage in collaboration to secure supply or reduce costs. One version of a joint venture is the current Daimler–BMW effort to develop and produce standard automobile components. Given the global consolidation of the auto industry, these two rivals in the luxury segment of the automobile market are at a disadvantage in volume. Their relatively low volume means fewer units over which to spread fixed costs, hence the interest in consolidating to cut development and production costs. As in all other such collaborations, the trick is to cooperate without diluting the brand or conceding a competitive advantage.

Keiretsu Networks

Many large Japanese manufacturers have found another strategy; it is part collaboration, part purchasing from few suppliers, and part vertical integration. These manufacturers are often financial supporters of suppliers through ownership or loans. The supplier becomes part of a company coalition known as a *keiretsu*. Members of the *keiretsu* are assured long-term relationships and are therefore expected to collaborate as partners, providing technical expertise and stable quality production to the manufacturer. Members of the *keiretsu* can also have suppliers farther down the chain, making second- and even third-tier suppliers part of the coalition.

Keiretsu
A Japanese term that describes suppliers who become part of a company coalition.

Virtual Companies

The limitations to vertical integration are severe. Our technological society continually demands more specialization, which complicates vertical integration. Moreover, a firm that has a department or division of its own for everything may be too bureaucratic to be world class. So rather than letting vertical integration lock an organization into businesses that it may not understand or be able to manage, another approach is to find good flexible suppliers. **Virtual companies** rely on a variety of supplier relationships to provide services on demand. Virtual companies have fluid, moving organizational boundaries that allow them to create a unique enterprise to meet changing market demands. Suppliers may provide a variety of services that include doing the payroll, hiring personnel, designing products, providing consulting services, manufacturing components, conducting tests, or distributing products. The relationships may be short or long term and may include true partners, collaborators, or simply able suppliers and subcontractors. Whatever the formal relationship, the result can be exceptionally lean performance. The advantages of virtual companies include specialized management expertise, low capital investment, flexibility, and speed. The result is efficiency.

Virtual companies
Companies that rely on a variety of supplier relationships to provide services on demand. Also known as hollow corporations or network companies.

The apparel business provides a *traditional* example of virtual organizations. The designers of clothes seldom manufacture their designs; rather, they license the manufacture. The manufacturer may then rent space, lease sewing machines, and contract for labor. The result is an organization that has low overhead, remains flexible, and can respond rapidly to the market.

A *contemporary* example is exemplified by Vizio, Inc., a California-based producer of LCD TVs that has only 85 employees but huge sales. Vizio uses modules to assemble its own brand of TVs. Because the key components of TVs are now readily available and sold almost as commodities, innovative firms such as Vizio can specify the components, hire a contract manufacturer, and market the TVs with very little startup cost. In a virtual company, the supply chain is the company. Managing it is dynamic and demanding.

MANAGING THE SUPPLY CHAIN

AUTHOR COMMENT
Trust, agreed-upon goals, and compatible cultures make supply-chain management easier.

As managers move toward integration of the supply chain, substantial efficiencies are possible. The cycle of materials—as they flow from suppliers, to production, to warehousing, to distribution, to the customer—takes place among separate and often very independent organizations. Therefore, there are significant management issues that may result in serious inefficiencies.

VIDEO 11.3
Arnold Palmer Hospital's Supply
Chain

Success begins with mutual agreement on goals, followed by mutual trust, and continues with compatible organizational cultures.

Mutual Agreement on Goals   An integrated supply chain requires more than just agreement on the contractual terms of a buy/sell relationship. Partners in the chain must appreciate that the only entity that puts money into a supply chain is the end customer. Therefore, establishing a mutual understanding of the mission, strategy, and goals of participating organizations is essential. The integrated supply chain is about adding economic value and maximizing the total content of the product.

Trust   Trust is critical to an effective and efficient supply chain. Members of the chain must enter into a relationship that shares information. Visibility throughout the supply chain—what Darden Restaurants calls a transparent supply chain—is a requirement. Supplier relationships are more likely to be successful if risk and cost savings are shared—and activities such as end-customer research, sales analysis, forecasting, and production planning are joint activities. Such relationships are built on mutual trust.

Compatible Organizational Cultures   A positive relationship between the purchasing and supplying organizations that comes with compatible organizational cultures can be a real advantage when making a supply chain hum. A champion within one of the two firms promotes both formal and informal contacts, and those contacts contribute to the alignment of the organizational cultures, further strengthening the relationship.

The operations manager is dealing with a supply chain that is made up of independent specialists, each trying to satisfy its own customers at a profit. This leads to actions that may not optimize the entire chain. On the other hand, the supply chain is replete with opportunities to reduce waste and enhance value. We now look at some of the significant issues and opportunities.

Issues in an Integrated Supply Chain

LO3: Explain issues and opportunities in the supply chain

Three issues complicate development of an efficient, integrated supply chain: local optimization, incentives, and large lots.

Local Optimization   Members of the chain are inclined to focus on maximizing local profit or minimizing immediate cost based on their limited knowledge. Slight upturns in demand are overcompensated for because no one wants to be caught short. Similarly, slight downturns are overcompensated for because no one wants to be caught holding excess inventory. So fluctuations are magnified. For instance, a pasta distributor does not want to run out of pasta for its retail customers; the natural response to an extra large order from the retailer is to compensate with an even larger order to the manufacturer on the assumption that retail sales are picking up. Neither the distributor nor the manufacturer knows that the retailer had a major one-time promotion that moved a lot of pasta. This is exactly the issue that complicated the implementation of efficient distribution at the Italian pasta maker Barilla.

Incentives (Sales Incentives, Quantity Discounts, Quotas, and Promotions)   Incentives push merchandise into the chain for sales that have not occurred. This generates fluctuations that are ultimately expensive to all members of the chain.

Large Lots   There is often a bias toward large lots because large lots tend to reduce unit costs. A logistics manager wants to ship large lots, preferably in full trucks, and a production manager wants long production runs. Both actions drive down unit shipping and production costs, but fail to reflect actual sales and increased holding costs.

These three common occurrences—local optimization, incentives, and large lots—contribute to distortions of information about what is really occurring in the supply chain. A well-running supply system needs to be based on accurate information about how many products are truly being pulled through the chain. The inaccurate information is unintentional, but it results in distortions and fluctuations in the supply chain and causes what is known as the bullwhip effect.

Bullwhip effect
The increasing fluctuation in orders that often occurs as orders move through the supply chain.

The **bullwhip effect** occurs as orders are relayed from retailers, to distributors, to wholesalers, to manufacturers, with fluctuations increasing at each step in the sequence. The "bullwhip" fluctuations in the supply chain increase the costs associated with inventory, transportation, shipping, and receiving, while decreasing customer service and profitability. Procter & Gamble found that although the use of Pampers diapers was steady and the retail-store orders had little fluctuation, as orders moved through the supply chain, fluctuations increased. By the time orders were initiated for raw material, the variability was substantial. Similar behavior has been observed and documented at many companies, including Campbell Soup, Hewlett-Packard, and Applied Materials.

The bullwhip effect can occur when orders decrease as well as when they increase. A number of opportunities exist for reducing the bullwhip effect and improving opportunities in the supply chain. These are discussed in the following section.

Opportunities in an Integrated Supply Chain

Opportunities for effective management in the supply chain include the following 11 items.

Accurate "Pull" Data Accurate **pull data** are generated by sharing (1) point-of-sales (POS) information so that each member of the chain can schedule effectively and (2) computer-assisted ordering (CAO). This implies using POS systems that collect sales data and then adjusting that data for market factors, inventory on hand, and outstanding orders. Then a net order is sent directly to the supplier who is responsible for maintaining the finished-goods inventory.

Pull data

Accurate sales data that initiate transactions to "pull" product through the supply chain.

Lot Size Reduction Lot sizes are reduced through aggressive management. This may include (1) developing economical shipments of less than truckload lots; (2) providing discounts based on total annual volume rather than size of individual shipments; and (3) reducing the cost of ordering through techniques such as standing orders and various forms of electronic purchasing.

Single-Stage Control of Replenishment **Single-stage control of replenishment** means designating a member in the chain as responsible for monitoring and managing inventory in the supply chain based on the "pull" from the end user. This approach removes distorted information and multiple forecasts that create the bullwhip effect. Control may be in the hands of:

Single-stage control of replenishment

Fixing responsibility for monitoring and managing inventory for the retailer.

- A sophisticated retailer who understands demand patterns. Walmart does this for some of its inventory with radio frequency ID (RFID) tags as shown in the *OM in Action* box "Radio Frequency Tags: Keeping the Shelves Stocked."

OM in Action ▶ Radio Frequency Tags: Keeping the Shelves Stocked

Supply chains work smoothly when sales are steady, but often break down when confronted by a sudden surge or rapid drop in demand. Radio frequency ID (or RFID) tags can change that by providing real-time information about what's happening on store shelves. Here's how the system works for Procter & Gamble's (P&G's) Pampers.

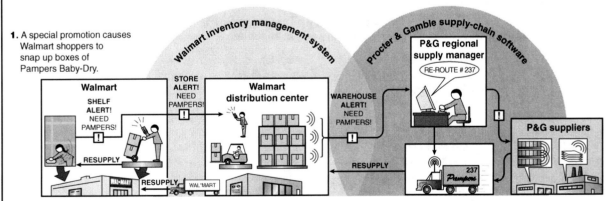

1. A special promotion causes Walmart shoppers to snap up boxes of Pampers Baby-Dry.

2. Each box of Pampers has an RFID tag. Shelf-mounted scanners alert the stockroom of urgent need for restock.

3. Walmart's inventory management system tracks and links its in-store stock and its warehouse stock, prompting quicker replenishment and providing accurate real-time data.

4. Walmart's systems are linked to the P&G supply-chain management system. Demand spikes reported by RFID tags are immediately visible throughout the supply chain.

5. P&G's logistics software tracks its trucks with GPS locators, and tracks their contents with RFID tag readers. Regional managers can reroute trucks to fill urgent needs.

6. P&G suppliers also use RFID tags and readers on their raw materials, giving P&G visibility several tiers down the supply chain, and giving suppliers the ability to accurately forecast demand and production.

Sources: *Financial Times* (August 22, 2008): 12; *Business 2.0* (May 2002): 86; and *Knight Ridder Tribune Business News* (August 6, 2006): 1.

- A distributor who manages the inventory for a particular distribution area. Distributors who handle grocery items, beer, and soft drinks may do this. Anheuser-Busch manages beer inventory and delivery for many of its customers.
- A manufacturer who has a well-managed forecasting, manufacturing, and distribution system. TAL Apparel Ltd., discussed in the *OM in Action* box, "The JCPenney Supply Chain for Dress Shirts," does this for JCPenney.

Vendor-managed inventory (VMI)

A system in which a supplier maintains material for the buyer, often delivering directly to the buyer's using department.

Vendor-Managed Inventory   Vendor-managed inventory (VMI) means the use of a local supplier (usually a distributor) to maintain inventory for the manufacturer or retailer. The supplier delivers directly to the purchaser's using department rather than to a receiving dock or stockroom. If the supplier can maintain the stock of inventory for a variety of customers who use the same product or whose differences are very minor (say, at the packaging stage), then there should be a net savings. These systems work without the immediate direction of the purchaser.

Collaborative planning, forecasting, and replenishment (CPFR)

A joint effort of members of a supply chain to share information in order to reduce supply-chain costs.

Collaborative Planning, Forecasting, and Replenishment (CPFR)   Like single-stage control and vendor-managed inventory, **CPFR** is another effort to manage inventory in the supply chain. With CPFR, members of the supply chain share planning, forecasting, and inventory information. Partners in a CPFR effort begin with collaboration on product definition and a joint marketing plan. Promotion, advertising, forecasts, and timing of shipments are all included in the plan in a concerted effort to drive down inventory and related costs.

Blanket order

A long-term purchase commitment to a supplier for items that are to be delivered against short-term releases to ship.

Blanket Orders   Blanket orders are unfilled orders with a vendor.[2] A **blanket order** is a contract to purchase certain items from a vendor. It is not an authorization to ship anything. Shipment is made only on receipt of an agreed-on document, perhaps a shipping requisition or shipment release.

Standardization   The purchasing department should make special efforts to increase levels of standardization. That is, rather than obtaining a variety of similar components with labeling, coloring, packaging, or perhaps even slightly different engineering specifications, the purchasing agent should try to have those components standardized.

Postponement

Delaying any modifications or customization to a product as long as possible in the production process.

Postponement   Postponement withholds any modification or customization to the product (keeping it generic) as long as possible. The concept is to minimize internal variety while maximizing external variety. For instance, after analyzing the supply chain for its printers, Hewlett-Packard (HP) determined that if the printer's power supply was moved out of the printer itself and into a power cord, HP could ship the basic printer anywhere in the world. HP modified the printer, its power cord, its packaging, and its documentation so that only the power cord and documentation needed to be added at the final distribution point. This modification allowed the

---

OM in Action ▶ The JCPenney Supply Chain for Dress Shirts

Purchase a white Stafford wrinkle-free dress shirt, size 17 neck, 34/35 sleeve at JCPenney at Atlanta's Northlake Mall on a Tuesday, and the supply chain responds. Within a day, TAL Apparel Ltd. in Hong Kong downloads a record of the sale. After a run through its forecasting model, TAL decides how many shirts to make and in what styles, colors, and sizes. By Wednesday afternoon, the replacement shirt is packed to be shipped directly to the JCPenney Northlake Mall store. The system bypasses the JCPenney warehouse—indeed all warehouses—as well as the JCPenney corporate decision makers.

In a second instance, two shirts are sold, leaving none in stock. TAL, after downloading the data, runs its forecasting model but comes to the decision that this store needs to have two in stock. Without consulting JCPenney, a TAL factory in Taiwan makes two new shirts. It sends one by ship, but because of the outage, the other goes by air.

As retailers deal with mass customization, fads, and seasonal swings they also strive to cut costs—making a responsive supply chain critical. Before globalization of the supply chain, JCPenney would have had thousands of shirts warehoused across the country. Now JCPenney stores, like those of many retailers, hold a very limited inventory of shirts.

JCPenney's supplier, TAL, is providing both sales forecasting and inventory management, a situation not acceptable to many retailers. But what is most startling is that TAL also places its own orders! A supply chain like this works only when there is trust between partners. The rapid changes in supply-chain management not only place increasing technical demands on suppliers but also increase demands for trust between the parties.

Sources: Apparel (April 2006): 14–18; The Wall Street Journal (September 11, 2003): A1, A9; and International Trade Forum (Issue 3, 2005): 12–13.

---

[2]Unfilled orders are also referred to as "open" orders, or "incomplete" orders.

firm to manufacture and hold centralized inventories of the generic printer for shipment as demand changed. Only the unique power system and documentation had to be held in each country. This understanding of the entire supply chain reduced both risk and investment in inventory.

Drop Shipping and Special Packaging   **Drop shipping** means the supplier will ship directly to the end consumer, rather than to the seller, saving both time and reshipping costs. Other cost-saving measures include the use of special packaging, labels, and optimal placement of labels and bar codes on containers. The final location down to the department and number of units in each shipping container can also be indicated. Substantial savings can be obtained through management techniques such as these. Some of these techniques can be of particular benefit to wholesalers and retailers by reducing shrinkage (lost, damaged, or stolen merchandise) and handling cost.

> **Drop shipping**
> Shipping directly from the supplier to the end consumer rather than from the seller, saving both time and reshipping costs.

For instance, Dell Computer has decided that its core competence is not in stocking peripherals, but in assembling PCs. So if you order a PC from Dell, with a printer and perhaps other components, the computer comes from Dell, but the printer and many of the other components will be drop shipped from the manufacturer.

Pass-through Facility   A **pass-through facility** is a distribution center where merchandise is held, but it functions less as a holding area and more as a shipping hub. These facilities, often run by logistics vendors, use the latest technology and automated systems to expedite orders. For instance, UPS works with Nike at such a facility in Louisville, Kentucky, to immediately handle orders. Similarly, FedEx's warehouse next to the airport in Memphis can receive an order after a store closes for the evening and can locate, package, and ship the merchandise that night. Delivery is guaranteed by 10 A.M. the next day.

> **Pass-through facility**
> Expedites shipment by holding merchandise and delivering from shipping hubs.

Channel Assembly   Channel assembly is an extension of the pass-through facility. **Channel assembly** sends individual components and modules, rather than finished products, to the distributor. The distributor then assembles, tests, and ships. Channel assembly treats distributors more as manufacturing partners than as distributors. This technique has proven successful in industries where products are undergoing rapid change, such as personal computers. With this strategy, finished-goods inventory is reduced because units are built to a shorter, more accurate forecast. Consequently, market response is better, with lower investment—a nice combination.

> **Channel assembly**
> Postpones final assembly of a product so the distribution channel can assemble it.

E-PROCUREMENT

E-procurement uses the Internet to facilitate purchasing. E-procurement speeds purchasing, reduces costs, and integrates the supply chain, enhancing an organization's competitive advantage. The traditional supply chain is full of paper transactions, such as requisitions, requests for bids, bid evaluations, purchase orders, order releases, receiving documents, invoices, and the issuance of checks. E-procurement reduces this barrage of paperwork and at the same time provides purchasing personnel with an extensive database of vendor, delivery, and quality data. With this history, vendor selection has improved.

> **AUTHOR COMMENT**
> The Internet has revolutionized procurement.

> **E-procurement**
> Purchasing facilitated through the Internet.

In this section, we discuss traditional techniques of electronic ordering and funds transfer and then move on to online catalogs, auctions, RFQs, and real-time inventory tracking.

Electronic Ordering and Funds Transfer   Electronic ordering and bank transfers are traditional approaches to speeding transactions and reducing paperwork. Transactions between firms often use **electronic data interchange (EDI)**, which is a standardized data-transmittal format for computerized communications between organizations. EDI provides data transfer for virtually any business application, including purchasing. Under EDI, data for a purchase order, such as order date, due date, quantity, part number, purchase order number, address, and so forth, are fitted into the standard EDI format. EDI also provides for the use of **advanced shipping notice (ASN)**, which notifies the purchaser that the vendor is ready to ship. Although some firms are still moving to EDI and ASN, the Internet's ease of use and lower cost is proving more popular.

> **Electronic data interchange (EDI)**
> A standardized data-transmittal format for computerized communications between organizations.

> **Advanced shipping notice (ASN)**
> A shipping notice delivered directly from vendor to purchaser.

Online Catalogs

Purchase of standard items is often accomplished via online catalogs. Such catalogs provide current information about products in electronic form. Online catalogs support cost comparisons and incorporate voice and video clips, making the process efficient for both buyers and sellers. Online catalogs are available in three versions:

1. Typical of *catalogs provided by vendors* are those of W. W. Grainger and Office Depot. W. W. Grainger is probably the world's largest seller of MRO items (items for maintenance, repair, and operations), while Office Depot provides the same service for office supplies.
2. *Catalogs provided by intermediaries* are Internet sites where business buyers and sellers can meet. These intermediaries typically create industry specific catalogs with content from many suppliers.
3. One of the first online *exchanges provided by buyers* was Avendra (**www.avendra.com**). Avendra was created by Marriott and Hyatt (and subsequently joined by other large hotel firms) to economically purchase the huge range of goods needed by the 2,800 hotels now in the exchange.

Such exchanges—and there are many—move companies from a multitude of individual phone calls, faxes, and e-mails to a centralized online system, and drive billions of dollars of waste out of the supply chain.

Auctions

Online auction sites can be maintained by sellers, buyers, or intermediaries. Operations managers find online auctions a fertile area for disposing of excess raw material and discontinued or excess inventory. Online auctions lower entry barriers, encouraging sellers to join and simultaneously increase the potential number of buyers.

The key for auction firms, such as Ariba of Sunnyvale, California (see the photo), is to find and build a huge base of potential bidders, improve client buying procedures, and qualify new suppliers.

RFQs

When purchasing requirements are nonstandard, time spent preparing requests for quotes (RFQs) and the related bid package can be substantial. Consequently, e-procurement has now moved these often expensive parts of the purchasing process online, allowing purchasing agents to inexpensively attach electronic copies of the necessary drawings to RFQs.

Real-Time Inventory Tracking

FedEx's pioneering efforts at tracking packages from pickup to delivery has shown the way for operations managers to do the same for their shipments and inventory. Because tracking cars and trucks has been a chronic and embarrassingly inexact science, Ford has hired UPS to track millions of vehicles as they move from factory to dealers. Using bar codes and the Internet, Ford dealers are now able to log onto a Web site and find out exactly where the ordered vehicles are in the distribution system. As operations managers move to an era of mass customization, with customers ordering exactly the cars they want, customers will expect to know where their cars are and

Here an Ariba team monitors an online market from the firm's Global Market Operations Center. Ariba provides support for the entire global sourcing process, including software, supplier development, competitive negotiations, and savings implementation. Online bidding leads to greater cost savings than more traditional procurement.

exactly when they can be picked up. E-procurement, supported by bar codes and RFID, can provide economical inventory tracking on the shop floor, in warehouses, and in logistics.

VENDOR SELECTION

LO4: Describe the steps in vendor selection

For those goods and services a firm buys, vendors must be selected. Vendor selection considers numerous factors, such as strategic fit, vendor competence, delivery, and quality performance. Because a firm may have some competence in all areas and may have exceptional competence in only a few, selection can be challenging. Procurement policies also need to be established. Those might address issues such as percent of business done with any one supplier or with minority businesses. We now examine vendor selection as a three-stage process: (1) vendor evaluation, (2) vendor development, and (3) negotiations.

Vendor Evaluation

The first stage of vendor selection, *vendor evaluation*, involves finding potential vendors and determining the likelihood of their becoming good suppliers. This phase requires the development of evaluation criteria such as criteria shown in Example 2. However, both the criteria and the weights selected vary depending on the supply-chain strategy being implemented. (Refer to Table 11.1, on page 453.)

◄ **EXAMPLE 2**

Weighted approach to vendor evaluation

Erin Davis, president of Creative Toys in Palo Alto, is interested in evaluating suppliers who will work with him to make nontoxic, environmentally friendly paints and dyes for his line of children's toys. This is a critical strategic element of his supply chain, and he desires a firm that will contribute to his product.

APPROACH ▶ Erin begins his analysis of one potential supplier, Faber Paint and Dye, by using the weighted approach to vendor evaluation.

SOLUTION ▶ Erin first reviews the supplier differentiation attributes in Table 11.1 and develops the following list of selection criteria. He then assigns the weights shown to help him perform an objective review of potential vendors. His staff assigns the scores shown and computes the total weighted score.

Criteria	Weights	Scores (1–5) (5 highest)	Weight × Score
Engineering/research/innovation skills	.20	5	1.0
Production process capability (flexibility/technical assistance)	.15	4	.6
Distribution/delivery capability	.05	4	.2
Quality systems and performance	.10	2	.2
Facilities/location	.05	2	.1
Financial and managerial strength (stability and cost structure)	.15	4	.6
Information systems capability (e-procurement, ERP)	.10	2	.2
Integrity (environmental compliance/ethics)	.20	5	1.0
	1.00		3.9 Total

Faber Paint and Dye receives an overall score of 3.9.

INSIGHT ▶ Erin now has a basis for comparison with other potential vendors, selecting the one with the highest overall rating.

LEARNING EXERCISE ▶ If Erin believes that the weight for "engineering/research/innovation skills" should be increased to .25 and the weight for "financial and managerial strength" reduced to .10, what is the new score? [Answer: Faber Paint and Dye now goes to 3.95.]

RELATED PROBLEMS ▶ 11.2, 11.3, 11.4

The selection of competent suppliers is critical. If good suppliers are not selected, then all other supply-chain efforts are wasted. As firms move toward using fewer longer-term suppliers, the issues of financial strength, quality, management, research, technical ability, and potential for a close long-term relationship play an increasingly important role. These attributes should be noted in the evaluation process.

Vendor Development

The second stage of vendor selection is *vendor development*. Assuming that a firm wants to proceed with a particular vendor, how does it integrate this supplier into its system? The buyer makes sure the vendor has an appreciation of quality requirements, product specifications, schedules and delivery, the purchaser's payment system, and procurement policies. *Vendor development* may include everything from training, to engineering and production help, to procedures for information transfer.

Negotiations

Negotiation strategies
Approaches taken by supply chain personnel to develop contractual relationships with suppliers.

Regardless of the supply chain strategy adopted, negotiations regarding the critical elements of the contractual relationship must take place. These negotiations often focus on quality, delivery, payment, and cost. We will look at three classic types of **negotiation strategies**: the cost-based model, the market-based price model, and competitive bidding.

Cost-Based Price Model The *cost-based price model* requires that the supplier open its books to the purchaser. The contract price is then based on time and materials or on a fixed cost with an escalation clause to accommodate changes in the vendor's labor and materials cost.

Market-Based Price Model In the market-based price model, price is based on a published, auction, or index price. Many commodities (agriculture products, paper, metal, etc.) are priced this way. Paperboard prices, for instance, are available via the *Official Board Markets* weekly publication (**www.advanstar.com**). Nonferrous metal prices are quoted in *Platt's Metals Week* (**www.platts.com/plattsmetals/**), and prices of other metals are quoted at **www.metalworld.com**.

Competitive Bidding When suppliers are not willing to discuss costs or where near-perfect markets do not exist, competitive bidding is often appropriate. Infrequent work (such as construction, tooling, and dies) is usually purchased based on a bid. Bidding may take place via mail, fax, or an Internet auction. Competitive bidding is the typical policy in many firms for the majority of their purchases. Bidding policies usually require that the purchasing agent have several potential suppliers of the product (or its equivalent) and quotations from each. The major disadvantage of this method, as mentioned earlier, is that the development of long-term relations between buyer and seller is hindered. Competitive bidding may effectively determine initial cost. However, it may also make difficult the communication and performance that are vital for engineering changes, quality, and delivery.

Yet a fourth approach is *to combine one or more* of the preceding negotiation techniques. The supplier and purchaser may agree on review of certain cost data, accept some form of market data for raw material costs, or agree that the supplier will "remain competitive." In any case, a good supplier relationship is one in which both partners have established a degree of mutual trust and a belief in each other's competence, honesty, and fair dealing.

> **AUTHOR COMMENT**
> Time, cost, and reliability variables make logistic decisions demanding.

LOGISTICS MANAGEMENT

Logistics management
An approach that seeks efficiency of operations through the integration of all material acquisition, movement, and storage activities.

Procurement activities may be combined with various shipping, warehousing, and inventory activities to form a logistics system. The purpose of **logistics management** is to obtain efficiency of operations through the integration of all material acquisition, movement, and storage activities. When transportation and inventory costs are substantial on both the input and output sides of the production process, an emphasis on logistics may be appropriate. When logistics issues are significant or expensive, many firms opt for outsourcing the logistics function. Logistics specialists can often bring expertise not available in-house. For instance, logistics companies often have tracking technology that reduces transportation losses and supports delivery schedules that adhere to precise delivery windows. The potential for competitive advantage is found via both reduced costs and improved customer service.

Firms recognize that the distribution of goods to and from their facilities can represent as much as 25% of the cost of products. In addition, the total distribution cost in the U.S. is over 10% of the gross national product (GNP). Because of this high cost, firms constantly evaluate their means of distribution. Five major means of distribution are trucking, railroads, airfreight, waterways, and pipelines.

Distribution Systems

Trucking   The vast majority of manufactured goods moves by truck. The flexibility of shipping by truck is only one of its many advantages. Companies that have adopted JIT programs in recent years have put increased pressure on truckers to pick up and deliver on time, with no damage, with paperwork in order, and at low cost. Trucking firms are using computers to monitor weather, find the most effective route, reduce fuel cost, and analyze the most efficient way to unload. In spite of these advances, the motor carrier industry averages a capacity utilization of only 50%. That under-utilized space costs the U.S. economy over $31 billion per year. To improve logistics efficiency, the industry is establishing Web sites such as Schneider National's connection (**www.schneider.com**), which lets shippers and truckers find each other to use some of this idle capacity. Shippers may pick from thousands of approved North American carriers that have registered with Schneider logistics.

Railroads   Railroads in the U.S. employ 187,000 people and ship 90% of all coal, 67% of autos, 68% of paper products, and about half of all food, lumber, and chemicals. Containerization has made intermodal shipping of truck trailers on railroad flat cars, often piggybacked as double-deckers, a popular means of distribution. More than 36 million trailer loads are moved in the U.S. each year by rail. With the growth of JIT, however, rail transport has been the biggest loser because small-batch manufacture requires frequent, smaller shipments that are likely to move via truck or air.

LO5: Explain major issues in logistics management

Airfreight   Airfreight represents only about 1% of tonnage shipped in the U.S. However, the recent proliferation of airfreight carriers such as FedEx, UPS, and DHL makes it the fastest-growing mode of shipping. Clearly, for national and international movement of lightweight items, such as medical and emergency supplies, flowers, fruits, and electronic components, air-freight offers speed and reliability.

Waterways   Waterways are one of the nation's oldest means of freight transportation, dating back to construction of the Erie Canal in 1817. Included in U.S. waterways are the nation's rivers, canals, the Great Lakes, coastlines, and oceans connecting to other countries. The usual cargo on waterways is bulky, low-value cargo such as iron ore, grains, cement, coal, chemicals, limestone, and petroleum products. Internationally, millions of containers are shipped at very low cost via huge oceangoing ships each year. Water transportation is important when shipping cost is more important than speed.

Pipelines   Pipelines are an important form of transporting crude oil, natural gas, and other petroleum and chemical products. An amazing 90% of the state of Alaska's budget is derived from the 1.5 million barrels of oil pumped daily through the pipeline at Prudhoe Bay.

Third-Party Logistics

Supply-chain managers may find that outsourcing logistics is advantageous in driving down inventory investment and costs while improving delivery reliability and speed. Specialized logistics firms support this goal by coordinating the supplier's inventory system with the service

As this photo of the port of Charleston suggests, with 16 million containers entering the U.S. annually, tracking location, content, and condition of trucks and containers is a challenge. But new technology may improve both security and JIT shipments.

Seven farms within a 2-hour drive of Kenya's Nairobi Airport supply 300 tons of fresh beans, bok choy, okra, and other produce that is packaged at the airport and shipped overnight to Europe. The time between harvest and arrival in Europe is 2 days. When a good supply chain and good logistics work together, the results can be startling—and fresh food.

capabilities of the delivery firm. FedEx, for example, has a successful history of using the Internet for online tracking. At **FedEx.com**, a customer can compute shipping costs, print labels, adjust invoices, and track package status all on the same Web site. FedEx, UPS, and DHL play a core role in other firms' logistics processes. In some cases, they even run the server for retailer Web sites. In other cases, such as for Dell Computer, FedEx operates warehouses that pick, pack, test, and assemble products, then it handles delivery and customs clearance when necessary. The *OM in Action* box "DHL's Role in the Supply Chain" provides another example of how outsourcing logistics can reduce costs while shrinking inventory and delivery times.

Cost of Shipping Alternatives

The longer a product is in transit, the longer the firm has its money invested. But faster shipping is usually more expensive than slow shipping. A simple way to obtain some insight into this trade-off is to evaluate holding cost against shipping options. We do this in Example 3.

OM in Action ▶ DHL's Role in the Supply Chain

It's the dead of night at DHL International's air express hub in Brussels, yet the massive building is alive with busy forklifts and sorting workers. The boxes going on and off the DHL plane range from Dell computers and Cisco routers to Caterpillar mufflers and Komatsu hydraulic pumps. Sun Microsystems computers from California are earmarked for Finland; DVDs from Teac's plant in Malaysia are destined for Bulgaria.

The door-to-door movement of time-sensitive packages is key to the global supply chain. JIT, short product life cycles, mass customization, and reduced inventories depend on logistics firms such as DHL, FedEx, and UPS. These powerhouses are in continuous motion.

With a decentralized network covering 225 countries and territories (more than are in the UN), DHL is a true multinational. The Brussels headquarters has only 450

of the company's 124,000 employees but includes 26 nationalities.

DHL has assembled an extensive global network of express logistics centers for strategic goods. In its Brussels logistics center, for instance, DHL upgrades, repairs, and configures Fijitsu computers, InFocus projectors, and Johnson & Johnson medical equipment. It stores and provides parts for EMC and Hewlett-Packard and replaces Nokia and Philips phones. "If something breaks down on a Thursday at 4 o'clock, the relevant warehouse knows at 4:05, and the part is on a DHL plane at 7 or 8 that evening," says Robert Kuijpers, DHL International's CEO.

Sources: Journal of Commerce (August 15, 2005): 1; *Hoover's Company Records* (May 1, 2009): 40126; and *Forbes* (October 18, 1999): 120–124.

◀ **EXAMPLE 3**

Determining daily cost of holding

A shipment of new connectors for semiconductors needs to go from San Jose to Singapore for assembly. The value of the connectors is $1,750 and holding cost is 40% per year. One airfreight carrier can ship the connectors 1 day faster than its competitor, at an extra cost of $20.00. Which carrier should be selected?

APPROACH ▶ First we determine the daily holding cost and then compare the daily holding cost with the cost of faster shipment.

SOLUTION ▶ Daily cost of holding the product = (Annual holding cost × Product value)/365

$$= (.40 \times \$1,750)/365$$

$$= \$1.92$$

Since the cost of saving one day is $20.00, which is much more than the daily holding cost of $1.92, we decide on the less costly of the carriers and take the extra day to make the shipment. This saves $18.08 ($20.00 − $1.92).

INSIGHT ▶ The solution becomes radically different if the 1-day delay in getting the connectors to Singapore delays delivery (making a customer angry) or delays payment of a $150,000 final product. (Even 1 day's interest on $150,000 or an angry customer makes a savings of $18.08 insignificant.)

LEARNING EXERCISE ▶ If the holding cost is 100% per year, what is the decision? [Answer: Even with a holding cost of $4.79 per day, the less costly carrier is selected.]

RELATED PROBLEMS ▶ 11.8, 11.9, 11.10

Example 3 looks only at holding costs versus shipping cost. For the operations or logistics manager there are many other considerations, including coordinating shipments to maintain a schedule, getting a new product to market, and keeping a customer happy. Estimates of these other costs can be added to the estimate of daily holding cost. Determining the impact and cost of these many other considerations makes the evaluation of shipping alternatives interesting.

Security and JIT

There is probably no society more open than the U.S. This includes its borders and ports—but they are swamped. About 7 million containers enter U.S. ports each year, along with thousands of planes, cars, and trucks each day. Even under the best of conditions, some 5% of the container movements are misrouted, stolen, damaged, or excessively delayed.

Since the September 11, 2001, terrorist attacks, supply chains have become more complex. Technological innovations, though, in the supply chain are improving security and JIT, making logistics more reliable. Technology is now capable of knowing truck and container location, content, and condition. New devices can detect whether someone has broken into a sealed container

Speed and accuracy in the supply chain are supported by bar-code tracking of shipments. At each step of a journey, from initial pickup to final destination, bar codes (left) are read and stored. Within seconds, this tracking information is available online to customers worldwide (right).

and can communicate that information to the shipper or receiver via satellite or radio. Motion detectors can also be installed inside containers. Other sensors can record interior data including temperature, shock, radioactivity, and whether a container is moving. Tracking lost containers, identifying delays, or just reminding individuals in the supply chain that a shipment is on its way will help expedite shipments. Improvements in security may aid JIT, and improvements in JIT may aid security—both of which can improve supply-chain logistics.

> **AUTHOR COMMENT**
> If you can't measure it, you can't control it.

MEASURING SUPPLY-CHAIN PERFORMANCE

Like all other managers, supply-chain managers require standards (or *metrics*, as they are often called) to evaluate performance. Evaluation of the supply chain is particularly critical for these managers because they spend most of the organization's money. In addition, they make scheduling and quantity decisions that determine the assets committed to inventory. Only with effective metrics can managers determine: (1) how well the *supply chain is performing* and (2) *the assets committed to inventory*. We will now discuss these two metrics.

LO6: Compute the percentage of assets committed to inventory and inventory turnover

Supply-Chain Performance   The benchmark metrics shown in Table 11.5 focus on procurement and vendor performance issues. World-class benchmarks are the result of well-managed supply chains that drive down costs, lead times, late deliveries, and shortages while improving quality.

Assets Committed to Inventory   Three specific measures can be helpful here. The first is the amount of money invested in inventory, usually expressed as a percentage of assets, as shown in Equation (11-1) and Example 4:

$$\text{Percentage invested in inventory} = (\text{Total inventory investment}/\text{Total assets}) \times 100 \quad \text{(11-1)}$$

EXAMPLE 4 ▶

Tracking Home Depot's inventory investment

Home Depot's management wishes to track its investment in inventory as one of its performance measures. Home Depot had $11.4 billion invested in inventory and total assets of $44.4 billion in 2006.

APPROACH ▶   Determine the investment in inventory and total assets and then use Equation (11-1).

SOLUTION ▶   Percent invested in inventory = $(11.4/44.4) \times 100 = 25.7\%$

INSIGHT ▶   Over one-fourth of Home Depot assets are committed to inventory.

LEARNING EXERCISE ▶   If Home Depot can drive its investment down to 20% of assets, how much money will it free up for other uses? [Answer: $11.4 - (44.4 \times .2) = \$2.52$ billion.]

RELATED PROBLEMS ▶   11.11b, 11.12b

Specific comparisons with competitors may assist evaluation. Total assets committed to inventory in manufacturing approach 15%, in wholesale 34%, and retail 27%—with wide variations, depending on the specific business model, the business cycle, and management (see Table 11.6).

The second common measure of supply chain performance is *inventory turnover* (see Table 11.7). Its reciprocal, *weeks of supply,* is the third. **Inventory turnover** is computed on an annual basis, using Equation (11-2):

Inventory turnover
Cost of goods sold divided by average inventory.

$$\text{Inventory turnover} = \text{Cost of goods sold}/\text{Inventory investment} \quad \text{(11-2)}$$

Cost of goods sold is the cost to produce the goods or services sold for a given period. Inventory investment is the average inventory value for the same period. This may be the average of several periods of inventory or beginning and ending inventory added together and divided by 2.

▶**TABLE 11.5**
Metrics for Supply-Chain Performance

	Typical Firms	**Benchmark Firms**
Lead time (weeks)	15	8
Time spent placing an order	42 minutes	15 minutes
Percent of late deliveries	33%	2%
Percent of rejected material	1.5%	.0001%
Number of shortages per year	400	4

Source: Adapted from a McKinsey & Company report.

▼ **TABLE 11.6**
Inventory as Percentage of Total Assets (with examples of exceptional performance)

Manufacturer	15%
(Toyota 5%)	
Wholesale	34%
(Coca-Cola 2.9%)	
Restaurants	2.9%
(McDonald's .05%)	
Retail	27%
(Home Depot 25.7%)	

▼ **TABLE 11.7**
Examples of Annual Inventory Turnover

Food, Beverage, Retail	
Anheuser Busch	15
Coca-Cola	14
Home Depot	5
McDonald's	112
Manufacturing	
Dell Computer	90
Johnson Controls	22
Toyota (overall)	13
Nissan (assembly)	150

Often, average inventory investment is based on nothing more than the inventory investment at the end of the period—typically at year-end.[3]

In Example 5, we look at inventory turnover applied to PepsiCo.

◄ **EXAMPLE 5**

Inventory turnover at PepsiCo, Inc.

PepsiCo, Inc., manufacturer and distributor of drinks, Frito-Lay, and Quaker Foods, provides the following in its 2005 annual report (shown here in $ billions). Determine PepsiCo's turnover.

Net revenue		$32.5
Cost of goods sold		$14.2
Inventory:		
Raw material inventory	$.74	
Work-in-process inventory	$.11	
Finished goods inventory	$.84	
Total inventory investment		$1.69

APPROACH ▶ Use the inventory turnover computation in Equation (11-2) to measure inventory performance. Cost of goods sold is $14.2 billion. Total inventory is the sum of raw material at $.74 billion, work-in-process at $.11 billion, and finished goods at $.84 billion, for total inventory investment of $1.69 billion.

SOLUTION ▶ Inventory Turnover = Cost of goods sold/Inventory investment

$$= 14.2/1.69$$

$$= 8.4$$

INSIGHT ▶ We now have a standard, popular measure by which to evaluate performance.

LEARNING EXERCISE ▶ If Coca-Cola's cost of goods sold is $10.8 billion and inventory investment is $.76 billion, what is its inventory turnover? [Answer: 14.2.]

RELATED PROBLEMS ▶ 11.11a, 11.12c, 11.13

Weeks of supply, as shown in Example 6, may have more meaning in the wholesale and retail portions of the service sector than in manufacturing. It is computed below as the reciprocal of inventory turnover:

Weeks of supply = Inventory investment/(Annual cost of goods sold/52 weeks) (11-3)

---

[3]Inventory quantities often fluctuate wildly, and various types of inventory exist (e.g., raw material, work-in-process, finished goods, and maintenance, repair, and operating supplies [MRO]). Therefore, care must be taken when using inventory values; they may reflect more than just supply-chain performance.

EXAMPLE 6 ▶

Determining weeks of supply at PepsiCo

Using the PepsiCo data in Example 5, management wants to know the weeks of supply.

APPROACH ▶   We know that inventory investment is $1.69 billion and that weekly sales equal annual cost of goods sold ($14.2 billion) divided by 52 = $14.2/52 = $.273 billion.

SOLUTION ▶   Using Equation (11-3), we compute weeks of supply as:

$$\text{Weeks of supply} = (\text{Inventory investment}/\text{Average weekly cost of goods sold})$$

$$= 1.69/.273 = 6.19 \text{ weeks}$$

INSIGHT ▶   We now have a standard measurement by which to evaluate a company's continuing performance or by which to compare companies.

LEARNING EXERCISE ▶   If Coca-Cola's average inventory investment is $.76 billion and its average weekly cost of goods sold is $.207 billion, what is the firm's weeks of supply? [Answer: 3.67 weeks.]

RELATED PROBLEMS ▶   11.12a, 11.14

Supply-chain management is critical in driving down inventory investment. The rapid movement of goods is key. Walmart, for example, has set the pace in the retailing sector with its world-renowned supply-chain management. By doing so, it has established a competitive advantage. With its own truck fleet, distribution centers, and a state-of-the-art communication system, Walmart (with the help of its suppliers) replenishes store shelves an average of twice per week. Competitors resupply every other week. Economical and speedy resupply means both rapid response to product changes and customer preferences, as well as lower inventory investment. Similarly, while many manufacturers struggle to move inventory turnover up to 10 times per year, Dell Computer has inventory turns exceeding 90 and supply measured in *days*—not weeks. Supply-chain management provides a competitive advantage when firms effectively respond to the demands of global markets and global sources.

The SCOR Model

Supply-Chain Operations Reference (SCOR) model

A set of processes, metrics, and best practices developed by the Supply-Chain Council.

In addition to the metrics presented above, the Supply-Chain Council (SCC) has developed 200 process elements, 550 metrics, and 500 best practices. The SCC (www.supply-chain.org) is a 900-member not-for-profit association for the improvement of supply-chain effectiveness. The council has developed the five-part **Supply-Chain Operations Reference (SCOR) model.** The five parts are Plan, Source, Make, Deliver, and Return, as shown in Figure 11.3.

The council believes the model provides a structure for its processes, metrics, and best practices to be (1) implemented for competitive advantage; (2) defined and communicated precisely; (3) measured, managed, and controlled; and (4) fine-tuned as necessary to a specific application.

▶ **FIGURE 11.3**
The Supply-Chain Operations Reference (SCOR) Model

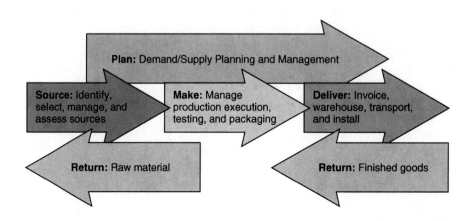

Plan: Demand/Supply Planning and Management

Source: Identify, select, manage, and assess sources

Make: Manage production execution, testing, and packaging

Deliver: Invoice, warehouse, transport, and install

Return: Raw material

Return: Finished goods

CHAPTER SUMMARY

Competition is no longer between companies but between supply chains. For many firms, the supply chain determines a substantial portion of product cost and quality, as well as opportunities for responsiveness and differentiation. Six supply-chain strategies have been identified: (1) many suppliers, (2) few suppliers, (3) vertical integration, (4) joint ventures, (5) *keiretsu* networks, and (6) virtual companies. Skillful supply-chain management provides a great strategic opportunity for competitive advantage.

Key Terms

Supply-chain management (p. 452)
Make-or-buy decision (p. 457)
Outsourcing (p. 457)
Vertical integration (p. 458)
Keiretsu (p. 459)
Virtual companies (p. 459)
Bullwhip effect (p. 460)
Pull data (p. 461)
Single-stage control of replenishment (p. 461)

Vendor-managed inventory (VMI) (p. 462)
Collaborative planning, forecasting, and replenishment (CPFR) (p. 462)
Blanket order (p. 462)
Postponement (p. 462)
Drop shipping (p. 463)
Pass-through facility (p. 463)
Channel assembly (p. 463)
E-procurement (p. 463)

Electronic data interchange (EDI) (p. 463)
Advanced shipping notice (ASN) (p. 463)
Negotiation strategies (p. 466)
Logistics management (p. 466)
Inventory turnover (p. 470)
Supply-Chain Operations Reference (SCOR) model (p. 472)

Ethical Dilemma

For generations, the policy of Sears Roebuck and Company, the granddaddy of retailers, was not to purchase more than 50% of any of its suppliers' output. The rationale of this policy was that it allowed Sears to move to other suppliers, as the market dictated, without destroying the supplier's ability to stay in business. In contrast, Walmart purchases more and more of a supplier's output. Eventually, Walmart can be expected to sit down with that supplier and explain why the supplier no longer needs a sales force and that the supplier should eliminate the sales force, passing the cost savings on to Walmart.

Sears is losing market share, has been acquired by K-Mart, and is eliminating jobs; Walmart is gaining market share and hiring. What are the ethical issues involved, and which firm has a more ethical position?

Discussion Questions

1. Define *supply-chain management*.
2. What are the objectives of supply-chain management?
3. What is the objective of logistics management?
4. How do we distinguish between the types of risk in the supply chain?
5. What is vertical integration? Give examples of backward and forward integration.
6. What are three basic approaches to negotiations?
7. How does a traditional adversarial relationship with suppliers change when a firm makes a decision to move to a few suppliers?
8. What is the difference between postponement and channel assembly?
9. What is CPFR?
10. What is the value of online auctions in e-commerce?
11. Explain how FedEx uses the Internet to meet requirements for quick and accurate delivery.
12. How does Walmart use drop shipping?
13. What are blanket orders? How do they differ from invoiceless purchasing?
14. What can purchasing do to implement just-in-time deliveries?
15. What is e-procurement?
16. How does Darden Restaurants, described in the *Global Company Profile*, find competitive advantage in its supply chain?
17. What is SCOR, and what purpose does it serve?

Solved Problems   Virtual Office Hours help is available at www.pearsonglobaleditions.com/myomlab

▼ SOLVED PROBLEM 11.1

Jack's Pottery Outlet has total end-of-year assets of $5 million. The first-of-the-year inventory was $375,000, with a year-end inventory of $325,000. The annual cost of goods sold was $7 million. The owner, Eric Jack, wants to evaluate his supply chain performance by measuring his percent of assets in inventory, his inventory turnover, and his weeks of supply. We use Equations (11-1), (11-2), and (11-3) to provide these measures.

▼ SOLUTION

First, determine *average inventory*:

$$(\$375,000 + \$325,000)/2 = \$350,000$$

Then, use Equation (11-1) to determine percent invested in inventory:

$$\text{Percent invested in inventory} = (\text{Total inventory investment}/\text{Total assets}) \times 100$$
$$= (350,000/5,000,000) \times 100$$
$$= 7\%$$

Third, determine inventory turnover, using Equation (11-2):

$$\text{Inventory turnover} = \text{Cost of goods sold}/\text{Inventory investment}$$
$$= 7,000,000/350,000$$
$$= 20$$

Finally, to determine weeks of inventory, use Equation (11-3), adjusted to weeks:

$$\text{Weeks of inventory} = \text{Inventory investment}/\text{Weekly cost of goods sold}$$
$$= 350,000/(7,000,000/52)$$
$$= 350,000/134,615$$
$$= 2.6$$

We conclude that Jack's Pottery Outlet has 7% of its assets invested in inventory, that the inventory turnover is 20, and that weeks of supply is 2.6.

Problems

•• **11.1** Choose a local establishment that is a member of a relatively large chain. From interviews with workers and information from the Internet, identify the elements of the supply chain. Determine whether the supply chain represents a low-cost, rapid response, or differentiation strategy (refer to Chapter 2). Are the supply-chain characteristics significantly different from one product to another?

•• **11.2** As purchasing agent for Woolsey Enterprises in Golden, Colorado, you ask your buyer to provide you with a ranking of "excellent," "good," "fair," or "poor" for a variety of characteristics for two potential vendors. You suggest that "Products" total be weighted 40% and the other three categories' totals be weighted 20% each. The buyer has returned the following ranking:

VENDOR RATING

Company	Excellent (4)	Good (3)	Fair (2)	Poor (1)
Financial Strength			K	D
Manufacturing Range			KD	
Research Facilities	K		D	
Geographical Locations		K	D	
Management		K	D	
Labor Relations			K	D
Trade Relations			KD	

Service	Excellent (4)	Good (3)	Fair (2)	Poor (1)
Deliveries on Time		KD		
Handling of Problems		KD		
Technical Assistance		K	D	

Products	Excellent (4)	Good (3)	Fair (2)	Poor (1)
Quality	KD			
Price			KD	
Packaging			KD	

Sales	Excellent (4)	Good (3)	Fair (2)	Poor (1)
Product Knowledge			D	K
Sales Calls			K	D
Sales Service			K	D

DONNA INC. = D
KAY CORP. = K

Which of the two vendors would you select?

•• **11.3** Using the data in Problem 11.2, assume that both Donna, Inc. and Kay Corp. are able to move all their "poor" ratings to "fair." How would you then rank the two firms?

•• **11.4** Develop a vendor-rating form that represents your comparison of the education offered by universities in which you considered (or are considering) enrolling. Fill in the necessary data, and identify the "best" choice. Are you attending that "best" choice? If not, why not?

•• **11.5** Using sources from the Internet, identify some of the problems faced by a company of your choosing as it moves toward, or operates as, a virtual organization. Does its operating as a virtual organization simply exacerbate old problems, or does it create new ones?

• **11.6** Using Table 11.4, determine the sales necessary to equal a dollar of savings on purchases for a company that has:
a) A net profit of 4% and spends 40% of its revenue on purchases.
b) A net profit of 6% and spends 80% of its revenue on purchases.

• **11.7** Using Table 11.4, determine the sales necessary to equal a dollar of savings on purchases for a company that has:
a) A net profit of 6% and spends 60% of its revenue on purchases.
b) A net profit of 8% and spends 80% of its revenue on purchases.

•• **11.8** Your options for shipping $100,000 of machine parts from Baltimore to Kuala Lumpur, Malaysia, are (1) use a ship that will take 30 days at a cost of $3,800, or (2) truck the parts to Los Angeles and then ship at a total cost of $4,800. The second option will take only 20 days. You are paid via a letter of credit the day the parts arrive. Your holding cost is estimated at 30% of the value per year.

a) Which option is more economical?
b) What customer issues are not included in the data presented?

•• **11.9** If you have a third option for the data in Problem 11.8, and it costs only $4,000 and also takes 20 days, what is your most economical plan?

•• **11.10** Monczka-Trent Shipping is the logistics vendor for Handfield Manufacturing Co. in Ohio. Handfield has daily shipments of a power-steering pump from its Ohio plant to an auto assembly line in Alabama. The value of the standard shipment is $250,000. Monczka-Trent has two options: (1) its standard 2-day shipment or (2) a subcontractor who will team drive overnight with an effective delivery of 1 day. The extra driver costs $175. Handfield's holding cost is 35% annually for this kind of inventory.
a) Which option is more economical?
b) What production issues are not included in the data presented?

•• **11.11** Baker Mfg Inc. (see Table 11.8) wishes to compare its inventory turnover to those of industry leaders, who have turnover of about 13 times per year and 8% of their assets invested in inventory.
a) What is Baker's inventory turnover?
b) What is Baker's percent of assets committed to inventory?
c) How does Baker's performance compare to the industry leaders?

▼ **TABLE 11.8**   For Problems 11.11 and 11.12

Arrow Distributing Corp.	
Net revenue	$16,500
Cost of sales	$13,500
Inventory	$ 1,000
Total assets	$ 8,600

Baker Mfg. Inc.	
Net revenue	$27,500
Cost of sales	$21,500
Inventory	$ 1,250
Total assets	$16,600

•• **11.12** Arrow Distributing Corp. (see Table 11.8) likes to track inventory by using weeks of supply as well as by inventory turnover.
a) What is its weeks of supply?
b) What percent of Arrow's assets are committed to inventory?
c) What is Arrow's inventory turnover?
d) Is Arrow's supply-chain performance, as measured by these inventory metrics, better than that of Baker, in Problem 11.11?

• **11.13** The grocery industry has an annual inventory turnover of about 14 times. Organic Grocers, Inc., had a cost of goods sold last year of $10.5 million; its average inventory was $1.0 million. What was Organic Grocers's inventory turnover, and how does that performance compare with that of the industry?

•• **11.14** Mattress Wholesalers, Inc. is constantly trying to reduce inventory in its supply chain. Last year, cost of goods sold was $7.5 million and inventory was $1.5 million. This year, costs of goods sold is $8.6 million and inventory investment is $1.6 million.
a) What were the weeks of supply last year?
b) What are the weeks of supply this year?
c) Is Mattress Wholesalers making progress in its inventory-reduction effort?

▶ **Refer to** myomlab◉ **for this additional homework problem: 11.15**

Case Studies

▶ Dell's Value Chain

Dell Computer, with close supplier relationships, encourages suppliers to focus on their individual technological capabilities to sustain leadership in their components. Research and development costs are too high and technological changes are too rapid for any one company to sustain leadership in every component. Suppliers are also pressed to drive down lead times, lot sizes, and inventories. Dell, in turn, keeps its research customer-focused and leverages that research to help itself and suppliers. Dell also constructs special Web pages for suppliers, allowing them to view orders for components they produce as well as current levels of inventory at Dell. This allows suppliers to plan based on actual end customer demand; as a result, it reduces the bullwhip effect. The intent is to work with suppliers to keep the supply chain moving rapidly, products current, and the customer order queue short. Then, with supplier collaboration, Dell can offer the latest options, can build-to-order, and can achieve rapid throughput. The payoff is a competitive advantage, growing market share, and low capital investment.

On the distribution side, Dell uses direct sales, primarily via the Internet, to increase revenues by offering a virtually unlimited variety of desktops, notebooks, and enterprise products. Options displayed over the Internet allow Dell to attract customers that value choice. Customers select recommended product configurations or customize them. Dell's customers place orders at any time of the day from anywhere in the world. And Dell's price is cheaper; retail stores have additional costs because of their brick-and-mortar model. Dell has also customized Web pages that enable large business customers to track past purchases and place orders consistent with their purchase history and current needs. Assembly begins immediately after receipt of a customer order. Competing firms have previously assembled products filling the distribution channels (including shelves at retailers) before a product reaches the customer. Dell, in contrast, introduces a new product to customers over the Internet as soon as the first of that model is ready. In an industry where products have life cycles measured in months, Dell enjoys a huge early-to-market advantage.

Dell's model also has cash flow advantages. Direct sales allow Dell to eliminate distributor and retailer margins and increase its own margin. Dell collects payment in a matter of days after products are sold. But Dell pays its suppliers according to the more traditional billing schedules. Given its low levels of inventory, Dell is able to operate its business with negative working capital because it manages to receive payment before it pays its suppliers for components. These more traditional supply chains often require 60 or more days for the cash to flow from customer to supplier—a huge demand on working capital.

Dell has designed its order processing, products, and assembly lines so that customized products can be assembled in a matter of hours. This allows Dell to postpone assembly until after a customer order has been placed. In addition, any inventory is often in the form of components that are common across a wide variety of finished products. Postponement, component modularity, and tight scheduling allow low inventory and support mass customization. Dell maximizes the benefit of postponement by focusing on new products for which demand is difficult to forecast. Manufacturers who sell via distributors and retailers find postponement virtually impossible. Therefore, traditional manufacturers are often stuck with product configurations that are not selling while simultaneously being out of the configurations that *are* selling. Dell is better able to match supply and demand.

One of the few negatives for Dell's model is that it results in higher outbound shipping costs than selling through distributors and retailers. Dell sends individual products directly to customers from its factories. But many of these shipments are small (often one or a few products), while manufacturers selling through distributors and retailers ship with some economy of scale, using large shipments via truck to warehouses and retailers, with the end user providing the final portion of delivery. As a result, Dell's outbound transportation costs are higher, but the relative cost is low (typically 2% to 3%), and thus the impact on the overall cost is low.

What Dell has done is build a collaborative supply chain and an innovative ordering and production system. The result is what Dell likes to refer to as its *value chain*—a chain that brings value from supplier to the customer and provides Dell with a competitive advantage.

Discussion Questions

1. How has Dell used its direct sales and build-to-order model to develop an exceptional supply chain?
2. How has Dell exploited the direct sales model to improve operations performance?
3. What are the main disadvantages of Dell's direct sales model?
4. How does Dell compete with a retailer who already has a stock?
5. How does Dell's supply chain deal with the bullwhip effect?

Sources: Adapted from S. Chopra and P. Meindl, *Supply Chain Management*, 3rd ed. (Upper Saddle River, NJ: Prentice Hall, 2007); R. Kapuscinski, et al., "Inventory Decisions in Dell's Supply Chain," *Interfaces* 34, no. 3 (May–June 2004): 191–205; and A. A. Thompson, A. J. Strickland, and J. E. Gamble, "Dell, Inc. in 2006: Can Rivals Beat Its Strategy?" *Crafting and Executing Strategy*, 15th ed. (New York: McGraw-Hill, 2007).

▶ Darden's Global Supply Chains

Video Case

Darden Restaurants (subject of the *Global Company Profile* at the beginning of this chapter), owner of popular brands such as Olive Garden and Red Lobster, requires unique supply chains to serve more than 300 million meals annually. Darden's strategy is operations excellence, and Senior VP Jim Lawrence's task is to ensure competitive advantage via Darden's supply chains. For a firm with

purchases exceeding $1.5 billion, managing the supply chains is a complex and challenging task.

Darden, like other casual dining restaurants, has unique supply chains that reflect its menu options. Darden's supply chains are rather shallow, often having just one tier of suppliers. But it has four distinct supply chains.

First, "smallware" is a restaurant industry term for items such as linens, dishes, tableware and kitchenware, and silverware. These are purchased, with Darden taking title as they are received at the Darden Direct Distribution (DDD) warehouse in Orlando, Florida. From this single warehouse, smallware items are shipped via common carrier (trucking companies) to Olive Garden, Red Lobster, Bahama Breeze, and Seasons 52 restaurants.

Second, frozen, dry, and canned food products are handled economically by Darden's 11 distribution centers in North America, which are managed by major U.S. food distributors, such as MBM, Maines, and Sygma. This is Darden's second supply line.

Third, the fresh food supply chain (not frozen and not canned), where life is measured in days, includes dairy products, produce, and meat. This supply chain is B2B, where restaurant managers directly place orders with a preselected group of independent suppliers.

Fourth, Darden's worldwide seafood supply chain is the final link. Here Darden has developed independent suppliers of salmon, shrimp, tilapia, scallops, and other fresh fish that are source inspected by Darden's overseas representatives to ensure quality. These fresh products are flown to the U.S. and shipped to 16 distributors, with 22 locations, for quick delivery to the restaurants. With suppliers in 35 countries, Darden must be on the cutting edge when it comes to collaboration, partnering, communication, and food safety. It does this with heavy travel schedules for purchasing and quality control personnel, native-speaking employees onsite, and aggressive communication. Communication is a critical element; Darden tries to develop as much forecasting transparency as possible. "Point of sale (POS) terminals," says Lawrence, "feed actual sales every night to suppliers."

Discussion Questions*

1. What are the advantages of each of Darden's four supply chains?
2. What are the complications of having four supply chains?
3. Where would you expect ownership/title to change in each of Darden's four supply chains?
4. How do Darden's four supply chains compare with those of other firms, such as Dell or an automobile manufacturer? Why do the differences exist, and how are they addressed?

*You may wish to view the video that accompanies this case before answering these questions.

▶ Arnold Palmer Hospital's Supply Chain

Video Case

Arnold Palmer Hospital, one of the nation's top hospitals dedicated to serving women and children, is a large business with over 2,000 employees working in a 431-bed facility totaling 676,000 square feet in Orlando, Florida. Like many other hospitals, and other companies, Arnold Palmer Hospital had been a long-time member of a large buying group, one servicing 900 members. But the group did have a few limitations. For example, it might change suppliers for a particular product every year (based on a new lower-cost bidder) or stock only a product that was not familiar to the physicians at Arnold Palmer Hospital. The buying group was also not able to negotiate contracts with local manufacturers to secure the best pricing.

So in 2003, Arnold Palmer Hospital, together with seven other partner hospitals in central Florida, formed its own much smaller, but still powerful (with $200 million in annual purchases) Healthcare Purchasing Alliance (HPA) corporation. The new alliance saved the HPA members $7 million in its first year with two main changes. First, it was structured and staffed to assure that the bulk of the savings associated with its contracting efforts went to its eight members. Second, it struck even better deals with vendors by guaranteeing a *committed* volume and signing not 1-year deals but 3- to 5-year contracts. "Even with a new internal cost of $400,000 to run HPA, the savings and ability to contract for what our member hospitals really want makes the deal a winner," says George DeLong, head of HPA.

Effective supply chain management in manufacturing often focuses on development of new product innovations and efficiency through buyer–vendor collaboration. However, the approach in a service industry has a slightly different emphasis. At Arnold Palmer Hospital, supply-chain opportunities often manifest themselves through the Medical Economic Outcomes Committee. This committee (and its subcommittees) consists of users (including the medical and nursing staff) who evaluate purchase options with a goal of better medicine while achieving economic targets. For instance, the heart pacemaker negotiation by the cardiology subcommittee allowed for the standardization to two manufacturers, with annual savings of $2 million for just this one product.

Arnold Palmer Hospital is also able to develop custom products that require collaboration down to the third tier of the supply chain. This is the case with custom packs that are used in the operating room. The custom packs are delivered by a distributor, McKesson General Medical, but assembled by a pack company that uses materials the hospital wanted purchased from specific manufacturers. The HPA allows Arnold Palmer Hospital to be creative in this way. With major cost savings, standardization, blanket purchase orders, long-term contracts, and more control of product development, the benefits to the hospital are substantial.

Discussion Questions*

1. How does this supply chain differ from that in a manufacturing firm?
2. What are the constraints on making decisions based on economics alone at Arnold Palmer Hospital?
3. What role do doctors and nurses play in supply-chain decisions in a hospital? How is this participation handled at Arnold Palmer Hospital?
4. Doctor Smith just returned from the Annual Physician's Orthopedic Conference, where she saw a new hip joint replacement demonstrated. She decides she wants to start using the replacement joint at Arnold Palmer Hospital. What process will Dr. Smith have to go through at the hospital to introduce this new product into the supply chain for future surgical use?

*You may wish to view the video that accompanies this case before answering the questions.

▶ Supply-Chain Management at Regal Marine

Video Case

Like most other manufacturers, Regal Marine finds that it must spend a huge portion of its revenue on purchases. Regal has also found that the better its suppliers understand its end users, the better are both the supplier's product and Regal's final product. As one of the 10 largest U.S. power boat manufacturers, Regal is trying to differentiate its products from the vast number of boats supplied by 300 other companies. Thus, the firm works closely with suppliers to ensure innovation, quality, and timely delivery.

Regal has done a number of things to drive down costs while driving up quality, responsiveness, and innovation. First, working on partnering relationships with suppliers ranging from providers of windshields to providers of instrument panel controls, Regal has brought timely innovation at reasonable cost to its product. Key vendors are so tightly linked with the company that they meet with designers to discuss material changes to be incorporated into new product designs.

Second, the company has joined about 15 other boat manufacturers in a purchasing group, known as American Boat Builders Association, to work with suppliers on reducing the costs of large purchases. Third, Regal is working with a number of local vendors to supply hardware and fasteners directly to the assembly line on a just-in-time basis. In some of these cases, Regal has worked out an arrangement with the vendor so that title does not transfer until parts are used by Regal. In other cases, title transfers when items are delivered to the property. This practice drives down total inventory and the costs associated with large-lot delivery.

Finally, Regal works with a personnel agency to outsource part of the recruiting and screening process for employees. In all these cases, Regal is demonstrating innovative approaches to supply-chain management that help the firm and, ultimately, the end user. The *Global Company Profile* featuring Regal Marine (which opens Chapter 5) provides further background on Regal's operations.

Discussion Questions*

1. What other techniques might Regal use to improve supply-chain management?
2. What kind of response might members of the supply chain expect from Regal in response to their "partnering" in the supply chain?
3. Why is supply-chain management important to Regal?

*You may wish to view the video that accompanies this case before answering the questions.

▶**Additional Case Study:** Visit **www.pearsonglobaleditions.com/myomlab** or **www.pearsonglobaleditions.com/heizer** for this free case study:

Amazon.com: Discusses opportunities and issues in an innovative business model for the Internet.

Bibliography

Blackburn, Joseph, and Gary Scudder. "Supply Chain Strategies for Perishable Products." *Production and Operations Management* 18, no. 2 (March–April 2009): 129–137.

Boyer, Kenneth K., and G. Tomas M. Hult. "Extending the Supply Chain: Integrating Operations and Marketing in the Online Grocery Industry." *Journal of Operations Management* 23, no. 6 (September 2005): 642–661.

Chopra, Sunil, and Peter Meindl. *Supply Chain Management*, 4th ed. Upper Saddle River, NJ: Prentice Hall (2010).

Crook, T. Russell, and James G. Combs. "Sources and Consequences of Bargaining Power in Supply Chains." *Journal of Operations Management* 25, no. 2 (March 2007): 546–555.

Hu, J., and C. L. Munson. "Speed versus Reliability Trade-offs in Supplier Selection." *International Journal Procurement Management* 1, no. 1/2 (2007): 238–259.

Kersten, Wolfgang, and Thorsten Blecker (eds.). *Managing Risk in Supply Chains*. Berlin: Erich Schmidt Verlag GmbH & Co. (2006).

Kreipl, Stephan, and Michael Pinedo. "Planning and Scheduling in Supply Chains." *Production and Operations Management* 13, no. 1 (Spring 2004): 77–92.

Linton, J. D., R. Klassen, and V. Jayaraman. "Sustainable Supply Chains: An Introduction." *Journal of Operations Management* 25, no. 6 (November, 2007): 1075–1082.

Monczka, R. M., R. B. Handfield, L. C. Gianipero, and J. L. Patterson. *Purchasing and Supply Chain Management*, 4th ed. Mason, OH: Cengage (2009).

Narayanan, Sriram, Ann S. Marucheck, and Robert B. Handfield. "Electronic Data Interchange: Research Review and Future Directions." *Decisions Sciences* 40, no. 1 (February 2009): 121–163.

Pisano, Gary P., and Roberto Verganti. "Which Kind of Collaboration Is Right for You?" *Harvard Business Review* 86, no. 12 (December, 2008): 78–86.

Sinha, K. K., and E. J. Kohnke. "Health Care Supply Chain Design." *Decision Sciences* 40, no. 2 (May 2009): 197–212.

Stanley, L. L., and V. R. Singhal. "Service Quality Along the Supply Chain." *Journal of Operations Management* 19, no. 3 (May 2001): 287–306.

Wisner, Joel, K. Tan, and G. Keong Leong. *Principles of Supply Chain Management*, 3rd ed., Mason, OH: Cengage (2009).

Main Heading	Review Material	PEARSON myomlab
THE SUPPLY CHAIN'S STRATEGIC IMPORTANCE	Most firms spend a huge portion of their sales dollars on purchases. ■ **Supply-chain management**—Management of activities related to procuring materials and services, transforming them into intermediate goods and final products, and delivering them through a distribution system. The *objective is to build a chain of suppliers that focuses on maximizing value to the ultimate customer.* Competition is no longer between companies; it is between supply chains.	**VIDEO 11.1** Darden's Global Supply Chain
ETHICS AND SUSTAINABILITY	Ethics includes personal ethics, ethics within the supply chain, and ethical behavior regarding the environment. The Institute for Supply Management has developed a set of Principles and Standards for ethical conduct.	
SUPPLY-CHAIN ECONOMICS	■ **Make-or-buy decision**—A choice between producing a component or service in-house or purchasing it from an outside source. ■ **Outsourcing**—Transferring to external suppliers a firm's activities that have traditionally been internal.	Problems: 11.6, 11.7
SUPPLY-CHAIN STRATEGIES	Six supply-chain strategies for goods and services to be obtained from outside sources are: 1. Negotiating with many suppliers and playing one supplier against another 2. Developing long-term partnering relationships with a few suppliers 3. Vertical integration 4. Joint ventures 5. Developing *keiretsu* networks 6. Developing virtual companies that use suppliers on an as-needed basis ■ **Vertical integration**—Developing the ability to produce goods or services previously purchased or actually buying a supplier or a distributor. ■ *Keiretsu*—A Japanese term that describes suppliers who become part of a company coalition. ■ **Virtual companies**—Companies that rely on a variety of supplier relationships to provide services on demand. Also known as hollow corporations or network companies.	**VIDEO 11.2** Supply-Chain Management at Regal Marine
MANAGING THE SUPPLY CHAIN	Supply-chain integration success begins with mutual agreement on goals, followed by mutual trust, and continues with compatible organizational cultures. Three issues complicate the development of an efficient, integrated supply chain: local optimization, incentives, and large lots. ■ **Bullwhip effect**—Increasing fluctuation in orders or cancellations that often occurs as orders move through the supply chain. ■ **Pull data**—Accurate sales data that initiate transactions to "pull" product through the supply chain. ■ **Single stage control of replenishment**—Fixing responsibility for monitoring and managing inventory for the retailer. ■ **Vendor-managed inventory (VMI)**—A system in which a supplier maintains material for the buyer, often delivering directly to the buyer's using department. ■ **Collaborative planning, forecasting, and replenishment (CPFR)**—A system in which members of a supply chain share information in a joint effort to reduce supply-chain costs. ■ **Blanket order**—A long-term purchase commitment to a supplier for items that are to be delivered against short-term releases to ship. The purchasing department should make special efforts to increase levels of standardization. ■ **Postponement**—Delaying any modifications or customization to a product as long as possible in the production process. Postponement strives to minimize internal variety while maximizing external variety. ■ **Drop shipping**—Shipping directly from the supplier to the end consumer rather than from the seller, saving both time and reshipping costs. ■ **Pass-through facility**—A facility that expedites shipment by holding merchandise and delivering from shipping hubs. ■ **Channel assembly**—A system that postpones final assembly of a product so the distribution channel can assemble it.	**VIDEO 11.3** Arnold Palmer Hospital's Supply Chain

Main Heading	Review Material	
E-PROCUREMENT	■ **E-procurement**—Purchasing facilitated through the Internet. ■ **Electronic data interchange (EDI)**—A standardized data-transmittal format for computerized communications between organizations. ■ **Advanced shipping notice (ASN)**—A shipping notice delivered directly from vendor to purchaser. Online catalogs move companies from a multitude of individual phone calls, faxes, and e-mails to a centralized online system and drive billions of dollars of waste out of the supply chain.	
VENDOR SELECTION	Vendor selection is a three-stage process: (1) vendor evaluation, (2) vendor development, and (3) negotiations. *Vendor evaluation* involves finding potential vendors and determining the likelihood of their becoming good suppliers. *Vendor development* may include everything from training, to engineering and production help, to procedures for information transfer. ■ **Negotiation strategies**—Approaches taken by supply-chain personnel to develop contractual relationships with suppliers. Three classic types of negotiation strategies are (1) the cost-based price model, (2) the market-based price model, and (3) competitive bidding.	Problems: 11.2, 11.3
LOGISTICS MANAGEMENT	■ **Logistics management**—An approach that seeks efficiency of operations through the integration of all material acquisition, movement, and storage activities. The total distribution cost in the United States is over 10% of the gross national product (GNP). Five major means of distribution are trucking, railroads, airfreight, waterways, and pipelines. The vast majority of manufactured goods move by truck.	Problems: 11.8–11.10
MEASURING SUPPLY-CHAIN PERFORMANCE	Typical supply-chain benchmark metrics include lead time, time spent placing an order, percent of late deliveries, percent of rejected material, and number of shortages per year: Percent invested in inventory = (Total inventory investment/Total assets) × 100 **(11-1)** ■ **Inventory turnover**—Cost of goods sold divided by average inventory: Inventory turnover = Cost of goods sold ÷ Inventory investment **(11-2)** Weeks of supply = Inventory investment ÷ (Annual cost of goods sold/52 weeks) **(11-3)** ■ **Supply Chain Operations Reference (SCOR) Model**—A set of processes, metrics, and best practices developed by the Supply Chain Council. The five parts of the SCOR model are Plan, Source, Make, Deliver, and Return.	Problems: 11.11–11.15 Virtual Office Hours for Solved Problem: 11.1

myomlab

Self Test

■ **Before taking the self-test,** refer to the learning objectives listed at the beginning of the chapter and the key terms listed at the end of the chapter.

LO1. The objective of supply-chain management is to _____.

LO2. The term *vertical integration* means to:
- a) develop the ability to produce products that complement or supplement the original product.
- b) produce goods or services previously purchased.
- c) develop the ability to produce the specified good more efficiently.
- d) all of the above.

LO3. The bullwhip effect can be aggravated by:
- a) local optimization.
- b) sales incentives.
- c) quantity discounts.
- d) promotions.
- e) all of the above.

LO4. Vendor selection requires:
- a) vendor evaluation and effective third-party logistics.
- b) vendor development and logistics.

- c) negotiations, vendor evaluation, and vendor development.
- d) an integrated supply chain.
- e) inventory and supply-chain management.

LO5. A major issue in logistics is:
- a) cost of purchases.
- b) vendor evaluation.
- c) product customization.
- d) cost of shipping alternatives.
- e) excellent suppliers.

LO6. Inventory turnover =
- a) Cost of goods sold ÷ Weeks of supply.
- b) Weeks of supply ÷ Annual cost of goods sold.
- c) Annual cost of goods sold ÷ 52 weeks.
- d) Inventory investment ÷ Cost of goods sold.
- e) Cost of goods sold ÷ Inventory investment.

Answers: LO1. build a chain of suppliers that focuses on maximizing value to the ultimate customer; LO2. b; LO3. e; LO4. c; LO5. d; LO6. e.

Outsourcing as a Supply-Chain Strategy

Supplement Outline

Contract manufacturers such as Flextronics provide outsourcing service to IBM, Cisco Systems, HP, Microsoft, Motorola, Sony, Nortel, Ericsson, and Sun, among many others. Flextronics is a high-quality producer that has won over 450 awards, including the Malcolm Baldrige Award. One of the side benefits of outsourcing is that client firms such as IBM can actually improve their performance by using the competencies of an outstanding firm like Flextronics. But there are risks involved in outsourcing. Outsourcing decisions, as part of the supply-chain strategy, are explored in this supplement.

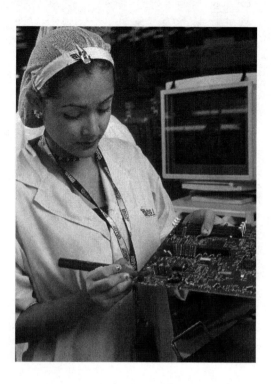

Supplement 11 **Learning Objectives**

LO1: Explain how core competencies relate to outsourcing   **484**

LO2: Describe the risks of outsourcing   **485**

LO3: Use factor rating to evaluate both country and provider outsourcers   **487**

LO4: List the advantages and disadvantages of outsourcing   **489**

> **AUTHOR COMMENT**
> Outsourcing is a supply-chain strategy that can deliver tremendous value to an organization.

WHAT IS OUTSOURCING?

Outsourcing is a creative management strategy. Indeed, some organizations use outsourcing to replace entire purchasing, information systems, marketing, finance, and operations departments. Outsourcing is applicable to firms throughout the world. And because outsourcing decisions are risky and many are not successful, making the right decision may mean the difference between success and failure.[1]

Because outsourcing grows by double digits every year, students and managers need to understand the issues, concepts, models, philosophies, procedures, and practices of outsourcing. This supplement describes current concepts, methodologies, and outsourcing strategies.

Outsourcing means procuring from external suppliers services or products that are normally a part of an organization. In other words, a firm takes functions it was performing in-house (such as accounting, janitorial, or call center functions) and has another company do the same job. If a company owns two plants and reallocates production from the first to the second, this is not considered outsourcing. If a company moves some of its business processes to a foreign country but retains control, we define this move as **offshoring**, not outsourcing. For example, China's Haier Group recently offshored a $40 million refrigerator factory to South Carolina (with huge savings in transportation costs). Or, as Thomas Friedman wrote in his book *The World is Flat*, "Offshoring is when a company takes one of its factories that it is operating in Canton, Ohio and moves the whole factory to Canton, China."

Outsourcing

Procuring from external sources services or products that are normally part of an organization.

Offshoring

Moving a business process to a foreign country but retaining control of it.

---

[1]The authors wish to thank Professor Marc J. Schneiderjans, of the University of Nebraska–Lincoln, for help with the development of this supplement. His book *Outsourcing and Insourcing in an International Context*, with Ashlyn Schniederjans and Dara Schniederjans (Armonk, NY: M.E. Sharpe, 2005), provided insight, content, and references that shaped our approach to the topic.

Early in their lives, many businesses handle their activities internally. As businesses mature and grow, however, they often find competitive advantage in the specialization provided by outside firms. They may also find limitations on locally available labor, services, materials, or other resources. So organizations balance the potential benefits of outsourcing with its potential risks. Outsourcing the wrong activities can cause major problems.

Outsourcing is not a new concept; it is simply an extension of the long-standing practice of *subcontracting* production activities. Indeed, the classic make-or-buy decision concerning products (which we discussed in Chapter 11) is an example of outsourcing.

So why has outsourcing expanded to become a major strategy in business the world over? From an economic perspective, it is due to the continuing move toward specialization in an increasingly technological society. More specifically, outsourcing's continuing growth is due to (1) increasing expertise, (2) reduced costs of more reliable transportation, and (3) the rapid development and deployment of advancements in telecommunications and computers. Low-cost communication, including the Internet, permits firms anywhere in the world to provide previously limited information services.

Examples of outsourcing include:

- Call centers for Brazil in Angola (a former Portuguese colony in Africa) and for the U.S. and England in India
- DuPont's legal services routed to the Philippines
- IBM handling travel services and payroll, and Hewlett-Packard providing IT services to P&G
- ADP providing payroll services for thousands of firms
- Production of the Audi A4 convertible and Mercedes CLK convertible by Wilheim Karmann in Osnabruck, Germany
- Blue Cross sending hip resurfacing surgery patients to India

Outsourced manufacturing, also known as *contract manufacturing*, is becoming standard practice in many industries, from computers to automobiles.

Paralleling the growth of outsourcing is the growth of international trade. With the passage of landmark trade agreements like the North American Free Trade Agreement (NAFTA), the work of the World Trade Organization and the European Union, and other international trade zones established throughout the world, we are witnessing the greatest expansion of international commerce in history.

Table S11.1 provides a ranking of the top five and bottom five outsourcing locations (out of 50 countries) in the annual A.T. Kearney Global Options survey. Scores are based on a Global Services Location Index tallying financial attractiveness, workforce availability, employee skill set, and business environment.

Types of Outsourcing   Nearly any business activity can be outsourced. A general contractor in the building industry, who subcontracts various construction activities needed to build a home, is a perfect example of an outsourcer. Every component of the building process, including the architect's design, a consultant's site location analysis, a lawyer's work to obtain the building permits, plumbing, electrical work, dry walling, painting, furnace installation, landscaping, and sales, is usually outsourced. Outsourcing implies an agreement (typically a legally binding contract) with an external organization.

Among the business processes outsourced are (1) purchasing, (2) logistics, (3) R&D, (4) operation of facilities, (5) management of services, (6) human resources, (7) finance/accounting, (8) customer relations, (9) sales/marketing, (10) training, and (11) legal processes. Note that the first six of these are OM functions that we discuss in this text.

VIDEO S11.1
Outsourcing Offshore at Darden

▼ TABLE S11.1
Desirable Outsourcing Destinations

Rank	Country	Score
1	India	6.9
2	China	6.6
3	Malaysia	6.1
4	Thailand	6.0
5	Brazil	5.9
⋮		
46	Ukraine	4.9
47	France	4.9
48	Turkey	4.8
49	Portugal	4.8
50	Ireland	4.2

Source: Based on A. T. Kearney, 2009.

STRATEGIC PLANNING AND CORE COMPETENCIES

As we saw in Chapter 2, organizations develop missions, long-term goals, and strategies as general guides for operating their businesses. The strategic planning process begins with a basic mission statement and establishing goals. Given the mission and goals, strategic planners next undertake an internal analysis of the organization to identify how much or little each business activity contributes to the achievement of the mission.

During such an analysis, firms identify their strengths—what they do well or better than their competitors. These unique skills, talents, and capabilities are called **core competencies**. Core

AUTHOR COMMENT
Ford Motor used to mine its own ore, make and ship its own steel, and sell cars directly, but those days are long gone.

Core competencies
An organization's unique skills, talents, and capabilities.

▶ **FIGURE S11.1**
Sony, an Outsourcing Company

Based on J. B. Quinn. "Outsourcing Innovation." *Sloan Management Review* (Summer 2000): 20.

Outsourcers *could* provide Sony with:

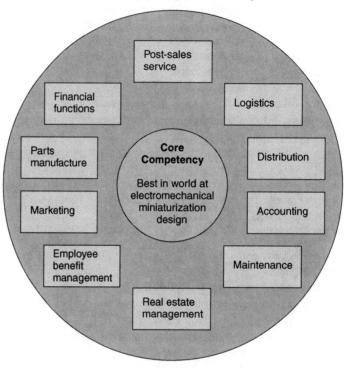

LO1: Explain how core competencies relate to outsourcing

competencies may include specialized knowledge, proprietary technology or information, and unique production methods. The trick is to identify what the organization does better than anyone else. Common sense dictates that core competencies are the activities that a firm should perform. By contrast, *non-core activities*, which can be a sizable portion of an organization's total business, are good candidates for outsourcing.

Sony's core competency, for example, is electromechanical design of chips. This is its core, and Sony is one of the best in the world when it comes to rapid response and specialized production of these chips. But, as Figure S11.1 suggests, outsourcing could offer Sony continuous innovation and flexibility. Leading specialized outsource providers are likely to come up with major innovations in such areas as software, human resources, and distribution. That is their business, not Sony's.

Managers evaluate their strategies and core competencies and ask themselves how to use the assets entrusted to them. Do they want to be the offshore company that does low-margin work at 3%–4% or the innovative firm that makes a 30%–40% margin? PC or iPod assemblers in China and Taiwan earn 3%–4%, but Apple, which innovates, designs, and sells, has a margin 10 times as large.

To summarize, management must be cautious in outsourcing those elements of the product or service that provide a competitive advantage.

AUTHOR COMMENT
Author James Champy writes, "Although you may be good at something tactically, someone else may do it better and at lower cost."

The Theory of Comparative Advantage

The motivation for international outsourcing comes from the **theory of comparative advantage**. This theory focuses on the basic economics of outsourcing internationally. According to the theory, if an external provider, regardless of its geographic location, can perform activities more productively than the purchasing firm, then the external provider should do the work. This allows the purchasing firm to focus on what it does best, its core competencies.

However, comparative advantage is not static. Companies, and indeed countries, strive to find comparative advantage. Countries such as India, China, and Russia have made it a government priority and set up agencies to support the easy transition of foreign firms into their outsourcing markets. Work and jobs go to countries that reduce risk through the necessary legal structures, effective infrastructure, and an educated workforce.

The dynamics of comparative advantage are evident from a recent study of five manufactured products. In an effort to meet "optimal" prices on auto parts in 2005, companies were moving work from Mexico to China. At that time China had a 22% price advantage on these parts over the U.S. But by 2009 that gap had dropped to 5.5%—and in some instances manufacturing in China was

Theory of comparative advantage

A theory which states that countries benefit from specializing in (and exporting) products and services in which they have relative advantage, and importing goods in which they have a relative disadvantage.

In the ultimate risk in outsourcing, NASA has awarded contracts of $3.5 billion to a team, led by Orbital Sciences Corp., to ship cargo to the International Space Station starting in 2011. The company will be solely responsible for designing, building, and launching rockets on a regular basis. NASA hopes to save time and money by outsourcing.

20% more expensive than Mexico. As a result, some manufacturing began migrating back to Mexico and the U.S.; the price gap wasn't large enough to merit the hassle of manufacturing halfway around the world.[2]

Nonetheless, consistent with the theory of comparative advantage, the trend toward outsourcing continues to grow. This does not mean all existing outsourcing decisions are perfect. The term **backsourcing** has been used to describe the return of business activity to the original firm. We will now discuss the risks associated with outsourcing.

Backsourcing
The return of business activity to the original firm.

RISKS OF OUTSOURCING

Risk management starts with a realistic analysis of risks and results in a strategy that minimizes the impact of these uncertainties. Indeed, outsourcing can look very risky. And it is. Perhaps half of all outsourcing agreements fail because of inappropriate planning and analysis. For one thing, few promoters of international outsourcing mention the erratic power grids in some foreign countries or the difficulties with local government officials, inexperienced managers, and unmotivated employees. On the other hand, when managers set an outsourcing goal of 75% cost reduction and receive only a 30%–40% cost reduction, they view the outsourcing as a failure, when, in fact, it may be a success.

> **AUTHOR COMMENT**
> The substantial risk in outsourcing requires managers to invest the effort to make sure they do it right.

Quality can also be at risk (See the *OM in Action box* "Revising Offshoring at M&S"). A recent survey of 150 North American companies found that, as a group, those that outsourced customer service saw a drop in their score on the American Consumer Satisfaction Index. We should point out that the declines were roughly the same whether companies outsourced domestically or overseas.[3]

Another risk is the political backlash that results from outsourcing to foreign countries. The perceived loss of U.S. jobs (as well as the loss of jobs and reputation in domestic market in US and Europe has fuelled anti-outsourcing rhetoric and action from companies) has fueled anti-outsourcing rhetoric and action from government officials.

LO2: Describe the risks of outsourcing

Despite the negative impression created by government actions, the press, and public opinion, data suggest that foreigners outsource far more services to the U.S. than U.S. companies send abroad. And while U.S. jobs are outsourced, a minuscule few are outsourced offshore. A recent Organization for Economic Cooperation and Development (OECD) report on the subject shows that outsourcing is not as big a cause in job losses as, say, improved technology, and has an overall positive effect.[4] It is also a two-way street. India's cartoon producer Jadoo Works, for example, outsources projects to U.S. animators.

[2]"China's Eroding Advantage" *Business Week* (June 15, 2009): 54:55. The report dealt with five categories of machined products, ranging from large engine parts requiring significant labor to small plastic components that need little.
[3]J. Whitaker, M. S. Krishnan, and C. Fornell. "How Offshore Outsourcing Affects Customer Satisfaction." *The Wall Street Journal* (July 7, 2008): R4.
[4]"Outsourcing: Old Assumptions Are Being Challenged as the Outsourcing Industry Matures," *The Economist* (July 28, 2007): 65–66.

OM in Action ▶ Revising Offshoring at M&S

European retailers continue their search for efficiency by outsourcing operations overseas (called offshoring). While offshoring the majority of operations to low-cost developing countries can bring considerable benefits to retailers, it may also involve significant risks.

Marks & Spencer (M&S), a leading British clothing retailer, tried offshoring during 1990s and early 2000s. M&S has been a reputable retailer for many middle-class British customers for years with a reputation of quality, reliability, and service. For decades, this combination proved to be a key to the success and working with local suppliers for years gave M&S a unique reputation as well.

In the 1990s, however, M&S began to have troubles as the company was competing with low-price retailers and high-street fashion market that was being dominated by fast-fashion retailers.

M&S decided to manage costs by following the lead of other retailers: it cut off sourcing from expensive local suppliers and outsourced almost every operation to Asian suppliers. This lead to a number of issues including unreliable delivery and quality issues. However this was not the only problem for M&S as the clothing market was getting more and more volatile. It needed to respond quickly to change the product mix, supply rate, distribution channels, and even

designs more frequently and quickly. This could not be achieved with overseas suppliers and because it no longer used local suppliers, jobs had been lost, and the reputation of M&S had been damaged.

Revising its initial outsourcing strategy, M&S studied European suppliers for its fast fashion products and reconsidered local suppliers for some its critical operations. Low-cost suppliers in eastern European countries and new members of the EU were alternatives. M&S also redeveloped its local design capabilities to leverage the benefits of global sourcing, manage the risks involved, and enhance its flexibility in quick response to market changes. It also returned some jobs to local and domestic suppliers.

M&S still offshores a considerable part of its operations. However, like other European retailers in the clothing and fashion market, M&S is searching for more reliable local and domestic sources to fulfill unstable demand, make products affordable for customers, and support job markets.

Sources: Lowson, R.H. (2001) "Analysing the Effectiveness of European Retail Sourcing Strategies," *European Management Journal,* 19, (5)543–551; Khan, O. and Christopher, M. (2008) "The Impact of Product Design on Supply Chain Risk: A Case Study," *International Journal of Physical Distribution & Logistics Management,* 38 (5) 412–432.

Table S11.2 lists some of the risks inherent in outsourcing.

In addition to the external risks, operations managers must deal with other issues that outsourcing brings. These include (1) changes in employment levels, (2) changes in facilities and processes needed to receive components in a different state of assembly, and (3) vastly expanded logistics issues, including insurance, customs, and timing.

What can be done to mitigate the risks of outsourcing? Research indicates that of all the reasons given for outsourcing failure, the most common is that the decision was made without sufficient understanding and analysis. The next section provides a methodology that helps analyze the outsourcing decision process.

▶ **TABLE S11.2**
The Outsourcing Process and Related Risks

Outsourcing Process	Examples of Possible Risks
Identify non-core competencies	Can be incorrectly identified as a non-core competency.
Identify non-core activities that should be outsourced	Just because the activity is not a core competency for your firm does not mean an outsource provider is more competent and efficient.
Identify impact on existing facilities, capacity, and logistics	Failing to understand the change in resources and talents needed internally.
Establish goals and draft outsourcing agreement specifications	Setting goals so high that failure is certain.
Identify and select outsource provider	Selecting the wrong outsource provider.
Negotiate goals and measures of outsourcing performance	Misinterpreting measures and goals, how they are measured, and what they mean.
Monitor and control current outsourcing program	Being unable to control product development, schedules, and quality.
Evaluate and give feedback to outsource provider	Having a non-responsive provider (i.e., one that ignores feedback).
Evaluate international political and currency risks	Country's currency may be unstable, a country may be politically unstable, or cultural and language differences may inhibit successful operations.
Evaluate coordination needed for shipping and distribution	Understanding of the timing necessary to manage flows to different facilities and markets.

AUTHOR COMMENT
Cultural differences may indeed be why companies are less frequently outsourcing their call centers.

EVALUATING OUTSOURCING RISK WITH FACTOR RATING

AUTHOR COMMENT
The factor-rating model adds objectivity to decision making.

The factor-rating method, first introduced in Chapter 8, is an excellent tool for dealing with both country risk assessment and provider selection problems.

Rating International Risk Factors

Suppose a company has identified for outsourcing an area of production that is a non-core competency. Example S1 shows how to rate several international risk factors using an *unweighted* factor-rating approach.

◀ **EXAMPLE S1**

Establishing risk factors for four countries

Toronto Airbags produces auto and truck airbags for Nissan, Chrysler, Mercedes, and BMW. It wants to conduct a risk assessment of outsourcing manufacturing. Four countries—England, Mexico, Spain, and Canada (the current home nation)—are being considered. Only English- or Spanish-speaking countries are included because they "fit" with organizational capabilities.

APPROACH: ▶ Toronto's management identifies nine factors, listed in Table S11.3, and rates each country on a 0–3 scale, where 0 is no risk and 3 is high risk. Risk ratings are added to find the lowest-risk location.

◀ **TABLE S11.3**
Toronto Airbag's International Risk Factors, by Country (an unweighted approach)*

Risk Factor	England	Mexico	Spain	Canada (home country)
Economic: Labor cost/laws	1	0	2	1
Economic: Capital availability	0	2	1	0
Economic: Infrastructure	0	2	2	0
Culture: Language	0	0	0	0
Culture: Social norms	2	0	1	2
Migration: Uncontrolled	0	2	0	0
Politics: Ideology	2	0	1	2
Politics: Instability	0	1	2	2
Politics: Legalities	3	0	2	3
Total risk rating scores	8	7	11	10

*Risk rating scale: 0 = no risk, 1 = minor risk, 2 = average risk, 3 = high risk

SOLUTION ▶ Based on these ratings, Mexico is the least risky of the four locations being considered.

INSIGHT ▶ As with many other quantitative methods, assessing risk factors is not easy and may require considerable research, but the technique adds objectivity to a decision.

LEARNING EXERCISE ▶ Social norms in England have just been rescored by an economist, and the new rating is "no risk." How does this affect Toronto's decision? [Answer: England now has the lowest rating, at 6, for risk.]

RELATED PROBLEMS ▶ S11.1, S11.3

In Example S1, Toronto Airbags considered only English- and Spanish-speaking countries. But it is worth mentioning that countries like China, India, and Russia have millions of English-speaking personnel. This may have an impact on the final decision.

Example S1 considered the home country of the outsourcing firm. This inclusion helps document the risks that a domestic outsourcing provider poses compared to the risks posed by international providers. Including the home country in the analysis also helps justify final strategy selection to stakeholders who might question it.

Indeed, **nearshoring** (i.e., choosing an outsource provider located in the home country or in a nearby country) can be a good strategy for businesses and governments seeking both control and cost advantages. U.S. firms are interested in nearshoring to Canada because of Canada's cultural similarity and geographic nearness to the U.S. This allows the company wanting to outsource to exert more control than would be possible when outsourcing to most other countries. Nearshoring represents a compromise in which some cost savings are sacrificed for greater control because Canada's smaller wage differential limits the labor cost reduction advantage.

LO3: Use factor rating to evaluate both country and provider outsourcers

Nearshoring
Choosing an outsource provider in the home country or in a nearby country.

Rating Outsource Providers

In Chapter 8 (see Example 1) we illustrated the factor-rating method's computations when each factor has its own importance weight. We now apply that concept in Example S2 to compare outsourcing providers being considered by a firm.

EXAMPLE S2 ▶

Rating provider selection criteria

National Architects, Inc., a San Francisco–based designer of high-rise buildings, has decided to outsource its information technology (IT) function. Three outsourcing providers are being actively considered: one in the U.S., one in India, and one in Israel.

APPROACH: ▶ National's VP–Operations, Susan Cholette, has made a list of seven criteria she considers critical. After putting together a committee of four other VPs, she has rated each firm (on a 1–5 scale, with 5 being highest) and has also placed an importance weight on each of the factors, as shown in Table S11.4.

▶**TABLE S11.4**
Factor Ratings Applied to National Architects's Potential IT Outsourcing Providers

Factor (criterion)*	Importance Weight	Outsource Providers		
		BIM (U.S.)	S.P.C. (India)	Telco (Israel)
1. Can reduce operating costs	.2	3	3	5
2. Can reduce capital investment	.2	4	3	3
3. Skilled personnel	.2	5	4	3
4. Can improve quality	.1	4	5	2
5. Can gain access to technology not in company	.1	5	3	5
6. Can create additional capacity	.1	4	2	4
7. Aligns with policy/ philosophy/culture	.1	2	3	5
Totals	1.0	3.9	3.3	3.8

* These seven major criteria are based on a survey of 165 procurement executives, as reported in J. Schildhouse, "Outsourcing Ins and Outs," *Inside Supply Management* (December 2005): 22–29.

SOLUTION: ▶ Susan multiplies each rating by the weight and sums the products in each column to generate a total score for each outsourcing provider. She selects BIM, which has the highest overall rating.

INSIGHT: ▶ When the total scores are as close (3.9 vs. 3.8) as they are in this case, it is important to examine the sensitivity of the results to inputs. For example, if one of the importance weights or factor scores changes even marginally, the final selection may change. Management preference may also play a role here.

LEARNING EXERCISE: ▶ Susan decides that "Skilled personnel" should instead get a weight of 0.1 and "Aligns with policy/philosophy/culture" should increase to 0.2. How do the total scores change? [Answer: BIM = 3.6, S.P.C. = 3.2, and Telco = 4.0, so Telco is selected.]

RELATED PROBLEMS: ▶ S11.2, S11.4, S11.5, S11.6, S11.7

Most U.S. toy companies now outsource their production to Chinese manufacturers. Cost savings are significant, but there are several downsides, including loss of control over such issues as quality. In 2007 alone, Mattel had to recall 10.5 million Elmos, Big Birds, and SpongeBobs. These made-in-China toys contained excessive levels of lead in their paint. In 2008 the quality headlines dealt with poisonous pet food from China, and in 2009 it was tainted milk products.

ADVANTAGES AND DISADVANTAGES OF OUTSOURCING

Advantages of Outsourcing

LO4: List the advantages and disadvantages of outsourcing

As mentioned earlier, companies outsource for five main reasons. They are, in order of importance: (1) cost savings, (2) gaining outside expertise, (3) improving operations and service, (4) focusing on core competencies, and (5) gaining outside technology.

Cost Savings   The number-one reason driving outsourcing for many firms is the possibility of significant cost savings, particularly for labor. (See the *OM in Action* box "Walmart's Link to China.")

Gaining Outside Expertise   In addition to gaining access to a broad base of skills that are unavailable in-house, an outsourcing provider may be a source of innovation for improving products, processes, and services.

Improving Operations and Service   An outsourcing provider may have production flexibility. This may allow the firm outsourcing its work to win orders by more quickly introducing new products and services.

Focusing on Core Competencies   An outsourcing provider brings *its* core competencies to the supply chain. This frees up a firm's human, physical, and financial resources to reallocate to core competencies.

Gaining Outside Technology   Firms can outsource to state-of-the-art providers instead of retaining old (legacy) systems. This means they do not have to invest in new technology, thereby cutting risks.

Other Advantages   There are additional advantages in outsourcing. For example, a firm may improve its performance and image by associating with an outstanding supplier. Outsourcing can also be used as a strategy for downsizing, or "reengineering," a firm.

Disadvantages of Outsourcing

There are a number of potential disadvantages in outsourcing. Here are just a few.

Increased Transportation Costs   Delivery costs may rise substantially if distance increases from an outsourcing provider to a firm using that provider.

Loss of Control   This disadvantage can permeate and link to all other problems with outsourcing. When managers lose control of some operations, costs may increase because it's harder to assess and control them. For example, production of most of the world's laptops is now outsourced. This means that companies like Dell and HP find themselves using the same contractor (Quanta) to make their machines in China. This can leave them struggling to maintain control over the supplier.

OM in Action ▶ Walmart's Link to China

No other company has a more efficient supply chain, and no other company has embraced outsourcing to China more vigorously than Walmart. Perhaps as much as 85% of Walmart's merchandise is made abroad, and Chinese factories are by far the most important and fastest growing of these sources.

A whopping 10%–13% of everything China sends to the U.S. ends up on Walmart's shelves—over $15 billion worth of goods a year. Walmart has almost 600 people on the ground in China just to negotiate and make purchases.

As much as Walmart has been demonized for its part in offshoring jobs, its critical mass allows Chinese firms to build assembly lines that are so huge that they drive prices down through economies of scale.

Walmart's Chinese suppliers achieve startling, market-shaking price cuts. For example, the price of portable DVDs with 7″ LCD screens dropped in half when Walmart found a Chinese factory to build in giant quantities. Walmart's success in going abroad and pressing suppliers for price breaks has forced both retailers and manufacturers to reevaluate their supply chains.

The company has also led the way to sustainability and product safety through its "Responsible Sourcing" program, announced in 2008. Because Chinese products have been riddled with safety issues, Walmart in 2009 required "an identifiable trail" from raw materials to suppliers.

It also told its top 200 Chinese suppliers that they have until 2012 to become energy and resource efficient, cutting energy use by 20%.

Sources: *The Wall Street Journal* (October 22, 2008): B1; **About.com**: Logistics/Supply Chain (November 26, 2008); and *Financial Times* (December 12, 2008): 9.

Creating Future Competition Intel, for example, outsourced a core competency, chip production, to AMD when it could not keep up with early demands. Within a few years, AMD became a leading competitor, manufacturing its own chips.

Negative Impact on Employees Employee morale may drop when functions are outsourced, particularly when friends lose their jobs. Employees believe they may be next, and indeed they may be. Productivity, loyalty, and trust—all of which are needed for a healthy, growing business—may suffer.

Longer-Term Impact Some disadvantages of outsourcing tend to be longer term than the advantages of outsourcing. In other words, many of the risks firms run by outsourcing may not show up on the bottom line until some time in the future. This permits CEOs who prefer short-term planning and are interested only in bottom-line improvements to use the outsourcing strategy to make quick gains at the expense of longer-term objectives.

The advantages and disadvantages of outsourcing may or may not occur but should be thought of as possibilities to be managed effectively.

AUDITS AND METRICS TO EVALUATE PERFORMANCE

Regardless of the techniques and success in selection of outsourcing providers, agreements must specify results and outcomes. Whatever the outsourced component or service, management needs an evaluation process to ensure satisfactory continuing performance. At a minimum, the product or service must be defined in terms of quality, customer satisfaction, delivery, cost, and improvement. The mix and detail of the performance measures will depend on the nature of the product.

In situations where the outsourced product or service plays a major role in strategy and winning orders, the relationship needs to be more than after-the-fact audits and reports. It needs to be based on continuing communication, understanding, trust, and performance. The relationship should manifest itself in the mutual belief that "we are in this together" and go well beyond the written agreement.

However, when outsourcing is for less critical components, agreements that include the traditional mix of audits and metrics (such as cost, logistics, quality, and delivery) may be reported weekly or monthly. When a *service* has been outsourced, more imaginative metrics may be necessary. For instance, in an outsourced call center, these metrics may deal with personnel evaluation and training, call volume, call type, and response time, as well as tracking complaints. In this dynamic environment, reporting of such metrics may be required daily.

> **AUTHOR COMMENT**
> Because outsourcing is rife with potential abuse, companies have to be careful not to harm individuals, societies, or nature.

ETHICAL ISSUES IN OUTSOURCING

Laws, trade agreements, and business practices are contributing to a growing set of international, ethical practices for the outsourcing industry. Table S11.5 presents several tenets of conduct that have fairly universal acceptance.

In the electronics industry, HP, Dell, IBM, Intel and twelve other companies have created the Electronics Industry Code of Conduct (EICC). The EICC sets environmental standards, bans child labor and excessive overtime, and audits outsourcing producers to ensure compliance.

▶**TABLE S11.5**
Ethical Principles and Related Outsourcing Linkages

Ethics Principle	Outsourcing Linkage
Do no harm to indigenous cultures	Avoid outsourcing in a way that violates religious holidays (e.g., making employees work during religious holidays).
Do no harm to the ecological systems	Don't use outsourcing to move pollution from one country to another.
Uphold universal labor standards	Don't use outsourcing to take advantage of cheap labor that leads to employee abuse.
Uphold basic human rights	Don't accept outsourcing that violates basic human rights.
Pursue long-term involvement	Don't use outsourcing as a short-term arrangement to reduce costs; view it as a long-term partnership.
Share knowledge and technology	Don't think outsourcing agreements will prevent loss of technology, but use the inevitable sharing to build good relationships.

SUPPLEMENT SUMMARY

Companies can give many different reasons why they outsource, but the reality is that outsourcing's most attractive feature is that it helps firms cut costs. Workers in low-cost countries simply work much more cheaply, with fewer fringe benefits, work rules, and legal restrictions, than their U.S. and European counterparts. For example, a comparable hourly wage of $20 in the U.S. and $30 in Europe is well above the $1.26 per hour in China. Yet China often achieves quality levels equivalent to (or even higher than) plants in the West.

There is a growing economic pressure to outsource. But there is also a need for planning outsourcing to make it acceptable to all participants. When outsourcing is done in the right way, it creates a win–win situation.

Key Terms

Outsourcing (p. 482)
Offshoring (p. 482)

Core competencies (p. 483
Theory of comparative advantage (p. 484)

Backsourcing (p. 485)
Nearshoring (p. 487)

Discussion Questions

1. How would you summarize outsourcing trends?
2. What potential cost saving advantages might firms experience by using outsourcing?
3. What internal issues must managers address when outsourcing?
4. How should a company select an outsourcing provider?
5. What are international risk factors in the outsourcing decision?
6. How can ethics be beneficial in an outsourcing organization?
7. What are some of the possible consequences of poor outsourcing?

Using Software to Solve Outsourcing Problems

Excel, Excel OM, and POM for Windows may be used to solve most of the problems in this supplement.

Excel OM and POM for Windows both contain Factor Rating modules that can address issues such as the ones we saw in Examples S1 and S2. The Factor-Rating module was illustrated earlier in Program 8.1 in Chapter 8.

Problems*

• **S11.1** Claudia Pragram Technologies, Inc., has narrowed its choice of outsourcing provider to two firms located in different countries. Pragram wants to decide which one of the two countries is the better choice, based on risk-avoidance criteria. She has polled her executives and established four criteria. The resulting ratings for the two countries are presented in the table below, where 1 is a lower risk and 3 is a higher risk.
a) Using the unweighted factor-rating method, which country would you select?
b) If the first two factors (price and nearness) are given a weight of 2, and the last two factors (technology and history) are given a weight of 1, how does your answer change? **Px**

Selection Criterion	England	Canada
Price of service from outsourcer	2	3
Nearness of facilities to client	3	1
Level of technology	1	3
History of successful outsourcing	1	2

*Note: **Px** means the problem may be solved with POM for Windows and/or Excel OM.

• **S11.2** Using the same ratings given in Problem S11.1, assume that the executives have determined four criteria weightings: Price, with a weight of 0.1; Nearness, with 0.6; Technology, with 0.2; and History, with 0.1.
a) Using the weighted factor-rating method, which country would you select?
b) Double each of the weights used in part (a) (to 0.2, 1.2, 0.4, and 0.2, respectively). What effect does this have on your answer? Why? **Px**

• **S11.3** Ranga Ramasesh is the operations manager for a firm that is trying to decide which one of four countries it should research for possible outsourcing providers. The first step is to select a country based on cultural risk factors, which are critical to eventual business success with the provider. Ranga has reviewed outsourcing provider directories and found that the four countries in the table that follows have an ample number of providers from which they can choose. To aid in the country selection step, he has enlisted the aid of a cultural expert, John Wang, who has provided ratings of the various criteria in the table that follows. The resulting ratings are on a 1 to 10 scale, where 1 is a low risk and 10 is a high risk.
a) Using the unweighted factor-rating method, which country should Ranga select based on risk avoidance?

b) If Peru's ratings for "Society value of quality work" and "Individualism attitudes" are each lowered by 50%, how does your answer to part (a) change? **Px**

Culture Selection Criterion	Mexico	Panama	Costa Rica	Peru
Trust	1	2	2	1
Society value of quality work	7	10	9	10
Religious attitudes	3	3	3	5
Individualism attitudes	5	2	4	8
Time orientation attitudes	4	6	7	3
Uncertainty avoidance attitudes	3	2	4	2

•• **S11.4** Using the same ratings given in Problem S11.3(a), assume that John Wang has determined six criteria weightings: Trust, with a weight of 0.4; Quality, with 0.2; Religious, with 0.1; Individualism, with 0.1; Time, with 0.1; and Uncertainty, with 0.1. Using the weighted factor-rating method, which country should Ranga select? **Px**

•• **S11.5** Charles Teplitz's firm wishes to use factor rating to help select an outsourcing provider of logistics services.
a) With weights from 1–5 (5 highest) and ratings 1–100 (100 highest), use the following table to help Teplitz make his decision:

		Rating of Logistics Providers		
Criterion	Weight	Atlanta Shipping	Seattle Delivery	Utah Freight
Quality	5	90	80	75
Delivery	3	70	85	70
Cost	2	70	80	95

b) Teplitz decides to increase the weights for quality, delivery, and cost to 10, 6, and 4, respectively. How does this change your conclusions? Why?
c) If Atlanta Shipping's ratings for each of the factors increase by 10%, what are the new results? **Px**

• **S11.6** Walker Accounting Software is marketed to small accounting firms throughout the U.S. and Canada. Owner George Walker has decided to outsource the company's help desk and is considering three providers: Manila Call Center (Philippines), Delhi Services (India), and Moscow Bell (Russia). The following table summarizes the data Walker has assembled. Which outsourcing firm has the best rating? (Higher weights imply higher importance and higher ratings imply more desirable providers.) **Px**

	Importance Weight	Provider Ratings		
Criterion		Manila	Delhi	Moscow
Flexibility	0.5	5	1	9
Trustworthiness	0.1	5	5	2
Price	0.2	4	3	6
Delivery	0.2	5	6	6

•••• **S11.7** Price Technologies, a California-based high-tech manufacturer, is considering outsourcing some of its electronics production. Four firms have responded to its request for bids, and CEO Willard Price has started to perform an analysis on the scores his OM team has entered in the table below.

		Ratings of Outsource Providers			
Factor	Weight	A	B	C	D
Labor	w	5	4	3	5
Quality procedures	30	2	3	5	1
Logistics system	5	3	4	3	5
Price	25	5	3	4	4
Trustworthiness	5	3	2	3	5
Technology in place	15	2	5	4	4
Management team	15	5	4	2	1

Weights are on a scale from 1 through 30, and the outsourcing provider scores are on a scale of 1 through 5. The weight for the labor factor is shown as a w because Price's OM team cannot agree on a value for this weight. For what range of values of w, if any, is company C a recommended outsourcing provider, according to the factor-rating method?

Case Studies

▶ Outsourcing to Tata

While some states, such as Tennessee, have been quick to ban or limit international outsourcing of government activities, other state governments have sought to take advantage of low-cost opportunities that international outsourcing can offer.

The state of New Mexico's Labor Department hired Tata Consultancy Services, an Indian outsourcing firm, to redo New Mexico's unemployment compensation computer system. While Tata had completed work for other states, including Pennsylvania and New York, it had never worked on an unemployment compensation system. Also, New Mexico agreed to allow Tata to do all computer software work in India, apparently with insufficient monitoring of progress by New Mexico officials responsible for the outsourcing project.

The new system should have been completed in 6 months, which put the due date in December 2001. Unfortunately, things did not work out well. The initial system was delivered 1 year later. But in late 2004 it was still not working. Also, the outsourcing project went way over the budget of $3.6 million, up to $13 million. The warranty for the system ended in 2003, leaving New Mexico with a situation of either suing Tata to complete the project (it was estimated at 80% complete) or hiring someone to fix it. Tata's position was that it had complied with the outsourcing agreement and was willing to continue fixing the system if it could receive additional compensation to justify additional work.

Discussion Questions

1. Use the process in Table S11.2 to analyze what New Mexico could have done to achieve a more successful outcome.
2. Is this a case of cultural misunderstanding, or could the same result have occurred if a U.S. firm, such as IBM, had been selected?
3. Conduct your own research to assess the risks of outsourcing any information technology project. (*Computerworld* is one good source.)

▶ Outsourcing Offshore at Darden   Video Case

Darden Restaurants, owner of popular brands such as Olive Garden and Red Lobster, serves more than 300 million meals annually in over 1,700 restaurants across the U.S. and Canada. To achieve competitive advantage via its supply chain, Darden must achieve excellence at each step. With purchases from 35 countries, and seafood products with a shelf life as short as 4 days, this is a complex and challenging task.

Those 300 million meals annually mean 40 million pounds of shrimp and huge quantities of tilapia, swordfish, and other fresh purchases. Fresh seafood is typically flown to the U.S. and monitored each step of the way to ensure that 34°F is maintained.

Darden's purchasing agents travel the world to find competitive advantage in the supply chain. Darden personnel from supply chain and development, quality assurance, and environmental relations contribute to developing, evaluating, and checking suppliers. Darden also has seven native-speaking representatives living on other continents to provide continuing support and evaluation of suppliers. All suppliers must abide by Darden's food standards, which typically exceed FDA and other industry standards. Darden expects continuous improvement in durable relationships that increase quality and reduce cost.

Darden's aggressiveness and development of a sophisticated supply chain provides an opportunity for outsourcing. Much food preparation is labor intensive and is often more efficient when handled in bulk. This is particularly true where large volumes may justify capital investment. For instance, Tyson and Iowa Beef prepare meats to Darden's specifications much more economically than can individual restaurants. Similarly, Darden has found that it can outsource both the cutting of salmon to the proper portion size and the cracking/peeling of shrimp more cost-effectively offshore than in U.S. distribution centers or individual restaurants.

Discussion Questions*

1. What are some outsourcing opportunities in a restaurant?
2. What supply-chain issues are unique to a firm sourcing from 35 countries?
3. Examine how other firms or industries develop international supply chains as compared to Darden.
4. Why does Darden outsource harvesting and preparation of much of its seafood?

*You may wish to view the video that accompanies this case study before answering these questions.

Bibliography

Aron, R., and J. V. Singh. "Getting Offshoring Right." *Harvard Business Review* (December 2005): 135–143.

Bravard, J., and R. Morgan. *Smarter Outsourcing.* Upper Saddle River, NJ: Pearson (2006).

Champy, James. *Avoiding the Seven Deadly Sins of Outsourcing Relationships.* Plano, TX: Perot Systems (2005).

Friedman, Thomas. *The World Is Flat: A Brief History of the 21st Century.* New York: Farrar, Straus, and Giroux (2005).

Greenwald, Bruce C., and Judd Kahn. *Globalization: The Irrational Fear That Someone in China Will Take Your Job.* New York: Wiley (2009).

Halvey, J. K., and B. M. Melby. *Business Process Outsourcing*, 2nd ed. New York: Wiley (2007).

Hirschheim, R., A. Heinzl, and J. Dibbern. *Information Systems Outsourcing.* Secaucus, NJ: Springer (2009).

Lee, Hau L., and Chung-Yee Lee. *Building Supply Chain Excellence in Emerging Economies.* Secaucus, NJ: Springer (2007).

Messner, W. *Working with India*, Secaucus, NJ: Springer (2009).

Midler, Paul. *Poorly Made in China: An Insider's Account of the Tactics behind China's Production Game.* New York: Wiley (2009).

Thomas, A. R., and T. J. Wilkinson. "The Outsourcing Compulsion." *MIT Sloan Management Review* 48, no. 1 (Fall 2006): 10.

Webb, L., and J. Laborde. "Crafting a Successful Outsourcing Vendor/Client Relationship." *Business Process Management Journal* 11, no. 5 (2005): 437–443.

Whitten, Dwayne, and Dorothy Leidner. "Bringing IT Back: An Analysis of the Decision to Backsource or Switch Vendors." *Decision Sciences* 37, no. 4 (November 2006): 605–621.

Yourdon, Edward. *Outsource: Competing in the Global Productivity Race.* Upper Saddle River, NJ: Prentice Hall (2005).

Supplement 11 *Rapid* Review

PEARSON
myomlab

Main Heading	Review Material	
WHAT IS OUTSOURCING?	■ **Outsourcing**—Procuring from external sources services or products that are normally part of an organization. Some organizations use outsourcing to replace entire purchasing, information systems, marketing, finance, and operations departments. ■ **Offshoring**—Moving a business process to a foreign country but retaining control of it. Outsourcing is not a new concept; it is simply an extension of the long-standing practice of *subcontracting* production activities. Outsourced manufacturing, also known as contract manufacturing, is becoming standard practice in many industries. Outsourcing implies an agreement (typically a legally binding contract) with an external organization.	**VIDEO S11.1** Outsourcing offshore at Darden
STRATEGIC PLANNING AND CORE COMPETENCIES	■ **Core competencies**—An organization's unique skills, talents, and capabilities. Core competencies may include specialized knowledge, proprietary technology or information, and unique production methods. *Non-core activities*, which can be a sizable portion of an organization's total business, are good candidates for outsourcing. ■ **Theory of comparative advantage**—A theory which states that countries benefit from specializing in (and exporting) products and services in which they have relative advantage and importing goods in which they have a relative disadvantage. ■ **Backsourcing**—The return of business activity to the original firm.	
RISKS OF OUTSOURCING	Perhaps half of all outsourcing agreements fail because of inappropriate planning and analysis. Potential risks of outsourcing include: • In some countries, erratic power grids, difficult local government officials, inexperienced managers, or unmotivated employees • A drop in quality or customer service • Political backlash that results from outsourcing to foreign countries • Changes in employment levels • Changes in facilities and processes needed to receive components in a different state of assembly • Vastly expanded logistics issues, including insurance, customs, and timing The most common reason given for outsourcing failure is that the decision was made without sufficient understanding and analysis.	
EVALUATING OUTSOURCING RISK WITH FACTOR RATING	The factor-rating method is an excellent tool for dealing with both country risk assessment and provider selection problems. Including the home country of the outsourcing firm in a factor-rating analysis helps document the risks that a domestic outsourcing provider poses compared to the risks posed by international providers. Including the home country in the analysis also helps justify final strategy selection to stakeholders who might question it. ■ **Nearshoring**—Choosing an outsource provider in the home country or in a nearby country. Nearshoring can be a good strategy for businesses and governments seeking both control and cost advantages.	Problems: S11.1–S11.7
ADVANTAGES AND DISADVANTAGES OF OUTSOURCING	Advantages of outsourcing include: • *Cost savings*: The number-one reason driving outsourcing for many firms is the possibility of significant cost savings, particularly for labor. • *Gaining outside expertise*: In addition to gaining access to a broad base of skills that are unavailable in-house, an outsourcing provider may be a source of innovation for improving products, processes, and services. • *Improving operations and service*: An outsourcing provider may have production flexibility. This may allow the client firm to win orders by more quickly introducing new products and services. • *Focusing on core competencies*: An outsourcing provider brings *its* core competencies to the supply chain. This frees up the firm's human, physical, and financial resources to reallocate to the firm's own core competencies.	

Main Heading	Review Material
	• *Gaining outside technology*: Firms can outsource to state-of-the-art providers instead of retaining old (legacy) systems. These firms do not have to invest in new technology, thereby cutting risks. • *Other advantages*: The client firm may improve its performance and image by associating with an outstanding supplier. Outsourcing can also be used as a strategy for downsizing, or "reengineering," a firm. Potential disadvantages of outsourcing include: • *Increased transportation costs*: Delivery costs may rise substantially if distance increases from an outsourcing provider to a client firm. • *Loss of control*: This disadvantage can permeate and link to all other problems with outsourcing. When managers lose control of some operations, costs may increase because it's harder to assess and control them. • *Creating future competitors* • *Negative impact on employees*: Employee morale may drop when functions are outsourced, particularly when friends lose their jobs. • *Longer-term impact*: Some disadvantages of outsourcing tend to be longer term than the advantages of outsourcing. In other words, many of the risks firms run by outsourcing may not show up on the bottom line until some time in the future.
AUDITS AND METRICS TO EVALUATE PERFORMANCE	Outsourcing agreements must specify results and outcomes. Management needs an evaluation process to ensure satisfactory continuing performance. At a minimum, the product or service must be defined in terms of quality, customer satisfaction, delivery, cost, and improvement. When the outsourced product or service plays a major role in strategy and winning orders, the relationship needs to be based on continuing communication, understanding, trust, and performance.
ETHICAL ISSUES IN OUTSOURCING	Some outsourcing policies linked to ethical principles include avoid outsourcing in a way that violates religious holidays; don't use outsourcing to move pollution from one country to another; don't use outsourcing to take advantage of cheap labor that leads to employee abuse; don't accept outsourcing that violates basic human rights; don't use outsourcing as a short-term arrangement to reduce costs—view it as a long-term partnership; and don't think an outsourcing agreement will prevent loss of technology, but use the inevitable sharing to build a good relationship with outsourcing firms.

Self Test

■ **Before taking the self-test,** refer to the learning objectives listed at the beginning of the supplement and the key terms listed at the end of the supplement.

LO1. Core competencies are those strengths in a firm that include:
  a) specialized skills.
  b) unique production methods.
  c) proprietary information/knowledge.
  d) things a company does better than others.
  e) all of the above.

LO2. Outsourcing can be a risky proposition because:
  a) about half of all outsourcing agreements fail.
  b) it saves only about 30% in labor costs.
  c) labor costs are increasing throughout the world.
  d) a non-core competency is outsourced.
  e) shipping costs are increasing.

LO3. Evaluating outsourcing providers by comparing their weighted average scores involves:
  a) factor-rating analysis.

  b) cost-volume analysis.
  c) transportation model analysis.
  d) linear regression analysis.
  e) crossover analysis.

LO4. Advantages of outsourcing include:
  a) focusing on core competencies and cost savings.
  b) gaining outside technology and creating new markets in India for U.S. products.
  c) improving operations by closing plants in Malaysia.
  d) employees wanting to leave the firm.
  e) reduced problems with logistics

Answers: LO1. e; LO2. a; LO3. a; LO4. a.

FORECASTING DEMAND

4 Forecasting Demand

Chapter Outline

GLOBAL COMPANY PROFILE: WALT DISNEY PARKS & RESORTS

FORECASTING PROVIDES A COMPETITIVE ADVANTAGE FOR DISNEY

When it comes to the world's most respected global brands, Walt Disney Parks & Resorts is a visible leader. Although the monarch of this magic kingdom is no man but a mouse—Mickey Mouse—it's CEO Robert Iger who daily manages the entertainment giant.

Disney's global portfolio includes Hong Kong Disneyland (opened 2005), Disneyland Paris (1992), and Tokyo Disneyland (1983). But it is Walt Disney World Resort (in Florida) and Disneyland Resort (in California) that drive profits in this $43 billion corporation, which is ranked 54th in the *Fortune* 500 and 79th in the *Financial Times* Global 500.

Revenues at Disney are all about people—how many visit the parks and how they spend money while there. When Iger receives a daily report from his four theme parks near Orlando, the report contains only two numbers: the *forecast* of yesterday's attendance at the parks (Magic Kingdom, Epcot, Disney's Animal Kingdom, Disney-MGM Studios, Typhoon Lagoon, and Blizzard Beach) and the *actual* attendance. An error close to zero is expected. Iger takes his forecasts very seriously.

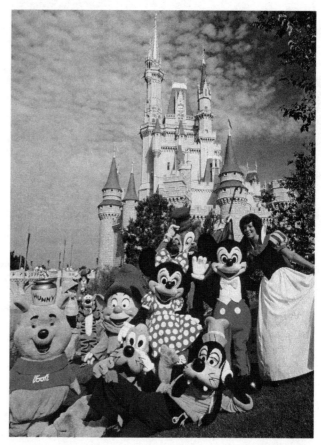

Mickey and Minnie Mouse, and other Disney characters, with Cinderella Castle in the background, provide the public image of Disney to the world. Forecasts drive the work schedules of 58,000 cast members working at Walt Disney World Resort near Orlando.

The giant sphere is the symbol of Epcot, one of Disney's four Orlando parks, for which forecasts of meals, lodging, entertainment, and transportation must be made. This Disney monorail moves guests among parks and the 20 hotels on the massive 47-square-mile property (about the size of San Francisco and twice the size of Manhattan).

▶ A daily forecast of attendance is made by adjusting Disney's annual operating plan for weather forecasts, the previous day's crowds, conventions, and seasonal variations. One of the two water parks at Walt Disney World Resort, Typhoon Lagoon, is shown here.

◀ Forecasts are critical to making sure rides are not overcrowded. Disney is good at "managing demand" with techniques such as adding more street activities to reduce long lines for rides.

The forecasting team at Walt Disney World Resort doesn't just do a daily prediction, however, and Iger is not its only customer. The team also provides daily, weekly, monthly, annual, and 5-year forecasts to the labor management, maintenance, operations, finance, and park scheduling departments. Forecasters use judgmental models, econometric models, moving-average models, and regression analysis.

With 20% of Walt Disney World Resort's customers coming from outside the United States, its economic model includes such variables as gross domestic product (GDP), cross-exchange rates, and arrivals into the U.S. Disney also uses 35 analysts and 70 field people to survey 1 million people each year. The surveys, administered to guests at the parks and its 20 hotels, to employees, and to travel industry professionals, examine future travel plans and experiences at the parks. This helps forecast not only attendance but behavior at each ride (e.g., how long people will wait, how many times they will ride). Inputs to the monthly forecasting model include airline specials, speeches by the chair of the Federal Reserve, and Wall Street trends. Disney even monitors 3,000 school districts inside and outside the U.S. for holiday/vacation schedules. With this approach, Disney's 5-year attendance forecast yields just a 5% error on average. Its annual forecasts have a 0% to 3% error.

▲ Disney uses characters such as Minnie Mouse to entertain guests when lines are forecast to be long. On slow days, Disney calls fewer cast members to work.

Attendance forecasts for the parks drive a whole slew of management decisions. For example, capacity on any day can be increased by opening at 8 A.M. instead of the usual 9 A.M., by opening more shows or rides, by adding more food/beverage carts (9 million hamburgers and 50 million Cokes are sold per year!), and by bringing in more employees (called "cast members"). Cast members are scheduled in 15-minute intervals throughout the parks for flexibility. Demand can be managed by limiting the number of guests admitted to the parks, with the "FAST PASS" reservation system, and by shifting crowds from rides to more street parades.

At Disney, forecasting is a key driver in the company's success and competitive advantage.

Chapter 4 **Learning Objectives**

> **AUTHOR COMMENT**
> An increasingly complex world economy makes forecasting challenging.

WHAT IS FORECASTING?

Every day, managers like those at Disney make decisions without knowing what will happen in the future. They order inventory without knowing what sales will be, purchase new equipment despite uncertainty about demand for products, and make investments without knowing what profits will be. Managers are always trying to make better estimates of what will happen in the future in the face of uncertainty. Making good estimates is the main purpose of forecasting.

In this chapter, we examine different types of forecasts and present a variety of forecasting models. Our purpose is to show that there are many ways for managers to forecast. We also provide an overview of business sales forecasting and describe how to prepare, monitor, and judge the accuracy of a forecast. Good forecasts are an *essential* part of efficient service and manufacturing operations.

Forecasting
The art and science of predicting future events.

Forecasting is the art and science of predicting future events. Forecasting may involve taking historical data and projecting them into the future with some sort of mathematical model. It may be a subjective or intuitive prediction. Or it may involve a combination of these—that is, a mathematical model adjusted by a manager's good judgment.

As we introduce different forecasting techniques in this chapter, you will see that there is seldom one superior method. What works best in one firm under one set of conditions may be a complete disaster in another organization, or even in a different department of the same firm. In addition, you will see that there are limits as to what can be expected from forecasts. They are seldom, if ever, perfect. They are also costly and time-consuming to prepare and monitor.

Few businesses, however, can afford to avoid the process of forecasting by just waiting to see what happens and then taking their chances. Effective planning in both the short run and long run depends on a forecast of demand for the company's products.

Forecasting Time Horizons

LO1: Understand the three time horizons and which models apply for each

A forecast is usually classified by the *future time horizon* that it covers. Time horizons fall into three categories:

1. *Short-range forecast:* This forecast has a time span of up to 1 year but is generally less than 3 months. It is used for planning purchasing, job scheduling, workforce levels, job assignments, and production levels.
2. *Medium-range forecast:* A medium-range, or intermediate, forecast generally spans from 3 months to 3 years. It is useful in sales planning, production planning and budgeting, cash budgeting, and analysis of various operating plans.
3. *Long-range forecast:* Generally 3 years or more in time span, long-range forecasts are used in planning for new products, capital expenditures, facility location or expansion, and research and development.

Medium and long-range forecasts are distinguished from short-range forecasts by three features:

1. First, intermediate and long-run forecasts *deal with more comprehensive issues* and support management decisions regarding planning and products, plants, and processes. Implementing some facility decisions, such as GM's decision to open a new Brazilian manufacturing plant, can take 5 to 8 years from inception to completion.
2. Second, short-term forecasting usually *employs different methodologies* than longer-term forecasting. Mathematical techniques, such as moving averages, exponential smoothing,

and trend extrapolation (all of which we shall examine shortly), are common to short-run projections. Broader, *less* quantitative methods are useful in predicting such issues as whether a new product, like the optical disk recorder, should be introduced into a company's product line.

3. Finally, as you would expect, short-range forecasts *tend to be more accurate* than longer-range forecasts. Factors that influence demand change every day. Thus, as the time horizon lengthens, it is likely that forecast accuracy will diminish. It almost goes without saying, then, that sales forecasts must be updated regularly to maintain their value and integrity. After each sales period, forecasts should be reviewed and revised.

The Influence of Product Life Cycle

Another factor to consider when developing sales forecasts, especially longer ones, is product life cycle. Products, and even services, do not sell at a constant level throughout their lives. Most successful products pass through four stages: (1) introduction, (2) growth, (3) maturity, and (4) decline.

Products in the first two stages of the life cycle (such as virtual reality and the Boeing 787 Dreamliner) need longer forecasts than those in the maturity and decline stages (such as large SUVs and skateboards). Forecasts that reflect life cycle are useful in projecting different staffing levels, inventory levels, and factory capacity as the product passes from the first to the last stage. The challenge of introducing new products is treated in more detail in Chapter 5.

Types of Forecasts

Organizations use three major types of forecasts in planning future operations:

1. **Economic forecasts** address the business cycle by predicting inflation rates, money supplies, housing starts, and other planning indicators.
2. **Technological forecasts** are concerned with rates of technological progress, which can result in the birth of exciting new products, requiring new plants and equipment.
3. **Demand forecasts** are projections of demand for a company's products or services. These forecasts, also called *sales forecasts*, drive a company's production, capacity, and scheduling systems and serve as inputs to financial, marketing, and personnel planning.

Economic and technological forecasting are specialized techniques that may fall outside the role of the operations manager. The emphasis in this book will therefore be on demand forecasting.

THE STRATEGIC IMPORTANCE OF FORECASTING

Good forecasts are of critical importance in all aspects of a business: *The forecast is the only estimate of demand until actual demand becomes known.* Forecasts of demand therefore drive decisions in many areas. Let's look at the impact of product demand forecast on three activities: (1) human resources, (2) capacity, and (3) supply-chain management.

Human Resources

Hiring, training, and laying off workers all depend on anticipated demand. If the human resources department must hire additional workers without warning, the amount of training declines and the quality of the workforce suffers. A large Louisiana chemical firm almost lost its biggest customer when a quick expansion to around-the-clock shifts led to a total breakdown in quality control on the second and third shifts.

Capacity

When capacity is inadequate, the resulting shortages can lead to loss of customers and market share. This is exactly what happened to Nabisco when it underestimated the huge demand for its new low-fat Snackwell Devil's Food Cookies. Even with production lines working overtime, Nabisco could not keep up with demand, and it lost customers. As the photo on the next page shows, Amazon made the same error with its Kindle. On the other hand, when excess capacity exists, costs can skyrocket.

Economic forecasts
Planning indicators that are valuable in helping organizations prepare medium- to long-range forecasts.

Technological forecasts
Long-term forecasts concerned with the rates of technological progress.

Demand forecasts
Projections of a company's sales for each time period in the planning horizon.

VIDEO 4.1
Forecasting at Hard Rock Cafe

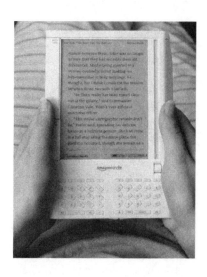

Even vaunted Amazon can make a major forecasting error, as it did in the case of its much-hyped Kindle e-book reader. With the holiday shopping season at hand, Amazon's Web page announced "Due to heavy customer demand, Kindle is sold out . . . ships in 11 to 13 weeks." Underforecasting demand for the product was the culprit, according to the Taiwanese manufacturer Prime View, which has since ramped up production.

Supply-Chain Management

Good supplier relations and the ensuing price advantages for materials and parts depend on accurate forecasts. In the global marketplace, where expensive components for Boeing 787 jets are manufactured in dozens of countries, coordination driven by forecasts is critical. Scheduling transportation to Seattle for final assembly at the lowest possible cost means no last-minute surprises that can harm already-low profit margins.

SEVEN STEPS IN THE FORECASTING SYSTEM

Forecasting follows seven basic steps. We use Disney World, the focus of this chapter's *Global Company Profile*, as an example of each step:

1. *Determine the use of the forecast:* Disney uses park attendance forecasts to drive decisions about staffing, opening times, ride availability, and food supplies.
2. *Select the items to be forecasted:* For Disney World, there are six main parks. A forecast of daily attendance at each is the main number that determines labor, maintenance, and scheduling.
3. *Determine the time horizon of the forecast:* Is it short, medium, or long term? Disney develops daily, weekly, monthly, annual, and 5-year forecasts.
4. *Select the forecasting model(s):* Disney uses a variety of statistical models that we shall discuss, including moving averages, econometrics, and regression analysis. It also employs judgmental, or nonquantitative, models.
5. *Gather the data needed to make the forecast:* Disney's forecasting team employs 35 analysts and 70 field personnel to survey 1 million people/businesses every year. Disney also uses a firm called Global Insights for travel industry forecasts and gathers data on exchange rates, arrivals into the U.S., airline specials, Wall Street trends, and school vacation schedules.
6. *Make the forecast.*
7. *Validate and implement the results:* At Disney, forecasts are reviewed daily at the highest levels to make sure that the model, assumptions, and data are valid. Error measures are applied; then the forecasts are used to schedule personnel down to 15-minute intervals.

These seven steps present a systematic way of initiating, designing, and implementing a forecasting system. When the system is to be used to generate forecasts regularly over time, data must be routinely collected. Then actual computations are usually made by computer.

Regardless of the system that firms like Disney use, each company faces several realities:

- Forecasts are seldom perfect. This means that outside factors that we cannot predict or control often impact the forecast. Companies need to allow for this reality.
- Most forecasting techniques assume that there is some underlying stability in the system. Consequently, some firms automate their predictions using computerized forecasting software, then closely monitor only the product items whose demand is erratic.
- Both product family and aggregated forecasts are more accurate than individual product forecasts. Disney, for example, aggregates daily attendance forecasts by park. This approach helps balance the over- and underpredictions of each of the six attractions.

FORECASTING APPROACHES

AUTHOR COMMENT
Forecasting is part science and part art.

There are two general approaches to forecasting, just as there are two ways to tackle all decision modeling. One is a quantitative analysis; the other is a qualitative approach. **Quantitative forecasts** use a variety of mathematical models that rely on historical data and/or associative variables to forecast demand. Subjective or **qualitative forecasts** incorporate such factors as the decision maker's intuition, emotions, personal experiences, and value system in reaching a forecast. Some firms use one approach and some use the other. In practice, a combination of the two is usually most effective.

Quantitative forecasts
Forecasts that employ mathematical modeling to forecast demand.

Qualitative forecasts
Forecasts that incorporate such factors as the decision maker's intuition, emotions, personal experiences, and value system.

Overview of Qualitative Methods

In this section, we consider four different *qualitative* forecasting techniques:

LO2: Explain when to use each of the four qualitative models

1. **Jury of executive opinion:** Under this method, the opinions of a group of high-level experts or managers, often in combination with statistical models, are pooled to arrive at a group estimate of demand. Bristol-Myers Squibb Company, for example, uses 220 well-known research scientists as its jury of executive opinion to get a grasp on future trends in the world of medical research.

2. **Delphi method:** There are three different types of participants in the Delphi method: decision makers, staff personnel, and respondents. Decision makers usually consist of a group of 5 to 10 experts who will be making the actual forecast. Staff personnel assist decision makers by preparing, distributing, collecting, and summarizing a series of questionnaires and survey results. The respondents are a group of people, often located in different places, whose judgments are valued. This group provides inputs to the decision makers before the forecast is made.

   The state of Alaska, for example, has used the Delphi method to develop its long-range economic forecast. An amazing 90% of the state's budget is derived from 1.5 million barrels of oil pumped daily through a pipeline at Prudhoe Bay. The large Delphi panel of experts had to represent all groups and opinions in the state and all geographic areas. Delphi was the perfect forecasting tool because panelist travel could be avoided. It also meant that leading Alaskans could participate because their schedules were not affected by meetings and distances.

3. **Sales force composite:** In this approach, each salesperson estimates what sales will be in his or her region. These forecasts are then reviewed to ensure that they are realistic. Then they are combined at the district and national levels to reach an overall forecast. A variation of this approach occurs at Lexus, where every quarter Lexus dealers have a "make meeting." At this meeting, they talk about what is selling, in what colors, and with what options, so the factory knows what to build.

4. **Consumer market survey:** This method solicits input from customers or potential customers regarding future purchasing plans. It can help not only in preparing a forecast but also in improving product design and planning for new products. The consumer market survey and sales force composite methods can, however, suffer from overly optimistic forecasts that arise from customer input. The 2001 crash of the telecommunication industry was the result of overexpansion to meet "explosive customer demand." Where did these data come from? Oplink Communications, a Nortel Networks supplier, says its "company forecasts over the last few years were based mainly on informal conversations with customers."[1]

Jury of executive opinion
A forecasting technique that uses the opinion of a small group of high-level managers to form a group estimate of demand.

Delphi method
A forecasting technique using a group process that allows experts to make forecasts.

Sales force composite
A forecasting technique based on salespersons' estimates of expected sales.

Consumer market survey
A forecasting method that solicits input from customers or potential customers regarding future purchasing plans.

Overview of Quantitative Methods

Five quantitative forecasting methods, all of which use historical data, are described in this chapter. They fall into two categories:

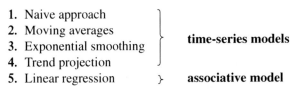

1. Naive approach
2. Moving averages
3. Exponential smoothing   **time-series models**
4. Trend projection
5. Linear regression   **associative model**

---

[1]"Lousy Sales Forecasts Helped Fuel the Telecom Mess," *The Wall Street Journal* (July 9, 2001): B1–B4.

Time series
A forecasting technique that uses a series of past data points to make a forecast.

Time-Series Models   Time-series models predict on the assumption that the future is a function of the past. In other words, they look at what has happened over a period of time and use a series of past data to make a forecast. If we are predicting sales of lawn mowers, we use the past sales for lawn mowers to make the forecasts.

Associative Models   Associative models, such as linear regression, incorporate the variables or factors that might influence the quantity being forecast. For example, an associative model for lawn mower sales might use factors such as new housing starts, advertising budget, and competitors' prices.

AUTHOR COMMENT
Here is the meat of this chapter. We now show you a wide variety of models that use time-series data.

TIME-SERIES FORECASTING

A time series is based on a sequence of evenly spaced (weekly, monthly, quarterly, and so on) data points. Examples include weekly sales of Nike Air Jordans, quarterly earnings reports of Microsoft stock, daily shipments of Coors beer, and annual consumer price indices. Forecasting time-series data implies that future values are predicted *only* from past values and that other variables, no matter how potentially valuable, may be ignored.

Decomposition of a Time Series

Analyzing time series means breaking down past data into components and then projecting them forward. A time series has four components:

1. *Trend* is the gradual upward or downward movement of the data over time. Changes in income, population, age distribution, or cultural views may account for movement in trend.
2. *Seasonality* is a data pattern that repeats itself after a period of days, weeks, months, or quarters. There are six common seasonality patterns:

AUTHOR COMMENT
The peak "seasons" for sales of Frito-Lay chips are the Super Bowl, Memorial Day, Labor Day, and the Fourth of July.

Period of Pattern	"Season" Length	Number of "Seasons" in Pattern
Week	Day	7
Month	Week	4–$4\frac{1}{2}$
Month	Day	28–31
Year	Quarter	4
Year	Month	12
Year	Week	52

Restaurants and barber shops, for example, experience weekly seasons, with Saturday being the peak of business. See the *OM in Action* box "Forecasting at Olive Garden and Red Lobster." Beer distributors forecast yearly patterns, with monthly seasons. Three "seasons"—May, July, and September—each contain a big beer-drinking holiday.

3. *Cycles* are patterns in the data that occur every several years. They are usually tied into the business cycle and are of major importance in short-term business analysis and planning. Predicting business cycles is difficult because they may be affected by political events or by international turmoil.
4. *Random variations* are "blips" in the data caused by chance and unusual situations. They follow no discernible pattern, so they cannot be predicted.

Figure 4.1 illustrates a demand over a 4-year period. It shows the average, trend, seasonal components, and random variations around the demand curve. The average demand is the sum of the demand for each period divided by the number of data periods.

Naive Approach

Naive approach
A forecasting technique which assumes that demand in the next period is equal to demand in the most recent period.

The simplest way to forecast is to assume that demand in the next period will be equal to demand in the most recent period. In other words, if sales of a product—say, Nokia cell phones—were 68 units in January, we can forecast that February's sales will also be 68 phones. Does this make any sense? It turns out that for some product lines, this **naive approach** is the most cost-effective

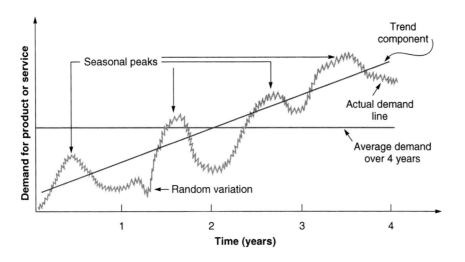

► **FIGURE 4.1**
Demand Charted over 4 Years with a Growth Trend and Seasonality Indicated

> **AUTHOR COMMENT**
> Forecasting is easy when demand is stable. But with trend, seasonality, and cycles considered, the job is a lot more interesting.

and efficient objective forecasting model. At least it provides a starting point against which more sophisticated models that follow can be compared.

Moving Averages

A **moving-average** forecast uses a number of historical actual data values to generate a forecast. Moving averages are useful *if we can assume that market demands will stay fairly steady over time*. A 4-month moving average is found by simply summing the demand during the past 4 months and dividing by 4. With each passing month, the most recent month's data are added to the sum of the previous 3 months' data, and the earliest month is dropped. This practice tends to smooth out short-term irregularities in the data series.

Mathematically, the simple moving average (which serves as an estimate of the next period's demand) is expressed as

$$\text{Moving average} = \frac{\Sigma \text{ demand in previous } n \text{ periods}}{n} \tag{4-1}$$

where n is the number of periods in the moving average—for example, 4, 5, or 6 months, respectively, for a 4-, 5-, or 6-period moving average.

Moving averages
A forecasting method that uses an average of the n most recent periods of data to forecast the next period.

OM in Action ► Forecasting at Olive Garden and Red Lobster

It's Friday night in the college town of Gainesville, Florida, and the local Olive Garden restaurant is humming. Customers may wait an average of 30 minutes for a table, but they can sample new wines and cheeses and admire scenic paintings of Italian villages on the Tuscan-style restaurant's walls. Then comes dinner with portions so huge that many people take home a doggie bag. The typical bill: under $15 per person.

Crowds flock to the Darden restaurant chain's Olive Garden, Red Lobster, Seasons 52, and Bahama Breeze for value and consistency—*and* they get it.

Every night, Darden's computers crank out forecasts that tell store managers what demand to anticipate the next day. The forecasting software generates a total meal forecast and breaks that down into specific menu items. The system tells a manager, for instance, that if 625 meals will be served the next day, "you will serve these items in these quantities. So before you go home, pull 25 pounds of shrimp and 30 pounds of crab out, and tell your operations

people to prepare 42 portion packs of chicken, 75 scampi dishes, 8 stuffed flounders, and so on." Managers often fine tune the quantities based on local conditions, such as weather or a convention, but they know what their customers are going to order.

By relying on demand history, the forecasting system has cut millions of dollars of waste out of the system. The forecast also reduces labor costs by providing the necessary information for improved scheduling. Labor costs decreased almost a full percent in the first year, translating into additional millions in savings for the Darden chain. In the low-margin restaurant business, every dollar counts.

Source: Interviews with Darden executives.

Example 1 shows how moving averages are calculated.

EXAMPLE 1 ▶

Determining the moving average

Donna's Garden Supply wants a 3-month moving-average forecast, including a forecast for next January, for shed sales.

APPROACH ▶   Storage shed sales are shown in the middle column of the table below. A 3-month moving average appears on the right.

Month	Actual Shed Sales	3-Month Moving Average
January	10	
February	12	
March	13	
April	16	$(10 + 12 + 13)/3 = 11\frac{2}{3}$
May	19	$(12 + 13 + 16)/3 = 13\frac{2}{3}$
June	23	$(13 + 16 + 19)/3 = 16$
July	26	$(16 + 19 + 23)/3 = 19\frac{1}{3}$
August	30	$(19 + 23 + 26)/3 = 22\frac{2}{3}$
September	28	$(23 + 26 + 30)/3 = 26\frac{1}{3}$
October	18	$(26 + 30 + 28)/3 = 28$
November	16	$(30 + 28 + 18)/3 = 25\frac{1}{3}$
December	14	$(28 + 18 + 16)/3 = 20\frac{2}{3}$

SOLUTION ▶   The forecast for December is $20\frac{2}{3}$. To project the demand for sheds in the coming January, we sum the October, November, and December sales and divide by 3: January forecast $= (18 + 16 + 14)/3 = 16$.

INSIGHT ▶   Management now has a forecast that averages sales for the last 3 months. It is easy to use and understand.

LEARNING EXERCISE ▶   If actual sales in December were 18 (rather than 14), what is the new January forecast? [Answer: $17\frac{1}{3}$.]

RELATED PROBLEMS ▶   4.1a, 4.2b, 4.5a, 4.6, 4.8a,b, 4.10a, 4.13b, 4.15, 4.47

EXCEL OM Data File **Ch04Ex1.xls** can be found at **www.pearsonglobaleditions.com/heizer**.

ACTIVE MODEL 4.1 This example is further illustrated in Active Model 4.1 at **www.pearsonglobaleditions.com/heizer**.

LO3: Apply the naive, moving-average, exponential smoothing, and trend methods

When a detectable trend or pattern is present, *weights* can be used to place more emphasis on recent values. This practice makes forecasting techniques more responsive to changes because more recent periods may be more heavily weighted. Choice of weights is somewhat arbitrary because there is no set formula to determine them. Therefore, deciding which weights to use requires some experience. For example, if the latest month or period is weighted too heavily, the forecast may reflect a large unusual change in the demand or sales pattern too quickly.

A weighted moving average may be expressed mathematically as:

$$\text{Weighted moving average} = \frac{\Sigma \,(\text{Weight for period } n)(\text{Demand in period } n)}{\Sigma \,\text{Weights}} \qquad (4\text{-}2)$$

Example 2 shows how to calculate a weighted moving average.

◄ **EXAMPLE 2**

**Determining the
weighted moving
average**

Donna's Garden Supply (see Example 1) wants to forecast storage shed sales by weighting the past 3 months, with more weight given to recent data to make them more significant.

APPROACH ►   Assign more weight to recent data, as follows:

Weights Applied	Period
3	Last month
2	Two months ago
$\frac{1}{6}$	Three months ago
	Sum of weights

Forecast for this month =

$$\frac{3 \times \text{Sales last mo.} + 2 \times \text{Sales 2 mos. ago} + 1 \times \text{Sales 3 mos. ago}}{\text{Sum of the weights}}$$

SOLUTION ►   The results of this weighted-average forecast are as follows:

Month	Actual Shed Sales	3-Month Weighted Moving Average
January	10	
February	12	
March	13	
April	16	$[(3 \times 13) + (2 \times 12) + (10)]/6 = 12\frac{1}{6}$
May	19	$[(3 \times 16) + (2 \times 13) + (12)]/6 = 14\frac{1}{3}$
June	23	$[(3 \times 19) + (2 \times 16) + (13)]/6 = 17$
July	26	$[(3 \times 23) + (2 \times 19) + (16)]/6 = 20\frac{1}{2}$
August	30	$[(3 \times 26) + (2 \times 23) + (19)]/6 = 23\frac{5}{6}$
September	28	$[(3 \times 30) + (2 \times 26) + (23)]/6 = 27\frac{1}{2}$
October	18	$[(3 \times 28) + (2 \times 30) + (26)]/6 = 28\frac{1}{3}$
November	16	$[(3 \times 18) + (2 \times 28) + (30)]/6 = 23\frac{1}{3}$
December	14	$[(3 \times 16) + (2 \times 18) + (28)]/6 = 18\frac{2}{3}$

INSIGHT ►   In this particular forecasting situation, you can see that more heavily weighting the latest month provides a much more accurate projection.

LEARNING EXERCISE ►   If the assigned weights were 0.50, 0.33, and 0.17 (instead of 3, 2, and 1) what is the forecast for January's weighted moving average? Why? [Answer: There is no change. These are the same *relative* weights. Note that Σ weights = 1 now, so there is no need for a denominator. When the weights sum to 1, calculations tend to be simpler.

RELATED PROBLEMS ►   4.1b, 4.2c, 4.5c, 4.6, 4.7, 4.10b

EXCEL OM Data File **Ch04Ex2.xls** can be found at **www.pearsonglobaleditions.com/heizer**.

Both simple and weighted moving averages are effective in smoothing out sudden fluctuations in the demand pattern to provide stable estimates. Moving averages do, however, present three problems:

1. Increasing the size of *n* (the number of periods averaged) does smooth out fluctuations better, but it makes the method less sensitive to *real* changes in the data.
2. Moving averages cannot pick up trends very well. Because they are averages, they will always stay within past levels and will not predict changes to either higher or lower levels. That is, they *lag* the actual values.
3. Moving averages require extensive records of past data.

Figure 4.2, a plot of the data in Examples 1 and 2, illustrates the lag effect of the moving-average models. Note that both the moving-average and weighted-moving-average lines lag the actual demand. The weighted moving average, however, usually reacts more quickly to demand

▶ **FIGURE 4.2**
Actual Demand vs. Moving-Average and Weighted-Moving-Average Methods for Donna's Garden Supply

AUTHOR COMMENT
Moving average methods always lag behind when there is a trend present, as shown by the blue line (actual sales) for January through August.

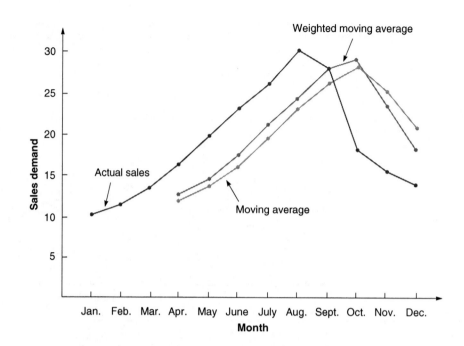

changes. Even in periods of downturn (see November and December), it more closely tracks the demand.

Exponential Smoothing

Exponential smoothing
A weighted-moving-average forecasting technique in which data points are weighted by an exponential function.

Exponential smoothing is a sophisticated weighted-moving-average forecasting method that is still fairly easy to use. It involves very *little* record keeping of past data. The basic exponential smoothing formula can be shown as follows:

New forecast = Last period's forecast
+ α (Last period's actual demand − Last period's forecast)   (4-3)

Smoothing constant
The weighting factor used in an exponential smoothing forecast, a number between 0 and 1.

where α is a weight, or **smoothing constant**, chosen by the forecaster, that has a value between 0 and 1. Equation (4-3) can also be written mathematically as:

$$F_t = F_{t-1} + \alpha(A_{t-1} - F_{t-1})$$ (4-4)

where F_t = new forecast
   F_{t-1} = previous period's forecast
   α = smoothing (or weighting) constant ($0 \le \alpha \le 1$)
   A_{t-1} = previous period's actual demand

The concept is not complex. The latest estimate of demand is equal to the old estimate adjusted by a fraction of the difference between the last period's actual demand and the old estimate. Example 3 shows how to use exponential smoothing to derive a forecast.

EXAMPLE 3 ▶
Determining a forecast via exponential smoothing

In January, a car dealer predicted February demand for 142 Ford Mustangs. Actual February demand was 153 autos. Using a smoothing constant chosen by management of α = .20, the dealer wants to forecast March demand using the exponential smoothing model.

APPROACH ▶   The exponential smoothing model in Equations (4-3) and (4-4) can be applied.

SOLUTION ▶   Substituting the sample data into the formula, we obtain:

New forecast (for Marche demand) = 142 + .2(153 − 142) = 142 + 2.2
= 144.2

Thus, the March demand forecast for Ford Mustangs is rounded to 144.

The *smoothing constant*, α, is generally in the range from .05 to .50 for business applications. It can be changed to give more weight to recent data (when α is high) or more weight to past data (when α is low). When α reaches the extreme of 1.0, then in Equation (4-4), $F_t = 1.0A_{t-1}$. All the older values drop out, and the forecast becomes identical to the naive model mentioned earlier in this chapter. That is, the forecast for the next period is just the same as this period's demand.

The following table helps illustrate this concept. For example, when $\alpha = .5$, we can see that the new forecast is based almost entirely on demand in the last three or four periods. When $\alpha = .1$, the forecast places little weight on recent demand and takes many periods (about 19) of historical values into account.

	Weight Assigned to				
Smoothing Constant	**Most Recent Period** (α)	**2nd Most Recent Period** $\alpha(1 - \alpha)$	**3rd Most Recent Period** $\alpha(1 - \alpha)^2$	**4th Most Recent Period** $\alpha(1 - \alpha)^3$	**5th Most Recent Period** $\alpha(1 - \alpha)^4$
$\alpha = .1$	.1	.09	.081	.073	.066
$\alpha = .5$	.5	.25	.125	.063	.031

Selecting the Smoothing Constant   The exponential smoothing approach is easy to use, and it has been successfully applied in virtually every type of business. However, the appropriate value of the smoothing constant, α, can make the difference between an accurate forecast and an inaccurate forecast. High values of α are chosen when the underlying average is likely to change. Low values of α are used when the underlying average is fairly stable. In picking a value for the smoothing constant, the objective is to obtain the most accurate forecast.

Measuring Forecast Error

The overall accuracy of any forecasting model—moving average, exponential smoothing, or other—can be determined by comparing the forecasted values with the actual or observed values. If F_t denotes the forecast in period t, and A_t denotes the actual demand in period t, the *forecast error* (or deviation) is defined as:

$$\text{Forecast error} = \text{Actual demand} - \text{Forecast value}$$
$$= A_t - F_t$$

Several measures are used in practice to calculate the overall forecast error. These measures can be used to compare different forecasting models, as well as to monitor forecasts to ensure they are performing well. Three of the most popular measures are mean absolute deviation (MAD), mean squared error (MSE), and mean absolute percent error (MAPE). We now describe and give an example of each.

Mean Absolute Deviation   The first measure of the overall forecast error for a model is the **mean absolute deviation (MAD)**. This value is computed by taking the sum of the absolute values of the individual forecast errors (deviations) and dividing by the number of periods of data (n):

$$\text{MAD} = \frac{\Sigma|\text{Actual} - \text{Forecast}|}{n} \tag{4-5}$$

> **AUTHOR COMMENT**
> The forecast error tells us how well the model performed against itself using past data.

LO4: Compute three measures of forecast accuracy

Mean absolute deviation (MAD)
A measure of the overall forecast error for a model.

Example 4 applies MAD, as a measure of overall forecast error, by testing two values of α.

EXAMPLE 4 ▶

Determining the mean absolute deviation (MAD)

During the past 8 quarters, the Port of Baltimore has unloaded large quantities of grain from ships. The port's operations manager wants to test the use of exponential smoothing to see how well the technique works in predicting tonnage unloaded. He guesses that the forecast of grain unloaded in the first quarter was 175 tons. Two values of α are to be examined: $\alpha = .10$ and $\alpha = .50$.

APPROACH ▶   Compare the actual data with the data we forecast (using each of the two α values) and then find the absolute deviation and MADs.

SOLUTION ▶   The following table shows the *detailed* calculations for $\alpha = .10$ only:

Quarter	Actual Tonnage Unloaded	Forecast with $\alpha = .10$	Forecast with $\alpha = .50$
1	180	175	175
2	168	$175.50 = 175.00 + .10(180 - 175)$	177.50
3	159	$174.75 = 175.50 + .10(168 - 175.50)$	172.75
4	175	$173.18 = 174.75 + .10(159 - 174.75)$	165.88
5	190	$173.36 = 173.18 + .10(175 - 173.18)$	170.44
6	205	$175.02 = 173.36 + .10(190 - 173.36)$	180.22
7	180	$178.02 = 175.02 + .10(205 - 175.02)$	192.61
8	182	$178.22 = 178.02 + .10(180 - 178.02)$	186.30
9	?	$178.59 = 178.22 + .10(182 - 178.22)$	184.15

To evaluate the accuracy of each smoothing constant, we can compute forecast errors in terms of absolute deviations and MADs:

Quarter	Actual Tonnage Unloaded	Forecast with $\alpha = .10$	Absolute Deviation for $\alpha = .10$	Forecast with $\alpha = .50$	Absolute Deviation for $\alpha = .50$
1	180	175	5.00	175	5.00
2	168	175.50	7.50	177.50	9.50
3	159	174.75	15.75	172.75	13.75
4	175	173.18	1.82	165.88	9.12
5	190	173.36	16.64	170.44	19.56
6	205	175.02	29.98	180.22	24.78
7	180	178.02	1.98	192.61	12.61
8	182	178.22	3.78	186.30	4.30
	Sum of absolute deviations:		82.45		98.62
	$MAD = \dfrac{\Sigma \lvert Deviations \rvert}{n}$		10.31		12.33

INSIGHT ▶   On the basis of this comparison of the two MADs, a smoothing constant of $\alpha = .10$ is preferred to $\alpha = .50$ because its MAD is smaller.

LEARNING EXERCISE ▶   If the smoothing constant is changed from $\alpha = .10$ to $\alpha = .20$, what is the new MAD? [Answer: 10.21.]

RELATED PROBLEMS ▶   4.5b, 4.8c, 4.9c, 4.14, 4.23, 4.37a

EXCEL OM Data File ChO4Ex4a.xls and ChO4Ex4b.xls can be found at **www.pearsonglobaleditions.com/heizer**.

ACTIVE MODEL 4.2 This example is further illustrated in Active Model 4.2 at **www.pearsonglobaleditions.com/heizer**.

Most computerized forecasting software includes a feature that automatically finds the smoothing constant with the lowest forecast error. Some software modifies the α value if errors become larger than acceptable.

Mean Squared Error　The **mean squared error (MSE)** is a second way of measuring overall forecast error. MSE is the average of the squared differences between the forecasted and observed values. Its formula is:

$$MSE = \frac{\Sigma(\text{Forecast errors})^2}{n} \qquad (4\text{-}6)$$

Example 5 finds the MSE for the Port of Baltimore introduced in Example 4.

The operations manager for the Port of Baltimore now wants to compute MSE for $\alpha = .10$.

APPROACH ▶　Use the same forecast data for $\alpha = .10$ from Example 4, then compute the MSE using Equation (4-6).

SOLUTION ▶

Quarter	Actual Tonnage Unloaded	Forecast for $\alpha = .10$	(Error)^2
1	180	175	$5^2 = 25$
2	168	175.50	$(-7.5)^2 = 56.25$
3	159	174.75	$(-15.75)^2 = 248.06$
4	175	173.18	$(1.82)^2 = 3.33$
5	190	173.36	$(16.64)^2 = 276.89$
6	205	175.02	$(29.98)^2 = 898.70$
7	180	178.02	$(1.98)^2 = 3.92$
8	182	178.22	$(3.78)^2 = 14.31$

Sum of errors squared = 1,526.46

$$MSE = \frac{\Sigma(\text{Forecast errors})^2}{n} = 1,526.54/8 = 190.8$$

INSIGHT ▶　Is this MSE = 190.8 good or bad? It all depends on the MSEs for other forecasting approaches. A low MSE is better because we want to minimize MSE. MSE exaggerates errors because it squares them.

LEARNING EXERCISE ▶　Find the MSE for $\alpha = .50$. [Answer: MSE = 195.24. The result indicates that $\alpha = .10$ is a better choice because we seek a lower MSE. Coincidentally, this is the same conclusion we reached using MAD in Example 4.]

RELATED PROBLEMS ▶　4.8d, 4.14, 4.20

A drawback of using the MSE is that it tends to accentuate large deviations due to the squared term. For example, if the forecast error for period 1 is twice as large as the error for period 2, the squared error in period 1 is four times as large as that for period 2. Hence, using MSE as the measure of forecast error typically indicates that we prefer to have several smaller deviations rather than even one large deviation.

Mean Absolute Percent Error　A problem with both the MAD and MSE is that their values depend on the magnitude of the item being forecast. If the forecast item is measured in thousands, the MAD and MSE values can be very large. To avoid this problem, we can use the **mean absolute percent error (MAPE)**. This is computed as the average of the absolute difference between the forecasted and actual values, expressed as a percentage of the actual values. That is, if we have forecasted and actual values for n periods, the MAPE is calculated as:

$$MAPE = \frac{\sum_{i=1}^{n} 100|\text{Actual}_i - \text{Forecast}_i|/\text{Actual}_i}{n} \qquad (4\text{-}7)$$

Example 6 illustrates the calculations using the data from Examples 4 and 5.

EXAMPLE 6 ▶

Determining the mean absolute percent error (MAPE)

The Port of Baltimore wants to now calculate the MAPE when $\alpha = .10$.

APPROACH ▶ Equation (4-7) is applied to the forecast data computed in Example 4.

SOLUTION ▶

Quarter	Actual Tonnage Unloaded	Forecast for $\alpha = .10$	Absolute Percent Error 100 (|error|/actual)
1	180	175.00	$100(5/180) = 2.78\%$
2	168	175.50	$100(7.5/168) = 4.46\%$
3	159	174.75	$100(15.75/159) = 9.90\%$
4	175	173.18	$100(1.82/175) = 1.05\%$
5	190	173.36	$100(16.64/190) = 8.76\%$
6	205	175.02	$100(29.98/205) = 14.62\%$
7	180	178.02	$100(1.98/180) = 1.10\%$
8	182	178.22	$100(3.78/182) = 2.08\%$
			Sum of % errors $= 44.75\%$

$$\text{MAPE} = \frac{\Sigma \text{ absolute percent errors}}{n} = \frac{44.75\%}{8} = 5.59\%$$

INSIGHT ▶ MAPE expresses the error as a percent of the actual values, undistorted by a single large value.

LEARNING EXERCISE ▶ What is MAPE when α is .50? [Answer: MAPE $= 6.75\%$. As was the case with MAD and MSE, the $\alpha = .1$ was preferable for this series of data.]

RELATED PROBLEMS ▶ 4.8e, 4.33c

The MAPE is perhaps the easiest measure to interpret. For example, a result that the MAPE is 6% is a clear statement that is not dependent on issues such as the magnitude of the input data.

Exponential Smoothing with Trend Adjustment

Simple exponential smoothing, the technique we just illustrated in Examples 3 to 6, is like any other moving-average technique: It fails to respond to trends. Other forecasting techniques that can deal with trends are certainly available. However, because exponential smoothing is such a popular modeling approach in business, let us look at it in more detail.

Here is why exponential smoothing must be modified when a trend is present. Assume that demand for our product or service has been increasing by 100 units per month and that we have been forecasting with $\alpha = 0.4$ in our exponential smoothing model. The following table shows a severe lag in the 2nd, 3rd, 4th, and 5th months, even when our initial estimate for month 1 is perfect:

Month	Actual Demand	Forecast for Month $T(F_T)$
1	100	$F_1 = 100$ (given)
2	200	$F_2 = F_1 + \alpha(A_1 - F_1) = 100 + .4(100 - 100) = 100$
3	300	$F_3 = F_2 + \alpha(A_2 - F_2) = 100 + .4(200 - 100) = 140$
4	400	$F_4 = F_3 + \alpha(A_3 - F_3) = 140 + .4(300 - 140) = 204$
5	500	$F_5 = F_4 + \alpha(A_4 - F_4) = 204 + .4(400 - 204) = 282$

To improve our forecast, let us illustrate a more complex exponential smoothing model, one that adjusts for trend. The idea is to compute an exponentially smoothed average of the data and then adjust for positive or negative lag in trend. The new formula is:

$$\text{Forecast including trend}(FIT_t) = \text{Exponentially smoothed forecast}(F_t)$$
$$+ \text{ Exponentially smoothed trend}(T_t) \qquad (4\text{-}8)$$

With trend-adjusted exponential smoothing, estimates for both the average and the trend are smoothed. This procedure requires two smoothing constants: α for the average and β for the trend. We then compute the average and trend each period:

$F_t = \alpha$(Actual demand last period) + $(1 - \alpha)$(Forecast last period + Trend estimate last period)

or:

$$F_t = \alpha(A_{t-1}) + (1 - \alpha)(F_{t-1} + T_{t-1}) \tag{4-9}$$

$T_t = \beta$(Forecast this period − Forecast last period) + $(1 - \beta)$(Trend estimate last period)

or:

$$T_t = \beta(F_t - F_{t-1}) + (1 - \beta)T_{t-1} \tag{4-10}$$

where F_t = exponentially smoothed forecast of the data series in period t
T_t = exponentially smoothed trend in period t
A_t = actual demand in period t
α = smoothing constant for the average $(0 \le \alpha \le 1)$
β = smoothing constant for the trend $(0 \le \beta \le 1)$

So the three steps to compute a trend-adjusted forecast are:

Step 1: Compute F_t, the exponentially smoothed forecast for period t, using Equation (4-9).
Step 2: Compute the smoothed trend, T_t, using Equation (4-10).
Step 3: Calculate the forecast including trend, FIT_t, by the formula $FIT_t = F_t + T_t$ (from Equation 4-8).

Example 7 shows how to use trend-adjusted exponential smoothing.

A large Portland manufacturer wants to forecast demand for a piece of pollution-control equipment. A review of past sales, as shown below, indicates that an increasing trend is present:

◄ **EXAMPLE 7**

Computing a trend-adjusted exponential smoothing forecast

Month (t)	Actual Demand (A_t)	Month (t)	Actual Demand (A_t)
1	12	6	21
2	17	7	31
3	20	8	28
4	19	9	36
5	24	10	?

Smoothing constants are assigned the values of $\alpha = .2$ and $\beta = .4$. The firm assumes the initial forecast for month 1 (F_1) was 11 units and the trend over that period (T_1) was 2 units.

APPROACH ▶   A trend-adjusted exponential smoothing model, using Equations (4-9), (4-10), and (4-8) and the three steps above, is employed.

SOLUTION ▶

Step 1:   Forecast for month 2:
$$F_2 = \alpha A_1 + (1 - \alpha)(F_1 + T_1)$$
$$F_2 = (.2)(12) + (1 - .2)(11 + 2)$$
$$= 2.4 + (.8)(13) = 2.4 + 10.4 = 12.8 \text{ units}$$

Step 2:   Compute the trend in period 2:
$$T_2 = \beta(F_2 - F_1) + (1 - \beta)T_1$$
$$= .4(12.8 - 11) + (1 - .4)(2)$$
$$= (.4)(1.8) + (.6)(2) = .72 + 1.2 = 1.92$$

Step 3:   Compute the forecast including trend (FIT_t):
$$FIT_2 = F_2 + T_2$$
$$= 12.8 + 1.92$$
$$= 14.72 \text{ units}$$

We will also do the same calculations for the third month:

Step 1: $F_3 = \alpha A_2 + (1 - \alpha)(F_2 + T_2) = (.2)(17) + (1 - .2)(12.8 + 1.92)$
$= 3.4 + (.8)(14.72) = 3.4 + 11.78 = 15.18$

Step 2: $T_3 = \beta(F_3 - F_2) + (1 - \beta)T_2 = (.4)(15.18 - 12.8) + (1 - .4)(1.92)$
$= (.4)(2.38) + (.6)(1.92) = .952 + 1.152 = 2.10$

Step 3: $FIT_3 = F_3 + T_3$
$= 15.18 + 2.10 = 17.28.$

Table 4.1 completes the forecasts for the 10-month period.

▶**TABLE 4.1**
Forecast with $\alpha = .2$ and $\beta = .4$

Month	Actual Demand	Smoothed Forecast, F_t	Smoothed Trend, T_t	Forecast Including Trend, FIT_t
1	12	11	2	13.00
2	17	12.80	1.92	14.72
3	20	15.18	2.10	17.28
4	19	17.82	2.32	20.14
5	24	19.91	2.23	22.14
6	21	22.51	2.38	24.89
7	31	24.11	2.07	26.18
8	28	27.14	2.45	29.59
9	36	29.28	2.32	31.60
10	—	32.48	2.68	35.16

INSIGHT ▶ Figure 4.3 compares actual demand (A_t) to an exponential smoothing forecast that includes trend (FIT_t). *FIT* picks up the trend in actual demand. A simple exponential smoothing model (as we saw in Examples 3 and 4) trails far behind.

▶ **FIGURE 4.3**
Exponential Smoothing with Trend-Adjustment Forecasts Compared to Actual Demand Data

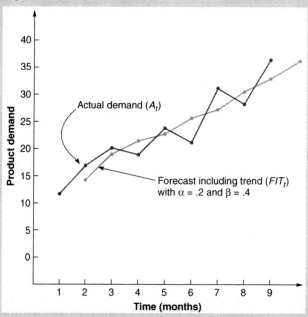

LEARNING EXERCISE ▶ Using the data for actual demand for the 9 months, compute the exponentially smoothed forecast *without* trend (using Equation (4-4) as we did earlier in Examples 3 and 4). Apply $\alpha = .2$ and assume an initial forecast for month 1 of 11 units. Then plot the months 2–10 forecast values on Figure 4.3. What do you notice? [Answer: Month 10 forecast = 24.65. All the points are below and lag the trend-adjusted forecast.]

RELATED PROBLEMS ▶ 4.19, 4.20, 4.21, 4.22, 4.44

ACTIVE MODEL 4.3 This example is further illustrated in Active Model 4.3 at **www.pearsonglobaleditions.com/heizer**.

The value of the trend-smoothing constant, β, resembles the α constant because a high β is more responsive to recent changes in trend. A low β gives less weight to the most recent trends and tends to smooth out the present trend. Values of β can be found by the trial-and-error approach or by using sophisticated commercial forecasting software, with the MAD used as a measure of comparison.

Simple exponential smoothing is often referred to as *first-order smoothing*, and trend-adjusted smoothing is called *second-order*, or *double smoothing*. Other advanced exponential-smoothing models are also used, including seasonal-adjusted and triple smoothing, but these are beyond the scope of this book.[2]

Trend Projections

The last time-series forecasting method we will discuss is **trend projection**. This technique fits a trend line to a series of historical data points and then projects the line into the future for medium to long-range forecasts. Several mathematical trend equations can be developed (for example, exponential and quadratic), but in this section, we will look at *linear* (straight-line) trends only.

If we decide to develop a linear trend line by a precise statistical method, we can apply the *least-squares method*. This approach results in a straight line that minimizes the sum of the squares of the vertical differences or deviations from the line to each of the actual observations. Figure 4.4 illustrates the least-squares approach.

A least-squares line is described in terms of its *y*-intercept (the height at which it intercepts the *y*-axis) and its expected change (slope). If we can compute the *y*-intercept and slope, we can express the line with the following equation:

$$\hat{y} = a + bx \tag{4-11}$$

where $\hat{y}$ (called "*y* hat") = computed value of the variable to be predicted (called the *dependent variable*)

a = *y*-axis intercept

b = slope of the regression line (or the rate of change in *y* for given changes in *x*)

x = the independent variable (which in this case is *time*)

Statisticians have developed equations that we can use to find the values of a and b for any regression line. The slope b is found by:

$$b = \frac{\Sigma xy - n\bar{x}\bar{y}}{\Sigma x^2 - n\bar{x}^2} \tag{4-12}$$

Trend projection
A time-series forecasting method that fits a trend line to a series of historical data points and then projects the line into the future for forecasts.

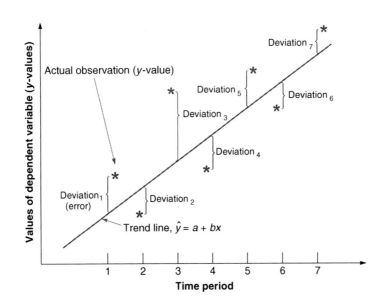

◀ **FIGURE 4.4**
The Least-Squares Method for Finding the Best-Fitting Straight Line, Where the Asterisks Are the Locations of the Seven Actual Observations or Data Points

---

[2]For more details, see D. Groebner, P. Shannon, P. Fry, and K. Smith, *Business Statistics*, 8th ed. (Upper Saddle River, NJ: Prentice Hall, 2011).

where b = slope of the regression line
Σ = summation sign
x = known values of the independent variable
y = known values of the dependent variable
$\bar{x}$ = average of the x-values
$\bar{y}$ = average of the y-values
n = number of data points or observations

We can compute the y-intercept a as follows:

$$a = \bar{y} - b\bar{x}$$ (4-13)

Example 8 shows how to apply these concepts.

EXAMPLE 8 ▶

Forecasting with least squares

The demand for electric power at N.Y. Edison over the period 2003 to 2009 is shown in the following table, in megawatts. The firm wants to forecast 2010 demand by fitting a straight-line trend to these data.

Year	Electrical Power Demand	Year	Electrical Power Demand
2003	74	2007	105
2004	79	2008	142
2005	80	2009	122
2006	90		

APPROACH ▶ With a series of data over time, we can minimize the computations by transforming the values of x (time) to simpler numbers. Thus, in this case, we can designate 2003 as year 1, 2004 as year 2, and so on. Then Equations (4-12) and (4-13) can be used to create the trend projection model.

SOLUTION ▶

Year	Time Period (x)	Electric Power Demand (y)	x^2	xy
2003	1	74	1	74
2004	2	79	4	158
2005	3	80	9	240
2006	4	90	16	360
2007	5	105	25	525
2008	6	142	36	852
2009	7	122	49	854
	$\Sigma x = 28$	$\Sigma y = 692$	$\Sigma x^2 = 140$	$\Sigma xy = 3{,}063$

$$\bar{x} = \frac{\Sigma x}{n} = \frac{28}{7} = 4 \qquad \bar{y} = \frac{\Sigma y}{n} = \frac{692}{7} = 98.86$$

$$b = \frac{\Sigma xy - n\bar{x}\bar{y}}{\Sigma x^2 - n\bar{x}^2} = \frac{3{,}063 - (7)(4)(98.86)}{140 - (7)(4^2)} = \frac{295}{28} = 10.54$$

$$a = \bar{y} - b\bar{x} = 98.86 - 10.54(4) = 56.70$$

Thus, the least squares trend equation is $\hat{y} = 56.70 + 10.54x$. To project demand in 2010, we first denote the year 2010 in our new coding system as $x = 8$:

$$\text{Demand in 2010} = 56.70 + 10.54(8)$$
$$= 141.02, \text{ or } 141 \text{ megawatts}$$

INSIGHT ▶ To evaluate the model, we plot both the historical demand and the trend line in Figure 4.5. In this case, we may wish to be cautious and try to understand the 2008 to 2009 swing in demand.

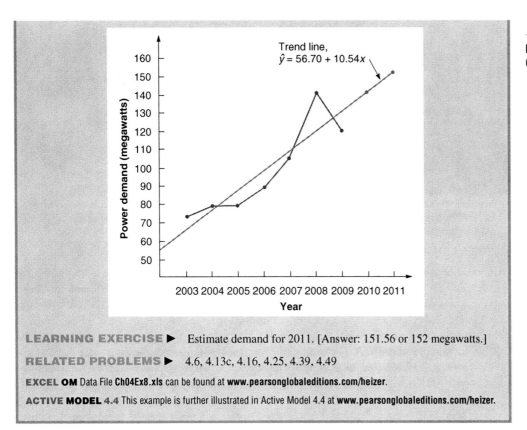

◄ **FIGURE 4.5**
Electrical Power and the Computed Trend Line

LEARNING EXERCISE ►   Estimate demand for 2011. [Answer: 151.56 or 152 megawatts.]

RELATED PROBLEMS ►   4.6, 4.13c, 4.16, 4.25, 4.39, 4.49

EXCEL OM Data File **Ch04Ex8.xls** can be found at **www.pearsonglobaleditions.com/heizer**.

ACTIVE MODEL 4.4 This example is further illustrated in Active Model 4.4 at **www.pearsonglobaleditions.com/heizer**.

Notes on the Use of the Least-Squares Method   Using the least-squares method implies that we have met three requirements:

1. We always plot the data because least-squares data assume a linear relationship. If a curve appears to be present, curvilinear analysis is probably needed.
2. We do not predict time periods far beyond our given database. For example, if we have 20 months' worth of average prices of Microsoft stock, we can forecast only 3 or 4 months into the future. Forecasts beyond that have little statistical validity. Thus, you cannot take 5 years' worth of sales data and project 10 years into the future. The world is too uncertain.
3. Deviations around the least-squares line (see Figure 4.4) are assumed to be random. They are normally distributed, with most observations close to the line and only a smaller number farther out.

Seasonal Variations in Data

Seasonal variations in data are regular up-and-down movements in a time series that relate to recurring events such as weather or holidays. Demand for coal and fuel oil, for example, peaks during cold winter months. Demand for golf clubs or sunscreen may be highest in summer.

Seasonality may be applied to hourly, daily, weekly, monthly, or other recurring patterns. Fast-food restaurants experience *daily* surges at noon and again at 5 P.M. Movie theaters see higher demand on Friday and Saturday evenings. The post office, Toys " Я " Us, The Christmas Store, and Hallmark Card Shops also exhibit seasonal variation in customer traffic and sales.

Similarly, understanding seasonal variations is important for capacity planning in organizations that handle peak loads. These include electric power companies during extreme cold and warm periods, banks on Friday afternoons, and buses and subways during the morning and evening rush hours.

Time-series forecasts like those in Example 8 involve reviewing the trend of data over a series of time periods. The presence of seasonality makes adjustments in trend-line forecasts necessary. Seasonality is expressed in terms of the amount that actual values differ from average values in the time series. Analyzing data in monthly or quarterly terms usually makes it easy for a statistician to spot seasonal patterns. Seasonal indices can then be developed by several common methods.

In what is called a *multiplicative seasonal model*, seasonal factors are multiplied by an estimate of average demand to produce a seasonal forecast. Our assumption in this section is that

AUTHOR COMMENT
John Deere understands seasonal variations: It has been able to obtain 70% of its orders in advance of seasonal use so it can smooth production.

Seasonal variations
Regular upward or downward movements in a time series that tie to recurring events.

Demand for many products is seasonal. Yamaha, the manufacturer of these jet skis and snowmobiles, produces products with complementary demands to address seasonal fluctuations.

trend has been removed from the data. Otherwise, the magnitude of the seasonal data will be distorted by the trend.

Here are the steps we will follow for a company that has "seasons" of 1 month:

1. Find the *average historical demand each season* (or month in this case) by summing the demand for that month in each year and dividing by the number of years of data available. For example, if, in January, we have seen sales of 8, 6, and 10 over the past 3 years, average January demand equals (8 + 6 + 10)/3 = 8 units.

2. Compute the *average demand over all months* by dividing the total average annual demand by the number of seasons. For example, if the total average demand for a year is 120 units and there are 12 seasons (each month), the average monthly demand is 120/12 = 10 units.

3. Compute a *seasonal index* for each season by dividing that month's actual historical demand (from step 1) by the average demand over all months (from step 2). For example, if the average historical January demand over the past 3 years is 8 units and the average demand over all months is 10 units, the seasonal index for January is 8/10 = .80. Likewise, a seasonal index of 1.20 for February would mean that February's demand is 20% larger than the average demand over all months.

4. Estimate next year's total annual demand.

5. Divide this estimate of total annual demand by the number of seasons, then multiply it by the seasonal index for that month. This provides the *seasonal forecast*.

LO5: Develop seasonal indices

Example 9 illustrates this procedure as it computes seasonal indices from historical data.

EXAMPLE 9 ▶

Determining seasonal indices

A Des Moines distributor of Sony laptop computers wants to develop monthly indices for sales. Data from 2007–2009, by month, are available.

APPROACH ▶   Follow the five steps listed above.

SOLUTION ▶

Month	Demand 2007	Demand 2008	Demand 2009	Average 2007–2009 Demand	Average Monthly Demand[a]	Seasonal Index[b]
Jan.	80	85	105	90	94	.957 (= 90/94)
Feb.	70	85	85	80	94	.851 (= 80/94)
Mar.	80	93	82	85	94	.904 (= 85/94)
Apr.	90	95	115	100	94	1.064 (= 100/94)
May	113	125	131	123	94	1.309 (= 123/94)
June	110	115	120	115	94	1.223 (= 115/94)
July	100	102	113	105	94	1.117 (= 105/94)
Aug.	88	102	110	100	94	1.064 (= 100/94)
Sept.	85	90	95	90	94	.957 (= 90/94)
Oct.	77	78	85	80	94	.851 (= 80/94)
Nov.	75	82	83	80	94	.851 (= 80/94)
Dec.	82	78	80	80	94	.851 (= 80/94)

Total average annual demand = 1,128

[a]Average monthly demand = $\dfrac{1,128}{12 \text{ months}}$ = 94.

[b]Seasonal index = $\dfrac{\text{Average 2007–2009 monthly demand}}{\text{Average monthly demand}}$.

If we expected the 2010 annual demand for computers to be 1,200 units, we would use these seasonal indices to forecast the monthly demand as follows:

Month	Demand	Month	Demand
Jan.	$\dfrac{1{,}200}{12} \times .957 = 96$	July	$\dfrac{1{,}200}{12} \times 1.117 = 112$
Feb.	$\dfrac{1{,}200}{12} \times .851 = 85$	Aug.	$\dfrac{1{,}200}{12} \times 1.064 = 106$
Mar.	$\dfrac{1{,}200}{12} \times .904 = 90$	Sept.	$\dfrac{1{,}200}{12} \times .957 = 96$
Apr.	$\dfrac{1{,}200}{12} \times 1.064 = 106$	Oct.	$\dfrac{1{,}200}{12} \times .851 = 85$
May	$\dfrac{1{,}200}{12} \times 1.309 = 131$	Nov.	$\dfrac{1{,}200}{12} \times .851 = 85$
June	$\dfrac{1{,}200}{12} \times 1.223 = 122$	Dec.	$\dfrac{1{,}200}{12} \times .851 = 85$

INSIGHT ▶ Think of these indices as percentages of average sales. The average sales (without seasonality) would be 94, but with seasonality, sales fluctuate from 85% to 131% of average.

LEARNING EXERCISE ▶ If 2010 annual demand is 1,150 laptops (instead of 1,200), what will the January, February, and March forecasts be? [Answer: 91.7, 81.5, and 86.6, which can be rounded to 92, 82, and 87]

RELATED PROBLEMS ▶ 4.27, 4.28

EXCEL OM Data File **Ch04Ex9.xls** can be found at **www.pearsonglobaleditions.com/heizer**.

For simplicity, only 3 periods are used for each monthly index in the preceding example. Example 10 illustrates how indices that have already been prepared can be applied to adjust trend-line forecasts for seasonality.

◀ EXAMPLE 10

Applying both trend and seasonal indices

San Diego Hospital wants to improve its forecasting by applying both trend and seasonal indices to 66 months of data it has collected. It will then forecast "patient-days" over the coming year.

APPROACH ▶ A trend line is created; then monthly seasonal indices are computed. Finally, a multiplicative seasonal model is used to forecast months 67 to 78.

SOLUTION ▶ Using 66 months of adult inpatient hospital days, the following equation was computed:

$$\hat{y} = 8{,}090 + 21.5x$$

where
$$\hat{y} = \text{patient days}$$
$$x = \text{time, in months}$$

Based on this model, which reflects only trend data, the hospital forecasts patient days for the next month (period 67) to be:

$$\text{Patient days} = 8{,}090 + (21.5)(67) = 9{,}530 \text{ (trend only)}$$

While this model, as plotted in Figure 4.6, recognized the upward trend line in the demand for inpatient services, it ignored the seasonality that the administration knew to be present.

▶ **FIGURE 4.6**
Trend Data for San Diego Hospital

Source: From "Modern Methods Improve Hospital Forecasting" by W. E. Sterk and E. G. Shryock from *Healthcare Financial Management*, Vol. 41, no. 3, p. 97. Reprinted by permission of Healthcare Financial Management Association.

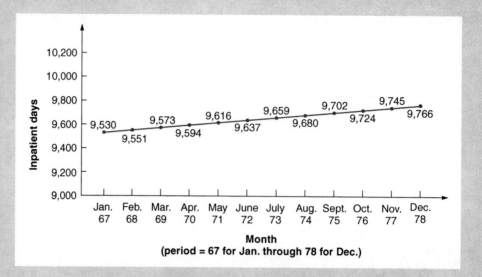

The following table provides seasonal indices based on the same 66 months. Such seasonal data, by the way, were found to be typical of hospitals nationwide.

Seasonality Indices for Adult Inpatient Days at San Diego Hospital

Month	Seasonality Index	Month	Seasonality Index
January	1.04	July	1.03
February	0.97	August	1.04
March	1.02	September	0.97
April	1.01	October	1.00
May	0.99	November	0.96
June	0.99	December	0.98

These seasonal indices are graphed in Figure 4.7. Note that January, March, July, and August seem to exhibit significantly higher patient days on average, while February, September, November, and December experience lower patient days.

However, neither the trend data nor the seasonal data alone provide a reasonable forecast for the hospital. Only when the hospital multiplied the trend-adjusted data times the appropriate seasonal index did it obtain good forecasts. Thus, for period 67 (January):

Patient days = (Trend-adjusted forecast) (Monthly seasonal index) = (9,530)(1.04) = 9,911

The patient days for each month are:

Period	67	68	69	70	71	72	73	74	75	76	77	78
Month	Jan.	Feb.	March	April	May	June	July	Aug.	Sept.	Oct.	Nov.	Dec.
Forecast with Trend & Seasonality	9,911	9,265	9,764	9,691	9,520	9,542	9,949	10,068	9,411	9,724	9,355	9,572

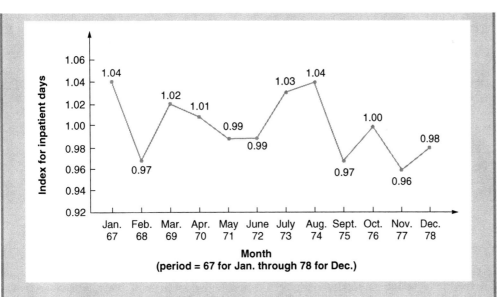

◄ **FIGURE 4.7**
Seasonal Index for San Diego Hospital

A graph showing the forecast that combines both trend and seasonality appears in Figure 4.8.

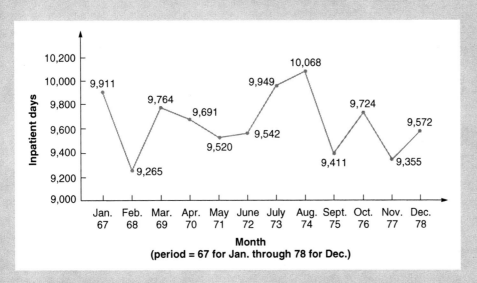

◄ **FIGURE 4.8**
Combined Trend and Seasonal Forecast

INSIGHT ▶ Notice that with trend only, the September forecast is 9,702, but with both trend and seasonal adjustments, the forecast is 9,411. By combining trend and seasonal data, the hospital was better able to forecast inpatient days and the related staffing and budgeting vital to effective operations.

LEARNING EXERCISE ▶ If the slope of the trend line for patient-days is 22.0 (rather than 21.5) and the index for December is .99 (instead of .98), what is the new forecast for December inpatient days? [Answer: 9,708.]

RELATED PROBLEMS ▶ 4.26, 4.29

Example 11 further illustrates seasonality for quarterly data at a department store.

◄ **EXAMPLE 11**

Adjusting trend data with seasonal indices

Management at Davis's Department Store has used time-series regression to forecast retail sales for the next 4 quarters. Sales estimates are $100,000, $120,000, $140,000, and $160,000 for the respective quarters. Seasonal indices for the 4 quarters have been found to be 1.30, .90, .70, and 1.10, respectively.

APPROACH ▶ To compute a seasonalized or adjusted sales forecast, we just multiply each seasonal index by the appropriate trend forecast:

$$\hat{y}_{seasonal} = \text{Index} \times \hat{y}_{trend\ forecast}$$

> **SOLUTION ▶**
> Quarter I: $\hat{y}_\text{I} = (1.30)(\$100,000) = \$130,000$
> Quarter II: $\hat{y}_\text{II} = (.90)(\$120,000) = \$108,000$
> Quarter III: $\hat{y}_\text{III} = (.70)(\$140,000) = \$98,000$
> Quarter IV: $\hat{y}_\text{IV} = (1.10)(\$160,000) = \$176,000$
>
> **INSIGHT ▶** The straight-line trend forecast is now adjusted to reflect the seasonal changes.
>
> **LEARNING EXERCISE ▶** If the sales forecast for Quarter IV was 180,000 (rather than 160,000), what would be the seasonally adjusted forecast? [Answer: $198,000.]
>
> **RELATED PROBLEMS ▶** 4.26, 4.29

Cyclical Variations in Data

Cycles
Patterns in the data that occur every several years.

Cycles are like seasonal variations in data but occur every several *years*, not weeks, months, or quarters. Forecasting cyclical variations in a time series is difficult. This is because cycles include a wide variety of factors that cause the economy to go from recession to expansion to recession over a period of years. These factors include national or industrywide overexpansion in times of euphoria and contraction in times of concern. Forecasting demand for individual products can also be driven by product life cycles—the stages products go through from introduction through decline. Life cycles exist for virtually all products; striking examples include floppy disks, video recorders, and the original Game Boy. We leave cyclical analysis to forecasting texts.

Developing associative techniques of variables that affect one another is our next topic.

AUTHOR COMMENT
We now deal with the same mathematical model that we saw earlier, the least-squares method. But we use any potential "cause-and-effect" variable as *x*.

ASSOCIATIVE FORECASTING METHODS: REGRESSION AND CORRELATION ANALYSIS

Unlike time-series forecasting, *associative forecasting* models usually consider *several* variables that are related to the quantity being predicted. Once these related variables have been found, a statistical model is built and used to forecast the item of interest. This approach is more powerful than the time-series methods that use only the historical values for the forecasted variable.

Linear-regression analysis
A straight-line mathematical model to describe the functional relationships between independent and dependent variables.

Many factors can be considered in an associative analysis. For example, the sales of Dell PCs may be related to Dell's advertising budget, the company's prices, competitors' prices and promotional strategies, and even the nation's economy and unemployment rates. In this case, PC sales would be called the *dependent variable*, and the other variables would be called *independent variables*. The manager's job is to develop *the best statistical relationship between PC sales and the independent variables*. The most common quantitative associative forecasting model is **linear-regression analysis**.

Using Regression Analysis for Forecasting

We can use the same mathematical model that we employed in the least-squares method of trend projection to perform a linear-regression analysis. The dependent variables that we want to forecast will still be $\hat{y}$. But now the independent variable, *x*, need no longer be time. We use the equation:

$$\hat{y} = a + bx$$

LO6: Conduct a regression and correlation analysis

where
$\hat{y}$ = value of the dependent variable (in our example, sales)
a = *y*-axis intercept
b = slope of the regression line
x = independent variable

Example 12 shows how to use linear regression.

Nodel Construction Company renovates old homes in West Bloomfield, Michigan. Over time, the company has found that its dollar volume of renovation work is dependent on the West Bloomfield area payroll. Management wants to establish a mathematical relationship to help predict sales.

APPROACH ▶ Nodel's VP of operations has prepared the following table, which lists company revenues and the amount of money earned by wage earners in West Bloomfield during the past 6 years:

Nodel's Sales (in $ millions), y	Area Payroll (in $ billions), x	Nodel's Sales (in $ millions), y	Area Payroll (in $ billions), x
2.0	1	2.0	2
3.0	3	2.0	1
2.5	4	3.5	7

The VP needs to determine whether there is a straight-line (linear) relationship between area payroll and sales. He plots the known data on a scatter diagram:

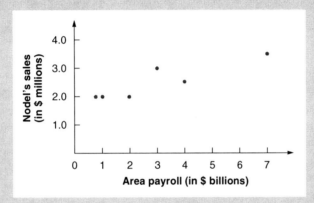

AUTHOR COMMENT
A scatter diagram is a powerful data analysis tool. It helps quickly size up the relationship between two variables.

From the six data points, there appears to be a slight positive relationship between the independent variable (payroll) and the dependent variable (sales): As payroll increases, Nodel's sales tend to be higher.

SOLUTION ▶ We can find a mathematical equation by using the least-squares regression approach:

Sales, y	Payroll, x	x^2	xy
2.0	1	1	2.0
3.0	3	9	9.0
2.5	4	16	10.0
2.0	2	4	4.0
2.0	1	1	2.0
3.5	7	49	24.5
$\Sigma y = 15.0$	$\Sigma x = 18$	$\Sigma x^2 = 80$	$\Sigma xy = 51.5$

$$\bar{x} = \frac{\Sigma x}{6} = \frac{18}{6} = 3$$

$$\bar{y} = \frac{\Sigma y}{6} = \frac{15}{6} = 2.5$$

$$b = \frac{\Sigma xy - n\bar{x}\bar{y}}{\Sigma x^2 - n\bar{x}^2} = \frac{51.5 - (6)(3)(2.5)}{80 - (6)(3^2)} = .25$$

$$a = \bar{y} - b\bar{x} = 2.5 - (.25)(3) = 1.75$$

The estimated regression equation, therefore, is:

$$\hat{y} = 1.75 + .25x$$

or:

$$\text{Sales} = 1.75 + .25 \text{ (payroll)}$$

If the local chamber of commerce predicts that the West Bloomfield area payroll will be $6 billion next year, we can estimate sales for Nodel with the regression equation:

$$\text{Sales (in \$ millions)} = 1.75 + .25(6)$$
$$= 1.75 + 1.50 = 3.25$$

or:

$$\text{Sales} = \$3,250,000$$

INSIGHT ▶   Given our assumptions of a straight-line relationship between payroll and sales, we now have an indication of the slope of that relationship: on average, sales increase at the rate of a million dollars for every quarter billion dollars in the local area payroll. This is because $b = .25$.

LEARNING EXERCISE ▶   What are Nodel's sales when the local payroll is $8 billion? [Answer: $3.75 million.]

RELATED PROBLEMS ▶   4.24, 4.30, 4.31, 4.32, 4.33, 4.35, 4.38, 4.40, 4.41, 4.46, 4.48, 4.49

EXCEL OM Data File Ch04Ex12.xls can be found at **www.pearsonglobaleditions.com/heizer**.

The final part of Example 12 shows a central weakness of associative forecasting methods like regression. Even when we have computed a regression equation, we must provide a forecast of the independent variable *x*—in this case, payroll—before estimating the dependent variable *y* for the next time period. Although this is not a problem for all forecasts, you can imagine the difficulty of determining future values of *some* common independent variables (such as unemployment rates, gross national product, price indices, and so on).

Standard Error of the Estimate

The forecast of $3,250,000 for Nodel's sales in Example 12 is called a *point estimate* of *y*. The point estimate is really the *mean*, or *expected value*, of a distribution of possible values of sales. Figure 4.9 illustrates this concept.

Standard error of the estimate

A measure of variability around the regression line—its standard deviation.

To measure the accuracy of the regression estimates, we must compute the **standard error of the estimate**, $S_{y,x}$. This computation is called the *standard deviation of the regression:* It measures the error from the dependent variable, *y*, to the regression line, rather than to the mean. Equation (4-14) is a similar expression to that found in most statistics books for computing the standard deviation of an arithmetic mean:

$$S_{y,x} = \sqrt{\frac{\Sigma(y - y_c)^2}{n - 2}} \tag{4-14}$$

where y = *y*-value of each data point
y_c = computed value of the dependent variable, from the regression equation
n = number of data points

▶ FIGURE 4.9
Distribution about the Point Estimate of $3.25 Million Sales

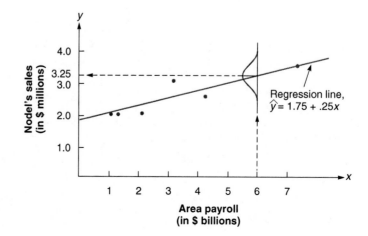

Glidden Paints' assembly lines fill thousands of cans per hour. To predict demand, the firm uses associative forecasting methods such as linear regression, with independent variables such as disposable personal income and GNP. Although housing starts would be a natural variable, Glidden found that it correlated poorly with past sales. It turns out that most Glidden paint is sold through retailers to customers who already own homes or businesses.

Equation (4-15) may look more complex, but it is actually an easier-to-use version of Equation (4-14). Both formulas provide the same answer and can be used in setting up prediction intervals around the point estimate[3]:

$$S_{y,x} = \sqrt{\frac{\Sigma y^2 - a\Sigma y - b\Sigma xy}{n - 2}} \qquad (4\text{-}15)$$

Example 13 shows how we would calculate the standard error of the estimate in Example 12.

◀ EXAMPLE 13

Computing the standard error of the estimate

Nodel's VP of operations now wants to know the error associated with the regression line computed in Example 12.

APPROACH ▶ Compute the standard error of the estimate, $S_{y,x}$, using Equation (4-15).

SOLUTION ▶ The only number we need that is not available to solve for $S_{y,x}$ is Σy^2. Some quick addition reveals $\Sigma y^2 = 39.5$. Therefore:

$$\begin{aligned} S_{y,x} &= \sqrt{\frac{\Sigma y^2 - a\Sigma y - b\Sigma xy}{n - 2}} \\ &= \sqrt{\frac{39.5 - 1.75(15.0) - .25(51.5)}{6 - 2}} \\ &= \sqrt{.09375} = .306 \text{ (in \$ millions)} \end{aligned}$$

The standard error of the estimate is then $306,000 in sales.

INSIGHT ▶ The interpretation of the standard error of the estimate is similar to the standard deviation; namely, ±1 standard deviation = .6827. So there is a 68.27% chance of sales being ±$306,000 from the point estimate of $3,250,000.

LEARNING EXERCISE ▶ What is the probability sales will exceed $3,556,000? [Answer: About 16%.]

RELATED PROBLEMS ▶ 4.41e, 4.48b

Correlation Coefficients for Regression Lines

The regression equation is one way of expressing the nature of the relationship between two variables. Regression lines are not "cause-and-effect" relationships. They merely describe the relationships among variables. The regression equation shows how one variable relates to the value and changes in another variable.

Another way to evaluate the relationship between two variables is to compute the **coefficient of correlation**. This measure expresses the degree or strength of the linear relationship. Usually

Coefficient of correlation
A measure of the strength of the relationship between two variables.

---

[3]When the sample size is large ($n > 30$), the prediction interval value of y can be computed using normal tables. When the number of observations is small, the t-distribution is appropriate. See D. Groebner et al., *Business Statistics*, 8th ed. (Upper Saddle River, NJ: Prentice Hall, 2011).

▶ **FIGURE 4.10**
**Four Values of the
Correlation Coefficient**

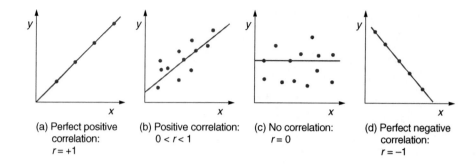

(a) Perfect positive
correlation:
$r = +1$

(b) Positive correlation:
$0 < r < 1$

(c) No correlation:
$r = 0$

(d) Perfect negative
correlation:
$r = -1$

identified as r, the coefficient of correlation can be any number between $+1$ and -1. Figure 4.10 illustrates what different values of r might look like.

To compute r, we use much of the same data needed earlier to calculate a and b for the regression line. The rather lengthy equation for r is:

$$r = \frac{n\Sigma xy - \Sigma x \Sigma y}{\sqrt{[n\Sigma x^2 - (\Sigma x)^2][n\Sigma y^2 - (\Sigma y)^2]}} \qquad (4\text{-}16)$$

Example 14 shows how to calculate the coefficient of correlation for the data given in Examples 12 and 13.

EXAMPLE 14 ▶

Determining the coefficient of correlation

In Example 12, we looked at the relationship between Nodel Construction Company's renovation sales and payroll in its hometown of West Bloomfield. The VP now wants to know the strength of the association between area payroll and sales.

APPROACH ▶ We compute the r value using Equation (4-16). We need to first add one more column of calculations—for y^2.

SOLUTION ▶ The data, including the column for y^2 and the calculations, are shown here:

y	x	x^2	xy	y^2
2.0	1	1	2.0	4.0
3.0	3	9	9.0	9.0
2.5	4	16	10.0	6.25
2.0	2	4	4.0	4.0
2.0	1	1	2.0	4.0
3.5	7	49	24.5	12.25
$\Sigma y = 15.0$	$\Sigma x = 18$	$\Sigma x^2 = 80$	$\Sigma xy = 51.5$	$\Sigma y^2 = 39.5$

$$r = \frac{(6)(51.5) - (18)(15.0)}{\sqrt{[(6)(80) - (18)^2][(6)(39.5) - (15.0)^2]}}$$

$$= \frac{309 - 270}{\sqrt{(156)(12)}} = \frac{39}{\sqrt{1,872}}$$

$$= \frac{39}{43.3} = .901$$

INSIGHT ▶ This r of .901 appears to be a significant correlation and helps confirm the closeness of the relationship between the two variables.

LEARNING EXERCISE ▶ If the coefficient of correlation was $-.901$ rather than $+.901$, what would this tell you? [Answer: The negative correlation would tell you that as payroll went up, Nodel's sales went down—a rather unlikely occurrence that would suggest you recheck your math.]

RELATED PROBLEMS ▶ 4.24d, 4.35d, 4.38c, 4.41f, 4.48b

Coefficient of determination

A measure of the amount of variation in the dependent variable about its mean that is explained by the regression equation.

Although the coefficient of correlation is the measure most commonly used to describe the relationship between two variables, another measure does exist. It is called the **coefficient of determination** and is simply the square of the coefficient of correlation—namely, r^2. The value of r^2 will always be a positive number in the range $0 \le r^2 \le 1$. The coefficient of determination is the percent of variation in the dependent variable (y) that is explained by the regression equation. In Nodel's case, the value of r^2 is .81, indicating that 81% of the total variation is explained by the regression equation.

Multiple-Regression Analysis

Multiple regression is a practical extension of the simple regression model we just explored. It allows us to build a model with several independent variables instead of just one variable. For example, if Nodel Construction wanted to include average annual interest rates in its model for forecasting renovation sales, the proper equation would be:

$$\hat{y} = a + b_1 x_1 + b_2 x_2 \tag{4-17}$$

> **Multiple regression**
> An associative forecasting method with more than one independent variable.

where

$\hat{y}$ = dependent variable, sales
a = a constant, the y intercept
x_1 and x_2 = values of the two independent variables, area payroll and interest rates, respectively
b_1 and b_2 = coefficients for the two independent variables

The mathematics of multiple regression becomes quite complex (and is usually tackled by computer), so we leave the formulas for a, b_1, and b_2 to statistics textbooks. However, Example 15 shows how to interpret Equation (4-17) in forecasting Nodel's sales.

Nodel Construction wants to see the impact of a second independent variable, interest rates, on its sales.

APPROACH ▶ The new multiple-regression line for Nodel Construction, calculated by computer software, is:

$$\hat{y} = 1.80 + .30x_1 - 5.0x_2$$

We also find that the new coefficient of correlation is .96, implying the inclusion of the variable x_2, interest rates, adds even more strength to the linear relationship.

SOLUTION ▶ We can now estimate Nodel's sales if we substitute values for next year's payroll and interest rate. If West Bloomfield's payroll will be $6 billion and the interest rate will be .12 (12%), sales will be forecast as:

$$\text{Sales(\$ millions)} = 1.80 + .30(6) - 5.0(.12)$$
$$= 1.8 + 1.8 - .6$$
$$= 3.00$$

or:

$$\text{Sales} = \$3,000,000$$

INSIGHT ▶ By using both variables, payroll and interest rates, Nodel now has a sales forecast of $3 million and a higher coefficient of correlation. This suggests a stronger relationship between the two variables and a more accurate estimate of sales.

LEARNING EXERCISE ▶ If interest rates were only 6%, what would be the sales forecast? [Answer: $1.8 + 1.8 - 5.0(.06) = 3.3$, or $3,300,000.]

RELATED PROBLEMS ▶ 4.34, 4.36

◀ EXAMPLE 15

Using a multiple-regression equation

MONITORING AND CONTROLLING FORECASTS

Once a forecast has been completed, it should not be forgotten. No manager wants to be reminded that his or her forecast is horribly inaccurate, but a firm needs to determine why actual demand (or whatever variable is being examined) differed significantly from that projected. If the forecaster is accurate, that individual usually makes sure that everyone is aware of his or her talents. Very seldom does one read articles in *Fortune*, *Forbes*, or *The Wall Street Journal*, however, about money managers who are consistently off by 25% in their stock market forecasts.

> **AUTHOR COMMENT**
> Using a tracking signal is a good way to make sure the forecasting system is continuing to do a good job.

Tracking signal

A measurement of how well a forecast is predicting actual values.

One way to monitor forecasts to ensure that they are performing well is to use a tracking signal. A **tracking signal** is a measurement of how well a forecast is predicting actual values. As forecasts are updated every week, month, or quarter, the newly available demand data are compared to the forecast values.

The tracking signal is computed as the cumulative error divided by the *mean absolute deviation (MAD)*:

$$\text{(Tracking signal)} = \frac{\text{Cumulative error}}{\text{MAD}}$$

$$= \frac{\Sigma(\text{Actual demand in period } i - \text{Forecast demand in period } i)}{\text{MAD}} \tag{4-18}$$

$$\text{where} \qquad \text{(MAD)} = \frac{\Sigma|\text{Actual} - \text{Forecast}|}{n}$$

as seen earlier, in Equation (4-5).

Positive tracking signals indicate that demand is *greater* than forecast. *Negative* signals mean that demand is *less* than forecast. A good tracking signal—that is, one with a low cumulative error—has about as much positive error as it has negative error. In other words, small deviations are okay, but positive and negative errors should balance one another so that the tracking signal centers closely around zero. A consistent tendency for forecasts to be greater or less than the actual values (that is, for a high absolute cumulative error) is called a **bias** error. Bias can occur if, for example, the wrong variables or trend line are used or if a seasonal index is misapplied.

Bias

A forecast that is consistently higher or consistently lower than actual values of a time series.

Once tracking signals are calculated, they are compared with predetermined control limits. When a tracking signal exceeds an upper or lower limit, there is a problem with the forecasting method, and management may want to reevaluate the way it forecasts demand. Figure 4.11 shows the graph of a tracking signal that is exceeding the range of acceptable variation. If the model being used is exponential smoothing, perhaps the smoothing constant needs to be readjusted.

LO7: Use a tracking signal

How do firms decide what the upper and lower tracking limits should be? There is no single answer, but they try to find reasonable values—in other words, limits not so low as to be triggered with every small forecast error and not so high as to allow bad forecasts to be regularly overlooked. One MAD is equivalent to approximately .8 standard deviation, ±2 MADs = ±1.6 standard deviations, ±3 MADs = ±2.4 standard deviations, and ±4 MADs = ±3.2 standard deviations. This fact suggests that for a forecast to be "in control," 89% of the errors are expected to fall within ±2 MADs, 98% within ±3 MADs, or 99.9% within ±4 MADs.[4]

Example 16 shows how the tracking signal and cumulative error can be computed.

▶ **FIGURE 4.11**
A Plot of Tracking Signals

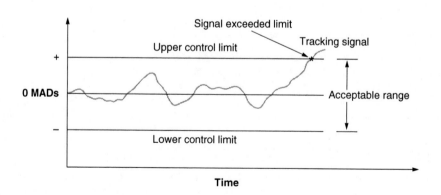

---

[4]To prove these three percentages to yourself, just set up a normal curve for ±1.6 standard deviations (*z*-values). Using the normal table in Appendix I, you find that the area under the curve is .89. This represents ±2 MADs. Likewise, ±3 MADs = ±2.4 standard deviations encompass 98% of the area, and so on for ±4 MADs.

Carlson's Bakery wants to evaluate performance of its croissant forecast.

APPROACH ▶ Develop a tracking signal for the forecast and see if it stays within acceptable limits, which we define as ±4 MADs.

SOLUTION ▶ Using the forecast and demand data for the past 6 quarters for croissant sales, we develop a tracking signal in the table below:

Quarter	Actual Demand	Forecast Demand	Error	Cumulative Error	|Absolute Forecast Error|	Cumulative Absolute Forecast Error	MAD	Tracking Signal (Cumulative Error/MAD)
1	90	100	−10	−10	10	10	10.0	−10/10 = −1
2	95	100	−5	−15	5	15	7.5	−15/7.5 = −2
3	115	100	+15	0	15	30	10.0	0/10 = 0
4	100	110	−10	−10	10	40	10.0	−10/10 = −1
5	125	110	+15	+5	15	55	11.0	+5/11 = +0.5
6	140	110	+30	+35	30	85	14.2	+35/14.2 = +2.5

$$\text{At the end of quarter 6, MAD} = \frac{\Sigma |\text{Forecast errors}|}{n} = \frac{85}{6} = 14.2$$

$$\text{and Tracking signal} = \frac{\text{Cumulative error}}{\text{MAD}} = \frac{35}{14.2} = 2.5 \text{ MADs}$$

INSIGHT ▶ Because the tracking signal drifted from −2 MAD to +2.5 MAD (between 1.6 and 2.0 standard deviations), we can conclude that it is within acceptable limits.

LEARNING EXERCISE ▶ If actual demand in quarter 6 was 130 (rather than 140), what would be the MAD and resulting tracking signal? [Answer: MAD for quarter 6 would be 12.5, and the tracking signal for period 6 would be 2 MADs.]

RELATED PROBLEMS ▶ 4.37, 4.45

Adaptive Smoothing

Adaptive forecasting refers to computer monitoring of tracking signals and self-adjustment if a signal passes a preset limit. For example, when applied to exponential smoothing, the α and β coefficients are first selected on the basis of values that minimize error forecasts and then adjusted accordingly whenever the computer notes an errant tracking signal. This process is called **adaptive smoothing**.

Adaptive smoothing
An approach to exponential smoothing forecasting in which the smoothing constant is automatically changed to keep errors to a minimum.

Focus Forecasting

Rather than adapt by choosing a smoothing constant, computers allow us to try a variety of forecasting models. Such an approach is called focus forecasting. **Focus forecasting** is based on two principles:

1. Sophisticated forecasting models are not always better than simple ones.
2. There is no single technique that should be used for all products or services.

Focus forecasting
Forecasting that tries a variety of computer models and selects the best one for a particular application.

Bernard Smith, inventory manager for American Hardware Supply, coined the term *focus forecasting*. Smith's job was to forecast quantities for 100,000 hardware products purchased by American's 21 buyers.[5] He found that buyers neither trusted nor understood the exponential smoothing model then in use. Instead, they used very simple approaches of their own. So Smith developed his new computerized system for selecting forecasting methods.

Smith chose to test seven forecasting methods. They ranged from the simple ones that buyers used (such as the naive approach) to statistical models. Every month, Smith applied the forecasts of all seven models to each item in stock. In these simulated trials, the forecast values were subtracted from the most recent actual demands, giving a simulated forecast error. The forecast

---

[5]Bernard T. Smith, *Focus Forecasting: Computer Techniques for Inventory Control* (Boston: CBI Publishing, 1978).

method yielding the least error is selected by the computer, which then uses it to make next month's forecast. Although buyers still have an override capability, American Hardware finds that focus forecasting provides excellent results.

AUTHOR COMMENT
Forecasting at McDonald's, FedEx, and Walmart is as important and complex as it is for manufacturers such as Toyota and Dell.

FORECASTING IN THE SERVICE SECTOR

Forecasting in the service sector presents some unusual challenges. A major technique in the retail sector is tracking demand by maintaining good short-term records. For instance, a barbershop catering to men expects peak flows on Fridays and Saturdays. Indeed, most barbershops are closed on Sunday and Monday, and many call in extra help on Friday and Saturday. A downtown restaurant, on the other hand, may need to track conventions and holidays for effective short-term forecasting. The *OM in Action* box "Forecasting at FedEx's Customer Service Centers" provides an example of a major service-sector industry, the call center.

Specialty Retail Shops   Specialty retail facilities, such as flower shops, may have other unusual demand patterns, and those patterns will differ depending on the holiday. When Valentine's Day falls on a weekend, for example, flowers can't be delivered to offices, and those romantically inclined are likely to celebrate with outings rather than flowers. If a holiday falls on a Monday, some of the celebration may also take place on the weekend, reducing flower sales. However, when Valentine's Day falls in midweek, busy midweek schedules often make flowers the optimal way to celebrate. Because flowers for Mother's Day are to be delivered on Saturday or Sunday, this holiday forecast varies less. Due to special demand patterns, many service firms maintain records of sales, noting not only the day of the week but also unusual events, including the weather, so that patterns and correlations that influence demand can be developed.

Fast-Food Restaurants   Fast-food restaurants are well aware not only of weekly, daily, and hourly but even 15-minute variations in demands that influence sales. Therefore, detailed forecasts of demand are needed. Figure 4.12(a) shows the hourly forecast for a typical fast-food restaurant. Note the lunchtime and dinnertime peaks. This contrasts to the mid-morning and mid-afternoon peaks at FedEx's call center in Figure 14.12(b).

Firms like Taco Bell now use point-of-sale computers that track sales every quarter hour. Taco Bell found that a 6-week moving average was the forecasting technique that minimized its mean squared error (MSE) of these quarter-hour forecasts. Building this forecasting methodology into each of Taco Bell's 6,500 stores' computers, the model makes weekly projections of customer

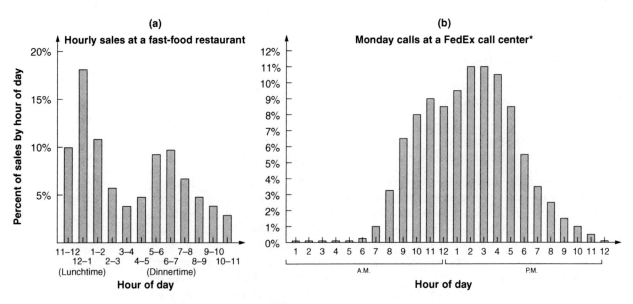

▲ **FIGURE 4.12**   **Forecasts Are Unique: Note the Variations between (a) Hourly Sales at a Fast-Food Restaurant and (b) Hourly Call Volume at FedEx**

*Based on historical data: see *Journal of Business Forecasting* (Winter 1999–2000): 6–11.

The world's largest express shipping company, FedEx, generates $38 billion in revenues, using 675 planes, 44,000 trucks, and a workforce of 145,000 in 220 countries. To support this global network, the company has 51 customer service call centers, whose service goal is to answer 90% of all calls within 20 seconds. With a half-million daily calls just in the U.S., FedEx makes extensive use of forecasting models for staffing decisions and to ensure that customer satisfaction levels stay the highest in the industry.

FedEx's Forecasting & Modeling department makes several different forecasts. *One-year* and *five-year* models predict number of calls, average handle time, and staffing needs. They break forecasts into weekday, Saturday, and Sunday and then use the Delphi method and time-series analysis.

FedEx's *tactical forecasts* are monthly and use 8 years of historical daily data. This time-series model addresses

month, day of week, and day of month to predict caller volume. Finally, the *operational forecast* uses a weighted moving average and 6 weeks of data to project the number of calls on a half-hourly basis.

FedEx's forecasts are consistently accurate to within 1% to 2% of actual call volumes. This means coverage needs are met, service levels are maintained, and costs are controlled.

Sources: Hoover's Company Records (July 1, 2009): 10552; *Baseline* (January 2005): 54; and *Journal of Business Forecasting* (Winter 1999–2000): 7–11.

---

transactions. These in turn are used by store managers to schedule staff, who begin in 15-minute increments, not 1-hour blocks as in other industries. The forecasting model has been so successful that Taco Bell has increased customer service while documenting more than $50 million in labor cost savings in 4 years of use.[6]

CHAPTER SUMMARY

Forecasts are a critical part of the operations manager's function. Demand forecasts drive a firm's production, capacity, and scheduling systems and affect the financial, marketing, and personnel planning functions.

There are a variety of qualitative and quantitative forecasting techniques. Qualitative approaches employ judgment, experience, intuition, and a host of other factors that are difficult to quantify. Quantitative forecasting uses historical data and causal, or associative, relations to project future demands. The Rapid Review for this chapter summarizes the formulas we introduced in quantitative forecasting.

Forecast calculations are seldom performed by hand. Most operations managers turn to software packages such as Forecast PRO, SAP, AFS, SAS, SPSS, or Excel.

No forecasting method is perfect under all conditions. And even once management has found a satisfactory approach, it must still monitor and control forecasts to make sure errors do not get out of hand. Forecasting can often be a very challenging, but rewarding, part of managing.

Key Terms

Forecasting
Economic forecasts
Technological forecasts
Demand forecasts
Quantitative forecasts
Qualitative forecasts
Jury of executive opinion
Delphi method
Sales force composite
Consumer market survey
Time series

Naive approach
Moving averages
Exponential smoothing
Smoothing constant
Mean absolute deviation (MAD)
Mean squared error (MSE)
Mean absolute percent error
   (MAPE)
Trend projection
Seasonal variations
Cycles

Linear-regression analysis
Standard error of the estimate
Coefficient of correlation
Coefficient of determination
Multiple regression
Tracking signal
Bias
Adaptive smoothing
Focus forecasting

---

[6]J. Hueter and W. Swart, "An Integrated Labor Management System for Taco Bell," *Interfaces* 28, no. 1 (January–February 1998): 75–91.

Ethical Dilemma

In 2009, the board of regents responsible for all public higher education funding in a large Midwestern state hired a consultant to develop a series of enrollment forecasting models, one for each college. These models used historical data and exponential smoothing to forecast the following year's enrollments. Based on the model, which included a smoothing constant (α) for each school, each college's budget was set by the board. The head of the board personally selected each smoothing constant based on what she called her "gut reactions and political acumen."

What do you think the advantages and disadvantages of this system are? Answer from the perspective of (a) the board of regents and (b) the president of each college. How can this model be abused and what can be done to remove any biases? How can a *regression model* be used to produce results that favor one forecast over another?

Discussion Questions

1. What is a qualitative forecasting model, and when is its use appropriate?
2. Identify and briefly describe the two general forecasting approaches.
3. Identify the three forecasting time horizons. State an approximate duration for each.
4. Briefly describe the steps that are used to develop a forecasting system.
5. A skeptical manager asks what medium-range forecasts can be used for. Give the manager three possible uses/purposes.
6. Explain why such forecasting devices as moving averages, weighted moving averages, and exponential smoothing are not well suited for data series that have trends.
7. What is the basic difference between a weighted moving average and exponential smoothing?
8. What three methods are used to determine the accuracy of any given forecasting method? How would you determine whether time-series regression or exponential smoothing is better in a specific application?
9. Research and briefly describe the Delphi technique. How would it be used by an employer you have worked for?
10. What is the primary difference between a time-series model and an associative model?
11. Define time series.
12. What effect does the value of the smoothing constant have on the weight given to the recent values?
13. Explain the value of seasonal indices in forecasting. How are seasonal patterns different from cyclical patterns?
14. Which forecasting technique can place the most emphasis on recent values? How does it do this?
15. In your own words, explain adaptive forecasting.
16. What is the purpose of a tracking signal?
17. Explain, in your own words, the meaning of the correlation coefficient. Discuss the meaning of a negative value of the correlation coefficient.
18. What is the difference between a dependent and an independent variable?
19. Give examples of industries that are affected by seasonality. Why would these businesses want to filter out seasonality?
20. Give examples of industries in which demand forecasting is dependent on the demand for other products.
21. What happens to the ability to forecast for periods farther into the future?

Using Software in Forecasting

This section presents three ways to solve forecasting problems with computer software. First, you can create your own Excel spreadsheets to develop forecasts. Second, you can use the Excel OM software that comes with the text and is found on our text web site. Third, POM for Windows is another program that is located on our web site at **www.pearsonglobaleditions.com/heizer**.

Creating Your Own Excel Spreadsheets

Excel spreadsheets (and spreadsheets in general) are frequently used in forecasting. Exponential smoothing, trend analysis, and regression analysis (simple and multiple) are supported by built-in Excel functions.

Program 4.1 illustrates how to build an Excel forecast for the data in Example 8. The goal for N.Y. Edison is to create a trend analysis of the 2003–2009 data. Note that in cell D4 you can enter either = $B$16 + $B$17 * C4 *or* = TREND ($B$4: $B$10, $C$4: $C$10, C4).

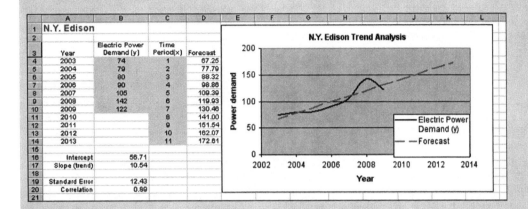

◀ **PROGRAM 4.1**

Using Excel to Develop Your Own Forecast, with Data from Example 8

	Computations		
Value	**Cell**	**Excel Formula**	**Action**
Trend line column	D4	=$B$16+$B$17*C4	Copy to D5:D14
		(or =TREND($B$4:$B$10,$C$4:$C$10,C4))	
Intercept	B16	=INTERCEPT(B4:B10, C4:C10)	
Slope (trend)	B17	=SLOPE(B4:B10, C4:C10)	
Standard error	B19	=STEYX(B4:B10, C4:C10)	
Correlation	B20	=CORREL(B4:B10, C4:C10)	

As an alternative, you may want to experiment with Excel's built-in regression analysis. To do so, under the *Data* menu bar selection choose *Data Analysis*, then *Regression*. Enter your *Y* and *X* data into two columns (say B and C). When the regression window appears, enter the *Y* and *X* ranges, then select *OK*. Excel offers several plots and tables to those interested in more rigorous analysis of regression problems.

✗ Using Excel OM

Excel OM's forecasting module has five components: (1) moving averages, (2) weighted moving averages, (3) exponential smoothing, (4) regression (with one variable only), and (5) decomposition. Excel OM's error analysis is much more complete than that available with the Excel add-in.

Program 4.2 illustrates Excel OM's input and output, using Example 2's weighted-moving-average data.

▶ Using POM for Windows

POM for Windows can project moving averages (both simple and weighted), handle exponential smoothing (both simple and trend adjusted), forecast with least squares trend projection, and solve linear-regression (associative) models. A summary screen of error analysis and a graph of the data can also be generated. As a special example of exponential smoothing adaptive forecasting, when using an α of 0, POM for Windows will find the α value that yields the minimum MAD.

Appendix IV provides further details.

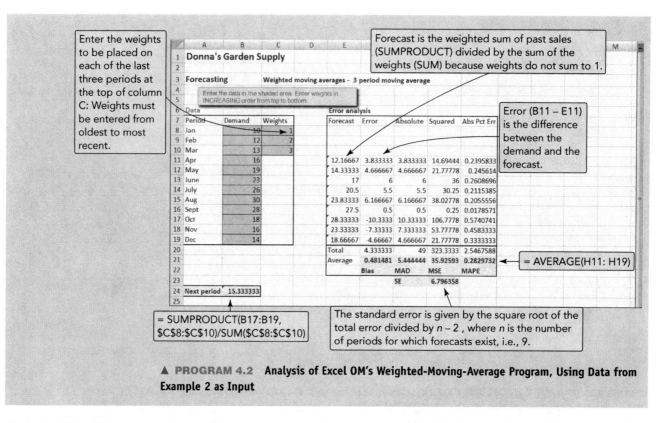

▲ **PROGRAM 4.2** Analysis of Excel OM's Weighted-Moving-Average Program, Using Data from Example 2 as Input

Solved Problems   Virtual Office Hours help is available at www.pearsonglobaleditions.com/myomlab

▼ SOLVED PROBLEM 4.1

Sales of Volkswagen's popular Beetle have grown steadily at auto dealerships in Nevada during the past 5 years (see table below). The sales manager had predicted in 2004 that 2005 sales would be 410 VWs. Using exponential smoothing with a weight of $\alpha = .30$, develop forecasts for 2006 through 2010.

Year	Sales	Forecast
2005	450	410
2006	495	
2007	518	
2008	563	
2009	584	
2010	?	

▼ SOLUTION

Year	Forecast
2005	410.0
2006	$422.0 = 410 + .3\,(450 - 410)$
2007	$443.9 = 422 + .3\,(495 - 422)$
2008	$466.1 = 443.9 + .3\,(518 - 443.9)$
2009	$495.2 = 466.1 + .3\,(563 - 466.1)$
2010	$521.8 = 495.2 + .3\,(584 - 495.2)$

▼ SOLVED PROBLEM 4.2

In Example 7, we applied trend-adjusted exponential smoothing to forecast demand for a piece of pollution-control equipment for months 2 and 3 (out of 9 months of data provided). Let us now continue this process for month 4. We want to confirm the forecast for month 4 shown in Table 4.1 (p. 150) and Figure 4.3 (p. 150).

For month 4, $A_4 = 19$, with $\alpha = .2$, and $\beta = .4$.

▼ SOLUTION

$$F_4 = \alpha A_3 + (1 - \alpha)(F_3 + T_3)$$
$$= (.2)(20) + (1 - .2)(15.18 + 2.10)$$
$$= 4.0 + (.8)(17.28)$$
$$= 4.0 + 13.82$$
$$= 17.82$$
$$T_4 = \beta(F_4 - F_3) + (1 - \beta)T_3$$
$$= (.4)(17.82 - 15.18) + (1 - .4)(2.10)$$
$$= (.4)(2.64) + (.6)(2.10)$$
$$= 1.056 + 1.26$$
$$= 2.32$$
$$FIT_4 = 17.82 + 2.32$$
$$= 20.14$$

▼ SOLVED PROBLEM 4.3

Room registrations in the Toronto Towers Plaza Hotel have been recorded for the past 9 years. To project future occupancy, management would like to determine the mathematical trend of guest registration. This estimate will help the hotel determine whether future expansion will be needed. Given the following time-series data, develop a regression equation relating registrations to time (e.g., a trend equation). Then forecast 2011 registrations. Room registrations are in the thousands:

2001: 17   2002: 16   2003: 16   2004: 21   2005: 20
2006: 20   2007: 23   2008: 25   2009: 24

▼ SOLUTION

Year	Transformed Year, x	Registrants, y (in thousands)	x^2	xy
2001	1	17	1	17
2002	2	16	4	32
2003	3	16	9	48
2004	4	21	16	84
2005	5	20	25	100
2006	6	20	36	120
2007	7	23	49	161
2008	8	25	64	200
2009	9	24	81	216
	$\Sigma x = 45$	$\Sigma y = 182$	$\Sigma x^2 = 285$	$\Sigma xy = 978$

$$b = \frac{\Sigma xy - n\bar{x}\bar{y}}{\Sigma x^2 - n\bar{x}^2} = \frac{978 - (9)(5)(20.22)}{285 - (9)(25)} = \frac{978 - 909.9}{285 - 225} = \frac{68.1}{60} = 1.135$$

$$a = \bar{y} - b\bar{x} = 20.22 - (1.135)(5) = 20.22 - 5.675 = 14.545$$

$$\hat{y} \text{ (registrations)} = 14.545 + 1.135x$$

The projection of registrations in the year 2011 (which is $x = 11$ in the coding system used) is:

$$\hat{y} = 14.545 + (1.135)(11) = 27.03$$
$$\text{or } 27,030 \text{ guests in 2011}$$

▼ SOLVED PROBLEM 4.4

Quarterly demand for Ford F150 pickups at a New York auto dealer is forecast with the equation:

$$\hat{y} = 10 + 3x$$

where x = quarters, and:

Quarter I of 2008 = 0
Quarter II of 2008 = 1
Quarter III of 2008 = 2
Quarter IV of 2008 = 3
Quarter I of 2009 = 4
and so on

and:

$$\hat{y} = \text{quarterly demand}$$

The demand for trucks is seasonal, and the indices for Quarters I, II, III, and IV are 0.80, 1.00, 1.30, and 0.90, respectively. Forecast demand for each quarter of 2010. Then, seasonalize each forecast to adjust for quarterly variations.

▼ SOLUTION

Quarter II of 2009 is coded $x = 5$; Quarter III of 2009, $x = 6$; and Quarter IV of 2009, $x = 7$. Hence, Quarter I of 2010 is coded $x = 8$; Quarter II, $x = 9$; and so on.

$$\hat{y}(2010 \text{ Quarter I}) = 10 + 3(8) = 34$$
$$\hat{y}(2010 \text{ Quarter II}) = 10 + 3(9) = 37$$
$$\hat{y}(2010 \text{ Quarter III}) = 10 + 3(10) = 40$$
$$\hat{y}(2010 \text{ Quarter IV}) = 10 + 3(11) = 43$$

Adjusted forecast = (.80)(34) = 27.2
Adjusted forecast = (1.00)(37) = 37
Adjusted forecast = (1.30)(40) = 52
Adjusted forecast = (.90)(43) = 38.7

Problems*

• 4.1 The following gives the number of pints of type A blood used at Woodlawn Hospital in the past 6 weeks:

Week Of	Pints Used
August 31	360
September 7	389
September 14	410
September 21	381
September 28	368
October 5	374

a) Forecast the demand for the week of October 12 using a 3-week moving average.
b) Use a 3-week weighted moving average, with weights of .1, .3, and .6, using .6 for the most recent week. Forecast demand for the week of October 12.
c) Compute the forecast for the week of October 12 using exponential smoothing with a forecast for August 31 of 360 and $\alpha = .2$. **P✗**

•• 4.2

Year	1	2	3	4	5	6	7	8	9	10	11
Demand	7	9	5	9	13	8	12	13	9	11	7

a) Plot the above data on a graph. Do you observe any trend, cycles, or random variations?
b) Starting in year 4 and going to year 12, forecast demand using a 3-year moving average. Plot your forecast on the same graph as the original data.
c) Starting in year 4 and going to year 12, forecast demand using a 3-year moving average with weights of .1, .3, and .6, using .6 for the most recent year. Plot this forecast on the same graph.
d) As you compare forecasts with the original data, which seems to give the better results? **P✗**

• 4.3 Refer to Problem 4.2. Develop a forecast for years 2 through 12 using exponential smoothing with $\alpha = .4$ and a forecast for year 1 of 6. Plot your new forecast on a graph with the actual data and the naive forecast. Based on a visual inspection, which forecast is better? **P✗**

• 4.4 A check-processing center uses exponential smoothing to forecast the number of incoming checks each month. The number of checks received in June was 40 million, while the forecast was 42 million. A smoothing constant of .2 is used.
a) What is the forecast for July?
b) If the center received 45 million checks in July, what would be the forecast for August?
c) Why might this be an inappropriate forecasting method for this situation? **P✗**

•• 4.5 The Carbondale Hospital is considering the purchase of a new ambulance. The decision will rest partly on the anticipated mileage to be driven next year. The miles driven during the past 5 years are as follows:

Year	Mileage
1	3,000
2	4,000
3	3,400
4	3,800
5	3,700

Note: **P✗** means the problem may be solved with POM for Windows and/or Excel OM.

a) Forecast the mileage for next year using a 2-year moving average.
b) Find the MAD based on the 2-year moving average forecast in part (a). (*Hint:* You will have only 3 years of matched data.)
c) Use a weighted 2-year moving average with weights of .4 and .6 to forecast next year's mileage. (The weight of .6 is for the most recent year.) What MAD results from using this approach to forecasting? (*Hint:* You will have only 3 years of matched data.)
d) Compute the forecast for year 6 using exponential smoothing, an initial forecast for year 1 of 3,000 miles, and $\alpha = .5$. **P✗**

•• 4.6 The monthly sales for Telco Batteries, Inc., were as follows:

Month	Sales
January	20
February	21
March	15
April	14
May	13
June	16
July	17
August	18
September	20
October	20
November	21
December	23

a) Plot the monthly sales data.
b) Forecast January sales using each of the following:
  i) Naive method.
  ii) A 3-month moving average.
  iii) A 6-month weighted average using .1, .1, .1, .2, .2, and .3, with the heaviest weights applied to the most recent months.
  iv) Exponential smoothing using an $\alpha = .3$ and a September forecast of 18.
  v) A trend projection.
c) With the data given, which method would allow you to forecast next March's sales? **P✗**

•• 4.7 The actual demand for the patients at Omaha Emergency Medical Clinic for the first six weeks of this year follows:

Week	Actual No. of Patients
1	65
2	62
3	70
4	48
5	63
6	52

Clinic administrator Marc Schniederjans wants you to forecast patient demand at the clinic for week 7 by using this data. You decide to use a weighted moving average method to find this forecast. Your method uses four actual demand levels, with weights of 0.333 on the present period, 0.25 one period ago, 0.25 two periods ago, and 0.167 three periods ago.
a) What is the value of your forecast? **P✗**
b) If instead the weights were 20, 15, 15, and 10, respectively, how would the forecast change? Explain why.
c) What if the weights were 0.40, 0.30, 0.20, and 0.10, respectively? Now what is the forecast for week 7?

· **4.8** Daily high temperatures in St. Louis for the last week were as follows: 93, 94, 93, 95, 96, 88, 90 (yesterday).

a) Forecast the high temperature today, using a 3-day moving average.

b) Forecast the high temperature today, using a 2-day moving average.

c) Calculate the mean absolute deviation based on a 2-day moving average.

d) Compute the mean squared error for the 2-day moving average.

e) Calculate the mean absolute percent error for the 2-day moving average. **Px**

··· **4.9** Dell uses the CR5 chip in some of its laptop computers. The prices for the chip during the past 12 months were as follows:

Month	Price per Chip	Month	Price per Chip
January	$1.80	July	1.80
February	1.67	August	1.83
March	1.70	September	1.70
April	1.85	October	1.65
May	1.90	November	1.70
June	1.87	December	1.75

a) Use a 2-month moving average on all the data and plot the averages and the prices.

b) Use a 3-month moving average and add the 3-month plot to the graph created in part (a).

c) Which is better (using the mean absolute deviation): the 2-month average or the 3-month average?

d) Compute the forecasts for each month using exponential smoothing, with an initial forecast for January of $1.80. Use $\alpha = .1$, then $\alpha = .3$, and finally $\alpha = .5$. Using MAD, which α is the best? **Px**

·· **4.10** Data collected on the yearly registrations for a Six Sigma seminar at the Quality College are shown in the following table:

Year	1	2	3	4	5	6	7	8	9	10	11
Registrations (000)	4	6	4	5	10	8	7	9	12	14	15

a) Develop a 3-year moving average to forecast registrations from year 4 to year 12.

b) Estimate demand again for years 4 to 12 with a 3-year weighted moving average in which registrations in the most recent year are given a weight of 2, and registrations in the other 2 years are each given a weight of 1.

c) Graph the original data and the two forecasts. Which of the two forecasting methods seems better? **Px**

· **4.11** a) Use exponential smoothing with a smoothing constant of 0.3 to forecast the registrations at the seminar given in Problem 4.10. To begin the procedure, assume that the forecast for year 1 was 5,000 people signing up.

b) What is the MAD? **Px**

·· **4.12** Consider the following actual and forecast demand levels for Big Mac hamburgers at a local McDonald's restaurant:

Day	Actual Demand	Forecast Demand
Monday	88	88
Tuesday	72	88
Wednesday	68	84
Thursday	48	80
Friday		

The forecast for Monday was derived by observing Monday's demand level and setting Monday's forecast level equal to this demand level. Subsequent forecasts were derived by using exponential smoothing with a smoothing constant of 0.25. Using this exponential smoothing method, what is the forecast for Big Mac demand for Friday? **Px**

··· **4.13** As you can see in the following table, demand for heart transplant surgery at Washington General Hospital has increased steadily in the past few years:

Year	1	2	3	4	5	6
Heart Transplants	45	50	52	56	58	?

The director of medical services predicted 6 years ago that demand in year 1 would be 41 surgeries.

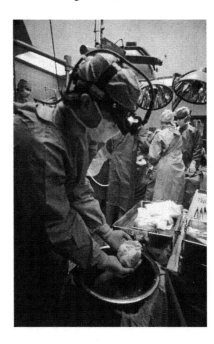

a) Use exponential smoothing, first with a smoothing constant of .6 and then with one of .9, to develop forecasts for years 2 through 6.

b) Use a 3-year moving average to forecast demand in years 4, 5, and 6.

c) Use the trend-projection method to forecast demand in years 1 through 6.

d) With MAD as the criterion, which of the four forecasting methods is best? **Px**

·· **4.14** Following are two weekly forecasts made by two different methods for the number of gallons of gasoline, in thousands, demanded at a local gasoline station. Also shown are actual demand levels, in thousands of gallons:

Week	Forecasts		Actual Demand
	Method 1	Method 2	
1	0.90	0.80	0.70
2	1.05	1.20	1.00
3	0.95	0.90	1.00
4	1.20	1.11	1.00

What are the MAD and MSE for each method?

4.15 Refer to Solved Problem 4.1 on page 170. Use a 3-year moving average to forecast the sales of Volkswagen Beetles in Nevada through 2010. What is the MAD? **PX**

4.16 Refer to Solved Problem 4.1. Using the trend projection method, develop a forecast for the sales of Volkswagen Beetles in Nevada through 2010. What is the MAD? **PX**

4.17 Refer to Solved Problem 4.1. Using smoothing constants of .6 and .9, develop forecasts for the sales of VW Beetles. What effect did the smoothing constant have on the forecast? Use MAD to determine which of the three smoothing constants (.3, .6, or .9) gives the most accurate forecast. **PX**

•••• **4.18** Consider the following actual (A_t) and forecast (F_t) demand levels for a product:

Time Period, t	Actual Demand, A_t	Forecast Demand, F_t
1	50	50
2	42	50
3	56	48
4	46	50
5		

The first forecast, F_1, was derived by observing A_1 and setting F_1 equal to A_1. Subsequent forecasts were derived by exponential smoothing. Using the exponential smoothing method, find the forecast for time period 5. (*Hint:* You need to first find the smoothing constant, α.)

••• **4.19** Income at the law firm Smith and Wesson for the period February to July was as follows:

Month	February	March	April	May	June	July
Income (in $ thousand)	70.0	68.5	64.8	71.7	71.3	72.8

Use trend-adjusted exponential smoothing to forecast the law firm's August income. Assume that the initial forecast for February is $65,000 and the initial trend adjustment is 0. The smoothing constants selected are $\alpha = .1$ and $\beta = .2$. **PX**

••• **4.20** Resolve Problem 4.19 with $\alpha = .1$ and $\beta = .8$. Using MSE, determine which smoothing constants provide a better forecast. **PX**

4.21 Refer to the trend-adjusted exponential smoothing illustration in Example 7 on pages 149–150. Using $\alpha = .2$ and $\beta = .4$, we forecast sales for 9 months, showing the detailed calculations for months 2 and 3. In Solved Problem 4.2, we continued the process for month 4.

In this problem, show your calculations for months 5 and 6 for F_t, T_t, and FIT_t. **PX**

4.22 Refer to Problem 4.21. Complete the trend-adjusted exponential-smoothing forecast computations for periods 7, 8, and 9. Confirm that your numbers for F_t, T_t, and FIT_t match those in Table 4.1 (p. 150). **PX**

•• **4.23** Sales of vegetable dehydrators at Bud Banis's discount department store in St. Louis over the past year are shown below. Management prepared a forecast using a combination of exponential smoothing and its collective judgment for the 4 months (March, April, May, and June of 2010):

Month	2009–2010 Unit Sales	Management's Forecast
July	100	
August	93	
September	96	
October	110	
November	124	
December	119	
January	92	
February	83	
March	101	120
April	96	114
May	89	110
June	108	108

a) Compute MAD and MAPE for management's technique.
b) Do management's results outperform (i.e., have smaller MAD and MAPE than) a naive forecast?
c) Which forecast do you recommend, based on lower forecast error?

•• **4.24** Howard Weiss, owner of a musical instrument distributorship, thinks that demand for bass drums may be related to the number of television appearances by the popular group Stone Temple Pilots during the previous month. Weiss has collected the data shown in the following table:

Demand for Bass Drums	3	6	7	5	10	7
Stone Temple Pilots' TV Appearances	3	4	7	6	8	5

a) Graph these data to see whether a linear equation might describe the relationship between the group's television shows and bass drum sales.
b) Use the least-squares regression method to derive a forecasting equation.
c) What is your estimate for bass drum sales if the Stone Temple Pilots performed on TV nine times last month?
d) What are the correlation coefficient (r) and the coefficient of determination (r^2) for this model, and what do they mean? **PX**

• **4.25** The following gives the number of accidents that occurred on Florida State Highway 101 during the past 4 months:

Month	Number of Accidents
January	30
February	40
March	60
April	90

Forecast the number of accidents that will occur in May, using least-squares regression to derive a trend equation. **PX**

• **4.26** In the past, Arup Mukherjee's tire dealership in Pensacola sold an average of 1,000 radials each year. In the past 2 years, 200 and 250, respectively, were sold in fall, 350 and 300 in winter, 150 and 165 in spring, and 300 and 285 in summer. With a major expansion planned, Mukherjee projects sales next year to increase to 1,200 radials. What will be the demand during each season?

•• **4.27** Mark Cotteleer owns a company that manufactures sailboats. Actual demand for Mark's sailboats during each season in 2006 through 2009 was as follows:

		Year		
Season	2006	2007	2008	2009
Winter	1,400	1,200	1,000	900
Spring	1,500	1,400	1,600	1,500
Summer	1,000	2,100	2,000	1,900
Fall	600	750	650	500

Mark has forecasted that annual demand for his sailboats in 2011 will equal 5,600 sailboats. Based on this data and the multiplicative seasonal model, what will the demand level be for Mark's sailboats in the spring of 2011?

•• **4.28** Attendance at Los Angeles's newest Disneylike attraction, Vacation World, has been as follows:

Quarter	Guests (in thousands)	Quarter	Guests (in thousands)
Winter '07	73	Summer '08	124
Spring '07	104	Fall '08	52
Summer '07	168	Winter '09	89
Fall '07	74	Spring '09	146
Winter '08	65	Summer '09	205
Spring '08	82	Fall '09	98

Compute seasonal indices using all of the data. **PX**

• **4.29** Central States Electric Company estimates its demand trend line (in millions of kilowatt hours) to be:

$$D = 77 + 0.43Q$$

where Q refers to the sequential quarter number and $Q = 1$ for winter 1986. In addition, the multiplicative seasonal factors are as follows:

Quarter	Factor (Index)
Winter	.8
Spring	1.1
Summer	1.4
Fall	.7

Forecast energy use for the four quarters of 2011, beginning with winter.

• **4.30** Brian Buckley has developed the following forecasting model:

$$\hat{y} = 36 + 4.3x$$

where $\hat{y}$ = demand for Aztec air conditioners and
       x = the outside temperature (°F)

a) Forecast demand for the Aztec when the temperature is 70°F.
b) What is demand when the temperature is 80°F?
c) What is demand when the temperature is 90°F? **PX**

•• **4.31** Coffee Palace's manager, Joe Felan, suspects that demand for mocha latte coffees depends on the price being charged. Based on historical observations, Joe has gathered the following data, which show the numbers of these coffees sold over six different price values:

Price	Number Sold
$2.70	760
$3.50	510
$2.00	980
$4.20	250
$3.10	320
$4.05	480

Using these data, how many mocha latte coffees would be forecast to be sold according to simple linear regression if the price per cup were $2.80? **PX**

• **4.32** The following data relate the sales figures of the bar in Marty and Polly Starr's small bed-and-breakfast inn in Marathon, Florida, to the number of guests registered that week:

Week	Guests	Bar Sales
1	16	$330
2	12	270
3	18	380
4	14	300

a) Perform a linear regression that relates bar sales to guests (not to time).
b) If the forecast is for 20 guests next week, what are the sales expected to be? **PX**

• **4.33** The number of transistors (in millions) made at a plant in Japan during the past 5 years follows:

Year	Transistors
1	140
2	160
3	190
4	200
5	210

a) Forecast the number of transistors to be made next year, using linear regression.
b) Compute the mean squared error (MSE) when using linear regression.
c) Compute the mean absolute percent error (MAPE). **PX**

• **4.34** The number of auto accidents in a certain region is related to the regional number of registered automobiles in thousands (X_1), alcoholic beverage sales in $10,000s (X_2), and rainfall in inches (X_3). Furthermore, the regression formula has been calculated as:

$$Y = a + b_1X_1 + b_2X_2 + b_3X_3$$

where Y = number of automobile accidents
      $a = 7.5$
      $b_1 = 3.5$
      $b_2 = 4.5$
      $b_3 = 2.5$

Calculate the expected number of automobile accidents under conditions a, b, and c:

	X_1	X_2	X_3
(a)	2	3	0
(b)	3	5	1
(c)	4	7	2	**PX**

•• **4.35** John Howard, a Mobile, Alabama, real estate developer, has devised a regression model to help determine residential housing prices in South Alabama. The model was developed using recent sales in a particular neighborhood. The price (Y) of the house is based on the size (square footage = X) of the house. The model is:

$$Y = 13,473 + 37.65X$$

The coefficient of correlation for the model is 0.63.
a) Use the model to predict the selling price of a house that is 1,860 square feet.
b) An 1,860-square-foot house recently sold for $95,000. Explain why this is not what the model predicted.

c) If you were going to use multiple regression to develop such a model, what other quantitative variables might you include?
d) What is the value of the coefficient of determination in this problem? **Px**

• **4.36** Accountants at the firm Michael Vest, CPAs, believed that several traveling executives were submitting unusually high travel vouchers when they returned from business trips. First, they took a sample of 200 vouchers submitted from the past year. Then they developed the following multiple-regression equation relating expected travel cost to number of days on the road (x_1) and distance traveled (x_2) in miles:

$$\hat{y} = \$90.00 + \$48.50x_1 + \$.40x_2$$

The coefficient of correlation computed was .68.
a) If Wanda Fennell returns from a 300-mile trip that took her out of town for 5 days, what is the expected amount she should claim as expenses?
b) Fennell submitted a reimbursement request for $685. What should the accountant do?
c) Should any other variables be included? Which ones? Why? **Px**

•• **4.37** Sales of music stands at Johnny Ho's music store in Columbus, Ohio, over the past 10 weeks are shown in the table below.
a) Forecast demand for each week, including week 10, using exponential smoothing with $\alpha = .5$ (initial forecast = 20).

Week	Demand	Week	Demand
1	20	6	29
2	21	7	36
3	28	8	22
4	37	9	25
5	25	10	28

b) Compute the MAD.
c) Compute the tracking signal. **Px**

•• **4.38** City government has collected the following data on annual sales tax collections and new car registrations:

Annual Sales Tax Collections (in millions)	1.0	1.4	1.9	2.0	1.8	2.1	2.3
New Car Registrations (in thousands)	10	12	15	16	14	17	20

Determine the following:
a) The least-squares regression equation.
b) Using the results of part (a), find the estimated sales tax collections if new car registrations total 22,000.
c) The coefficients of correlation and determination. **Px**

•• **4.39** Dr. Susan Sweeney, a Providence, Rhode Island, psychologist, specializes in treating patients who are agoraphobic (i.e., afraid to leave their homes). The following table indicates how many patients Dr. Sweeney has seen each year for the past 10 years. It also indicates what the robbery rate was in Providence during the same year:

Year	1	2	3	4	5	6	7	8	9	10
Number of Patients	36	33	40	41	40	55	60	54	58	61
Robbery Rate per 1,000 Population	58.3	61.1	73.4	75.7	81.1	89.0	101.1	94.8	103.3	116.2

Using trend analysis, predict the number of patients Dr. Sweeney will see in years 11 and 12 as a function of time. How well does the model fit the data? **Px**

•• **4.40** Using the data in Problem 4.39, apply linear regression to study the relationship between the robbery rate and Dr. Sweeney's patient load. If the robbery rate increases to 131.2 in year 11, how many phobic patients will Dr. Sweeney treat? If the robbery rate drops to 90.6, what is the patient projection? **Px**

••• **4.41** Bus and subway ridership for the summer months in London, England, is believed to be tied heavily to the number of tourists visiting the city. During the past 12 years, the following data have been obtained:

Year (summer months)	Number of Tourists (in millions)	Ridership (in millions)
1	7	1.5
2	2	1.0
3	6	1.3
4	4	1.5
5	14	2.5
6	15	2.7
7	16	2.4
8	12	2.0
9	14	2.7
10	20	4.4
11	15	3.4
12	7	1.7

a) Plot these data and decide if a linear model is reasonable.
b) Develop a regression relationship.
c) What is expected ridership if 10 million tourists visit London in a year?
d) Explain the predicted ridership if there are no tourists at all.
e) What is the standard error of the estimate?
f) What is the model's correlation coefficient and coefficient of determination? **Px**

••• **4.42** Des Moines Power and Light has been collecting data on demand for electric power in its western subregion for only the past 2 years. Those data are shown in the table at the top of the next page.
To plan for expansion and to arrange to borrow power from neighboring utilities during peak periods, the utility needs to be able to forecast demand for each month next year. However, the standard

Demand in Megawatts		
Month	Last Year	This Year
January	5	17
February	6	14
March	10	20
April	13	23
May	18	30
June	15	38
July	23	44
August	26	41
September	21	33
October	15	23
November	12	26
December	14	17

forecasting models discussed in this chapter will not fit the data observed for the 2 years.
a) What are the weaknesses of the standard forecasting techniques as applied to this set of data?
b) Because known models are not appropriate here, propose your own approach to forecasting. Although there is no perfect solution to tackling data such as these (in other words, there are no 100% right or wrong answers), justify your model.
c) Forecast demand for each month next year using the model you propose.

••• **4.43** Emergency calls to the 911 system of Gainesville, Florida, for the past 24 weeks are shown in the following table:

Week	1	2	3	4	5	6	7	8	9	10	11	12
Calls	50	35	25	40	45	35	20	30	35	20	15	40
Week	13	14	15	16	17	18	19	20	21	22	23	24
Calls	55	35	25	55	55	40	35	60	75	50	40	65

a) Compute the exponentially smoothed forecast of calls for each week. Assume an initial forecast of 50 calls in the first week, and use $\alpha = .2$. What is the forecast for week 25?
b) Reforecast each period using $\alpha = .6$.
c) Actual calls during week 25 were 85. Which smoothing constant provides a superior forecast? Explain and justify the measure of error you used. **Px**

••• **4.44** Using the 911 call data in Problem 4.43, forecast calls for weeks 2 through 25 with a trend-adjusted exponential smoothing model. Assume an initial forecast for 50 calls for week 1 and an initial trend of zero. Use smoothing constants of $\alpha = .3$ and $\beta = .2$. Is this model better than that of Problem 4.43? What adjustment might be useful for further improvement? (Again, assume that actual calls in week 25 were 85.) **Px**

••• **4.45** The following are monthly actual and forecast demand levels for May through December for units of a product manufactured by the N. Tamimi Pharmaceutical Company:

Month	Actual Demand	Forecast Demand
May	100	100
June	80	104
July	110	99
August	115	101
September	105	104
October	110	104
November	125	105
December	120	109

What is the value of the tracking signal as of the end of December?

•• **4.46** Thirteen students entered the business program at Hillcrest College 2 years ago. The following table indicates what each student scored on the high school SAT math exam and their grade-point averages (GPAs) after students were in the Hillcrest program for 2 years.

Student	A	B	C	D	E	F	G
SAT Score	421	377	585	690	608	390	415
GPA	2.90	2.93	3.00	3.45	3.66	2.88	2.15
Student	H	I	J	K	L	M	
SAT Score	481	729	501	613	709	366	
GPA	2.53	3.22	1.99	2.75	3.90	1.60	

a) Is there a meaningful relationship between SAT math scores and grades?
b) If a student scores a 350, what do you think his or her GPA will be?
c) What about a student who scores 800?

••• **4.47** City Cycles has just started selling the new Z-10 mountain bike, with monthly sales as shown in the table. First, co-owner Amit wants to forecast by exponential smoothing by initially setting February's forecast equal to January's sales with $\alpha = .1$. Co-owner Barbara wants to use a three-period moving average.

	Sales	Amit	Barbara	Amit's Error	Barbara's Error
January	400	—			
February	380	400			
March	410				
April	375				
May					

a) Is there a strong linear trend in sales over time?
b) Fill in the table with what Amit and Barbara each forecast for May and the earlier months, as relevant.
c) Assume that May's actual sales figure turns out to be 405. Complete the table's columns and then calculate the mean absolute deviation for both Amit's and Barbara's methods.
d) Based on these calculations, which method seems more accurate? **Px**

•• **4.48** Sundar Balakrishnan, the general manager of Precision Engineering Corporation (PEC), thinks that his firm's engineering services contracted to highway construction firms are directly related to the volume of highway construction business contracted with companies in his geographic area. He wonders if this is really so, and if it is, can this information help him plan his operations better by forecasting the quantity of his engineering services required by construction firms in each quarter of the year? The following table presents the sales of his services and total amounts of contracts for highway construction over the past 8 quarters:

Quarter	1	2	3	4	5	6	7	8
Sales of PEC Services (in $ thousands)	8	10	15	9	12	13	12	16
Contracts Released (in $ thousands)	153	172	197	178	185	199	205	226

a) Using this data, develop a regression equation for predicting the level of demand of Precision's services.

b) Determine the coefficient of correlation and the standard error of the estimate. **Px**

•••• **4.49**   Salinas Savings and Loan is proud of its long tradition in Topeka, Kansas. Begun by Teresita Salinas 20 years after World War II, the S&L has bucked the trend of financial and liquidity problems that has repeatedly plagued the industry. Deposits have increased slowly but surely over the years, despite recessions in 1983, 1988, 1991, 2001, and 2008. Ms. Salinas believes it is necessary to have a long-range strategic plan for her firm, including a 1-year forecast and preferably even a 5-year forecast of deposits. She examines the past deposit data and also peruses Kansas's gross state product (GSP), over the same 44 years. (GSP is analogous to gross national product [GNP] but on the state level.) The resulting data are in the following table:

a) Using exponential smoothing, with α = .6, then trend analysis, and finally linear regression, discuss which forecasting model fits best for Salinas's strategic plan. Justify the selection of one model over another.

b) Carefully examine the data. Can you make a case for excluding a portion of the information? Why? Would that change your choice of model? **Px**

▶ Refer to myomlab🌐 for these additional homework problems: 4.50–4.62

Year	Deposits[a]	GSP[b]	Year	Deposits[a]	GSP[b]
1966	.25	.4	1988	6.2	2.5
1967	.24	.4	1989	4.1	2.8
1968	.24	.5	1990	4.5	2.9
1969	.26	.7	1991	6.1	3.4
1970	.25	.9	1992	7.7	3.8
1971	.30	1.0	1993	10.1	4.1
1972	.31	1.4	1994	15.2	4.0
1973	.32	1.7	1995	18.1	4.0
1974	.24	1.3	1996	24.1	3.9
1975	.26	1.2	1997	25.6	3.8
1976	.25	1.1	1998	30.3	3.8
1977	.33	.9	1999	36.0	3.7
1978	.50	1.2	2000	31.1	4.1
1979	.95	1.2	2001	31.7	4.1
1980	1.70	1.2	2002	38.5	4.0
1981	2.3	1.6	2003	47.9	4.5
1982	2.8	1.5	2004	49.1	4.6
1983	2.8	1.6	2005	55.8	4.5
1984	2.7	1.7	2006	70.1	4.6
1985	3.9	1.9	2007	70.9	4.6
1986	4.9	1.9	2008	79.1	4.7
1987	5.3	2.3	2009	94.0	5.0

[a]In $ millions.
[b]In $ billions.

Case Studies

▶ Southwestern University: (B)*

Southwestern University (SWU), a large state college in Stephenville, Texas, enrolls close to 20,000 students. The school is a dominant force in the small city, with more students during fall and spring than permanent residents.

Always a football powerhouse, SWU is usually in the top 20 in college football rankings. Since the legendary Bo Pitterno was hired as its head coach in 2003 (in hopes of reaching the elusive number 1 ranking), attendance at the five Saturday home games each year increased. Prior to Pitterno's arrival, attendance generally averaged 25,000 to 29,000 per game. Season ticket sales bumped up by 10,000 just with the announcement of the new coach's arrival. Stephenville and SWU were ready to move to the big time!

The immediate issue facing SWU, however, was not NCAA ranking. It was capacity. The existing SWU stadium, built in 1953, has seating for 54,000 fans. The following table indicates attendance at each game for the past 6 years.

One of Pitterno's demands upon joining SWU had been a stadium expansion, or possibly even a new stadium. With attendance increasing, SWU administrators began to face the issue head-on. Pitterno had wanted dormitories solely for his athletes in the stadium as an additional feature of any expansion.

SWU's president, Dr. Joel Wisner, decided it was time for his vice president of development to forecast when the existing stadium would "max out." The expansion was, in his mind, a given. But Wisner needed to know how long he could wait. He also sought a revenue projection, assuming an average ticket price of $50 in 2010 and a 5% increase each year in future prices.

Discussion Questions

1. Develop a forecasting model, justifying its selection over other techniques, and project attendance through 2011.
2. What revenues are to be expected in 2010 and 2011?
3. Discuss the school's options.

* This integrated case study runs throughout the text. Other issues facing Southwestern's football stadium include (A) managing the stadium project (Chapter 3); (C) quality of facilities (Chapter 6); (D) break-even analysis of food services (Supplement 7 web site); (E) locating the new stadium (Chapter 8 web site); (F) inventory planning of football programs (Chapter 12 web site); and (G) scheduling of campus security officers/staff for game days (Chapter 13).

Southwestern University Football Game Attendance, 2004–2009

Game	2004 Attendees	Opponent	2005 Attendees	Opponent	2006 Attendees	Opponent
1	34,200	Baylor	36,100	Oklahoma	35,900	TCU
2[a]	39,800	Texas	40,200	Nebraska	46,500	Texas Tech
3	38,200	LSU	39,100	UCLA	43,100	Alaska
4[b]	26,900	Arkansas	25,300	Nevada	27,900	Arizona
5	35,100	USC	36,200	Ohio State	39,200	Rice

Game	2007 Attendees	Opponent	2008 Attendees	Opponent	2009 Attendees	Opponent
1	41,900	Arkansas	42,500	Indiana	46,900	LSU
2[a]	46,100	Missouri	48,200	North Texas	50,100	Texas
3	43,900	Florida	44,200	Texas A&M	45,900	Prairie View A&M
4[b]	30,100	Miami	33,900	Southern	36,300	Montana
5	40,500	Duke	47,800	Oklahoma	49,900	Arizona State

[a]Homecoming games.

[b]During the 4th week of each season, Stephenville hosted a hugely popular southwestern crafts festival. This event brought tens of thousands of tourists to the town, especially on weekends, and had an obvious negative impact on game attendance.

▶ Digital Cell Phone, Inc.

Paul Jordan has just been hired as a management analyst at Digital Cell Phone, Inc. Digital Cell manufactures a broad line of phones for the consumer market. Paul's boss, John Smithers, chief operations officer, has asked Paul to stop by his office this morning. After a brief exchange of pleasantries over a cup of coffee, he says he has a special assignment for Paul: "We've always just made an educated guess about how many phones we need to make each month. Usually we just look at how many we sold last month and plan to produce about the same number. This sometimes works fine. But most months we either have too many phones in inventory or we are out of stock. Neither situation is good."

Handing Paul the table shown here, Smithers continues, "Here are our actual orders entered for the past 36 months. There are 144 phones per case. I was hoping that since you graduated recently from the University of Alaska, you might have studied some techniques that would help us plan better. It's been awhile since I was in college—I think I forgot most of the details I learned then. I'd like you to analyze these data and give me an idea of what our business will look like over the next 6 to 12 months. Do you think you can handle this?"

"Of course," Paul replies, sounding more confident than he really is. "How much time do I have?"

"I need your report on the Monday before Thanksgiving—that would be November 20th. I plan to take it home with me and read it during the holiday. Since I'm sure you will not be around during the holiday, be sure that you explain things carefully so that I can understand your recommendation without having to ask you any more questions. Since you are new to the company, you should know that I like to see all the details and complete justification for recommendations from my staff."

Source: Professor Victor E. Sower, Sam Houston State University.

With that, Paul was dismissed. Arriving back at his office, he began his analysis.

Orders Received, by Month

Month	Cases 2007	Cases 2008	Cases 2009
January	480	575	608
February	436	527	597
March	482	540	612
April	448	502	603
May	458	508	628
June	489	573	605
July	498	508	627
August	430	498	578
September	444	485	585
October	496	526	581
November	487	552	632
December	525	587	656

Discussion Question

1. Prepare Paul Jordan's report to John Smithers using regression analysis. Provide a summary of the cell phone industry outlook as part of Paul's response.
2. Adding seasonality into your model, how does the analysis change?

▶ Forecasting at Hard Rock Cafe

Video Case

With the growth of Hard Rock Cafe—from one pub in London in 1971 to more than 129 restaurants in more than 40 countries today—came a corporatewide demand for better forecasting. Hard Rock uses long-range forecasting in setting a capacity plan and intermediate-term forecasting for locking in contracts for leather goods (used in jackets) and for such food items as beef, chicken, and pork. Its short-term sales forecasts are conducted each month, by cafe, and then aggregated for a headquarters view.

The heart of the sales forecasting system is the point-of-sale system (POS), which, in effect, captures transaction data on nearly every person who walks through a cafe's door. The sale of each entrée represents one customer; the entrée sales data are transmitted daily to the Orlando corporate headquarters' database. There, the financial team, headed by Todd Lindsey, begins the forecast process. Lindsey forecasts monthly guest counts, retail sales, banquet sales, and concert sales (if applicable) at each cafe. The general managers of individual cafes tap into the same database to prepare a daily forecast for their sites. A cafe manager pulls up prior years' sales for that day, adding information from the local Chamber of Commerce or Tourist Board on upcoming events such as a major convention, sporting event, or concert in the city where the cafe is located. The daily forecast is further broken into hourly sales, which drives employee scheduling. An hourly forecast of $5,500 in sales translates into 19 workstations, which are further broken down into a specific number of wait staff, hosts, bartenders, and kitchen staff. Computerized scheduling software plugs in people based on their availability. Variances between forecast and actual sales are then examined to see why errors occurred.

Hard Rock doesn't limit its use of forecasting tools to sales. To evaluate managers and set bonuses, a 3-year weighted moving average is applied to cafe sales. If cafe general managers exceed their targets, a bonus is computed. Todd Lindsey, at corporate headquarters, applies weights of 40% to the most recent year's sales, 40% to the year before, and 20% to sales 2 years ago in reaching his moving average.

An even more sophisticated application of statistics is found in Hard Rock's menu planning. Using multiple regression, managers can compute the impact on demand of other menu items if the price of one item is changed. For example, if the price of a cheeseburger increases from $7.99 to $8.99, Hard Rock can predict the effect this will have on sales of chicken sandwiches, pork sandwiches, and salads. Managers do the same analysis on menu placement, with the center section driving higher sales volumes. When an item such as a hamburger is moved off the center to one of the side flaps, the corresponding effect on related items, say french fries, is determined.

Hard Rock's Moscow Cafe[a]

Month	1	2	3	4	5	6	7	8	9	10
Guest count (in thousands)	21	24	27	32	29	37	43	43	54	66
Advertising (in $ thousand)	14	17	25	25	35	35	45	50	60	60

[a]These figures are used for purposes of this case study.

Discussion Questions*

1. Describe three different forecasting applications at Hard Rock. Name three other areas in which you think Hard Rock could use forecasting models.
2. What is the role of the POS system in forecasting at Hard Rock?
3. Justify the use of the weighting system used for evaluating managers for annual bonuses.
4. Name several variables besides those mentioned in the case that could be used as good predictors of daily sales in each cafe.
5. At Hard Rock's Moscow restaurant, the manager is trying to evaluate how a new advertising campaign affects guest counts. Using data for the past 10 months (see the table) develop a least squares regression relationship and then forecast the expected guest count when advertising is $65,000.

*You may wish to view the video that accompanies this case before answering these questions.

▶**Additional Case Study:** Visit www.pearsonglobaleditions.com/myomlab or www.pearsonglobaleditions.com/heizer for this free case study: **North-South Airlines:** Reflects the merger of two airlines and addresses their maintenance costs.

Bibliography

Balakrishnan, R., B. Render, and R. M. Stair. *Managerial Decision Modeling with Spreadsheets*, 2nd ed. Upper Saddle River, NJ: Prentice Hall, 2007.

Berenson, Mark, Tim Krehbiel, and David Levine. *Basic Business Statistics*, 11th ed. Upper Saddle River, NJ: Prentice Hall, 2009.

Campbell, Omar. "Forecasting in Direct Selling Business: Tupperware's Experience." *The Journal of Business Forecasting* 27, no. 2 (Summer 2008): 18–19.

Diebold, F. X. *Elements of Forecasting*, 5th ed. Cincinnati: South-Western College Publishing, 2010.

Fildes, Robert, and Paul Goodwin. "Against Your Better Judgment? How Organizations Can Improve Their Use of Management Judgment in Forecasting." *Decision Sciences* 37, no. 6 (November–December 2007): 570–576.

Georgoff, D. M., and R. G. Murdick. "Manager's Guide to Forecasting." *Harvard Business Review* 64 (January–February 1986): 110–120.

Gilliland, M., and M. Leonard. "Forecasting Software—The Past and the Future." *The Journal of Business Forecasting* 25, no. 1 (Spring 2006): 33–36.

Hanke, J. E. and D. W. Wichern. *Business Forecasting*, 9th ed. Upper Saddle River, NJ: Prentice Hall, 2009.

Heizer, Jay. "Forecasting with Stagger Charts." *IIE Solutions* 34 (June 2002): 46–49.

Jain, Chaman L. "Benchmarking Forecasting Software and Systems." *The Journal of Business Forecasting* 26, no. 4 (Winter 2007/2008): 30–34.

Onkal, D., M. S. Gonul, and M. Lawrence. "Judgmental Adjustments of Previously Adjusted Forecasts." *Decision Sciences* 39, no. 2 (May 2008): 213–238.

Render, B., R. M. Stair, and M. Hanna. *Quantitative Analysis for Management*, 10th ed. Upper Saddle River, NJ: Prentice Hall, 2009.

Shah, Piyush. "Techniques to Support Better Forecasting." *APICS Magazine* (November/December 2008): 49–50.

Tabatabai, Bijan. "Improving Forecasting." *Financial Management* (October, 2008): 48–49.

Urs, Rajiv. "How to Use a Demand Planning System for Best Forecasting and Planning Results." *The Journal of Business Forecasting* 27, no. 2 (Summer 2008): 22–25.

Wilson, J. H., B. Keating, and J. Galt. *Business Forecasting*, 6th ed. New York: McGraw-Hill, 2009.

Yurklewicz, Jack. "Forecasting at Steady State." *Analytics* (Summer 2008): 42–45.

Chapter 4 *Rapid* Review

Main Heading	Review Material	myomlab
WHAT IS FORECASTING?	■ **Forecasting**—The art and science of predicting future events. ■ **Economic forecasts**—Planning indicators that are valuable in helping organizations prepare medium- to long-range forecasts. ■ **Technological forecasts**—Long-term forecasts concerned with the rates of technological progress. ■ **Demand forecasts**—Projections of a company's sales for each time period in the planning horizon.	
THE STRATEGIC IMPORTANCE OF FORECASTING	*The forecast is the only estimate of demand until actual demand becomes known.* Forecasts of demand drive decisions in many areas, including: *Human resources, Capacity, Supply-chain management.*	**VIDEO 4.1** Forecasting at Hard Rock Cafe
SEVEN STEPS IN THE FORECASTING SYSTEM	Forecasting follows seven basic steps: 1. Determine the use of the forecast; 2. Select the items to be forecasted; 3. Determine the time horizon of the forecast; 4. Select the forecasting model(s); 5. Gather the data needed to make the forecast; 6. Make the forecast; 7. Validate and implement the results.	
FORECASTING APPROACHES	■ **Quantitative forecasts**—Forecasts that employ mathematical modeling to forecast demand. ■ **Qualitative forecast**—Forecasts that incorporate such factors as the decision maker's intuition, emotions, personal experiences, and value system. ■ **Jury of executive opinion**—Takes the opinion of a small group of high-level managers and results in a group estimate of demand. ■ **Delphi method**—Uses an interactive group process that allows experts to make forecasts. ■ **Sales force composite**—Based on salespersons' estimates of expected sales. ■ **Consumer market survey**—Solicits input from customers or potential customers regarding future purchasing plans. ■ **Time series**—Uses a series of past data points to make a forecast.	
TIME-SERIES FORECASTING	■ **Naïve approach**—Assumes that demand in the next period is equal to demand in the most recent period. ■ **Moving averages**—Uses an average of the *n* most recent periods of data to forecast the next period.	Problems: 4.1, 4.2, 4.3, 4.4, 4.5, 4.6, 4.7, 4.8, 4.9, 4.10, 4.11-4.23, 4.25-4.29, 4.33, 4.37, 4.39, 4.43, 4.44, 4.47, 4.49 Virtual Office Hours for Solved Problems: 4.1–4.4 **ACTIVE MODELS: 4.1–4.4**

$$\text{Moving average} = \frac{\Sigma \text{Demand in previous } n \text{ periods}}{n} \qquad (4\text{-}1)$$

$$\text{Weighted moving average} = \frac{\Sigma(\text{Weight for period } n)\,(\text{Demand in period } n)}{\Sigma \text{Weights}} \qquad (4\text{-}2)$$

■ **Exponential smoothing**—A weighted-moving-average forecasting technique in which data points are weighted by an exponential function.
■ **Smoothing constant**—The weighting factor, α, used in an exponential smoothing forecast, a number between 0 and 1.

Exponential smoothing formula: $F_t = F_{t-1} + \alpha(A_{t-1} - F_{t-1})$ $\qquad (4\text{-}4)$

■ **Mean absolute deviation (MAD)**—A measure of the overall forecast error for a model.

$$MAD = \frac{\sum |\text{Actual} - \text{Forecast}|}{n} \qquad (4\text{-}5)$$

■ **Mean squared error (MSE)**—The average of the squared differences between the forecast and observed values.

$$MSE = \frac{\sum (\text{Forecast errors})^2}{n} \qquad (4\text{-}6)$$

■ **Mean absolute percent error (MAPE)**—The average of the absolute differences between the forecast and actual values, expressed as a percentage of actual values.

$$MAPE = \frac{\sum_{i=1}^{n} 100\,|\text{Actual}_t - \text{Forecast}_t|\,/\,\text{Actual}_t}{n} \qquad (4\text{-}7)$$

Main Heading	Review Material	myomlab
	Exponential Smoothing with Trend Adjustment	

Forecast including trend (FIT_t) = Exponentially smoothed forecast (F_t)
$\qquad$ + Exponentially smoothed trend (T_t) $\qquad$ (4-8)

- **Trend projection**—A time-series forecasting method that fits a trend line to a series of historical data points and then projects the line into the future for forecasts.

Trend Projection and Regression Analysis

$$\hat{y} = a + bx, \text{ where } b = \frac{\Sigma xy - n\bar{x}\bar{y}}{\Sigma x^2 - n\bar{x}^2}, \text{ and } a = \bar{y} - b\bar{x} \qquad \text{(4-11),(4-12),(4-13)}$$

- **Seasonal variations**—Regular upward or downward movements in a time series that tie to recurring events.
- **Cycles**—Patterns in the data that occur every several years.

Main Heading	Review Material	Problems
ASSOCIATIVE FORECASTING METHODS: REGRESSION AND CORRELATION ANALYSIS	- **Linear-regression analysis**—A straight-line mathematical model to describe the functional relationships between independent and dependent variables. - **Standard error of the estimate**—A measure of variability around the regression line. - **Coefficient of correlation**—A measure of the strength of the relationship between two variables. - **Coefficient of determination**—A measure of the amount of variation in the dependent variable about its mean that is explained by the regression equation. - **Multiple regression**—An associative forecasting method with > 1 independent variable. $\qquad$ Multiple regression forecast: $\hat{y} = a + b_1 x_1 + b_2 x_2$ $\qquad$ (4-17)	Problems: 4.24, 4.30–4.32, 4.34–4.36, 4.38, 4.40, 4.41, 4.46, 4.48
MONITORING AND CONTROLLING FORECASTS	- **Tracking signal**—A measurement of how well the forecast is predicting actual values. $\qquad$ Tracking signal $= \dfrac{\sum(\text{Actual demand in period } i - \text{Forecast demand in period } i)}{\text{MAD}}$ $\qquad$ (4-18) - **Bias**—A forecast that is consistently higher or lower than actual values of a time series. - **Adaptive smoothing**—An approach to exponential smoothing forecasting in which the smoothing constant is automatically changed to keep errors to a minimum. - **Focus forecasting**—Forecasting that tries a variety of computer models and selects the best one for a particular application.	Problems: 4.37, 4.45
FORECASTING IN THE SERVICE SECTOR	Service-sector forecasting may require good short-term demand records, even per 15-minute intervals. Demand during holidays or specific weather events may also need to be tracked.	

Self Test

- **Before taking the self-test,** refer to the learning objectives listed at the beginning of the chapter and the key terms listed at the end of the chapter.

LO1. Forecasting time horizons include:
    a) long range.   **b)** medium range.
    c) short range.   **d)** all of the above.

LO2. Qualitative methods of forecasting include:
    a) sales force composite.   **b)** jury of executive opinion.
    c) consumer market survey.   **d)** exponential smoothing.
    e) all except (d).

LO3. The difference between a *moving-average* model and an *exponential smoothing* model is that _____.

LO4. Three popular measures of forecast accuracy are:
    a) total error, average error, and mean error.
    b) average error, median error, and maximum error.
    c) median error, minimum error, and maximum absolute error.
    d) mean absolute deviation, mean squared error, and mean absolute percent error.

LO5. Average demand for iPods in the Rome, Italy, Apple store is 800 units per month. The May monthly index is 1.25. What is the seasonally adjusted sales forecast for May?
    a) 640 units   **b)** 798.75 units   **c)** 800 units   **d)** 1,000 units
    e) cannot be calculated with the information given

LO6. The main difference between simple and multiple regression is _____.

LO7. The tracking signal is the:
    a) standard error of the estimate.
    b) cumulative error.
    c) mean absolute deviation (MAD).
    d) ratio of the cumulative error to MAD.
    e) mean absolute percent error (MAPE).

Answers: LO1. d; LO2. e; LO3. exponential smoothing is a weighted moving-average model in which all prior values are weighted with a set of exponentially declining weights; LO4. d; LO5. d ; LO6. simple regression has only one independent variable ; LO7. d.

DESIGNING OPERATIONS

Process design

Key questions

➤ What is process design?
➤ What objectives should process design have?
➤ How do volume and variety affect process design?
➤ How are processes designed in detail?

Introduction

Say you are a 'designer' and most people will assume that you are someone who is concerned with how a product looks. But the design activity is much broader than that and while there is no universally recognized definition of 'design', we take it to mean 'the process by which some functional requirement of people is satisfied through the shaping or configuration of the resources and/or activities that compose a product, or a service, or the transformation process that produces them'. All operations managers are designers. When they purchase or rearrange the position of a piece of equipment, or when they change the way of working within a process, it is a design decision because it affects the physical shape and nature of their processes. This chapter examines the design of processes. Figure 4.1 shows where this topic fits within the overall model of operations management.

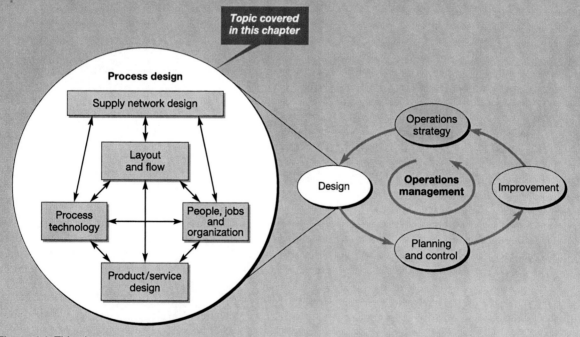

Figure 4.1 This chapter examines process design

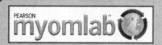

Check and improve your understanding of this chapter using self assessment questions and a personalised study plan, audio and video downloads, and an eBook – all at www.myomlab.com.

Operations in practice Fast-food drive-throughs[1]

The quick-service restaurant (QSR) industry reckons that the very first drive-through dates back to 1928 when Royce Hailey first promoted the drive-through service at his Pig Stand restaurant in Los Angeles. Customers would simply drive by the back door of the restaurant where the chef would come out and deliver the restaurant's famous 'Barbequed Pig' sandwiches. Today, drive-through processes are slicker and faster. They are also more common. In 1975, McDonald's did not have any drive-throughs, but now more than 90 per cent of its US restaurants incorporate a drive-through process. In fact 80 per cent of recent fast-food growth has come through the growing number of drive-throughs. Says one industry specialist, *'There are a growing number of customers for whom fast-food is not fast enough. They want to cut waiting time to the very minimum without even getting out of their car. Meeting their needs depends on how smooth we can get the process.'*

The competition to design the fastest and most reliable drive-through process is fierce. Starbucks drive-throughs have strategically placed cameras at the order boards so that servers can recognize regular customers and start making their order even before it's placed. Burger King has experimented with sophisticated sound systems, simpler menu boards and see-through food bags to ensure greater accuracy (no point in being fast if you don't deliver what the customer ordered). These details matter. McDonald's reckon that their sales increase one per cent for every six seconds saved at a drive-through, while a single Burger King restaurant calculated that its takings increased by 15,000 dollars a year each time it reduced queuing time by one second.

Source: Getty Images

Menu items must be easy to read and understand. Designing 'combo meals' (burger, fries and a cola), for example, saves time at the ordering stage. Perhaps the most remarkable experiment in making drive-through process times slicker is being carried out by McDonald's in the USA. On California's central coast 150 miles from Los Angeles, a call centre takes orders remotely from 40 McDonald's outlets around the country. The orders are then sent back to the restaurants through the Internet and the food is assembled only a few metres from where the order was placed. It may only save a few seconds on each order, but that can add up to extra sales at busy times of the day. But not everyone is thrilled by the boom in drive-throughs. People living in the vicinity may complain of the extra traffic they attract and the unhealthy image of fast food combined with a process that does not even make customers get out of their car, is, for some, a step too far.

What is process design?

Design happens before creation

To 'design' is to conceive the looks, arrangement, and workings of something *before it is created*. In that sense it is a conceptual exercise. Yet it is one which must deliver a solution that will work in practice. Design is also an activity that can be approached at different levels of detail. One may envisage the general shape and intention of something before getting down to defining its details. This is certainly true for process design. At the start of the process design activity it is important to understand the design objectives, especially at first, when the overall shape and nature of the process is being decided. The most common way of doing this is by positioning it according to its volume and variety characteristics. Eventually the details of the process must be analysed to ensure that it fulfils its objectives effectively.

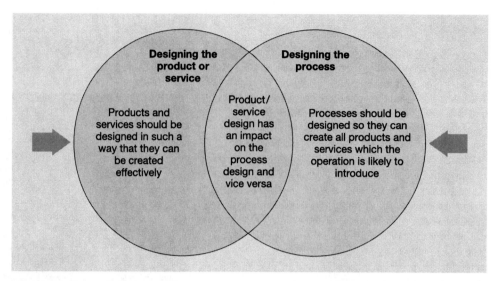

Figure 4.2 The design of products/services and processes are interrelated and should be treated together

Yet, it is often only through getting to grips with the detail of a design that the feasibility of its overall shape can be assessed. But don't think of this as a simple sequential process. There may be aspects concerned with the objectives or the broad positioning of the process that will need to be modified following its more detailed analysis.

Process design and product/service design are interrelated

Often we will treat the design of products and services, on the one hand, and the design of the processes which make them, on the other, as though they were separate activities. Yet they are clearly interrelated. It would be foolish to commit to the detailed design of any product or service without some consideration of how it is to be produced. Small changes in the design of products and services can have profound implications for the way the operation eventually has to produce them. Similarly, the design of a process can constrain the freedom of product and service designers to operate as they would wish (*see* Fig. 4.2). This holds good whether the operation is producing products or services. However, the overlap between the two design activities is generally greater in operations which produce **services**. Because many services involve the customer in being part of the transformation process, the service, as far as the customer sees it, cannot be separated from the process to which the customer is subjected. Overlapping product and process design has implications for the organization of the design activity, as will be discussed in Chapter 5. Certainly, when product designers also have to make or use the things which they design, it can concentrate their minds on what is important. For example, in the early days of flight, the engineers who designed the aircraft were also the test pilots who took them out on their first flight. For this reason, if no other, safety was a significant objective in the design activity.

Process design and product/service design should be considered together

What objectives should process design have?

The whole point of process design is to make sure that the performance of the process is appropriate for whatever it is trying to achieve. For example, if an operation competed primarily on its ability to respond quickly to customer requests, its processes would need to be designed to give fast throughput times. This would minimize the time between customers

Table 4.1 The impact of strategic performance objectives on process design objectives and performance

Operations performance objective	Typical process design objectives	Some benefits of good process design
Quality	• Provide appropriate resources, capable of achieving the specification of product of services • Error-free processing	• Products and services produced 'on-specification' • Less recycling and wasted effort within the process
Speed	• Minimum throughput time • Output rate appropriate for demand	• Short customer waiting time • Low in-process inventory
Dependability	• Provide dependable process resources • Reliable process output timing and volume	• On-time deliveries of products and services • Less disruption, confusion and rescheduling within the process
Flexibility	• Provide resources with an appropriate range of capabilities • Change easily between processing states (what, how, or how much is being processed)	• Ability to process a wide range of products and services • Low cost/fast product and service change • Low cost/fast volume and timing changes • Ability to cope with unexpected events (e.g. supply or a processing failure)

Cost	• Appropriate capacity to meet demand
	• Eliminate process waste in terms of
	  – excess capacity
	  – excess process capability
	  – in-process delays
	  – in-process errors
	  – inappropriate process inputs
		• Low processing costs
		• Low resource costs (capital costs)
		• Low delay and inventory costs (working capital costs)

requesting a product or service and their receiving it. Similarly, if an operation competed on low price, cost-related objectives are likely to dominate its process design. Some kind of logic should link what the operation as a whole is attempting to achieve and the **performance objectives** of its individual processes. This is illustrated in Table 4.1.

Process design should reflect process objectives

Operations performance objectives translate directly to process design objectives as shown in Table 4.1. But, because processes are managed at a very operational level, process design also needs to consider a more 'micro' and detailed set of objectives. These are largely concerned with flow through the process. When whatever are being 'processed' enter a process they will progress through a series of activities where they are 'transformed' in some way. Between these activities they may dwell for some time in inventories, waiting to be transformed by the next activity. This means that the time that a unit spends in the process (its throughput time) will be longer than the sum of all the transforming activities that it passes through. Also the resources that perform the processes activities may not be used all the time because not all units will necessarily require the same activities and the capacity of each resource may not match the demand placed upon it. So neither the units moving through the process, nor the resources performing the activities may be fully utilized. Because of this the way that units leave the process is unlikely to be exactly the same as the way they arrive at the process. It is common for more 'micro' performance flow objectives to be used that describe process flow performance. For example:

Throughput rate

- **Throughput rate** (or flow rate) is the rate at which units emerge from the process, i.e. the number of units passing through the process per unit of time.

Throughput time

- **Throughput time** is the average elapsed time taken for inputs to move through the process and become outputs.

Work in process

- The number of units in the process (also called the '**work in process**' or in-process inventory), as an average over a period of time.

Utilization

- The **utilization** of process resources is the proportion of available time that the resources within the process are performing useful work.

Environmentally sensitive design

With the issues of environmental protection becoming more important, both process and product/service designers have to take account of 'green' issues. In many developed countries, legislation has already provided some basic standards which restrict the use of toxic materials, limit discharges to air and water, and protect employees and the public from immediate and long-term harm. Interest has focused on some fundamental issues:

- *The sources of inputs* to a product or service. (Will they damage rainforests? Will they use up scarce minerals? Will they exploit the poor or use child labour?)
- *Quantities and sources of energy* consumed in the process. (Do plastic beverage bottles use more energy than glass ones? Should waste heat be recovered and used in fish farming?)
- *The amounts and type of waste material* that are created in the manufacturing processes. (Can this waste be recycled efficiently, or must it be burnt or buried in landfill sites? Will the waste have a long-term impact on the environment as it decomposes and escapes?)
- *The life of the product itself*. It is argued that if a product has a useful life of, say, twenty years, it will consume fewer resources than one that only lasts five years, which must therefore be replaced four times in the same period. However, the long-life product may require more initial inputs, and may prove to be inefficient in the latter part of its use, when the latest products use less energy or maintenance to run.
- *The end-of-life of the product*. (Will the redundant product be difficult to dispose of in an environmentally friendly way? Could it be recycled or used as a source of energy? Could it still be useful in third-world conditions? Could it be used to benefit the environment, such as old cars being used to make artificial reefs for sea life?)

Short case
Ecologically smart[2]

Source: Getty Images

When Daimler-Chrysler started to examine the feasibility of the Smart town car, the challenge was not just to examine the economic feasibility of the product but also to build in environmental sensitivity to the design of the product and the process that was to make it. This is why environmental protection is now a fundamental part of all production activities in its 'Smartville' plant at Hambach near France's border with Germany. The product itself is designed on environmentally compatible principles. Even before assembly starts, the product's disassembly must be considered. In fact the modular construction of the Smart car helped to guarantee economical dismantling at the end of its life. This also helps with the recycling of materials. Over 85 per cent of the Smart's components are recyclable and recycled material is used in its initial construction. For example, the Smart's instrument panel comprises 12 per cent recycled plastic material. Similarly, production processes are designed to be ecologically sustainable. The plant's environmentally friendly painting technique allows less paint to be used while maintaining a high quality of protection. It also involves no solvent emission and no hazardous waste, as well as the recycling of surplus material. But it is not only the use of new technology that contributes to the plant's ecological credentials. Ensuring a smooth and efficient movement of materials within the plant also saves time, effort and, above all, energy. So, traffic flow outside and through the building has been optimized, buildings are made accessible to suppliers delivering to the plant, and conveyor systems are designed to be loaded equally in both directions so as to avoid empty runs. The company even claims that the buildings themselves are a model for ecological compatibility. No construction materials contain formaldehyde or CFCs and the outside of the buildings are lined with 'TRESPA', a raw material made from European timber that is quick to regenerate.

Designers are faced with complex trade-offs between these factors, although it is not always easy to obtain all the information that is needed to make the 'best' choices. For example, it is relatively straightforward to design a long-life product, using strong material, over-designed components, ample corrosion protection, and so on. But its production might use more materials and energy and it could create more waste on disposal. To help make more rational

Life cycle analysis
decisions in the design activity, some industries are experimenting with *life cycle analysis*. This technique analyses all the production inputs, the life-cycle use of the product and its final disposal, in terms of total energy used (and more recently, of all the emitted wastes such as carbon dioxide, sulphurous and nitrous gases, organic solvents, solid waste, etc.). The inputs and wastes are evaluated at *every* stage in its creation, beginning with the extraction or farming of the basic raw materials. The short case 'Ecologically smart' demonstrates that it is possible to include ecological considerations in all aspects of product and process design.

Process types – the volume–variety effect on process design

In Chapter 1 we saw how processes in operations can range from producing a very high volume of products or services (for example, a food canning factory) to a very low volume (for example, major project consulting engineers). Also they can range from producing a very low variety of products or services (for example, in an electricity utility) to a very high variety (as, for example, in an architects' practice). Usually the two dimensions of volume and variety go together. Low-volume operations processes often have a high variety of products and services, and high-volume operations processes often have a narrow variety of products and services. Thus there is a continuum from low volume and high variety through to high volume and low variety, on which we can position operations. Different operations, even those in the same operation, may adopt different types of processes. Many manufacturing plants will have a large area, organized on a 'mass-production' basis, in which it makes its high-volume 'best-selling' products. In another part of the plant it may also have an area where it makes a wide variety of products in much smaller volumes. The design of each of these processes is likely to be different. Similarly, in a medical service, compare the approach taken during mass medical treatments, such as large-scale immunization programmes, with that taken for a transplant operation where the treatment is designed specifically to meet the needs of one person. These differences go well beyond their differing technologies or the processing requirements of their products or services. They are explained by the fact that no one type of process design is best for all types of operation in all circumstances. The differences are explained largely by

Volume–variety positions
the different **volume–variety positions** of the operations.

Process types

The position of a process on the volume–variety continuum shapes its overall design and the general approach to managing its activities. These 'general approaches' to designing and

Process types
managing processes are called **process types**. Different terms are sometimes used to identify process types depending on whether they are predominantly manufacturing or service processes, and there is some variation in the terms used. For example, it is not uncommon to find the 'manufacturing' terms used in service industries. Figure 4.3 illustrates how these 'process types' are used to describe different positions on the volume–variety spectrum.

Project processes

Project processes
Project processes are those which deal with discrete, usually highly customized products. Often the timescale of making the product or service is relatively long, as is the interval between the completion of each product or service. So low volume and high variety are characteristics of project processes. The activities involved in making the product can be ill-defined and uncertain, sometimes changing during the production process itself. Examples of project

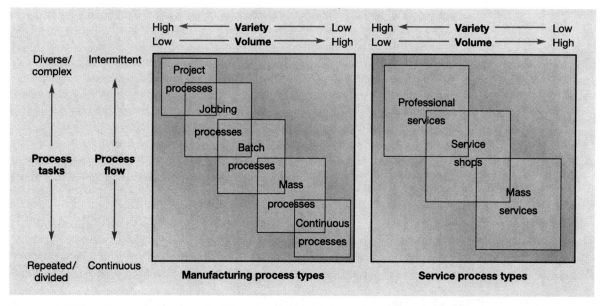

Figure 4.3 Different process types imply different volume–variety characteristics for the process

processes include shipbuilding, most construction companies, movie production companies, large fabrication operations such as those manufacturing turbo generators, and installing a computer system. The essence of project processes is that each job has a well-defined start and finish, the time interval between starting different jobs is relatively long and the transforming resources which make the product will probably have been organized especially for each product. The process map for project processes will almost certainly be complex, partly because each unit of output is so large with many activities occurring at the same time and partly because the activities in such processes often involve significant discretion to act according to professional judgement.

Jobbing processes

Jobbing processes

Jobbing processes also deal with very high variety and low volumes. Whereas in project processes each product has resources devoted more or less exclusively to it, in jobbing processes each product has to share the operation's resources with many others. The resources of the operation will process a series of products but, although all the products will require the same kind of attention, each will differ in its exact needs. Examples of jobbing processes include many precision engineers such as specialist tool-makers, furniture restorers, bespoke tailors, and the printer who produces tickets for the local social event. Jobbing processes produce more

The major construction site shown in this picture is a project process. Each 'product' (project) is different and poses different challenges to those running the process (civil engineers).

This craftsperson is using general purpose wood-cutting technology to make a product for an individual customer. The next product he makes will be different (although it may be similar), possibly for a different customer.

and usually smaller items than project processes but, like project processes, the degree of repetition is low. Many jobs will probably be 'one-offs'. Again, any process map for a jobbing process could be relatively complex for similar reasons to project processes. However, jobbing processes usually produce physically smaller products and, although sometimes involving considerable skill, such processes often involve fewer unpredictable circumstances.

Batch processes

Batch processes can often look like jobbing processes, but batch does not have quite the degree of variety associated with jobbing. As the name implies, each time batch processes produce a product they produce more than one. So each part of the operation has periods when it is repeating itself, at least while the 'batch' is being processed. The size of the batch could be just two or three, in which case the batch process would differ little from jobbing, especially if each batch is a totally novel product. Conversely, if the batches are large, and especially if the products are familiar to the operation, batch processes can be fairly repetitive. Because of this, the batch type of process can be found over a wide range of volume and variety levels. Examples of batch processes include machine tool manufacturing, the production of some special gourmet frozen foods, and the manufacture of most of the component parts which go into mass-produced assemblies such as automobiles.

In this kitchen, food is being prepared in batches. All batches go through the same sequence (preparation, cooking, storing), but each batch is a different dish.

Mass processes

Mass processes are those which produce goods in high volume and relatively narrow variety – narrow, that is, in terms of the fundamentals of the product design. An automobile plant, for example, might produce several thousand variants of car if every option of engine size, colour, extra equipment, etc. is taken into account. Yet essentially it is a mass operation because the different variants of its product do not affect the basic process of production. The activities in the automobile plant, like all mass operations, are essentially repetitive and largely predictable. Examples of mass processes include the automobile plant, a television factory, most food processes and DVD production. Several variants of a product could be produced on a mass process such as an assembly line, but the process itself is unaffected. The equipment used at each stage of the process can be designed to handle several different types of components loaded into the assembly equipment. So, provided the sequence of components in the equipment is synchronized with the sequence of models moving through the process, the process seems to be almost totally repetitive.

This automobile plant is everyone's' idea of a mass process. Each product is almost (but not quite) the same, and is made in large quantities.

Continuous processes

Continuous processes are one step beyond mass processes insomuch as they operate at even higher volume and often have even lower variety. They also usually operate for longer periods of time. Sometimes they are literally continuous in that their products are inseparable, being produced in an endless flow. Continuous processes are often associated with relatively inflexible, capital-intensive technologies with highly predictable flow. Examples of continuous processes include petrochemical refineries, electricity utilities, steel making and some paper making. There are often few elements of discretion in this type of process and although products may be stored during the process, the predominant characteristic of most continuous processes is of smooth flow from one part of the process to another. Inspections are likely to form part of the process, although the control applied as a consequence of those inspections is often automatic rather than requiring human discretion.

Professional services

Professional services are defined as high-contact organizations where customers spend a considerable time in the service process. Such services provide high levels of customization, the service process being highly adaptable in order to meet individual customer needs. A great deal of staff time is spent in the front office and contact staff are given considerable discretion in servicing customers. Professional services tend to be people-based rather than equipment-based, with emphasis placed on the process (how the service is delivered) rather than the 'product' (what is delivered). Professional services include management consultants, lawyers' practices, architects, doctors' surgeries, auditors, health and safety inspectors and some computer field service operations. A typical example would be OEE, a consultancy that sells the problem-solving expertise of its skilled staff to tackle clients' problems. Typically, the problem will first be discussed with clients and the boundaries of the project defined. Each 'product' is different, and a high proportion of work takes place at the client's premises, with frequent contact between consultants and the client.

Service shops

Service shops are characterized by levels of customer contact, customization, volumes of customers and staff discretion, which position them between the extremes of professional and mass services (see next paragraph). Service is provided via mixes of front- and back-office activities. Service shops include banks, high-street shops, holiday tour operators, car rental companies, schools, most restaurants, hotels and travel agents. For example, an equipment hire and sales organization may have a range of products displayed in front-office outlets, while back-office operations look after purchasing and administration. The front-office staff have

This continuous water treatment process almost never stops (it only stops for maintenance) and performs a narrow range of tasks (filters impurities). Often we only notice the process if it goes wrong!

Here consultants are preparing to start a consultancy assignment. They are discussing how they might approach the various stages of the assignment, from understanding the real nature of the problem through to the implementation of their recommended solutions. This is a process map, although a very high level one. It guides the nature and sequence of the consultants' activities.

The health club shown in the picture has front-office staff who can give advice on exercise programmes and other treatments. To maintain a dependable service the staff need to follow defined processes every day.

some technical training and can advise customers during the process of selling the product. Essentially the customer is buying a fairly standardized product but will be influenced by the process of the sale which is customized to the customer's individual needs.

Mass services

Mass services

Mass services have many customer transactions, involving limited contact time and little customization. Such services may be equipment-based and 'product'-oriented, with most value added in the back office and relatively little judgement applied by front-office staff. Staff are likely to have a closely defined division of labour and to follow set procedures. Mass services include supermarkets, a national rail network, an airport, telecommunications services, libraries, television stations, the police service and the enquiry desk at a utility. For example, rail services such as Virgin Trains in the UK or SNCF in France

This is an account management centre for a large retail bank. It deals with thousands of customer requests every day. Although each customer request is different, they are all of the same type – involving customers' accounts.

all move a large number of passengers with a variety of rolling stock on an immense infrastructure of railways. Passengers pick a journey from the range offered. One of the most common types of mass service is the call centres used by almost all companies that deal directly with consumers. Coping with a very high volume of enquiries requires some kind of structuring of the process of communicating with customers. This is often achieved by using a carefully designed enquiry process (sometimes known as a 'script').

Critical commentary

Although the idea of process types is useful insomuch as it reinforces the, sometimes important, distinctions between different types of process, it is in many ways simplistic. In reality there is no clear boundary between process types. For example, many processed foods are manufactured using mass-production processes but in batches. So, a 'batch' of one type of cake (say) can be followed by a 'batch' of a marginally different cake (perhaps with different packaging), followed by yet another, etc. Essentially this is still a mass process, but not quite as pure a version of mass processing as a manufacturing process that only makes one type of cake. Similarly, the categories of service processes are likewise blurred. For example, a specialist camera retailer would normally be categorized as a service shop, yet it also will give, sometimes very specialized, technical advice to customers. It is not a professional service like a consultancy of course, but it does have elements of a professional service process within its design. This is why the volume and variety characteristics of a process are sometimes seen as being a more realistic way of describing processes. The product–process matrix described next adopts this approach.

The product–process matrix

Making comparisons between different processes along a spectrum which goes, for example, from shipbuilding at one extreme to electricity generation at the other has limited value. No one grumbles that yachts are so much more expensive than electricity. The real point is that because the different process types overlap, organizations often have a choice of what type of process to employ. This choice will have consequences to the operation, especially in terms of its cost and flexibility. The classic representation of how cost and flexibility vary

Product–process matrix

with process choice is the **product–process matrix** that comes from Professors Hayes and Wheelwright of Harvard University.[3] They represent process choices on a matrix with the

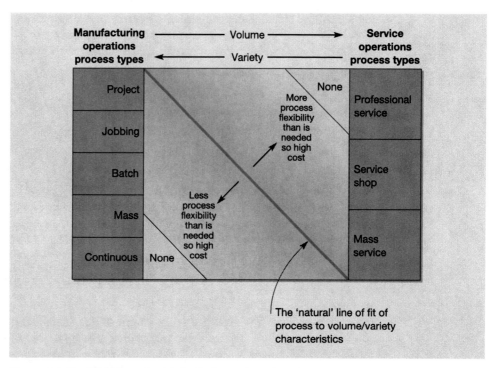

Figure 4.4 Deviating from the 'natural' diagonal on the product–process matrix has consequences for cost and flexibility
Source: Based on Hayes and Wheelwright[4]

The 'natural' diagonal

volume–variety as one dimension, and process types as the other. Figure 4.4 shows their matrix adapted to fit with the terminology used here. Most operations stick to **the 'natural' diagonal** of the matrix, and few, if any, are found in the extreme corners of the matrix. However, because there is some overlap between the various process types, operations might be positioned slightly off the diagonal.

The diagonal of the matrix shown in Figure 4.4 represents a 'natural' lowest cost position for an operation. Operations which are on the right of the 'natural' diagonal have processes which would normally be associated with lower volumes and higher variety. This means that their processes are likely to be more flexible than seems to be warranted by their actual volume–variety position. Put another way, they are not taking advantage of their ability to standardize their processes. Because of this, their costs are likely to be higher than they would be with a process that was closer to the diagonal. Conversely, operations that are on the left of the diagonal have adopted processes which would normally be used in a higher-volume and lower-variety situation. Their processes will therefore be 'over-standardized' and probably too inflexible for their volume–variety position. This lack of flexibility can also lead to high costs because the process will not be able to change from one activity to another as efficiently as a more flexible process.

Detailed process design

After the overall design of a process has been determined, its individual activities must be configured. At its simplest this detailed design of a process involves identifying all the individual activities that are needed to fulfil the objectives of the process and deciding on the sequence in which these activities are to be performed and who is going to do them.

There will, of course, be some constraints on this. Some activities must be carried out before others and some activities can only be done by certain people or machines. Nevertheless, for a process of any reasonable size, the number of alternative process designs is usually large. Because of this, process design is often done using some simple visual approach such as **process mapping**.

Process mapping

Process mapping

Process mapping simply involves describing processes in terms of how the activities within the process relate to each other. There are many techniques which can be used for *process mapping* (or **process blueprinting**, or **process analysis**, as it is sometimes called). However, all the techniques identify the different *types of* activity that take place during the process and show the flow of materials or people or information through the process.

Process blueprinting
Process analysis

Process mapping symbols

Process mapping
symbols

Process mapping symbols are used to classify different types of activity. And although there is no universal set of symbols used all over the world for any type of process, there are some that are commonly used. Most of these derive either from the early days of 'scientific' management around a century ago (see Chapter 9) or, more recently, from information system flowcharting. Figure 4.5 shows the symbols we shall use here.

These symbols can be arranged in order, and in series or in parallel, to describe any process. For example, the retail catering operation of a large campus university has a number of outlets around the campus selling sandwiches. Most of these outlets sell 'standard' sandwiches that are made in the university's central kitchens and transported to each outlet every day. However, one of these outlets is different; it is a kiosk that makes more expensive 'customized' sandwiches to order. Customers can specify the type of bread they want and a very wide combination of different fillings. Because queues for this customized service are becoming excessive, the catering manager is considering redesigning the process to speed it up. This new process design is based on the findings from a recent student study of the current process which proved that 95 per cent of all customers ordered only two types of bread (soft roll and Italian bread) and three types of protein filling (cheese, ham and chicken). Therefore the six 'sandwich bases' (2 types of bread × 3 protein fillings) could be prepared

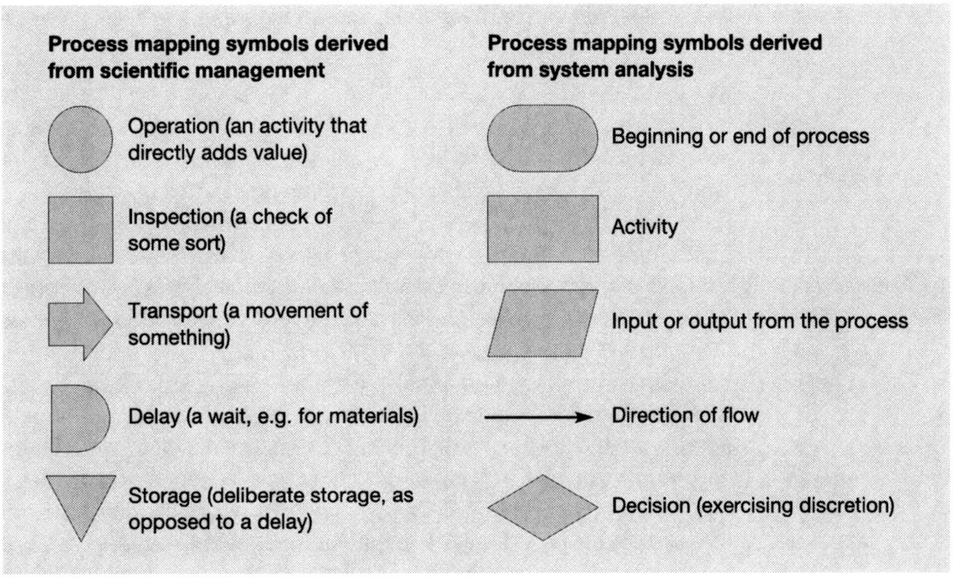

Figure 4.5 Some common process mapping symbols

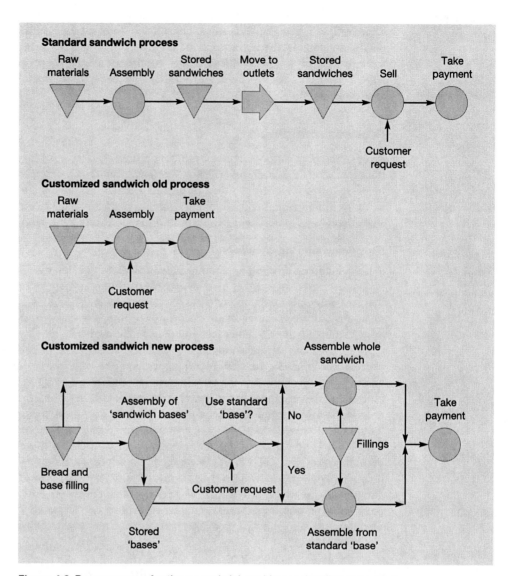

Figure 4.6 Process maps for three sandwich making and selling processes

in advance and customized with salad, mayonnaise, etc. as customers ordered them. The process maps for making and selling the standard sandwiches, the current customized sandwiches and the new customized process are shown in Figure 4.6.

Note how the introduction of some degree of discretion in the new process makes it more complex to map at this detailed level. This is one reason why processes are often mapped at a more aggregated level, called **high-level process mapping**, before more detailed maps are drawn. Figure 4.7 illustrates this for the new customized sandwich operation. At the highest level the process can be drawn simply as an input–transformation–output process with sandwich materials and customers as its input resources and satisfied customers 'assembled' to their sandwich as outputs. No details of how inputs are transformed into outputs are included. At a slightly lower, or more detailed level, what is sometimes called an **outline process map** (or chart) identifies the sequence of activities but only in a general way. So the activity of finding out what type of sandwich a customer wants, deciding if it can be assembled from a sandwich 'base' and then assembling it to meet the customer's request, is all contained in the general activity 'assemble as required'. At the more detailed level, all the activities are shown (we have shown the activities within 'assemble as required').

High-level process
mapping

Outline process map

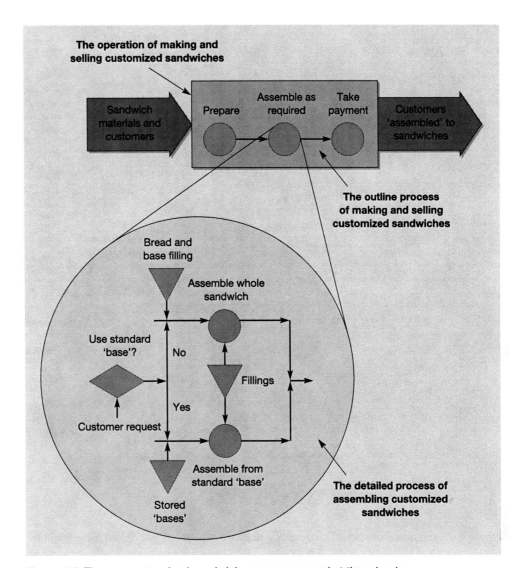

Figure 4.7 The new customized sandwich process mapped at three levels

Using process maps to improve processes

One significant advantage of mapping processes is that each activity can be systematically challenged in an attempt to improve the process. For example, Figure 4.8 shows the flow process chart which Intel Corporation, the computer chip company, drew to describe its method of processing expense reports (claims forms). It also shows the process chart for the same process after critically examining and improving the process. The new process cut the number of activities from 26 down to 15. The accounts payable's activities were combined with the cash-receipt's activities of checking employees' past expense accounts (activities 8, 10 and 11) which also eliminated activities 5 and 7. After consideration, it was decided to eliminate the activity of checking items against company rules, because it seemed '*more trouble than it was worth*'. Also, logging the batches was deemed unnecessary. All this combination and elimination of activities had the effect of removing several 'delays' from the process. The end-result was a much-simplified process which reduced the staff time needed to do the job by 28 per cent and considerably speeded up the whole process.

In the case of the customized sandwich process, the new design was attempting to offer as wide a range of sandwiches as were previously offered, without the slow service of the old

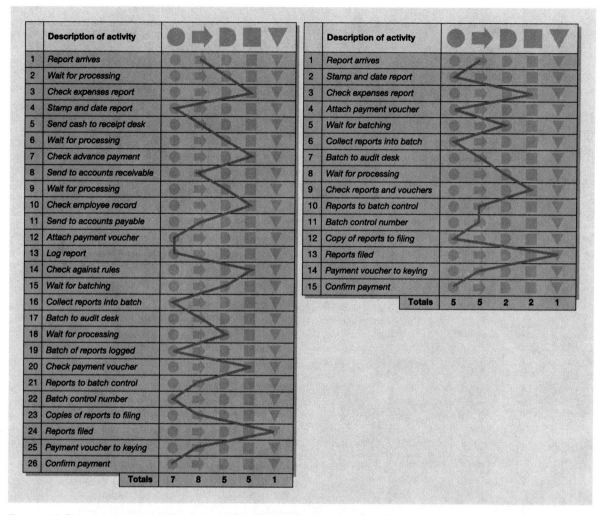

Figure 4.8 Flow process charts for processing expense reports at Intel before and after improving the process

process. In other words, it was maintaining similar levels of flexibility (to offer the same variety) while improving the speed of service. The new process would probably also increase the efficiency of the process because the sandwich 'bases' could be assembled during periods of low demand. This would balance the load on staff and so cost performance would improve. The quality of the sandwiches would presumably not suffer, although pre-assembling the sandwich bases may detract from the fresh appearance and taste. The dependability of the new process is less easy to assess. With the old process the time between requesting a sandwich and its delivery was long but reasonably predictable. The new process, however, will deliver fairly quickly 95 per cent of the time but take longer if the sandwich is non-standard. Table 4.2 summarizes the performance of the new design.

Throughput, cycle time and work-in-process

The new customized sandwich process has one indisputable advantage over the old process: it is faster in the sense that customers spend less time in the process. The additional benefit this brings is a reduction in cost per customer served (because more customers can be served without increasing resources). Note, however, that the total amount of work needed to make and sell a sandwich has not reduced. All the new process has done is to move some of the work to a less busy time. So the **work content** (the total amount of work required to produce a unit of output) has not changed but customer **throughput time** (the time for a unit to move through the process) has improved.

Work content
Throughput time

Table 4.2 Assessing the performance of the new customized sandwich process

Performance objective	Change with new process	Comments
Quality	No change?	Check to make sure that sandwich bases do not deteriorate in storage
Speed	Faster for 95 per cent of customers	
Dependability	Less predictable delivery time	Need to manage customer expectations regarding delivery time for non-standard sandwiches
Flexibility	No change	
Cost	Potentially lower cost	Need to forecast the number of each type of sandwich 'base' to pre-assemble

For example, suppose that the time to assemble and sell a sandwich (the work content) using the old process was two minutes and that two people were staffing the process during the busy period. Each person could serve a customer every two minutes, therefore every two minutes two customers were being served, so on average a customer is emerging from the process every minute. This is called the **cycle time** of the process, the average time between units of output emerging from the process. When customers join the queue in the process they become **work-in-process** (or work-in-progress) sometimes written as WIP. If the queue is ten people long (including that customer) when the customer joins it, he or she will have to wait ten minutes to emerge from the process. Or put more succinctly:

Cycle time

Work-in-process

$$\text{Throughput time} = \text{Work-in-process} \times \text{Cycle time}$$

In this case,

$$10 \text{ minutes wait} = 10 \text{ people in the system} \times 1 \text{ minute per person}$$

Little's law

This mathematical relationship (throughput time = work-in-process × cycle time) is called **Little's law**. It is simple but very useful, and it works for any stable process. For example, suppose it is decided that, when the new process is introduced, the average number of customers in the process should be limited to around ten and the maximum time a customer is in the process should be on average four minutes. If the time to assemble and sell a sandwich (from customer request to the customer leaving the process) in the new process has reduced to 1.2 minutes, how many staff should be serving?

Little's law

Putting this into Little's law:

$$\text{Throughput time} = 4 \text{ minutes}$$

and

$$\text{Work-in-progress, WIP} = 10$$

So, since

$$\text{Throughput time} = \text{WIP} \times \text{Cycle time}$$

$$\text{Cycle time} = \frac{\text{Throughput time}}{\text{WIP}}$$

$$\text{Cycle time for the process} = \frac{4}{10} = 0.4 \text{ minute}$$

That is, a customer should emerge from the process every 0.4 minute, on average.

Given that an individual can be served in 1.2 minutes,

$$\text{Number of servers required} = \frac{1.2}{0.4} = 3$$

In other words, three servers would serve three customers in 1.2 minutes. Or one customer in 0.4 minute.

Worked example

Mike was totally confident in his judgement, '*You'll never get them back in time*', he said. '*They aren't just wasting time, the process won't allow them to all have their coffee and get back for 11 o'clock.*' Looking outside the lecture theatre, Mike and his colleague Dick were watching the 20 business people who were attending the seminar queuing to be served coffee and biscuits. The time was 10.45 and Dick knew that unless they were all back in the lecture theatre at 11 o'clock there was no hope of finishing his presentation before lunch. '*I'm not sure why you're so pessimistic*', said Dick. '*They seem to be interested in what I have to say and I think they will want to get back to hear how operations management will change their lives.*' Mike shook his head. '*I'm not questioning their motivation*', he said, '*I'm questioning the ability of the process out there to get through them all in time. I have been timing how long it takes to serve the coffee and biscuits. Each coffee is being made fresh and the time between the server asking each customer what they want and them walking away with their coffee and biscuits is taking 48 seconds. Remember that, according to Little's law, throughput equals work-in-process multiplied by cycle time. If the work-in-process is the 20 managers in the queue and cycle time is 48 seconds, the total throughput time is going to be 20 multiplied by 0.8 minute which equals 16 minutes. Add to that sufficient time for the last person to drink their coffee and you must expect a total throughput time of a bit over 20 minutes. You just haven't allowed long enough for the process.*' Dick was impressed. '*Err . . . what did you say that law was called again?*' '*Little's law*', said Mike.

Worked example

Every year it was the same. All the workstations in the building had to be renovated (tested, new software installed, etc.) and there was only one week in which to do it. The one week fell in the middle of the August vacation period when the renovation process would cause minimum disruption to normal working. Last year the company's 500 work-stations had all been renovated within one working week (40 hours). Each renovation last year took on average 2 hours and 25 technicians had completed the process within the week. This year there would be 530 workstations to renovate but the company's IT support unit had devised a faster testing and renovation routine that would only take on average $1\frac{1}{2}$ hours instead of 2 hours. How many technicians will be needed this year to complete the renovation processes within the week?

Last year:

$$\text{Work-in-progress (WIP)} = 500 \text{ workstations}$$

$$\text{Time available } (T_t) = 40 \text{ hours}$$

$$\text{Average time to renovate} = 2 \text{ hours}$$

$$\text{Therefore throughput rate } (T_r) = \frac{1}{2} \text{ hour per technician}$$

$$= 0.5N$$

where N = Number of technicians

Little's law:

$$WIP = T_t \times T_r$$

$$500 = 40 \times 0.5N$$

$$N = \frac{500}{40 \times 0.5}$$

$$= 25 \text{ technicians}$$

This year:

Work-in-progress (WIP) = 530 workstations

Time available = 40 hours

Average time to renovate = 1.5 hours

Throughput rate (T_r) = 1/1.5 per technician

$$= 0.67N$$

where N = Number of technicians

Little's law:

$$WIP = T_t \times T_r$$

$$530 = 40 \times 0.67N$$

$$N = \frac{530}{40 \times 0.67}$$

$$= 19.88 \text{ technicians}$$

Throughput efficiency

This idea that the throughput time of a process is different from the work content of whatever it is processing has important implications. What it means is that for significant amounts of time no useful work is being done to the materials, information or customers that are progressing through the process. In the case of the simple example of the sandwich process described earlier, customer throughput time is restricted to 4 minutes, but the work content of the task (serving the customer) is only 1.2 minutes. So, the item being processed (the customer) is only being 'worked on' for 1.2/4 = 30 per cent of its time. This is called the **throughput efficiency** of the process.

Throughput efficiency

$$\text{Percentage throughput efficiency} = \frac{\text{Work content}}{\text{Throughput time}} \times 100$$

In this case the throughput efficiency is very high, relative to most processes, perhaps because the 'items' being processed are customers who react badly to waiting. In most material and information transforming processes, throughput efficiency is far lower, usually in single percentage figures.

Worked example

A vehicle licensing centre receives application documents, keys in details, checks the information provided on the application, classifies the application according to the type of licence required, confirms payment and then issues and mails the licence. It is currently processing an average of 5,000 licences every 8-hour day. A recent spot check found 15,000 applications that were 'in progress' or waiting to be processed. The sum of all activities that are required to process an application is 25 minutes. What is the throughput efficiency of the process?

→

Work-in-progress = 15,000 applications

Cycle time = Time producing

$$\frac{\text{Time producing}}{\text{Number produced}} = \frac{8 \text{ hours}}{5,000} = \frac{480 \text{ minutes}}{5,000} = 0.096 \text{ minute}$$

From Little's law,

Throughput time = WIP × Cycle time

Throughput time = 15,000 × 0.096

= 1,440 minutes = 24 hours = 3 days of working

$$\text{Throughput efficiency} = \frac{\text{Work content}}{\text{Throughput time}} = \frac{25}{1,440} = 1.74 \text{ per cent}$$

Although the process is achieving a throughput time of 3 days (which seems reasonable for this kind of process) the applications are only being worked on for 1.7 per cent of the time they are in the process.

Value-added throughput efficiency

The approach to calculating throughput efficiency that is described above assumes that all the 'work content' is actually needed. Yet we have already seen from the Intel expense report example that changing a process can significantly reduce the time that is needed to complete the task. Therefore, work content is actually dependent upon the methods and technology used to perform the task. It may be also that individual elements of a task may not be considered 'value-added'. In the Intel expense report example the new method eliminated some steps because they were 'not worth it', that is, they were not seen as adding value. So, **value-added throughput efficiency** restricts the concept of work content to only those tasks that are actually adding value to whatever is being processed. This often eliminates activities such as movement, delays and some inspections.

For example, if in the licensing worked example, of the 25 minutes of work content only 20 minutes were actually adding value, then

$$\text{Value-added throughput efficiency} = \frac{20}{1,440} = 1.39 \text{ per cent}$$

Value-added throughput efficiency

Workflow[5]

When the transformed resources in a process is information (or documents containing information), and when information technology is used to move, store and manage the information, process design is sometimes called 'workflow' or 'workflow management'. It is defined as 'the automation of procedures where documents, information or tasks are passed between participants according to a defined set of rules to achieve, or contribute to, an overall business goal'. Although workflow may be managed manually, it is almost always managed using an IT system. The term is also often associated with business process re-engineering (see Chapter 1 and Chapter 18). More specifically, workflow is concerned with the following:

- Analysis, modelling, definition and subsequent operational implementation of business processes;
- The technology that supports the processes;
- The procedural (decision) rules that move information or documents through processes;
- Defining the process in terms of the sequence of work activities, the human skills needed to perform each activity and the appropriate IT resources.

The effects of process variability

So far in our treatment of process design we have assumed that there is no significant variability either in the demand to which the process is expected to respond or in the time taken for the process to perform its various activities. Clearly, this is not the case in reality. So, it is important to look at the variability that can affect processes and take account of it.

Process variability There are many reasons why **variability** occurs in processes. These can include: the late (or early) arrival of material, information or customers, a temporary malfunction or breakdown of process technology within a stage of the process, the recycling of 'mis-processed' materials, information or customers to an earlier stage in the process, variation in the requirements of items being processed. All these sources of variation interact with each other, but result in two fundamental types of variability.

- Variability in the demand for processing at an individual stage within the process, usually expressed in terms of variation in the inter-arrival times of units to be processed.
- Variation in the time taken to perform the activities (i.e. process a unit) at each stage.

To understand the effect of arrival variability on process performance it is first useful to examine what happens to process performance in a very simple process as arrival time changes under conditions of no variability. For example, the simple process shown in Figure 4.9 is composed of one stage that performs exactly 10 minutes of work. Units arrive at the process at a constant and predictable rate. If the arrival rate is one unit every 30 minutes, then the process will be utilized for only 33.33% of the time, and the units will never have to wait to be processed. This is shown as point A on Figure 4.9. If the arrival rate increases to one arrival every 20 minutes, the utilization increases to 50%, and again the units will not have to wait to be processed. This is point B on Figure 4.9. If the arrival rate increases to one arrival every 10 minutes, the process is now fully utilized, but, because a

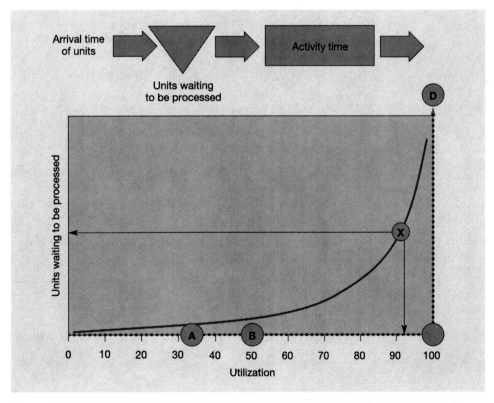

Figure 4.9 The relationship between process utilization and number of units waiting to be processed for constant, and variable, arrival and process times

unit arrives just as the previous one has finished being processed, no unit has to wait. This is point C on Figure 4.9. However, if the arrival rate ever exceeded one unit every 10 minutes, the waiting line in front of the process activity would build up indefinitely, as is shown as point D in Figure 4.9. So, in a perfectly constant and predictable world, the relationship between process waiting time and utilization is a rectangular function as shown by the red dotted line in Figure 4.9.

However, when arrival and process times are variable, then sometimes the process will have units waiting to be processed, while at other times the process will be idle, waiting for units to arrive. Therefore the process will have both a 'non-zero' average queue and be under-utilized in the same period. So, a more realistic point is that shown as point X in Figure 4.9. If the average arrival time were to be changed with the same variability, the blue line in Figure 4.9 would show **the relationship between average waiting time and process utilization.** As the process moves closer to 100% utilization the higher the average waiting time will become. Or, to put it another way, the only way to guarantee very low waiting times for the units is to suffer low process utilization.

> The relationship between average waiting time and process utilization is a particularly important one

The greater the variability in the process, the more the waiting time utilization deviates from the simple rectangular function of the 'no variability' conditions that was shown in Figure 4.9. A set of curves for a typical process is shown in Figure 4.10(a). This phenomenon has important implications for the design of processes. In effect it presents three options to process designers wishing to improve the waiting time or utilization performance of their processes, as shown in Figure 4.10(b):

- Accept long average waiting times and achieve high utilization (point X);
- Accept low utilization and achieve short average waiting times (point Y); or
- Reduce the variability in arrival times, activity times, or both, and achieve higher utilization and short waiting times (point Z).

To analyse processes with both inter-arrival and activity time variability, queuing or 'waiting line' analysis can be used. This is treated in the supplement to Chapter 11. But, do not dismiss the relationship shown in Figures 4.9 and 4.10 as some minor technical phenomenon. It is far more than this. It identifies an important choice in process design that could have strategic implications. Which is more important to a business, fast throughput time or high utilization of its resources? The only way to have both of these simultaneously

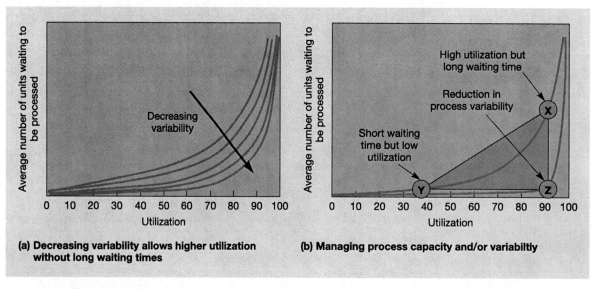

(a) Decreasing variability allows higher utilization without long waiting times

(b) Managing process capacity and/or variabiltiy

Figure 4.10 The relationship between process utilization and number of units waiting to be processed for variable arrival and activity times

is to reduce variability in its processes, which may itself require strategic decisions such as limiting the degree of customization of products or services, or imposing stricter limits on how products or services can be delivered to customers, and so on. It also demonstrates an important point concerned with the day-to-day management of process – the only way to absolutely guarantee a hundred per cent utilization of resources is to accept an infinite amount of work-in-progress and/or waiting time.

Short case
Heathrow delays caused by capacity utilization[6]

Source: Alamy Images

It may be the busiest international airport in the world, but it is unlikely to win any prizes for being the most loved. Long delays, overcrowding and a shortage of capacity has meant that Heathrow is often a cause of frustration to harassed passengers. Yet to the airlines it is an attractive hub. Its size and location give it powerful 'network effects'. This means that it can match incoming passengers with outgoing flights to hundreds of different cities. Actually it is its attractiveness to the airlines that is one of its main problems. Heathrow's runways are in such demand that they are almost always operating at, or close to, their maximum capacity. In fact, its runways operate at 99% of capacity. This compares with about 70% at most other large airports. This means that the slightest variability (bad weather or an unscheduled landing such as a plane having to turn back with engine trouble) causes delays, which in turn cause more delays. (See Figure 4.10 for the theoretical explanation of this effect.) The result is that a third of all flights at Heathrow are delayed by at least 15 minutes. This is poor when compared with other large European airports such as Amsterdam and Frankfurt, which have 21% and 24% of flights delayed respectively.

Simulation in design

Designing processes often involves making decisions in advance of the final process being created, and so the designer is often not totally sure of the consequences of his or her decisions. To increase their own confidence in their design decision, however, they will probably try to *simulate* how the process might work in practice. In some ways simulation is one of the most fundamental approaches to decision-making. Children play games and 'pretend' so as to extend their experience of novel situations; likewise, managers can gain insights and explore possibilities through the formalized 'pretending' involved in using simulation models. These **simulation models** can take many forms. In designing the various processes within a football stadium, the architect could devise a computer-based 'model' which would simulate the movement of people through the stadium's various processes according to the probability distribution which describes their random arrival and movement. This could then be used to predict where the layout might become overcrowded or where extra space might be reduced.

Simulation models

Summary answers to key questions

Check and improve your understanding of this chapter using self assessment questions and a personalised study plan, audio and video downloads, and an eBook – all at www.myomlab.com.

➤ What is process design?

■ Design is the activity which shapes the physical form and purpose of both products and services and the processes that produce them.

■ This design activity is more likely to be successful if the complementary activities of product or service design and process design are coordinated.

➤ What objectives should process design have?

■ The overall purpose of process design is to meet the needs of customers through achieving appropriate levels of quality, speed, dependability, flexibility and cost.

■ The design activity must also take account of environmental issues. These include examination of the source and suitability of materials, the sources and quantities of energy consumed, the amount and type of waste material, the life of the product itself, and the end-of-life state of the product.

➤ How do volume and variety affect process design?

■ The overall nature of any process is strongly influenced by the volume and variety of what it has to process.

■ The concept of process types summarizes how volume and variety affect overall process design.

■ In manufacturing, these process types are (in order of increasing volume and decreasing variety) project, jobbing, batch, mass and continuous processes. In service operations, although there is less consensus on the terminology, the terms often used (again in order of increasing volume and decreasing variety) are professional services, service shops and mass services.

➤ How are processes designed in detail?

■ Processes are designed initially by breaking them down into their individual activities. Often common symbols are used to represent types of activity. The sequence of activities in a process is then indicated by the sequence of symbols representing activities. This is called 'process mapping'. Alternative process designs can be compared using process maps and improved processes considered in terms of their operations performance objectives.

■ Process performance in terms of throughput time, work-in-progress, and cycle time are related by a formula known as Little's law: throughput time equals work-in-progress multiplied by cycle time.

■ Variability has a significant effect on the performance of processes, particularly the relationship between waiting time and utilization.

Case study
The Central Evaluation Unit

The Central Evaluation Unit (CEU) of the XIII Directorate evaluated applications from academics bidding for research grants available under the 'cooperation and foundations' scheme of the European Union. This scheme distributed relatively small grants (less than €100,000) to fund the early stages of cooperative research between universities in the European Union. Based in Brussels, the CEU's objectives were to make decisions that were consistently in line with directory guide rules, but also to give as speedy a response as possible to applicants. All new applications are sent to the CEU's applications processing unit (CEUPU) by University Liaison Officers (ULOs) who were based at around 150 universities around the EU. Any academic who wanted to apply for a grant needed to submit an application form (downloadable online) and other signed documentation through the local ULO. The CEUPU employs three 'checkers' with three support and secretarial staff, a pool of twelve clerks who are responsible for data entry and filing, ten auditors (staff who prepare and issue the grant approval documents), and a special advisor (who is a senior ex-officer employed part-time to assess non-standard applications).

Véronique Fontan was the manager in charge of the Central Evaluation Unit's applications processing unit (CEUPU). She had been invited by the Directory chief executive, Leda Grumman, to make a presentation to senior colleagues about the reasons for the success of her unit. The reason for her invitation to the meeting was, first, that the systems used for handling new grant applications were well proven and robust, and, secondly, that her operation was well known for consistently meeting, and in many cases exceeding, its targets.

Véronique set a day aside to collect some information about the activities of the CEUPU. She first reviewed her monthly management reports. The information system provided an update of number of applications (by week, month and year), the number and percentage of applications approved, number and percentage of those declined, the cumulative amount of money allocated, and the value of applications processed during the month. These reports identified that the Unit dealt with about 200 to 300 applications per week (the Unit operated a five-day 35-hour week) and all the Unit's financial targets were being met. In addition most operational performance criteria were being exceeded. The targets for turnaround of an application, from receipt of an application to the applicant being informed (excluding time spent waiting for additional information from ULOs) was 40 working days. The average time taken by the CEUPU was 36 working days. Accuracy had never been an issue as all files were thoroughly assessed to ensure

that all the relevant and complete data were collected before the applications were processed. Staff productivity was high and there was always plenty of work waiting for processing at each section. A cursory inspection of the sections' in-trays revealed about 130 files in each with just two exceptions. The 'receipt' clerks' tray had about 600 files in it and the checkers' tray contained about 220 files.

Processing grant applications

The processing of applications is a lengthy procedure requiring careful examination by checkers trained to make assessments. All applications arriving at the Unit are placed in an in-tray. The incoming application is then opened by one of the eight 'receipt' clerks who will check that all the necessary forms have been included in the application. This is then placed in an in-tray pending collection by the coding staff. The two clerks with special responsibility for coding allocate a unique identifier to each application and code the information on the application into the information system.

The application is then given a front sheet, a pro forma, with the identifier in the top left corner. The files are then placed in a tray on the senior checker's secretary's desk. As a checker becomes available, the senior secretary provides the next job in the line to the checker. In the case of about half of the applications, the checker returns the file to the checkers' secretaries to request the collection of any information that is missing or additional information that is required. The secretaries then write to the applicant and return the file to the 'receipt' clerks who place the additional information into the file as it arrives. Once the file is complete it is returned to the checkers for a decision on →

the grant application. The file is then taken to auditors who prepare the acceptance or rejection documents.

These documents are then sent, with the rest of the file, to the two 'dispatch' clerks who complete the documents and mail them to the ULO for delivery to the academic who made the application. Each section, clerical, coding, checkers, secretarial, auditing or issuing, have trays for incoming work. Files are taken from the bottom of the pile when someone becomes free to ensure that all documents are dealt with in strict order.

Véronique's confidence in her operation was somewhat eroded when she asked for comments from some university liaison officers and staff. One ULO told her of frequent complaints about the delays over the processing of the applications and she felt there was a danger of alienating some of the best potential applicants to the point where they 'just would not bother applying'. A second ULO complained that when he telephoned to ascertain the status of an application, the CEUPU staff did not seem to know where it was or how long it might be before a decision would be made. Furthermore he felt that this lack of information was eroding his relationship with potential applicants, some of whom had already decided to apply elsewhere for research funding. Véronique reviewed the levels of applications over the last few years which revealed a decline of five per cent last year and two per cent the year before that on the number of applications made. Véronique then spent about ten minutes with four of the clerks. They said their work was clear and routine, but their life was made difficult by university liaison officers who rang in expecting them to be able to tell them the status of an application they had submitted. It could take them hours, sometimes days, to find any individual file. Indeed, two of the 'receipt' clerks now worked full-time on this activity. They also said that university liaison officers frequently complained that decision-making seemed to be unusually slow, given the relatively small amounts of money being applied for. Véronique wondered whether, after all, she should agree to make the presentation.

Questions

1 Analyse and evaluate the processing of new applications at the CEUPU:
   - Create a process map for new applications
   - Calculate the time needed to process an individual application cycle time for the process
   - Calculate the number of people involved in the processing of an application
   - Explain why it is difficult to locate an individual file.

2 Summarize the problems of the CEUPU process.

3 What suggestions would you make to Véronique to improve her process?

Problems and applications

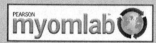

These problems and applications will help to improve your analysis of operations. You can find more practice problems as well as worked examples and guided solutions on MyOMLab at www.myomlab.com.

1 Read again the description of fast-food drive-through processes at the beginning of this chapter. (a) Draw a process map that reflects the types of process described. (b) What advantage do you think is given to McDonald's through its decision to establish a call centre for remote order-taking for some of its outlets?

2 A laboratory process receives medical samples from hospitals in its area and then subjects them to a number of tests that take place in different parts of the laboratory. The average response time for the laboratory to complete all its tests and mail the results back to the hospital (measured from the time that the sample for analysis arrives) is 3 days. A recent process map has shown that, of the 60 minutes that are needed to complete all the tests, the tests themselves took 30 minutes, moving the samples between each test area took 10 minutes, and double-checking the results took a further 20 minutes. What is the throughput efficiency of this process? What is the value-added throughput efficiency of the process? (State any assumptions that you are making.) If the process is rearranged so that all the tests are performed in the same area, thus eliminating the time to move between test areas, and the tests themselves are improved to halve the amount of time needed for double-checking, what effect would this have on the value-added throughput efficiency?

3 A regional government office that deals with passport applications is designing a process that will check applications and issue the documents. The number of applications to be processed is 1,600 per week and the time available to process the applications is 40 hours per week. What is the required cycle time for the process?

4 For the passport office, described above, the total work content of all the activities that make up the total task of checking, processing and issuing a passport is, on average, 30 minutes. How many people will be needed to meet demand?

5 The same passport office has a 'clear desk' policy that means that all desks must be clear of work by the end of the day. How many applications should be loaded onto the process in the morning in order to ensure that every one is completed and desks are clear by the end of the day? (Assume a 7.5-hour (450-minute) working day.)

6 Visit a drive-through quick-service restaurant and observe the operation for half an hour. You will probably need a stop watch to collect the relevant timing information. Consider the following questions.

   (a) Where are the bottlenecks in the service (in other words, what seems to take the longest time)?
   (b) How would you measure the efficiency of the process?
   (c) What appear to be the key design principles that govern the effectiveness of this process?
   (d) Using Little's law, how long would the queue have to be before you think it would be not worth joining the queue?

Selected further reading

Chopra, S., Anupindi, R., Deshmukh, S.D., Van Mieghem, J.A. and Zemel, E. (2006) *Managing Business Process Flows*, Prentice-Hall, Upper Saddle River NJ. An excellent, although mathematical, approach to process design in general.

Hammer, M. (1990) Reengineering work: don't automate, obliterate, *Harvard Business Review*, July–August. This is the paper that launched the whole idea of business processes and process management in general to a wider managerial audience. Slightly dated but worth reading.

Hopp, W.J. and Spearman, M.L. (2001) *Factory Physics*, 2nd edn, McGraw-Hill. Very technical so don't bother with it if you aren't prepared to get into the maths. However, there is some fascinating analysis, especially concerning Little's law.

Smith, H. and Fingar, P. (2003) *Business Process Management: The Third Wave*, Meghan-Kiffer Press, Tampa, Fla. A popular book on process management from a BPR perspective.

Useful web sites

www.bpmi.org Site of the Business Process Management Initiative. Some good resources including papers and articles.
www.bptrends.com News site for trends in business process management generally. Some interesting articles.
www.bls.gov/oes/ US Department of Labor employment statistics.
www.fedee.com/hrtrends Federation of European Employers guide to employment and job trends in Europe.

www.iienet.org The American Institute of Industrial Engineers site. This is an important professional body for process design and related topics.
www.opsman.org Lots of useful stuff.
www.waria.com A Workflow and Reengineering Association web site. Some useful topics.

Now that you have finished reading this chapter, why not visit MyOMLab at www.myomlab.com where you'll find more learning resources to help you make the most of your studies and get a better grade?

9

Layout Decisions

10

OM Strategy Decisions

- ► Design of Goods and Services
- ► Managing Quality
- ► Process Strategy
- ► Location Strategies
- ► Layout Strategies
- ► Human Resources
- ► Supply-Chain Management
- ► Inventory Management
- ► Scheduling
- ► Maintenance

GLOBAL COMPANY PROFILE: McDONALD'S

McDONALD'S LOOKS FOR COMPETITIVE ADVANTAGE THROUGH LAYOUT

n its half-century of existence, McDonald's revolutionized the restaurant industry by inventing the limited-menu fast-food restaurant. It has also made seven major innovations. The first, the introduction of *indoor seating* (1950s), was a layout issue, as was the second, *drive-through windows* (1970s). The third, adding *breakfasts* to the menu (1980s), was a product strategy. The fourth, *adding play areas* (late 1980s), was again a layout decision.

In the 1990s, McDonald's completed its fifth innovation, a radically new *redesign of the kitchens* in its 14,000 North America outlets to facilitate a mass customization process. Dubbed the "Made by You" kitchen system, sandwiches were assembled to order with the revamped layout.

In 2004, the chain began the rollout of its sixth innovation, a new food ordering layout: the *self-service kiosk*. Self-service kiosks have been infiltrating the service sector since the introduction of ATMs in 1985 (there are over 1.5 million ATMs in banking). Alaska Airlines was the first airline to provide self-service airport check-in, in 1996. Most passengers of the major airlines now check themselves in for flights. Kiosks take up less space than an employee and reduce waiting line time.

Now, McDonald's is working on its seventh innovation, and not surprisingly, it also deals with restaurant layout. The company, on an unprecedented scale, is redesigning all 30,000 eateries around the globe to take on a *21st century look*. The dining area will be separated into three sections with distinct personalities: (1) the "linger" zone focuses on young adults and offers comfortable furniture and Wi-Fi connections; (2) the "grab and go" zone features tall counters, bar stools, and plasma TVs; and (3) the "flexible" zone has colorful family booths, flexible seating, and kid-oriented music. The cost per outlet: a whopping $300,000–$400,000 renovation fee.

As McDonald's has discovered, facility layout is indeed a source of competitive advantage.

McDonald's finds that kiosks reduce both space requirements and waiting; order taking is faster. An added benefit is that customers like them. Also, kiosks are reliable—they don't call in sick. And, most importantly, sales are up 10%–15% (an average of $1) when a customer orders from a kiosk, which consistently recommends the larger size and other extras.

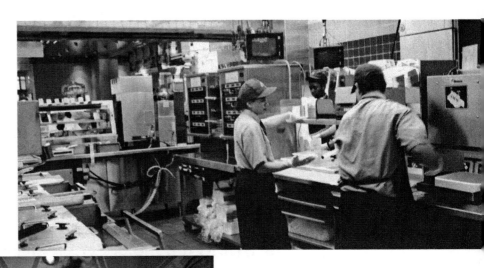

▶ The redesigned kitchen of a McDonald's in Manhattan. The more efficient layout requires less labor, reduces waste, and provides faster service. A graphic of this "assembly line" is shown in Figure 9.12

Linger Zone ▼
Cozy armchairs and sofas, plus Wi-Fi connections, make these areas attractive to those who want to hang out and socialize.

Grab & Go Zone ▼
This section has tall counters with bar stools for customers who eat alone. Plasma TVs keep them company.

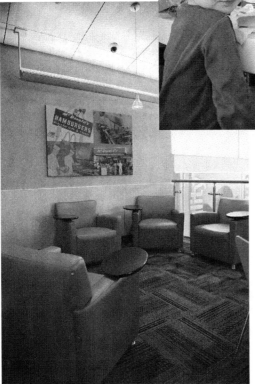

Flexible Zone ▲
Booths with colorful fabric cushions make up the area geared to family and larger groups. Tables and chairs are movable.

Chapter 9 **Learning Objectives**

THE STRATEGIC IMPORTANCE OF LAYOUT DECISIONS

Layout is one of the key decisions that determines the long-run efficiency of operations. Layout has numerous strategic implications because it establishes an organization's competitive priorities in regard to capacity, processes, flexibility, and cost, as well as quality of work life, customer contact, and image. An effective layout can help an organization achieve a strategy that supports differentiation, low cost, or response. Benetton, for example, supports a *differentiation* strategy by heavy investment in warehouse layouts that contribute to fast, accurate sorting and shipping to its 5,000 outlets. Wal-Mart store layouts support a strategy of *low cost*, as do its warehouse layouts. Hallmark's office layouts, where many professionals operate with open communication in work cells, support *rapid development* of greeting cards. *The objective of layout strategy is to develop an effective and efficient layout that will meet the firm's competitive requirements.* These firms have done so.

In all cases, layout design must consider how to achieve the following:

- Higher utilization of space, equipment, and people
- Improved flow of information, materials, or people
- Improved employee morale and safer working conditions
- Improved customer/client interaction
- Flexibility (whatever the layout is now, it will need to change).

In our increasingly short-life-cycle, mass-customized world, layout designs need to be viewed as dynamic. This means considering small, movable, and flexible equipment. Store displays need to be movable, office desks and partitions modular, and warehouse racks prefabricated. To make quick and easy changes in product models and in production rates, operations managers must design flexibility into layouts. To obtain flexibility in layout, managers cross train their workers, maintain equipment, keep investments low, place workstations close together, and use small, movable equipment. In some cases, equipment on wheels is appropriate, in anticipation of the next change in product, process, or volume.

TYPES OF LAYOUT

Layout decisions include the best placement of machines (in production settings), offices and desks (in office settings), or service centers (in settings such as hospitals or department stores). An effective layout facilitates the flow of materials, people, and information within and between areas. To achieve these objectives, a variety of approaches has been developed. We will discuss seven of them in this chapter:

1. *Office layout:* Positions workers, their equipment, and spaces/offices to provide for movement of information.
2. *Retail layout:* Allocates shelf space and responds to customer behavior.
3. *Warehouse layout:* Addresses trade-offs between space and material handling.
4. *Fixed-position layout:* Addresses the layout requirements of large, bulky projects such as ships and buildings.
5. *Process-oriented layout:* Deals with low-volume, high-variety production (also called "job shop," or intermittent production).

▼ TABLE 9.1 Layout Strategies

	Objectives	Examples
Office	Locate workers requiring frequent contact close to one another	Allstate Insurance Microsoft Corp.
Retail	Expose customer to high-margin items	Kroger's Supermarket Walgreen's Bloomingdale's
Warehouse (storage)	Balance low-cost storage with low cost material handling	Federal-Mogul's warehouse The Gap's distribution center
Project (fixed position)	Move material to the limited storage areas around the site	Ingall Ship Building Corp. Trump Plaza Pittsburgh Airport
Job Shop (process oriented)	Manage varied material flow for each product	Arnold Palmer Hospital Hard Rock Cafe Olive Garden
Work Cell (product families)	Identify a product family, build teams, cross train team members	Hallmark Cards Wheeled Coach Standard Aero
Repetitive/Continuous (product oriented)	Equalize the task time at each workstation	Sony's TV assembly line Toyota Scion

6. *Work-cell layout:* Arranges machinery and equipment to focus on production of a single product or group of related products.
7. *Product-oriented layout:* Seeks the best personnel and machine utilization in repetitive or continuous production.

Examples for each of these classes of layouts are noted in Table 9.1.

Because only a few of these seven classes can be modeled mathematically, layout and design of physical facilities are still something of an art. However, we do know that a good layout requires determining the following:

- *Material handling equipment:* Managers must decide about equipment to be used, including conveyors, cranes, automated storage and retrieval systems, and automatic carts to deliver and store material.
- *Capacity and space requirements:* Only when personnel, machines, and equipment requirements are known can managers proceed with layout and provide space for each component. In the case of office work, operations managers must make judgments about the space require-

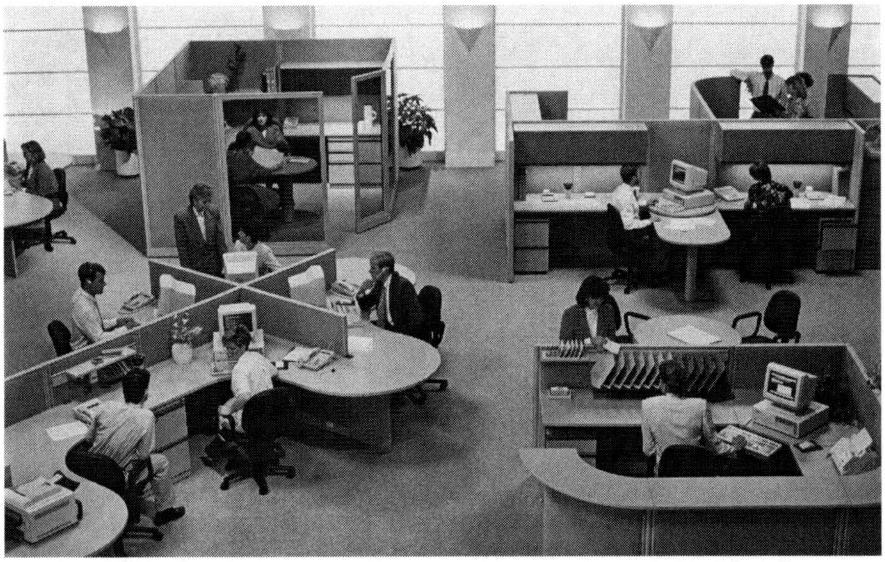

This open office offers a large shared space that encourages employees to interact. Before Steelcase, the office furniture maker, went to an open office system, 80% of its office space was private; now it is just 20% private. The CEO even went from a private 700-square-foot office to a 48-square-foot enclosure in an open area. This dramatically increases unplanned and spontaneous communication between employees.

ments for each employee. It may be a 6 × 6-foot cubicle plus allowance for hallways, aisles, rest rooms, cafeterias, stairwells, elevators, and so forth, or it may be spacious executive offices and conference rooms. Management must also consider allowances for requirements that address safety, noise, dust, fumes, temperature, and space around equipment and machines.

- *Environment and aesthetics:* Layout concerns often require decisions about windows, planters, and height of partitions to facilitate air flow, reduce noise, provide privacy, and so forth.
- *Flows of information:* Communication is important to any organization and must be facilitated by the layout. This issue may require decisions about proximity as well as decisions about open spaces versus half-height dividers versus private offices.
- *Cost of moving between various work areas:* There may be unique considerations related to moving materials or to the importance of having certain areas next to each other. For example, moving molten steel is more difficult than moving cold steel.

OFFICE LAYOUT

Office layout

The grouping of workers, their equipment, and spaces/offices to provide for comfort, safety, and movement of information.

Office layouts require the grouping of workers, their equipment, and spaces to provide for comfort, safety, and movement of information. The main distinction of office layouts is the importance placed on the flow of information. Office layouts are in constant flux as the technological change sweeping society alters the way offices function.

Even though the movement of information is increasingly electronic, analysis of office layouts still requires a task-based approach. Paper correspondence, contracts, legal documents, confidential patient records, and hard-copy scripts, artwork, and designs still play a major role in many offices. Managers therefore examine both electronic and conventional communication patterns, separation needs, and other conditions affecting employee effectiveness. A useful tool for such an analysis is the *relationship chart* shown in Figure 9.1. This chart, prepared for an office of product designers, indicates that the chief marketing officer must be (1) near the designers' area, (2) less near the secretary and central files, and (3) not at all near the copy center or accounting department.

LO1: Discuss important issues in office layout

General office-area guidelines allot an average of about 100 square feet per person (including corridors). A major executive is allotted about 400 square feet, and a conference room area is based on 25 square feet per person.

On the other hand, some layout considerations are universal (many of which apply to factories as well as to offices). They have to do with working conditions, teamwork, authority, and status. Should offices be private or open cubicles, have low file cabinets to foster informal communication or high cabinets to reduce noise and contribute to privacy? (See the Steelcase photo on the previous page). Should all employees use the same entrance, rest rooms, lockers, and cafeteria? As mentioned earlier, layout decisions are part art and part science.

As a final comment on office layout, we note two major trends. First, technology, such as cell phones, iPods, faxes, the Internet, laptop computers, and PDAs, allows increasing layout flexibility by moving information electronically and allowing employees to work offsite. Second, modern firms create dynamic needs for space and services.

▶ **FIGURE 9.1**
Office Relationship Chart

Source: Adapted from Richard Muther, *Simplified Systematic Layout Planning*, 3rd ed. (Kansas City, Mgt. & Ind'l Research Publications). Used by permission of the publisher.

Value	CLOSENESS
A	Absolutely necessary
E	Especially important
I	Important
O	Ordinary OK
U	Unimportant
X	Not desirable

Here are two examples:[1]

- When Deloitte & Touche found that 30% to 40% of desks were empty at any given time, the firm developed its "hoteling programs." Consultants lost their permanent offices; anyone who plans to be in the building (rather than out with clients) books an office through a "concierge," who hangs that consultant's name on the door for the day and stocks the space with requested supplies.
- Cisco Systems cut rent and workplace service costs by 37% and saw productivity benefits of $2.4 billion per year by reducing square footage, reconfiguring space, creating movable, everything-on-wheels offices, and designing "get away from it all" innovation areas.

RETAIL LAYOUT

Retail layouts are based on the idea that sales and profitability vary directly with customer exposure to products. Thus, most retail operations managers try to expose customers to as many products as possible. Studies do show that the greater the rate of exposure, the greater the sales and the higher the return on investment. The operations manager can change exposure with store arrangement and the allocation of space to various products within that arrangement.

Five ideas are helpful for determining the overall arrangement of many stores:

1. Locate the high-draw items around the periphery of the store. Thus, we tend to find dairy products on one side of a supermarket and bread and bakery products on another. An example of this tactic is shown in Figure 9.2.
2. Use prominent locations for high-impulse and high-margin items. Best Buy puts fast-growing, high-margin digital goods—such as cameras and DVDs—in the front and center of its stores.
3. Distribute what are known in the trade as "power items"—items that may dominate a purchasing trip—to both sides of an aisle, and disperse them to increase the viewing of other items.
4. Use end-aisle locations because they have a very high exposure rate.
5. Convey the mission of the store by carefully selecting the position of the lead-off department. For instance, if prepared foods are part of a supermarket's mission, position the bakery and deli up front to appeal to convenience-oriented customers. Wal-Mart's push to increase sales of clothes means those departments are in broad view upon entering a store.

Once the overall layout of a retail store has been decided, products need to be arranged for sale. Many considerations go into this arrangement. However, the main *objective of retail layout is to maximize profitability per square foot of floor space* (or, in some stores, on linear foot of shelf space). Big-ticket, or expensive, items may yield greater dollar sales, but the profit per square foot may be lower. Computerized programs are available to assist managers in evaluating the profitability of various merchandising plans for hundreds of categories: this technique is known as category management.

An additional, and somewhat controversial, issue in retail layout is called slotting. **Slotting fees** are fees manufacturers pay to get their goods on the shelf in a retail store or supermarket

> **AUTHOR COMMENT**
> The goal in a retail layout is to maximize profit per square foot of store space.

> **Retail layout**
> An approach that addresses flow, allocates space, and responds to customer behavior

> **LO 2:** Define the objectives of retail layout

> **Slotting fees**
> Fees manufacturers pay to get shelf space for their products.

> ◀ **FIGURE 9.2**
> **Store Layout with Dairy and Bakery, High-Draw Items, in Different Areas of the Store**

[1]"Square Feet. Oh, How Square!" *Business Week* (July 3, 2006): 100–101.

Trying to penetrate urban areas that have lofty land prices and strong antidevelopment movements, Wal-Mart is changing its layout to up, not out. A new generation of multi-level stores take only one-third the space of the traditional 25-acre swaths. Here, in the El Cajon, California, store, Wal-Mart trained workers to help shoppers confused by the device next to the escalator that carries shopping carts from one floor to another.

chain. The result of massive new-product introductions, retailers can now demand up to $25,000 to place an item in their chain. During the last decade, marketplace economics, consolidations, and technology have provided retailers with this leverage. The competition for shelf space is advanced by POS systems and scanner technology, which improve supply-chain management and inventory control. Many small firms question the legality and ethics of slotting fees, claiming the fees stifle new products, limit their ability to expand, and cost consumers money. Wal-Mart is one of the few major retailers that does not demand slotting fees. This removes the barrier to entry that small companies usually face. (See the *Ethical Dilemma* at the end of this chapter.)

Servicescapes

Servicescape

The physical surroundings in which a service takes place, and how they affect customers and employees.

Although the main objective of retail layout is to maximize profit through product exposure, there are other aspects of the service that managers consider. The term **servicescape** describes the physical surroundings in which the service is delivered and how the surroundings have a humanistic effect on customers and employees. To provide a good service layout, a firm considers three elements:

1. *Ambient conditions*, which are background characteristics such as lighting, sound, smell, and temperature. All these affect workers *and* customers and can affect how much is spent and how long a person stays in the building.
2. *Spatial layout and functionality*, which involve customer circulation path planning, aisle characteristics (such as width, direction, angle, and shelf spacing), and product grouping.
3. *Signs, symbols, and artifacts*, which are characteristics of building design that carry social significance (such as carpeted areas of a department store that encourage shoppers to slow down and browse).

A critical element contributing to the bottom line at Hard Rock Cafe is the layout of each cafe's retail shop space. The retail space, from 600 to 1,300 square feet in size, is laid out in conjunction with the restaurant area to create the maximum traffic flow before and after eating. The payoffs for cafes like this one in London are huge. Almost half of a cafe's annual sales are generated from these small shops, which have very high retail sales per square foot.

Examples of each of these three elements of servicescape are:

- *Ambient conditions:* Fine-dining restaurants with linen tablecloths and candlelit atmosphere; Mrs. Field's Cookie bakery smells permeating the shopping mall; leather chairs at Starbucks.
- *Layout/functionality:* Kroger's long aisles and high shelves; Best Buy's wide center aisle.
- *Signs, symbols, and artifacts:* Wal-Mart's greeter at the door; Hard Rock Cafe's wall of guitars; Disneyland's entrance looking like hometown heaven.

WAREHOUSING AND STORAGE LAYOUTS

The objective of **warehouse layout** *is to find the optimum trade-off between handling cost and costs associated with warehouse space.* Consequently, management's task is to maximize the utilization of the total "cube" of the warehouse—that is, utilize its full volume while maintaining low material handling costs. We define *material handling costs* as all the costs related to the transaction. This consists of incoming transport, storage, and outgoing transport of the materials to be warehoused. These costs include equipment, people, material, supervision, insurance, and depreciation. Effective warehouse layouts do, of course, also minimize the damage and spoilage of material within the warehouse.

Management minimizes the sum of the resources spent on finding and moving material plus the deterioration and damage to the material itself. The variety of items stored and the number of items "picked" has direct bearing on the optimum layout. A warehouse storing a few unique items lends itself to higher density than a warehouse storing a variety of items. Modern warehouse management is, in many instances, an automated procedure using *automated storage and retrieval systems* (ASRSs).

The Stop & Shop grocery chain, with 350 supermarkets in New England, has recently completed the largest ASRS in the world. The 1.3-million-square-foot distribution center in Freetown, Massachusetts, employs 77 rotating-fork automated storage and retrieval machines. These 77 cranes each access 11,500 pick slots on 90 aisles—a total of 64,000 pallets of food. The Wolfsburg, Germany parking garage photo (below) indicates that an ASRS can take many forms.

An important component of warehouse layout is the relationship between the receiving/unloading area and the shipping/loading area. Facility design depends on the type of supplies unloaded, what they are unloaded from (trucks, rail cars, barges, and so on), and where they are unloaded. In some companies, the receiving and shipping facilities, or *docks*, as they are called, are even in the same area; sometimes they are receiving docks in the morning and shipping docks in the afternoon.

Warehouse layout
A design that attempts to minimize total cost by addressing trade-offs between space and material handing.

LO3: Discuss modern warehouse management and terms such as ASRS, cross-docking, and random stocking

Automated storage and retrieval systems are not found only in traditional warehouses. This parking garage in Wolfsburg, Germany, occupies only 20% of the space of a traditionally designed garage. The ASRS "retrieves" autos in less time, without the potential of the cars being damaged by an attendant.

Cross-Docking

Cross-docking means to avoid placing materials or supplies in storage by processing them as they are received. In a manufacturing facility, product is received directly to the assembly line. In a distribution center, labeled and presorted loads arrive at the shipping dock for immediate rerouting, thereby avoiding formal receiving, stocking/storing, and order-selection activities. Because these activities add no value to the product, their elimination is 100% cost savings. Wal-Mart, an early advocate of cross-docking, uses the technique as a major component of its continuing low-cost strategy. With cross-docking, Wal-Mart reduces distribution costs and speeds restocking of stores, thereby improving customer service. Although cross-docking reduces product handling, inventory, and facility costs, it requires both (1) tight scheduling and (2) accurate inbound product identification.

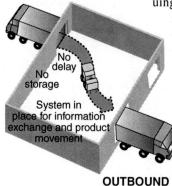

INBOUND

No delay
No storage
System in place for information exchange and product movement

OUTBOUND

Random Stocking

Automatic identification systems (AISs), usually in the form of bar codes, allow accurate and rapid item identification. When automatic identification systems are combined with effective management information systems, operations managers know the quantity and location of every unit. This information can be used with human operators or with automatic storage and retrieval systems to load units anywhere in the warehouse—randomly. Accurate inventory quantities and locations mean the potential utilization of the whole facility because space does not need to be reserved for certain stock-keeping units (SKUs) or part families. Computerized **random stocking** systems often include the following tasks:

1. Maintaining a list of "open" locations
2. Maintaining accurate records of existing inventory and its locations
3. Sequencing items to minimize the travel time required to "pick" orders
4. Combining orders to reduce picking time
5. Assigning certain items or classes of items, such as high-usage items, to particular warehouse areas so that the total distance traveled within the warehouse is minimized

Random stocking systems can increase facility utilization and decrease labor cost, but they require accurate records.

Customizing

Although we expect warehouses to store as little product as possible and hold it for as short a time as possible, we are now asking warehouses to customize products. Warehouses can be places where value is added through **customizing**. Warehouse customization is a particularly useful way to generate competitive advantage in markets where products have multiple configurations. For instance, a warehouse can be a place where computer components are put together, software loaded, and repairs made. Warehouses may also provide customized labeling and packaging for retailers so items arrive ready for display.

Increasingly, this type of work goes on adjacent to major airports, in facilities such as the FedEx terminal in Memphis. Adding value at warehouses adjacent to major airports also facilitates overnight delivery. For example, if your computer has failed, the replacement may be sent to you from such a warehouse for delivery the next morning. When your old machine arrives back at the warehouse, it is repaired and sent to someone else. These value-added activities at "quasi-warehouses" contribute to strategies of differentiation, low cost, and rapid response.

FIXED-POSITION LAYOUT

In a **fixed-position layout**, the project remains in one place and workers and equipment come to that one work area. Examples of this type of project are a ship, a highway, a bridge, a house, and an operating table in a hospital operating room.

The techniques for addressing the fixed-position layout are complicated by three factors. First, there is limited space at virtually all sites. Second, at different stages of a project, different materials are needed; therefore, different items become critical as the project develops. Third, the volume of materials needed is dynamic. For example, the rate of use of steel panels for the hull of a ship changes as the project progresses.

Here are three versions of the fixed-position layout.

A house built via traditional fixed-position layout would be constructed onsite, with equipment, materials, and workers brought to the site. Then a "meeting of the trades" would assign space for various time periods. However, the home pictured here can be built at a much lower cost. The house is built in two movable modules in a factory. Scaffolding and hoists make the job easier, quicker, and cheaper, and the indoor work environment aids labor productivity.

A service example of a fixed-position layout is an operating room; the patient remains stationary on the table, and medical personnel and equipment are brought to the site.

In shipbuilding, there is limited space next to the fixed-position layout. Shipyards call these loading areas platens, and they are assigned for various time periods to each contractor.

Because problems with fixed-position layouts are so difficult to solve well onsite, an alternative strategy is to complete as much of the project as possible offsite. This approach is used in the shipbuilding industry when standard units—say, pipe-holding brackets—are assembled on a nearby assembly line (a product-oriented facility). In an attempt to add efficiency to shipbuilding, Ingall Ship Building Corporation has moved toward product-oriented production when sections of a ship (modules) are similar or when it has a contract to build the same section of several similar ships. Also, as the top photo on the page shows, many home builders are moving from a fixed-position layout strategy to one that is more product oriented. About one-third of all new homes in the U.S. are built this way. In addition, many houses that are built onsite (fixed position) have the majority of components such as doors, windows, fixtures, trusses, stairs, and wallboard built as modules with more efficient offsite processes.

LO4: Identify when fixed-position layouts are appropriate

PROCESS-ORIENTED LAYOUT

A **process-oriented layout** can simultaneously handle a wide variety of products or services. This is the traditional way to support a product differentiation strategy. It is most efficient when making products with different requirements or when handling customers, patients, or clients with different

Process-oriented layout
A layout that deals with low-volume, high-variety production in which like machines and equipment are grouped together.

► **FIGURE 9.3**

An Emergency Room Process Layout Showing the Routing of Two Patients

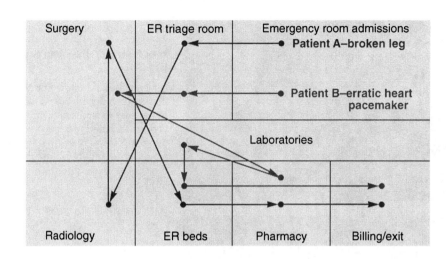

AUTHOR COMMENT
Patient A (broken leg) proceeds (blue arrow) to ER triage, to radiology, to surgery, to a bed, to pharmacy, to billing. Patient B (pacemaker problem) moves (red arrow) to ER triage, to surgery, to pharmacy, to lab, to a bed, to billing.

VIDEO 9.1
Layout at Arnold Palmer Hospital

Job lots
Groups or batches of parts processed together.

LO5: Explain how to achieve a good process-oriented facility layout

needs. A process-oriented layout is typically the low-volume, high-variety strategy discussed in Chapter 7. In this job-shop environment, each product or each small group of products undergoes a different sequence of operations. A product or small order is produced by moving it from one department to another in the sequence required for that product. A good example of the process-oriented layout is a hospital or clinic. Figure 9.3 illustrates the process for two patients, A and B, at an emergency clinic in Chicago. An inflow of patients, each with his or her own needs, requires routing through admissions, laboratories, operating rooms, radiology, pharmacies, nursing beds, and so on. Equipment, skills, and supervision are organized around these processes.

A big advantage of process-oriented layout is its flexibility in equipment and labor assignments. The breakdown of one machine, for example, need not halt an entire process; work can be transferred to other machines in the department. Process-oriented layout is also especially good for handling the manufacture of parts in small batches, or **job lots**, and for the production of a wide variety of parts in different sizes or forms.

The disadvantages of process-oriented layout come from the general-purpose use of the equipment. Orders take more time to move through the system because of difficult scheduling, changing setups, and unique material handling. In addition, general-purpose equipment requires high labor skills, and work-in-process inventories are higher because of imbalances in the production process. High labor-skill needs also increase the required level of training and experience, and high work-in-process levels increase capital investment.

When designing a process layout, the most common tactic is to arrange departments or work centers so as to minimize the costs of material handling. In other words, departments with large flows of parts or people between them should be placed next to one another. Material handling costs in this approach depend on (1) the number of loads (or people) to be moved between two departments during some period of time and (2) the distance-related costs of moving loads (or people) between departments. Cost is assumed to be a function of distance between departments. The objective can be expressed as follows:

$$\text{Minimize cost} = \sum_{i=1}^{n} \sum_{j=1}^{n} X_{ij} C_{ij} \tag{9-1}$$

where n = total number of work centers or departments
i, j = individual departments
X_{ij} = number of loads moved from department i to department j
C_{ij} = cost to move a load between department i and department j

Process-oriented facilities (and fixed-position layouts as well) try to minimize loads, or trips, times distance-related costs. The term C_{ij} combines distance and other costs into one factor. We thereby assume not only that the difficulty of movement is equal but also that the pickup and setdown costs are constant. Although they are not always constant, for simplicity's sake we summarize these data (that is, distance, difficulty, and pickup and setdown costs) in this one variable, cost. The best way to understand the steps involved in designing a process layout is to look at an example.

Walters Company management wants to arrange the six departments of its factory in a way that will minimize interdepartmental material handling costs. They make an initial assumption (to simplify the problem) that each department is 20×20 feet and that the building is 60 feet long and 40 feet wide.

APPROACH AND SOLUTION ▶   The process layout procedure that they follow involves six steps:

STEP 1: *Construct a "from–to matrix"* showing the flow of parts or materials from department to department (see Figure 9.4).

◀ FIGURE 9.4

Interdepartmental Flow of Parts

Number of loads per week

Department	Assembly (1)	Painting (2)	Machine Shop (3)	Receiving (4)	Shipping (5)	Testing (6)
Assembly (1)		50	100	0	0	20
Painting (2)			30	50	10	0
Machine Shop (3)				20	0	100
Receiving (4)					50	0
Shipping (5)						0
Testing (6)						

AUTHOR COMMENT
The high flows between 1 and 3 and between 3 and 6 are immediately apparent. Departments 1, 3, and 6, therefore, should be close together.

STEP 2: *Determine the space requirements* for each department. (Figure 9.5 shows available plant space.)

◀ FIGURE 9.5

Building Dimensions and One Possible Department Layout

Area A	Area B	Area C
Assembly Department (1)	Painting Department (2)	Machine Shop Department (3)
Receiving Department (4)	Shipping Department (5)	Testing Department (6)
Area D	Area E	Area F

40'

60'

AUTHOR COMMENT
Think of this as a starting, initial, layout. Our goal is to improve it, if possible.

STEP 3: *Develop an initial schematic diagram* showing the sequence of departments through which parts must move. Try to place departments with a heavy flow of materials or parts next to one another. (See Figure 9.6.)

◀ FIGURE 9.6

Interdepartmental Flow Graph Showing Number of Weekly Loads

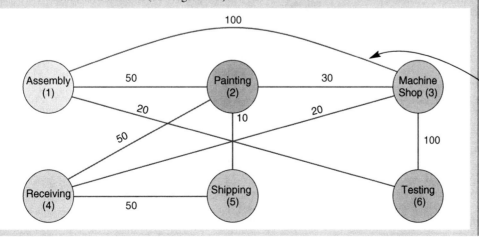

AUTHOR COMMENT
This shows that 100 loads also move weekly between Assembly and the Machine Shop. We will probably want to move these two departments closer to one another to minimize the flow of parts through the factory.

STEP 4: *Determine the cost of this layout* by using the material-handling cost equation:

$$\text{Cost} = \sum_{i=1}^{n} \sum_{j=1}^{n} X_{ij} C_{ij}$$

For this problem, Walters Company assumes that a forklift carries all interdepartmental loads. The cost of moving one load between adjacent departments is estimated to be $1. Moving a load between nonadjacent departments costs $2. Looking at Figures 9.4 and 9.5, we thus see that the handling cost between departments 1 and 2 is $50 ($1 × 50 loads), $200 between departments 1 and 3 ($2 × 100 loads), $40 between departments 1 and 6 ($2 × 20 loads), and so on. Work areas that are diagonal to one another, such as 2 and 4, are treated as adjacent. The total cost for the layout shown in Figure 9.6 is:

$$\begin{aligned}
\text{Cost} = \quad &\$50 \quad + \quad \$200 \quad + \quad \$40 \quad + \quad \$30 \quad + \quad \$50 \\
&(1 \text{ and } 2) \quad (1 \text{ and } 3) \quad (1 \text{ and } 6) \quad (2 \text{ and } 3) \quad (2 \text{ and } 4) \\
&+ \quad \$10 \quad + \quad \$40 \quad + \quad \$100 \quad + \quad \$50 \\
&(2 \text{ and } 5) \quad (3 \text{ and } 4) \quad (3 \text{ and } 6) \quad (4 \text{ and } 5) \\
= \quad &\$570
\end{aligned}$$

STEP 5. By trial and error (or by a more sophisticated computer program approach that we discuss shortly), *try to improve the layout* pictured in Figure 9.5 to establish a better arrangement of departments.

By looking at both the flow graph (Figure 9.6) and the cost calculations, we see that placing departments 1 and 3 closer together appears desirable. They currently are nonadjacent, and the high volume of flow between them causes a large handling expense. Looking the situation over, we need to check the effect of shifting departments and possibly raising, instead of lowering, overall costs.

One possibility is to switch departments 1 and 2. This exchange produces a second departmental flow graph (Figure 9.7), which shows a reduction in cost to $480, a savings in material handling of $90:

$$\begin{aligned}
\text{Cost} = \quad &\$50 \quad + \quad \$100 \quad + \quad \$20 \quad + \quad \$60 \quad + \quad \$50 \\
&(1 \text{ and } 2) \quad (1 \text{ and } 3) \quad (1 \text{ and } 6) \quad (2 \text{ and } 3) \quad (2 \text{ and } 4) \\
&+ \quad \$10 \quad + \quad \$40 \quad + \quad \$100 \quad + \quad \$50 \\
&(2 \text{ and } 5) \quad (3 \text{ and } 4) \quad (3 \text{ and } 6) \quad (4 \text{ and } 5) \\
= \quad &\$480
\end{aligned}$$

▶ **FIGURE 9.7**

Second Interdepartmental Flow Graph

AUTHOR COMMENT
Notice how Assembly and Machine Shop are now adjacent. Testing stayed close to the Machine Shop also.

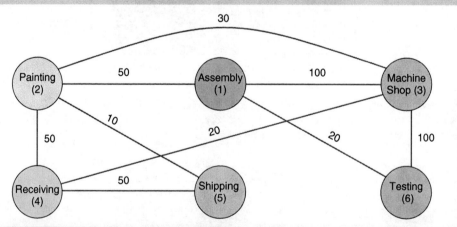

Suppose Walters Company is satisfied with the cost figure of $480 and the flow graph of Figure 9.7. The problem may not be solved yet. Often, a sixth step is necessary:

STEP 6: *Prepare a detailed plan* arranging the departments to fit the shape of the building and its nonmovable areas (such as the loading dock, washrooms, and stairways). Often this step involves ensuring that the final plan can be accommodated by the electrical system, floor loads, aesthetics, and other factors.

In the case of Walters Company, space requirements are a simple matter (see Figure 9.8).

► **FIGURE 9.8**

A Feasible Layout for Walters Company

	Area A	Area B	Area C
	Painting Department (2)	Assembly Department (1)	Machine Shop Department (3)
	Receiving Department (4)	Shipping Department (5)	Testing Department (6)
	Area D	Area E	Area F

AUTHOR COMMENT
Here we see the departments moved to areas A–F to try to improve the flow.

INSIGHT ▶ This switch of departments is only one of a large number of possible changes. For a six-department problem, there are actually 720 (or 6! = 6 × 5 × 4 × 3 × 2 × 1) potential arrangements! In layout problems, we may not find the optimal solution and may have to be satisfied with a "reasonable" one.

LEARNING EXERCISE ▶ Can you improve on the layout in Figures 9.7 and 9.8? [Answer: Yes, it can be lowered to $430 by placing Shipping in area A, Painting in area B, Assembly in area C, Receiving in area D (no change), Machine Shop in area E, and Testing in area F (no change).]

RELATED PROBLEMS ▶ 9.1, 9.2, 9.3, 9.4, 9.5, 9.6, 9.7, 9.8, 9.9

EXCEL OM Data File **Ch09Ex1.xls** can be found at **www.pearsonglobaleditions.com/heizer**.

ACTIVE MODEL 9.1 Example 1 is further illustrated in Active Model 9.1 at **www.pearsonglobaleditions.com/heizer**.

Computer Software for Process-Oriented Layouts

The graphic approach in Example 1 is fine for small problems. It does not, however, suffice for larger problems. When 20 departments are involved in a layout problem, more than 600 *trillion* different department configurations are possible. Fortunately, computer programs have been written to handle large layouts. These programs often add sophistication with flowcharts, multiple-story capability, storage and container placement, material volumes, time analysis, and cost comparisons. Such programs include **CRAFT** (Computerized Relative Allocation of Facilities Technique) (see Figure 9.9), Automated Layout Design program (ALDEP), Computerized Relationship Layout Planning (CORELAP), and Factory Flow. These programs tend to be interactive—that is, require participation by the user. And most only claim to provide "good," not "optimal," solutions.

Legend:

■ A = X-ray/MRI rooms

☐ B = laboratories

☐ C = admissions

■ D = exam rooms

☐ E = operating rooms

☐ F = recovery rooms

(a)

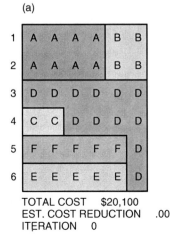

TOTAL COST $20,100
EST. COST REDUCTION   .00
ITERATION   0

(b)

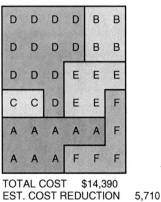

TOTAL COST $14,390
EST. COST REDUCTION   5,710
ITERATION   3

◄ **FIGURE 9.9**

In This Six-Department Outpatient Hospital Example, (a) CRAFT Has Rearranged the Initial Layout, with a Cost of $20,100, into (b) the New Layout with a Lower Cost of $14,390.

AUTHOR COMMENT
CRAFT does this by systematically testing pairs of departments to see if moving them closer to each other lowers total cost.

AUTHOR COMMENT
Using work cells is a big step toward manufacturing efficiency. They can make jobs more interesting, save space, and cut inventory.

Work cell

An arrangement of machines and personnel that focuses on making a single product or family of related products.

WORK CELLS

A **work cell** reorganizes people and machines that would ordinarily be dispersed in various departments into a group so that they can focus on making a single product or a group of related products (Figure 9.10). Cellular work arrangements are used when volume warrants a special arrangement of machinery and equipment. In a manufacturing environment, *group technology* (Chapter 5) identifies products that have similar characteristics and lend themselves to being processed in a particular work cell. These work cells are reconfigured as product designs change or volume fluctuates. Although the idea of work cells was first presented by R. E. Flanders in 1925, only with the increasing use of group technology has the technique reasserted itself. The advantages of work cells are:

1. *Reduced work-in-process inventory* because the work cell is set up to provide one-piece flow from machine to machine.
2. *Less floor space* required because less space is needed between machines to accommodate work-in-process inventory.
3. *Reduced raw material and finished goods inventories* because less work-in-process allows more rapid movement of materials through the work cell.
4. *Reduced direct labor cost* because of improved communication among employees, better material flow, and improved scheduling.
5. *Heightened sense of employee participation* in the organization and the product: employees accept the added responsibility of product quality because it is directly associated with them and their work cell.
6. *Increased equipment and machinery utilization* because of better scheduling and faster material flow.
7. *Reduced investment in machinery and equipment* because good utilization reduces the number of machines and the amount of equipment and tooling.

LO6: Define work cell and the requirements of a work cell

Requirements of Work Cells

The requirements of cellular production include:

- Identification of families of products, often through the use of group technology codes or equivalents
- A high level of training, flexibility, and empowerment of employees
- Being self-contained, with its own equipment and resources.
- Test (poka-yoke) at each station in the cell

Work cells have at least five advantages over assembly lines and process facilities: (1) because tasks are grouped, inspection is often immediate; (2) fewer workers are needed; (3) workers can reach more of the work area; (4) the work area can be more efficiently

Contemporary software such as this from e-factory (UGS Corp.) allows operations managers to quickly place and connect symbols for factory equipment for a full three-dimensional view of the layout. Such presentations provide added insight into the issues of facility layout in terms of process, material handling, efficiency, and safety.

Note in both (a) and (b) that U-shaped work cells can reduce material and employee movement. The U shape may also reduce space requirements, enhance communication, cut the number of workers, and make inspection easier.

(a)

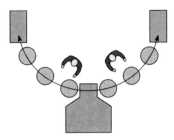

Current layout–workers in small closed areas.

Improved layout—cross-trained workers can assist each other. May be able to add a third worker as added output is needed.

(b)

Current layout—straight lines make it hard to balance tasks because work may not be divided evenly.

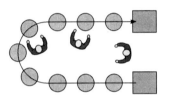

Improved layout—in U shape, workers have better access. Four cross-trained workers were reduced to three.

balanced; and (5) communication is enhanced. Work cells are sometimes organized in a U shape, as shown on the right side of Figure 9.10.

About half of U.S. plants with fewer than 100 employees use some sort of cellular system, whereas 75% of larger plants have adopted cellular production methods. Bayside Controls in Queens, New York, for example, has in the past decade increased sales from $300,000 per year to $11 million. Much of the gain was attributed to its move to cellular manufacturing. As noted in the *OM in Action* box, Canon has had similar success with work cells.

Staffing and Balancing Work Cells

Once the work cell has the appropriate equipment located in the proper sequence, the next task is to staff and balance the cell. Efficient production in a work cell requires appropriate staffing.

OM in Action ▶ Work Cells Increase Productivity at Canon

Look quickly at Canon's factory near Tokyo, and you might think you stepped back a few decades. Instead of the swiftly moving assembly lines you might expect to see in a high-cost, sophisticated digital camera and photo copier giant, you see workers gathered in small groups called *work cells*. Each cell is responsible for one product or a small family of products. The product focus encourages employees to exchange ideas about how to improve the assembly process. They also accept more responsibility for their work.

Canon's work cells have increased productivity by 30%. But how?

First, conveyor belts and their spare parts take up space, an expensive commodity in Japan. The shift to the cell system has freed 12 miles of conveyor-belt space at 54 plants and allowed Canon to close 29 parts warehouses, saving $280 million in real estate costs.

Employees are encouraged to work in ever-tighter cells, with prizes given to those who free up the most space.

Second, the cells enable Canon to change the product mix more quickly to meet market demands for innovative products—a big advantage as product life cycles become shorter and shorter.

Third, staff morale has increased because instead of performing a single task over and over, employees are trained to put together whole machines. Some of Canon's fastest workers are so admired that they have become TV celebrities.

A layout change that improves morale while increasing productivity is a win–win for Canon.

Sources: The Wall Street Journal (September 27, 2004): R11; and *Financial Times* (September 23, 2003): 14.

Takt time

Pace of production to meet customer demands.

This involves two steps. First, determine the **takt time**,[2] which is the pace (frequency) of production units necessary to meet customer orders:

$$\text{Takt time} = \text{Total work time available/Units required} \qquad (9\text{-}2)$$

Second, determine the number of operators required. This requires dividing the total operation time in the work cell by the takt time:

$$\text{Workers required} = \text{Total operation time required/Takt time} \qquad (9\text{-}3)$$

Example 2 considers these two steps when staffing work cells.

EXAMPLE 2 ▶

Staffing work cells

Stephen Hall's company in Dayton makes auto mirrors. The major customer is the Honda plant nearby. Honda expects 600 mirrors delivered daily, and the work cell producing the mirrors is scheduled for 8 hours. Hall wants to determine the takt time and the number of workers required.

APPROACH ▶ Hall uses Equations (9-2) and (9-3) and develops a work balance chart to help determine the time for each operation in the work cell, as well as total time.

SOLUTION ▶

Takt time = (8 hours × 60 minutes)/600 units = 480/600 = .8 minute = 48 seconds

Therefore, the customer requirement is one mirror every 48 seconds.

The *work balance chart* in Figure 9.11 shows that 5 operations are necessary, for a total operation time of 140 seconds:

Workers required = Total operation time required/Takt time
= (50 + 45 + 10 + 20 + 15)/48
= 140/48 = 2.92

▶ **FIGURE 9.11**
Work Balance Chart for Mirror Production

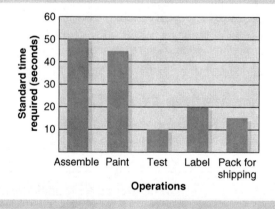

INSIGHT ▶ To produce one unit every 48 seconds will require 2.92 people. With three operators this work cell will be producing one unit each 46.67 seconds (140 seconds/3 employees = 46.67) and 617 units per day (480 minutes available × 60 seconds)/46.67 seconds for each unit = 617).

LEARNING EXERCISE ▶ If testing time is expanded to 20 seconds, what is the staffing requirement? [Answer: 3.125 employees.]

RELATED PROBLEM ▶ 9.10

A *work balance chart* (like the one in Example 2) is also valuable for evaluating the operation times in work cells. Some consideration must be given to determining the bottleneck operation. Bottleneck operations can constrain the flow through the cell. Imbalance in a work cell is seldom an issue if the operation is manual, as cell members by definition are part of a cross-trained team.

---

[2]*Takt* is German for "time," "measure," or "beat" and is used in this context as the rate at which completed units must be produced to satisfy customer demand.

Consequently, the inherent flexibility of work cells typically overcome modest imbalance issues within a cell. However, if the imbalance is a machine constraint, then an adjustment in machinery, process, or operations may be necessary. In such situations the use of traditional assembly-line-balancing analysis, the topic of our next section, may be helpful.

In many arrangements, without cells and without cross training, if one operation is halted for whatever reason (reading a drawing, getting a tool, machine maintenance, etc.), the entire flow stops. Multiple-operator cells are therefore preferred. However, we should note that the increasing capability of multitasking machines can complicate work cell design and staffing.

The success of work cells is not limited to manufacturing. Kansas City's Hallmark, which has over half the U.S. greeting card market and produces some 40,000 different cards, has modified the offices into a cellular design. In the past, its 700 creative professionals would take up to 2 years to develop a new card. Hallmark's decision to create work cells consisting of artists, writers, lithographers, merchandisers, and accountants, all located in the same area, has resulted in card preparation in a fraction of the time that the old layout required. Work cells have also yielded higher performance and better service for the American Red Cross blood donation process.[3]

Commercial software, such as ProPlanner and Factory Flow, is available to aid managers in their move to work cells. These programs typically require information that includes AutoCAD layout drawings; part routing data; and cost, times, and speeds of material handling systems.

The Focused Work Center and the Focused Factory

When a firm has *identified a family of similar products that have a large and stable demand*, it may organize a focused work center. A **focused work center** moves production from a general-purpose, process-oriented facility to a large work cell that remains part of the present plant. If the focused work center is in a separate facility, it is often called a **focused factory**. A fast-food restaurant is a focused factory—most are easily reconfigured for adjustments to product mix and volume. Burger King, for example, changes the number of personnel and task assignments rather than moving machines and equipment. In this manner, Burger King balances the assembly line to meet changing production demands. In effect, the "layout" changes numerous times each day.

Focused work center
A permanent or semi-permanent product-oriented arrangement of machines and personnel.

Focused factory
A facility designed to produce similar products or components.

The term *focused factories* may also refer to facilities that are focused in ways other than by product line or layout. For instance, facilities may be focused in regard to meeting quality, new product introduction, or flexibility requirements.

Focused facilities in both manufacturing and services appear to be better able to stay in tune with their customers, to produce quality products, and to operate at higher margins. This is true whether they are steel mills like CMC, Nucor, or Chaparral; restaurants like McDonald's and Burger King; or a hospital like Arnold Palmer.

Table 9.2 summarizes our discussion of work cells, focused work centers, and focused factories.

	Work Cell	Focused Work Center	Focused Factory
Description	A work cell is a temporary product-oriented arrangement of machines and personnel in what is ordinarily a process-oriented facility	A focused work center is a permanent product-oriented arrangement of machines and personnel in what is ordinarily a process-oriented facility	A focused factory is a permanent facility to produce a product or component in a product-oriented facility. Many of the focused factories currently being built were originally part of a process-oriented facility
Example	A job shop with machinery and personnel rearranged to produce 300 unique control panels	Pipe bracket manufacturing at a shipyard	A plant to produce window mechanisms or seat belts for automobiles

◀ **TABLE 9.2**
Work Cells, Focused Work Centers, and the Focused Factory

[3]Mark Pagell and Steven A. Melnyk, "Assessing the Impact of Alternative Manufacturing Layouts in a Service Setting," *Journal of Operations Management* 22 (2004): 413–429.

AUTHOR COMMENT
The traditional assembly line handles repetitive production.

REPETITIVE AND PRODUCT-ORIENTED LAYOUT

Product-oriented layouts are organized around products or families of similar high-volume, low-variety products. Repetitive production and continuous production, which are discussed in Chapter 7, use product layouts. The assumptions are that:

LO7: Define product-oriented layout

1. Volume is adequate for high equipment utilization
2. Product demand is stable enough to justify high investment in specialized equipment
3. Product is standardized or approaching a phase of its life cycle that justifies investment in specialized equipment
4. Supplies of raw materials and components are adequate and of uniform quality (adequately standardized) to ensure that they will work with the specialized equipment

Fabrication line

A machine-paced, product-oriented facility for building components.

Assembly line

An approach that puts fabricated parts together at a series of workstations; used in repetitive processes.

Two types of a product-oriented layout are fabrication and assembly lines. The **fabrication line** builds components, such as automobile tires or metal parts for a refrigerator, on a series of machines, while an **assembly line** puts the fabricated parts together at a series of workstations. However, both are repetitive processes, and in both cases, the line must be "balanced": That is, the time spent to perform work on one machine must equal or "balance" the time spent to perform work on the next machine in the fabrication line, just as the time spent at one workstation by one assembly-line employee must "balance" the time spent at the next workstation by the next employee. The same issues arise when designing the "disassembly lines" of slaughterhouses and automobile makers (see the *OM in Action* box "From Assembly Lines to Green Disassembly Lines").

Fabrication lines tend to be machine-paced and require mechanical and engineering changes to facilitate balancing. Assembly lines, on the other hand, tend to be paced by work tasks assigned to individuals or to workstations. Assembly lines, therefore, can be balanced by moving tasks from one individual to another. The central problem, then, in product-oriented layout planning is to balance the tasks at each workstation on the production line so that it is nearly the same while obtaining the desired amount of output.

Management's goal is to create a smooth, continuing flow along the assembly line with a minimum of idle time at each workstation. A well-balanced assembly line has the advantage of high

---

OM in Action ▶ From Assembly Lines to Green Disassembly Lines

Almost 100 years have passed since assembly lines were developed to *make* automobiles—and now we're developing disassembly lines to take them apart. Sprawling graveyards of rusting cars and trucks bear testimony to the need for automotive disassembly lines. But those graveyards are slowly beginning to shrink as we learn the art of automobile disassembly. New *disassembly* lines now take apart so many automobiles that recycling is the 16th-largest industry in the U.S. The motivation for this disassembly comes from many sources, including mandated industry recycling standards and a growing consumer interest in purchasing cars based on how "green" they are.

New car designs have traditionally been unfriendly to recyclers, with little thought given to disassembly. However, manufacturers now design in such a way that materials can be easily reused in the next generation of cars. The 2009 Mercedes S-class is 95% recyclable and already meets the 2015 EU standard. BMW has disassembly plants in Europe and Japan as well as U.S. salvage centers in New York, Los Angeles, and Orlando. A giant 200,000-square-foot facility in Baltimore (called CARS) can disassemble up to 30,000 vehicles per year. At CARS's initial "greening

station," special tools puncture tanks and drain fluids, and the battery and gas tank are removed. Then on a semi-automated track, which includes a giant steel vise that can flip a 7,500-pound car upside-down, wheels, doors, hood, and trunk are removed; next come the interior items; then plastic parts are removed and sorted for recycling; then glass and interior and trunk materials. Eventually the chassis is in a bale and sold as a commodity to minimills that use scrap steel.

Disassembly lines are not easy. Some components, like air bags, are hard to handle, dangerous, and take time to disassemble. Reusable parts are bar coded and entered into a database. Various color-coded plastics must be recycled differently to support being remelted and turned into new parts, such as intake manifolds. After the engines, transmissions, radios, and exhausts have been removed, the remaining metal parts of the disassembly line are easier: with shredders and magnets, baseball-sized chunks of metal are sorted. Assembly lines put cars together, and disassembly lines take them apart.

Sources: The Wall Street Journal (April 29, 2008): A1, A9; *The New York Times* (September 19, 2005): D5; and *Automotive Industry Trends* (March 2004).

personnel and facility utilization and equity among employees' work loads. Some union contracts require that work loads be nearly equal among those on the same assembly line. The term most often used to describe this process is **assembly-line balancing**. Indeed, the *objective of the product-oriented layout is to minimize imbalance in the fabrication or assembly line.*

The main advantages of product-oriented layout are:

1. The low variable cost per unit usually associated with high-volume, standardized products
2. Low material handling costs
3. Reduced work-in-process inventories
4. Easier training and supervision
5. Rapid throughput

The disadvantages of product layout are:

1. The high volume required because of the large investment needed to establish the process
2. Work stoppage at any one point ties up the whole operation
3. A lack of flexibility when handling a variety of products or production rates

Because the problems of fabrication lines and assembly lines are similar, we focus our discussion on assembly lines. On an assembly line, the product typically moves via automated means, such as a conveyor, through a series of workstations until completed. This is the way fast-food hamburgers are made (see Figure 9.12), automobiles and some planes (see the photo of the Boeing 737 on the next page) are assembled, television sets and ovens are produced. Product-oriented layouts use more automated and specially designed equipment than do process layouts.

Assembly-Line Balancing

Line balancing is usually undertaken to minimize imbalance between machines or personnel while meeting a required output from the line. To produce at a specified rate, management must know the tools, equipment, and work methods used. Then the time requirements for each assembly task (e.g., drilling a hole, tightening a nut, or spray-painting a part) must be determined. Management also needs to know the *precedence relationship* among the activities—that is, the sequence in which various tasks must be performed. Example 3 shows how to turn these task data into a precedence diagram.

Assembly-line balancing

Obtaining output at each workstation on a production line so delay is minimized.

VIDEO 9.2
Facility Layout at Wheeled Coach Ambulances

LO8: Explain how to balance production flow in a repetitive or product-oriented facility

Elapsed time	0:00	0:11	0:31	0:45		1:30
Task time (seconds)		11	20	14	0	45
Task	1. Order	2. Bun toasting	3. Assembly with condiments	4. Wrapping of patty with bun	5. Order picked up immediately to keep it fresh	6. Customer service (order and payment)

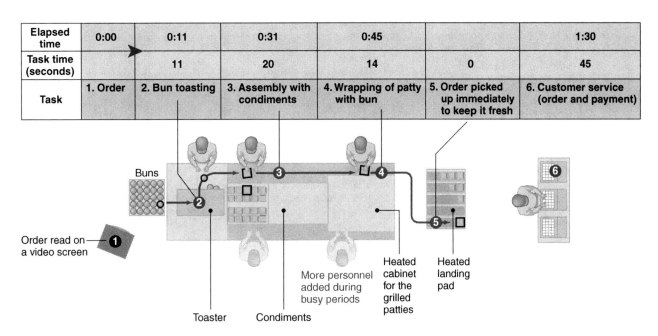

Buns

Order read on a video screen

More personnel added during busy periods

Heated cabinet for the grilled patties

Heated landing pad

Toaster   Condiments

▲ **FIGURE 9.12** **McDonald's Hamburger Assembly Line**

The Boeing 737, the world's most popular commercial airplane, is produced on a moving production line, traveling at 2 inches a minute through the final assembly process. The moving line, one of several lean manufacturing innovations at the Renton, Washington, facility, has enhanced quality, reduced flow time, slashed inventory levels, and cut space requirements. Final assembly is only 11 days—a time savings of 50%—and inventory is down more than 55%. Boeing has expanded the moving line concept to its 747 jumbo jet.

EXAMPLE 3 ▶

Developing a precedence diagram for an assembly line

Boeing wants to develop a precedence diagram for an electrostatic wing component that requires a total assembly time of 66 minutes.

APPROACH ▶ Staff gather tasks, assembly times, and sequence requirements for the component in Table 9.3.

▶ **TABLE 9.3**
Precedence Data for Wing Component

Task	Assembly Time (minutes)	Task Must Follow Task Listed Below	
A	10	—	This means that
B	11	A	tasks B and E
C	5	B	cannot be done
D	4	B	until task A has
E	12	A	been completed.
F	3	C, D	
G	7	F	
H	11	E	
I	3	G, H	
	Total time 66		

SOLUTION ▶ Figure 9.13 shows the precedence diagram.

▶ **FIGURE 9.13**
Precedence Diagram

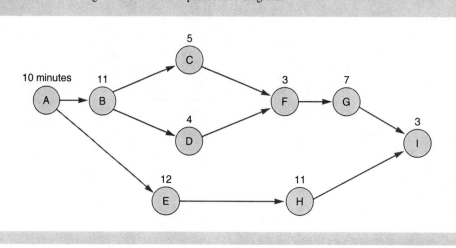

Once we have constructed a precedence chart summarizing the sequences and performance times, we turn to the job of grouping tasks into job stations so that we can meet the specified production rate. This process involves three steps:

1. Take the units required (demand or production rate) per day and divide it into the productive time available per day (in minutes or seconds). This operation gives us what is called the **cycle time**[4]—namely, the maximum time allowed at each workstation if the production rate is to be achieved:

$$\text{Cycle time} = \frac{\text{Production time available per day}}{\text{Units required per day}} \quad (9\text{-}4)$$

Cycle time
The maximum time that a product is allowed at each workstation.

2. Calculate the theoretical minimum number of workstations. This is the total task-duration time (the time it takes to make the product) divided by the cycle time. Fractions are rounded to the next higher whole number:

$$\text{Minimum number of workstations} = \frac{\sum_{i=1}^{n} \text{Time for task } i}{\text{Cycle time}} \quad (9\text{-}5)$$

where n is the number of assembly tasks.

3. Balance the line by assigning specific assembly tasks to each workstation. An efficient balance is one that will complete the required assembly, follow the specified sequence, and keep the idle time at each workstation to a minimum. A formal procedure for doing this is the following:
   a. Identify a master list of tasks.
   b. Eliminate those tasks that have been assigned.
   c. Eliminate those tasks whose precedence relationship has not been satisfied.
   d. Eliminate those tasks for which inadequate time is available at the workstation.
   e. Use one of the line-balancing "heuristics" described in Table 9.4. The five choices are (1) longest task time, (2) most following tasks, (3) ranked positional weight, (4) shortest

1. *Longest task (operation) time*	From the available tasks, choose the task with the largest (longest) time.
2. *Most following tasks*	From the available tasks, choose the task with the largest number of following tasks.
3. *Ranked positional weight*	From the available tasks, choose the task for which the sum of the times for each following task is longest. (In Example 4 we see that the ranked positional weight of task C = 5(C) + 3(F) + 7(G) + 3(I) = 18, whereas the ranked positional weight of task D = 4(D) + 3(F) + 7(G) + 3(I) =17; therefore, C would be chosen first, using this heuristic.)
4. *Shortest task (operations) time*	From the available tasks, choose the task with the shortest task time.
5. *Least number of following tasks*	From the available tasks, choose the task with the least number of subsequent tasks.

◀ **TABLE 9.4**
Layout Heuristics That May Be Used to Assign Tasks to Workstations in Assembly-Line Balancing

[4]*Cycle time* is the actual time to accomplish a task or process step. Several process steps may be necessary to complete the product. *Takt time*, discussed earlier, is determined by the customer and is the speed at which completed units must be produced to satisfy customer demand.

Heuristic

Problem solving using procedures and rules rather than mathematical optimization.

task time, and (5) least number of following tasks. You may wish to test several of these **heuristics** to see which generates the "best" solution—that is, the smallest number of workstations and highest efficiency. Remember, however, that although heuristics provide solutions, they do not guarantee an optimal solution.

Example 4 illustrates a simple line-balancing procedure.

EXAMPLE 4 ▶

Balancing the assembly line

On the basis of the precedence diagram and activity times given in Example 3, Boeing determines that there are 480 productive minutes of work available per day. Furthermore, the production schedule requires that 40 units of the wing component be completed as output from the assembly line each day. It now wants to group the tasks into workstations.

APPROACH ▶ Following the three steps above, we compute the cycle time using Equation (9-4) and minimum number of workstations using Equation (9-5), and we assign tasks to workstations—in this case using the *most following tasks* heuristic.

SOLUTION ▶

$$\text{Cycle time (in minutes)} = \frac{480 \text{ minutes}}{40 \text{ units}}$$
$$= 12 \text{ minutes/unit}$$

$$\text{Minimum number of workstations} = \frac{\text{Total task time}}{\text{Cycle time}} = \frac{66}{12}$$
$$= 5.5 \text{ or } 6 \text{ stations}$$

Figure 9.14 shows one solution that does not violate the sequence requirements and that groups tasks into six one-person stations. To obtain this solution, activities with the most following tasks were moved into workstations to use as much of the available cycle time of 12 minutes as possible. The first workstation consumes 10 minutes and has an idle time of 2 minutes.

▶ **FIGURE 9.14**
A Six-Station Solution to the Line-Balancing Problem

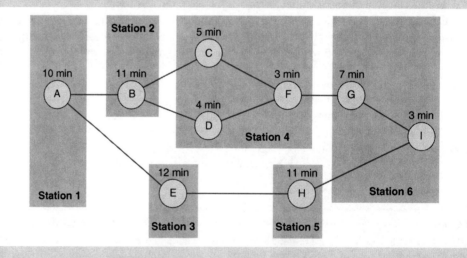

AUTHOR COMMENT
Tasks C, D, and F can be grouped together in one workstation, provided that the physical facilities and skill levels meet the work requirements.

INSIGHT ▶ This is a reasonably well-balanced assembly line. The second workstation uses 11 minutes, and the third consumes the full 12 minutes. The fourth workstation groups three small tasks and balances perfectly at 12 minutes. The fifth has 1 minute of idle time, and the sixth (consisting of tasks G and I) has 2 minutes of idle time per cycle. Total idle time for this solution is 6 minutes per cycle.

LEARNING EXERCISE ▶ If task I required 6 minutes (instead of 3 minutes), how would this change the solution? [Answer: The cycle time would not change, and the *theoretical* minimum number of workstations would still be 6 (rounded up from 5.75), but it would take 7 stations to balance the line.]

RELATED PROBLEMS ▶ 9.11, 9.12, 9.13, 9.14, 9.15, 9.16, 9.17, 9.18, 9.19, 9.20, 9.21, 9.22, 9.23

We can compute the efficiency of a line balance by dividing the total task time by the product of the number of workstations required times the assigned (actual) cycle time of the longest workstation:

$$\text{Efficiency} = \frac{\Sigma \text{ Task times}}{(\text{Actual number of workstations}) \times (\text{Largest assigned cycle time})} \quad \text{(9-6)}$$

Operations managers compare different levels of efficiency for various numbers of workstations. In this way, a firm can determine the sensitivity of the line to changes in the production rate and workstation assignments.

Determining line efficiency

Boeing needs to calculate the balance efficiency for Example 4.

APPROACH ▶ Equation (9-6) is applied.

SOLUTION ▶ $\text{Efficiency} = \dfrac{66 \text{ minutes}}{(6 \text{ stations}) \times (12 \text{ minutes})} = \dfrac{66}{72} = 91.7\%$

Note that opening a seventh workstation, for whatever reason, would decrease the efficiency of the balance to 78.6% (assuming that at least one of the workstations still required 12 minutes):

$$\text{Efficiency} = \frac{66 \text{ minutes}}{(7 \text{ stations}) \times (12 \text{ minutes})} = 78.6\%$$

INSIGHT ▶ Increasing efficiency may require that some tasks be divided into smaller elements and reassigned to other tasks. This facilitates a better balance between workstations and means higher efficiency.

LEARNING EXERCISE ▶ What is the efficiency if an eighth workstation is opened? [Answer: Efficiency = 68.75%.]

RELATED PROBLEMS ▶ 9.12f, 9.13c, 9.14f, 9.16c, 9.17b, 9.18b, 9.19e,g

---

Large-scale line-balancing problems, like large process-layout problems, are often solved by computers. Several computer programs are available to handle the assignment of workstations on assembly lines with 100 (or more) individual work activities. Two computer routines, COM-SOAL (Computer Method for Sequencing Operations for Assembly Lines) and ASYBL (General Electric's Assembly Line Configuration program), are widely used in larger problems to evaluate the thousands, or even millions, of possible workstation combinations much more efficiently than could ever be done by hand.

In the case of slaughtering operations, the assembly line is actually a disassembly line. The line-balancing procedures described in this chapter are the same as for an assembly line. The chicken-processing plant shown here must balance the work of several hundred employees. The total labor content in each of the chickens processed is a few minutes.

CHAPTER SUMMARY

Layouts make a substantial difference in operating efficiency. The seven layout situations discussed in this chapter are (1) office, (2) retail, (3) warehouse, (4) fixed position, (5) process oriented, (6) work cells, and (7) product oriented. A variety of techniques have been developed to solve these layout problems. Office layouts often seek to maximize information flows, retail firms focus on product exposure, and warehouses attempt to optimize the trade-off between storage space and material handling cost.

The fixed-position layout problem attempts to minimize material handling costs within the constraint of limited space at the site. Process layouts minimize travel distances times the number of trips. Product layouts focus on reducing waste and the imbalance in an assembly line. Work cells are the result of identifying a family of products that justify a special configuration of machinery and equipment that reduces material travel and adjusts imbalances with cross-trained personnel.

Often, the issues in a layout problem are so wide-ranging that finding an optimal solution is not possible. For this reason, layout decisions, although the subject of substantial research effort, remain something of an art.

Key Terms

Office layout	Customizing	Focused factory
Retail layout	Fixed-position layout	Fabrication line
Slotting fees	Process-oriented layout	Assembly line
Servicescape	Job lots	Assembly-line balancing
Warehouse layout	Work cell	Cycle time
Cross-docking	Takt time	Heuristic
Random stocking	Focused work center	

Ethical Dilemma

Although buried by mass customization and a proliferation of new products of numerous sizes and variations, grocery chains continue to seek to maximize payoff from their layout. Their layout includes a marketable commodity—shelf space—and they charge for it. This charge is known as a *slotting fee.** Recent estimates are that food manufacturers now spend some 13% of sales on trade promotions, which is paid to grocers to get them to promote and discount the manufacturer's products. A portion of these fees is for slotting; but slotting fees drive up the manufacturer's cost. They also put the small company with a new product at a disadvantage, because small companies with limited resources are squeezed out of the market place. Slotting fees may also mean that customers may no longer be able to find the special local brand. How ethical are slotting fees?

Discussion Questions

1. What are the seven layout strategies presented in this chapter?
2. What are the three factors that complicate a fixed-position layout?
3. What are the advantages and disadvantages of process layout?
4. How would an analyst obtain data and determine the number of trips in:
   (a) a hospital?
   (b) a machine shop?
   (c) an auto-repair shop?
5. What are the advantages and disadvantages of product layout?
6. What are the four assumptions (or preconditions) of establishing layout for high-volume, low-variety products?
7. What are the three forms of work cells discussed in the textbook?
8. What are the advantages and disadvantages of work cells?
9. What are the requirements for a focused work center or focused factory to be appropriate?
10. What are the two major trends influencing office layout?

*For an interesting discussion of slotting fees, see J. G. Kaikati and A. M. Kaikati, "Slotting and Promotional Allowances," *Supply Chain Management* 11, no. 2 (2006): 140–147; or J. L. Stanton and K. C. Herbst, "Slotting Allowances," *International Journal of Retail & Distribution Management* 34, no. 2/3 (2006): 187–197.

11. What layout variables would you consider particularly important in an office layout where computer programs are written?

12. What layout innovations have you noticed recently in retail establishments?

13. What are the variables that a manager can manipulate in a retail layout?

14. Visit a local supermarket and sketch its layout. What are your observations regarding departments and their locations?

15. What is random stocking?

16. What information is necessary for random stocking to work?

17. Explain the concept of cross-docking.

18. What is a heuristic? Name several that can be used in assembly-line balancing.

Using Software to Solve Layout Problems

In addition to the many commercial software packages available for addressing layout problems, Excel OM and POM for Windows, both of which accompany this text, contain modules for the process problem and the assembly-line-balancing problem.

✕ Using Excel OM

Excel OM can assist in evaluating a series of department work assignments like the one we saw for the Walters Company in Example 1. The layout module can generate an optimal solution by enumeration or by computing the "total movement" cost for each layout you wish to examine. As such, it provides a speedy calculator for each flow–distance pairing.

Program 9.1 illustrates our inputs in the top two tables. We first enter department flows, then provide distances between work areas. Entering area assignments on a trial-and-error basis in the upper left of the top table generates movement computations at the bottom of the screen. Total movement is recalculated each time we try a new area assignment. It turns out that the assignment shown is optimal at 430 feet of movement.

▼ **PROGRAM 9.1**   Using Excel OM's Process Layout Module to Solve the Walters Company Problem in Example 1

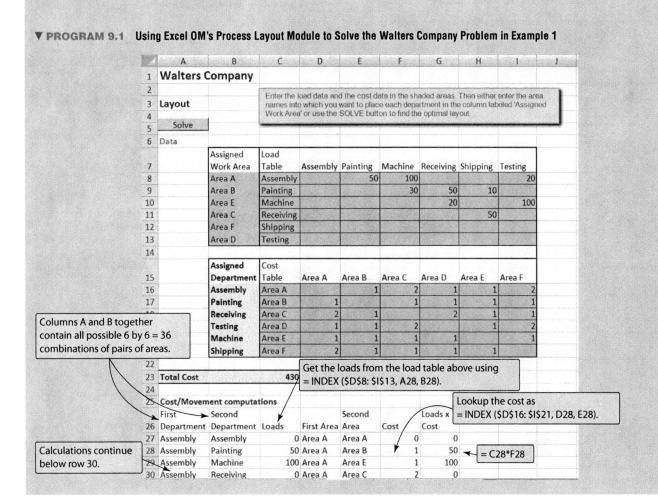

P Using POM for Windows

The POM for Windows facility layout module can be used to place up to 10 departments in 10 rooms to minimize the total distance traveled as a function of the distances between the rooms and the flow between departments. The program exchanges departments until no exchange will reduce the total amount of movement, meaning an optimal solution has been reached.

The POM for Windows and Excel OM modules for line balancing can handle a line with up to 99 tasks, each with up to 6 immediate predecessors. In this program, cycle time can be entered either (1) *given*, if known, or (2) the *demand* rate can be entered with time available as shown. All five "heuristic rules" are used: (1) longest operation (task) time, (2) most following tasks, (3) ranked positional weight, (4) shortest operation (task) time, and (5) least number of following tasks. No one rule can guarantee an optimal solution, but POM for Windows displays the number of stations needed for each rule.

Appendix IV discusses further details regarding POM for Windows.

Solved Problems   Virtual Office Hours help is available at www.pearsonglobaleditions.com/myomlab

▼ SOLVED PROBLEM 9.1

Aero Maintenance is a small aircraft engine maintenance facility located in Wichita, Kansas. Its new administrator, Ann Daniel, decides to improve material flow in the facility, using the process-layout method she studied at Wichita State University. The current layout of Aero Maintenance's eight departments is shown in Figure 9.15.

The only physical restriction perceived by Daniel is the need to keep the entrance in its current location. All other departments can be moved to a different work area (each 10 feet square) if layout analysis indicates a move would be beneficial.

First, Daniel analyzes records to determine the number of material movements among departments in an average month. These data are shown in Figure 9.16. Her objective, Daniel decides, is to lay out the departments so as to minimize the total movement (distance traveled) of material in the facility. She writes her objective as:

$$\text{Minimize material movement} = \sum_{i=1}^{8} \sum_{j=1}^{8} X_{ij} C_{ij}$$

where X_{ij} = number of material movements per month (loads or trips) moving from department i to department j

C_{ij} = distance in feet between departments i and j (which, in this case, is the equivalent of cost per load to move between departments)

Note that this is only a slight modification of the cost-objective equation shown earlier in the chapter.

Current Aero Maintenance Layout

Area A	Area B	Area C	Area D	
Entrance (1)	Receiving (2)	Parts (3)	Metallurgy (4)	10'
Breakdown (5)	Assembly (6)	Inspection (7)	Test (8)	10'
Area E	Area F	Area G	Area H	

← 40' →

▲ **FIGURE 9.15**   **Aero Maintenance Layout**

▶ **FIGURE 9.16**
Number of Material Movements (Loads) between Departments in One Month

	Entrance (1)	Receiving (2)	Parts (3)	Metallurgy (4)	Breakdown (5)	Assembly (6)	Inspection (7)	Test (8)	Department
		100	100	0	0	0	0	0	Entrance (1)
			0	50	20	0	0	0	Receiving (2)
				30	30	0	0	0	Parts (3)
					20	0	0	20	Metallurgy (4)
						20	0	10	Breakdown (5)
							30	0	Assembly (6)
								0	Inspection (7)
									Test (8)

Daniel assumes that adjacent departments, such as entrance (now in work area A) and receiving (now in work area B), have a walking distance of 10 feet. Diagonal departments are also considered adjacent and assigned a distance of 10 feet. Nonadjacent departments, such as the entrance and parts (now in area C) or the entrance and inspection (area G) are 20 feet apart, and nonadjacent rooms, such as entrance and metallurgy (area D), are 30 feet apart. (Hence, 10 feet is considered 10 units of cost, 20 feet is 20 units of cost, and 30 feet is 30 units of cost.)

Given the above information, redesign Aero Maintenance's layout to improve its material flow efficiency.

▼ SOLUTION

First, establish Aero Maintenance's current layout, as shown in Figure 9.17. Then, by analyzing the current layout, compute material movement:

$$
\begin{aligned}
\text{Total movement} = \quad & \underset{\text{1 to 2}}{(100 \times 10')} + \underset{\text{1 to 3}}{(100 \times 20')} + \underset{\text{2 to 4}}{(50 \times 20')} + \underset{\text{2 to 5}}{(20 \times 10')} \\
+ \quad & \underset{\text{3 to 4}}{(30 \times 10')} + \underset{\text{3 to 5}}{(30 \times 20')} + \underset{\text{4 to 5}}{(20 \times 30')} + \underset{\text{4 to 8}}{(20 \times 10')} \\
+ \quad & \underset{\text{5 to 6}}{(20 \times 10')} + \underset{\text{5 to 8}}{(10 \times 30')} + \underset{\text{6 to 7}}{(30 \times 10')} \\
= \quad & 1{,}000 + 2{,}000 + 1{,}000 + 200 + 300 + 600 + 600 \\
& + 200 + 200 + 300 + 300 \\
= \quad & 6{,}700 \text{ feet}
\end{aligned}
$$

▶ **FIGURE 9.17**
Current Material Flow

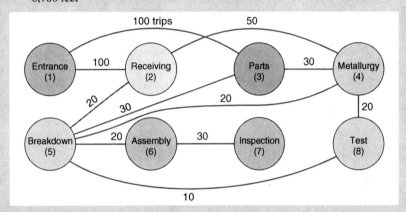

Propose a new layout that will reduce the current figure of 6,700 feet. Two useful changes, for example, are to switch departments 3 and 5 and to interchange departments 4 and 6. This change would result in the schematic shown in Figure 9.18:

$$
\begin{aligned}
\text{Total movement} = \quad & \underset{\text{1 to 2}}{(100 \times 10')} + \underset{\text{1 to 3}}{(100 \times 10')} + \underset{\text{2 to 4}}{(50 \times 10')} + \underset{\text{2 to 5}}{(20 \times 10')} \\
+ \quad & \underset{\text{3 to 4}}{(30 \times 10')} + \underset{\text{3 to 5}}{(30 \times 20')} + \underset{\text{4 to 5}}{(20 \times 10')} + \underset{\text{4 to 8}}{(20 \times 20')} \\
+ \quad & \underset{\text{5 to 6}}{(20 \times 10')} + \underset{\text{5 to 8}}{(10 \times 10')} + \underset{\text{6 to 7}}{(30 \times 10')} \\
= \quad & 1{,}000 + 1{,}000 + 500 + 200 + 300 + 600 + 200 \\
& + 400 + 200 + 100 + 300 \\
= \quad & 4{,}800 \text{ feet}
\end{aligned}
$$

Do you see any room for further improvement?

▶ **FIGURE 9.18**
Improved Layout

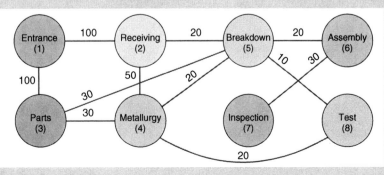

▼ SOLVED PROBLEM 9.2

The assembly line whose activities are shown in Figure 9.19 has an 8-minute cycle time. Draw the precedence graph and find the minimum possible number of one-person workstations. Then arrange the work activities into workstations so as to balance the line. What is the efficiency of your line balance?

Task	Performance Time (minutes)	Task Must Follow This Task
A	5	—
B	3	A
C	4	B
D	3	B
E	6	C
F	1	C
G	4	D, E, F
H	$\underline{2}$	G
	28	

▶ **FIGURE 9.19**
Four-Station Solution to the Line-Balancing Problem

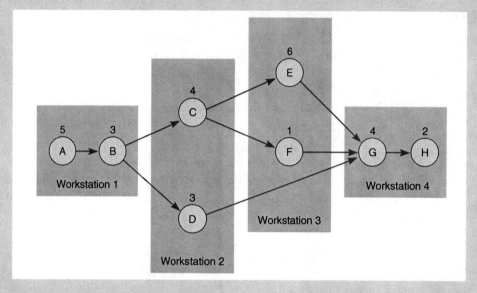

▼ SOLUTION

The theoretical minimum number of workstations is:

$$\frac{\Sigma t_i}{\text{Cycle time}} = \frac{28 \text{ minutes}}{8 \text{ minutes}} = 3.5, \text{ or 4 stations}$$

The precedence graph and one good layout are shown in Figure 9.19.

$$\text{Efficiency} = \frac{\text{Total task time}}{(\text{Number of workstations}) \times (\text{Largest cycle time})} = \frac{28}{(4)(8)} = 87.5\%$$

Problems*

•• **9.1** Michael Plumb's job shop has four work areas, A, B, C, and D. Distances in feet between centers of the work areas are:

	A	B	C	D
A	—	4	9	7
B	—	—	6	8
C	—	—	—	10
D	—	—	—	—

*Note: **PX** means the problem may be solved with POM for Windows and/or Excel OM.

Workpieces moved, in 100s of workpieces per week, between pairs of work areas, are:

	A	B	C	D
A	—	8	7	4
B	—	—	3	2
C	—	—	—	6
D	—	—	—	—

It costs Michael $1 to move 1 work piece 1 foot. What is the weekly total material handling cost of the layout? **PX**

•• **9.2** A Missouri job shop has four departments—machining (M), dipping in a chemical bath (D), finishing (F), and plating (P)—

assigned to four work areas. The operations manager, Mary Marrs, has gathered the following data for this job shop as it is currently laid out (Plan A).

100s of Workpieces Moved Between Work Areas Each Year
Plan A

	M	D	F	P
M	—	6	18	2
D	—	—	4	2
F	—	—	—	18
P	—	—	—	—

Distances Between Work Areas (Departments) in Feet

	M	D	F	P
M	—	20	12	8
D	—	—	6	10
F	—	—	—	4
P	—	—	—	—

It costs $0.50 to move 1 workpiece 1 foot in the job shop. Marrs's goal is to find a layout that has the lowest material handling cost.

a) Determine cost of the current layout, Plan A, from the data above.

b) One alternative is to switch those departments with the high loads, namely, finishing (F) and plating (P), which alters the distance between them and machining (M) and dipping (D), as follows:

Distances Between Work Areas (Departments) in Feet
Plan B

	M	D	F	P
M	—	20	8	12
D	—	—	10	6
F	—	—	—	4
P	—	—	—	—

What is the cost of *this* layout?

c) Marrs now wants you to evaluate Plan C, which also switches milling (M) and drilling (D), below.

Distance Between Work Areas (Departments) in Feet
Plan C

	M	D	F	P
M	—	20	10	6
D	—	—	8	12
F	—	—	—	4
P	—	—	—	—

What is the cost of *this* layout?

d) Which layout is best from a cost perspective? **P✗**

• **9.3** Three departments—milling (M), drilling (D), and sawing (S)—are assigned to three work areas in Samuel Smith's machine shop in Baltimore. The number of work pieces moved per day and the distances between the centers of the work areas, in feet, are shown in the next column.

Pieces Moved Between Work Areas Each Day

	M	D	S
M	—	23	32
D	—	—	20
S	—	—	—

Distances Between Centers of Work Areas (Departments) in Feet

	M	D	S
M	—	10	5
D	—	—	8
S	—	—	—

It costs $2 to move 1 workpiece 1 foot.
What is the cost? **P✗**

•• **9.4** Roy Creasey Enterprises, a machine shop, is planning to move to a new, larger location. The new building will be 60 feet long by 40 feet wide. Creasey envisions the building as having six distinct production areas, roughly equal in size. He feels strongly about safety and intends to have marked pathways throughout the building to facilitate the movement of people and materials. See the following building schematic.

Building Schematic (with work areas 1–6)

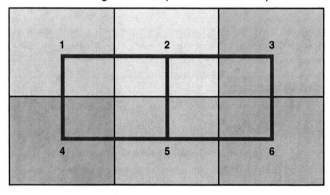

His foreman has completed a month-long study of the number of loads of material that have moved from one process to another in the current building. This information is contained in the following flow matrix.

Flow Matrix between Production Processes

To From	Materials	Welding	Drills	Lathes	Grinders	Benders
Materials	0	100	50	0	0	50
Welding	25	0	0	50	0	0
Drills	25	0	0	0	50	0
Lathes	0	25	0	0	20	0
Grinders	50	0	100	0	0	0
Benders	10	0	20	0	0	0

Finally, Creasey has developed the following matrix to indicate distances between the work areas shown in the building schematic.

Distance between Work Areas						
	1	2	3	4	5	6
1		20	40	20	40	60
2			20	40	20	40
3				60	40	20
4					20	40
5						20
6						

What is the appropriate layout of the new building? **Px**

•• **9.5** Registration at Southern University has always been a time of emotion, commotion, and lines. Students must move among four stations to complete the trying semiannual process. Last semester's registration, held in the fieldhouse, is described in Figure 9.20. You can see, for example, that 450 students moved from the paperwork station (A) to advising (B), and 550 went directly from A to picking up their class cards (C). Graduate students, who for the most part had preregistered, proceeded directly from A to the station where registration is verified and payment collected (D). The layout used last semester is also shown in Figure 9.20. The registrar is preparing to set up this semester's stations and is anticipating similar numbers.

Interstation Activity Mix

	Pick up paperwork and forms	Advising station	Pick up class cards	Verification of status and payment
	(A)	(B)	(C)	(D)
Paperwork/forms (A)	—	450	550	50
Advising (B)	350	—	200	0
Class cards (C)	0	0	—	750
Verification/payment (D)	0	0	0	—

Existing Layout

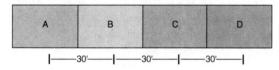

▲ **FIGURE 9.20   Registration Flow of Students**

a) What is the "load × distance," or "movement cost," of the layout shown?

b) Provide an improved layout and compute its movement cost. **Px**

••• **9.6** You have just been hired as the director of operations for Reid Chocolates, a purveyor of exceptionally fine candies. Reid Chocolates has two kitchen layouts under consideration for its recipe making and testing department. The strategy is to provide the best kitchen layout possible so that food scientists can devote their time and energy to product improvement, not wasted effort in the kitchen. You have been asked to evaluate these two kitchen layouts and to prepare a recommendation for your boss, Mr. Reid, so that he can proceed to place the contract for building the kitchens. (See Figure 9.21(a), and Figure 9.21(b).) **Px**

▼ **FIGURE 9.21(a)   Layout Options**

Number of trips between work centers:

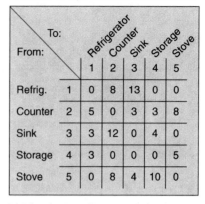

▼ **FIGURE 9.21(b)**

Kitchen layout #1

Walking distance in feet

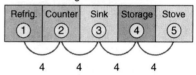

Kitchen layout #2

Walking distance in feet

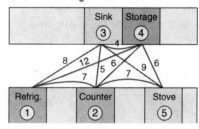

•• **9.7** Reid Chocolates (see Problem 9.6) is considering a third layout, as shown below. Evaluate its effectiveness in trip-distance feet. **Px**

Kitchen layout #3

Walking distance in feet

•• **9.8** Reid Chocolates (see Problems 9.6 and 9.7) has yet two more layouts to consider.

a) Layout 4 is shown on the next page. What is the total trip distance?

b) Layout 5, which also follows, has what total trip distance?

Kitchen layout #4
Walking distance in feet

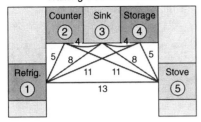

Kitchen layout #5
Walking distance in feet

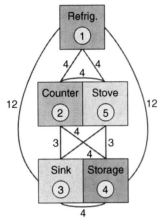

Operation	Standard time (min)
Shear	1.1
Bend	1.1
Weld	1.7
Clean	3.1
Paint	1.0

•• **9.11** Stanford Rosenberg Electronics wants to establish an assembly line for producing a new product, the Personal Little Assistant (PLA). The tasks, task times, and immediate predecessors for the tasks are as follows:

Task	Time (sec)	Immediate Predecessors
A	12	—
B	15	A
C	8	A
D	5	B, C
E	20	D

Rosenberg's goal is to produce 180 PLAs per hour.
a) What is the cycle time?
b) What is the theoretical minimum for the number of workstations that Rosenberg can achieve in this assembly line?
c) Can the theoretical minimum actually be reached when workstations are assigned? **Px**

••• **9.12** South Carolina Furniture, Inc., produces all types of office furniture. The "Executive Secretary" is a chair that has been designed using ergonomics to provide comfort during long work hours. The chair sells for $130. There are 480 minutes available during the day, and the average daily demand has been 50 chairs. There are eight tasks:

Task	Performance Time (min)	Task Must Follow Task Listed Below
A	4	—
B	7	—
C	6	A, B
D	5	C
E	6	D
F	7	E
G	8	E
H	6	F, G

•• **9.9** Six processes are to be laid out in six areas along a long corridor at Linda Babat Accounting Services. The distance between adjacent work centers is 40 feet. The number of trips between work centers is given in the following table:

From	To					
	A	**B**	**C**	**D**	**E**	**F**
A		18	25	73	12	54
B			96	23	31	45
C				41	22	20
D					19	57
E						48
F						

a) Assign the processes to the work areas in a way that minimizes the total flow, using a method that places processes with highest flow adjacent to each other.
b) What assignment minimizes the total traffic flow? **Px**

•• **9.10** After an extensive product analysis using group technology, Bob Buerlein has identified a product he believes should be pulled out of his process facility and handled in a work cell. Bob has identified the following operations as necessary for the work cell. The customer expects delivery of 250 units per day, and the work day is 420 minutes.
a) What is the takt time?
b) How many employees should be cross-trained for the cell?
c) Which operations may warrant special consideration?

a) Draw a precedence diagram of this operation.
b) What is the cycle time for this operation?
c) What is the *theoretical* minimum number of workstations?
d) Assign tasks to workstations.
e) What is the idle time per cycle?
f) How much total idle time is present each day?
g) What is the overall efficiency of the assembly line? **Px**

•• **9.13** Rita Gibson Appliances wants to establish an assembly line to manufacture its new product, the Mini-Me Microwave Oven. The goal is to produce five Mini-Me Microwave Ovens per hour. The tasks, task times, and immediate predecessors for producing one Mini-Me Microwave Oven are as follows:

Task	Time (min)	Immediate Predecessors
A	10	—
B	12	A
C	8	A, B
D	6	B, C
E	6	C
F	6	D, E

a) What is the *theoretical* minimum for the smallest number of workstations that Gibson can achieve in this assembly line?
b) Graph the assembly line and assign workers to workstations. Can you assign them with the theoretical minimum?
c) What is the efficiency of *your* assignment? **Px**

•• **9.14** The Temple Toy Company has decided to manufacture a new toy tractor, the production of which is broken into six steps. The demand for the tractor is 4,800 units per 40-hour workweek:

Task	Performance Time (sec)	Predecessors
A	20	None
B	30	A
C	15	A
D	15	A
E	10	B, C
F	30	D, E

a) Draw a precedence diagram of this operation.
b) Given the demand, what is the cycle time for this operation?
c) What is the *theoretical* minimum number of workstations?
d) Assign tasks to workstations.
e) How much total idle time is present each cycle?
f) What is the overall efficiency of the assembly line with five stations; and with six stations? **Px**

•• **9.15** The following table details the tasks required for Dallas-based T. Liscio Industries to manufacture a fully portable industrial vacuum cleaner. The times in the table are in minutes. Demand forecasts indicate a need to operate with a cycle time of 10 minutes.

Activity	Activity Description	Immediate Predecessors	Time
A	Attach wheels to tub	—	5
B	Attach motor to lid	—	1.5
C	Attach battery pack	B	3
D	Attach safety cutoff	C	4
E	Attach filters	B	3
F	Attach lid to tub	A, E	2
G	Assemble attachments	—	3
H	Function test	D, F, G	3.5
I	Final inspection	H	2
J	Packing	I	2

a) Draw the appropriate precedence diagram for this production line.
b) Assign tasks to workstations and determine how much idle time is present each cycle?
c) Discuss how this balance could be improved to 100%.
d) What is the *theoretical* minimum number of workstations? **Px**

•• **9.16** Tailwind, Inc., produces high-quality but expensive training shoes for runners. The Tailwind shoe, which sells for $210, contains both gas- and liquid-filled compartments to provide more

stability and better protection against knee, foot, and back injuries. Manufacturing the shoes requires 10 separate tasks. There are 400 minutes available for manufacturing the shoes in the plant each day. Daily demand is 60. The information for the tasks is as follows:

Task	Performance Time (min)	Task Must Follow Task Listed Below
A	1	—
B	3	A
C	2	B
D	4	B
E	1	C, D
F	3	A
G	2	F
H	5	G
I	1	E, H
J	3	I

a) Draw the precedence diagram.
b) Assign tasks to the minimum feasible number of workstations according to the "ranked positioned weight" decision rule.
c) What is the efficiency of the process?
d) What is the idle time per cycle? **Px**

•• **9.17** The Mach 10 is a one-person sailboat manufactured by Creative Leisure. The final assembly plant is in Cupertino, California. The assembly area is available for production of the Mach 10 for 200 minutes per day. (The rest of the time it is busy making other products.) The daily demand is 60 boats. Given the following information,
a) Draw the precedence diagram and assign tasks using five workstations.
b) What is the efficiency of the assembly line, using your answer to (a)?
c) What is the *theoretical* minimum number of workstations?
d) What is the idle time per boat produced? **Px**

Task	Performance Time (min)	Task Must Follow Task Listed Below
A	1	—
B	1	A
C	2	A
D	1	C
E	3	C
F	1	C
G	1	D, E, F
H	2	B
I	1	G, H

•• **9.18** Because of the expected high demand for Mach 10, Creative Leisure has decided to increase manufacturing time available to produce the Mach 10 (see Problem 9.17).
a) If demand remained the same but 300 minutes were available each day on the assembly line, how many workstations would be needed?
b) What would be the efficiency of the new system?
c) What would be the impact on the system if 400 minutes were available? **Px**

••• **9.19** Dr. Lori Baker, operations manager at Nesa Electronics, prides herself on excellent assembly-line balancing. She has been told that the firm needs to complete 96 instruments per 24-hour day. The assembly-line activities are:

Task	Time (min)	Predecessors
A	3	—
B	6	—
C	7	A
D	5	A, B
E	2	B
F	4	C
G	5	F
H	7	D, E
I	1	H
J	6	E
K	$\underline{\quad 4 \quad}$	G, I, J
	50	

a) Draw the precedence diagram.

b) If the daily (24-hour) production rate is 96 units, what is the highest allowable cycle time?

c) If the cycle time after allowances is given as 10 minutes, what is the daily (24-hour) production rate?

d) With a 10-minute cycle time, what is the theoretical minimum number of stations with which the line can be balanced?

e) With a 10-minute cycle time and six workstations, what is the efficiency?

f) What is the total idle time per cycle with a 10-minute cycle time and six workstations?

g) What is the best work station assignment you can make without exceeding a 10-minute cycle time and what is its efficiency? **Px**

•• **9.20** Suppose production requirements in Solved Problem 9.2 (see page 402) increase and require a reduction in cycle time from 8 minutes to 7 minutes. Balance the line once again, using the new cycle time. Note that it is not possible to combine task times so as to group tasks into the minimum number of workstations. This condition occurs in actual balancing problems fairly often. **Px**

•• **9.21** The preinduction physical examination given by the U.S. Army involves the following seven activities:

Activity	Average Time (min)
Medical history	10
Blood tests	8
Eye examination	5
Measurements (i.e., weight, height, blood pressure)	7
Medical examination	16
Psychological interview	12
Exit medical evaluation	10

These activities can be performed in any order, with two exceptions: Medical history must be taken first, and Exit medical evaluation is last. At present, there are three paramedics and two physicians on duty during each shift. Only physicians can perform exit evaluations and conduct psychological interviews. Other activities can be carried out by either physicians or paramedics.

a) Develop a layout and balance the line.

b) How many people can be processed per hour?

c) Which activity accounts for the current bottleneck?

d) What is the total idle time per cycle?

e) If one more physician and one more paramedic can be placed on duty, how would you redraw the layout? What is the new throughput?

••• **9.22** Frank Pianki's company wants to establish an assembly line to manufacture its new product, the iScan phone. Frank's goal is to produce 60 iScans per hour. Tasks, task times, and immediate predecessors are as follows:

Task	Time (sec)	Immediate Predecessors	Task	Time (sec)	Immediate Predecessors
A	40	—	F	25	C
B	30	A	G	15	C
C	50	A	H	20	D, E
D	40	B	I	18	F, G
E	6	B	J	30	H, I

a) What is the theoretical minimum for the number of workstations that Frank can achieve in this assembly line?

b) Use the *most following tasks* heuristic to balance an assembly line for the iScan phone.

c) How many workstations are in your answer to (b)?

d) What is the efficiency of your answer to (b)? **Px**

•••• **9.23** As the Cottrell Bicycle Co. of St. Louis completes plans for its new assembly line, it identifies 25 different tasks in the production process. VP of Operations Jonathan Cottrell now faces the job of balancing the line. He lists precedences and provides time estimates for each step based on work-sampling techniques. His goal is to produce 1,000 bicycles per standard 40-hour workweek.

Task	Time (sec)	Precedence Tasks	Task	Time (sec)	Precedence Tasks
K3	60	—	E3	109	F3
K4	24	K3	D6	53	F4
K9	27	K3	D7	72	F9, E2, E3
J1	66	K3	D8	78	E3, D6
J2	22	K3	D9	37	D6
J3	3	—	C1	78	F7
G4	79	K4, K9	B3	72	D7, D8, D9, C1
G5	29	K9, J1	B5	108	C1
F3	32	J2	B7	18	B3
F4	92	J2	A1	52	B5
F7	21	J3	A2	72	B5
F9	126	G4	A3	114	B7, A1, A2
E2	18	G5, F3			

a) Balance this operation, using various heuristics. Which is best and why?

b) What happens if the firm can change to a 41-hour workweek? **Px**

▶ **Refer to** myomlab ⊙ **for these additional homework problems: 9.24–9.27**

Case Studies

▶ State Automobile License Renewals

Henry Coupe, the manager of a metropolitan branch office of the state department of motor vehicles, attempted to analyze the driver's license–renewal operations. He had to perform several steps. After examining the license-renewal process, he identified those steps and associated times required to perform each step, as shown in the following table:

State Automobile License–Renewal Process Times

Step	Average Time to Perform (seconds)
1. Review renewal application for correctness	15
2. Process and record payment	30
3. Check file for violations and restrictions	60
4. Conduct eye test	40
5. Photograph applicant	20
6. Issue temporary license	30

Coupe found that each step was assigned to a different person. Each application was a separate process in the sequence shown. He determined that his office should be prepared to accommodate a maximum demand of processing 120 renewal applicants per hour.

He observed that work was unevenly divided among clerks and that the clerk responsible for checking violations tended to shortcut her task to keep up with the others. Long lines built up during the maximum-demand periods.

Coupe also found that Steps 1 to 4 were handled by general clerks who were each paid $12 per hour. Step 5 was performed by a photographer paid $16 per hour. (Branch offices were charged $10 per hour for each camera to perform photography.) Step 6, issuing temporary licenses, was required by state policy to be handled by uniformed motor vehicle officers. Officers were paid $18 per hour but could be assigned to any job except photography.

A review of the jobs indicated that Step 1, reviewing applications for correctness, had to be performed before any other step could be taken. Similarly, Step 6, issuing temporary licenses, could not be performed until all the other steps were completed.

Henry Coupe was under severe pressure to increase productivity and reduce costs, but he was also told by the regional director that he must accommodate the demand for renewals. Otherwise, "heads would roll."

Discussion Questions

1. What is the maximum number of applications per hour that can be handled by the present configuration of the process?
2. How many applications can be processed per hour if a second clerk is added to check for violations?
3. If the second clerk could be added *anywhere* you choose (and not necessarily to check for violations, as in question 2), what is the maximum number of applications the process can handle? What is the new configuration?
4. How would you suggest modifying the process to accommodate 120 applications per hour? What is the cost per application of this new configuration?

Source: Modified from a case by W. Earl Sasser, Paul R. Olson, and D. Daryl Wyckoff, *Management of Services Operations: Text, Cases, and Readings* (Boston: Allyn & Bacon).

▶ Laying Out Arnold Palmer Hospital's New Facility

Video Case

When Orlando's Arnold Palmer Hospital began plans to create a new 273-bed, 11-story hospital across the street from its existing facility, which was bursting at the seams in terms of capacity, a massive planning process began. The $100 million building, opened in 2006, was long overdue, according to Executive Director Kathy Swanson: "We started Arnold Palmer Hospital in 1989, with a mission to provide quality services for children and women in a comforting, family-friendly environment. Since then we have served well over 1.5 million women and children and now deliver more than 12,000 babies a year. By 2001, we simply ran out of room, and it was time for us to grow."

The new hospital's unique, circular pod design provides a maximally efficient layout in all areas of the hospital, creating a patient-centered environment. *Servicescape* design features include a serene environment created through the use of warm colors, private rooms with pull-down Murphy beds for family members, 14-foot ceilings, and natural lighting with oversized windows in patient rooms. But these radical new features did not come easily. "This pod concept with a central nursing area and pie-shaped rooms resulted from over 1,000 planning meetings of 35 user groups, extensive motion and time studies, and computer simulations of the daily movements of nurses," says Swanson.

In a traditional linear hospital layout, called the *racetrack* design, patient rooms line long hallways, and a nurse might walk 2.7 miles per day serving patient needs at Arnold Palmer. "Some nurses spent 30% of their time simply walking. With the nursing shortage and the high cost of health care professionals, efficiency is a major concern," added Swanson. With the nursing station in the center of 10- or 12-bed circular pods, no patient room is more than 14 feet from a station. The time savings are in the 20% range. Swanson pointed to Figures 9.22 and 9.23 as examples of the old and new walking and trip distances.*

"We have also totally redesigned our neonatal rooms," says Swanson. "In the old system, there were 16 neonatal beds in a large and often noisy rectangular room. The new building features

*Layout and walking distances, including some of the numbers in Figures 9.22 and 9.23, have been simplified for purposes of this case.

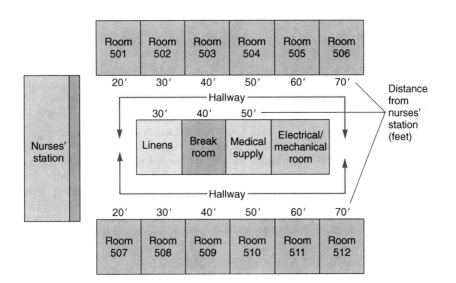

◀ FIGURE 9.22
Traditional Hospital Layout
Patient rooms are on two linear hallways with exterior windows. Supply rooms are on interior corridors. This layout is called a "racetrack" design.

semiprivate rooms for these tiny babies. The rooms are much improved, with added privacy and a quiet, simulated night atmosphere, in addition to pull-down beds for parents to use. Our research shows that babies improve and develop much more quickly with this layout design. Layout and environment indeed impact patient care!"

Discussion Questions*

1. Identify the many variables that a hospital needs to consider in layout design.
2. What are the advantages of the circular pod design over the traditional linear hallway layout found in most hospitals?
3. Figure 9.22 illustrates a sample linear hallway layout. During a period of random observation, nurse Thomas Smith's day includes 6 trips from the nursing station to each of the 12 patient rooms (back and forth), 20 trips to the medical supply room, 5 trips to the break room, and 12 trips to the linen supply room. What is his total distance traveled in miles?
4. Figure 9.23 illustrates an architect's drawing of Arnold Palmer Hospital's new circular pod system. If nurse Susan Jones's day includes 7 trips from the nursing pod to each of the 12 rooms (back and forth), 20 trips to central medical supply, 6 trips to the break room, and 12 trips to the pod linen supply, how many miles does she walk during her shift? What are the differences in the travel times between the two nurses for this random day?
5. The concept of *servicescapes* is discussed in this chapter. Describe why this is so important at Arnold Palmer Hospital and give examples of its use in layout design.

*You may wish to view the video that accompanies this case before addressing these questions.

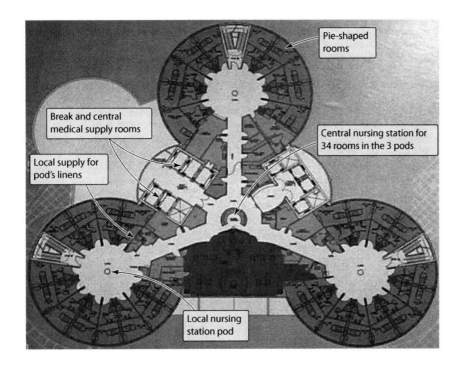

◀ FIGURE 9.23
New Pod Design for Hospital Layout
Note that each room is 14 feet from the pod's *local* nursing station. The *break rooms* and the *central medical station* are each about 60 feet from the local nursing pod. Pod *linen supply* rooms are also 14 feet from the local nursing station.

▶ Facility Layout at Wheeled Coach

Video Case

When President Bob Collins began his career at Wheeled Coach, the world's largest manufacturer of ambulances, there were only a handful of employees. Now the firm's Florida plant has a workforce of 350. The physical plant has also expanded, with offices, R&D, final assembly, and wiring, cabinetry, and upholstery work cells in one large building. Growth has forced the painting work cell into a separate building, aluminum fabrication and body installation into another, inspection and shipping into a fourth, and warehousing into yet another.

Like many other growing companies, Wheeled Coach was not able to design its facility from scratch. And although management realizes that material handling costs are a little higher than an ideal layout would provide, Collins is pleased with the way the facility has evolved and employees have adapted. The aluminum cutting work cell lies adjacent to body fabrication, which, in turn, is located next to the body-installation work cell. And while the vehicle must be driven across a street to one building for painting and then to another for final assembly, at least the ambulance is on wheels. Collins is also satisfied with the flexibility shown in design of the work cells. Cell construction is flexible and can accommodate changes in product mix and volume. In addition, work cells are typically small and movable, with many work benches and staging racks borne on wheels so that they can be easily rearranged and products transported to the assembly line.

Assembly-line balancing is one key problem facing Wheeled Coach and every other repetitive manufacturer. Produced on a schedule calling for four 10-hour work days per week, once an ambulance is on one of the six final assembly lines, it *must* move forward each day to the next workstation. Balancing just enough workers and tasks at each of the seven workstations is a never-ending challenge. Too many workers end up running into each other; too few can't finish an ambulance in 7 days. Constant shifting of design and mix and improved analysis has led to frequent changes.

Discussion Questions*

1. What analytical techniques are available to help a company like Wheeled Coach deal with layout problems?
2. What suggestions would you make to Bob Collins about his layout?
3. How would you measure the "efficiency" of this layout?

*You may wish to view the video that accompanies this case before addressing these questions.

▶**Additional Case Study:** Visit **www.pearsonglobaleditions.com/myomlab** or **www.pearsonglobaleditions.com/heizer** *for this free case study:*

Microfix, Inc.: This company needs to balance its PC manufacturing assembly line and deal with sensitivity analysis of time estimates.

Bibliography

Birchfield, J. C., and J. Birchfield. *Design and Layout of Foodservice Facilities*, 3rd ed. New York, Wiley & Sons, 2007.

Francis, R. L., L. F. McGinnis, and J. A. White. *Facility Layout and Location*, 3rd ed. Upper Saddle River, NJ: Prentice Hall, 1998.

Gultekin, H., O. Y. Karasan, and M. S. Akturk. "Pure Cycles in Flexible Robotic Cells." *Computers & Operations Research* 36, no. 2 (February 2009): 329.

Heragu, S. S. *Facilities Design,* 3rd ed. New York: CRC Press, 2008.

Heyer, N., and U. Wemmerlöv. *Reorganizing the Factory: Competing through Cellular Manufacturing*. Portland, OR: Productivity Press, 2002.

Johnson, Alan. "Getting the Right Factory Layout." *Manufacturer's Monthly* (July 2008): 16.

Kator, C. "Crossdocking on the Rise." *Modern Materials Handling* 63, no. 6 (June 2008): 15.

Kee, Micah R. "The Well-Ordered Warehouse." *APICS: The Performance Advantage* (March 2003): 20–24.

Keeps, David A. "Out-of-the-Box Offices." *Fortune* 159, no.1 (January 19, 2009): 45.

Larson, S. "Extreme Makeover—OR Edition." *Nursing Management* (November 2005): 26.

Panchalavarapu, P. R., and V. Chankong. "Design of Cellular Manufacturing System with Assembly Considerations." *Computers & Industrial Engineering* 48, no. 3 (May 2005): 448.

Roodbergen, K. J., and I. F. A. Vis. "A Model for Warehouse Layout." *IIE Transactions* 38, no. 10 (October 2006): 799–811.

Stanowy, A. "Evolutionary Strategy for Manufacturing Cell Design." *Omega* 34, no. 1 (January 2006): 1.

Tompkins, James A. *Facility Planning*, 4th ed. New York: Wiley, 2009.

Upton, David. "What Really Makes Factories Flexible?" *Harvard Business Review* 73, no. 4 (July–August 1995): 74–84.

Zeng, A. Z., M. Mahan, and N. Fleut. "Designing an Efficient Warehouse Layout to Facilitate the Order-Filling Process." *Production and Inventory Management Journal* 43, no. 3–4 (3rd/4th Quarter 2002): 83–88.

Zhao, T., and C. L. Tseng. "Flexible Facility Interior Layout." *The Journal of the Operational Research Society* 58, no. 6 (June 2007): 729–740.

Main Heading	Review Material	myomlab
THE STRATEGIC IMPORTANCE OF LAYOUT DECISIONS	Layout has numerous strategic implications because it establishes an organization's competitive priorities in regard to capacity, processes, flexibility, and cost, as well as quality of work life, customer contact, and image. *The objective of layout strategy is to develop an effective and efficient layout that will meet the firm's competitive requirements.*	
TYPES OF LAYOUT	Types of layout and examples of their typical objectives include: 1. *Office layout:* Locate workers requiring frequent contact close to one another. 2. *Retail layout:* Expose customers to high-margin items. 3. *Warehouse layout:* Balance low-cost storage with low-cost material handling. 4. *Fixed-position layout:* Move material to the limited storage areas around the site. 5. *Process-oriented layout:* Manage varied material flow for each product. 6. *Work-cell layout:* Identify a product family, build teams, and cross-train team members. 7. *Product-oriented layout:* Equalize the task time at each workstation.	
OFFICE LAYOUT	■ **Office layout**—The grouping of workers, their equipment, and spaces/offices to provide for comfort, safety, and movement of information. A *relationship chart* displays a "closeness value" between each pair of people and/or departments that need to be placed in the office layout.	
RETAIL LAYOUT	■ **Retail layout**—An approach that addresses flow, allocates space, and responds to customer behavior. Retail layouts are based on the idea that sales and profitability vary directly with customer exposure to products. The main *objective of retail layout is to maximize profitability per square foot of floor space* (or, in some stores, per linear foot of shelf space). ■ **Slotting fees**—Fees manufacturers pay to get shelf space for their products. ■ **Servicescape**—The physical surroundings in which a service takes place and how they affect customers and employees.	
WAREHOUSING AND STORAGE LAYOUT	■ **Warehouse layout**—A design that attempts to minimize total cost by addressing trade-offs between space and material handling. The variety of items stored and the number of items "picked" has direct bearing on the optimal layout. Modern warehouse management is often an automated procedure using *automated storage and retrieval systems* (ASRSs). ■ **Cross-docking**—Avoiding the placement of materials or supplies in storage by processing them as they are received for shipment. Cross-docking requires both tight scheduling and accurate inbound product identification. ■ **Random stocking**—Used in warehousing to locate stock wherever there is an open location. ■ **Customizing**—Using warehousing to add value to a product through component modification, repair, labeling, and packaging.	
FIXED-POSITION LAYOUT	■ **Fixed-position layout**—A system that addresses the layout requirements of stationary projects. Fixed-position layouts involve three complications: (1) There is limited space at virtually all sites, (2) different materials are needed at different stages of a project, and (3) the volume of materials needed is dynamic.	
PROCESS-ORIENTED LAYOUT	■ **Process-oriented layout**—A layout that deals with low-volume, high-variety production in which like machines and equipment are grouped together. ■ **Job lots**—Groups or batches of parts processed together. $$\text{Material handling cost minimization} = \sum_{i=1}^{n} \sum_{j=1}^{n} X_{ij} C_{ij} \qquad (9\text{-}1)$$	Problems: 9.1–9.9 Virtual Office Hours for Solved Problem: 9.1 **VIDEO 9.1** Arnold Palmer Hospital **ACTIVE MODEL 9.1**

Main Heading	Review Material	PEARSON myomlab
WORK CELLS	■ **Work cell**—An arrangement of machines and personnel that focuses on making a single product or family of related products. ■ **Takt time**—Pace of production to meet customer demands. $$\text{Takt time} = \text{Total work time available/Units required} \quad (9\text{-}2)$$ $$\text{Workers required} = \text{Total operation time required/Takt time} \quad (9\text{-}3)$$ ■ **Focused work center**—A permanent or semi-permanent product-oriented arrangement of machines and personnel. ■ **Focused factory**—A facility designed to produce similar products or components.	Problem: 9.10
REPETITIVE AND PRODUCT-ORIENTED LAYOUT	■ **Fabrication line**—A machine-paced, product-oriented facility for building components. ■ **Assembly line**—An approach that puts fabricated parts together at a series of workstations; a repetitive process. ■ **Assembly-line balancing**—Obtaining output at each workstation on a production line in order to minimize delay. $$\text{Cycle time} = \text{Production time available per day} \div \text{Units required per day} \quad (9\text{-}4)$$ $$\text{Minimum number of workstations} = \sum_{i=1}^{n} \text{Time for task } i \div \text{Cycle time} \quad (9\text{-}5)$$ ■ **Heuristic**—Problem solving using procedures and rules rather than mathematical optimization. Line balancing heuristics include *longest task (operation) time, most following tasks, ranked positional weight, shortest task (operation) time, and least number of following tasks.* $$\text{Efficiency} = \frac{\sum \text{Task times}}{(\text{Actual number of workstations}) \times (\text{Largest assigned cycle time})} \quad (9\text{-}6)$$	Problems: 9.11–9.22 **VIDEO 9.2** Facility Layout at Wheeled Coach Ambulances Virtual Office Hours for Solved Problem: 9.2

Self Test

■ **Before taking the self-test,** refer to the learning objectives listed at the beginning of the chapter and the key terms listed at the end of the chapter.

LO1. Which of the statements below best describes *office layout*?
   a) Groups workers, their equipment, and spaces/offices to provide for movement of information.
   b) Addresses the layout requirements of large, bulky projects such as ships and buildings.
   c) Seeks the best personnel and machine utilization in repetitive or continuous production.
   d) Allocates shelf space and responds to customer behavior.
   e) Deals with low-volume, high-variety production.

LO2. Which of the following does *not* support the retail layout objective of maximizing customer exposure to products?
   a) Locate high-draw items around the periphery of the store.
   b) Use prominent locations for high-impulse and high-margin items.
   c) Maximize exposure to expensive items.
   d) Use end-aisle locations.
   e) Convey the store's mission with the careful positioning of the lead-off department.

LO3. The major problem addressed by the warehouse layout strategy is:
   a) minimizing difficulties caused by material flow varying with each product.
   b) requiring frequent contact close to one another.
   c) addressing trade-offs between space and material handling.
   d) balancing product flow from one workstation to the next.
   e) none of the above.

LO4. A fixed-position layout:
   a) groups workers to provide for movement of information.
   b) addresses the layout requirements of large, bulky projects such as ships and buildings.
   c) seeks the best machine utilization in continuous production.

   d) allocates shelf space based on customer behavior.
   e) deals with low-volume, high-variety production.

LO5. A process-oriented layout:
   a) groups workers to provide for movement of information.
   b) addresses the layout requirements of large, bulky projects such as ships and buildings.
   c) seeks the best machine utilization in continuous production.
   d) allocates shelf space based on customer behavior.
   e) deals with low-volume, high-variety production.

LO6. For a focused work center or focused factory to be appropriate, the following three factors are required:
   a) _____
   b) _____
   c) _____

LO7. Before considering a product-oriented layout, it is important to be certain that:
   a) _____
   b) _____
   c) _____
   d) _____

LO8. An assembly line is to be designed for a product whose completion requires 21 minutes of work. The factory works 400 minutes per day. Can a production line with five workstations make 100 units per day?
   a) Yes, with exactly 100 minutes to spare.
   b) No, but four workstations would be sufficient.
   c) No, it will fall short even with a perfectly balanced line.
   d) Yes, but the line's efficiency is very low.
   e) Cannot be determined from the information given.

Answers: LO1. a; LO2. c; LO3. c; LO4. b; LO5. e; LO6. family of products, stable forecast (demand), volume; LO7. adequate volume, stable demand, standardized product, adequate/quality supplies; LO8. c.

Capacity Management

Chapter 11

Capacity planning and control

Key questions

➤ What is capacity planning and control?

➤ How are demand and capacity measured?

➤ What are the alternative ways of coping with demand fluctuation?

➤ How can operations plan and control their capacity level?

➤ How can queuing theory be used to plan capacity?

Introduction

Providing the capability to satisfy current and future demand is a fundamental responsibility of operations management. Get the balance between capacity and demand right and the operation can satisfy its customers cost-effectively. Get it wrong and it will fail to satisfy demand, and have excessive costs. Capacity planning and control is also sometimes referred to as *aggregate* planning and control. This is because, at this level of the planning and control, demand and capacity calculations are usually performed on an aggregated basis which does not discriminate between the different products and services that an operation might produce. The essence of the task is to reconcile, at a general and aggregated level, the supply of capacity with the level of demand which it must satisfy (*see* Figure 11.1). This chapter also has a supplement that deals with analytical queuing models, one way of considering capacity planning and control, especially in some service operations.

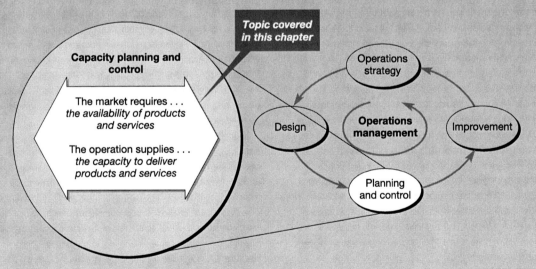

Figure 11.1 This chapter covers capacity planning and control

Operations in practice Britvic – delivering drinks to demand[1]

Britvic is amongst Europe's leading soft-drink manufacturers, a major player in a market consuming nearly ten billion litres a year. Annually, Britvic bottles, distributes and sells over 1 billion litres of ready-to-drink soft drinks in around 400 different flavours, shapes and sizes, including brands such as Pepsi, Tango, Robinsons, Aqua Libra, Purdey's and J2O. Every year, Britvic produce enough cans of soft drinks to stretch three times around the world, so it has to be a high-volume and high-speed business. Its six UK factories contain factory lines producing up to 1,500 cans a minute, with distribution organized on a giant scale. At the centre of its distribution network is a National Distribution Centre (NDC) located at Lutterworth, UK. It is designed to operate 24 hours a day throughout the year, handling up to 620 truckloads of soft drinks daily and, together with a national network of 12 depots, it has to ensure that 250,000 outlets in the UK receive their orders on time. Designed and built in collaboration with Wincanton, a specialist supply chain solutions company, which now manages Britvic's NDC, it is capable of holding up to 140 million cans in its 50,000-pallet 'High Bay' warehouse. All information, from initial order to final delivery, is held electronically. Loads are scanned at Britvic factories and fed into the *'Business Planning and Control System'* that creates a schedule of receipts. This information is then fed to the *Warehouse Management System* and when hauliers arrive at the NDC, data are passed over to the *Movement Control System* that controls the retrieval of pallets from the High Bay.

Source: Wincanton

Over the year Britvic distribute over 100 million cases. However, the demand pattern for soft drinks is seasonal, with short-term changes caused by both weather and marketing campaigns. Furthermore, Britvic's service policy of responding whenever customers want them to deliver has a dramatic impact on the NDC and its capacity planning. *'Our busiest periods are during the summer and in the run-up to Christmas, where we expect over 200 trailers in and out each day – that equates to about 3 million cases per week. In the quiet periods, especially after Christmas, we have less than a million cases per week'* (Distribution Manager).

Not only is demand on the NDC seasonal in a general sense, it can vary from 2,000 pallets one day, to 6,000 the next, as a result of short-term weather patterns and variable order patterns from large customers (supermarkets). Given the lack of space in the High Bay, it is not possible to simply stock up for the busy periods, so flexibility and efficiency are the keys to success.

The NDC uses a number of methods to cope with demand fluctuation. Most importantly is the use and development of technology both within the NDC and out in Britvic's supply chain. High levels of throughput and the ability to respond quickly to demand fluctuations depend on the use of integrated information technology linked to automated 'High Bay' handling technology. *'Without the automation this plant simply couldn't function. You realize how much you need this system when it breaks down! The other day, multiple errors in the system meant that in the space of 6 hours we went from being ahead to having 50 loads waiting to be processed. That equates to 1,350 pallets or nearly 4 million cans.'*

Human resource management is also key in managing capacity. Every morning the shift manager receives orders for the day, although further orders can be placed at any time during the day. The order information allows the multi-skilled workforce to be allocated effectively. The daily meetings also allow any problems to be addressed and dealt with before they become critical. Finally, by outsourcing the NDC management to Wincanton, the site is able to second employees from other Wincanton-owned sites when demand is high. *'Our other sites around the country have different peaks and troughs throughout the year which helps us utilize employee numbers.'*

What is capacity management?

Capacity

The most common use of the word **capacity** is in the static, physical sense of the fixed *volume* of a container, or the space in a building. This meaning of the word is also sometimes used by operations managers. For example, a pharmaceutical manufacturer may invest in new 1,000-litre capacity reactor vessels, a property company purchases a 500-vehicle capacity city-centre car park, and a 'multiplex' cinema is built with 10 screens and a total capacity of 2,500 seats. Although these capacity measures describe the *scale* of these operations, they do not reflect the processing capacities of these investments. To do this we must incorporate a *time* dimension appropriate to the use of assets. So the pharmaceutical company will be concerned with the level of output that can be achieved using the 1,000-litre reactor vessel. If a batch of standard products can be produced every hour, the planned processing capacity could be as high as 24,000 litres per day. If the reaction takes four hours, and two hours are used for cleaning between batches, the vessel may only produce 4,000 litres per day. Similarly, the car park may be fully occupied by office workers during the working day, 'processing' only 500 cars per day. Alternatively, it may be used for shoppers staying on average only one hour, and theatre-goers occupying spaces for three hours in the evening. The processing capacity would then be up to 5,000 cars per day. Thus the definition of the capacity of an operation is the *maximum level of value-added activity over a period of time* that the process can achieve under normal operating conditions.

Capacity constraints

Many organizations operate at below their maximum processing capacity, either because there is insufficient demand completely to 'fill' their capacity, or as a deliberate policy, so that the operation can respond quickly to every new order. Often, though, organizations find themselves with some parts of their operation operating below their capacity while other parts are at their capacity 'ceiling'. It is the parts of the operation that are operating at their capacity 'ceiling'
Capacity constraint
which are the **capacity constraint** for the whole operation. It is these parts of the operation that are pushed to their capacity ceiling that act as the constraint on the whole operation. For example, a retail superstore might offer a gift-wrapping service which at normal times can cope with all requests for its services without delaying customers unduly. At Christmas, however, the demand for gift wrapping might increase proportionally far more than the overall increase in custom for the store as a whole. Unless extra resources are provided to increase the capacity of this micro-operation, it could constrain the capacity of the whole store.

Planning and controlling capacity

Capacity planning and control is the task of setting the effective capacity of the operation so that it can respond to the demands placed upon it. This usually means deciding how the operation should react to fluctuations in demand. We have faced this issue before in Chapter 6 where we examined long-term changes in demand and the alternative capacity strategies for dealing with the changes. These strategies were concerned with introducing
Long-term capacity strategy
(or deleting) major increments of physical capacity. We called this task **long-term capacity strategy**. In this chapter we are treating the shorter timescale where capacity decisions are being made largely within the constraints of the physical capacity limits set by the operation's long-term capacity strategy.

Medium- and short-term capacity

Having established long-term capacity, operations managers must decide how to adjust the
Medium term capacity planning and control
capacity of the operation in the **medium term**. This usually involves an assessment of the demand forecasts over a period of 2–18 months ahead, during which time planned output

Short-term capacity
planning and control

can be varied, for example, by changing the number of hours the equipment is used. In practice, however, few forecasts are accurate, and most operations also need to respond to changes in demand which occur over a shorter timescale. Hotels and restaurants have unexpected and apparently random changes in demand from night to night, but also know from experience that certain days are on average busier than others. So operations managers also have to make **short-term capacity** adjustments, which enable them to flex output for a short period, either on a predicted basis (for example, bank checkouts are always busy at lunchtimes) or at short notice (for example, a sunny warm day at a theme park).

Aggregate demand and capacity

Aggregate planning and
control

The important characteristic of capacity planning and control, as we are treating it here, is that it is concerned with setting capacity levels over the medium and short terms in **aggregated** terms. That is, it is making overall, broad capacity decisions, but is not concerned with all of the detail of the individual products and services offered. This is what 'aggregated' means – different products and services are bundled together in order to get a broad view of demand and capacity. This may mean some degree of approximation, especially if the mix of products or services being produced varies significantly (as we shall see later in this chapter). Nevertheless, as a first step in planning and control, aggregation is necessary. For example, a hotel might think of demand and capacity in terms of 'room nights per month', which ignores the number of guests in each room and their individual requirements, but is a good first approximation. A woollen knitwear factory might measure demand and capacity in the number of units (garments) it is capable of making per month, ignoring size, colour or style variations. Aluminium producers could use tonnes per month, ignoring types of alloy, gauge and batch size variation. The ultimate aggregation measure is money. For example, retail stores, which sell an exceptionally wide variety of products, use revenue per month, ignoring variation in spend, number of items bought, the gross margin of each item and the number of items per customer transaction. If all this seems very approximate, remember that most operations have sufficient experience of dealing with aggregated data to find it useful.

The objectives of capacity planning and control

The decisions taken by operations managers in devising their capacity plans will affect several different aspects of performance:

- *Costs* will be affected by the balance between capacity and demand (or output level if that is different). Capacity levels in excess of demand could mean under-utilization of capacity and therefore high unit cost.
- *Revenues* will also be affected by the balance between capacity and demand, but in the opposite way. Capacity levels equal to or higher than demand at any point in time will ensure that all demand is satisfied and no revenue lost.
- *Working capital* will be affected if an operation decides to build up finished goods inventory prior to demand. This might allow demand to be satisfied, but the organization will have to fund the inventory until it can be sold.
- *Quality* of goods or services might be affected by a capacity plan which involved large fluctuations in capacity levels, by hiring temporary staff for example. The new staff and the disruption to the routine working of the operation could increase the probability of errors being made.
- *Speed* of response to customer demand could be enhanced, either by the build-up of inventories (allowing customers to be satisfied directly from the inventory rather than having to wait for items to be manufactured) or by the deliberate provision of surplus capacity to avoid queuing.
- *Dependability* of supply will also be affected by how close demand levels are to capacity. The closer demand gets to the operation's capacity ceiling, the less able it is to cope with any unexpected disruptions and the less dependable its deliveries of goods and services could be.

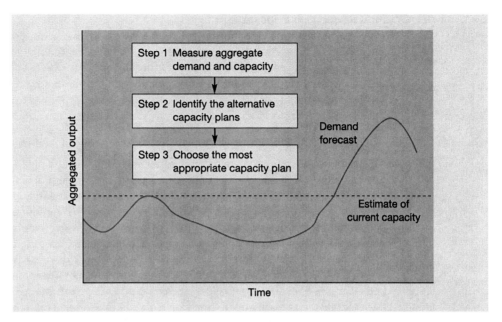

Figure 11.2 **The steps in capacity planning and control**

- *Flexibility*, especially volume flexibility, will be enhanced by surplus capacity. If demand and capacity are in balance, the operation will not be able to respond to any unexpected increase in demand.

The steps of capacity planning and control

The sequence of capacity planning and control decisions which need to be taken by operations managers is illustrated in Figure 11.2. Typically, operations managers are faced with a forecast of demand which is unlikely to be either certain or constant. They will also have some idea of their own ability to meet this demand. Nevertheless, before any further decisions are taken, they must have quantitative data on both capacity and demand. So the first step will be to *measure the aggregate demand and capacity* levels for the planning period. The second step will be to *identify the alternative capacity plans* which could be adopted in response to the demand fluctuations. The third step will be to *choose the most appropriate capacity plan* for their circumstances.

Measuring demand and capacity

Forecasting demand fluctuations

Forecasting is a key input to capacity planning and control

Although demand forecasting is usually the responsibility of the sales and/or marketing functions, it is a very important input into the **capacity planning and control** decision, and so is of interest to operations managers. After all, without an estimate of future demand it is not possible to plan effectively for future events, only to react to them. It is therefore important to understand the basis and rationale for these demand forecasts. (See the supplement on forecasting at the end of Chapter 6.) As far as capacity planning and control is concerned, there are three requirements from a demand forecast.

It is expressed in terms which are useful for capacity planning and control

If forecasts are expressed only in money terms and give no indication of the demands that will be placed on an operation's capacity, they will need to be translated into realistic expectations of demand, expressed in the same units as the capacity (for example, machine hours per year, operatives required, space, etc.).

It is as accurate as possible

In capacity planning and control, the accuracy of a forecast is important because, whereas demand can change instantaneously, there is a lag between deciding to change capacity and the change taking effect. Thus many operations managers are faced with a dilemma. In order to attempt to meet demand, they must often decide output in advance, based on a forecast which might change before the demand occurs, or worse, prove not to reflect actual demand at all.

It gives an indication of relative uncertainty

Decisions to operate extra hours and recruit extra staff are usually based on forecast levels of demand, which could in practice differ considerably from actual demand, leading to unnecessary costs or unsatisfactory customer service. For example, a forecast of demand levels in a supermarket may show initially slow business that builds up to a lunchtime rush. After this, demand slows, only to build up again for the early evening rush, and it finally falls again at the end of trading. The supermarket manager can use this forecast to adjust (say) checkout capacity throughout the day. But although this may be an accurate average demand forecast, no single day will exactly conform to this pattern. Of equal importance is an estimate of how much actual demand could differ from the average. This can be found by examining demand statistics to build up a distribution of demand at each point in the day. The importance of this is that the manager now has an understanding of when it will be important to have reserve staff, perhaps filling shelves, but on call to staff the checkouts should demand warrant it. Generally, the advantage of probabilistic forecasts such as this is that it allows operations managers to make a judgement between possible plans that would virtually guarantee the operation's ability to meet actual demand, and plans that minimize costs. Ideally, this judgement should be influenced by the nature of the way the business wins orders: price-sensitive markets may require a risk-avoiding cost minimization plan that does not always satisfy peak demand, whereas markets that value responsiveness and service quality may justify a more generous provision of operational capacity.

Seasonality of demand

Demand seasonality
Supply seasonality

In many organizations, capacity planning and control is concerned largely with coping with seasonal demand fluctuations. Almost all products and services have some **demand seasonality** and some also have **supply seasonality**, usually where the inputs are seasonal agricultural products – for example, in processing frozen vegetables. These fluctuations in demand or supply may be reasonably forecastable, but some are usually also affected by unexpected variations in the weather and by changing economic conditions. Figure 11.3 gives some examples of seasonality, and the short case 'Producing while the sun shines' discusses the sometimes unexpected link between weather conditions and demand levels.

Consider the four different types of operation described previously: a wool knitwear factor, a city hotel, a supermarket and an aluminium producer. Their demand patterns are shown in Figure 11.4. The woollen knitwear business and the city hotel both have seasonal sales demand patterns, but for different reasons: the woollen knitwear business because of climatic patterns (cold winters, warm summers) and the hotel because of demand from business people, who take vacations from work at Christmas and in the summer. The retail supermarket is a little less seasonal, but is affected by pre-vacation peaks and reduced sales during vacation periods. The aluminium producer shows virtually no seasonality, but is showing a steady growth in sales over the forecast period.

Weekly and daily demand fluctuations

Seasonality of demand occurs over a year, but similar predictable variations in demand can also occur for some products and services on a shorter cycle. The daily and weekly demand patterns of a supermarket will fluctuate, with some degree of predictability. Demand might be low in the morning, higher in the afternoon, with peaks at lunchtime and after work in the evening. Demand might be low on Monday and Tuesday, build up during the latter part

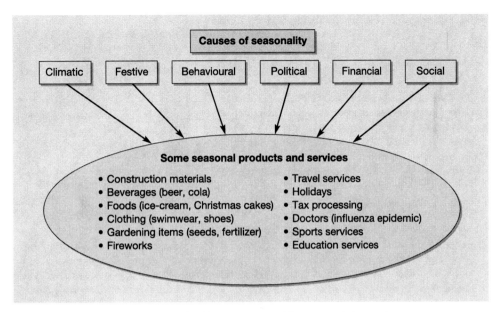

Figure 11.3 Many types of operation have to cope with seasonal demand

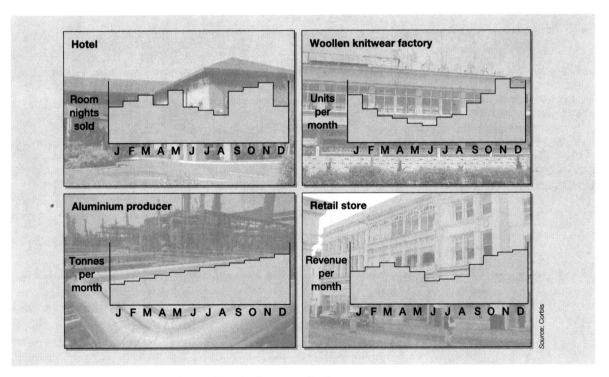

Figure 11.4 Aggregate demand fluctuations for four organizations

of the week and reach a peak on Friday and Saturday. Banks, public offices, telephone sales organizations and electricity utilities all have weekly and daily, or even hourly, demand patterns which require capacity adjustment. The extent to which an operation will have to cope with very short-term demand fluctuations is partly determined by how long its customers are prepared to wait for their products or services. An operation whose customers are incapable of, or unwilling to, wait will have to plan for very short-term demand fluctuations. Emergency services, for example, will need to understand the hourly variation in the demand for their services and plan capacity accordingly.

Short case
Producing while the sun shines[2]

The sales of some products are profoundly affected by the weather. Sunglasses, sunscreen, waterproof clothing and ice cream are all obvious examples. Yet the range of operations interested in weather forecasting has expanded significantly. Energy utilities, soft drink producers and fresh food producers and retailers are all keen to purchase the latest weather forecasts. But so are operations such as banking call centres and mobile phone operators. It would appear that the demand for telephone banking falls dramatically when the sun shines, as does the use of mobile phones. A motorway catering group was surprised to find that their sales of hot meals fell predictably by €110,000 per day for each degree temperature rise above 20 °C. Similarly, insurance companies have found it wise to sell their products when the weather is poor and likely customers are trapped indoors rather than relaxing outside in the sun, refusing to worry about the future. In the not-for-profit sector new understanding is being developed on the link between various illnesses and temperature. Here temperature is often used as a predictor of demand. So, for example, coronary thrombosis cases peak two days after a drop in temperature, for strokes the delay is around five days, while deaths from respiratory infections peak twelve days from a temperature drop. Knowing this, hospital managers can plan for changes in their demand.

Because of this, meteorological services around the world now sell increasingly sophisticated forecasts to a wide range of companies. In the UK, the Meteorological Office offers an internet-based service for its customers.

It is also used to help insurance specialists price insurance policies to provide compensation against weather-related risk. Complex financial products called 'weather derivates' are now available to compensate for weather-related uncertainty. So, for example, an energy company could buy a financial option before winter where the seller pays the company a guaranteed sum of money if the temperature rises above a certain level. If the weather is mild and energy sales are low, the company gets compensation. If the weather is cold, the company loses the premium it has paid to the seller but makes up for it by selling more power at higher prices. However, as meteorologists point out, it is up to the individual businesses to use the information wisely. Only they have the experience to assess the full impact of weather on their operation. So, for example, supermarkets know that a rise in temperature will impact on the sales of cottage cheese (whereas, unaccountably, the sales of cottage cheese with pineapple chunks are not affected).

Measuring capacity

The main problem with measuring capacity is the complexity of most operations. Only when the operation is highly standardized and repetitive is capacity easy to define unambiguously. So if a television factory produces only one basic model, the weekly capacity could be described as 2,000 Model A televisions. A government office may have the capacity to print and post 500,000 tax forms per week. A fast ride at a theme park might be designed to process batches of 60 people every three minutes – a capacity to convey 1,200 people per hour. In each case, an **output capacity measure** is the most appropriate measure because the output from the operation does not vary in its nature. For many operations, however, the definition of capacity is not so obvious. When a much wider range of outputs places varying demands on the process, for instance, output measures of capacity are less useful. Here **input capacity measures** are frequently used to define capacity. Almost every type of operation could use a mixture of both input and output measures, but in practice, most choose to use one or the other (*see* Table 11.1).

Output capacity measure

Input capacity measures

Capacity depends on activity mix

The hospital measures its capacity in terms of its resources, partly because there is not a clear relationship between the number of beds it has and the number of patients it treats. If all

Table 11.1 Input and output capacity measures for different operations

Operation	Input measure of capacity	Output measure of capacity
Air-conditioner plant	Machine hours available	**Number of units per week**
Hospital	**Beds available**	Number of patients treated per week
Theatre	**Number of seats**	Number of customers entertained per week
University	**Number of students**	Students graduated per year
Retail store	**Sales floor area**	Number of items sold per day
Airline	**Number of seats available on the sector**	Number of passengers per week
Electricity company	Generator size	**Megawatts of electricity generated**
Brewery	Volume of fermentation tanks	**Litres per week**

Note: The most commonly used measure is shown in bold.

its patients required relatively minor treatment with only short stays in hospital, it could treat many people per week. Alternatively, if most of its patients required long periods of observation or recuperation, it could treat far fewer. Output depends on the mix of activities in which the hospital is engaged and, because most hospitals perform many different types of activities, output is difficult to predict. Certainly it is difficult to compare directly the capacity of hospitals which have very different activities.

Worked example

Suppose an air-conditioner factory produces three different models of air-conditioner unit: the de luxe, the standard and the economy. The de luxe model can be assembled in 1.5 hours, the standard in 1 hour and the economy in 0.75 hour. The assembly area in the factory has 800 staff hours of assembly time available each week.

If demand for de luxe, standard and economy units is in the ratio 2:3:2, the time needed to assemble $2 + 3 + 2 = 7$ units is:

$$(2 \times 1.5) + (3 \times 1) + (2 \times 0.75) = 7.5 \text{ hours}$$

The number of units produced per week is:

$$\frac{800}{7.5} \times 7 = 746.7 \text{ units}$$

If demand changes to a ratio of de luxe, economy, standard units of 1:2:4, the time needed to assemble $1 + 2 + 4 = 7$ units is:

$$(1 \times 1.5) + (2 \times 1) + (4 \times 0.75) = 6.5 \text{ hours}$$

Now the number of units produced per week is:

$$\frac{800}{6.5} \times 7 = 861.5 \text{ units}$$

Design capacity and effective capacity

The theoretical capacity of an operation – the capacity which its technical designers had in mind when they commissioned the operation – cannot always be achieved in practice. For example, a company coating photographic paper will have several coating lines which deposit thin layers of chemicals onto rolls of paper at high speed. Each line will be capable of running at a particular speed. Multiplying the maximum coating speed by the operating time of the plant gives the theoretical **design capacity** of the line. But in reality the line cannot be

Design capacity

run continuously at its maximum rate. Different products will have different coating requirements, so the line will need to be stopped while it is changed over. Maintenance will need to be performed on the line, which will take out further productive time. Technical scheduling difficulties might mean further lost time. Not all of these losses are the operations manager's fault; they have occurred because of the market and technical demands on the operation. The actual capacity which remains, after such losses are accounted for, is called the **effective capacity** of operation. These causes of reduction in capacity will not be the only losses in the operation. Such factors as quality problems, machine breakdowns, absenteeism and other avoidable problems will all take their toll. This means that the *actual output* of the line will be even lower than the effective capacity. The ratio of the output actually achieved by an operation to its design capacity, and the ratio of output to effective capacity are called, respectively, the **utilization** and the **efficiency** of the plant:

Margin notes: Effective capacity; Utilization; Efficiency

$$\text{Utilization} = \frac{\text{actual output}}{\text{design capacity}}$$

$$\text{Efficiency} = \frac{\text{actual output}}{\text{effective capacity}}$$

Worked example

Suppose the photographic paper manufacturer has a coating line with a design capacity of 200 square metres per minute, and the line is operated on a 24-hour day, 7 days per week (168 hours per week) basis.

Design capacity is $200 \times 60 \times 24 \times 7 = 2.016$ million square metres per week. The records for a week's production show the following lost production time:

1	Product changeovers (set-ups)	20 hrs
2	Regular preventative maintenance	16 hrs
3	No work scheduled	8 hrs
4	Quality sampling checks	8 hrs
5	Shift change times	7 hrs
6	Maintenance breakdown	18 hrs
7	Quality failure investigation	20 hrs
8	Coating material stockouts	8 hrs
9	Labour shortages	6 hrs
10	Waiting for paper rolls	6 hrs

During this week the actual output was only 582,000 square metres.

The first five categories of lost production occur as a consequence of reasonably unavoidable, planned occurrences and amount to a total of 59 hours. The last five categories are unplanned, and avoidable, losses and amount to 58 hours.

Measured in hours of production.

$$\text{Design capacity} = 168 \text{ hours per week}$$

$$\text{Effective capacity} = 168 - 59 = 109 \text{ hrs}$$

$$\text{Actual output} = 168 - 59 - 58 = 51 \text{ hrs}$$

$$\text{Utilization} = \frac{\text{actual output}}{\text{design capacity}} = \frac{51 \text{ hrs}}{168 \text{ hrs}} = 0.304 (30\%)$$

$$\text{Efficiency} = \frac{\text{actual output}}{\text{effective capacity}} = \frac{51 \text{ hrs}}{109 \text{ hrs}} = 0.468 (47\%)$$

Critical commentary

For such an important topic, there is surprisingly little standardization in how capacity is measured. Not only is a reasonably accurate measure of capacity needed for operations planning and control, it is also needed to decide whether it is worth investing in extra physical capacity such as machines. Yet not all practitioners would agree with the way in which design and effective capacity have been defined or measured in the previous worked example. For example, some would argue that the first five categories do *not* occur as 'a consequence of reasonably unavoidable, planned occurrences'. Product changeover set-ups can be reduced, allocating work in a different manner between processes could reduce the amount of time when no work is scheduled, even re-examining preventive maintenance schedules could lead to a reduction in lost time. One school of thought is that whatever capacity efficiency measures are used, they should be useful as diagnostic measures which can highlight the root causes of inefficient use of capacity. The idea of overall equipment effectiveness (OEE) described next is often put forward as a useful way of measuring capacity efficiencies.

Overall equipment effectiveness[3]

Overall equipment effectiveness

The **overall equipment effectiveness** (OEE) measure is an increasingly popular method of judging the effectiveness of operations equipment. It is based on three aspects of performance:

- *the time* that equipment is available to operate;
- *the quality* of the product or service it produces;
- *the speed,* or throughput rate, of the equipment.

Overall equipment effectiveness is calculated by multiplying an availability rate by a performance (or speed) rate multiplied by a quality rate. Figure 11.5 uses the same categories of 'lost' time as were used in Figure 10.5 in the previous chapter. Some of the reduction in available capacity of a piece of equipment (or any process) is caused by time losses such as set-up and changeover losses (when the equipment or process is being prepared for its next

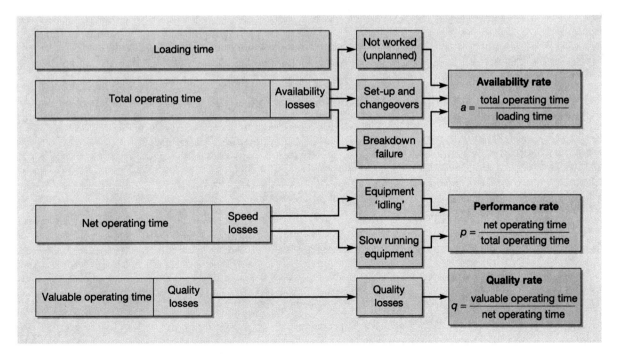

Figure 11.5 Operating equipment effectiveness

activity), and breakdown failures when the machine is being repaired. Some capacity is lost through speed losses such as when equipment is idling (for example when it is temporarily waiting for work from another process) and when equipment is being run below its optimum work rate. Finally, not everything processed by a piece of equipment will be error-free. So some capacity is lost through quality losses.

Taking the notation in Figure 11.5,

$$OEE = a \times p \times q$$

For equipment to operate effectively, it needs to achieve high levels of performance against all three of these dimensions. Viewed in isolation, these individual metrics are important indicators of plant performance, but they do not give a complete picture of the machine's *overall* effectiveness. This can only be understood by looking at the combined effect of the three measures, calculated by multiplying the three individual metrics together. All these losses to the OEE performance can be expressed in terms of units of time – the design cycle time to produce one good part. So, a reject of one part has an equivalent time loss. In effect, this means that an OEE represents the valuable operating time as a percentage of the design capacity.

Worked example

In a typical 7-day period, the planning department programmes a particular machine to work for 150 hours – its loading time. Changeovers and set-ups take an average of 10 hours and breakdown failures average 5 hours every 7 days. The time when the machine cannot work because it is waiting for material to be delivered from other parts of the process is 5 hours on average and during the period when the machine is running, it averages 90 per cent of its rated speed. Three per cent of the parts processed by the machine are subsequently found to be defective in some way.

$$\text{Maximum time available} = 7 \times 24 \text{ hours}$$
$$= 168 \text{ hours}$$

$$\text{Loading time} = 150 \text{ hours}$$

$$\text{Availability losses} = 10 \text{ hours (set-ups)} + 5 \text{ hrs (breakdowns)}$$
$$= 15 \text{ hours}$$

$$\text{So, Total operating time} = \text{Loading time} - \text{Availability}$$
$$= 150 \text{ hours} - 15 \text{ hours}$$
$$= 135 \text{ hours}$$

$$\text{Speed losses} = 5 \text{ hours (idling)} + ((135 - 5) \times 0.1)(10\% \text{ of remaining time})$$
$$= 18 \text{ hours}$$

$$\text{So, Net operating time} = \text{Total operating time} - \text{Speed losses}$$
$$= 135 - 18$$
$$= 117 \text{ hours}$$

$$\text{Quality losses} = 117 \text{ (Net operating time)} \times 0.03 \text{ (Error rate)}$$
$$= 3.51 \text{ hours}$$

$$\text{So, Valuable operating time} = \text{Net operating time} - \text{Quality losses}$$
$$= 117 - 3.51$$
$$= 113.49 \text{ hours}$$

$$\text{Therefore, availability rate} = a = \frac{\text{Total operating time}}{\text{Loading time}}$$
$$= \frac{135}{150} = 90\%$$

$$\text{and, performance rate} = p = \frac{\text{Net operating time}}{\text{Total operating time}}$$

$$= \frac{117}{135} = 86.67$$

$$\text{and quality rate} = q = \frac{\text{Valuable operating time}}{\text{Net operating time}}$$

$$= \frac{113.49}{117} = 97\%$$

$$\text{OEE } (a \times p \times q) = 75.6\%$$

Short case
British Airways London Eye

The British Airways London Eye is the world's largest observation wheel and one of the UK's most spectacular tourist attractions. The 32 passenger capsules, fixed on the perimeter of the 135 metre diameter rim, each hold 25 people. The wheel rotates continuously, so entry requires customers to step into the capsules which are moving at 0.26 metre per second, which is a quarter of normal walking speed. One complete 360 degree rotation takes 30 minutes, at the end of which the doors open and passengers disembark. Boarding and disembarkation are separated on the specially designed platform which is built out over the river. The attraction has a 'timed admissions booking system' (TABS) for both individual and group bookings. This allocates requests for 'flights' on the basis of half-hour time slots. At the time of writing, the BA London Eye is open every day except Christmas Day. Admission is from 10.00 am to 9.30 pm (for the 9.30 to 10.00 pm slot) in the summer, from the beginning of April to mid-September. For the rest of the year, the winter season, admission begins at 10.00 am, and last admissions are for the 5.30 to 6.00 pm slot.

The BA London Eye forecasts anticipated that 2.2 million passengers would fly the London Eye in 2000, excluding January, which was reserved for final testing and admission of invited guests only. An early press release told journalists that the London Eye would rotate an average of 6,000 revolutions per year.

The alternative capacity plans

With an understanding of both demand and capacity, the next step is to consider the alternative methods of responding to demand fluctuations. There are three 'pure' options available for coping with such variation:

Level capacity plan
Chase demand plan
Demand management

- Ignore the fluctuations and keep activity levels constant (**level capacity plan**).
- Adjust capacity to reflect the fluctuations in demand (**chase demand plan**).
- Attempt to change demand to fit capacity availability (**demand management**).

In practice, most organizations will use a mixture of all of these 'pure' plans, although often one plan might dominate. The Short case 'Seasonal salads' describes how one operation pursues some of these options.

Short case
Seasonal salads

Source: Corbis

Lettuce is an all-year-round ingredient for most salads, but both the harvesting of the crop and its demand are seasonal. Lettuces are perishable and must be kept in cold stores and transported in refrigerated vehicles. Even then the product only stays fresh for a maximum of a week. In most north European countries, demand continues throughout the winter at around half the summer levels, but outdoor crops cannot be grown during the winter months. Glasshouse cultivation is possible but expensive.

One of Europe's largest lettuce growers is G's Fresh Salads, based in the UK. Their supermarket customers require fresh produce to be delivered 364 days a year, but because of the limitations of the English growing season, the company has developed other sources of supply in Europe. It acquired a farm and packhouse in the Murcia region of south-eastern Spain, which provides the bulk of salad crops during the winter, transported daily to the UK by a fleet of refrigerated trucks. Further top-up produce is imported by air from around the world.

Sales forecasts are agreed with the individual supermarkets well in advance, allowing the planting and growing programmes to be matched to the anticipated level of sales. However, the programme is only a rough guide. The supermarkets may change their orders right up to the afternoon of the preceding day. Weather is a

dominant factor. First, it determines supply – how well the crop grows and how easy it is to harvest. Second, it influences sales – cold, wet periods during the summer discourage the eating of salads, whereas hot spells boost demand greatly.

Figure 11.6 illustrates this. The Iceberg lettuce sales programme is shown, and compared with the actual English-grown and Spanish-grown sales. The fluctuating nature of the actual sales is the result of a combination of weather-related availability and supermarket demand. These do not always match. When demand is higher than expected, the picking rigs and their crews continue

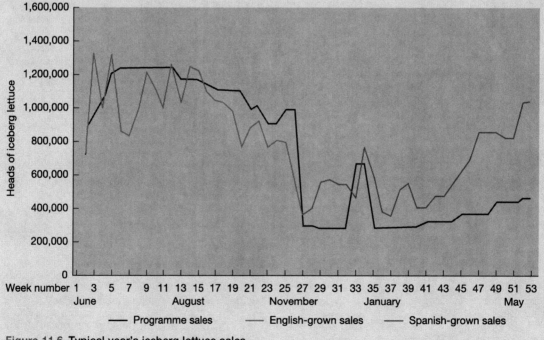

Figure 11.6 Typical year's iceberg lettuce sales

to work into the middle of night, under floodlights. Another capacity problem is the operation's staffing levels. It relies on temporary seasonal harvesting and packing staff to supplement the full-time employees for both the English and Spanish seasons. Since most of the crop is transported to the UK in bulk, a large permanent staff is maintained for packing and distribution in the UK. The majority of the Spanish workforce is temporary, with only a small number retained during the

extremely hot summer to grow and harvest other crops such as melons.

The specialist lettuce harvesting machines (the 'rigs') are shipped over to Spain every year at the end of the English season, so that the company can achieve maximum utilization from all this expensive capital equipment. These rigs not only enable very high productivity of the pickers, but also ensure the best possible conditions for quality packing and rapid transportation to the cold stores.

Level capacity plan

In a level capacity plan, the processing capacity is set at a uniform level throughout the planning period, regardless of the fluctuations in forecast demand. This means that the same number of staff operate the same processes and should therefore be capable of producing the same aggregate output in each period. Where non-perishable materials are processed, but not immediately sold, they can be transferred to finished goods inventory in anticipation of sales at a later time. Thus this plan is feasible (but not necessarily desirable) for our examples of the woollen knitwear company and the aluminium producer (*see* Fig. 11.7).

Level capacity plans of this type can achieve the objectives of stable employment patterns, high process utilization, and usually also high productivity with low unit costs. Unfortunately, they can also create considerable inventory which has to be financed and stored. Perhaps the biggest problem, however, is that decisions have to be taken as to what to produce for inventory rather than for immediate sale. Will green woollen sweaters knitted in July still be fashionable in October? Could a particular aluminium alloy in a specific sectional shape still be sold months after it has been produced? Most firms operating this plan, therefore, give priority to only creating inventory where future sales are relatively certain and unlikely to be affected by changes in fashion or design. Clearly, such plans are not suitable for 'perishable' products, such as foods and some pharmaceuticals, for products where fashion changes rapidly and unpredictably (for example, popular music CDs, fashion garments), or for customized products.

A level capacity plan could also be used by the hotel and supermarket, although this would not be the usual approach of such organizations, because it usually results in a waste of staff resources, reflected in low productivity. Because service cannot be stored as inventory, a level capacity plan would involve running the operation at a uniformly high level of capacity

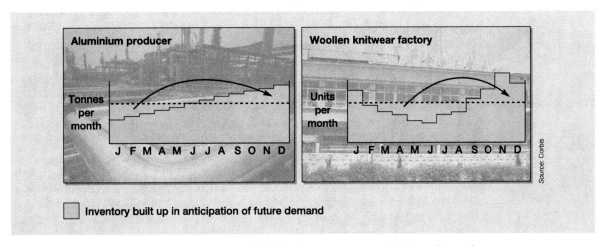

Figure 11.7 Level capacity plans which use anticipation inventory to supply future demand

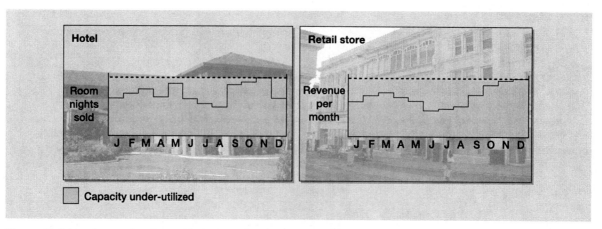

Figure 11.8 Level capacity plans with under-utilization of capacity

availability. The hotel would employ sufficient staff to service all the rooms, to run a full restaurant, and to staff the reception even in months when demand was expected to be well below capacity. Similarly, the supermarket would plan to staff all the checkouts, warehousing operations, and so on, even in quiet periods (*see* Fig. 11.8).

Low utilization can make level capacity plans prohibitively expensive in many service operations, but may be considered appropriate where the opportunity costs of individual lost sales are very high. For example, in the high-margin retailing of jewellery and in (real) estate agents. It is also possible to set the capacity somewhat below the forecast peak demand level in order to reduce the degree of under-utilization. However, in the periods where demand is expected to exceed planned capacity, customer service may deteriorate. Customers may have to queue for long periods or may be 'processed' faster and less sensitively. While this is obviously far from ideal, the benefits to the organization of stability and productivity may outweigh the disadvantages of upsetting some customers.

Chase demand plan

The opposite of a level capacity plan is one which attempts to match capacity closely to the varying levels of forecast demand. This is much more difficult to achieve than a level capacity plan, as different numbers of staff, different working hours, and even different amounts of equipment may be necessary in each period. For this reason, pure chase demand plans are unlikely to appeal to operations which manufacture standard, non-perishable products. Also, where manufacturing operations are particularly capital-intensive, the chase demand policy would require a level of physical capacity, all of which would only be used occasionally. It is for this reason that such a plan is less likely to be appropriate for the aluminium producer than for the woollen garment manufacturer (*see* Fig. 11.9). A pure chase demand plan is more usually adopted by operations which cannot store their output, such as customer-processing operations or manufacturers of perishable products. It avoids the wasteful provision of excess staff that occurs with a level capacity plan, and yet should satisfy customer demand throughout the planned period. Where output can be stored, the chase demand policy might be adopted in order to minimize or eliminate finished goods inventory.

Sometimes it is difficult to achieve very large variations in capacity from period to period. If the changes in forecast demand are as large as those in the hotel example (*see* Fig. 11.10), significantly different levels of staffing will be required throughout the year. This would mean employing part-time and temporary staff, requiring permanent employees to work longer hours, or even bringing in contract labour. The operations managers will then have the difficult task of ensuring that quality standards and safety procedures are still adhered to, and that the customer service levels are maintained.

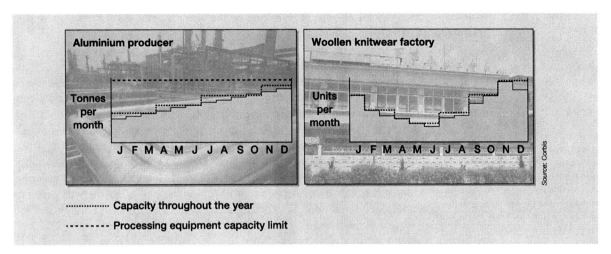

Figure 11.9 Chase demand capacity plans with changes in capacity which reflect changes in demand

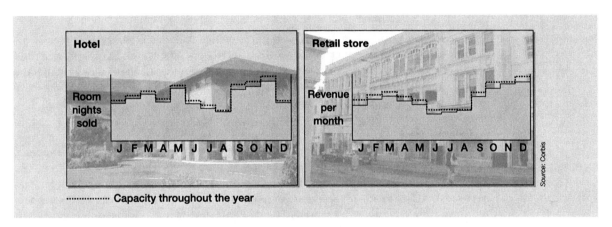

Figure 11.10 Chase demand capacity plans with changes in capacity which reflect changes in demand

Methods of adjusting capacity

The chase demand approach requires that capacity is adjusted by some means. There are a number of different methods for achieving this, although they may not all be feasible for all types of operation. Some of these methods are listed below.

Overtime and idle time

Often the quickest and most convenient method of adjusting capacity is by varying the number of productive hours worked by the staff in the operation. When demand is higher than nominal capacity, **overtime** is worked, and when demand is lower than nominal capacity the amount of time spent by staff on productive work can be reduced. In the latter case, it may be possible for staff to engage in some other activity such as cleaning or maintenance. This method is only useful if the timing of the extra productive capacity matches that of the demand. For example, there is little to be gained in asking a retail operation's staff to work extra hours in the evening if all the extra demand is occurring during their normal working period. The costs associated with this method are either the extra payment which is normally necessary to secure the agreement of staff to work overtime, or in the case of **idle time**, the costs of paying staff who are not engaged in direct productive work. Further, there might be costs associated with the fixed costs of keeping the operation heated, lit and secure over the extra period staff are working. There is also a limit to the amount of extra working time which any workforce can deliver before productivity levels decrease. **Annualized hours** approaches,

Overtime

Idle time

Annualized hours

as described below in the Short case 'Working by the year', are one way of flexing working hours without excessive extra costs.

Varying the size of the workforce

Hire and fire

If capacity is largely governed by workforce size, one way to adjust it is to adjust the size of the workforce. This is done by hiring extra staff during periods of high demand and laying them off as demand falls, or **hire and fire**. However, there are cost and ethical implications to be taken into account before adopting such a method. The costs of hiring extra staff include those associated with recruitment, as well as the costs of low productivity while new staff go through the learning curve. The costs of lay-off may include possible severance payments, but might also include the loss of morale in the operation and loss of goodwill in the local labour market. At a micro-operation level, one method of coping with peaks in demand in one area of an operation is to build sufficient flexibility into job design and job demarcation so that staff can transfer across from less busy parts of the operation. For example, the French hotel chain Novotel has trained some of its kitchen staff to escort customers from the reception area up to their rooms. The peak times for registering new customers coincide with the least busy times in the kitchen and restaurant areas.

Using part-time staff

Part-time staff

A variation on the previous strategy is to recruit **part-time staff**, that is, for less than the normal working day. This method is extensively used in service operations such as supermarkets and fast-food restaurants but is also used by some manufacturers to staff an evening shift after the normal working day. However, if the fixed costs of employment for each employee, irrespective of how long he or she works, are high then using this method may not be worthwhile.

Subcontracting

Subcontracting

In periods of high demand, an operation might buy capacity from other organizations, called **subcontracting**. This might enable the operation to meet its own demand without the extra expense of investing in capacity which will not be needed after the peak in demand has passed. Again, there are costs associated with this method. The most obvious one is that subcontracting can be very expensive. The subcontractor will also want to make sufficient margin out of the business. A subcontractor may not be as motivated to deliver on time or to the desired levels of quality. Finally, there is the risk that the subcontractors might themselves decide to enter the same market.

Critical commentary

To many, the idea of fluctuating the workforce to match demand, either by using part-time staff or by hiring and firing, is more than just controversial. It is regarded as unethical. It is any business's responsibility, they argue, to engage in a set of activities which are capable of sustaining employment at a steady level. Hiring and firing merely for seasonal fluctuations, which can be predicted in advance, is treating human beings in a totally unacceptable manner. Even hiring people on a short-term contract, in practice, leads to them being offered poorer conditions of service and leads to a state of permanent anxiety as to whether they will keep their jobs. On a more practical note, it is pointed out that, in an increasingly global business world where companies may have sites in different countries, those countries that allow hiring and firing are more likely to have their plants 'downsized' than those where legislation makes this difficult.

Manage demand plan

Demand management
Change demand

The most obvious mechanism of **demand management** is to **change demand** through price. Although this is probably the most widely applied approach in demand management, it is less common for products than for services. For example, some city hotels offer low-cost 'city break' vacation packages in the months when fewer business visitors are expected. Skiing and camping holidays are cheapest at the beginning and end of the season and are particularly expensive during school vacations. Discounts are given by photo-processing firms during winter periods, but never around summer holidays. Ice cream is 'on offer' in many supermarkets during the winter. The objective is invariably to stimulate off-peak demand and to constrain peak demand, in order to smooth demand as much as possible. Organizations can also attempt to increase demand in low periods by appropriate advertising. For example, turkey growers in the UK and the USA make vigorous attempts to promote their products at times other than Christmas and Thanksgiving.

Short case
Working by the year[4]

One method of fluctuating capacity as demand varies throughout the year without many of the costs associated with overtime or hiring temporary staff is called the Annual Hours Work Plan. This involves staff contracting to work a set number of hours per year rather than a set number of hours per week. The advantage of this is that the amount of staff time available to an organization can be varied throughout the year to reflect the real state of demand. Annual hours plans can also be useful when supply varies throughout the year. For example, a UK cheese factory of Express Foods, like all cheese factories, must cope with processing very different quantities of milk at different times of the year. In spring and during early summer, cows produce large quantities of milk, but in late summer and autumn the supply of milk slows to a trickle. Before the introduction of annualized hours, the factory

had relied on overtime and hiring temporary workers during the busy season. Now the staff are contracted to work a set number of hours a year with rotas agreed more than a year in advance and after consultation with the union. This means that at the end of July staff broadly know what days and hours they will be working up to September of the following year. If an emergency should arise, the company can call in people from a group of 'super crew' who work more flexible hours in return for higher pay but can do any job in the factory.

However, not all experiments with annualized hours have been as successful as that at Express Foods. In cases where demand is very unpredictable, staff can be asked to come in to work at very short notice. This can cause considerable disruption to social and family life. For example, at one news-broadcasting company, the scheme caused problems. Journalists and camera crew who went to cover a foreign crisis found that they had worked so many hours they were asked to take the whole of one month off to compensate. Since they had no holiday plans, many would have preferred to work.

Alternative products and services

Alternative products

Sometimes, a more radical approach is required to fill periods of low demand such as developing **alternative products** or services which can be produced on existing processes, but have different demand patterns throughout the year (see the Short case 'Getting the message' for an example of this approach). Most universities fill their accommodation and lecture theatres with conferences and company meetings during vacations. Ski resorts provide organized mountain activity holidays in the summer. Some garden tractor companies in the US now make snow movers in the autumn and winter. The apparent benefits of filling capacity in this way must be weighted against the risks of damaging the core product or service, and the operation must be fully capable of serving both markets. Some universities have been criticized for providing sub-standard, badly decorated accommodation which met the needs of impecunious undergraduates, but which failed to impress executives at a trade conference.

Mixed plans

Each of the three 'pure' plans is applied only where its advantages strongly outweigh its disadvantages. For many organizations, however, these 'pure' approaches do not match their required combination of competitive and operational objectives. Most operations managers are required simultaneously to reduce costs and inventory, to minimize capital investment, and yet to provide a responsive and customer-oriented approach at all times. For this reason, most organizations choose to follow a mixture of the three approaches. This can be best illustrated by the woollen knitwear company example (*see* Fig. 11.11). Here some of the peak demand has been brought forward by the company offering discounts to selected retail

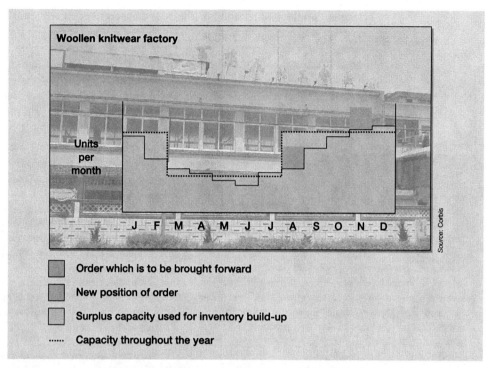

Figure 11.11 A mixed capacity plan for the woollen knitwear factory

customers (manage demand plan). Capacity has also been adjusted at two points in the year to reflect the broad changes in demand (chase demand plan). Yet the adjustment in capacity is not sufficient to avoid totally the build-up of inventories (level capacity plan).

Yield management

Yield management

In operations which have relatively fixed capacities, such as airlines and hotels, it is important to use the capacity of the operation for generating revenue to its full potential. One approach used by such operations is called **yield management**.[5] This is really a collection of methods, some of which we have already discussed, which can be used to ensure that an operation maximizes its potential to generate profit. Yield management is especially useful where:

● capacity is relatively fixed;
● the market can be fairly clearly segmented;
● the service cannot be stored in any way;
● the services are sold in advance;
● the marginal cost of making a sale is relatively low.

Airlines, for example, fit all these criteria. They adopt a collection of methods to try to maximize the yield (i.e. profit) from their capacity. These include the following:

● *Over-booking capacity.* Not every passenger who has booked a place on a flight will actually show up for the flight. If the airline did not fill this seat it would lose the revenue from it. Because of this, airlines regularly book more passengers onto flights than the capacity of the aircraft can cope with. If they over-book by the exact number of passengers who fail to show up, they have maximized their revenue under the circumstances. Of course, if more passengers show up than they expect, the airline will have a number of upset passengers to deal with (although they may be able to offer financial inducements for the passengers to take another flight). If they fail to over-book sufficiently, they will have empty seats. By studying past data on flight demand, airlines try to balance the risks of over-booking and under-booking.

Short case
Getting the message[6]

Companies which traditionally operate in seasonal markets can demonstrate some considerable ingenuity in their attempts to develop counter-seasonal products. One of the most successful industries in this respect has been the greetings card industry. Mother's Day, Father's Day, Halloween, Valentine's Day and other occasions have all been promoted as times to send (and buy) appropriately designed cards. Now, having run out of occasions to promote, greetings card manufacturers have moved on to 'non-occasion' cards, which can be sent at any time. These have the considerable advantage of being less seasonal, thus making the companies' seasonality less marked.

Hallmark Cards, the market leader in North America, has been the pioneer in developing non-occasion cards. Their cards include those intended to be sent from a parent to a child with messages such as 'Would a hug help?', 'Sorry I made you feel bad' and 'You're perfectly wonderful – it's your room that's a mess'. Other cards deal with more serious adult themes such as friendship ('You're more than a friend, you're just like family') or even alcoholism ('This is hard to say, but I think you're a much neater person when you're not drinking'). Now Hallmark Cards has founded a 'loyalty marketing group' that 'helps companies communicate with their customers at an emotional level'. It promotes the use of greetings cards for corporate use, to show that customers and

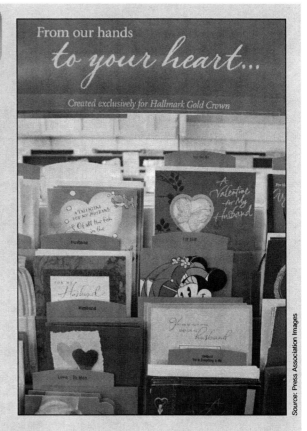

Source: Press Association Images

employees are valued. Whatever else these products may be, they are not seasonal!

- *Price discounting.* At quiet times, when demand is unlikely to fill capacity, airlines will also sell heavily discounted tickets to agents who then themselves take the risk of finding customers for them. In effect, this is using the price mechanism to affect demand.

- *Varying service types.* Discounting and other methods of affecting demand are also adjusted depending on the demand for particular types of service. For example, the relative demand for first-, business- and economy-class seats varies throughout the year. There is no point discounting tickets in a class for which demand will be high. Yield management also tries to adjust the availability of the different classes of seat to reflect their demand. They will also vary the number of seats available in each class by upgrading or even changing the configuration of airline seats.

Choosing a capacity planning and control approach

Before an operation can decide which of the capacity plans to adopt, it must be aware of the consequences of adopting each plan in its own set of circumstances. Two methods are particularly useful in helping to assess the consequences of adopting particular capacity plans:

Cumulative
representations

Queuing theory

- **cumulative representations** of demand and capacity;
- **queuing theory.**

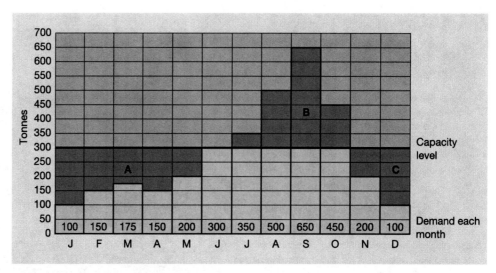

Figure 11.12 If the over-capacity areas (A+C) are greater than the under-capacity area (B), the capacity level seems adequate to meet demand. This may not necessarily be the case, however

Cumulative representations

Figure 11.12 shows the forecast aggregated demand for a chocolate factory which makes confectionery products. Demand for its products in the shops is greatest at Christmas. To meet this demand and allow time for the products to work their way through the distribution system, the factory must supply a demand which peaks in September, as shown. One method of assessing whether a particular level of capacity can satisfy the demand would be to calculate the degree of over-capacity below the graph which represents the capacity levels (areas A and C) and the degree of under-capacity above the graph (area B). If the total over-capacity is greater than the total under-capacity for a particular level of capacity, then that capacity could be regarded as adequate to satisfy demand fully, the assumption being that inventory has been accumulated in the periods of over-capacity. However, there are two problems with this approach. The first is that each month shown in Figure 11.12 may not have the same amount of productive time. Some months (August, for example) may contain vacation periods which reduce the availability of capacity. The second problem is that a capacity level which seems adequate may only be able to supply products *after* the demand for them has occurred. For example, if the period of under-capacity occurred at the beginning of the year, no inventory could have accumulated to meet demand. A far superior way of assessing capacity plans is first to plot demand on a *cumulative* basis. This is shown as the thicker line in Figure 11.13.

The cumulative representation of demand immediately reveals more information. First, it shows that although total demand peaks in September, because of the restricted number of available productive days, the peak demand per productive day occurs a month earlier in August. Second, it shows that the fluctuation in demand over the year is even greater than it seemed. The ratio of monthly peak demand to monthly lowest demand is 6.5:1, but the ratio of peak to lowest demand per productive day is 10:1. Demand per productive day is more relevant to operations managers, because productive days represent the time element of capacity.

The most useful consequence of plotting demand on a cumulative basis is that, by plotting capacity on the same graph, the feasibility and consequences of a capacity plan can be assessed. Figure 11.13 also shows a level capacity plan which produces at a rate of 14.03 tonnes per productive day. This meets cumulative demand by the end of the year. It would also pass our earlier test of total over-capacity being the same as or greater than under-capacity.

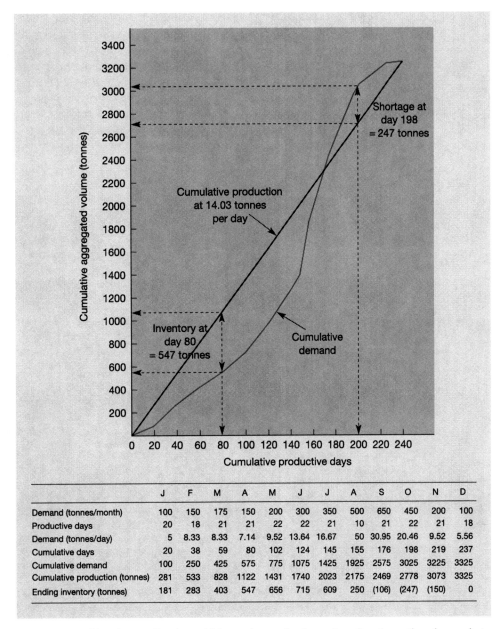

Figure 11.13 A level capacity plan which produces shortages in spite of meeting demand at the end of the year

However, if one of the aims of the plan is to supply demand when it occurs, the plan is inadequate. Up to around day 168, the line representing cumulative production is above that representing cumulative demand. This means that at any time during this period, more product has been produced by the factory than has been demanded from it. In fact the vertical distance between the two lines is the level of inventory at that point in time. So by day 80, 1,122 tonnes have been produced but only 575 tonnes have been demanded. The surplus of production above demand, or inventory, is therefore 547 tonnes. When the cumulative demand line lies above the cumulative production line, the reverse is true. The vertical distance between the two lines now indicates the shortage, or lack of supply. So by day 198, 3,025 tonnes have been demanded but only 2,778 tonnes produced. The shortage is therefore 247 tonnes.

For any capacity plan to meet demand as it occurs, its cumulative production line must always lie above the cumulative demand line. This makes it a straightforward task to judge the adequacy of a plan, simply by looking at its cumulative representation. An impression of the inventory implications can also be gained from a cumulative representation by judging the area between the cumulative production and demand curves. This represents the amount of inventory carried over the period. Figure 11.14 illustrates an adequate level capacity plan for the chocolate manufacturer, together with the costs of carrying inventory. It is assumed that inventory costs £2 per tonne per day to keep in storage. The average inventory each month is taken to be the average of the beginning- and end-of-month inventory levels, and the

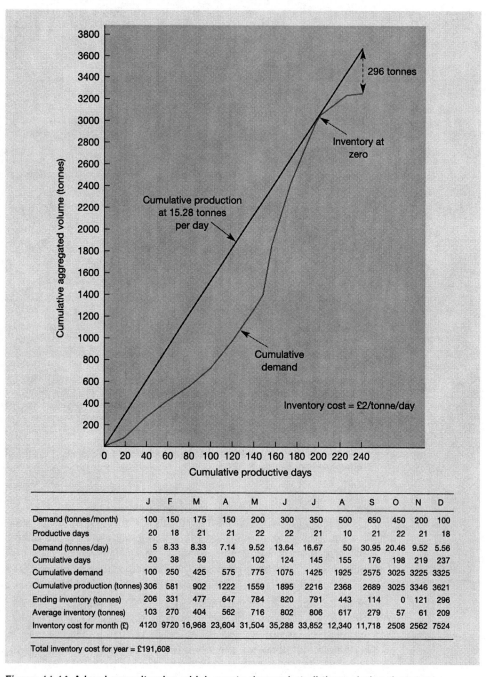

	J	F	M	A	M	J	J	A	S	O	N	D
Demand (tonnes/month)	100	150	175	150	200	300	350	500	650	450	200	100
Productive days	20	18	21	21	22	22	21	10	21	22	21	18
Demand (tonnes/day)	5	8.33	8.33	7.14	9.52	13.64	16.67	50	30.95	20.46	9.52	5.56
Cumulative days	20	38	59	80	102	124	145	155	176	198	219	237
Cumulative demand	100	250	425	575	775	1075	1425	1925	2575	3025	3225	3325
Cumulative production (tonnes)	306	581	902	1222	1559	1895	2216	2368	2689	3025	3346	3621
Ending inventory (tonnes)	206	331	477	647	784	820	791	443	114	0	121	296
Average inventory (tonnes)	103	270	404	562	716	802	806	617	279	57	61	209
Inventory cost for month (£)	4120	9720	16,968	23,604	31,504	35,288	33,852	12,340	11,718	2508	2562	7524

Total inventory cost for year = £191,608

Figure 11.14 A level capacity plan which meets demand at all times during the year

inventory-carrying cost each month is the product of the average inventory, the inventory cost per day per tonne and the number of days in the month.

Comparing plans on a cumulative basis

Chase demand plans can also be illustrated on a cumulative representation. Rather than the cumulative production line having a constant gradient, it would have a varying gradient representing the production rate at any point in time. If a pure demand chase plan was adopted, the cumulative production line would match the cumulative demand line. The gap between the two lines would be zero and hence inventory would be zero. Although this would eliminate inventory-carrying costs, as we discussed earlier, there would be costs associated with changing capacity levels. Usually, the marginal cost of making a capacity change increases with the size of the change. For example, if the chocolate manufacturer wishes to increase capacity by 5 per cent, this can be achieved by requesting its staff to work overtime – a simple, fast and relatively inexpensive option. If the change is 15 per cent, overtime cannot provide sufficient extra capacity and temporary staff will need to be employed – a more expensive solution which also would take more time. Increases in capacity of above 15 per cent might only be achieved by subcontracting some work out. This would be even more expensive. The cost of the change will also be affected by the point from which the change is being made, as well as the direction of the change. Usually, it is less expensive to change capacity towards what is regarded as the 'normal' capacity level than away from it.

Worked example

Suppose the chocolate manufacturer, which has been operating the level capacity plan as shown in Figure 11.15, is unhappy with the inventory costs of this approach. It decides to explore two alternative plans, both involving some degree of demand chasing.

Plan 1

- Organize and staff the factory for a 'normal' capacity level of 8.7 tonnes per day.
- Produce at 8.7 tonnes per day for the first 124 days of the year, then increase capacity to 29 tonnes per day by heavy use of overtime, hiring temporary staff and some subcontracting.
- Produce at 29 tonnes per day until day 194, then reduce capacity back to 8.7 tonnes per day for the rest of the year.

The costs of changing capacity by such a large amount (the ratio of peak to normal capacity is 3.33:1) are calculated by the company as being:

Cost of changing from 8.7 tonnes/day to 29 tonnes/day = £110,000
Cost of changing from 29 tonnes/day to 8.7 tonnes/day = £60,000

Plan 2

- Organize and staff the factory for a 'normal' capacity level of 12.4 tonnes per day.
- Produce at 12.4 tonnes per day for the first 150 days of the year, then increase capacity to 29 tonnes per day by overtime and hiring some temporary staff.
- Produce at 29 tonnes/day until day 190, then reduce capacity back to 12.4 tonnes per day for the rest of the year.

The costs of changing capacity in this plan are smaller because the degree of change is smaller (a peak to normal capacity ratio of 2.34:1), and they are calculated by the company as being:

Cost of changing from 12.4 tonnes/day to 29 tonnes/day = £35,000
Cost of changing from 29 tonnes/day to 12.4 tonnes/day = £15,000

→

Figure 11.15 illustrates both plans on a cumulative basis. Plan 1, which envisaged two drastic changes in capacity, has high capacity change costs but, because its production levels are close to demand levels, it has low inventory carrying costs. Plan 2 sacrifices some of the inventory cost advantage of Plan 1 but saves more in terms of capacity change costs.

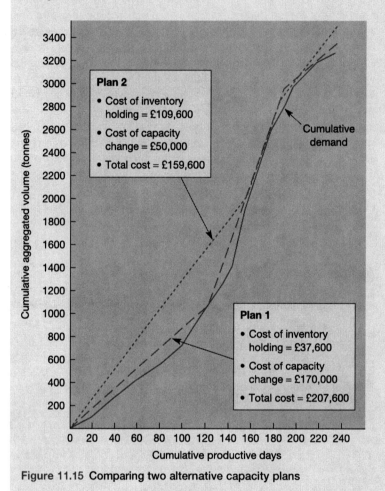

Figure 11.15 Comparing two alternative capacity plans

Capacity planning as a queuing problem

Cumulative representations of capacity plans are useful where the operation has the ability to store its finished goods as inventory. However, for operations where it is not possible to produce products and services *before* demand for them has occurred, a cumulative representation would tell us relatively little. The cumulative 'production' could never be above the cumulative demand line. At best, it could show when an operation failed to meets its demand. So the vertical gap between the cumulative demand and production lines would indicate the amount of demand unsatisfied. Some of this demand would look elsewhere to be satisfied, but some would wait. This is why, for operations which, by their nature, cannot store their output, such as most service operations, capacity planning and control is best considered using waiting or **queuing theory**.

Queuing theory

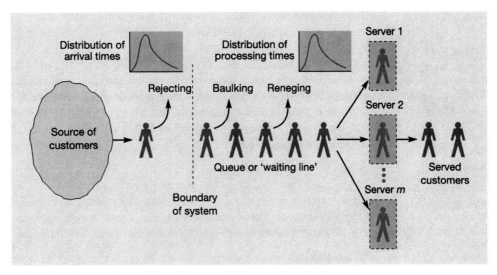

Figure 11.16 The general form of the capacity decision in queuing systems

Queuing or 'waiting line' management

When we were illustrating the use of cumulative representations for capacity planning and control, our assumption was that, generally, any production plan should aim to meet demand at any point in time (the cumulative production line must be above the cumulative demand line). Looking at the issue as a queuing problem (in many parts of the world queuing concepts are referred to as 'waiting line' concepts) accepts that, while sometime demand may be satisfied instantly, at other times customers may have to wait. This is particularly true when the arrival of individual demands on an operation are difficult to predict, or the time to produce a product or service is uncertain, or both. These circumstances make providing adequate capacity at all points in time particularly difficult. Figure 11.16 shows the general form of this capacity issue. Customers arrive according to some probability distribution and wait to be processed (unless part of the operation is idle); when they have reached the front of the queue, they are processed by one of the *n* parallel 'servers' (their processing time also being described by a probability distribution), after which they leave the operation. There are many examples of this kind of system. Table 11.2 illustrates some of these. All of these examples can be described by a common set of elements that define their queuing behaviour.

Calling population

The source of customers – sometimes called the **calling population** – is the source of supply of customers. In queue management 'customers' are not always human. 'Customers' could for example be trucks arriving at a weighbridge, orders arriving to be processed or machines waiting to be serviced, etc. The source of customers for queuing system can be either *finite* or *infinite*. A finite source has a known number of possible customers. For example, if one

Table 11.2 Examples of operations which have parallel processors

Operation	Arrivals	Processing capacity
Bank	Customers	Tellers
Supermarket	Shoppers	Checkouts
Hospital clinic	Patients	Doctors
Graphic artist	Commissions	Artists
Custom cake decorators	Orders	Cake decorators
Ambulance service	Emergencies	Ambulances with crews
Telephone switchboard	Calls	Telephonists
Maintenance department	Breakdowns	Maintenance staff

maintenance person serves four assembly lines, the number of customers for the maintenance person is known, i.e. four. There will be a certain probability that one of the assembly lines will break down and need repairing. However, if one line really does break down the probability of another line needing repair is reduced because there are now only three lines to break down. So, with a finite source of customers the probability of a customer arriving depends on the number of customers already being serviced. By contrast, an infinite customer source assume that there is a large number of potential customers so that it is always possible for another customer to arrive no matter how many are being serviced. Most queuing systems that deal with outside markets have infinite, or 'close-to-infinite', customer sources.

Arrival rate

The arrival rate is the rate at which customers needing to be served arrive at the server or servers. Rarely do customers arrive at a steady and predictable rate. Usually there is variability in their arrival rate. Because of this it is necessary to describe arrival rates in terms of probability distributions. The important issue here is that, in queuing systems, it is normal that at times no customers will arrive and at other times many will arrive relatively close together.

Queue

The queue – customers waiting to be served form the queue or waiting line itself. If there is relatively little limit on how many customers can queue at any time, we can assume that, for all practical purposes, an infinite queue is possible. Sometimes, however, there is a limit to how many customers can be in the queue at any one time.

Rejecting

Rejecting – if the number of customers in a queue is already at the maximum number allowed, then the customer could be rejected by the system. For example, during periods of heavy demand some web sites will not allow customers to access part of the site until the demand on its services has declined.

Baulking

Baulking – when a customer is a human being with free will (and the ability to get annoyed) he or she may refuse to join the queue and wait for service if it is judged to be too long. In queuing terms this is called baulking.

Reneging

Reneging – this is similar to baulking but here the customer has queued for a certain length of time and then (perhaps being dissatisfied with the rate of progress) leaves the queue and therefore the chance of being served.

Queue discipline

Queue discipline – this is the set of rules that determine the order in which customers waiting in the queue are served. Most simple queues, such as those in a shop, use a *first-come first-served* queue discipline. The various sequencing rules described in Chapter 10 are examples of different queue disciplines.

Servers

Servers – a server is the facility that processes the customers in the queue. In any queuing system there may be any number of servers configured in different ways. In Figure 11.16 servers are configured in parallel, but some may have servers in a series arrangement. For example, on entering a self-service restaurant you may queue to collect a tray and cutlery, move on to the serving area where you queue again to order and collect a meal, move on to a drinks area where you queue once more to order and collect a drink, and then finally queue to pay for the meal. In this case you have passed through four servers (even though the first one was not staffed) in a series arrangement. Of course, many queue systems are complex arrangements of series and parallel connections. There is also likely to be variation in how long it takes to process each customer. Even if customers do not have differing needs, human servers will vary in the time they take to perform repetitive serving tasks. Therefore processing time, like arrival time, is usually described by a probability distribution.

Balancing capacity and demand

The dilemma in managing the capacity of a queuing system is how many servers to have available at any point in time in order to avoid unacceptably long queuing times or unacceptably low utilization of the servers. Because of the probabilistic arrival and processing times, only rarely will the arrival of customers match the ability of the operation to cope with them. Sometimes, if several customers arrive in quick succession and require longer-than-average processing times, queues will build up in front of the operation. At other times, when customers arrive less frequently than average and also require shorter-than-average processing times, some of the servers in the system will be idle. So even when the average capacity (processing capability) of the operation matches the average demand (arrival rate) on the system, both queues and idle time will occur.

If the operation has too few servers (that is, capacity is set at too low a level), queues will build up to a level where customers become dissatisfied with the time they are having to wait, although the utilization level of the servers will be high. If too many servers are in place (that is, capacity is set at too high a level), the time which customers can expect to wait will not be long but the utilization of the servers will be low. This is why the capacity planning and control problem for this type of operation is often presented as a trade-off between customer waiting time and system utilization. What is certainly important in making capacity decisions is being able to predict both of these factors for a given queuing system. The supplement to this chapter details some of the more simple mathematical approaches to understanding queue behaviour.

Variability in demand or supply

Variability reduces effective capacity

The variability, either in demand or capacity, as discussed above, will reduce the ability of an operation to process its inputs. That is, it will **reduce its effective capacity**. This effect was explained in Chapter 4 when the consequences of variability in individual processes were discussed. As a reminder, the greater the variability in arrival time or activity time at a process the more the process will suffer both high throughput times and reduced utilization. This principle holds true for whole operations, and because long throughput times mean that queues will build up in the operation, high variability also affects inventory levels. This is illustrated in Figure 11.17. The implication of this is that the greater the variability, the more extra capacity will need to be provided to compensate for the reduced utilization of available capacity. Therefore, operations with high levels of variability will tend to set their base level of capacity relatively high in order to provide this extra capacity.

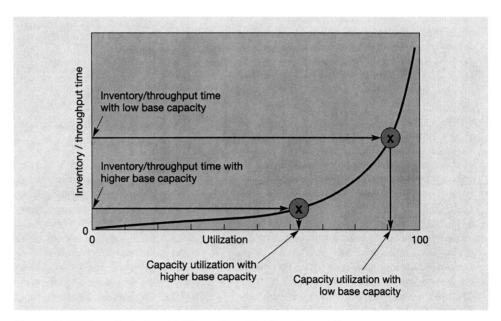

Figure 11.17 The effect of variability on the utilization of capacity

Customer perceptions of queuing

If the 'customers' waiting in a queue are real human customers, an important aspect of how they judge the service they receive from a queuing system is how they perceive the time spent queuing. It is well known that if you are told that you'll be waiting in a queue for twenty minutes and you are actually serviced in ten minutes, your perception of the queuing experience will be more positive than if you were told that you would be waiting ten minutes but the queue actually took twenty minutes. Because of this, the management of queuing systems usually involves attempting to manage customers' perceptions and expectations in some way (see the Short case on Madame Tussaud's for an example of this). One expert in queuing has come up with a number of principles that influence how customers perceive waiting times.[7]

- Time spent idle is perceived as longer than time spent occupied.
- The wait before a service starts is perceived as more tedious than a wait within the service process.
- Anxiety and/or uncertainty heightens the perception that time spent waiting is long.
- A wait of unknown duration is perceived as more tedious than a wait whose duration is known.
- An unexplained wait is perceived as more tedious than a wait that is explained.
- The higher the value of the service for the customer, the longer the wait that will be tolerated.
- Waiting on one's own is more tedious than waiting in a group (unless you really don't like the others in the group).

Short case
Managing queues at Madame Tussaud's, Amsterdam

A short holiday in Amsterdam would not be complete without a visit to Madame Tussaud's, located on four upper floors of the city's most prominent department store in Dam Square. With 600,000 visitors each year, this is the third most popular tourist attraction in Amsterdam, after the flower market and canal trips. On busy days in the summer, the centre can just manage to handle 5,000 visitors. On a wet day in January, however, there may only be 300 visitors throughout the whole day. The centre is open for admission, seven days a week, from 10.00 am to 5.30 pm. In the streets outside, orderly queues of expectant tourists snake along the pavement, looking in at the displays in the store windows. In this public open space, Tussaud's can do little to entertain the visitors, but entrepreneurial buskers and street artists are quick to capitalize on a captive market. On reaching the entrance lobby, individuals, families and groups purchase their admission tickets. The lobby is in the shape of a large horseshoe, with the ticket sales booth in the centre. On winter days or at quiet spells, there will only be one sales assistant, but on busier days, visitors can pay at either side of the ticket booth, to speed up the process. Having paid, the visitors assemble in the

Source: Madame Tussaud's

lobby outside the two lifts. While waiting in this area, a photographer wanders around offering to take photos of the visitors standing next to life-sized wax figures of famous people. They may also be entertained by living look-alikes of famous personalities who act as guides to groups of visitors in batches of around 25 customers (the capacity of each of the two lifts which takes visitors up to the facility). The lifts arrive every four minutes and customers simultaneously disembark, forming one group of about 50 customers, who stay together throughout the session.

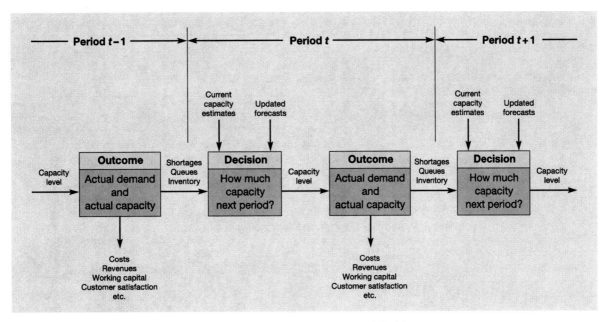

Figure 11.18 Capacity planning and control as a dynamic sequence of decisions

The dynamics of capacity planning and control

Our emphasis so far has been on the planning aspects of capacity management. In practice, the management of capacity is a far more dynamic process which involves controlling and reacting to *actual* demand and *actual* capacity as it occurs. The capacity control process can be seen as a sequence of partially reactive capacity decision processes as shown in Figure 11.18. At the beginning of each period, operations management considers its forecasts of demand, its understanding of current capacity and, if appropriate, how much inventory has been carried forward from the previous period. Based on all this information, it makes plans for the following period's capacity. During the next period, demand might or might not be as forecast and the actual capacity of the operation might or might not turn out as planned. But whatever the actual conditions during that period, at the beginning of the next period the same types of decisions must be made, in the light of the new circumstances.

Summary answers to key questions

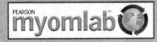 *Check and improve your understanding of this chapter using self assessment questions and a personalised study plan, audio and video downloads, and an eBook – all at www.myomlab.com.*

➤ What is capacity planning and control?

- It is the way operations organize the level of value-added activity which they can achieve under normal operating conditions over a period of time.

- It is usual to distinguish between long-, medium- and short-term capacity decisions. Medium- and short-term capacity management where the capacity level of the organization is adjusted within the fixed physical limits which are set by long-term capacity decisions is sometimes called aggregate planning and control.

- Almost all operations have some kind of fluctuation in demand (or seasonality) caused by some combination of climatic, festive, behavioural, political, financial or social factors.

➤ How are demand and capacity measured?

- Either by the availability of its input resources or by the output which is produced. Which of these measures is used partly depends on how stable is the mix of outputs. If it is difficult to aggregate the different types of output from an operation, input measures are usually preferred.
- The usage of capacity is measured by the factors 'utilization' and 'efficiency'. A more recent measure is that of overall operations effectiveness (OEE).

➤ What are the alternative ways of coping with demand fluctuation?

- Output can be kept level, in effect ignoring demand fluctuations. This will result in under-utilization of capacity where outputs cannot be stored, or the build-up of inventories where output can be stored.
- Output can chase demand by fluctuating the output level through some combination of over-time, varying the size of the workforce, using part-time staff and subcontracting.
- Demand can be changed, either by influencing the market through such measures as advertising and promotion, or by developing alternative products with a counter-seasonal demand pattern.
- Most operations use a mix of all these three 'pure' strategies.

➤ How can operations plan and control their capacity level?

- Representing demand and output in the form of cumulative representations allows the feasibility of alternative capacity plans to be assessed.
- In many operations, especially service operations, a queuing approach can be used to explore capacity strategies.

➤ How can queuing theory be used to plan capacity?

- By considering the capacity decision as a dynamic decision which periodically updates the decisions and assumptions upon which decisions are based.

Case study
Holly farm

In 2003, Charles and Gillian Giles decided to open up their farm to the paying public, in response to diminishing profits from their milk and cereals activities. They invested all their savings into building a 40-space car park and an area with spaces for six 40-seater buses, a safe viewing area for the milking parlour, special trailers for passengers to be transported around the farm on guided tours, a permanent exhibition of equipment, a 'rare breeds' paddock, a children's adventure playground, a picnic area, a maize maze and a farm shop. Behind the farm shop they built a small 'factory' making real dairy ice cream, which also provided for public viewing. Ingredients for the ice cream, pasteurized cream and eggs, sugar, flavourings, etc., were bought out, although this was not obvious to the viewing public.

Source: Wistow Maze, Leicestershire

Source: Sue Williams

The maize maze at Holly Farm

Gillian took responsibility for all these new activities and Charles continued to run the commercial farming business. Through advertising, giving lectures to local schools and local organizations, the number of visitors to the farm increased steadily. By 2006 Gillian became so involved in running her business that she was unable to give so much time to these promotional activities, and the number of paying visitors levelled out at around 15,000 per year. Although the farm opened to the public at 11.00 am and closed at 7.00 pm after milking was finished, up to 90 per cent of visitors in cars or coaches would arrive later than 12.30 pm, picnic until around 2.00 pm, and tour the farm until about 4.00 pm. By that time, around 20 per cent would have visited the farm shop and left, but the remainder would wait to view the milking, then visit the shop to purchase ice cream and other produce, and then depart.

Gillian opened the farm to the public each year from April to October inclusive. Demand would be too low outside this period, the conditions were often unsuitable for regular tractor rides, and most of the animals had to be kept inside. Early experience had confirmed that mid-week demand was too low to justify opening, but Friday to Monday was commercially viable, with almost exactly twice as many visitors on Saturdays and Sundays as on Fridays or Mondays. Gillian summed up the situation. *'I have decided to attempt to increase the number of farm visitors in 2008 by 50 per cent. This would not only improve our return on "farm tours" assets, but also would help the farm shop to achieve its targets, and the extra sales of ice cream would help to keep the "factory" at full output. The real problem is whether to promote sales to coach firms or to intensify local advertising to attract more families in cars. We could also consider tie-ups with schools for educational visits, but I would not want to use my farm guide staff on any extra weekdays, as Charles needs them three days per week for "real" farming work. However, most of the farm workers are glad of this extra of work as if fits in well with their family life, and helps them to save up for the luxuries most farm workers cannot afford.'*

The milking parlour

With 150 cows to milk, Charles invested in a 'carousel' parlour where cows are milked on a slow-moving turntable. Milking usually lasts from 4.30 pm to 7.00 pm, during which time visitors can view from a purpose-built gallery which has space and explanatory tape recordings, via headphones, for twelve people. Gillian has found that on average spectators like to watch for ten minutes, including five minutes for the explanatory tape. *'We're sometimes a bit busy on Saturdays and Sundays and a queue often develops before 4.00 pm as some people want to see the milking and then go home. Unfortunately, neither Charles nor the cows are prepared to start earlier. However, most people are patient and everybody gets their turn to see this bit of high technology. In a busy period, up to 80 people per hour pass through the gallery.'*

The ice cream 'factory'

The factory is operated 48 weeks per year, four days per week, eight hours per day, throughout the year. The three employees, farm workers' wives, are expected to work in line with farm opening from April to October, but hours and days are by negotiation in other months. All output is in one-litre plastic boxes, of which 350 are made every day, which is the maximum mixing and fast-freezing capacity. Although extra mixing hours would create more unfrozen ice cream, the present equipment cannot safely and fully fast-freeze more than 350 litres over a 24-hour period. Ice cream that is not fully frozen cannot be transferred to the finished goods freezer, as slower freezing spoils the texture of the product. As it takes about one hour to clean out between flavours, only one of the four flavours is made on any day. The finished goods freezer holds a maximum of 10,000 litres, but to allow stock rotation, it cannot in practice be loaded to above 7,000 litres. Ideally no ice cream should be held more than six weeks at the factory, as the total recommended storage time is only twelve weeks prior to retail sale (there is no preservative used). Finished goods inventory at the end of December 2007 was 3,600 litres.

Gillian's most recent figures indicated that all flavours cost about £4.00 per litre to produce (variable cost of materials, packaging and labour). The factory layout is by process with material preparation and weighing sections, mixing area, packing equipment, and separate freezing equipment. It is operated as a batch process.

Ice cream sales

The majority of output is sold through regional special-ity shops and food sections of department stores. These outlets are given a standard discount of 25 per cent to allow a 33 per cent mark-up to the normal retail price of £8.00 per litre. Minimum order quantity is 100 litres, and deliveries are made by Gillian in the van on Tuesdays. Also, having been shown around the farm and 'factory', a large proportion of visitors buy ice cream at the farm shop, and take it away in well-insulated containers that keep it from melting for up to two hours in the summer. Gillian commented 'These are virtually captive customers. We have analysed this demand and found that on aver-age one out of two coach customers buys a one-litre box. On average, a car comes with four occupants, and two 1-litre boxes are purchased. The farm shop retail price is £2.00 per box, which gives us a much better margin than for our sales to shops.'

In addition, a separate, fenced, road entrance allows local customers to purchase goods at a separate counter of the farm shop without payment for, or access to, the other farm facilities. 'This is a surprisingly regular source of sales. We believe this is because householders make very infrequent visits to stock up their freezers almost regard-less of the time of year, or the weather. We also know that local hotels also buy a lot this way, and their use of ice cream is year-round, with a peak only at Christmas when there are a larger number of banquets.' All sales in this category are at the full retail price (£8.00). The finished product is sold to three categories of buyers. See Table 11.3. (Note – (a) no separate record is kept of those sales to the paying farm visitors and those to the 'Farm Shop only', (b) the selling prices and discounts for 2008 will be as for 2007, (c) Gillian considered that 2007 was reasonably typical in terms of weather, although rainfall was a little higher than average during July and August.)

Table 11.3 Analysis of annual sales of ice cream (£000s) from 2003 to 2007, and forecast sales for 2008

	2003	2004	2005	2006	2007	2008 forecast
Retail shops	32	104	156	248	300	260
Farm shop total	40	64	80	100	108	160
Total	72	168	236	348	408	420

Table 11.4 gives details of visitors to the farm and ice cream sales in 2007. Gillian's concluding comments were 'We have a long way to go to make this enterprise meet our expectations. We will probably make only a small return on capital employed in 2007, so must do all we can to increase our profitability. Neither of us wants to put more capital into the business, as we would have to borrow at interest rates of up to 15 per cent. We must make our investment work better. As a first step, I have decided to increase the num-ber of natural flavours of our ice cream to ten in 2008 (currently only four) to try and defend the delicatessen trade against a competitor's aggressive marketing campaign. I don't expect that to fully halt the decline in our sales to these outlets, and this is reflected in our sales forecast.'

Questions

1 Evaluate Gillian's proposal to increase the number of farm visitors in 2008 by 50 per cent. (You may wish to consider: What are the main capacity constraints within these businesses? Should she promote coach company visits, even if this involves offering a discount on the admission charges? Should she pursue increasing visitors by car or school parties? In what other ways is Gillian able to manage capacity? What other information would help Gillian to take these decisions?)

2 What factors should Gillian consider when deciding to increase the number of flavours from four to ten?

(Note: For any calculations, assume that each month consists of four weeks. The effects of statutory holidays should be ignored for the purpose of this initial analysis.)

Table 11.4 Records of farm visitors and ice cream sales (in £000) in 2007

	Jan	Feb	Mar	Apr	May	June	July	Aug	Sept	Oct	Nov	Dec	TOTAL
Total number of paying farm visitors	0	0	0	1,200	1,800	2,800	3,200	3,400	1,800	600	0	0	14,800
Monthly ice cream sales	18	20.2	35	26.8	36	50.2	50.6	49.2	39	25.6	17.4	40	408.8

Problems and applications

These problems and applications will help to improve your analysis of operations. You can find more practice problems as well as worked examples and guided solutions on MyOMLab at www.myomlab.com.

1 A local government office issues hunting licences. Demand for these licences is relatively slow in the first part of the year but then increases after the middle of the year before slowing down again towards the end of the year. The department works a 220-day year on a 5-days-a-week basis. Between working days 0 and 100, demand is 25 per cent of demand during the peak period which lasts between day 100 and day 150. After 150 demand reduces to about 12 per cent of the demand during the peak period. In total, the department processes 10,000 applications per year. The department has 2 permanent members of staff who are capable of processing 15 licence applications per day. If an untrained temporary member of staff can only process 10 licences per day, how many temporary staff should the department recruit between days 100 and 150?

2 In the example above, if a new computer system is installed that allows experienced staff to increase their work rate to 20 applications per day, and untrained staff to 15 applications per day, (a) does the department still need 2 permanent staff, and (b) how many temporary members of staff will be needed between days 100 and 150?

3 A field service organization repairs and maintains printing equipment for a large number of customers. It offers one level of service to all its customers and employs 30 staff. The operation's marketing vice-president has decided that in future the company will offer 3 standards of service, platinum, gold and silver. It is estimated that platinum-service customers will require 50 per cent more time from the company's field service engineers than the current service. The current service is to be called 'the gold service'. The silver service is likely to require about 80 per cent of the time of the gold service. If future demand is estimated to be 20 per cent platinum, 70 per cent gold and 10 per cent silver service, how many staff will be needed to fulfil demand?

4 Look again at the principles which govern customers' perceptions of the queuing experience. For the following operations, apply the principles to minimize the perceived negative effects of queuing.

(a) A cinema
(b) A doctor's surgery
(c) Waiting to board an aircraft.

5 Consider how airlines cope with balancing capacity and demand. In particular, consider the role of yield management. Do this by visiting the web site of a low-cost airline, and for a number of flights price the fare that is being charged by the airline from tomorrow onwards. In other words, how much would it cost if you needed to fly tomorrow, how much if you needed to fly next week, how much if you needed to fly in 2 weeks, etc. Plot the results for different flights and debate the findings.

6 Calculate the overall equipment efficiency (OEE) of the following facilities by investigating their use.

(a) A lecture theatre
(b) A cinema
(c) A coffee machine

Discuss whether it is worth trying to increase the OEE of these facilities and, if it is, how you would go about it.

Selected further reading

Brandimarte, P. and Villa, A. (1999) *Modelling Manufacturing Systems: From Aggregate Planning to Real Time Control*, Springer, New York, NY. Very academic although it does contain some interesting pieces if you need to get 'under the skin' of the subject.

Hopp, W.J. and Spearman, M.L. (2000) *Factory Physics*, 2nd edn, McGraw-Hill, New York, NY. Very mathematical indeed, but includes some interesting maths on queuing theory.

Olhager, J., Rudberg, M. and Wikner, J. (2001) Long-term capacity management: linking the perspectives from manufacturing strategy and sales and operations planning, *International Journal of Production Economics*, vol. 69, issue 2, 215–25. Academic article, but interesting.

Vollmann, T., Berry, W., Whybark, D.C. and Jacobs, F.R. (2004) *Manufacturing Planning and Control Systems for Supply Chain Management: The Definitive Guide for Professionals*, McGraw-Hill Higher Education. The latest version of the 'bible' of manufacturing planning and control. It's exhaustive in its coverage of all aspects of planning and control including aggregate planning.

Useful web sites

www.dti.gov.uk/er/index Web site of the Employment Relations Directorate which has developed a framework for employers and employees which promotes a skilled and flexible labour market founded on principles of partnership.

www.worksmart.org.uk/index.php This site is from the Trades Union Congress. Its aim is 'to help today's working people get the best out of the world of work'.

www.opsman.org Lots of useful stuff.

www.eoc-law.org.uk/ This web site aims to provide a resource for legal advisers and representatives who are conducting claims on behalf of applicants in sex discrimination and equal pay cases in England and Wales. This site covers employment-related sex discrimination only.

www.dol.gov/index.htm US Department of Labor's site with information regarding using part-time employees.

www.downtimecentral.com/ Lots of information on operational equipment efficiency (OEE).

Now that you have finished reading this chapter, why not visit MyOMLab at www.myomlab.com where you'll find more learning resources to help you make the most of your studies and get a better grade?

Analytical queuing models

Introduction

In the main part of Chapter 11 we described how the queuing approach (in the United States it would be called the 'waiting line approach') can be useful in thinking about capacity, especially in service operations. It is useful because it deals with the issue of variability, both of the arrival of customers (or items) at a process and of how long each customer (or item) takes to process. And where variability is present in a process (as it is in most processes, but particularly in service processes) the capacity required by an operation cannot easily be based on averages but must include the effects of the variation. Unfortunately, many of the formulae that can be used to understand queuing are extremely complicated, especially for complex systems, and are beyond the scope of this book. In fact, computer programs are almost always now used to predict the behaviour of queuing systems. However, studying queuing formulae can illustrate some useful characteristics of the way queuing systems behave.

Notation

Unfortunately there are several different conventions for the notation used for different aspects of queuing system behaviour. It is always advisable to check the notation used by different authors before using their formulae. We shall use the following notation:

$$t_a = \text{average time between arrival}$$
$$r_a = \text{arrival rate (items per unit time)} \quad = 1/t_a$$
$$c_a = \text{coefficient of variation of arrival times}$$
$$m = \text{number of parallel servers at a station}$$
$$t_e = \text{mean processing time}$$
$$r_e = \text{processing rate (items per unit time)} \quad = m/t_e$$
$$c_e = \text{coefficient of variation of process time}$$
$$u = \text{utilization of station} \quad = r_a/r_e = (r_a\, t_e)/m$$
$$\text{WIP} = \text{average work-in-progress (number of items) in the queue}$$
$$\text{WIP}_q = \text{expected work-in-progress (number of times) in the queue}$$
$$W_q = \text{expected waiting time in the queue}$$
$$W = \text{expected waiting time in the system (queue time + processing time)}$$

Some of these factors are explained later.

Variability

The concept of variability is central to understanding the behaviour of queues. If there were no variability there would be no need for queues to occur because the capacity of a process could be relatively easily adjusted to match demand. For example, suppose one member of staff (a server) serves at a bank counter customers who always arrive exactly every five minutes (i.e. 12 per hour). Also suppose that every customer takes exactly five minutes to be served, then because,

(a) the arrival rate is $\leq$ processing rate, and
(b) there is no variation

no customer need ever wait because the next customer will arrive when, or before, the previous customer. That is, $WIP_q = 0$.

Also, in this case, the server is working all the time, again because exactly as one customer leaves the next one is arriving. That is, $u = 1$.

Even with more than one server, the same may apply. For example, if the arrival time at the counter is five minutes (12 per hour) and the processing time for each customer is now always exactly 10 minutes, the counter would need two servers, and because,

(a) arrival rate is $\leq$ processing rate m, and
(b) there is no variation

again, $WIP_q = 0$, and $u = 1$.

Of course, it is convenient (but unusual) if arrival rate/processing rate = a whole number. When this is not the case (for this simple example with no variation),

$$Utilization = processing\ rate/(arrival\ rate\ multiplied\ by\ m)$$
For example, if arrival rate, $r_a = 5$ minutes
processing rate, $r_e = 8$ minutes
number of servers, $m = 2$
then, utilization, $u = 8 / (5 \times 2) = 0.8$ or 80%

Incorporating variability

The previous examples were not realistic because the assumption of no variation in arrival or processing times very rarely occurs. We can calculate the average or mean arrival and process times but we also need to take into account the variation around these means. To do that we need to use a probability distribution. Figure S11.1 contrasts two processes with different arrival distributions. The units arriving are shown as people, but they could be jobs arriving at a machine, trucks needing servicing, or any other uncertain event. The top example shows low variation in arrival time where customers arrive in a relatively predictable manner. The bottom example has the same average number of customer arriving but this time they arrive unpredictably with sometimes long gaps between arrivals and at other times two or three customers arriving close together. Of course, we could do a similar analysis to describe processing times. Again, some would have low variation, some higher variation and others be somewhere in between.

In Figure S11.1 high arrival variation has a distribution with a wider spread (called 'dispersion') than the distribution describing lower variability. Statistically the usual measure for indicating the spread of a distribution is its standard deviation, σ. But variation does not only depend on standard deviation. For example, a distribution of arrival times may have a standard deviation of 2 minutes. This could indicate very little variation when the average arrival time is 60 minutes. But it would mean a very high degree of variation when the

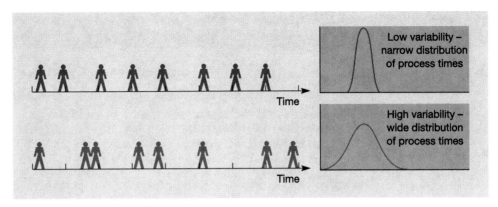

Figure S11.1 Low and high arrival variation

average arrival time is 3 minutes. Therefore to normalize standard deviation, it is divided by the mean of its distribution. This measure is called the coefficient of variation of the distribution. So,

$$c_a = \text{coefficient of variation of arrival times} = \sigma_a/t_a$$
$$c_e = \text{coefficient of variation of processing times} = \sigma_e/t_e$$

Incorporating Little's law

In Chapter 4 we discussed on of the fundamental laws of processes that describes the relationship between the cycle time of a process (how often something emerges from the process), the working in progress in the process and the throughput time of the process (the total time it takes for an item to move through the whole process including waiting time). It was called Little's law and it was denoted by the following simple relationship.

$$\text{Work-in-progress} = \text{cycle time} \times \text{throughput time}$$

Or,

$$\text{WIP} = C \times T$$

We can make use of Little's law to help understand queuing behaviour. Consider the queue in front of a station.

Work-in-progress in the queue = the arrival rate at the queue (equivalent to cycle time) × waiting time in the queue (equivalent to throughput time)

$$\text{WIP}_q = r_a \times W_q$$

and

Waiting time in the whole system = the waiting time in the queue + the average process time at the station

$$W = W_q + t_e$$

We will use this relationship later to investigate queuing behaviour.

Types of queuing system

Conventionally queuing systems are characterized by four parameters.

A – the distribution of arrival times (or more properly interarrival times, the elapsed times between arrivals)
B – the distribution of process times
m – the number of servers at each station
b – the maximum number of items allowed in the system.

The most common distributions used to describe A or B are either

(a) the exponential (or Markovian) distribution denoted by M; or
(b) the general (for example normal) distribution denoted by G.

So, for example, an M/G/1/5 queuing system would indicate a system with exponentially distributed arrivals, process times described by a general distribution such as a normal distribution, with one server and a maximum number of items allowed in the system of 5. This type of notation is called Kendall's notation.

Queuing theory can help us investigate any type of queuing system, but in order to simplify the mathematics, we shall here deal only with the two most common situations. Namely,

M/M/m queues

● **M/M/m** – the exponential arrival and processing times with m servers and no maximum limit to the queue.

G/G/m queues

● **G/G/m** – general arrival and processing distributions with m servers and no limit to the queue.

And first we will start by looking at the simple case when $m = 1$.

For M/M/1 queuing systems

The formulae for this type of system are as follows.

$$\text{WIP} = \frac{u}{1 - u}$$

Using Little's law,

$$\text{WIP} = \text{cycle time} \times \text{throughput time}$$
$$\text{Throughput time} = \text{WIP} / \text{cycle time}$$

Then,

$$\text{Throughput time} = \frac{u}{1 - u} \times \frac{1}{r_a} = \frac{t_e}{1 - u}$$

and since, throughput time in the queue = total throughput time − average processing time,

$$W_q = W - t_e$$

$$= \frac{t_e}{1 - u} - t_e$$

$$= \frac{t_e - t_e(1 - u)}{1 - u} = \frac{t_e - t_e - ut_e}{1 - u}$$

$$= \frac{u}{(1 - u)} t_e$$

again, using Little's law

$$\text{WIP}_q = r_a \times W_q = \frac{u}{(1-u)} t_e r_a$$

and since

$$u = \frac{r_a}{r_e} = r_a t_e$$

$$r_a = \frac{u}{t_e}$$

then,

$$\text{WIP}_q = \frac{u}{(1-u)} \times t_e \times \frac{u}{t_e}$$

$$= \frac{u^2}{(1-u)}$$

For M/M/*m* systems

When there are *m* servers at a station the formula for waiting time in the queue (and therefore all other formulae) needs to be modified. Again, we will not derive these formulae but just state them.

$$W_q = \frac{u^{\sqrt{2(m+1)}-1}}{m(1-u)} t_e$$

From which the other formulae can be derived as before.

For G/G/1 systems

The assumption of exponential arrival and processing times is convenient as far as the mathematical derivation of various formulae are concerned. However, in practice, process times in particular are rarely truly exponential. This is why it is important to have some idea of how a G/G/1 and G/G/*m* queue behaves. However, exact mathematical relationships are not possible with such distributions. Therefore some kind of approximation is needed. The one here is in common use, and although it is not always accurate, it is for practical purposes. For G/G/1 systems the formula for waiting time in the queue is as follows.

$$W_q = \left(\frac{c_a^2 + c_e^2}{2} \right) \left(\frac{u}{(1-u)} \right) t_e$$

There are two points to make about this equation. The first is that it is exactly the same as the equivalent equation for an M/M/1 system but with a factor to take account of the variability of the arrival and process times. The second is that this formula is sometimes known as the **VUT formula** because it describes the waiting time in a queue as a function of:

VUT formula

V – the variability in the queuing system
U – the utilization of the queuing system (that is demand versus capacity), and
T – the processing times at the station.

In other words, we can reach the intuitive conclusion that queuing time will increase as variability, utilization or processing time increases.

For G/G/*m* systems

The same modification applies to queuing systems using general equations and *m* servers. The formula for waiting time in the queue is now as follows.

$$W_q = \left(\frac{c_a^2 + c_e^2}{2}\right)\left(\frac{u^{\sqrt{2(m+1)}-1}}{m(1-u)}\right)t_e$$

Worked example 1

'I can't understand it. We have worked out our capacity figures and I am sure that one member of staff should be able to cope with the demand. We know that customers arrive at a rate of around 6 per hour and we also know that any trained member of staff can process them at a rate of 8 per hour. So why is the queue so large and the wait so long? Have at look at what is going on there please.'

Sarah knew that it was probably the variation, both in customers arriving and in how long it took each of them to be processed, that was causing the problem. Over a two-day period when she was told that demand was more or less normal, she timed the exact arrival times and processing times of every customer. Her results were as follows.

The coefficient of variation, c_a of customer arrivals = 1
The coefficient of variation, c_e of processing time   = 3.5
The average arrival rate of customers, r_a = 6 per hour
therefore, the average inter-arrival time   = 10 minutes
The average processing rate, r_e = 8 per hour
therefore, the average processing time   = 7.5 minutes
Therefore the utilization of the single server, u = 6/8 = 0.75

Using the waiting time formula for a G/G/1 queuing system

$$W_q = \left(\frac{1+12.25}{2}\right)\left(\frac{0.75}{1-0.75}\right)7.5$$

$$= 6.625 \times 3 \times 7.5 = 149.06 \text{ mins}$$

$$= 2.48 \text{ hours}$$

Also because,

$$WIP_q = \text{cycle time} \times \text{throughput time}$$

$$WIP_q = 6 \times 2.48 = 14.68$$

So, Sarah had found out that the average wait that customers could expect was 2.48 hours and that there would be an average of 14.68 people in the queue.

'Ok, so I see that it's the very high variation in the processing time that is causing the queue to build up. How about investing in a new computer system that would standardize processing time to a greater degree? I have been talking with our technical people and they reckon that, if we invested in a new system, we could cut the coefficient of variation of processing time down to 1.5. What kind of a different would this make?'

Under these conditions with $c_e = 1.5$

$$W_q = \left(\frac{1+2.25}{2}\right)\left(\frac{0.75}{1-0.75}\right)7.5$$

$$= 1.625 \times 3 \times 7.5 = 36.56 \text{ mins}$$

$$= 0.61 \text{ hour}$$

Therefore,

$$WIP_q = 6 \times 0.61 = 3.66$$

In other words, reducing the variation of the process time has reduced average queuing time from 2.48 hours down to 0.61 hour and has reduced the expected number of people in the queue from 14.68 down to 3.66.

Worked example 2

A bank wishes to decide how many staff to schedule during its lunch period. During this period customers arrive at a rate of 9 per hour and the enquiries that customers have (such as opening new accounts, arranging loans, etc.) take on average 15 minutes to deal with. The bank manager feels that four staff should be on duty during this period but wants to make sure that the customers do not wait more than 3 minutes on average before they are served. The manager has been told by his small daughter that the distributions that describe both arrival and processing times are likely to be exponential. Therefore,

$r_a = 9$ per hour, therefore
$t_a = 6.67$ minutes
$r_e = 4$ per hour, therefore
$t_e = 15$ minutes

The proposed number of servers, $m = 4$

therefore, the utilization of the system, $u = 9/(4 \times 4) = 0.5625$.

From the formula for waiting time for a M/M/m system,

$$W_q = \frac{u^{\sqrt{2(m+1)}-1}}{m(1-u)}t_e$$

$$W_q = \frac{0.5625^{\sqrt{10}-1}}{4(1-0.5625)} \times 0.25$$

$$= \frac{0.5625^{2.162}}{1.75} \times 0.25$$

$$= 0.042 \text{ hour}$$

$$= 2.52 \text{ minutes}$$

Therefore the average waiting time with 4 servers would be 2.52 minutes, which is well within the manager's acceptable waiting tolerance.

INVENTORY MANAGEMENT

12 MANAGING INVENTORIES

State-of-the-art technology, including new RFID tags, help move merchandise efficiently through Wal-Mart's distribution centers.

INVENTORY MANAGEMENT AT WAL-MART

In the market for shaver blade replacements? A printer? First-aid supplies? Dog food? Hair spray? If so, you expect that the store you shop at will have what you want. However, making sure that the shelves are stocked with tens of thousands of products is no simple matter for inventory managers at Wal-Mart, which has 7,357 Wal-Mart stores and Sam's Club locations in 14 markets, employs more than 2 million associates, serves 180 million customers per week worldwide, and uses 56,000 suppliers. You can imagine in an operation this large that some things can get lost. Linda Dillman, CIO at Wal-Mart, recounts the story of the missing hair spray at one of the stores. The shelf needed to be restocked with a specific hair spray; however, it took three days to find the case in the backroom. Most customers will not swap hair sprays, so Wal-Mart lost three days of sales on that product.

Knowing what is in stock, in what quantity, and where it is being held is critical to effective inventory management. Without accurate inventory information, companies can make major mistakes by ordering too much, not enough, or shipping products to the wrong location. Companies can have large inventories and still have stockouts of product because they have too much inventory of some products and not enough of others. Wal-Mart, with inventories in excess of $36 billion, is certainly aware of the potential benefits from improved inventory management and is constantly experimenting with ways to reduce inventory investment. Knowing when

LEARNING GOALS

After reading this chapter, you should be able to:

1. Determine the items deserving most attention and tightest inventory control.
2. Calculate the economic order quantity and apply it to various situations.
3. Determine the order quantity and reorder point for a continuous review inventory control system.
4. Determine the review interval and target inventory level for a periodic review inventory control system.
5. Define the key factors that determine the appropriate choice of an inventory system.

to replenish inventory stocks and how much to order each time is critical when dealing with so much inventory investment. The application of technology is also important, such as using radio frequency identification (RFID) to track inventory shipments and stock levels at stores and warehouses throughout the supply chain. One handheld RFID reader could have found the missing case of hair spray in a few minutes.

Sources: Laurie Sullivan, "Wal-Mart's Way," Informationweek.com (September 27, 2004), pp. 36–50; Gus Whitcomb and Christi Gallagher, "Wal-Mart Begins Roll-Out of Electronic Product Codes in Dallas/Fort Worth Area," www.walmartstores.com (June, 2008), and Investor Information, 2008 Financial Reports.

myomlab and the Companion Website at **www.pearsonglobaleditions.com/krajewski** contain many tools, activities, and resources designed for this chapter.

Inventory management, the planning and controlling of inventories in order to meet the competitive priorities of the organization, is an important concern for managers in all types of businesses. Effective inventory management is essential for realizing the full potential of any supply chain. The challenge is not to pare inventories to the bone to reduce costs or to have plenty around to satisfy all demands, but to have the right amount to achieve the competitive priorities of the business most efficiently. This type of efficiency can only happen if the right amount of inventory is flowing through the supply chain—through suppliers, the firm, warehouses or distribution centers, and customers. These decisions were so important for Wal-Mart that it decided to use RFID to improve the information flows in the supply chain. Much of inventory management involves *lot sizing*, which is the determination of how frequently and in what quantity to order inventory. We make ample reference to the term **lot size**, which is the quantity of an inventory item management either buys from a supplier or manufactures using internal processes. In this chapter we focus on the decision-making aspects of inventory management. We begin with an overview of the importance of inventory management to the organization and how to choose the items most deserving of management attention. We then introduce the basics of inventory decision making by exploring the economic order quantity and how it can be used to balance inventory holding costs with ordering costs. A major segment of the chapter is devoted to retail and distribution inventory control systems and how to use them.

INVENTORY MANAGEMENT ACROSS THE ORGANIZATION

Inventories are important to all types of organizations, their employees, and their supply chains. Inventories profoundly affect everyday operations because they must be counted, paid for, used in operations, used to satisfy customers, and managed. Inventories require an investment of funds, as does the purchase of a new machine. Monies invested in inventory are not available for investment in other things; thus, they represent a drain on the cash flows of an organization. Nonetheless, companies realize that the availability of products is a key selling point in many markets and downright critical in many more.

So, is inventory a boon or a bane? Certainly, too much inventory on hand reduces profitability, and too little inventory on hand creates shortages in the supply chain and ultimately damages customer confidence. Inventory management, therefore, involves trade-offs. Let us discover how companies can effectively manage inventories across the organization.

ABC Analysis

Thousands of items, often referred to as stock-keeping units, are held in inventory by a typical organization, but only a small percentage of them deserve management's closest attention and tightest control. A **stock-keeping unit (SKU)** is an individual item or product that has an identifying code and is held in inventory somewhere along the supply chain. **ABC analysis** is the process of dividing SKUs into three classes according to their dollar usage so that managers can focus on items that have the highest dollar value. This method is the equivalent of creating a *Pareto chart* except that it is applied to inventory rather than to process errors. As Figure 12.1 shows, class A items typically represent only about 20 percent of the SKUs but account for 80 percent of the dollar usage. Class B items account for another 30 percent of the SKUs but only 15 percent of the dollar usage. Finally, 50 percent of the SKUs fall in class C, representing a mere 5 percent of the dollar usage. The goal of ABC analysis is to identify the class A SKUs so management can control their inventory levels.

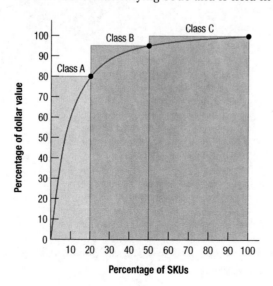

FIGURE 12.1 ▶
Typical Chart Using ABC Analysis

The analysis begins by multiplying the annual demand rate for an SKU by the dollar value (cost) of one unit of that SKU to determine its dollar usage. After ranking the SKUs on the basis of dollar usage and creating the Pareto chart, the analyst looks for "natural" changes in slope. The dividing lines in Figure 12.1 between classes are inexact. Class A SKUs could be somewhat higher or lower than 20 percent of all SKUs but normally account for the bulk of the dollar usage.

Class A SKUs are reviewed frequently to reduce the average lot size and to ensure timely deliveries from suppliers. It is important to maintain high inventory turnover for these items. By contrast, class B SKUs require an intermediate level of control. Here, less frequent monitoring of suppliers coupled with adequate safety stocks can provide cost-effective coverage of demands. For class C SKUs, much looser control is appropriate. While a stockout of a class C SKU can be as crucial as for a class A SKU, the inventory holding cost of class C SKUs tends to be low. These features suggest that higher inventory levels can be tolerated and that more safety stock and larger lot sizes may suffice for class C SKUs. See Solved Problem 4 for a detailed example of ABC analysis.

Creating ABC inventory classifications is useless unless inventory records are accurate. Technology can help; many companies are going to RFID to track inventory wherever it exists in the supply chain. Chips imbedded in product packaging contain information on the product and send signals that can be accessed by sensitive receivers and transmitted to a central location for processing. There are other, less sophisticated approaches of achieving accuracy that can be used. One way is to assign responsibility to specific employees for issuing and receiving materials and accurately reporting each transaction. Another method is to secure inventory behind locked doors or gates to prevent unauthorized or unreported withdrawals. This method also guards against accidentally storing newly received inventory in the wrong locations, where it can be lost for months. **Cycle counting** can also be used, whereby storeroom personnel physically count a small percentage of the total number of SKUs each day, correcting errors that they find. Class A SKUs are counted most frequently. A final method, for computerized systems, is to make logic error checks on each transaction reported and fully investigate any discrepancies. The discrepancies can include (1) actual receipts when no receipts are scheduled, (2) disbursements that exceed the current on-hand inventory balance, and (3) receipts with an inaccurate (nonexistent) SKU number.

Now that we have identified the inventory items deserving of most attention, we devote the remainder of the chapter to the decisions of how much to order and when.

ECONOMIC ORDER QUANTITY

Recall from our discussion in Chapter 9, "Designing Effective Supply Chains," that managers face conflicting pressures to keep inventories low enough to avoid excess inventory holding costs but high enough to reduce ordering and setup costs. *Inventory holding cost* is the sum of the cost of capital and the variable costs of keeping items on hand, such as storage and handling, taxes, insurance, and shrinkage. *Ordering cost* is the cost of preparing a purchase order for a supplier or a production order for the shop, while *setup cost* is the cost of changing over a machine to produce a different item. In this section we will address the *cycle inventory*, which is that portion of total inventory that varies directly with lot size. A good starting point for balancing these conflicting pressures and determining the best cycle-inventory level for an item is finding the **economic order quantity (EOQ)**, which is the lot size that minimizes total annual cycle-inventory holding and ordering costs. The approach to determining the EOQ is based on the following assumptions:

1. The demand rate for the item is constant (for example, always 10 units per day) and known with certainty.

2. No constraints are placed (such as truck capacity or materials handling limitations) on the size of each lot.

3. The only two relevant costs are the inventory holding cost and the fixed cost per lot for ordering or setup.

4. Decisions for one item can be made independently of decisions for other items. In other words, no advantage is gained in combining several orders going to the same supplier.

5. The lead time is constant (e.g., always 14 days) and known with certainty. The amount received is exactly what was ordered and it arrives all at once rather than piecemeal.

Tutor 12.1 in my**om**lab provides a new example to practice ABC analysis.

cycle counting

An inventory control method, whereby storeroom personnel physically count a small percentage of the total number of items each day, correcting errors that they find.

economic order quantity (EOQ)

The lot size that minimizes total annual inventory holding and ordering costs.

The economic order quantity will be optimal when all five assumptions are satisfied. In reality, few situations are so simple. Nonetheless, the EOQ is often a reasonable approximation of the appropriate lot size, even when several of the assumptions do not quite apply. Here are some guidelines on when to use or modify the EOQ.[1]

- **Do not use the EOQ**
  - If you use the "make-to-order" strategy and your customer specifies that the entire order be delivered in one shipment
  - If the order size is constrained by capacity limitations such as the size of the firm's ovens, amount of testing equipment, or number of delivery trucks
- **Modify the EOQ**
  - If significant quantity discounts are given for ordering larger lots
  - If replenishment of the inventory is not instantaneous, which can happen if the items must be used or sold as soon as they are finished without waiting until the entire lot has been completed (see Supplement D, "Special Inventory Models," for several useful modifications to the EOQ)
- **Use the EOQ**
  - If you follow a "make-to-stock" strategy and the item has relatively stable demand
  - If your carrying costs per unit and setup or ordering costs are known and relatively stable

The EOQ was never intended to be an optimizing tool. Nonetheless, if you need to determine a reasonable lot size, it can be helpful in many situations.

Calculating the EOQ

We begin by formulating the total cost for any lot size Q for a given SKU. Next, we derive the EOQ, which is the Q that minimizes total annual cycle-inventory cost. Finally, we describe how to convert the EOQ into a companion measure, the elapsed time between orders.

When the EOQ assumptions are satisfied, cycle inventory behaves as shown in Figure 12.2. A cycle begins with Q units held in inventory, which happens when a new order is received. During the cycle, on-hand inventory is used at a constant rate and, because demand is known with certainty and the lead time is a constant, a new lot can be ordered so that inventory falls to 0 precisely when the new lot is received. Because inventory varies uniformly between Q and 0, the average cycle inventory equals half the lot size, Q.

FIGURE 12.2 ▶
Cycle-Inventory Levels

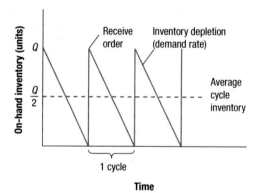

The annual holding cost for this amount of inventory, which increases linearly with Q, as Figure 12.3(a)shows, is

Annual holding cost = (Average cycle inventory)(Unit holding cost)

The annual ordering cost is

Annual ordering cost = (Number of orders/Year)(Ordering or setup cost)

The average number of orders per year equals annual demand divided by Q. For example, if 1,200 units must be ordered each year and the average lot size is 100 units, then 12 orders will be placed during the year. The annual ordering or setup cost decreases nonlinearly as Q increases, as shown in Figure 12.3(b), because fewer orders are placed.

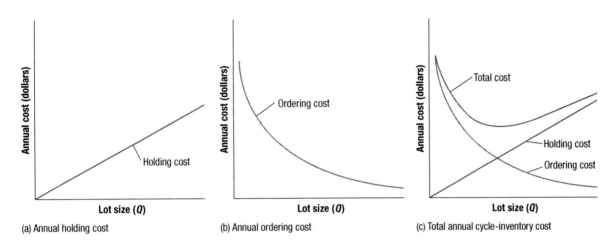

(a) Annual holding cost   (b) Annual ordering cost   (c) Total annual cycle-inventory cost

▲ FIGURE 12.3
Graphs of Annual Holding, Ordering, and Total Costs

The total annual cycle-inventory cost,[2] as graphed in Figure 12.4(c), is the sum of the two cost components:

Total cost = Annual holding cost + Annual ordering or setup cost[3]

$$C = \frac{Q}{2}(H) + \frac{D}{Q}(S)$$

where

C = total annual cycle-inventory cost

Q = lot size, in units

H = cost of holding one unit in inventory for a year, often expressed as a percentage of the item's value

D = annual demand, in units per year

S = cost of ordering or setting up one lot, in dollars per lot

---

[2] Expressing the total cost on an annual basis usually is convenient (although not necessary). Any time horizon can be selected, as long as D and H cover the same time period. If the total cost is calculated on a monthly basis, D must be monthly demand and H must be the cost of holding a unit for 1 month.

[3] The number of orders actually placed in any year is always a whole number, although the formula allows the use of fractional values. However, rounding is not needed because what is being calculated is an average for multiple years. Such averages often are nonintegers.

EXAMPLE 12.1   The Cost of a Lot-Sizing Policy

A museum of natural history opened a gift shop two years ago. Managing inventories has become a problem. Low inventory turnover is squeezing profit margins and causing cash-flow problems.

One of the top-selling SKUs in the container group at the museum's gift shop is a bird feeder. Sales are 18 units per week, and the supplier charges $60 per unit. The cost of placing an order with the supplier is $45. Annual holding cost is 25 percent of a feeder's value, and the museum operates 52 weeks per year. Management chose a 390-unit lot size so that new orders could be placed less frequently. What is the annual cycle-inventory cost of the current policy of using a 390-unit lot size? Would a lot size of 468 be better?

SOLUTION

We begin by computing the annual demand and holding cost as

$$D = (18 \text{ units/week})(52 \text{ weeks/year}) = 936 \text{ units}$$
$$H = 0.25(\$60/\text{unit}) = \$15$$

The total annual cycle-inventory cost for the current policy is

$$C = \frac{Q}{2}(H) + \frac{D}{Q}(S)$$

$$= \frac{390}{2}(\$15) + \frac{936}{390}(\$45) = \$2{,}925 + \$108 = \$3{,}033$$

The total annual cycle-inventory cost for the alternative lot size is

$$C = \frac{468}{2}(\$15) + \frac{936}{468}(\$45) = \$3{,}510 + \$90 = \$3{,}600$$

DECISION POINT

The lot size of 468 units, which is a half-year supply, would be a more expensive option than the current policy. The savings in ordering costs are more than offset by the increase in holding costs. Management should use the total annual cycle-inventory cost function to explore other lot-size alternatives.

Figure 12.4 displays the impact of using several Q values for the bird feeder in Example 12.1. Eight different lot sizes were evaluated in addition to the current one. Both holding and ordering costs were plotted, but their sum—the total annual cycle-inventory cost curve—is the important feature. The graph shows that the best lot size, or EOQ, is the lowest point on the total annual cost curve, or between 50 and 100 units. Obviously, reducing the current lot-size policy ($Q = 390$) can result in significant savings.

A more efficient approach is to use the EOQ formula:

$$EOQ = \sqrt{\frac{2DS}{H}}$$

We use calculus to obtain the EOQ formula from the total annual cycle-inventory cost function. We take the first derivative of the total annual cycle-inventory cost function with respect to Q, set it equal to 0, and solve for Q. As Figure 12.4 indicates, the EOQ is the order quantity for which annual holding cost equals annual ordering cost. Using this insight, we can also obtain the EOQ formula by equating the formulas for annual ordering cost and annual holding cost and solving for Q. The graph in

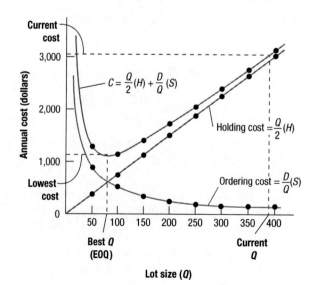

FIGURE 12.4 ▶
Total Annual Cycle-Inventory Cost
Function for the Bird Feeder

Figure 12.4 also reveals that when the annual holding cost for any Q exceeds the annual ordering cost, as with the 390-unit order, we can immediately conclude that Q is too big. A smaller Q reduces holding cost and increases ordering cost, bringing them into balance. Similarly, if the annual ordering cost exceeds the annual holding cost, Q should be increased.

Sometimes, inventory policies are based on the time between replenishment orders, rather than on the number of units in the lot size. The **time between orders (TBO)** for a particular lot size is the average elapsed time between receiving (or placing) replenishment orders of Q units. Expressed as a fraction of a year, the TBO is simply Q divided by annual demand. When we use the EOQ and express time in terms of months, the TBO is

time between orders (TBO)

The average elapsed time between receiving (or placing) replenishment orders of Q units for a particular lot size.

$$\text{TBO}_{\text{EOQ}} = \frac{\text{EOQ}}{D}(12 \text{ months/year})$$

In Example 12.2, we show how to calculate TBO for years, months, weeks, and days.

EXAMPLE 12.2   Finding the EOQ, Total Cost, and TBO

For the bird feeders in Example 12.1, calculate the EOQ and its total annual cycle-inventory cost. How frequently will orders be placed if the EOQ is used?

Tutor 12.2 in myomlab provides a new example to practice the application of the EOQ model.

SOLUTION

Using the formulas for EOQ and annual cost, we get

$$\text{EOQ} = \sqrt{\frac{2DS}{H}} = \sqrt{\frac{2(936)(45)}{15}} = 74.94 \text{ or } 75 \text{ units}$$

Figure 12.5 shows that the total annual cost is much less than the $3,033 cost of the current policy of placing 390-unit orders.

Parameters

Current Lot Size (Q)	390	
Demand (D)	936	
Order Cost (S)	$45	
Unit Holding Cost (H)	$15	

Economic Order Quantity	75

◀ **FIGURE 12.5**
Total Annual Cycle-Inventory Costs Based on EOQ Using Tutor 12.2

Annual Costs

Orders per Year	2.4
Annual Ordering Cost	$108.00
Annual Holding Cost	$2,925.00
Annual Inventory Cost	$3,033.00

Annual Costs based on EOQ

Orders per Year	12.48
Annual Ordering Cost	$561.60
Annual Holding Cost	$562.50
Annual Inventory Cost	$1,124.10

When the EOQ is used, the TBO can be expressed in various ways for the same time period.

$$\text{TBO}_{\text{EOQ}} = \frac{\text{EOQ}}{D} = \frac{75}{936} = 0.080 \text{ year}$$

$$\text{TBO}_{\text{EOQ}} = \frac{\text{EOQ}}{D}(12 \text{ months/year}) = \frac{75}{936}(12) = 0.96 \text{ month}$$

$$\text{TBO}_{\text{EOQ}} = \frac{\text{EOQ}}{D}(52 \text{ weeks/year}) = \frac{75}{936}(52) = 4.17 \text{ weeks}$$

$$\text{TBO}_{\text{EOQ}} = \frac{\text{EOQ}}{D}(365 \text{ days/year}) = \frac{75}{936}(365) = 29.25 \text{ days}$$

Active Model 12.1 in myomlab provides additional insight on the EOQ model and its uses.

DECISION POINT

Using the EOQ, about 12 orders per year will be required. Using the current policy of 390 units per order, an average of 2.4 orders will be needed each year (every 5 months). The current policy saves on ordering costs but incurs a much larger cost for carrying the cycle inventory. Although it is easy to see which option is best on the basis of total ordering and holding costs, other factors may affect the final decision. For example, if the supplier would reduce the price per unit for large orders, it may be better to order the larger quantity.

Managerial Insights from the EOQ

Subjecting the EOQ formula to *sensitivity analysis* can yield valuable insights into the management of inventories. Sensitivity analysis is a technique for systematically changing crucial parameters to determine the effects of a change. Table 12.1 shows the effects on the EOQ when we substitute different values into the numerator or denominator of the formula.

TABLE 12.1			SENSITIVITY ANALYSIS OF THE EOQ	
Parameter	**EOQ**	**Parameter Change**	**EOQ Change**	**Comments**
Demand	$\sqrt{\dfrac{2\,D\,S}{H}}$	↑	↑	Increase in lot size is in proportion to the square root of D.
Order/Setup Costs	$\sqrt{\dfrac{2\,D\,S}{H}}$	↓	↓	Weeks of supply decreases and inventory turnover increases because the lot size decreases.
Holding Costs	$\sqrt{\dfrac{2\,D\,S}{H}}$	↓	↑	Larger lots are justified when holding costs decrease.

As Table 12.1 shows, the EOQ provides support for some of the intuition you may have about inventory management. However, the effect of ordering or setup cost changes on inventories is especially important for *lean systems*. This relationship explains why manufacturers are so concerned about reducing setup time and costs; it makes small lot production economic. Actually, lean systems provide an environment conducive to the use of the EOQ. For example, yearly, monthly, daily, or hourly demand rates are known with reasonable certainty in lean systems, and the rate of demand is relatively uniform. Lean systems (see Chapter 8, "Designing Lean Systems") may have few process constraints if the firm practices *constraint management* (see Chapter 7, "Managing Process Constraints"). In addition, lean systems strive for constant delivery lead times and dependable delivery quantities from suppliers, both of which are assumptions of the EOQ. Consequently, the EOQ as a lot sizing tool is quite compatible with the principles of lean systems.

INVENTORY CONTROL SYSTEMS

The EOQ and other lot-sizing methods answer the important question: *How much* should we order? Another important question that needs an answer is: *When* should we place the order? An inventory control system responds to both questions. In selecting an inventory control system for a particular application, the nature of the demands imposed on the inventory items is crucial. An important distinction between types of inventory is whether an item is subject to dependent or independent demand. Retailers, such as JCPenney, and distributors must manage **independent demand items**—that is, items for which demand is influenced by market conditions and is not related to the inventory decisions for any other item held in stock or produced. Independent demand inventory includes

independent demand items

Items for which demand is influenced by market conditions and is not related to the inventory decisions for any other item held in stock or produced.

- Wholesale and retail merchandise
- Service support inventory, such as stamps and mailing labels for post offices, office supplies for law firms, and laboratory supplies for research universities
- Product and replacement-part distribution inventories
- Maintenance, repair, and operating (MRO) supplies—that is, items that do not become part of the final service or product, such as employee uniforms, fuel, paint, and machine repair parts

Managing independent demand inventory can be tricky because demand is influenced by external factors. For example, the owner of a bookstore may not be sure how many copies of the latest best-seller novel customers will purchase during the coming month. As a result, the manager may decide to stock extra copies as a safeguard. Independent demand, such as the demand for various book titles, must be *forecasted*.

In this chapter, we focus on inventory control systems for independent demand items, which is the type of demand the bookstore owner, other retailers, service providers, and distributors face. Even though demand from any one customer is difficult to predict, low demand from some customers for a particular item often is offset by high demand from others. Thus, total demand for any independent demand item may follow a relatively smooth pattern, with some random fluctuations. *Dependent demand items* are those required as components or inputs to a service or product. Dependent demand exhibits a pattern very different from that of independent demand and must be managed with different techniques (see Chapter 15, "Planning Sufficient Resources").

In this section, we discuss and compare two inventory control systems: (1) the continuous review system, called a *Q* system, and (2) the periodic review system, called a *P* system. We close with a look at hybrid systems, which incorporate features of both the *P* and *Q* systems.

A shopper peruses the shoes display at a Macy's Department Store. Shoes experience an independent demand at the retail level.

Continuous Review System

A **continuous review (Q) system**, sometimes called a **reorder point (ROP) system** or *fixed order-quantity system*, tracks the remaining inventory of a SKU each time a withdrawal is made to determine whether it is time to reorder. In practice, these reviews are done frequently (e.g., daily) and often continuously (after each withdrawal). The advent of computers and electronic cash registers linked to inventory records has made continuous reviews easy. At each review, a decision is made about a SKU's inventory position. If it is judged to be too low, the system triggers a new order. The **inventory position (IP)** measures the SKU's ability to satisfy future demand. It includes **scheduled receipts (SR)**, which are orders that have been placed but have not yet been received, plus on-hand inventory (OH) minus backorders (BO). Sometimes scheduled receipts are called **open orders**. More specifically,

Inventory position = On-hand inventory + Scheduled receipts − Backorders

$$IP = OH + SR - BO$$

When the inventory position reaches a predetermined minimum level, called the **reorder point (R)**, a fixed quantity *Q* of the SKU is ordered. In a continuous review system, although the order quantity *Q* is fixed, the time between orders can vary. Hence, *Q* can be based on the EOQ, a price break quantity (the minimum lot size that qualifies for a quantity discount), a container size (such as a truckload), or some other quantity selected by management.

Selecting the Reorder Point When Demand and Lead Time Are Constant   To demonstrate the concept of a reorder point, suppose that the demand for feeders at the museum gift shop in Example 12.2 is always 18 per week, the lead time is a constant 2 weeks, and the supplier always ships the exact number ordered on time. With both demand and lead time constant, the museum's buyer can wait until the inventory position drops to 36 units, or (18 units/week) (2 weeks), to place a new order. Thus, in this case, the reorder point, *R*, equals the *total demand during lead time*, with no added allowance for safety stock.

Figure 12.6 shows how the system operates when demand and lead time are constant. The

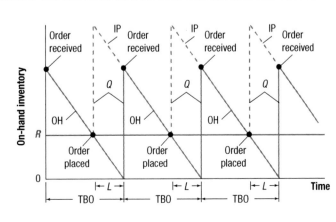

◀ **FIGURE 12.6**
Q System When Demand and Lead Time Are Constant and Certain

continuous review (Q) system

A system designed to track the remaining inventory of a SKU each time a withdrawal is made to determine whether it is time to reorder.

reorder point (ROP) system

See continuous review (Q) system.

inventory position (IP)

The measurement of a SKU's ability to satisfy future demand.

scheduled receipts (SR)

Orders that have been placed but have not yet been received.

open orders

See scheduled receipts (SR).

reorder point (R)

The predetermined minimum level that an inventory position must reach before a fixed quantity *Q* of the SKU is ordered.

downward-sloping line represents the on-hand inventory, which is being depleted at a constant rate. When it reaches reorder point R (the horizontal line), a new order for Q units is placed. The on-hand inventory continues to drop throughout lead time L until the order is received. At that time, which marks the end of the lead time, on-hand inventory jumps by Q units. A new order arrives just when inventory drops to 0. The TBO is the same for each cycle.

The inventory position, IP, shown in Figure 12.6 corresponds to the on-hand inventory, except during the lead time. Just after a new order is placed, at the start of the lead time, IP increases by Q, as shown by the dashed line. The IP exceeds OH by this same margin through-out the lead time.[4] At the end of the lead time, when the scheduled receipts convert to on-hand inventory, IP = OH once again. The key point here is to compare IP, not OH, with R in deciding whether to reorder. A common error is to ignore scheduled receipts or backorders.

EXAMPLE 12.3   Placing a New Order When Demand and Lead Time Are Constant

Demand for chicken soup at a supermarket is always 25 cases a day and the lead time is always 4 days. The shelves were just restocked with chicken soup, leaving an on-hand inventory of only 10 cases. No backorders currently exist, but there is one open order in the pipeline for 200 cases. What is the inventory position? Should a new order be placed?

SOLUTION

$$R = \text{Total demand during lead time} = (25)(4) = 100 \text{ cases}$$
$$\text{IP} = \text{OH} + \text{SR} - \text{BO}$$
$$= 10 + 200 - 0 = 210 \text{ cases}$$

DECISION POINT

Because IP exceeds R (210 versus 100), do not reorder. Inventory is almost depleted, but a new order need not be placed because the scheduled receipt is in the pipeline.

Selecting the Reorder Point When Demand Is Variable and Lead Time Is Constant   In reality demand is not always predictable. For instance, the museum's buyer knows that *average* demand is 18 feeders per week. That is, a variable number of feeders may be purchased during the lead time, with an average demand during lead time of 36 feeders (assuming that each week's demand is identically distributed and lead time is a constant 2 weeks). This situation gives rise to the need for safety stocks. Suppose that the museum's buyer sets R at 46 units, thereby placing orders before they typically are needed. This approach will create a safety stock, or stock held in excess of expected demand, of 10 units (46 – 36) to buffer against uncertain demand. In general

$$\text{Reorder point} = \text{Average demand during lead time} + \text{Safety stock}$$
$$= \bar{d}\,L + \text{safety stock}$$

where

$$\bar{d} = \text{average demand per week (or day or month)}$$
$$L = \text{constant lead time in weeks (or days or months)}$$

Figure 12.7 shows how the Q system operates when demand is variable and lead time is constant. The wavy downward-sloping line indicates that demand varies from day to day. Its slope is steeper in the second cycle, which means that the demand rate is higher during this time period. The changing demand rate means that the time between orders changes, so $\text{TBO}_1 \neq \text{TBO}_2 \neq \text{TBO}_3$. Because of uncertain demand, sales during the lead time are unpredictable, and safety stock is added to hedge against lost sales. This addition is why R is

---

[4] A possible exception is the unlikely situation when more than one scheduled receipt is open at the same time because of long lead times.

higher in Figure 12.7 than in Figure 12.6. It also explains why the on-hand inventory usually does not drop to 0 by the time a replenishment order arrives. The greater the safety stock and thus the higher reorder point R, the less likely a stockout.

Because the average demand during lead time is variable, the real decision to be made when selecting R concerns the safety stock level. Deciding on a small or large safety stock is a trade-off between customer service and inventory holding costs. Cost minimization models can be used to find the best safety stock, but they require estimates of stockout and back-order costs, which are usually difficult to make with any precision because it is hard to estimate the effect of lost sales, lost customer confidence, future loyalty of customers, and market share because the customer went to a competitor. The usual approach for determining R is for management—based on judgment—to set a reasonable service-level policy for the inventory and then determine the safety stock level that satisfies this policy. There are three steps to arrive at a reorder point:

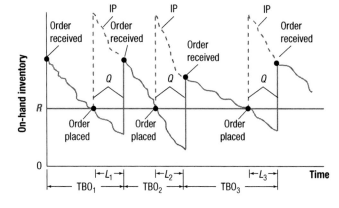

▲ FIGURE 12.7
Q System When Demand Is Uncertain

1. Choose an appropriate service-level policy.
2. Determine the demand during lead time probability distribution.
3. Determine the safety stock and reorder point levels.

Step 1: Service level policy.   Select a **service level**, or **cycle-service level** (the desired probability of not running out of stock in any one ordering cycle), which begins at the time an order is placed and ends when it arrives in stock. The intent is to provide coverage over the **protection interval**, or the period over which safety stock must protect the user from running out of stock. For the Q system, the lead time is the protection interval. For example, in a bookstore the manager may select a 90 percent cycle-service level for a book. In other words, the probability is 90 percent that demand will not exceed the supply during the lead time. The probability of running short *during the protection interval*, creating a stockout or backorder, is only 10 percent $(100 - 90)$ in our example. This stockout risk, which occurs only during the lead time in the Q system, is greater than the overall risk of a stockout because the risk is nonexistent outside the ordering cycle.

Step 2: Demand during lead time distribution.   Determine the demand during lead time probability distribution, which requires the specification of its mean and standard deviation. To translate a cycle-service level policy into a specific safety stock level, we must know how demand during the lead time is distributed. If demand and lead times vary little around their averages, the safety stock can be small. Conversely, if they vary greatly from one order cycle to the next, the safety stock must be large. Variability is measured by the demand during lead time distribution. Sometimes average demand during the lead time and the standard deviation of demand during the lead time are not directly available and must be calculated by combining information on the demand rate with information on the lead time. Suppose that lead time is constant and demand is variable, but records on demand are not collected for a time interval that is exactly the same as the lead time. The same inventory control system may be used to manage thousands of different SKUs, each with a different lead time. For example, if demand is reported *weekly*, these records can be used directly to compute the average and the standard deviation of demand during the lead time if the lead time is exactly one week. However, if the lead time is three weeks, the computation is more difficult.

We can determine the demand during the lead time distribution by making some reasonable assumptions. Suppose that the average demand, $\overline{d}$, is known along with the standard deviation of demand, σ_d, over some time interval such as days or weeks. Also, suppose that the probability distributions of demand for each time interval are identical and independent of each other. For example, if the time interval is a week, the probability distributions of demand are assumed to be the same each week (identical $\overline{d}$ and σ_d), and the total demand in one week does not affect the total demand in another week. Let L be the constant lead time, expressed in the same time units as the demand. Under these assumptions, average demand during the lead time will be the sum of the averages for each of the L identical and independent distributions of demand, or $\overline{d} + \overline{d} + \overline{d} + \ldots = \overline{d}L$. In addition, the variance of the demand during lead time distribution will be the sum of the variances of the L identical and independent distributions of demand, or

$$\sigma_d^2 + \sigma_d^2 + \sigma_d^2 + \ldots = \sigma_d^2 L$$

service level

The desired probability of not running out of stock in any one ordering cycle, which begins at the time an order is placed and ends when it arrives in stock.

cycle-service level

See service level.

protection interval

The period over which safety stock must protect the user from running out of stock.

Finally, the standard deviation of the demand during lead time distribution is

$$\sigma_{dLT} = \sqrt{\sigma_d^2 L} = \sigma_d \sqrt{L}$$

Figure 12.8 shows how the demand distribution of the lead time is developed from the individual distributions of weekly demands, where $\bar{d} = 75$, $\sigma_d = 15$, and $L = 3$ weeks. In this example, average demand during the lead time is $(75)(3) = 225$ units and $\sigma_{dLT} = 15\sqrt{3} = 25.98$.

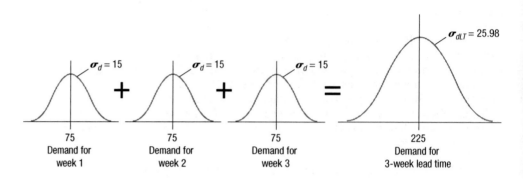

FIGURE 12.8 ▲
Development of Demand Distribution for the Lead Time

Step 3: Safety stock and reorder point. When selecting the safety stock, the inventory planner often assumes that demand during the lead time is normally distributed, as shown in Figure 12.9. The average demand during the lead time is the centerline of the graph, with 50 percent of the area under the curve to the left and 50 percent to the right. Thus, if a cycle-service level of 50 percent were chosen, the reorder point R would be the quantity represented by this centerline. Because R equals the average demand during the lead time plus the safety stock, the safety stock is 0 when R equals this average demand. Demand is less than average 50 percent of the time and, thus, having no safety stock will be sufficient only 50 percent of the time.

To provide a service level above 50 percent, the reorder point must be greater than the average demand during the lead time. As Figure 12.9 shows, that requires moving the reorder point to the right of the centerline so that more than 50 percent of the area under the curve is to the left of R. An 85 percent cycle-service level is achieved in Figure 12.9 with 85 percent of the area under the curve to the left of R (in blue) and only 15 percent to the right (in pink). We compute the safety stock as follows:

$$\text{Safety stock} = z\sigma_{dLT}$$

where

z = the number of standard deviations needed to achieve the cycle-service level

σ_{dLT} = standard deviation of demand during the lead time

The reorder point becomes

$$R = \bar{d}L + \text{safety stock}$$

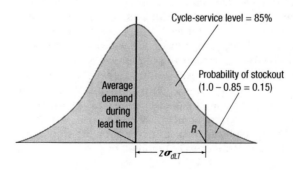

FIGURE 12.9 ▶
Finding Safety Stock with a Normal Probability Distribution for an 85 Percent Cycle-Service Level

The higher the value of z, the higher the safety stock and the cycle-service level should be. If $z = 0$, there is no safety stock, and stockouts will occur during 50 percent of the order cycles. For a cycle-service level of 85 percent, $z = 1.04$. Example 12.4 shows how to use the Normal Distribution appendix to find the appropriate z value, safety stock, and reorder point.

EXAMPLE 12.4	**Reorder Point for Variable Demand and Constant Lead Time**

Let us return to the bird feeder in Example 12.2. The EOQ is 75 units. Suppose that the average demand is 18 units per week with a standard deviation of 5 units. The lead time is constant at two weeks. Determine the safety stock and reorder point if management wants a 90 percent cycle-service level.

SOLUTION

In this case, $\sigma_d = 5$, $\bar{d} = 18$ units, and $L = 2$ weeks, so $\sigma_{dLT} = \sigma_d\sqrt{L} = 5\sqrt{2} = 7.07$. Consult the body of the table in the Normal Distribution appendix for 0.9000, which corresponds to a 90 percent cycle-service level. The closest number is 0.8997, which corresponds to 1.2 in the row heading and 0.08 in the column heading. Adding these values gives a z value of 1.28. With this information, we calculate the safety stock and reorder point as follows:

$$\text{Safety stock} = z\sigma_{dLT} = 1.28(7.07) = 9.05 \text{ or } 9 \text{ units}$$
$$\text{Reorder point} = \bar{d}L + \text{Safety stock}$$
$$= 2(18) + 9 = 45 \text{ units}$$

DECISION POINT

The Q system for the bird feeder operates as follows: Whenever the inventory position reaches 45 units, order the EOQ of 75 units. Various order quantities and safety stock levels can be used in a Q system. For example, management could specify a different order quantity (because of shipping constraints) or a different safety stock (because of storage limitations).

Selecting the Reorder Point When Both Demand and Lead Time Are Variable In practice it is often the case that both the demand and the lead time are variable. Unfortunately, the equations for the safety stock and reorder point become more complicated. In the model below we make two simplifying assumptions. First, the demand distribution and the lead time distribution are measured in the same time units. For example, both demand and lead time are measured in weeks. Second, demand and lead time are *independent*. That is, demand per week is not affected by the length of the lead time.

$$\text{Safety stock} = z\sigma_{dLT}$$
$$R = (\text{Average weekly demand} \times \text{Average lead time in weeks}) + \text{Safety stock}$$
$$= \bar{d}\,\bar{L} + \text{Safety stock}$$

where

$\bar{d}$ = Average weekly (or daily or monthly) demand

$\bar{L}$ = Average weekly (or daily or monthly) lead time

σ_d = Standard deviation of weekly (or daily or monthly) demand

σ_{LT} = Standard deviation of the lead time, and

$\sigma_{dLT} = \sqrt{\bar{L}\sigma_d^2 + \bar{d}^2\sigma_{LT}^2}$

Now that we have determined the mean and standard deviation of the demand during lead time distribution under these more complicated conditions, we can select the reorder point as we did before for the case where the lead time was constant.

EXAMPLE 12.5	**Reorder Point for Variable Demand and Variable Lead Time**

The Office Supply Shop estimates that the average demand for a popular ball-point pen is 12,000 pens per week with a standard deviation of 3,000 pens. The current inventory policy calls for replenishment orders of 156,000 pens. The average lead time from the distributor is 5 weeks, with a standard deviation of 2 weeks. If management wants a 95 percent cycle-service level, what should the reorder point be?

Tutor 12.3 in my**om**lab provides a new example to determine the safety stock and the reorder point for a Q system.

SOLUTION

We have $\bar{d} = 12{,}000$ pens, $\sigma_d = 3{,}000$ pens, $\bar{L} = 5$ weeks, and $\sigma_{LT} = 2$ weeks.

$$\sigma_{dLT} = \sqrt{\bar{L}\sigma_d^2 + \bar{d}^{\,2}\sigma_{LT}^2} = \sqrt{(5)(3{,}000)^2 + (12{,}000)^2(2)^2} = 24{,}919.87 \text{ pens}$$

Consult the body of the Normal Distribution appendix for 0.9500, which corresponds to a 95 percent cycle-service level. That value falls exactly in the middle of the tabular values of 0.9495 (for a z value of 1.64) and 0.9505 (for a z value of 1.65). Consequently, we will use the more conservative value of 1.65. We calculate the safety stock and reorder point as follows:

$$\text{Safety stock} = z\sigma_{dLT} = (1.65)(24{,}919.87) = 41{,}117.79, \text{ or } 41{,}118 \text{ pens}$$

$$\text{Reorder point} = \bar{d}\bar{L} + \text{Safety stock} = (12{,}000)(5) + 41{,}118 = 101{,}118 \text{ pens}$$

DECISION POINT

Whenever the stock of ball-point pens drops to 101,118, management should place another replenishment order of 156,000 pens to the distributor.

Sometimes the theoretical distributions for demand and lead time are not known. In those cases, we can use simulation to find the distribution of demand during lead time using discrete distributions for demand and lead times. Simulation can also be used to estimate the performance of an inventory system. Solved Problems 6 and 7 show how the Demand During Lead Time Simulator and the Q System Simulator in OM Explorer can be used to determine the appropriate inventory system parameters and to see how the system might work in practice. More discussion, and an example, can be found in my**om**lab.

visual system

A system that allows employees to place orders when inventory visibly reaches a certain marker.

two-bin system

A visual system version of the Q system in which a SKU's inventory is stored at two different locations.

Two-Bin System   The concept of a Q system can be incorporated in a **visual system**, that is, a system that allows employees to place orders when inventory visibly reaches a certain marker. Visual systems are easy to administer because records are not kept on the current inventory position. The historical usage rate can simply be reconstructed from past purchase orders. Visual systems are intended for use with low-value SKUs that have a steady demand, such as nuts and bolts or office supplies. Overstocking is common, but the extra inventory holding cost is minimal because the items have relatively little value.

A visual system version of the Q system is the **two-bin system** in which a SKU's inventory is stored at two different locations. Inventory is first withdrawn from one bin. If the first bin is empty, the second bin provides backup to cover demand until a replenishment order arrives. An empty first bin signals the need to place a new order. Premade order forms placed near the bins let workers send one to purchasing or even directly to the supplier. When the new order arrives, the second bin is restored to its normal level and the rest is put in the first bin. The two-bin system operates like a Q system, with the normal level in the second bin being the reorder point R. The system also may be implemented with just one bin by marking the bin at the reorder point level.

Calculating Total Q System Costs   Total costs for the continuous review (Q) system is the sum of three cost components:

Total cost = Annual cycle inventory holding cost + annual ordering cost

+ annual safety stock holding cost

$$C = \frac{Q}{2}(H) + \frac{D}{Q}(S) + (H)(\text{Safety stock})$$

The annual cycle-inventory holding cost and annual ordering cost are the same equations we used for computing the total annual cycle-inventory cost in Example 12.1. The annual cost of holding the safety stock is computed under the assumption that the safety stock is on hand at all times. Referring to Figure 12.7 in each order cycle, we will sometimes experience a demand greater than the average demand during lead time, and sometimes we will experience less. On average over the year, we can assume the safety stock will be on hand. See Solved Problem 1 at the end of this chapter for an example of calculating the total costs for a Q system.

Periodic Review System

An alternative inventory control system is the **periodic review (*P*) system**, sometimes called a *fixed interval reorder system* or *periodic reorder system*, in which an item's inventory position is reviewed periodically rather than continuously. Such a system can simplify delivery scheduling because it establishes a routine. A new order is always placed at the end of each review, and the time between orders (TBO) is fixed at *P*. Demand is a random variable, so total demand between reviews varies. In a *P* system, the lot size, *Q*, may change from one order to the next, but the time between orders is fixed. An example of a periodic review system is that of a soft-drink supplier making weekly rounds of grocery stores. Each week, the supplier reviews the store's inventory of soft drinks and restocks the store with enough items to meet demand and safety stock requirements until the next week.

periodic review (*P*) sytem

A system in which an item's inventory position is reviewed periodically rather than continuously.

Under a *P* system, four of the original EOQ assumptions are maintained: (1) no constraints are placed on the size of the lot, (2) the relevant costs are holding and ordering costs, (3) decisions for one SKU are independent of decisions for other SKUs, and (4) lead times are certain and supply is known. However, demand uncertainty is again allowed for. Figure 12.10 shows the periodic review system under these assumptions. The downward-sloping line again represents on-hand inventory. When the predetermined time, *P*, has elapsed since the last review, an order is placed to bring the inventory position, represented by the dashed line, up to the target inventory level, *T*. The lot size for the first review is Q_1, or the difference between inventory position IP_1 and *T*. As with the continuous review system, IP and OH differ only during the lead time. When the order arrives at the end of the lead time, OH and IP again are identical. Figure 12.10 shows that lot sizes vary from one order cycle to the next. Because the inventory position is lower at the second review, a greater quantity is needed to achieve an inventory level of *T*.

▼ FIGURE 12.10
P System When Demand Is Uncertain

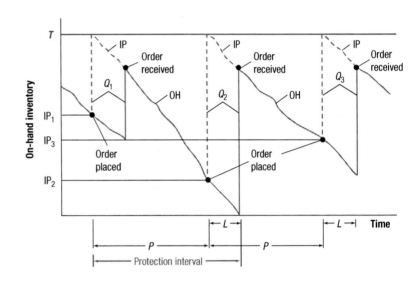

EXAMPLE 12.6   Determining How Much to Order in a *P* System

A distribution center has a backorder for five 46-inch LCD TV sets. No inventory is currently on hand, and now is the time to review. How many should be reordered if *T* = 400 and no receipts are scheduled?

SOLUTION

$$IP = OH + SR - BO$$
$$= 0 + 0 - 5 = -5 \text{ sets}$$
$$T - IP = 400 - (-5) = 405 \text{ sets}$$

That is, 405 sets must be ordered to bring the inventory position up to *T* sets.

Selecting the Time between Reviews   To run a *P* system, managers must make two decisions: the length of time between reviews, *P*, and the target inventory level, *T*. Let us first consider the time between reviews, *P*. It can be any convenient interval, such as each Friday or every other Friday. Another option is to base *P* on the cost trade-offs of the EOQ. In other words, *P* can be set equal to the average time between orders for the economic order quantity, or TBO_{EOQ}. Because demand is variable, some orders will be larger than the EOQ and some will be smaller. However, over an extended period of time, the average lot size should be close to the EOQ. If other models are used to determine the lot size (e.g., those described in Supplement D, "Special Inventory Models"), we divide the lot size chosen by the annual demand, *D*, and use this ratio as *P*. It will be expressed as the fraction of a year between orders, which can be converted into months, weeks, or days as needed.

Selecting the Target Inventory Level When Demand Is Variable and Lead Time Is Constant   Now let us calculate the target inventory level, *T*, when demand is variable but the lead time is constant. Figure 12.10 reveals that an order must be large enough to make the inventory position, IP, last beyond the next review, which is P time periods away. The checker must wait P periods to revise, correct, and reestablish the inventory position. Then, a new order is placed, but it does not arrive until after the lead time, L. Therefore, as Figure 12.10 shows, a protection interval of $P + L$ periods is needed. A fundamental difference between the Q and P systems is the length of time needed for stockout protection. A Q system needs stockout protection only during the lead time because orders can be placed as soon as they are needed and will be received L periods later. A P system, however, needs stockout protection for the longer $P + L$ protection interval because orders are placed only at fixed intervals, and the inventory is not checked until the next designated review time.

As with the Q system, we need to develop the appropriate distribution of demand during the protection interval to specify the system fully. In a P system, we must develop the distribution of demand for $P + L$ time periods. The target inventory level T must equal the expected demand during the protection interval of $P + L$ periods, plus enough safety stock to protect against demand uncertainty over this same protection interval. We assume that lead time is constant and that demand in one period is independent of demand in the next period. Thus, the average demand during the protection interval is $\bar{d}(P + L)$, or

$$T = \bar{d}(P + L) + \text{Safety stock for the protection interval}$$

We compute safety stock for a P system much as we did for the Q system. However, the safety stock must cover demand uncertainty for a longer period of time. When using a normal probability distribution, we multiply the desired standard deviations to implement the cycle-service level, z, by the standard deviation of demand during the protection interval, σ_{P+L}. The value of z is the same as for a Q system with the same cycle-service level. Thus,

$$\text{Safety stock} = z\sigma_{P+L}$$

Based on our earlier logic for calculating σ_{dLT}, we know that the standard deviation of the distribution of demand during the protection interval is

$$\sigma_{P+L} = \sigma_d \sqrt{P + L}$$

Because a P system requires safety stock to cover demand uncertainty over a longer time period than a Q system, a P system requires more safety stock; that is, σ_{P+L} exceeds σ_{dLT}. Hence, to gain the convenience of a P system requires that overall inventory levels be somewhat higher than those for a Q system.

EXAMPLE 12.7	**Calculating P and T**

Tutor 12.4 in my**om**lab provides a new example to determine the review interval and the target inventory for a P system.

Again, let us return to the bird feeder example. Recall that demand for the bird feeder is normally distributed with a mean of 18 units per week and a standard deviation in weekly demand of 5 units. The lead time is 2 weeks, and the business operates 52 weeks per year. The Q system developed in Example 12.4 called for an EOQ of 75 units and a safety stock of 9 units for a cycle-service level of 90 percent. What is the equivalent P system? Answers are to be rounded to the nearest integer.

SOLUTION

We first define D and then P. Here, P is the time between reviews, expressed in weeks because the data are expressed in demand *per week*:

$$D = (18 \text{ units/week})(52 \text{ weeks/year}) = 936 \text{ units}$$

$$P = \frac{\text{EOQ}}{D}(52) = \frac{75}{936}(52) = 4.2 \quad \text{or} \quad 4 \text{ weeks}$$

With $\bar{d} = 18$ units per week, an alternative approach is to calculate P by dividing the EOQ by $\bar{d}$ to get 75/18=4.2 or 4 weeks. Either way, we would review the bird feeder inventory every 4 weeks. We now find the standard deviation of demand over the protection interval ($P + L = 6$):

$$\sigma_{P+L} = \sigma_d \sqrt{P + L} = 5\sqrt{6} = 12.25 \text{ units}$$

Before calculating T, we also need a z value. For a 90 percent cycle-service level, $z = 1.28$ (see the Normal Distribution appendix). The safety stock becomes

$$\text{safety stock} = z\sigma_{P+L} = 1.28(12.25) = 15.68, \text{ or } 16 \text{ units}$$

We now solve for T:

$$T = \text{Average demand during the protection interval} + \text{Safety stock}$$
$$= \bar{d}(P + L) + \text{safety stock}$$
$$= (18 \text{ units/week})(6 \text{ weeks}) + 16 \text{ units} = 124 \text{ units}$$

DECISION POINT

Every 4 weeks we would order the number of units needed to bring inventory position IP (counting the new order) up to the target inventory level of 124 units. The P system requires 16 units in safety stock, while the Q system only needs 9 units. If cost were the only criterion, the Q system would be the choice for the bird feeder. As we discuss later, other factors may sway the decision in favor of the P system.

Selecting the Target Inventory Level When Demand and Lead Time Are Variable A useful approach for finding P and T in practice is simulation. Given discrete probability distributions for demand and lead time, simulation can be used to estimate the demand during the protection interval distribution. The Demand During the Protection Interval Simulator in OM Explorer can be used to determine the distribution. Once determined, the distribution can be used to select a value for T, given a desired cycle-service level. Solved Problem 7 demonstrates this approach. More discussion, and an example, can be found in my**om**lab.

Managerial Practice 12.1 shows how the use of periodic inventory review systems is important in supply chains in the chemical industry.

Single-Bin System The concept of a P system can be translated into a simple visual system of inventory control. In the **single-bin system**, a maximum level is marked on the storage shelf or bin, and the inventory is brought up to the mark periodically—say, once a week. The single bin may be, for example, a gasoline storage tank at a service station or a storage bin for small parts at a manufacturing plant.

single-bin system

A system of inventory control in which a maximum level is marked on the storage shelf or bin, and the inventory is brought up to the mark periodically.

Calculating Total P System Costs The total costs for the P system are the sum of the same three cost elements for the Q system. The differences are in the calculation of the order quantity and the safety stock. As shown in Figure 12.10, the average order quantity will be the average consumption of inventory during the P periods between orders. Consequently, $Q = \bar{d}P$. Total costs for the P system are

$$C = \frac{\bar{d}P}{2}(H) + \frac{D}{\bar{d}P}(S) + (H)(\text{Safety stock})$$

See Solved Problem 1 at the end of this chapter for an example of calculating total P system costs.

Comparative Advantages of the Q and P Systems

Neither the Q nor the P system is best for all situations. Three P-system advantages must be balanced against three Q-system advantages. The advantages of one system are implicitly disadvantages of the other system.

The primary advantages of P systems are the following:

1. The system is convenient because replenishments are made at fixed intervals. Fixed replenishment intervals allow for standardized pickup and delivery times.

2. Orders for multiple items from the same supplier can be combined into a single purchase order. This approach reduces ordering and transportation costs and can result in a price break from the supplier.

3. The inventory position, IP, needs to be known only when a review is made (not continuously, as in a Q system). However, this advantage is moot for firms using computerized record-keeping systems, in which a transaction is reported upon each receipt or withdrawal. When inventory records are always current, the system is called a **perpetual inventory system**.

perpetual inventory system

A system of inventory control in which the inventory records are always current.

MANAGERIAL PRACTICE 12.1 — The Supply Chain Implications of Periodic Review Inventory Systems at Celanese

What do products such as paints, adhesives, coatings, plastics, medicines, cosmetics, detergents, textiles, or fragrances have in common? All of these products use acetic acid as a major component. Celanese, a $6.5 billion chemical company with $640 million in total inventories, is a major supplier of acetic acid in the world. The large investment in inventory forces Celanese to take a hard look at inventory policies for all products, including acetic acid. The key to successful management of the inventories was to acknowledge the interaction between the inventory policies at each stage of the supply chain with the realities of material flows and logistics in the chemical industry.

The supply chain for acetic acid is complex, involving 90 stages. For example, the supply chain is comprised of stages such as vendors supplying a liner to transport the acid, manufacturing sites producing the acid, transportation modes moving acid, warehouses storing it, and customer demand locations to which the acid is finally shipped. There are four manufacturing facilities, three in the United States and one in Singapore, each of which supplies several storage locations worldwide. Transportation stages correspond to rail, barges, trucks, and ocean vessels. Material typically moves in large quantities because of economies of scale and transportation schedules. Storage facilities may be supplied by multiple upstream facilities as well as the manufacturing plant itself.

The use of periodic review inventory systems at the storage and demand locations in this supply chain scenario makes sense for several reasons. First, the transportation modes have defined schedules of operation. Review periods at storage facilities reflect the schedule of the supplying transportation mode. Second, customer orders are typically batched and timed with weekly, bi-weekly, or monthly frequencies. Celanese often assigns customers and storage facilities specific days to place orders so that their own production schedules can be coordinated. Finally, the cyclic ordering is often a function of the capital intensity of the industry. Long production runs are scheduled to gain production efficiency; it is costly to set up the equipment for another product.

Specifying the best review period and target inventory levels for the various stages of the supply chain takes sophisticated mathematical models. Regardless of the effort required, it is important to recognize the implications of the supply chain when determining inventory policies.

Large manufacturers of chemicals often assign schedules to customers and storage facilities for ordering and picking up chemicals. Such a practice facilitates the coordination of the manufacturer's production schedules. Here a tank truck is loaded at its assigned time.

Source: John M. Bossert and Sean P. Williams, "A Periodic-Review Modeling Approach for Guaranteed Service Supply Chains," *Interfaces*, Vol. 37, No. 5 (September/October 2007), pp. 420–435; http://finance.yahoo.com; www.Celanese.com, 2008.

The primary advantages of Q systems are the following:

1. The review frequency of each SKU may be individualized. Tailoring the review frequency to the SKU can reduce total ordering and holding costs.
2. Fixed lot sizes, if large enough, can result in quantity discounts. The firm's physical limitations, such as its truckload capacities, materials handling methods, and shelf space might also necessitate a fixed lot size.
3. Lower safety stocks result in savings.

In conclusion, the choice between Q and P systems is not clear cut. Which system is better depends on the relative importance of its advantages in various situations.

Hybrid Systems

Various hybrid inventory control systems merge some but not all the features of the *P* and *Q* systems. We briefly examine two such systems: (1) optional replenishment and (2) base stock.

Optional Replenishment System   Sometimes called the optional review, min–max, or (*s*, *S*) system, the **optional replenishment system** is much like the *P* system. It is used to review the inventory position at fixed time intervals and, if the position has dropped to (or below) a predetermined level, to place a variable-sized order to cover expected needs. The new order is large enough to bring the inventory position up to a target inventory, similar to *T* for the *P* system. However, orders are not placed after a review unless the inventory position has dropped to the predetermined minimum level. The minimum level acts as the reorder point *R* does in a *Q* system. If the target is 100 and the minimum level is 60, the minimum order size is 40 (or 100 − 60). Because continuous reviews need not be made, this system is particularly attractive when both review and ordering costs are high.

optional replenishment system

A system used to review the inventory position at fixed time intervals and, if the position has dropped to (or below) a predetermined level, to place a variable-sized order to cover expected needs.

Base-Stock System   In its simplest form, the **base-stock system** issues a replenishment order, *Q*, each time a withdrawal is made, for the same amount as the withdrawal. This one-for-one replacement policy maintains the inventory position at a base-stock level equal to expected demand during the lead time plus safety stock. The base-stock level, therefore, is equivalent to the reorder point in a *Q* system. However, order quantities now vary to keep the inventory position at *R* at all times. Because this position is the lowest IP possible that will maintain a specified service level, the base-stock system may be used to minimize cycle inventory. More orders are placed, but each order is smaller. This system is appropriate for expensive items, such as replacement engines for jet airplanes. No more inventory is held than the maximum demand expected until a replacement order can be received.

base-stock system

An inventory control system that issues a replenishment order, *Q*, each time a withdrawal is made, for the same amount of the withdrawal.

Inventory management is a critical activity for the efficient operation of supply chains. Whether the firm is a service provider or a manufacturer, inventories are a necessity. In this chapter we focused on the systems firms can use to maintain levels of inventory that balance cost with customer service. ABC analysis identifies inventory categories so that management can focus attention on the most critical items. We explored the economic order quantity (EOQ) as a starting point for the determination of the best cycle-inventory level, its assumptions, and it usefulness for gaining insight into the management of inventory. We then showed how to develop and use the continuous review system and the periodic review system and identified the benefits and shortcomings of each one. There are also visual systems and hybrid systems that managers can use to fit certain situations. In Supplement D, "Special Inventory Models," we show models that can be useful for quantity discounts, production lot sizes, and one-period decisions.

INTERNET RESOURCES

myom**lab** and the Companion Website at **www.pearsonglobaleditions.com/krajewski** contain many tools, activities, and resources designed for this chapter.

KEY EQUATIONS

1. Total annual cycle-inventory cost = Annual holding cost + Annual ordering or setup cost

$$C = \frac{Q}{2}(H) + \frac{D}{Q}(S)$$

2. Economic order quantity:

$$EOQ = \sqrt{\frac{2DS}{H}}$$

3. Time between orders, expressed in weeks:

$$TBO_{EOQ} = \frac{EOQ}{D}(52 \text{ weeks/year})$$

4. Inventory position = On-hand inventory + Scheduled receipts − Backorders

$$IP = OH + SR - BO$$

5. Continuous review system:

Protection interval = Lead time (L)

Standard deviation of demand during the lead time (constant L) = $\sigma_{dLT} = \sigma_d \sqrt{L}$

Standard deviation of demand during the lead time (variable L) =
$$\sigma_{dLT} = \sqrt{L\sigma_d^2 + \bar{d}^2 \sigma_{LT}^2}$$

Safety stock = $z\sigma_{dLT}$

Reorder point (R) for constant lead time = $\bar{d}L$ + Safety stock

Reorder point (R) for variable lead time   = $\bar{d}\bar{L}$ + Safety stock

Order quantity = EOQ

Replenishment rule: Order EOQ units when IP ≤ R

Total Q system cost: $C = \dfrac{Q}{2}(H) + \dfrac{D}{Q}(S) + (H)(\text{Safety stock})$

6. Periodic review system:

Review interval = Time between orders = P

Protection interval = Time between orders + Lead time

$$= P + L$$

Standard deviation of demand during the protection interval = $\sigma_{P+L} = \sigma_d \sqrt{P + L}$

Safety stock = $z\sigma_{P+L}$

Target inventory level (T) = Average demand during the protection interval + Safety stock

$$= \bar{d}(P + L) + \text{Safety stock}$$

Order quantity = Target inventory level − Inventory position = T − IP

Replenishment rule: Every P time periods, order T − IP units

Total P system cost: $C = \dfrac{\bar{d}P}{2}(H) + \dfrac{D}{\bar{d}P}(S) + (H)(\text{Safety stock})$

KEY TERMS

ABC analysis	inventory position (IP)	reorder point (ROP) system
base-stock system	lot size	scheduled receipts (SR)
continuous review (Q) system	open orders	service level
cycle counting	optional replenishment system	single-bin system
cycle-service level	periodic review (P) system	stock-keeping unit (SKU)
economic order quantity (EOQ)	perpetual inventory system	time between orders (TBO)
independent demand items	protection interval	two-bin system
inventory management	reorder point (R)	visual system

SOLVED PROBLEM 1

A regional distributor purchases discontinued appliances from various suppliers and then sells them on demand to retailers in the region. The distributor operates 5 days per week, 52 weeks per year. Only when it is open for business can orders be received. Management wants to reevaluate its current inventory policy, which calls for order quantities of 440 counter-top mixers. The following data are estimated for the mixer:

Average daily demand $(\bar{d})$ = 100 mixers

Standard deviation of daily demand (σ_d) = 30 mixers

Lead time (L) = 3 days

Holding cost $(H) = \$9.40/\text{unit}/\text{year}$

Ordering cost $(S) = \$35/\text{order}$

Cycle-service level = 92 percent

The distributor uses a continuous review (Q) system.

a. What order quantity Q, and reorder point, R, should be used?

b. What is the total annual cost of the system?

c. If on-hand inventory is 40 units, one open order for 440 mixers is pending, and no backorders exist, should a new order be placed?

SOLUTION

a. Annual demand is

$$D = (5 \text{ days/week})(52 \text{ weeks/year})(100 \text{ mixers/day}) = 26,000 \text{ mixers/year}$$

The order quantity is

$$\text{EOQ} = \sqrt{\frac{2DS}{H}} = \sqrt{\frac{2(26,000)(\$35)}{\$9.40}} = \sqrt{193,167} = 440.02 \text{ or } 440 \text{ mixers}$$

The standard deviation of the demand during lead time distribution is

$$\sigma_{dLT} = \sigma_d \sqrt{L} = 30\sqrt{3} = 51.96$$

A 92 percent cycle-service level corresponds to $z = 1.41$ (see the Normal Distribution appendix). Therefore,

$$\text{Safety stock} = z\sigma_{dLT} = 1.41(51.96 \text{ mixers}) = 73.26 \text{ or } 73 \text{ mixers}$$
$$\text{Average demand during the lead time} = \bar{d}L = 100(3) = 300 \text{ mixers}$$
$$\text{Reorder point } (R) = \text{Average demand during the lead time} + \text{Safety stock}$$
$$= 300 \text{ mixers} + 73 \text{ mixers} = 373 \text{ mixers}$$

With a continuous review system, $Q = 440$ and $R = 373$.

b. The total annual cost for the Q systems is

$$C = \frac{Q}{2}(H) + \frac{D}{Q}(S) + (H)(\text{Safety stock})$$

$$C = \frac{440}{2}(\$9.40) + \frac{26,000}{440}(35) + (\$9.40)(73) = \$4,822.38$$

c. Inventory position = On-hand inventory + Scheduled receipts − Backorders

$$\text{IP} = \text{OH} + \text{SR} - \text{BO} = 40 + 440 - 0 = 480 \text{ mixers}$$

Because IP (480) exceeds R (373), do not place a new order.

SOLVED PROBLEM 2

Suppose that a periodic review (P) system is used at the distributor in Solved Problem 2, but otherwise the data are the same.

a. Calculate the P (in workdays, rounded to the nearest day) that gives approximately the same number of orders per year as the EOQ.

b. What is the target inventory level, T? Compare the P system to the Q system in Solved Problem 2.

c. What is the total annual cost of the P system?

d. It is time to review the item. On-hand inventory is 40 mixers; receipt of 440 mixers is scheduled, and no backorders exist. How much should be reordered?

SOLUTION

a. The time between orders is

$$P = \frac{\text{EOQ}}{D}(260 \text{ days/year}) = \frac{440}{26,000}(260) = 4.4 \text{ or } 4 \text{ days}$$

b. Figure 12.11 shows that $T = 812$ and safety stock $= (1.41)(79.37) = 111.91$ or about 112 mixers. The corresponding Q system for the counter-top mixer requires less safety stock.

c. The total annual cost of the P system is

$$C = \frac{\overline{d}P}{2}(H) + \frac{D}{\overline{d}P}(S) + (H)(\text{Safety stock})$$

$$C = \frac{(100)(4)}{2}(\$9.40) + \frac{26,000}{(100)(4)}(\$35) + (\$9.40)(1.41)(79.37)$$

$$= \$5,207.80$$

d. Inventory position is the amount on hand plus scheduled receipts minus backorders, or

$$\text{IP} = \text{OH} + \text{SR} - \text{BO} = 40 + 440 - 0 = 480 \text{ mixers}$$

The order quantity is the target inventory level minus the inventory position, or

$$Q = T - \text{IP} = 812 \text{ mixers} - 480 \text{ mixers} = 332 \text{ mixers}$$

An order for 332 mixers should be placed.

FIGURE 12.11 ▶
OM Explorer Solver for Inventory Systems

Continuous Review (Q) System		Periodic Review (P) System	
z	1.41	Time Between Reviews (P)	4.00 Days
Safety Stock	73	☑ Enter manually	
Reorder Point	373	Standard Deviation of Demand During Protection Interval	79.37
Annual Cost	$4,822.38	Safety Stock	112
		Average Demand During Protection Interval	700
		Target Inventory Level (T)	812
		Annual Cost	$5,207.80

SOLVED PROBLEM 3

Nelson's Hardware Store stocks a 19.2 volt cordless drill that is a popular seller. Annual demand is 5,000 units, the ordering cost is $15, and the inventory holding cost is $4/unit/year.

a. What is the economic order quantity?

b. What is the total annual cost for this inventory item?

SOLUTION

a. The order quantity is

$$\text{EOQ} = \sqrt{\frac{2DS}{H}} = \sqrt{\frac{2(5,000)(\$15)}{\$4}} = \sqrt{37,500} = 193.65 \text{ or } 194 \text{ drills}$$

b. The total annual cost is

$$C = \frac{Q}{2}(H) + \frac{D}{Q}(S) = \frac{194}{2}(\$4) + \frac{5,000}{194}(\$15) = \$774.60$$

SOLVED PROBLEM 4

Booker's Book Bindery divides SKUs into three classes, according to their dollar usage. Calculate the usage values of the following SKUs and determine which is most likely to be classified as class A.

SOLUTION

The annual dollar usage for each SKU is determined by multiplying the annual usage quantity by the value per unit. As shown in Figure 12.12, the SKUs are then sorted by annual dollar

SKU Number	Description	Quantity Used per Year	Unit Value ($)
1	Boxes	500	3.00
2	Cardboard (square feet)	18,000	0.02
3	Cover stock	10,000	0.75
4	Glue (gallons)	75	40.00
5	Inside covers	20,000	0.05
6	Reinforcing tape (meters)	3,000	0.15
7	Signatures	150,000	0.45

usage, in declining order. Finally, A–B and B–C class lines are drawn roughly, according to the guidelines presented in the text. Here, class A includes only one SKU (signatures), which represents only 1/7, or 14 percent, of the SKUs but accounts for 83 percent of annual dollar usage. Class B includes the next two SKUs, which taken together represent 28 percent of the SKUs and account for 13 percent of annual dollar usage. The final four SKUs, class C, represent over half the number of SKUs but only 4 percent of total annual dollar usage.

SKU Number	Description	Quantity Used per Year		Unit Value($)		Annual Dollar Usage($)
1	Boxes	500	×	3.00	=	1,500
2	Cardboard (square feet)	18,000	×	0.02	=	360
3	Cover stock	10,000	×	0.75	=	7,500
4	Glue (gallons)	75	×	40.00	=	3,000
5	Inside covers	20,000	×	0.05	=	1,000
6	Reinforcing tape (meters)	3,000	×	0.15	=	450
7	Signatures	150,000	×	0.45	=	67,500
					Total	81,310

SKU #	Description	Qty Used/Year	Value	Dollar Usage	Pct of Total	Cumulative % of Dollar Value	Cumulative % of SKU	Class
7	Signatures	150,000	$0.45	$67,500	83.0%	83.0%	14.3%	A
3	Cover stock	10,000	$0.75	$7,500	9.2%	92.2%	28.6%	B
4	Glue	75	$40.00	$3,000	3.7%	95.9%	42.9%	B
1	Boxes	500	$3.00	$1,500	1.8%	97.8%	57.1%	C
5	Inside covers	20,000	$0.05	$1,000	1.2%	99.0%	71.4%	C
6	Reinforcing tape	3,000	$0.15	$450	0.6%	99.6%	85.7%	C
2	Cardboard	18,000	$0.02	$360	0.4%	100.0%	100.0%	C
Total				$81,310				

◀ FIGURE 12.12
Annual Dollar Usage for Class A, B, and C SKUs Using Tutor 12.2

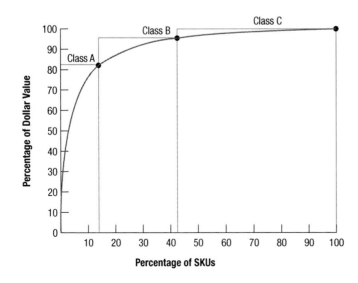

SOLVED PROBLEM 5

A distribution center experiences an average weekly demand of 60 units for one of its items. The product is valued at $700 per unit. Average inbound shipments from the factory warehouse average 350 units. Average lead time (including ordering delays and transit time) is 2 weeks. The distribution center operates 52 weeks per year. It carries a 1-week supply of inventory as safety stock and no anticipation inventory. What is the average aggregate inventory that the distribution center holds?

SOLUTION

Type of Inventory	Calculation of Average Inventory	Quantity
Cycle	$\frac{Q}{2} = \frac{350}{2} =$	175 units
Safety stock	1-week supply =	60 units
Anticipation	None	
Pipeline	$dL = $ (60 units/week)(2 weeks) =	120 units
	Average aggregate inventory =	355 units

SOLVED PROBLEM 6

Zeke's Hardware Store sells furnace filters. The cost to place an order to the distributor is $25 and the annual cost to hold a filter in stock is $2. The average demand per week for the filters is 32 units, and the store operates 50 weeks per year. The weekly demand for filters has the probability distribution shown on the left below. The delivery lead time from the distributor is uncertain and has the probability distribution shown on the right below.

Suppose Zeke wants to use a P system with $P = 6$ weeks and a cycle-service level of 90 percent. What is the appropriate value for T and the associated annual cost of the system?

Demand	Probability
24	0.15
28	0.20
32	0.30
36	0.20
40	0.15

Lead Time (wks)	Probability
1	0.05
2	0.25
3	0.40
4	0.25
5	0.05

SOLUTION

Figure 12.13 contains output from the Demand During the Protection Interval Simulator from OM Explorer.

FIGURE 12.13 ▶
OM Explorer Solver for Demand during the Protection Interval Simulator

Demand During Protection Interval Distribution

Bin Upper Bound	Demand	Frequency	Cumulative Percentage
196	182	0	0.0%
224	210	17	3.4%
252	138	66	16.6%
280	266	135	43.6%
308	294	140	71.6%
336	322	109	93.4%
364	350	30	99.4%
392	378	3	100.0%
420	406	0	100.0%
448	More	0	100.0%
Total		**500**	

Average Demand During Protection Interval
289

Given the desired cycle-service level of 90 percent, the appropriate T value is 322 units. The simulation estimated the average demand during the protection interval to be 289 units, consequently the safety stock is $322 - 289 = 33$ units.

The annual cost of this P system is

$$C = \frac{6(32)}{2}(\$2) + \frac{50(32)}{6(32)}(\$25) + 33(\$2) = \$192.00 + \$208.33 + \$66.00 = \$466.33$$

SOLVED PROBLEM 7

Consider Zeke's inventory in Solved Problem 7. Suppose that he wants to use a continuous review (Q) system for the filters, with an order quantity of 200 and a reorder point of 140. Initial inventory is 170 units. If the stockout cost is \$5 per unit, and all of the other data in Solved Problem 7 are the same, what is the expected cost per week of using the Q system?

SOLUTION

Figure 12.14 shows output from the Q System Simulator in OM Explorer. Only weeks 1 through 13 and weeks 41 through 50 are shown in the figure. The average total cost per week is \$305.62. Notice that no stockouts occurred in this simulation. These results are dependent on Zeke's choices for the reorder point and lot size. It is possible that stockouts would occur if the simulation were run for more than 50 weeks.

	D	E	F	G	H	I	J	K	L	M	N	O
14	Week	Beginning Inventory	Simulated Demand	Ending Inventory	Stockout Units	Place Order?	Simulated Lead Time	Weeks to Receive Order	Holding Cost	Ordering Cost	Stockout Cost	Total Cost
15	1	170	36	134	0	Yes	4	4	$ 304	$ 25	$ -	$ 329
16	2	134	32	102	0	No	-	3	$ 236	$ -	$ -	$ 236
17	3	102	40	62	0	No	-	2	$ 164	$ -	$ -	$ 164
18	4	62	28	34	0	No	-	1	$ 96	$ -	$ -	$ 96
19	5	234	32	202	0	No	-	0	$ 436	$ -	$ -	$ 436
20	6	202	40	162	0	No	-	-	$ 364	$ -	$ -	$ 364
21	7	162	28	134	0	Yes	2	2	$ 296	$ 25	$ -	$ 321
22	8	134	40	94	0	No	-	1	$ 228	$ -	$ -	$ 228
23	9	294	32	262	0	No	-	0	$ 556	$ -	$ -	$ 556
24	10	262	24	238	0	No	-	-	$ 500	$ -	$ -	$ 500
25	11	238	32	206	0	No	-	-	$ 444	$ -	$ -	$ 444
26	12	206	40	166	0	No	-	-	$ 372	$ -	$ -	$ 372
27	13	166	24	142	0	No	-	-	$ 308	$ -	$ -	$ 308
55	41	262	28	234	0	No	-	0	$ 496	$ -	$ -	$ 496
56	42	234	40	194	0	No	-	-	$ 428	$ -	$ -	$ 428
57	43	194	36	158	0	No	-	-	$ 352	$ -	$ -	$ 352
58	44	158	36	122	0	Yes	3	3	$ 280	$ 25	$ -	$ 305
59	45	122	36	86	0	No	-	2	$ 208	$ -	$ -	$ 208
60	46	86	28	58	0	No	-	1	$ 144	$ -	$ -	$ 144
61	47	258	36	222	0	No	-	0	$ 480	$ -	$ -	$ 480
62	48	222	36	186	0	No	-	-	$ 408	$ -	$ -	$ 408
63	49	186	40	146	0	No	-	-	$ 332	$ -	$ -	$ 332
64	50	146	32	114	0	Yes	2	2	$ 260	$ 25	$ -	$ 285
65	**Averages**	**167.12**	**33.12**	**134.00**	**0.00**		**3.00**		**$301.12**	**$4.50**	**$0.00**	**$305.62**

▲ FIGURE 12.14
OM Explorer Q System Simulator

DISCUSSION QUESTIONS

1. Will organizations ever get to the point where they will no longer need inventories? Why or why not?

2. What is the relationship between inventory and the nine competitive priorities we discussed in Chapter 1, "Using Operations to Compete?" Suppose that two competing manufacturers, Company H and Company L, are similar except that Company H has much higher investments in raw materials, work-in-process, and finished goods inventory than Company L. In which of the nine competitive priorities will Company H have an advantage?

3. Suppose that a large discount retailer with a lot of purchasing power in a supply chain requires that all suppliers incorporate a new information system that will reduce the cost of placing orders between the retailer and its suppliers as well as between the suppliers and their suppliers. Suppose also that order quantities and lead times are related; the smaller the order quantity the shorter the lead time from suppliers. Assume that all members of the supply chain use a continuous review system and EOQ order quantities. Explain the implications of the new information system for the supply chain in general and the inventory systems of the supply chain members in particular.

PROBLEMS

It will be helpful to review the section Inventory and Supply Chains in Chapter 9, "Designing Effective Supply Chains" before attempting these problems. Software, such as OM Explorer, Active Models, and POM for Windows, is in myomlab. Check with your instructor on how best to use it. In many cases, the instructor wants you to understand how to do the calculations by hand. At most, the software provides a check on your calculations. When calculations are particularly complex and the goal is interpreting the results in making decisions, the software replaces entirely the manual calculations.

1. Stock-Rite, Inc., is considering the use of ABC analysis to focus on the most critical SKUs in its inventory. For a random sample of eight SKUs, the following table shows the SKU's unit value and annual demand. Categorize these SKUs as A, B, and C classes.

SKU Code	Unit Value	Demand (units)
A104	$40.25	80
D205	80.75	120
X104	10.00	150
U404	40.50	150
L205	60.70	50
S104	80.20	20
X205	80.15	20
L104	20.05	100

2. Lockwood Industries is considering the use of ABC analysis to focus on the most critical SKUs in its inventory. For a random sample of eight SKUs, the following table shows the annual dollar usage. Rank the SKUs, and assign them to the A, B, or C class.

SKU	Dollar Value	Annual Usage
1	$0.01	1,200
2	$0.03	120,000
3	$0.45	100
4	$1.00	44,000
5	$4.50	900
6	$0.90	350
7	$0.30	70,000
8	$1.50	200

3. Leaky Pipe, a local retailer of plumbing supplies, faces demand for one of its SKUs at a constant rate of 30,000 units per year. It costs Leaky Pipe $10 to process an order to replenish stock and $1 per unit per year to carry the item in stock. Stock is received four working days after an order is placed. No backordering is allowed. Assume 300 working days a year.

   a. What is Leaky Pipe's optimal order quantity?

   b. What is the optimal number of orders per year?

c. What is the optimal interval (in working days) between orders?

d. What is the demand during the lead time?

e. What is the reorder point?

f. What is the inventory position immediately after an order has been placed?

4. At Dot Com, a large retailer of popular books, demand is constant at 32,000 books per year. The cost of placing an order to replenish stock is $10, and the annual cost of holding is $4 per book. Stock is received five working days after an order has been placed. No backordering is allowed. Assume 300 working days a year.

a. What is Dot Com's optimal order quantity?

b. What is the optimal number of orders per year?

c. What is the optimal interval (in working days) between orders?

d. What is demand during the lead time?

e. What is the reorder point?

f. What is the inventory position immediately after an order has been placed?

5. Babble, Inc., buys 400 blank cassette tapes per month for use in producing foreign language courseware. The ordering cost is $12.50. Holding cost is $0.12 per cassette per year.

a. How many tapes should Babble order at a time?

b. What is the time between orders?

6. Yellow Press, Inc., buys paper in 1,500-pound rolls for printing. Annual demand is 2,500 rolls. The cost per roll is $800, and the annual holding cost is 15 percent of the cost. Each order costs $50.

a. How many rolls should Yellow Press order at a time?

b. What is the time between orders?

7. Sam's Cat Hotel operates 52 weeks per year, 6 days per week, and uses a continuous review inventory system. It purchases kitty litter for $11.70 per bag. The following information is available about these bags.

Demand = 90 bags/week

Order cost = $54/order

Annual holding cost = 27 percent of cost

Desired cycle-service level= 80 percent

Lead time = 3 weeks (18 working days)

Standard deviation of weekly demand = 15 bags

Current on-hand inventory is 320 bags, with no open orders or backorders.

a. What is the EOQ? What would be the average time between orders (in weeks)?

b. What should R be?

c. An inventory withdrawal of 10 bags was just made. Is it time to reorder?

d. The store currently uses a lot size of 500 bags (i.e., $Q = 500$). What is the annual holding cost of this policy? Annual ordering cost? Without calculating the EOQ, how can you conclude from these two calculations that the current lot size is too large?

e. What would be the annual cost saved by shifting from the 500-bag lot size to the EOQ?

8. In a Q system, the demand rate for strawberry ice cream is normally distributed, with an average of 300 pints *per week*. The lead time is 9 weeks. The standard deviation of *weekly* demand is 15 pints.

a. What is the standard deviation of demand during the 9-week lead time?

b. What is the average demand during the 9-week lead time?

c. What reorder point results in a cycle-service level of 99 percent?

9. Consider again the kitty litter ordering policy for Sam's Cat Hotel in Problem 7.

a. Suppose that the weekly demand forecast of 90 bags is incorrect and actual demand averages only 60 bags per week. How much higher will total costs be, owing to the distorted EOQ caused by this forecast error?

b. Suppose that actual demand is 60 bags but that ordering costs are cut to only $6 by using the Internet to automate order placing. However, the buyer does not tell anyone, and the EOQ is not adjusted to reflect this reduction in S. How much higher will total costs be, compared to what they could be if the EOQ were adjusted?

10. Suppose that Sam's Cat Hotel in Problem 7 uses a P system instead of a Q system. The average daily demand is 15 bags (90/6), and the standard deviation of *daily* demand is 6.124 bags $(15/\sqrt{6})$.

a. What P (in working days) and T should be used to approximate the cost trade-offs of the EOQ?

b. How much more safety stock is needed than with a Q system?

c. It is time for the periodic review. How much kitty litter should be ordered?

11. You are in charge of inventory control of a highly successful product retailed by your firm. Weekly demand for this item varies, with an average of 200 units and a standard deviation of 16 units. It is purchased from a wholesaler at a cost of $12.50 per unit. The supply lead time is 4 weeks. Placing an order costs $50, and the inventory carrying rate per year is 20 percent of the item's cost. Your firm operates 5 days per week, 50 weeks per year.

a. What is the optimal ordering quantity for this item?

b. How many units of the item should be maintained as safety stock for 99 percent protection against stockouts during an order cycle?

c. If supply lead time can be reduced to 2 weeks, what is the percent reduction in the number of units maintained as safety stock for the same 99 percent stockout protection?

d. If through appropriate sales promotions, the demand variability is reduced so that the standard deviation of weekly demand is 8 units instead of 16, what is the percent reduction (compared to that in part [b]) in the number of units maintained as safety stock for the same 99 percent stockout protection?

12. In a *P* system, the lead time for a box of weed-killer is two weeks and the review period is one week. Demand during the protection interval averages 218 boxes, with a standard deviation of 40 boxes. What is the cycle-service level when the target inventory level is set at 300 boxes?

13. Nationwide Auto Parts uses a periodic review inventory control system for one of its stock items. The review interval is six weeks, and the lead time for receiving the materials ordered from its wholesaler is three weeks. Weekly demand is normally distributed, with a mean of 100 units and a standard deviation of 20 units.

a. What is the average and the standard deviation of demand during the protection interval?

b. What should be the target inventory level if the firm desires 97.5 percent stockout protection?

c. If 350 units were in stock at the time of a periodic review, how many units should be ordered?

14. In a two-bin inventory system, the demand for three-inch lag bolts during the two-week lead time is normally distributed, with an average of 53 units per week. The standard deviation of weekly demand is 5 units. What cycle-service level is provided when the normal level in the second bin is set at 120 units?

15. In a continuous review inventory system, the lead time for door knobs is five weeks. The standard deviation of demand during the lead time is 85 units. The desired cycle-service level is 99 percent. The supplier of door knobs streamlined its operations and now quotes a one-week lead time. How much can safety stock be reduced without reducing the 99 percent cycle-service level?

16. Petromax Enterprises uses a continuous review inventory control system for one of its SKUs. The following information is available on the item. The firm operates 50 weeks in a year.

Demand = 50,000 units/year

Ordering cost = $35/order

Holding cost = $2/unit/year

Average lead time = 3 weeks

Standard deviation of weekly demand = 125 units

a. What is the economic order quantity for this item?

b. If Petromax wants to provide a 90 percent cycle-service level, what should be the safety stock and the reorder point?

17. Your firm uses a continuous review system and operates 52 weeks per year. One of the SKUs has the following characteristics.

Demand (*D*) = 20,000 units/year

Ordering cost (*S*) = $40/order

Holding cost (*H*) = $2/unit/year

Lead time (*L*) = 2 weeks

Cycle-service level = 95%

Demand is normally distributed, with a standard deviation of *weekly* demand of 100 units.

Current on-hand inventory is 1,040 units, with no scheduled receipts and no backorders.

a. Calculate the item's EOQ. What is the average time, in weeks, between orders?

b. Find the safety stock and reorder point that provide a 95 percent cycle-service level.

c. For these policies, what are the annual costs of (i) holding the cycle inventory and (ii) placing orders?

d. A withdrawal of 15 units just occurred. Is it time to reorder? If so, how much should be ordered?

18. Suppose that your firm uses a periodic review system, but otherwise the data are the same as in Problem 17.

a. Calculate the *P* that gives approximately the same number of orders per year as the EOQ. Round your answer to the nearest week.

b. Find the safety stock and the target inventory level that provide a 95 percent cycle-service level.

c. How much larger is the safety stock than with a *Q* system?

19. A company begins a review of ordering policies for its continuous review system by checking the current policies for a sample of SKUs. Following are the characteristics of one item.

Demand (*D*) = 64 units/week (Assume 52 weeks per year)

Ordering and setup cost (*S*) = $50/order

Holding cost (*H*) = $13/unit/year

Lead time (*L*) = 2 weeks

Standard deviation of *weekly* demand = 12 units

Cycle-service level = 88 percent

a. What is the EOQ for this item?

b. What is the desired safety stock?

c. What is the reorder point?

d. What are the cost implications if the current policy for this item is $Q = 200$ and $R = 180$?

20. Using the same information as in Problem 19, develop the best policies for a periodic review system.

a. What value of P gives the same approximate number of orders per year as the EOQ? Round to the nearest week.

b. What safety stock and target inventory level provide an 88 percent cycle-service level?

21. The Farmer's Wife is a country store specializing in knick-knacks suitable for a farm-house décor. One item experiencing a considerable buying frenzy is a miniature Holstein cow. Average weekly demand is 30 cows, with a standard deviation of 5 cows. The cost to place a replenishment order is $15 and the holding coast is $0.75/cow/year. The supplier, however, is in China. The lead time for new orders is 8 weeks, with a standard deviation of 2 weeks. The Farmer's Wife, which is open only 50 weeks a year, wants to develop a continuous review inventory system for this item with a cycle-service level of 90 percent.

a. Specify the continuous review system for the cows. Explain how it would work in practice.

b. What is the total annual cost for the system you developed?

22. Osprey Sports stocks everything that a musky fisherman could want in the Great North Woods. A particular musky lure has been very popular with local fishermen as well as those who buy lures on the Internet from Osprey Sports. The cost to place orders with the supplier is $30/order; the demand averages 4 lures per day, with a standard deviation of 1 lure; and the inventory holding cost is $1.00/lure/year. The lead time form the supplier is 10 days, with a standard deviation of 3 days. It is important to maintain a 97 percent cycle-service level to properly balance service with inventory holding costs. Osprey Sports is open 350 days a year to allow the owners the opportunity to fish for muskies during the prime season.

The owners want to use a continuous review inventory system for this item.

a. What order quantity should be used?

b. What reorder point should be used?

c. What is the total annual cost for this inventory system?

23. A golf specialty wholesaler operates 50 weeks per year. Management is trying to determine an inventory policy for its 1-irons, which have the following characteristics:

Demand (D) = 2,000 units/year

Demand is normally distributed

Standard deviation of *weekly* demand = 3 units

Ordering cost = $40/order

Annual holding cost (H) = $5/units

Desired cycle-service level = 90%

Lead time (L) = 4 weeks

a. If the company uses a periodic review system, what should P and T be? Round P to the nearest week.

b. If the company uses a continuous review system, what should R be?

24. Wood County Hospital consumes 1,000 boxes of bandages per week. The price of bandages is $35 per box, and the hospital operates 52 weeks per year. The cost of processing an order is $15, and the cost of holding one box for a year is 15 percent of the value of the material.

a. The hospital orders bandages in lot sizes of 900 boxes. What *extra* cost does the hospital incur, which it could save by using the EOQ method?

b. Demand is normally distributed, with a standard deviation of weekly demand of 100 boxes. The lead time is 2 weeks. What safety stock is necessary if the hospital uses a continuous review system and a 97 percent cycle-service level is desired? What should be the reorder point?

c. If the hospital uses a periodic review system, with $P = 2$ weeks, what should be the target inventory level, T?

ADVANCED PROBLEMS

It may be helpful to review Supplement B, "Simulation Models," before working Problem 25.

25. The Georgia Lighting Center stocks more than 3,000 lighting fixtures, including chandeliers, swags, wall lamps, and track lights. The store sells at retail, operates six days per week, and advertises itself as the "brightest spot in town." One expensive fixture is selling at an average rate of five units per day. The reorder policy is $Q = 40$ and $R = 15$. A new order is placed on the day the reorder point is reached. The lead time is three business days. For example, an order placed on Monday will be delivered on Thursday. Simulate the performance of this Q system for the next 3 weeks (18 workdays). Any stockouts result in lost sales (rather than backorders). The beginning inventory is 19 units, and no receipts are scheduled. Table 12.2 simulates the first week of operation. Extend Table 12.2 to simulate operations for the next 2 weeks if demand for the next 12 business days is 7, 4, 2, 7, 3, 6, 10, 0, 5, 10, 4, and 7.

   a. What is the average daily ending inventory over the 18 days?

   b. How many stockouts occurred?

26. Muscle Bound is chain of fitness stores located in many large shopping centers. Recently, an internal memo from the CEO to all operations personnel complained about the budget overruns at Muscle Bound's central warehouse. In particular, she said that inventories were too high and that the budget will be cut dramatically and proportionately equal for all items in stock. Consequently, warehouse management set up a pilot study to see what effect the budget cuts would have on customer service. They chose 5-pound barbells, which are a high volume SKU and consume considerable warehouse space. Daily demand for the barbells is 1,000 units, with a standard deviation of 150 units. Ordering costs are $40 per order. Holding costs are $2/unit/year. The supplier is located in the Philippines; consequently, the lead time is 35 days with a standard deviation of 5 days. Muscle Bound stores operate 313 days a year (no Sundays).

   Suppose that the barbells are allocated a budget of $16,000 for total annual costs. If Muscle Bound uses a continuous review system for the barbells and cannot change the ordering costs and holding costs or the distributions of demand or lead time, what is the best cycle-service level management can expect from their system?

TABLE 12.2	FIRST WEEK OF OPERATION					
Workday	**Beginning Inventory**	**Orders Received**	**Daily Demand**	**Ending Inventory**	**Inventory Position**	**Order Quantity**
1. Monday	19	—	5	14	14	40
2. Tuesday	14	—	3	11	51	—
3. Wednesday	11	—	4	7	47	—
4. Thursday	7	40	1	46	46	—
5. Friday	46	—	10	36	36	—
6. Saturday	36	—	9	27	27	—

ACTIVE MODEL EXERCISE

This Active Model appears in myomlab. It allows you to evaluate the sensitivity of the EOQ and associated costs to changes in the demand and cost parameters.

QUESTIONS

1. What is the EOQ and what is the lowest total cost?

2. How much does the total cost increase if the store manager orders twice as many bird feeders as the EOQ? How much does the total cost increase if the store manager orders half as many bird feeders as the EOQ?

3. From the graph, what can you conclude about the relationship between the lowest total cost and the costs of ordering and holding inventory?

4. What is the annual cost of holding inventory at the EOQ and the annual cost of ordering inventory at the EOQ?

5. What happens to the EOQ and the total cost when demand is doubled? What happens to the EOQ and the total cost when unit price is doubled?

6. Comment on the sensitivity of the EOQ model to errors in demand or cost estimates.

7. Scroll through the lower order cost values and describe the changes to the graph. What happens to the EOQ?

Economic Order Quantity (EOQ) Model

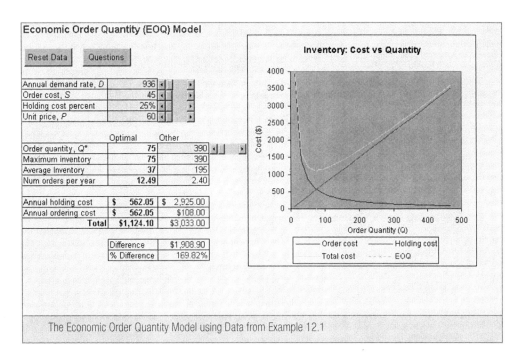

	Reset Data	Questions

Annual demand rate, D	936	
Order cost, S	45	
Holding cost percent	25%	
Unit price, P	60	

	Optimal	Other
Order quantity, Q^*	75	390
Maximum inventory	75	390
Average Inventory	37	195
Num orders per year	12.49	2.40

Annual holding cost	$ 562.05	$ 2,925.00
Annual ordering cost	$ 562.05	$108.00
Total	**$1,124.10**	**$3,033.00**

Difference	$1,908.90
% Difference	169.82%

Inventory: Cost vs Quantity

The Economic Order Quantity Model using Data from Example 12.1

EXPERIENTIAL LEARNING   Swift Electronic Supply, Inc.

It was a typical fall afternoon in Southern California, with thousands of tourists headed to the beaches to have fun. About 40 miles away, however, Steven Holland, the CEO of the Swift Electronic Supply, Inc., faced a severe problem with Swift's inventory management.

An Intel veteran, Steven Holland worked in the electronic components distribution industry for more than 20 years. Seven years ago, he founded the Swift Electronic Supply, Inc., an electronic distributor. After several successful years, the company is now troubled with eroding profit margins. Recent economic downturns worsened the situation further. Factors such as the growth of B2B e-commerce, the globalization of markets, the increased popularity of value-added services, and ongoing consolidations among electronic distributors affect the future of Swift.

To reverse these influences, Holland talked to a prestigious local university. After consultation, Holland found the most effective way to increase profitability is to cut inventory costs. As a starting point, he studied in detail a representative product, dynamic random access memory (DRAM), as the basis for his plan.

Industry and Company Preview

Owing to a boom in the telecommunications industry and the information technology revolution, electronics distributors experienced double-digit annual growth over the last decade. To cut the cost of direct purchasing forces, large component manufacturers such as Intel, Cisco, and Texas Instruments decided to outsource their procurement so that they could focus on product development and manufacturing. Therefore, independent electronic distributors like Swift started offering procurement services to these companies.

Swift serves component manufacturers in California and Arizona. Working as the intermediary between its customers and overseas original equipment manufacturers (OEMs), Swift's business model is quite simple. Forecasting customer demand, Swift places orders to a number of OEMs, stocks those products, breaks the quantities down, and delivers the products to its end customers.

Recently, due to more intense competition and declines in demand, Swift offered more flexible delivery schedules and was willing to accommodate small order quantities. However, customers can always shift to Swift's competitors should Swift not fulfill their orders. Steven Holland was in a dilemma: The intangible costs of losing customers can be enormous; however, maintaining high levels of inventory can also be costly.

DRAM

Holland turned his attention to DRAM as a representative product. Previously, the company ordered a big amount every time it felt it was necessary. Holland's assistant developed a table (Table 12.3) that has two months of demand history. From Holland's experience, the demand for DRAM is relatively stable in the company's product line and it had no sales seasonality. The sales staff agrees that conditions in the current year will not be different from those of past years, and historical demand will be a good indicator of what to expect in the future.

TABLE 12.3	HISTORICAL DEMAND DATA FOR THE DRAM (UNITS)				
Day	Demand	Day	Demand	Day	Demand
1	869	21	663	41	959
2	902	22	1,146	42	703
3	1,109	23	1,016	43	823
4	947	24	1,166	44	862
5	968	25	829	45	966
6	917	26	723	46	1,042
7	1,069	27	749	47	889
8	1,086	28	766	48	1,002
9	1,066	29	996	49	763
10	929	30	1,122	50	932
11	1,022	31	962	51	1,052
12	959	32	829	52	1,062
13	756	33	862	53	989
14	882	34	793	54	1,029
15	829	35	1,039	55	823
16	726	36	1,009	56	942
17	666	37	979	57	986
18	879	38	976	58	736
19	1,086	39	856	59	1,009
20	992	40	1,036	60	852

The primary manufacturers of DRAM are those in Southeast Asia. Currently, Swift can purchase one unit of 128M DRAM for $10. After negotiation with a reputable supplier, Holland managed to sign a long-term agreement, which kept the price at $10 and allowed Swift to place orders at any time. The supplier also supplies other items in Swift's inventory. In addition, it takes the supplier of the DRAM two days to deliver the goods to Swift's warehouse using air carriers.

When Swift does not have enough inventory to fill a customer's order, the sales are lost; that is, Swift is not able to backorder the shortage because its customers fill their requirements through competitors. The customers will accept partial shipments, however.

It costs Swift $200 to place an order with the suppliers. This amount covers the corresponding internal ordering costs and the costs of delivering the products to the company. Holland estimates that the cost of lost sales amounts to $2 per unit of DRAM. This rough estimate includes the loss of profits, as well as the intangible damage to customer goodwill.

To simplify its inventory management system, Swift has a policy of maintaining a cycle-service level of 95 percent. The holding cost per day per unit is estimated to be 0.5 percent of the cost of goods, regardless of the product. Inventory holding costs are calculated on the basis of the ending inventory each day. The current balance is 1,700 units of DRAM in stock.

The daily purchasing routine is as follows. Orders are placed at the *beginning* of the day, before Swift is open for customer business. The orders arrive at the beginning of the day, two days later, and can be used for sales that day. For example, an order placed at the beginning of day 1 will arrive at Swift before Swift is open for business on day 3. The actual daily demand is always recorded at the *end* of the day, after Swift has closed for customer business. All cost computations are done at the end of the day after the total demand has been recorded.

Simulation

Holland believes that simulation is a useful approach to assess various inventory control alternatives. The historical data from Table 12.3 could be used to develop attractive inventory policies. The table was developed to record various costs and evaluate different alternatives. An example showing some recent DRAM inventory decisions is shown in Table 12.4.

1. Design a new inventory system for Swift Electronic Supply, Inc., using the data provided.

2. Provide the rationale for your system, which should include the decision rules you would follow to determine how much to order and when.

3. Simulate the use of your inventory system and record the costs. Develop a table such as Table 12.4 to record your results. Your instructor will provide actual demands on a day-to-day basis during the simulation.

TABLE 12.4 | EXAMPLE SIMULATION

Day	1	2	3	4	5	6	7	8	9	10
Beginning inventory position	1,700	831	1,500	391	3,000	3,232	2,315			
Number ordered	1,500		3,000	1,200			1,900			
Daily demand	869	902	1,109	947	968	917	1,069			
Day-ending inventory	831	−71	391	−556	2,032	2,315	1,246			
Ordering costs ($200 per order)	200		200	200			200			
Holding costs ($0.05 per piece per day)	41.55	0.00	19.55	0.00	101.60	115.75	62.30			
Shortage costs ($2 per piece)	0	142	0	1,112	0	0	0			
Total cost for day	241.55	142.00	219.55	1,312.00	101.60	115.75	262.30			
Cumulative cost from last day	0.00	241.55	383.55	603.10	1,915.10	2,016.70	2,132.45			
Cumulative costs to date	241.55	383.55	603.10	1,915.10	2,016.70	2,132.45	2,394.75			

CASE Parts Emporium

Parts Emporium, Inc., is a wholesale distributor of automobile parts formed by two disenchanted auto mechanics, Dan Block and Ed Spriggs. Originally located in Block's garage, the firm showed slow but steady growth for 7 years before it relocated to an old, abandoned meat-packing warehouse on Chicago's South Side. With increased space for inventory storage, the company was able to begin offering an expanded line of auto parts. This increased selection, combined with the trend toward longer car ownership, led to an explosive growth of the business. Fifteen years later, Parts Emporium was the largest independent distributor of auto parts in the north central region.

Recently, Parts Emporium relocated to a sparkling new office and warehouse complex off Interstate 55 in suburban Chicago. The warehouse space alone occupied more than 100,000 square feet. Although only a handful of new products have been added since the warehouse was constructed, its utilization increased from 65 percent to more than 90 percent of capacity. During this same period, however, sales growth stagnated. These conditions motivated Block and Spriggs to hire the first manager from outside the company in the firm's history.

It is June 6, Sue McCaskey's first day in the newly created position of materials manager for Parts Emporium. A recent graduate of a prominent business school, McCaskey is eagerly awaiting her first real-world problem. At approximately 8:30 A.M., it arrives in the form of status reports on inventory and orders shipped. At the top of an extensive computer printout is a hand-written note from Joe Donnell, the purchasing manager: "Attached you will find the inventory and customer service performance data. Rest assured that the individual inventory levels are accurate because we took a complete physical inventory count at the end of last week. Unfortunately, we do not keep compiled records in some of the areas as you requested. However, you are welcome to do so yourself. Welcome aboard!"

A little upset that aggregate information is not available, McCaskey decides to randomly select a small sample of approximately 100 items and compile inventory and customer service characteristics to get a feel for the "total picture." The results of this experiment reveal to her why Parts Emporium decided to create the position she now fills. It seems that the inventory is in all the wrong places. Although an *average* of approximately

60 days of inventory is on hand, the firm's customer service is inadequate. Parts Emporium tries to backorder the customer orders not immediately filled from stock, but some 10 percent of demand is being lost to competing distributorships. Because stockouts are costly, relative to inventory holding costs, McCaskey believes that a cycle-service level of at least 95 percent should be achieved.

McCaskey knows that although her influence to initiate changes will be limited, she must produce positive results immediately. Thus, she decides to concentrate on two products from the extensive product line: the EG151 exhaust gasket and the DB032 drive belt. If she can demonstrate significant gains from proper inventory management for just two products, perhaps Block and Spriggs will give her the backing needed to change the total inventory management system.

The EG151 exhaust gasket is purchased from an overseas supplier, Haipei, Inc. Actual demand for the first 21 weeks of this year is shown in the following table:

Week	Actual Demand	Week	Actual Demand
1	104	12	97
2	103	13	99
3	107	14	102
4	105	15	99
5	102	16	103
6	102	17	101
7	101	18	101
8	104	19	104
9	100	20	108
10	100	21	97
11	103		

A quick review of past orders, shown in another document, indicates that a lot size of 150 units is being used and that the lead time from Haipei is fairly constant at 2 weeks. Currently, at the end of week 21, no inventory is on hand, 11 units are backordered, and the company is awaiting a scheduled receipt of 150 units.

The DB032 drive belt is purchased from the Bendox Corporation of Grand Rapids, Michigan. Actual demand so far this year is shown in the following table:

Week	Actual Demand	Week	Actual Demand
11	18	17	50
12	33	18	53
13	53	19	54
14	54	20	49
15	51	21	52
16	53		

Because this product is new, data are available only since its introduction in week 11. Currently, 324 units are on hand, with no backorders and no scheduled receipts. A lot size of 1,000 units is being used, with the lead time fairly constant at 3 weeks.

The wholesale prices that Parts Emporium charges its customers are $12.99 for the EG151 exhaust gasket and $8.89 for the DB032 drive belt. Because no quantity discounts are offered on these two highly profitable items, gross margins based on current purchasing practices are 32 percent of the wholesale price for the exhaust gasket and 48 percent of the wholesale price for the drive belt.

Parts Emporium estimates its cost to hold inventory at 21 percent of its inventory investment. This percentage recognizes the opportunity cost of tying money up in inventory and the variable costs of taxes, insurance, and shrinkage. The annual report notes other warehousing expenditures for utilities and maintenance and debt service on the 100,000-square-foot warehouse, which was built for $1.5 million. However, McCaskey reasons that these warehousing costs can be ignored because they will not change for the range of inventory policies that she is considering.

Out-of-pocket costs for Parts Emporium to place an order with suppliers are estimated to be $20 per order for exhaust gaskets and $10 per order for drive belts. On the outbound side, the company can charge a delivery fee. Although most customers pick up their parts at Parts Emporium, some orders are delivered to customers. To provide this service, Parts Emporium contracts with a local company for a flat fee of $21.40 per order, which is added to the customer's bill. McCaskey is unsure whether to increase the ordering costs for Parts Emporium to include delivery charges.

QUESTIONS

1. Put yourself in Sue McCaskey's position and prepare a detailed report to Dan Block and Ed Spriggs on managing the inventory of the EG151 exhaust gasket and the DB032 drive belt. Be sure to present a proper inventory system and recognize all relevant costs.

2. By how much do your recommendations for these two items reduce annual cycle inventory, stockout, and ordering costs?

SELECTED REFERENCES

Bastow, B. J. "Metrics in the Material World." *APICS—The Performance Advantage* (May 2005), pp. 49–52.

Berlin, Bob. "Solving the OEM Puzzle at Valleylab." *APICS—The Performance Advantage* (March 1997), pp. 58–63.

Callioni, Gianpaolo, Xavier de Montgros, Regine Slagmulder, Luk N. Van Wassenhove, and Linda Wright. "Inventory-Driven Costs." *Harvard Business Review* (March 2005), pp. 135–141.

Cannon, Alan R., and Richard E. Crandall. "The Way Things Never Were." *APICS—The Performance Advantage* (January 2004), pp. 32–35.

Chikan, A., A. Milne, and L. G. Sprague. "Reflections on Firm and National Inventories." Budapest: International Society for Inventory Research, 1996.

Greene, James H. *Production and Inventory Control Handbook*, 3d ed. New York: McGraw-Hill, 1997.

Hartvigsen, David. *SimQuick: Process Simulation with Excel*, 2d ed. Upper Saddle River, NJ: Prentice Hall, 2004.

Inventory Management Reprints. Falls Church, VA: American Production and Inventory Control Society, 1993.

Krupp, James A. G. "Are ABC Codes an Obsolete Technology?" *APICS—The Performance Advantage* (April 1994), pp. 34–35.

Silver, Edward A. "Changing the Givens in Modeling Inventory Problems: The Example of Just-in-Time Systems." *International Journal of Production Economics*, vol. 26 (1996), pp. 347–351.

Silver, Edward A., D. E. Pyke, and Rein Peterson. *Inventory Management, Production Planning, and Scheduling*, 3d ed. New York: John Wiley & Sons, 1998.

Tersine, Richard J. *Principles of Inventory and Materials Management*, 4th ed. Upper Saddle River, NJ: Prentice Hall, 1994.

Timme, Stephen G., and Christine Williams-Timme. "The Real Cost of Holding." *Supply Chain Management Review* (July/August 2003), pp. 30–37.

D SPECIAL INVENTORY MODELS

LEARNING GOALS

After reading this supplement, you should be able to:

1. Define the relevant costs that should be considered to determine the order quantity when discounts are available.

2. Identify the situations where the economic lot size should be used rather than the economic order quantity.

3. Calculate the optimal lot size when replenishment is not instantaneous.

4. Determine the optimal order quantity when materials are subject to quantity discounts.

5. Calculate the order quantity that maximizes the expected profits for a one-period inventory decision.

Many real world problems require relaxation of certain assumptions on which the economic order quantity (EOQ) model is based. This supplement addresses three realistic situations that require going beyond the simple EOQ formulation.

1. Noninstantaneous Replenishment. Particularly in situations in which manufacturers use a continuous process to make a primary material, such as a liquid, gas, or powder, production is not instantaneous. Thus, inventory is replenished gradually, rather than in lots.

2. Quantity Discounts. Three annual costs are the inventory holding cost, the fixed cost for ordering and setup, and the cost of materials. For service providers and for manufacturers alike, the unit cost of purchased materials sometimes depends on the order quantity.

3. One-Period Decisions. Retailers and manufacturers of fashion goods often face a situation in which demand is uncertain and occurs during just one period or season.

This supplement assumes you have read Chapter 12, "Managing Inventories," and Supplement A, "Decision Making Models."

my**om**lab and the Companion Website at **www.pearsonglobaleditions.com/krajewski** contain many tools, activities, and resources designed for this supplement.

NONINSTANTANEOUS REPLENISHMENT

If an item is being produced internally rather than purchased, finished units may be used or sold as soon as they are completed, without waiting until a full lot is completed. For example, a restaurant that bakes its own dinner rolls begins to use some of the rolls from the first pan even before the baker finishes a five-pan batch. The inventory of rolls never reaches the full five-pan level, the way it would if the rolls all arrived at once on a truck sent by a supplier.

Figure D.1 depicts the usual case, in which the production rate, p, *exceeds* the demand rate, d.[1] *Cycle* inventory accumulates faster than demand occurs; that is, a buildup *of $p - d$* units occurs per time period. For example, if the production rate is 100 units per day and the demand is 5 units per day, the buildup is 95 (or 100 − 5) units each day. This buildup continues until the lot size, Q, has been produced, after which the inventory depletes at a rate of 5 units per day. Just as the inventory reaches 0, the next production interval begins. To be consistent, both p and d must be expressed in units of the same time period, such as units per day or units per week. Here, we assume that they are expressed in units per day.

The $p - d$ buildup continues for Q/p days because Q is the lot size and p units are produced each day. In our example, if the lot size is 300 units, the production interval is 3 days (300/100). For the given rate of buildup over the production interval, the maximum cycle inventory, I_{max}, is

$$I_{max} = \frac{Q}{p}(p - d) = Q\left(\frac{p - d}{p}\right)$$

Cycle inventory is no longer $Q/2$, as it was with the basic EOQ method; instead, it is $I_{max}/2$. Setting up the total annual cost equation for this production situation, where D is annual demand, as before, and d is daily demand, we get

$$\text{Total annual cost} = \text{Annual holding cost} + \text{Annual ordering or setup cost}$$

$$C = \frac{I_{max}}{2}(H) + \frac{D}{Q}(S) = \frac{Q}{2}\left(\frac{p - d}{p}\right)(H) + \frac{D}{Q}(S)$$

Based on this cost function, the optimal lot size, often called the **economic production lot size (ELS)**, is

$$\text{ELS} = \sqrt{\frac{2DS}{H}}\sqrt{\frac{p}{p - d}}$$

Because the second term is a ratio greater than 1, the ELS results in a larger lot size than the EOQ.

economic production lot size (ELS)

The optimal lot size in a situation in which replenishment is not instantaneous.

◀ FIGURE D.1
Lot Sizing with Noninstantaneous Replenishment

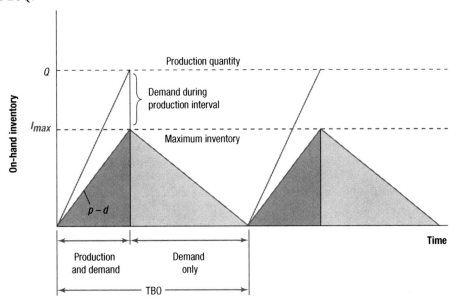

---

[1] If demand and production were equal, production would be continuous with no buildup of cycle inventory. If the production rate is lower than the demand rate, sales opportunities are being missed on an ongoing basis. We assume that $p > d$ in this supplement.

EXAMPLE D.1	Finding the Economic Production Lot Size

Tutor D.1 in my**om**lab provides a new example to determine the ELS.

Active Model D.1 in my**om**lab provides additional insight on the ELS model and its uses.

A plant manager of a chemical plant must determine the lot size for a particular chemical that has a steady demand of 30 barrels per day. The production rate is 190 barrels per day, annual demand is 10,500 barrels, setup cost is $200, annual holding cost is $0.21 per barrel, and the plant operates 350 days per year.

a.   Determine the economic production lot size (ELS).

b.   Determine the total annual setup and inventory holding cost for this item.

c.   Determine the time between orders (TBO), or cycle length, for the ELS.

d.   Determine the production time per lot.

What are the advantages of reducing the setup time by 10 percent?

SOLUTION

a.   Solving first for the ELS, we get

$$\text{ELS} = \sqrt{\frac{2DS}{H}}\sqrt{\frac{p}{p-d}} = \sqrt{\frac{2(10,500)(\$200)}{\$0.21}}\sqrt{\frac{190}{190-30}}$$

$$= 4,873.4 \text{ barrels}$$

b.   The total annual cost with the ELS is

$$C = \frac{Q}{2}\left(\frac{p-d}{p}\right)(H) + \frac{D}{Q}(S)$$

$$= \frac{4,873.4}{2}\left(\frac{190-30}{190}\right)(\$0.21) + \frac{10,500}{4,873.4}(\$200)$$

$$= \$430.91 + \$430.91 = \$861.82$$

c.   Applying the TBO formula to the ELS, we get

$$\text{TBO}_{\text{ELS}} = \frac{\text{ELS}}{D}(350 \text{ days/year}) = \frac{4,873.4}{10,500}(350)$$

$$= 162.4 \quad \text{or} \quad 162 \text{ days}$$

d.   The production time during each cycle is the lot size divided by the production rate:

$$\frac{\text{ELS}}{p} = \frac{4,873.4}{190} = 25.6 \quad \text{or} \quad 26 \text{ days}$$

DECISION POINT

As OM Explorer shows in Figure D.2, the net effect of reducing the setup cost by 10 percent is to reduce the lot size, the time between orders, and the production cycle time. Consequently, total annual costs are also reduced. This adds flexibility to the manufacturing process because items can be made more quickly with less expense. Management must decide whether the added cost of improving the setup process is worth the added flexibility and inventory cost reductions.

FIGURE D.2 ▶
OM Explorer Solver for the Economic Production Lot Size Showing the Effect of a 10 Percent Reduction in Setup Cost

Period Used in Calculations	Day ▼
Demand per Day	30
Production Rate/Day	190
Annual Demand	10,500
Setup Cost	$180
Annual Holding Cost ($)	$0.21
Operating Days per Year	350

● Enter Holding Cost Manually   ○ Holding Cost As % of Value

Economic Lot Size (ELS)	4,623
Annual Total Cost	$817.60
Time Between Orders (days)	154.1
Production Time	24.3

QUANTITY DISCOUNTS

Quantity discounts, which are price incentives to purchase large quantities, create pressure to maintain a large inventory. For example, a supplier may offer a price of $4.00 per unit for orders between 1 and 99 units, a price of $3.50 per unit for orders between 100 and 199 units, and a price of $3.00 per unit for orders of 200 or more units. The item's price is no longer fixed, as assumed in the EOQ derivation; instead, if the order quantity is increased enough, the price is discounted. Hence, a new approach is needed to find the best lot size—one that balances the advantages of lower prices for purchased materials and fewer orders (which are benefits of large order quantities) against the disadvantage of the increased cost of holding more inventory.

The total annual cost now includes not only the holding cost, $(Q/2)(H)$, and the ordering cost, $(D/Q)(S)$, but also the cost of purchased materials. For any per-unit price level, P, the total cost is

Total annual cost = Annual holding cost + Annual ordering or setup cost

+ Annual cost of materials

$$C = \frac{Q}{2}(H) \ + \ \frac{D}{Q}(S) \ + \ PD$$

The unit holding cost, H, usually is expressed as a percent of the unit price because the more valuable the item held in inventory, the higher the holding cost is. Thus, the lower the unit price, P, the lower H is. Conversely, the higher P is, the higher H is.

The total cost equation yields U-shaped total cost curves. Adding the annual cost of materials to the total cost equation raises each total cost curve by a fixed amount, as shown in Figure D.3(a). The three cost curves illustrate each of the price levels. The top curve applies when no discounts are received; the lower curves reflect the discounted price levels. No single curve is relevant to all purchase quantities. The relevant, or feasible, total cost begins with the top curve, then drops down, curve by curve, at the price breaks. A price break is the minimum quantity needed to get a discount. In Figure D.3, two price breaks occur at $Q = 100$ and $Q = 200$. The result is a total cost curve, with steps at the price breaks.

Figure D.3(b) also shows three additional points—the minimum point on each curve—obtained with the EOQ formula at each price level. These EOQs do not necessarily produce the best lot size for two reasons.

1. The EOQ at a particular price level may not be feasible. The lot size may not lie in the range corresponding to its per-unit price. Figure D.3(b) illustrates two instances of an infeasible EOQ. First, the minimum point for the $3.00 curve appears to be fewer than 200 units. However, the supplier's quantity discount schedule does not allow purchases of that small a quantity at the $3.00 unit price. Similarly, the EOQ for the $4.00 price level is greater than the first price break, so the price charged would be only $3.50.

▼ FIGURE D.3
Total Cost Curves with Quantity Discounts

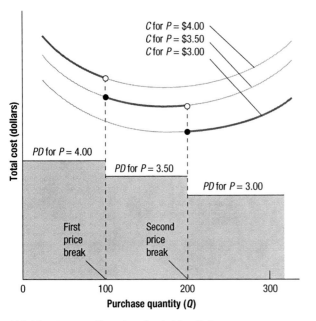

(a) Total cost curves with purchased materials added

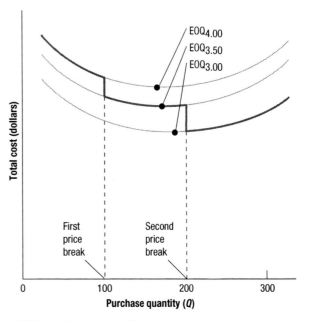

(b) EOQs and price break quantities

2. The EOQ at a particular price level may be feasible but may not be the best lot size. The feasible EOQ may have a higher cost than is achieved by the EOQ or price break quantity on a lower price curve. In Figure D.3(b), for example, the 200-unit price break quantity for the $3.00 price level has a lower total cost than the feasible EOQ for the $3.50 price level. A feasible EOQ always is better than any feasible point on cost curves with higher price levels, but not necessarily those with lower levels. Thus, the only time we can immediately conclude, without comparing total costs, that a feasible EOQ is the best order quantity is when it is on the curve for the lowest price level. This conclusion is not possible in Figure D.3(b) because the only feasible EOQ is at the middle price level, $P = \$3.50$.

We must, therefore, pay attention only to feasible price–quantity combinations, shown as solid lines in Figure D.3(b), as we search for the best lot size. The following two-step procedure may be used to find the best lot size.

Step 1. Beginning with the lowest price, calculate the EOQ for each price level until a feasible EOQ is found. It is feasible if it lies in the range corresponding to its price. Each subsequent EOQ is smaller than the previous one because P, and thus H, gets larger and because the larger H is in the denominator of the EOQ formula.

Step 2. If the first feasible EOQ found is for the lowest price level, this quantity is the best lot size. Otherwise, calculate the total cost for the first feasible EOQ and for the larger price break quantity at each lower price level. The quantity with the lowest total cost is optimal.

EXAMPLE D.2	Finding Q with Quantity Discounts at St. LeRoy Hospital

Tutor D.2 in my**om**lab provides a new example for choosing the best order quantity when discounts are available.

Active Model D.2 in my**om**lab provides additional insight on the quantity discount model and its uses.

A supplier for St. LeRoy Hospital has introduced quantity discounts to encourage larger order quantities of a special catheter. The price schedule is

Order Quantity	Price per Unit
0 to 299	$60.00
300 to 499	$58.80
500 or more	$57.00

The hospital estimates that its annual demand for this item is 936 units, its ordering cost is $45.00 per order, and its annual holding cost is 25 percent of the catheter's unit price. What quantity of this catheter should the hospital order to minimize total costs? Suppose the price for quantities between 300 and 499 is reduced to $58.00. Should the order quantity change?

SOLUTION

Step 1: Find the first feasible EOQ, starting with the lowest price level:

$$EOQ_{57.00} = \sqrt{\frac{2DS}{H}} = \sqrt{\frac{2(936)(\$45.00)}{0.25(\$57.00)}} = 77 \text{ units}$$

A 77-unit order actually costs $60.00 per unit, instead of the $57.00 per unit used in the EOQ calculation, so this EOQ is infeasible. Now try the $58.80 level:

$$EOQ_{58.80} = \sqrt{\frac{2DS}{H}} = \sqrt{\frac{2(936)(\$45.00)}{0.25(\$58.80)}} = 76 \text{ units}$$

This quantity also is infeasible because a 76-unit order is too small to qualify for the $58.80 price. Try the highest price level:

$$EOQ_{60.00} = \sqrt{\frac{2DS}{H}} = \sqrt{\frac{2(936)(\$45.00)}{0.25(\$60.00)}} = 75 \text{ units}$$

This quantity is feasible because it lies in the range corresponding to its price, $P = \$60.00$.

Step 2: The first feasible EOQ of 75 does not correspond to the lowest price level. Hence, we must compare its total cost with the price break quantities (300 and 500 units) at the lower price levels ($58.80 and $57.00):

$$C = \frac{Q}{2}(H) + \frac{D}{Q}(S) + PD$$

$$C_{75} = \frac{75}{2}[(0.25)(\$60.00)] + \frac{936}{75}(\$45.00) + \$60.00(936) = \$57,284$$

$$C_{300} = \frac{300}{2}[(0.25)(\$58.80)] + \frac{936}{300}(\$45.00) + \$58.80(936) = \$57,382$$

$$C_{500} = \frac{500}{2}[(0.25)(\$57.00)] + \frac{936}{500}(\$45.00) + \$57.00(936) = \$56,999$$

The best purchase quantity is 500 units, which qualifies for the deepest discount.

DECISION POINT

If the price per unit for the range of 300 to 499 units is reduced to $58.00, the best decision is to order 300 catheters, as shown by OM Explorer in Figure D.4. This result shows that the decision is sensitive to the price schedule. A reduction of slightly more than 1 percent is enough to make the difference in this example. In general, however, it is not always the case that you should order more than the economic order quantity when given price discounts. When discounts are small, holding cost H is large, and demand D is small, small lot sizes are better even though price discounts are forgone.

◀ FIGURE D.4
OM Explorer Solver for Quantity Discounts Showing the Best Order Quantity

Min. Amount Req'd for Price Point	Lot Sizes	Price/Unit		
	More	Fewer		
...	0–299	$60.00		
300	300–499	$58.00		
500	500 or more	$57.00		

Annual Demand	936	
Order Cost	$45	
Holding Cost (% or price)	25%	

Best Order Quantity	300

	Price Point	EOQ or Req'd Order for Price Point	Inventory Cost	Order Cost	Purchase Cost	Total Cost	
>>	$60.00	75	$562.50	$561.60	$56,160	$57,284	
	$58.00	300	$2,175	$140.40	$54,288	$56,603	<<
	$57.00	500	$3,563	$84.24	$53,352	$56,999	

ONE-PERIOD DECISIONS

One of the dilemmas facing many retailers is how to handle seasonal goods, such as winter coats. Often, they cannot be sold at full markup the next year because of changes in styles. Furthermore, the lead time can be longer than the selling season, allowing no second chance to rush through another order to cover unexpectedly high demand. A similar problem exists for manufacturers of fashion goods.

This type of situation is often called the newsboy problem. If the newspaper seller does not buy enough newspapers to resell on the street corner, sales opportunities are lost. If the seller buys too many newspapers, the overage cannot be sold because nobody wants yesterday's newspaper.

The following process is a straightforward way to analyze such problems and decide on the best order quantity.

1. List the different levels of demand that are possible, along with the estimated probability of each.

2. Develop a *payoff* table that shows the profit for each purchase quantity, *Q*, at each assumed demand level, *D*. Each row in the table represents a different order quantity, and each column represents a different demand level. The payoff for a given quantity–demand combination depends on whether all units are sold at the regular profit margin during the regular season, which results in two possible cases.

a. If demand is high enough $(Q \leq D)$, then all units are sold at the full profit margin, p, during the regular season,

$$\text{Payoff} = (\text{Profit per unit})(\text{Purchase quantity}) = pQ$$

b. If the purchase quantity exceeds the eventual demand $(Q > D)$, only D units are sold at the full profit margin, and the remaining units purchased must be disposed of at a loss, l, after the season. In this case,

$$\text{Payoff} = \left(\begin{array}{c}\text{Profit per unit sold}\\ \text{during season}\end{array}\right)(\text{Demand}) - \left(\begin{array}{c}\text{Loss per}\\ \text{unit}\end{array}\right)\left(\begin{array}{c}\text{Amount disposed of}\\ \text{after season}\end{array}\right)$$

$$= pD - l(Q - D)$$

3. Calculate the expected payoff for each Q (or row in the payoff table) by using the *expected value* decision rule. For a specific Q, first multiply each payoff in the row by the demand probability associated with the payoff, and then add these products.

4. Choose the order quantity Q with the highest expected payoff.

Using this decision process for all such items over many selling seasons will maximize profits. However, it is not foolproof, and it can result in an occasional bad outcome.

EXAMPLE D.3   Finding Q for One-Period Inventory Decisions

Tutor D.3 in my**om**lab provides a new example to practice the one-period inventory decision.

Active Model D.3 in my**om**lab provides additional insight on the one-period inventory decision model and its uses.

One of many items sold at a museum of natural history is a Christmas ornament carved from wood. The gift shop makes a $10 profit per unit sold during the season, but it takes a $5 loss per unit after the season is over. The following discrete probability distribution for the season's demand has been identified:

Demand	10	20	30	40	50
Demand Probability	0.2	0.3	0.3	0.1	0.1

How many ornaments should the museum's buyer order?

SOLUTION

Each demand level is a candidate for best order quantity, so the payoff table should have five rows. For the first row, where $Q = 10$, demand is at least as great as the purchase quantity. Thus, all five payoffs in this row are

$$\text{Payoff} = pQ = (\$10)(10) = \$100$$

This formula can be used in other rows but only for those quantity–demand combinations where all units are sold during the season. These combinations lie in the upper-right portion of the payoff table, where $Q \leq D$. For example, the payoff when $Q = 40$ and $D = 50$ is

$$\text{Payoff} = pQ = (\$10)(40) = \$400$$

The payoffs in the lower-left portion of the table represent quantity–demand combinations where some units must be disposed of after the season $(Q > D)$. For this case, the payoff must be calculated with the second formula. For example, when $Q = 40$ and $D = 30$,

$$\text{Payoff} = pD - l(Q - D) = (\$10)(30) - (\$5)(40 - 30) = \$250$$

Using OM Explorer, we obtain the payoff table in Figure D.5.

FIGURE D.5 ▼
OM Explorer Solver for One-Period Inventory Decisions Showing the Payoff Table

Profit	$10.00	(if sold during preferred period)
Loss	$5.00	(if sold after preferred period)

Enter the possible demands along with the probability of each occuring. Use the buttons to increase or decrease the number of allowable demand forecasts. NOTE: Be sure to enter demand forecasts and probablities in all tinted cells, and be sure probabilities add up to 1.

		<	>			
Demand		10	20	30	40	50
Profitability		0.2	0.3	0.3	0.1	0.1

Payoff Table

		Demand				
		10	20	30	40	50
Quantity	10	100	100	100	100	100
	20	50	200	200	200	200
	30	0	150	300	300	300
	40	−50	100	250	400	400
	50	−100	50	200	350	500

Now we calculate the expected payoff for each Q by multiplying the payoff for each demand quantity by the probability of that demand and then adding the results. For example, for $Q = 30$,

$$\text{Payoff} = 0.2(\$0) + 0.3(\$150) + 0.3(\$300) + 0.1(\$300) + 0.1(\$300) = \$195$$

Using OM Explorer, Figure D.6 shows the expected payoffs.

Weighted Payoffs

Order Quantity	Expected Payoff
10	100
20	170
30	195
40	175
50	140

Greatest Expected Payoff   195

Associated with Order Quantity   30

◀ FIGURE D.6
OM Explorer Solver Showing the Expected Payoffs

DECISION POINT

Because $Q = 30$ has the highest payoff at $195, it is the best order quantity. Management can use OM Explorer to do sensitivity analysis on the demands and their probabilities to see how confident they are with that decision.

The need for one-time inventory decisions also can arise in manufacturing plants when (1) customized items are made (or purchased) to a single order, and (2) scrap quantities are high.[2] A customized item produced for a single order is never intentionally held in stock because the demand for it is too unpredictable. In fact, it may never be ordered again so the manufacturer would like to make just the amount requested by the customer—no more, no less. The manufacturer also would like to satisfy an order in just one run to avoid an extra setup and a delay in delivering goods ordered. These two goals may conflict if the likelihood of some units being scrapped is high. Suppose that a customer places an order for 20 units. If the manager orders 20 units from the shop or from the supplier, one or two units may have to be scrapped. This shortage will force the manager to place a second (or even third) order to replace the defective units. Replacement can be costly if setup time is high and can also delay shipment to the customer. To avoid such problems, the manager could order more than 20 units the first time. If some units are left over, the customer might be willing to buy the extras or the manager might find an internal use for them. For example, some manufacturing companies set up a special account for obsolete materials. These materials can be "bought" by departments within the company at less than their normal cost, as an incentive to use them.

INTERNET RESOURCES

my**om**lab and the Companion Website at **www.pearsonglobaleditions.com/krajewski** contain many tools, activities, and resources designed for this supplement.

KEY EQUATIONS

1. Noninstantaneous replenishment:

   Maximum inventory: $I_{\max} = Q\left(\dfrac{p - d}{p}\right)$

   Total annual cost = Annual holding cost + Annual ordering or setup cost

   $$C = \frac{Q}{2}\left(\frac{p - d}{p}\right)(H) + \frac{D}{Q}(S)$$

---

[2] One goal of total quality management (TQM) and Six Sigma is to eliminate scrap. Achievement of that goal makes this discussion moot.

$$\text{Economic production lot size:} \quad \text{ELS} = \sqrt{\frac{2\,D\,S}{H}}\sqrt{\frac{p}{p-d}}$$

$$\text{Time between orders, expressed in years:} \quad \text{TBO}_{\text{ELS}} = \frac{\text{ELS}}{D}$$

2. Quantity discounts:

Total annual cost = Annual holding cost + Annual ordering
or setup cost + Annual cost of material

$$C = \frac{Q}{2}(H) \ + \ \frac{D}{Q}(S) \ + \ PD$$

3. One-period decisions:

$$\text{Payoff matrix: Payoff} = \begin{cases} pQ & \text{if } Q \le D \\ pD - l(Q{-}D) & \text{if } Q > D \end{cases}$$

SOLVED PROBLEM 1

A hospital buys disposable surgical packages from Pfisher, Inc. Pfisher's price schedule is $50.25 per package on orders of 1 to 199 packages and $49.00 per package on orders of 200 or more packages. Ordering cost is $64 per order, and annual holding cost is 20 percent of the per-unit purchase price. Annual demand is 490 packages. What is the best purchase quantity?

SOLUTION

We first calculate the EOQ at the *lowest* price:

$$\text{EOQ}_{49.00} = \sqrt{\frac{2\,D\,S}{H}} = \sqrt{\frac{2(490)\,(\$64.00)}{0.20(\$49.00)}} = \sqrt{6{,}400} = 80 \text{ packages}$$

This solution is infeasible because, according to the price schedule, we cannot purchase 80 packages at a price of $49.00 each. Therefore, we calculate the EOQ at the next lowest price ($50.25):

$$\text{EOQ}_{50.25} = \sqrt{\frac{2\,D\,S}{H}} = \sqrt{\frac{2(490)\,(\$64.00)}{0.20(\$50.00)}} = \sqrt{6{,}241} = 79 \text{ packages}$$

This EOQ is feasible, but $50.25 per package is not the lowest price. Hence, we have to determine whether total costs can be reduced by purchasing 200 units and thereby obtaining a quantity discount.

$$C = \frac{Q}{2}(H) \ + \ \frac{D}{Q}(S) \ + \ PD$$

$$C_{79} = \frac{79}{2}(0.20 \ \times \ \$50.25) \ + \ \frac{490}{79}(\$64.00) \ + \ \$50.25(490)$$

$$= \$396.98/\text{year} \ + \ \$396.68/\text{year} \ + \ \$24{,}622.50/\text{year} = \$25{,}416.44/\text{year}$$

$$C_{200} = \frac{200}{2}(0.20 \ \times \ \$49.00) \ + \ \frac{490}{200}(\$64.00) \ + \ \$49.00(490)$$

$$= \$980.00/\text{year} \ + \ \$156.80/\text{year} \ + \ \$24{,}010.00/\text{year} \ = \ \$25{,}146.80/\text{year}$$

Purchasing 200 units per order will save $269.64/year, compared to buying 79 units at a time.

SOLVED PROBLEM 2

Peachy Keen, Inc., makes mohair sweaters, blouses with Peter Pan collars, pedal pushers, poodle skirts, and other popular clothing styles of the 1950s. The average demand for mohair sweaters is 100 per week. Peachy's production facility has the capacity to sew 400 sweaters per week. Setup cost is $351. The value of finished goods inventory is $40 per sweater. The annual per-unit inventory holding cost is 20 percent of the item's value.

a. What is the economic production lot size (ELS)?
b. What is the average time between orders (TBO)?
c. What is the total of the annual holding cost and setup cost?

SOLUTION

a. The production lot size that minimizes total cost is

$$ELS = \sqrt{\frac{2\,D\,S}{H}}\sqrt{\frac{p}{p-d}} = \sqrt{\frac{2(100 \times 52)(\$351)}{0.20(\$40)}}\sqrt{\frac{400}{(400-100)}}$$

$$= \sqrt{456{,}300}\sqrt{\frac{4}{3}} = 780 \text{ sweaters}$$

b. The average time between orders is

$$TBO_{ELS} = \frac{ELS}{D} = \frac{780}{5{,}200} = 0.15 \text{ year}$$

Converting to weeks, we get

$$TBO_{ELS} = (0.15 \text{ year})(52 \text{ weeks/year}) = 7.8 \text{ weeks}$$

c. The minimum total of setup and holding costs is

$$C = \frac{Q}{2}\left(\frac{p-d}{p}\right)(H) + \frac{D}{Q}(S) = \frac{780}{2}\left(\frac{400-100}{400}\right)(0.20 \times \$40) + \frac{5{,}200}{780}(\$351)$$

$$= \$2{,}340/\text{year} + \$2{,}340/\text{year} = \$4{,}680/\text{year}$$

SOLVED PROBLEM 3

Swell Productions is sponsoring an outdoor conclave for owners of collectible and classic Fords. The concession stand in the T-Bird area will sell clothing such as T-shirts and official Thunderbird racing jerseys. Jerseys are purchased from Columbia Products for $40 each and are sold during the event for $75 each. If any jerseys are left over, they can be returned to Columbia for a refund of $30 each. Jersey sales depend on the weather, attendance, and other variables. The following table shows the probability of various sales quantities. How many jerseys should Swell Productions order from Columbia for this one-time event?

Sales Quantity	Probability	Quantity Sales	Probability
100	0.05	400	0.34
200	0.11	500	0.11
300	0.34	600	0.05

SOLUTION

Table D.1 is the payoff table that describes this one-period inventory decision. The upper-right portion of the table shows the payoffs when the demand, D, is greater than or equal to

TABLE D.1   PAYOFFS

Q	100	200	300	400	500	600	Expected Payoff
			Demand, D				
100	$3,500	$3,500	$ 3,500	$ 3,500	$ 3,500	$ 3,500	$ 3,500
200	$2,500	$7,000	$ 7,000	$ 7,000	$ 7,000	$ 7,000	$ 6,775
300	$1,500	$6,000	$10,500	$10,500	$10,500	$10,500	$ 9,555
400	$ 500	$5,000	$ 9,500	$14,000	$14,000	$14,000	$10,805
500	($ 500)	$4,000	$ 8,500	$13,000	$17,500	$17,500	$10,525
600	($1,500)	$3,000	$ 7,500	$12,000	$16,500	$21,000	$ 9,750

the order quantity, Q. The payoff is equal to the per-unit profit (the difference between price and cost) multiplied by the order quantity. For example, when the order quantity is 100 and the demand is 200,

$$\text{Payoff} = (p-c)\,Q = (\$75 - \$40)100 = \$3,500$$

The lower-left portion of the payoff table shows the payoffs when the order quantity exceeds the demand. Here the payoff is the profit from sales, pD, minus the loss associated with returning overstock, $l(Q-D)$, where l is the difference between the cost and the amount refunded for each jersey returned and $Q-D$ is the number of jerseys returned. For example, when the order quantity is 500 and the demand is 200,

$$\text{Payoff} = pD - l(Q-D) = (\$75 - \$40)200 - (\$40 - \$30)(500 - 200) = \$4,000$$

The highest expected payoff occurs when 400 jerseys are ordered:

$$\text{Expected payoff}_{400} = (\$500 \times 0.05) + (\$5,000 \times 0.11) + (\$9,500 \times 0.34)$$
$$+ (\$14,000 \times 0.34) + (\$14,000 \times 0.11) + (\$14,000 \times 0.05)$$
$$= \$10,805$$

PROBLEMS

Software, such as OM Explorer, Active Models, and POM for Windows, is available in my**om**lab. Check with your instructor on how best to use it. In many cases, the instructor wants you to understand how to do the calculations by hand. At most, the software provides a check on your calculations. When calculations are particularly complex and the goal is interpreting the results in making decisions, the software replaces entirely the manual calculations. The software also can be a valuable resource well after your course is completed.

1. Based on advance ticket sales, the athletic department has forecast hot dog sales for an upcoming football game to be as shown in the following table. The school buys premium hot dogs for $1.50 and sells them during the game at $3.00 each. Hot dogs left over after the game will be sold for $0.50 each to the Aggie student cafeteria to be used in making hotdog casserole.

Sales Quantity	Probability
2,000	0.10
3,000	0.30
4,000	0.30
5,000	0.20
6,000	0.10

Use a payoff matrix to determine the number of hot dogs to buy for the game.

2. Dorothy's pastries are freshly baked and sold at several specialty shops throughout Perth. When they are a day old, they must be sold at reduced prices. Daily demand is distributed as follows:

Demand	Probability
50	0.25
150	0.50
200	0.25

Each pastry sells for $1.00 and costs $0.60 to make. Each one not sold at the end of the day can be sold the next day for $0.30 as day-old merchandise. How many pastries should be baked each day?

3. National Printing Company must decide how many wall calendars it should produce for sale during the upcoming sale season. Each calendar sells for $8.50 and costs $2.50 to produce. The local school district has agreed to buy all unsold calendars at a unit price of $1.50. National estimates the following probability distribution for the season's demand:

Demand	Probability
2,000	0.05
3,000	0.20
4,000	0.25
5,000	0.40
6,000	0.10

How many calendars should National produce to maximize its expected profit?

4. As inventory manager, you must decide on the order quantity for an item that has an annual demand of 2,000 units. Placing an order costs you $20 each time. Your annual holding cost, expressed as a percentage of average inventory value, is 20 percent. Your supplier has provided the following price schedule:

Minimum Order Quantity	Price per Unit
1	$2.50
200	$2.40
300	$2.25
1,000	$2.00

What ordering policy do you recommend?

5. Mac-in-the-Box, Inc., sells computer equipment by mail and telephone order. Mac sells 1,200 flat-bed scanners per year. Ordering cost is $300, and annual holding cost is 16 percent of the item's price. The scanner manufacturer offers the following price structure to Mac-in-the-Box:

Order Quantity	Price per Unit
0 to 11	$520
12 to 143	$500
144 or more	$400

What order quantity minimizes total annual costs?

6. The University Bookstore at a prestigious private university buys mechanical pencils from a wholesaler. The wholesaler offers discounts for large orders according to the following price schedule:

Order Quantity	Price per Unit
0 to 200	$4.00
201 to 2,000	$3.50
2,001 or more	$3.25

The bookstore expects an annual demand of 2,500 units. It costs $10 to place an order, and the annual cost of holding a unit in stock is 30 percent of the unit's price. Determine the best order quantity.

7. To boost sales, Pfisher (refer to Solved Problem 1) announces a new price structure for disposable surgical packages. Although the price break no longer is available at 200 units, Pfisher now offers an even greater discount if larger quantities are purchased. On orders of 1 to 499 packages, the price is $50.25 per package. For orders of 500 or more, the price per unit is $47.80. Ordering costs, annual holding costs, and annual demand remain at $64 per order, 20 percent of the per-unit cost, and 490 packages per year, respectively. What is the new lot size?

8. The Bucks Grande major league baseball team breaks an average of four bats per week. The team orders baseball bats from Corky's, a bat manufacturer noted for its access to the finest hardwood. The order cost is $70, and the annual holding cost per bat per year is 38 percent of the purchase price. Corky's price structure is

Order Quantity	Price per Unit
0 to 11	$54.00
12 to 143	$51.00
144 or more	$48.50

a. How many bats should the team buy per order?

b. What are the total annual costs associated with the best order quantity?

c. Corky discovers that, owing to special manufacturing processes required for the Bucks's bats, it has underestimated setup costs. Rather than raise prices, Corky adds another category to the price structure to provide an incentive for larger orders and reduce the number of setups required. If the Bucks buy 180 bats or more, the price will drop to $45.00 each. Should the Bucks revise the order quantity to 180 bats?

9. Suds's Bottling Company does bottling, labeling, and distribution work for several local microbreweries. The demand rate for Wortman's beer is 600 cases (24 bottles each) per week. Suds's bottling production rate is 2,400 cases per week, and the setup cost is $800. The value of inventory is $12.50 per case, and the annual holding cost is 30 percent of the inventory value. What is the economic production lot size?

10. Sharpe Cutter is a small company that produces specialty knives for paper cutting machinery. The annual demand for a particular type of knife is 100,000 units. The demand is uniform over the 250 working days in a year. Sharpe Cutter produces this type of knife in lots and, on average, can produce 450 knives a day. The cost to set up a production lot is $300, and the annual holding cost is $1.20 per knife.

a. Determine the economic production lot size (ELS).

b. Determine the total annual setup and inventory holding cost for this item.

c. Determine the TBO, or cycle length, for the ELS.

d. Determine the production time per lot.

11. Bold Vision, Inc., makes laser printer and photocopier toner cartridges. The demand rate is 625 EP cartridges per week. The production rate is 1,736 EP cartridges per week, and the setup cost is $100. The value of inventory is $130 per unit, and the holding cost is 20 percent of the inventory value. What is the economic production lot size?

Selected References

"Factors That Make or Break Season Sales." *Wall Street Journal* (December 9, 1991).

Greene, James H. *Production and Inventory Control Handbook*, 3d ed. New York: McGraw-Hill, 1997.

Inventory Management Reprints. Falls Church, VA: American Production and Inventory Control Society, 1993.

Manikas, Andrew. "Fighting Pests with the EOQ," *APICS Magazine* (April 2007), pp. 34–37.

Silver, Edward A., D. F. Pyke, and Rein Peterson. *Inventory Management, Production Planning, and Scheduling*, 3d ed. New York: John Wiley & Sons, 1998.

Sipper, Daniel, and Robert L. Bulfin, Jr. *Production Planning, Control, and Integration*. New York: McGraw-Hill, 1997.

Tersine, Richard J. *Principles of Inventory and Materials Management*, 4th ed. Upper Saddle River, NJ: Prentice Hall, 1994.

MRP, ERP and Scheduling

10

OM Strategy Decisions

▶ Design of Goods and Services
▶ Managing Quality
▶ Process Strategy
▶ Location Strategies
▶ Layout Strategies
▶ Human Resources
▶ Supply-Chain Management
▶ Inventory Management
  ■ Independent Demand
  ■ Dependent Demand
  ■ JIT and Lean Operations
▶ Scheduling
▶ Maintenance

GLOBAL COMPANY PROFILE: WHEELED COACH

MRP PROVIDES A COMPETITIVE ADVANTAGE FOR WHEELED COACH

Wheeled Coach, headquartered in Winter Park, Florida, is the largest manufacturer of ambulances in the world. The $200 million firm is an international competitor that sells more than 25% of its vehicles to markets outside the U.S. Twelve major ambulance designs are produced on assembly lines (i.e., a repetitive process) at the Florida plant, using 18,000 different inventory items, of which 6,000 are manufactured and 12,000 purchased. Most of the product line is custom designed and assembled to meet the specific and often unique requirements

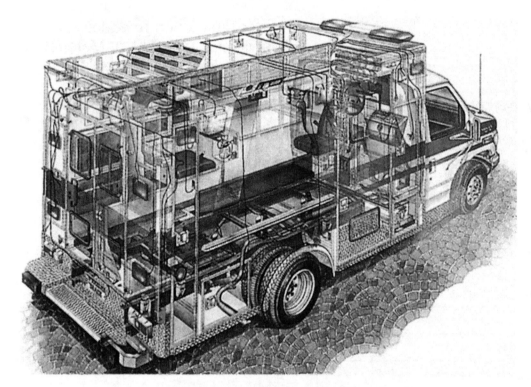

This cutaway of one ambulance interior indicates the complexity of the product, which for some rural locations may be the equivalent of a hospital emergency room in miniature. To complicate production, virtually every ambulance is custom ordered. This customization necessitates precise orders, excellent bills of materials, exceptional inventory control from supplier to assembly, and an MRP system that works.

Wheeled Coach uses work cells to feed the assembly line. It maintains a complete carpentry shop (to provide interior cabinetry), a paint shop (to prepare, paint, and detail each vehicle), an electrical shop (to provide for the complex electronics in a modern ambulance), an upholstery shop (to make interior seats and benches), and as shown here, a metal fabrication shop (to construct the shell of the ambulance).

demanded by the ambulance's application and customer preferences.

This variety of products and the nature of the process demand good material requirements planning. Effective use of an MRP system requires accurate bills of material and inventory records. The Wheeled Coach system, which uses MAPICS DB software, provides daily updates and has reduced inventory by more than 30% in just 2 years.

Wheeled Coach insists that four key tasks be performed properly. First, the material plan must meet both the requirements of the master schedule and the capabilities of the production facility. Second, the plan must be executed as designed. Third, inventory investment must be minimized through effective "time-phased" material deliveries, consignment inventories, and a constant review of purchase methods. Finally, excellent record integrity must be maintained. Record accuracy is recognized as a fundamental ingredient of Wheeled Coach's successful MRP program. Its cycle counters are charged with material audits that not only correct errors but also investigate and correct problems.

Wheeled Coach Industries uses MRP as the catalyst for low inventory, high quality, tight schedules, and accurate records. Wheeled Coach has found competitive advantage via MRP.

On six parallel lines, ambulances move forward each day to the next workstation. The MRP system makes certain that just the materials needed at each station arrive overnight for assembly the next day.

VIDEO 14.1
MRP at Wheeled Coach
Ambulances

Here an employee is installing the wiring for an ambulance. There are an average of 15 miles of wire in a Wheeled Coach vehicle. This compares to 17 miles of wire in a sophisticated F-16 fighter jet.

Chapter 14 **Learning Objectives**

> **AUTHOR COMMENT**
> "Dependent demand" means the demand for one item is related to the demand for another item.

DEPENDENT DEMAND

Wheeled Coach, the subject of the *Global Company Profile*, and many other firms have found important benefits in MRP. These benefits include (1) better response to customer orders as the result of improved adherence to schedules, (2) faster response to market changes, (3) improved utilization of facilities and labor, and (4) reduced inventory levels. Better response to customer orders and to the market wins orders and market share. Better utilization of facilities and labor yields higher productivity and return on investment. Less inventory frees up capital and floor space for other uses. These benefits are the result of a strategic decision to use a *dependent* inventory scheduling system. Demand for every component of an ambulance is dependent.

Demand for items is dependent when the relationship between the items can be determined. Therefore, once management receives an order or makes a forecast for the final product, quantities for all components can be computed. All components are dependent items. The Boeing Aircraft operations manager who schedules production of one plane per week, for example, knows the requirements down to the last rivet. For any product, all components of that product are dependent demand items. *More generally, for any product for which a schedule can be established, dependent techniques should be used.*

> **Material requirements planning (MRP)**
> A dependent demand technique that uses a bill-of-material, inventory, expected receipts, and a master production schedule to determine material requirements.

When the requirements of MRP are met, dependent models are preferable to the EOQ models described in Chapter 12.[1] Dependent models are better not only for manufacturers and distributors but also for a wide variety of firms from restaurants to hospitals. The dependent technique used in a production environment is called **material requirements planning (MRP)**.

Because MRP provides such a clean structure for dependent demand, it has evolved as the basis for Enterprise Resource Planning (ERP). ERP is an information system for identifying and planning the enterprise-wide resources needed to take, make, ship, and account for customer orders. We will discuss ERP in the latter part of this chapter.

DEPENDENT INVENTORY MODEL REQUIREMENTS

Effective use of dependent inventory models requires that the operations manager know the following:

1. Master production schedule (what is to be made and when)
2. Specifications or bill of material (materials and parts required to make the product)
3. Inventory availability (what is in stock)
4. Purchase orders outstanding (what is on order, also called expected receipts)
5. Lead times (how long it takes to get various components)

We now discuss each of these requirements in the context of material requirements planning.

Master Production Schedule

> **Master production schedule (MPS)**
> A timetable that specifies what is to be made and when.

A **master production schedule (MPS)** specifies what is to be made (i.e., the number of finished products or items) and when. The schedule must be in accordance with a production plan. The production plan sets the overall level of output in broad terms (e.g., product families, standard

---

[1]The inventory models (EOQ) discussed in Chapter 12 assumed that the demand for one item was independent of the demand for another item. For example, EOQ assumes the demand for refrigerator parts is *independent* of the demand for refrigerators and that demand for parts is constant.

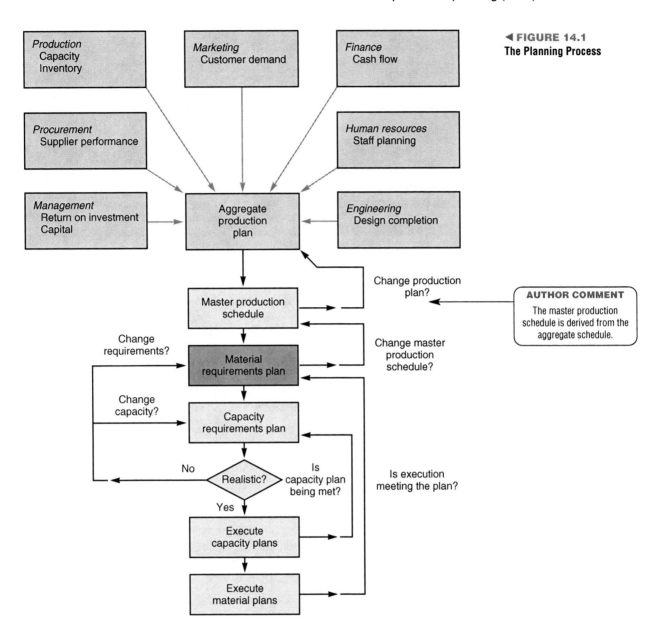

hours, or dollar volume). The plan also includes a variety of inputs, including financial plans, customer demand, engineering capabilities, labor availability, inventory fluctuations, supplier performance, and other considerations. Each of these inputs contributes in its own way to the production plan, as shown in Figure 14.1

As the planning process moves from the production plan to execution, each of the lower-level plans must be feasible. When one is not, feedback to the next higher level is used to make the necessary adjustment. One of the major strengths of MRP is its ability to determine precisely the feasibility of a schedule within aggregate capacity constraints. This planning process can yield excellent results. The production plan sets the upper and lower bounds on the master production schedule. The result of this production planning process is the master production schedule.

The master production schedule tells us what is required to satisfy demand and meet the production plan. This schedule establishes what items to make and when: It *disaggregates* the aggregate production plan. While the *aggregate production plan* (as discussed in Chapter 13) is established in gross terms such as families of products or tons of steel, the *master production schedule* is established in terms of specific products. Figure 14.2 shows the master production schedules for three stereo models that flow from the aggregate production plan for a family of stereo amplifiers.

Managers must adhere to the schedule for a reasonable length of time (usually a major portion of the production cycle—the time it takes to produce a product). Many organizations establish a master production schedule and establish a policy of not changing ("fixing") the near-term portion of the plan. This near-term portion of the plan is then referred to as the "fixed," "firm," or "frozen"

Months		January				February			
Aggregate Production Plan (Shows the total quantity of amplifiers)		1,500				1,200			
Weeks	1	2	3	4	5	6	7	8	
Master Production Schedule (Shows the specific type and quantity of amplifier to be produced)									
240-watt amplifier	100		100		100		100		
150-watt amplifier		500		500		450		450	
75-watt amplifier			300				100		

schedule. Wheeled Coach, the subject of the *Global Company Profile* for this chapter, fixes the last 14 days of its schedule. Only changes farther out, beyond the fixed schedule, are permitted. The master production schedule is a "rolling" production schedule. For example, a fixed 7-week plan has an additional week added to it as each week is completed, so a 7-week fixed schedule is maintained. Note that the master production schedule is a statement of *what is to be produced*, not a forecast of demand. The master schedule can be expressed in any of the following terms:

1. A *customer order in a job shop* (make-to-order) company
2. *Modules in a repetitive* (assemble-to-order or forecast) company
3. An *end item in a continuous* (stock-to-forecast) company

This relationship of the master production schedule to the processes is shown in Figure 14.3.

A master production schedule for two of Nancy's Specialty Foods' products, crabmeat quiche and spinach quiche, might look like Table 14.1.

Bills of Material

Bill of material (BOM)
A listing of the components, their description, and the quantity of each required to make one unit of a product.

Defining what goes into a product may seem simple, but it can be difficult in practice. As we noted in Chapter 5, to aid this process, manufactured items are defined via a bill of material. A **bill of material (BOM)** is a list of quantities of components, ingredients, and materials required to make a product. Individual drawings describe not only physical dimensions but also any special processing as well as the raw material from which each part is made. Nancy's Specialty

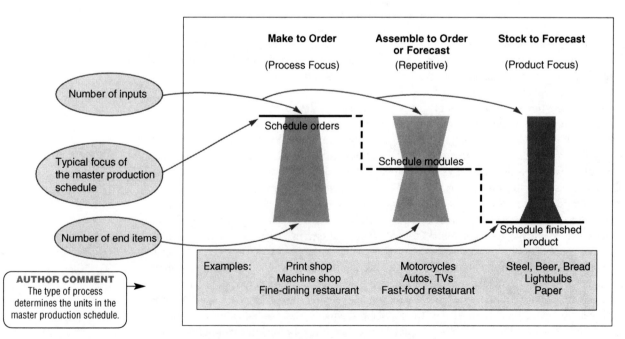

▲ **FIGURE 14.3**   **Typical Focus of the Master Production Schedule in Three Process Strategies**

Gross Requirements for Crabmeat Quiche									
Day	6	7	8	9	10	11	12	13	14	and so on
Amount	50		100	47	60		110	75	

Gross Requirements for Spinach Quiche									
Day	7	8	9	10	11	12	13	14	15	16	and so on
Amount	100	200	150			60	75		100	

◀ **TABLE 14.1**
Master Production Schedule for Crabmeat Quiche and Spinach Quiche at Nancy's Specialty Foods

Foods has a recipe for quiche, specifying ingredients and quantities, just as Wheeled Coach has a full set of drawings for an ambulance. Both are bills of material (although we call one a recipe, and they do vary somewhat in scope).

Because there is often a rush to get a new product to market, however, drawings and bills of material may be incomplete or even nonexistent. Moreover, complete drawings and BOMs (as well as other forms of specifications) often contain errors in dimensions, quantities, or countless other areas. When errors are identified, engineering change notices (ECNs) are created, further complicating the process. An *engineering change notice* is a change or correction to an engineering drawing or bill of material.

One way a bill of material defines a product is by providing a product structure. Example 1 shows how to develop the product structure and "explode" it to reveal the requirements for each component. A bill of material for item A in Example 1 consists of items B and C. Items above any level are called *parents*; items below any level are called *components* or *children*. By convention, the top level in a BOM is the 0 level.

Speaker Kits, Inc., packages high-fidelity components for mail order. Components for the top-of-the-line speaker kit, "Awesome" (A), include 2 standard 12-inch speaker kits (Bs) and 3 speaker kits with amp-boosters (Cs).

Each B consists of 2 speakers (Ds) and 2 shipping boxes each with an installation kit (E). Each of the three 300-watt speaker kits (Cs) has 2 speaker boosters (Fs) and 2 installation kits (Es). Each speaker booster (F) includes 2 speakers (Ds) and 1 amp-booster (G). The total for each Awesome is 4 standard 12-inch speakers and twelve 12-inch speakers with the amp-booster. (Most purchasers require hearing aids within 3 years, and at least one court case is pending because of structural damage to a men's dormitory.) As we can see, the demand for B, C, D, E, F, and G is completely dependent on the master production schedule for A—the Awesome speaker kits.

APPROACH ▶ Given the above information, we construct a product structure and "explode" the requirements.

SOLUTION ▶ This structure has four levels: 0, 1, 2, and 3. There are four parents: A, B, C, and F. Each parent item has at least one level below it. Items B, C, D, E, F, and G are components because each item has at least one level above it. In this structure, B, C, and F are both parents and components. The number in parentheses indicates how many units of that particular item are needed to make the item immediately above it. Thus, $B_{(2)}$ means that it takes two units of B for every unit of A, and $F_{(2)}$ means that it takes two units of F for every unit of C.

◀ **EXAMPLE 1**

Developing a product structure and gross requirements

LO1: Develop a product structure.

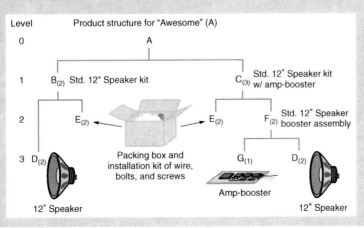

Level   Product structure for "Awesome" (A)

0 — A

1 — $B_{(2)}$ Std. 12" Speaker kit $C_{(3)}$ Std. 12" Speaker kit w/ amp-booster

2 — $E_{(2)}$ $E_{(2)}$ $F_{(2)}$ Std. 12" Speaker booster assembly

3 — $D_{(2)}$ Packing box and installation kit of wire, bolts, and screws $G_{(1)}$ $D_{(2)}$

12" Speaker   Amp-booster   12" Speaker

Once we have developed the product structure, we can determine the number of units of each item required to satisfy demand for a new order of 50 Awesome speaker kits. We "explode" the requirements as shown:

Part B:	$2 \times$ number of As $=$	$(2)(50) =$	100
Part C:	$3 \times$ number of As $=$	$(3)(50) =$	150
Part D:	$2 \times$ number of Bs $+ 2 \times$ number of Fs $=$	$(2)(100) + (2)(300) =$	800
Part E:	$2 \times$ number of Bs $+ 2 \times$ number of Cs $=$	$(2)(100) + (2)(150) =$	500
Part F:	$2 \times$ number of Cs $=$	$(2)(150) =$	300
Part G:	$1 \times$ number of Fs $=$	$(1)(300) =$	300

INSIGHT ▶ We now have a visual picture of the Awesome speaker kit requirements and knowledge of the quantities required. Thus, for 50 units of A, we will need 100 units of B, 150 units of C, 800 units of D, 500 units of E, 300 units of F, and 300 units of G.

LEARNING EXERCISE ▶ If there are 100 Fs in stock, how many Ds do you need? [Answer: 600.]

RELATED PROBLEMS ▶ 14.1, 14.3a, 14.13a, 14.25a

EXCEL OM Data File **Ch14Ex1.xls** can be found at **www.pearsonglobaleditions.com/heizer**.

Bills of material not only specify requirements but also are useful for costing, and they can serve as a list of items to be issued to production or assembly personnel. When bills of material are used in this way, they are usually called *pick lists*.

Modular bills

Bills of material organized by major subassemblies or by product options.

Modular Bills Bills of material may be organized around product modules (see Chapter 5). *Modules* are not final products to be sold but are components that can be produced and assembled into units. They are often major components of the final product or product options. Bills of material for modules are called **modular bills**. Bills of material are sometimes organized as modules (rather than as part of a final product) because production scheduling and production are often facilitated by organizing around relatively few modules rather than a multitude of final assemblies. For instance, a firm may make 138,000 different final products but may have only 40 modules that are mixed and matched to produce those 138,000 final products. The firm builds an aggregate production plan and prepares its master production schedule for the 40 modules, not the 138,000 configurations of the final product. This approach allows the MPS to be prepared for a reasonable number of items (the narrow portion of the middle graphic in Figure 14.3) and to postpone assembly. The 40 modules can then be configured for specific orders at final assembly.

Planning bills (or kits)

A material grouping created in order to assign an artificial parent to a bill of material; also called "pseudo" bills.

Phantom bills of material

Bills of material for components, usually assemblies, that exist only temporarily; they are never inventoried.

Planning Bills and Phantom Bills Two other special kinds of bills of material are planning bills and phantom bills. **Planning bills** (sometimes called "pseudo" bills or super bills) are created in order to assign an artificial parent to the bill of material. Such bills are used (1) when we want to group subassemblies so the number of items to be scheduled is reduced and (2) when we want to issue "kits" to the production department. For instance, it may not be efficient to issue inexpensive items such as washers and cotter pins with each of numerous subassemblies, so we call this a *kit* and generate a planning bill. The planning bill specifies the *kit* to be issued. Consequently, a planning bill may also be known as **kitted material**, or **kit**. **Phantom bills of material** are bills of material for components, usually subassemblies, that exist only temporarily. These components go directly into another assembly and are never inventoried. Therefore, components of phantom bills of material are coded to receive special treatment; lead times are zero, and they are handled as an integral part of their parent item. An example is a transmission shaft with gears and bearings assembly that is placed directly into a transmission.

Low-level coding

A number that identifies items at the lowest level at which they occur.

Low-Level Coding Low-level coding of an item in a BOM is necessary when identical items exist at various levels in the BOM. **Low-level coding** means that the item is coded at the lowest level at which it occurs. For example, item D in Example 1 is coded at the lowest level at which it is used. Item D could be coded as part of B and occur at level 2. However, because D is also part of F, and F is level 2, item D becomes a level-3 item. Low-level coding is a convention to allow easy computing of the requirements of an item. When the BOM has thousands of items or when requirements are frequently recomputed, the ease and speed of computation become a major concern.

Accurate Inventory Records

As we saw in Chapter 12, knowledge of what is in stock is the result of good inventory management. Good inventory management is an absolute necessity for an MRP system to work. If the firm does not exceed 99% record accuracy, then material requirements planning will not work.[2]

Purchase Orders Outstanding

Knowledge of outstanding orders exists as a by-product of well-managed purchasing and inventory-control departments. When purchase orders are executed, records of those orders and their scheduled delivery dates must be available to production personnel. Only with good purchasing data can managers prepare meaningful production plans and effectively execute an MRP system.

Lead Times for Components

Once managers determine when products are needed, they determine when to acquire them. The time required to acquire (that is, purchase, produce, or assemble) an item is known as **lead time**. Lead time for a manufactured item consists of *move*, *setup*, and *assembly* or *run times* for each component. For a purchased item, the lead time includes the time between recognition of need for an order and when it is available for production.

When the bill of material for Awesome speaker kits (As), in Example 1, is turned on its side and modified by adding lead times for each component (see Table 14.2), we then have a *time-phased product structure*. Time in this structure is shown on the horizontal axis of Figure 14.4 with item A due for completion in week 8. Each component is then offset to accommodate lead times.

MRP STRUCTURE

Although most MRP systems are computerized, the MRP procedure is straightforward and we can illustrate a small one by hand. A master production schedule, a bill of material, inventory and purchase records, and lead times for each item are the ingredients of a material requirements planning system (see Figure 14.5).

Lead time

In purchasing systems, the time between recognition of the need for an order and receiving it; in production systems, it is the order, wait, move, queue, setup, and run times for each component.

▼ **TABLE 14.2**
Lead Times for Awesome Speaker Kits (As)

Component	Lead Time
A	1 week
B	2 weeks
C	1 week
D	1 week
E	2 weeks
F	3 weeks
G	2 weeks

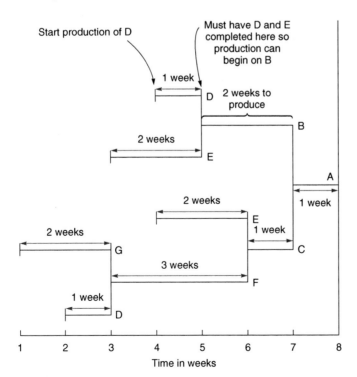

> **AUTHOR COMMENT**
> This is a product structure on its side, with lead times.

◄ **FIGURE 14.4**
Time-Phased Product Structure

[2]Record accuracy of 99% may sound good, but note that even when each component has an availability of 99% and a product has only seven components, the likelihood of a product being completed is only .932 (because $.99^7 = .932$).

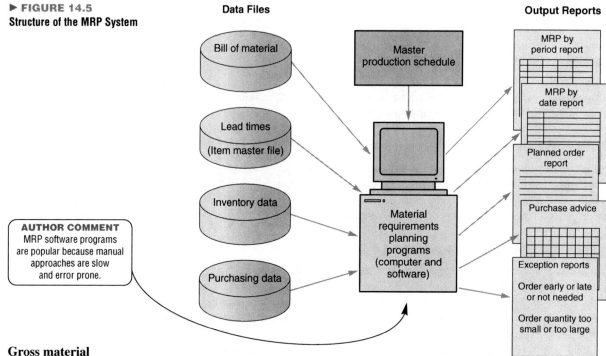

AUTHOR COMMENT
MRP software programs are popular because manual approaches are slow and error prone.

Gross material requirements plan

A schedule that shows the total demand for an item (prior to subtraction of on-hand inventory and scheduled receipts) and (1) when it must be ordered from suppliers, or (2) when production must be started to meet its demand by a particular date.

Once these ingredients are available and accurate, the next step is to construct a gross material requirements plan. The **gross material requirements plan** is a schedule, as shown in Example 2. It combines a master production schedule (that requires one unit of A in week 8) and the time-phased schedule (Figure 14.4). It shows when an item must be ordered from suppliers if there is no inventory on hand or when the production of an item must be started to satisfy demand for the finished product by a particular date.

EXAMPLE 2 ▶

Building a gross requirements plan

Each Awesome speaker kit (item A of Example 1) requires all the items in the product structure for A. Lead times are shown in Table 14.2.

APPROACH ▶ Using the information in Example 1 and Table 14.2, we construct the gross material requirements plan with a production schedule that will satisfy the demand of 50 units of A by week 8.

SOLUTION ▶ We prepare a schedule as shown in Table 14.3.

▶ **TABLE 14.3**
Gross Material Requirements Plan for 50 Awesome Speaker Kits (As)

					Week				
	1	**2**	**3**	**4**	**5**	**6**	**7**	**8**	**Lead Time**
A. Required date								50	
Order release date							50		1 week
B. Required date							100		
Order release date					100				2 weeks
C. Required date							150		
Order release date						150			1 week
E. Required date					200	300			
Order release date			200	300					2 weeks
F. Required date					300				
Order release date			300						3 weeks
D. Required date			600	200					
Order release date		600		200					1 week
G. Required date			300						
Order release date	300								2 weeks

LO2: Build a gross requirements plan

You can interpret the gross material requirements shown in Table 14.3 as follows: If you want 50 units of A at week 8, you must start assembling A in week 7. Thus, in week 7, you will need 100 units of B and 150 units of C. These two items take 2 weeks and 1 week, respectively, to produce. Production of B, therefore, should start in week 5, and production of C should start in week 6 (lead time subtracted from the required date for these items). Working backward, we can perform the same computations for all of the other items. Because D and E are used in two different places in Awesome speaker kits, there are two entries in each data record.

INSIGHT ▶   The gross material requirements plan shows when production of each item should begin and end in order to have 50 units of A at week 8. Management now has an initial plan.

LEARNING EXERCISE ▶   If the lead time for G decreases from 2 weeks to 1 week, what is the new order release date for G? [Answer: 300 in week 2.]

RELATED PROBLEMS ▶   14.2, 14.4, 14.6, 14.8b, 14.9, 14.10a, 14.11a, 14.13b, 14.25b

So far, we have considered *gross material requirements*, which assumes that there is no inventory on hand. When there is inventory on hand, we prepare a **net requirements plan**. When considering on-hand inventory, we must realize that many items in inventory contain subassemblies or parts. If the gross requirement for Awesome speaker kits (As) is 100 and there are 20 of those speakers on hand, the net requirement for Awesome speaker kits (As) is 80 (that is, 100 − 20). However, each Awesome speaker kit on hand contains 2 Bs. As a result, the requirement for Bs drops by 40 Bs (20 A kits on hand × 2 Bs per A). Therefore, if inventory is on hand for a parent item, the requirements for the parent item and all its components decrease because each Awesome kit contains the components for lower-level items. Example 3 shows how to create a net requirements plan.

Net material requirements
The result of adjusting gross requirements for inventory on hand and scheduled receipts.

◀ **EXAMPLE 3**
Determining net requirements

Speaker Kits, Inc., developed a product structure from a bill of material in Example 1. Example 2 developed a gross requirements plan. Given the following on-hand inventory, Speaker Kits, Inc., now wants to construct a net requirements plan.

Item	On Hand	Item	On Hand
A	10	E	10
B	15	F	5
C	20	G	0
D	10		

APPROACH ▶   A net material requirements plan includes gross requirements, on-hand inventory, net requirements, planned order receipt, and planned order release for each item. We begin with A and work backward through the components.

SOLUTION ▶   Shown in the chart on the next page is the net material requirements plan for product A.

Constructing a net requirements plan is similar to constructing a gross requirements plan. Starting with item A, we work backward to determine net requirements for all items. To do these computations, we refer to the product structure, on-hand inventory, and lead times. The gross requirement for A is 50 units in week 8. Ten items are on hand; therefore, the net requirements and the scheduled **planned order receipt** are both 40 items in week 8. Because of the 1-week lead time, the **planned order release** is 40 items in week 7 (see the arrow connecting the order receipt and order release). Referring to week 7 and the product structure in Example 1, we can see that 80 (2 × 40) items of B and 120 (3 × 40) items of C are required in week 7 to have a total for 50 items of A in week 8. The letter superscripted A to the right of the gross figure for items B and C was generated as a result of the demand for the parent, A. Performing the same type of analysis for B and C yields the net requirements for D, E, F, and G. Note the on-hand inventory in row E in week 6 is zero. It is zero because the on-hand inventory (10 units) was used to make B in week 5. By the same token, the inventory for D was used to make F in week 3.

Planned order receipt
The quantity planned to be received at a future date.

Planned order release
The scheduled date for an order to be released.

INSIGHT ▶   Once a net requirement plan is completed, management knows the quantities needed, an ordering schedule, and a production schedule for each component.

▼ Net Material Requirements Plan for Product A   *(the superscript is the source of the demand)*

Lot Size	Lead Time (weeks)	On Hand	Safety Stock	Allo-cated	Low-Level Code	Item Identi-fication		Week							
								1	2	3	4	5	6	7	8
Lot-for-Lot	1	10	—	—	0	A	Gross Requirements								50
							Scheduled Receipts								
							Projected On Hand	10	10	10	10	10	10	10	10	10
							Net Requirements								40
							Planned Order Receipts								40
							Planned Order Releases							40	
Lot-for-Lot	2	15	—	—	1	B	Gross Requirements							80^A	
							Scheduled Receipts								
							Projected On Hand	15	15	15	15	15	15	15	15	
							Net Requirements							65	
							Planned Order Receipts							65	
							Planned Order Releases						65		
Lot-for-Lot	1	20	—	—	1	C	Gross Requirements							120^A	
							Scheduled Receipts								
							Projected On Hand	20	20	20	20	20	20	20	20	
							Net Requirements							100	
							Planned Order Receipts							100	
							Planned Order Releases						100		
Lot-for-Lot	2	10	—	—	2	E	Gross Requirements					130^B	200^C		
							Scheduled Receipts								
							Projected On Hand	10	10	10	10	10	10			
							Net Requirements					120	200		
							Planned Order Receipts					120	200		
							Planned Order Releases			120	200				
Lot-for-Lot	3	5	—	—	2	F	Gross Requirements						200^C		
							Scheduled Receipts								
							Projected On Hand	5	5	5	5	5	5	5		
							Net Requirements						195		
							Planned Order Receipts						195		
							Planned Order Releases			195					
Lot-for-Lot	1	10	—	—	3	D	Gross Requirements				390^F		130^B		
							Scheduled Receipts								
							Projected On Hand	10	10	10	10					
							Net Requirements				380		130		
							Planned Order Receipts				380		130		
							Planned Order Releases			380		130			
Lot-for-Lot	2	0	—	—	3	G	Gross Requirements				195^F				
							Scheduled Receipts								
							Projected On Hand				0				
							Net Requirements				195				
							Planned Order Receipts				195				
							Planned Order Releases		195						

LEARNING EXERCISE ▶   If the on-hand inventory quantity of component F is 95 rather than 5, how many units of G will need to be ordered in week 1? [Answer: 105 units.]

RELATED PROBLEMS ▶   14.5, 14.7, 14.8c, 14.10b, 14.11b, 14.12, 14.13c, 14.14b, 14.15a,b,c, 14.16a, 14.25c, 14.27

ACTIVE MODEL 14.1 This example is further illustrated in Active Model 14.1 at **www.pearsonglobaleditions.com/heizer**.

Examples 2 and 3 considered only product A, the Awesome speaker kit, and its completion only in week 8. Fifty units of A were required in week 8. Normally, however, there is a demand for many products over time. For each product, management must prepare a master production schedule (as we saw earlier in Table 14.1). Scheduled production of each product is added to the

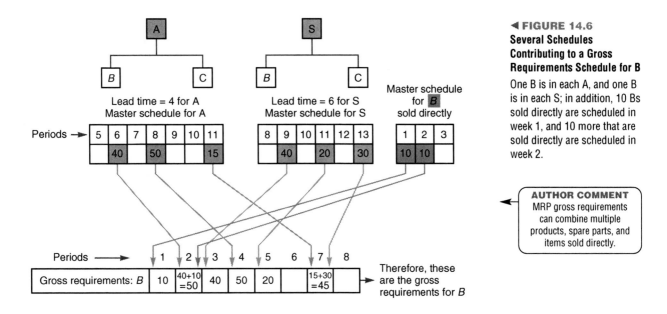

One B is in each A, and one B is in each S; in addition, 10 Bs sold directly are scheduled in week 1, and 10 more that are sold directly are scheduled in week 2.

AUTHOR COMMENT
MRP gross requirements can combine multiple products, spare parts, and items sold directly.

master schedule and ultimately to the net material requirements plan. Figure 14.6 shows how several product schedules, including requirements for components sold directly, can contribute to one gross material requirements plan.

Most inventory systems also note the number of units in inventory that have been assigned to specific future production but not yet used or issued from the stockroom. Such items are often referred to as *allocated* items. Allocated items increase requirements and may then be included in an MRP planning sheet, as shown in Figure 14.7.

The allocated quantity has the effect of increasing the requirements (or, alternatively, reducing the quantity on hand). The logic, then, of a net requirements MRP is:

$$\underbrace{[(\text{Gross requirements}) + (\text{Allocations})]}_{\text{Total requirements}} - \underbrace{[(\text{On hand}) + (\text{Scheduled receipts})]}_{\text{Available inventory}} = \begin{matrix} \text{Net} \\ \text{requirements} \end{matrix}$$

LO3: Build a net requirements plan

Safety Stock The continuing task of operations managers is to remove variability. This is the case in MRP systems as in other operations systems. Realistically, however, managers need to realize that bills of material and inventory records, like purchase and production quantities, as well as lead times, may not be perfect. This means that some consideration of safety stock may be prudent. Because of the significant domino effect of any change in requirements, safety stock should be minimized, with a goal of ultimate elimination. When safety stock is deemed absolutely necessary, the usual policy is to build it into the projected on-hand inventory of the MRP logic. Distortion can be minimized when safety stock is held at the finished goods level and at the purchased component or raw material level.

▼ **FIGURE 14.7**   **Sample MRP Planning Sheet for Item Z**

Lot Size	Lead Time	On Hand	Safety Stock	Allocated	Low-Level Code	Item ID		Period							
								1	2	3	4	5	6	7	8
Lot For Lot	1	0	0	10	0	Z	Gross Requirements								80 90
							Scheduled Receipts								0
							Projected On Hand 0	0	0	0	0	0	0	0	0
							Net Requirements								90
							Planned Order Receipts								90
							Planned Order Releases							90	

MRP MANAGEMENT

The material requirements plan is not static. And since MRP systems increasingly are integrated with just-in-time (JIT) techniques, we now discuss these two issues.

MRP Dynamics

Bills of material and material requirements plans are altered as changes in design, schedules, and production processes occur. In addition, changes occur in material requirements whenever the master production schedule is modified. Regardless of the cause of any changes, the MRP model can be manipulated to reflect them. In this manner, an up-to-date requirements schedule is possible.

The inputs to MRP (the master schedule, BOM, lead times, purchasing, and inventory) frequently change. Conveniently, a central strength of MRP systems is timely and accurate replanning. This occurs in one of two ways: by recomputing (also known as "regenerating") the requirement and schedule periodically, often weekly, or via a "net change" calculation. Net change in an MRP system means the MRP system creates new requirements in response to transactions. However, many firms find they do not want to respond to minor scheduling or quantity changes even if they are aware of them. These frequent changes generate what is called **system nervousness** and can create havoc in purchasing and production departments if implemented. Consequently, OM personnel reduce such nervousness by evaluating the need and impact of changes prior to disseminating requests to other departments. Two tools are particularly helpful when trying to reduce MRP system nervousness.

System nervousness
Frequent changes in an MRP system.

The first is time fences. **Time fences** allow a segment of the master schedule to be designated as "not to be rescheduled." This segment of the master schedule is therefore not changed during the periodic regeneration of schedules. The second tool is pegging. **Pegging** means tracing upward in the BOM from the component to the parent item. By pegging upward, the production planner can determine the cause for the requirement and make a judgment about the necessity for a change in the schedule.

Time fences
A means for allowing a segment of the master schedule to be designated as "not to be rescheduled."

Pegging
In material requirements planning systems, tracing upward in the bill of material from the component to the parent item.

With MRP, the operations manager *can* react to the dynamics of the real world. How frequently the manager wishes to impose those changes on the firm requires professional judgment. Moreover, if the nervousness is caused by legitimate changes, then the proper response may be to investigate the production environment—not adjust via MRP.

MRP and JIT

MRP does not do detailed scheduling—it plans. MRP will tell you that a job needs to be completed on a certain week or day but does not tell you that Job X needs to run on Machine A at 10:30 A.M. and be completed by 11:30 A.M. so that Job X can then run on machine B. MRP is also a planning technique with *fixed* lead times. Fixed lead times can be a limitation. For instance, the lead time to produce 50 units may vary substantially from the lead time to produce 5 units. These limitations complicate the marriage of MRP and just-in-time (JIT). What is needed is a way to make MRP more responsive to moving material rapidly in small batches. An MRP system combined with JIT can provide the best of both worlds. MRP provides the plan and an accurate picture of requirements; then JIT rapidly moves material in small batches, reducing work-in-process inventory. Let's look at four approaches for integrating MRP and JIT: finite capacity scheduling, small buckets, balanced flow, and supermarkets.

Finite Capacity Scheduling (FCS) Most MRP software loads work into infinite size "buckets." The **buckets** are time units, usually one week. Traditionally, when work is to be done in a given week, MRP puts the work there without regard to capacity. Consequently, MRP is considered an *infinite* scheduling technique. Frequently, as you might suspect, this is not realistic. Finite capacity scheduling (FCS), which we discuss in Chapter 15, considers department and machine capacity, which is *finite*, hence the name. FCS provides the precise scheduling needed for rapid material movement. We are now witnessing a convergence of FCS and MRP. Sophisticated FCS systems modify the output from MRP systems to provide a finite schedule.

Buckets
Time units in a material requirements planning system.

Small Bucket Approach MRP is an excellent tool for resource and scheduling management in process-focused facilities, that is, in job shops. Such facilities include machine shops, hospitals, and restaurants, where lead times are relatively stable and poor balance between work centers is expected. Schedules are often driven by work orders, and lot sizes are the exploded bill-of-material size. In these enterprises, MRP can be integrated with JIT through the following steps.

STEP 1: Reduce MRP "buckets" from weekly to daily to perhaps hourly. Buckets are time units in an MRP system. Although the examples in this chapter have used weekly *time buckets*, many firms now use daily or even fraction-of-a-day time buckets. Some systems use a **bucketless system** in which all time-phased data have dates attached rather than defined time periods or buckets.

STEP 2: The planned receipts that are part of a firm's planned orders in an MRP system are communicated to the work areas for production purposes and used to sequence production.

STEP 3: Inventory is moved through the plant on a JIT basis.

STEP 4: As products are completed, they are moved into inventory (typically finished-goods inventory) in the normal way. Receipt of these products into inventory reduces the quantities required for subsequent planned orders in the MRP system.

STEP 5: A system known as *back flush* is used to reduce inventory balances. **Back flushing** uses the bill of material to deduct component quantities from inventory as each unit is completed.

Bucketless system
Time-phased data are referenced using dated records rather than defined time periods, or buckets.

Back flush
A system to reduce inventory balances by deducting everything in the bill of material on completion of the unit.

The focus in these facilities becomes one of maintaining schedules. Nissan achieves success with this approach by computer communication links to suppliers. These schedules are confirmed, updated, or changed every 15 to 20 minutes. Suppliers provide deliveries 4 to 16 times per day. Master schedule performance is 99% on time, as measured every hour. On-time delivery from suppliers is 99.9% and for manufactured piece parts, 99.5%.

Balanced Flow Approach   MRP supports the planning and scheduling necessary for repetitive operations, such as the assembly lines at Harley-Davidson, Whirlpool, and a thousand other places. In these environments, the planning portion of MRP is combined with JIT execution. The JIT portion uses kanbans, visual signals, and reliable suppliers to pull the material through the facility. In these systems, execution is achieved by maintaining a carefully balanced flow of material to assembly areas with small lot sizes.

Supermarket   Another technique that joins MRP and JIT is the use of a "supermarket." In many firms, subassemblies, their components, and hardware items are common to a variety of products. In such cases, releasing orders for these common items with traditional lead-time offset, as is done in an MRP system, is not necessary. The subassemblies, components, and hardware items can be maintained in a common area, sometimes called a **supermarket**, adjacent to the production areas where they are used. For instance, Ducati, Italy's high-performance motorcycle manufacturer, pulls "kits" with the materials needed for one engine or vehicle from the supermarket and delivers them to the assembly line on a JIT basis. Items in the supermarket are replenished by a JIT/kanban system.

Supermarket
An inventory area that holds common items that are replenished by a kanban system.

LOT-SIZING TECHNIQUES

An MRP system is an excellent way to determine production schedules and net requirements. However, whenever we have a net requirement, a decision must be made about *how much* to order. This decision is called a **lot-sizing decision**. There are a variety of ways to determine lot sizes in an MRP system; commercial MRP software usually includes the choice of several lot-sizing techniques. We now review a few of them.

AUTHOR COMMENT
Managers need to know how to group/order the "planned order releases."

Lot-sizing decision
The process of, or techniques used in, determining lot size.

Lot-for-Lot   In Example 3, we used a lot-sizing technique known as **lot-for-lot**, which produced exactly what was required. This decision is consistent with the objective of an MRP system, which is to meet the requirements of *dependent* demand. Thus, an MRP system should produce units only as needed, with no safety stock and no anticipation of further orders. When frequent orders are economical and just-in-time inventory techniques implemented, lot-for-lot can be very efficient. However, when setup costs are significant or management has been unable to implement JIT, lot-for-lot can be expensive. Example 4 uses the lot-for-lot criteria and determines cost for 10 weeks of demand.

Lot-for-lot
A lot-sizing technique that generates exactly what is required to meet the plan.

EXAMPLE 4 ▶

Lot sizing with lot-for-lot

Speaker Kits, Inc., wants to compute its ordering and carrying cost of inventory on lot-for-lot criteria.

APPROACH ▶   With lot-for-lot, we order material only as it is needed. Once we have the cost of ordering (setting up), the cost of holding each unit for a given time period, and the production schedule, we can assign orders to our net requirements plan.

SOLUTION ▶   Speaker Kits has determined that, for the 12-inch speaker unit, setup cost is $100 and holding cost is $1 per period. The production schedule, as reflected in net requirements for assemblies, is as follows:

MRP Lot Sizing: Lot-for-Lot Technique*

		1	2	3	4	5	6	7	8	9	10
Gross requirements		35	30	40	0	10	40	30	0	30	55
Scheduled receipts											
Projected on hand	35	35	0	0	0	0	0	0	0	0	0
Net requirements		0	30	40	0	10	40	30	0	30	55
Planned order receipts			30	40		10	40	30		30	55
Planned order releases		30	40		10	40	30		30	55	

*Holding costs = $1/unit/week; setup cost = $100; gross requirements average per week = 27; lead time = 1 week.

The lot-sizing solution using the lot-for-lot technique is shown in the table. The holding cost is zero as there is never any inventory. (Inventory in the first period is used immediately and therefore has no holding cost.) But seven separate setups (one associated with each order) yield a total cost of $700. (Holding cost = 0 × 1 = 0; ordering cost = 7 × 100 = 700.)

INSIGHT ▶   When supply is reliable and frequent orders are inexpensive, but holding cost or obsolescence is high, lot-for-lot ordering can be very efficient.

LEARNING EXERCISE ▶   What is the impact on total cost if holding cost is $2 per period rather than $1? [Answer: Total holding cost remains zero, as no units are held from one period to the next with lot-for-lot.]

RELATED PROBLEMS ▶   14.17, 14.20, 14.21, 14.22

LO4: Determine lot sizes for lot-for-lot, EOQ, and PPB

Economic Order Quantity   As discussed in Chapter 12, EOQ can be used as a lot-sizing technique. But as we indicated there, EOQ is preferable when *relatively constant* independent demand exists, not when we *know* the demand. EOQ is a statistical technique using averages (such as average demand for a year), whereas the MRP procedure assumes *known* (dependent)

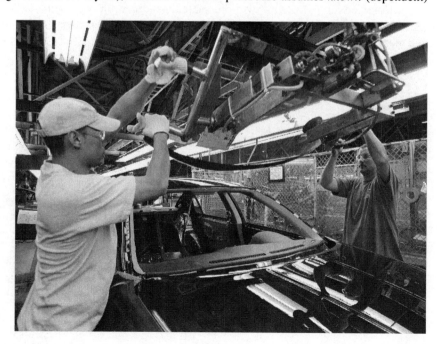

This Nissan line in Smyrna, Tennessee, has little inventory because Nissan schedules to a razor's edge. At Nissan, MRP helps reduce inventory to world-class standards. World-class automobile assembly requires that purchased parts have a turnover of slightly more than once a day and that overall turnover approaches 150 times per year.

demand reflected in a master production schedule. Operations managers should take advantage of demand information when it is known, rather than assuming a constant demand. EOQ is examined in Example 5.

◀ **EXAMPLE 5**

Lot sizing with EOQ

With a setup cost of $100 and a holding cost per week of $1, Speaker Kits, Inc., wants to examine its cost with lot sizes based on an EOQ criteria.

APPROACH ▶ Using the same cost and production schedule as in Example 4, we determine net requirements and EOQ lot sizes.

SOLUTION ▶ Ten-week usage equals a gross requirement of 270 units; therefore, weekly usage equals 27, and 52 weeks (annual usage) equals 1,404 units. From Chapter 12, the EOQ model is:

$$Q^* = \sqrt{\frac{2DS}{H}}$$

where

D = annual usage = 1,404
S = setup cost = $100
H = holding (carrying) cost, on an annual basis per unit
    = $1 × 52 weeks = $52

$$Q^* = 73 \text{ units}$$

MRP Lot Sizing: EOQ Technique*

		1	2	3	4	5	6	7	8	9	10
Gross requirements		35	30	40	0	10	40	30	0	30	55
Scheduled receipts											
Projected on hand	35	35	0	43	3	3	66	26	69	69	39
Net requirements		0	30	0	0	7	0	4	0	0	16
Planned order receipts			73			73		73			73
Planned order releases		73			73		73		73		

*Holding costs = $1/unit/week; setup cost = $100; gross requirements average per week = 27; lead time = 1 week.

Setups = 1,404/73 = 19 per year
Annual Setup cost = 19 × $100 = $1,900
Annual Holding cost = $\frac{73}{2}$ × ($1 × 52 weeks) = $1,898
Annual Setup cost + Holding cost = $1,900 + 1,898 = $3,798

The EOQ solution yields a computed 10-week cost of $730 [$3,798 × (10 weeks/52 weeks) = $730].

INSIGHT ▶ EOQ can be an effective lot-sizing technique when demand is relatively constant. However, notice that actual holding cost will vary from the computed $730, depending on the rate of actual usage. From the preceding table, we can see that in our 10-week example, costs really are $400 for four setups, plus a holding cost of 375 units (includes 57 remaining at the end of the period) at $1 per week for a total of $775. Because usage was not constant, the actual computed cost was in fact more than the theoretical EOQ ($730) and the lot-for-lot rule ($700). If any stockouts had occurred, these costs too would need to be added to our actual EOQ cost of $775.

LEARNING EXERCISE ▶ What is the impact on total cost if holding cost is $2 per period rather than $1? [Answer: The EOQ quantity becomes 52, the theoretical annual total cost becomes $5,404, and the 10-week cost is $1,039 ($5,404 × (10/52).]

RELATED PROBLEMS ▶ 14.18, 14.20, 14.21, 14.22

Part Period Balancing   Part period balancing (PPB) is a more dynamic approach to balance setup and holding cost.[3] PPB uses additional information by changing the lot size to reflect requirements of the next lot size in the future. PPB attempts to balance setup and holding cost for

Part period balancing (PPB)

An inventory ordering technique that balances setup and holding costs by changing the lot size to reflect requirements of the next lot size in the future.

[3]J. J. DeMatteis, "An Economic Lot-Sizing Technique: The Part-Period Algorithms," *IBM Systems Journal* 7 (1968): 30–38.

Economic part period (EPP)

A period of time when the ratio of setup cost to holding cost is equal.

known demands. Part period balancing develops an **economic part period (EPP)**, which is the ratio of setup cost to holding cost. For our Speaker Kits example, EPP = $100/$1 = 100 units. Therefore, holding 100 units for one period would cost $100, exactly the cost of one setup. Similarly, holding 50 units for two periods also costs $100 (2 periods $\times$ $1 $\times$ 50 units). PPB merely adds requirements until the number of part periods approximates the EPP—in this case, 100. Example 6 shows the application of part period balancing.

EXAMPLE 6 ▶

Lot sizing with part period balancing

Speaker Kits, Inc., wants to compute the costs associated with lot sizing using part period balancing. It will use a setup cost of $100 and a $1 holding cost.

APPROACH ▶ Using the same costs and production schedule as Examples 3 and 4, we develop a format that helps us compute the PPB quantity and apply that to our net requirements plan.

SOLUTION ▶ The procedure for computing the order releases of 80, 100, and 55 is shown in the following PPB calculation. In the second table, we apply the PPB order quantities to the net requirements plan.

PPB Calculations

Periods Combined	Trial Lot Size (cumulative net requirements)	Part Periods	Setup	Holding	Total
2	30	0			
2, 3	70	$40 = 40 \times 1$			
2, 3, 4	70	40			
2, 3, 4, 5	80	$70 = 40 \times 1 + 10 \times 3$	100 +	70	= 170
2, 3, 4, 5, 6	120	$230 = 40 \times 1 + 10 \times 3 + 40 \times 4$			

40 units held for 1 period = $40
10 units held for 3 periods = $30

(Therefore, combine periods 2 through 5; 70 is as close to our EPP of 100 as we are going to get.)

6	40	0			
6, 7	70	$30 = 30 \times 1$			
6, 7, 8	70	$30 = 30 \times 1 + 0 \times 2$			
6, 7, 8, 9	100	$120 = 30 \times 1 + 30 \times 3$	100 +	120	= 220

(Therefore, combine periods 6 through 9; 120 is as close to our EPP of 100 as we are going to get.)

10	55	0	100 +	0	= 100
			300 +	190	= 490

MRP Lot Sizing: PPB Technique*

		1	2	3	4	5	6	7	8	9	10
Gross requirements		35	30	40	0	10	40	30	0	30	55
Scheduled receipts											
Projected on hand	35	35	0	50	10	10	0	60	30	30	0
Net requirements		0	30	0	0	0	40	0	0	0	55
Planned order receipts			80				100				55
Planned order releases		80				100				55	

*Holding costs = $1/unit/week; setup cost = $100; gross requirements average per week = 27; lead time = 1 week.

EPP is 100 (setup cost divided by holding cost = $100/$1). The first lot is to cover periods 2, 3, 4, and 5 and is 80.

The total costs are $490, with setup costs totaling $300 and holding costs totaling $190.

INSIGHT ▶ Both the EOQ and PPB approaches to lot sizing balance holding cost and ordering cost. But PPB places an order each time holding cost equals ordering cost, while EOQ takes a longer averaging approach.

LEARNING EXERCISE ▶ What is the impact on total cost if holding cost is $2 per period rather than $1? [Answer: With higher holding costs [PPB becomes 100/2 = 50], reorder points become more frequent, with orders now being placed for 70 units in period 1, 50 in period 4, 60 in period 6, and 55 in period 9.]

RELATED PROBLEMS ▶ 14.19, 14.20, 14.21, 14.22

Wagner-Whitin Algorithm   The **Wagner-Whitin procedure** is a dynamic programming model that adds some complexity to the lot-size computation. It assumes a finite time horizon beyond which there are no additional net requirements. It does, however, provide good results.[4]

Wagner-Whitin procedure
A technique for lot-size computation that assumes a finite time horizon beyond which there are no additional net requirements to arrive at an ordering strategy.

Lot-Sizing Summary   In the three Speaker Kits lot-sizing examples, we found the following costs:

Lot-for-lot	$700
EOQ	$730
Part period balancing	$490

These examples should not, however, lead operations personnel to hasty conclusions about the preferred lot-sizing technique. In theory, new lot sizes should be computed whenever there is a schedule or lot-size change anywhere in the MRP hierarchy. However, in practice, such changes cause the instability and system nervousness referred to earlier in this chapter. Consequently, such frequent changes are not made. This means that all lot sizes are wrong because the production system cannot respond to frequent changes.

In general, the lot-for-lot approach should be used whenever low-cost deliveries can be achieved. Lot-for-lot is the goal. Lots can be modified as necessary for scrap allowances, process constraints (for example, a heat-treating process may require a lot of a given size), or raw material purchase lots (for example, a truckload of chemicals may be available in only one lot size). However, caution should be exercised prior to any modification of lot size because the modification can cause substantial distortion of actual requirements at lower levels in the MRP hierarchy. When setup costs are significant and demand is reasonably smooth, part period balancing (PPB), Wagner-Whitin, or even EOQ should provide satisfactory results. Too much concern with lot sizing yields false accuracy because of MRP dynamics. A correct lot size can be determined only after the fact, based on what actually happened in terms of requirements.

EXTENSIONS OF MRP

In this section, we review three extensions of MRP.

Material Requirements Planning II (MRP II)

Material requirements planning II is an extremely powerful technique. Once a firm has MRP in place, requirements data can be enriched by resources other than just components. When MRP is used this way, *resource* is usually substituted for *requirements,* and MRP becomes **MRP II**. It then stands for material *resource* planning.

Material requirements planning II (MRP II)
A system that allows, with MRP in place, inventory data to be augmented by other resource variables; in this case, MRP becomes *material resource planning.*

Many MRP programs, such as *Resource Manager for Excel* and *DB,* are commercially available. *Resource Manager's* initial menu screen is shown here.

A demo program is available for student use at **www.usersolutions.com**.

[4]We leave discussion of the algorithm to mathematical programming texts. The Wagner-Whitin algorithm yields a cost of $455 for the data in Examples 4, 5, and 6.

▶ **TABLE 14.4**
Material Resource Planning (MRP II)

By utilizing the logic of MRP, resources such as labor, machine-hours, scrap, and cost can be accurately determined and scheduled. Weekly demand for labor, machine-hours, scrap, and payables for 100 computers are shown.

	Lead Time	WEEKS			
		5	6	7	8
Computer	1				100
Labor-hours: .2 each					20
Machine-hours: .2 each					20
Scrap: 1 ounce fiberglass each					6.25 lbs
Payables: $0					$0
PC board (1 each)	2			100	
Labor-hours: .15 each				15	
Machine-hours: .1 each				10	
Scrap: .5 ounces copper each				3.125 lb	
Payables: raw material at $5 each				$500	
Processors (5 each)	4	500			
Labor-hours: .2 each		100			
Machine-hours: .2 each		100			
Scrap: .01 ounces of acid waste each		0.3125 lb			
Payables: processors at $10 each		$5,000			

So far in our discussion of MRP, we have scheduled products and their components. However, products require many resources, such as energy and money, beyond the product's tangible components. In addition to these resource inputs, *outputs* can be generated as well. Outputs can include such things as scrap, packaging waste, effluent, and carbon emissions. As OM becomes increasingly sensitive to the environmental and sustainability issues, identifying and managing byproducts becomes increasingly important. MRP II provides a vehicle for doing so. Table 14.4 provides an example of labor-hours, machine-hours, pounds of scrap, and cash, in the format of a gross requirements plan. With MRP II, management can identify both the inputs and outputs as well as the relevant schedule. MRP II provides another tool in OM's battle for sustainable operations.

MRP II systems are seldom stand-alone programs. Most are tied into other computer software that provide data to the MRP system or receive data from the MRP system. Purchasing, production scheduling, capacity planning, inventory, and warehouse management are a few examples of this data integration.

LO5: Describe MRP II

Closed-loop MRP system
A system that provides feedback to the capacity plan, master production schedule, and production plan so planning can be kept valid at all times.

LO6: Describe closed-loop MRP

Closed-Loop MRP

Closed-loop material requirements planning implies an MRP system that provides feedback to scheduling from the inventory control system. Specifically, a **closed-loop MRP system** provides information to the capacity plan, master production schedule, and ultimately to the production plan (as shown in Figure 14.8). Virtually all commercial MRP systems are closed-loop.

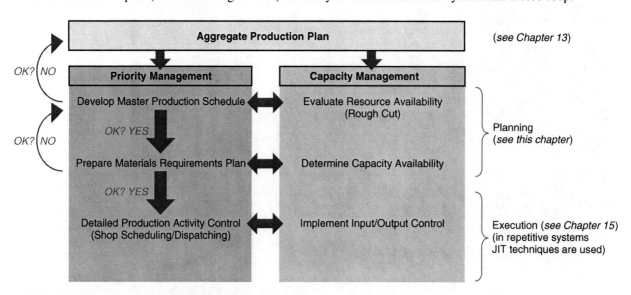

▲ **FIGURE 14.8** **Closed-Loop Material Requirements Planning**

Capacity Planning

In keeping with the definition of closed-loop MRP, feedback about workload is obtained from each work center. **Load reports** show the resource requirements in a work center for all work currently assigned to the work center, all work planned, and expected orders. Figure 14.9(a) shows that the initial load in the milling center exceeds capacity on days 2, 3, and 5. Closed-loop MRP systems allow production planners to move the work between time periods to smooth the load or at least bring it within capacity. (This is the "capacity planning" part of Figure 14.8.) The closed-loop MRP system can then reschedule all items in the net requirements plan (see Figure 14.9[b]).

Load report

A report for showing the resource requirements in a work center for all work currently assigned there as well as all planned and expected orders.

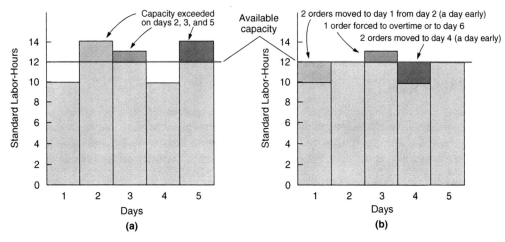

◄ **FIGURE 14.9**
(a) Initial Resource Requirements Profile for a Work Center (b) Smoothed Resource Requirements Profile for a Work Center

Tactics for smoothing the load and minimizing the impact of changed lead time include the following:

1. *Overlapping,* which reduces the lead time, sends pieces to the second operation before the entire lot is completed on the first operation.
2. *Operations splitting* sends the lot to two different machines for the same operation. This involves an additional setup, but results in shorter throughput times, because only part of the lot is processed on each machine.
3. *Order* or, *lot splitting,* involves breaking up the order and running part of it earlier (or later) in the schedule.

Example 7 shows a brief detailed capacity scheduling example using order splitting to improve utilization.

| ◄ **EXAMPLE 7** |
| **Order splitting** |

Kevin Watson, the production planner at Wiz Products, needs to develop a capacity plan for a work center. He has the production orders shown below for the next 5 days. There are 12 hours available in the work cell each day. The parts being produced require 1 hour each.

Day	1	2	3	4	5
Orders	10	14	13	10	14

APPROACH ►   Compute the time available in the work center and the time necessary to complete the production requirements.

SOLUTION ►

Day	Units Ordered	Capacity Required (hours)	Capacity Available (hours)	Utilization: Over/ (Under) (hours)	Production Planner's Action	New Production Schedule
1	10	10	12	(2)		12
2	14	14	12	2	Split order: move 2 units to day 1	12
3	13	13	12	1	Split order: move 1 unit to day 6 or request overtime	13
4	10	10	12	(2)		12
5	14	14	12	2	Split order: move 2 units to day 4	12
	61					

When the workload consistently exceeds work-center capacity, the tactics just discussed are not adequate. This may mean adding capacity. Options include adding capacity via personnel, machinery, overtime, or subcontracting.

MRP IN SERVICES

The demand for many services or service items is classified as dependent demand when it is directly related to or derived from the demand for other services. Such services often require product-structure trees, bills-of-material and labor, and scheduling. MRP can make a major contribution to operational performance in such services. Examples from restaurants, hospitals, and hotels follow.

Restaurants In restaurants, ingredients and side dishes (bread, vegetables, and condiments) are typically meal components. These components are dependent on the demand for meals. The meal is an end item in the master schedule. Figure 14.10 shows (a) a product-structure tree and (b) a bill of material for veal picante, a top-selling entrée in a New Orleans restaurant. Note that the various components of veal picante (that is, veal, sauce, spinach, and linguini) are prepared by different kitchen personnel (see part [a] of Figure 14.10). These preparations also require different amounts of time to complete. Figure 14.10(c) shows a bill-of-labor for the veal dish. It lists the operations to be performed, the order of operations, and the labor requirements for each operation (types of labor and labor-hours).

Hospitals MRP is also applied in hospitals, especially when dealing with surgeries that require known equipment, materials, and supplies. Houston's Park Plaza Hospital and many hospital suppliers, for example, use the technique to improve the scheduling and management of expensive surgical inventory.

Hotels Marriott develops a bill of material (BOM) and a bill of labor when it renovates each of its hotel rooms. Marriott managers explode the BOM to compute requirements for materials, furniture, and decorations. MRP then provides net requirements and a schedule for use by purchasing and contractors.

Distribution Resource Planning (DRP)

Distribution resource planning (DRP)

A time-phased stock-replenishment plan for all levels of a distribution network.

When dependent techniques are used in the supply chain, they are called distribution resource planning (DRP). **Distribution resource planning (DRP)** is a time-phased stock-replenishment plan for all levels of the supply chain.

DRP procedures and logic are analogous to MRP. With DRP, expected demand becomes gross requirements. Net requirements are determined by allocating available inventory to gross requirements. The DRP procedure starts with the forecast at the retail level (or the most distant point of the distribution network being supplied). All other levels are computed. As is the case with MRP, inventory is then reviewed with an aim to satisfying demand. So that stock will arrive when it is needed, net requirements are offset by the necessary lead time. A planned order release quantity becomes the gross requirement at the next level down the distribution chain.

DRP *pulls* inventory through the system. Pulls are initiated when the retail level orders more stock. Allocations are made to the retail level from available inventory and production after being adjusted to obtain shipping economies. Effective use of DRP requires an integrated information system to rapidly convey planned order releases from one level to the next. The goal of the DRP system is small and frequent replenishment within the bounds of economical ordering and shipping.[5]

[5]For an expanded discussion of time-phased stock-replenishment plans, see the section "Opportunities in an Integrated Supply Chain" in Chapter 11 of this text.

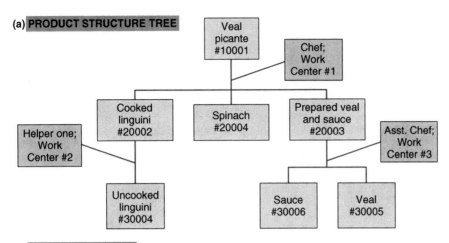

(a) PRODUCT STRUCTURE TREE

◄ **FIGURE 14.10**
Product Structure Tree, Bill-of-Material, and Bill-of-Labor for Veal Picante

Source: Adapted from John G. Wacker, "Effective Planning and Cost Control for Restaurants," *Production and Inventory Management* (Vol. 26, no. 1): 60. Reprinted by permission of American Production and Inventory Control Society.

(b) BILL OF MATERIALS

Part Number	Description	Quantity	Unit of Measure	Unit Cost
10001	Veal picante	1	Serving	—
20002	Cooked linguini	1	Serving	—
20003	Prepared veal and sauce	1	Serving	—
20004	Spinach	0.1	Bag	0.94
30004	Uncooked linguini	0.5	Pound	—
30005	Veal	1	Serving	2.15
30006	Sauce	1	Serving	0.80

(c) BILL OF LABOR FOR VEAL PICANTE

Work Center	Operation	Labor Type	Labor-Hours Setup Time	Labor-Hours Run Time
1	Assemble dish	Chef	.0069	.0041
2	Cook linguini	Helper one	.0005	.0022
3	Cook veal and sauce	Assistant chef	.0125	.0500

ENTERPRISE RESOURCE PLANNING (ERP)

AUTHOR COMMENT
ERP tries to integrate all of a firm's information.

Advances in MRP II systems that tie customers and suppliers to MRP II have led to the development of enterprise resource planning (ERP) systems. **Enterprise resource planning (ERP)** is software that allows companies to (1) automate and integrate many of their business processes, (2) share a common database and business practices throughout the enterprise, and (3) produce information in real time. A schematic showing some of these relationships for a manufacturing firm appears in Figure 14.11.

Enterprise resource planning (ERP)
An information system for identifying and planning the enterprise-wide resources needed to take, make, ship, and account for customer orders.

The objective of an ERP system is to coordinate a firm's whole business, from supplier evaluation to customer invoicing. This objective is seldom achieved, but ERP systems are evolving as umbrella systems that tie together a variety of specialized systems. This is accomplished by using a centralized database to assist the flow of information among business functions. Exactly what is tied together, and how, varies on a case-by-case basis. In addition to the traditional components of MRP, ERP systems usually provide financial and human resource (HR) management information. ERP systems also include:

- *Supply chain management (SCM)* software to support sophisticated vendor communication, e-commerce, and those activities necessary for efficient warehousing and logistics. The idea is to tie operations (MRP) to procurement, to materials management, and to suppliers, providing the tools necessary for effective management of all four areas.
- *Customer relationship management (CRM)* software for the incoming side of the business. CRM is designed to aid analysis of sales, target the most profitable customers, and manage the sales force.

LO7: Describe ERP

In addition to data integration, ERP software promises reduced transaction costs and fast, accurate information. A strategic emphasis on just-in-time systems and supply chain integration

► **FIGURE 14.11**
MRP and ERP Information Flows, Showing Customer Relationship Management (CRM), Supply-Chain Management (SCM), and Finance/Accounting
Other functions such as human resources are often also included in ERP systems.

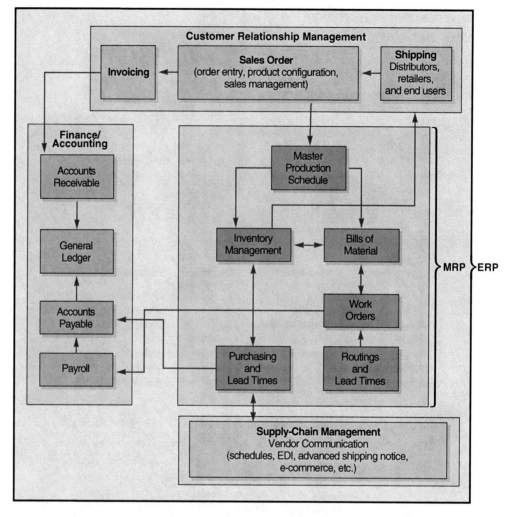

drives the desire for enterprise-wide software. The *OM in Action* box "Managing Benetton with ERP Software" provides an example of how ERP software helps integrate company operations.

OM in Action ► Managing Benetton with ERP Software

Thanks to ERP, the Italian sportswear company Benetton can probably claim to have the world's fastest factory and the most efficient distribution in the garment industry. Located in Ponzano, Italy, Benetton makes and ships 50 million pieces of clothing each year. That is 30,000 boxes every day—boxes that must be filled with exactly the items ordered going to the correct store of the 5,000 Benetton outlets in 60 countries. This highly automated distribution center uses only 19 people. Without ERP, hundreds of people would be needed.

Here is how ERP software works:

1. *Ordering:* A salesperson in the south Boston store finds that she is running out of a best-selling blue sweater. Using a laptop PC, her local Benetton sales agent taps into the ERP sales module.
2. *Availability:* ERP's inventory software simultaneously forwards the order to the mainframe in Italy and finds that half the order can be filled immediately from the Italian warehouse. The rest will be manufactured and shipped in 4 weeks.

3. *Production:* Because the blue sweater was originally created by computer-aided design (CAD), ERP manufacturing software passes the specifications to a knitting machine. The knitting machine makes the sweaters.
4. *Warehousing:* The blue sweaters are boxed with a radio frequency ID (RFID) tag addressed to the Boston store and placed in one of the 300,000 slots in the Italian warehouse. A robot flies by, reading RFID tags, picks out any and all boxes ready for the Boston store, and loads them for shipment.
5. *Order tracking:* The Boston salesperson logs onto the ERP system through the Internet and sees that the sweater (and other items) are completed and being shipped.
6. *Planning:* Based on data from ERP's forecasting and financial modules, Benetton's chief buyer decides that blue sweaters are in high demand and quite profitable. She decides to add three new hues.

Sources: The Wall Street Journal (April 10, 2007): B1; *Frontline Solutions* (April 2003): 54; and *MIT Sloan Management Review* (Fall 2001): 46–53.

In an ERP system, data are entered only once into a common, complete, and consistent database shared by all applications. For example, when a Nike salesperson enters an order into his ERP system for 20,000 pairs of sneakers for Foot Locker, the data are instantly available on the manufacturing floor. Production crews start filling the order if it is not in stock, accounting prints Foot Locker's invoice, and shipping notifies the Foot Locker of the future delivery date. The salesperson, or even the customer, can check the progress of the order at any point. This is all accomplished using the same data and common applications. To reach this consistency, however, the data fields must be defined identically across the entire enterprise. In Nike's case, this means integrating operations at production sites from Vietnam to China to Mexico, at business units across the globe, in many currencies, and with reports in a variety of languages.

Each ERP vendor produces unique products. The major vendors, SAP AG (a German firm), BEA (Canada), SSAGlobal, American Software, PeopleSoft/Oracle, CMS Software (all of the U.S.), sell software or modules designed for specific industries (a set of SAP's modules is shown in Figure 14.12). However, companies must determine if their way of doing business will fit the standard ERP module. If they determine that the product will not fit the standard ERP product, they can change the way they do business to accommodate the software. But such a change can have an adverse impact on their business process, reducing a competitive advantage. Alternatively, ERP software can be customized to meet their specific process requirements. Although the vendors build the software to keep the customization process simple, many companies spend up to five times the cost of the software to customize it. In addition to the expense, the major downside of customization is that when ERP vendors provide an upgrade or enhancement to the software, the customized part of the code must be rewritten to fit into the new version. ERP programs cost from a minimum of $300,000 for a small company to hundreds of millions of dollars for global giants like Ford and Coca-Cola. It is easy to see, then, that ERP systems are expensive, full of hidden issues, and time-consuming to install.

▼ FIGURE 14.12   **SAP's Modules for ERP**

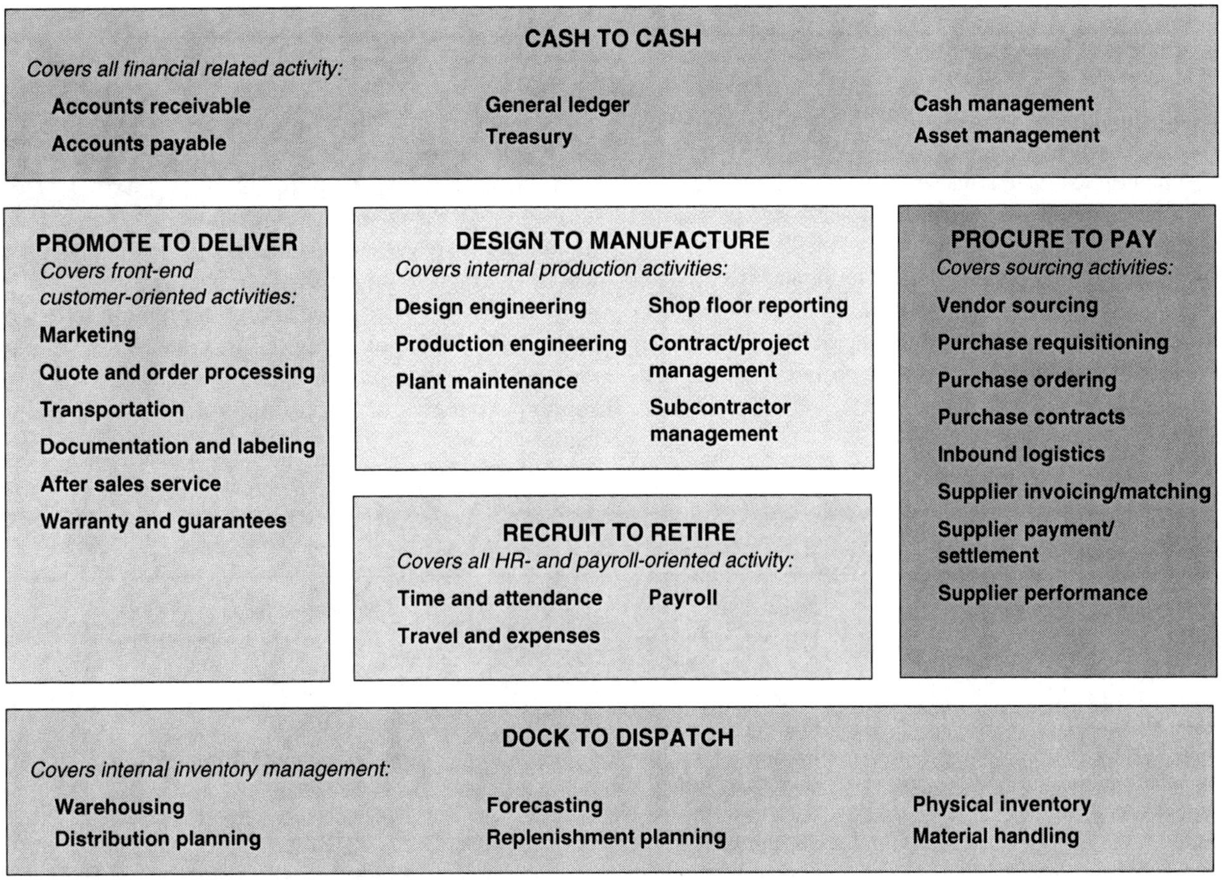

CASH TO CASH
Covers all financial related activity:

| Accounts receivable | General ledger | Cash management |
| Accounts payable | Treasury | Asset management |

PROMOTE TO DELIVER
Covers front-end customer-oriented activities:

Marketing

Quote and order processing

Transportation

Documentation and labeling

After sales service

Warranty and guarantees

DESIGN TO MANUFACTURE
Covers internal production activities:

Design engineering	Shop floor reporting
Production engineering	Contract/project management
Plant maintenance	
	Subcontractor management

RECRUIT TO RETIRE
Covers all HR- and payroll-oriented activity:

| Time and attendance | Payroll |
| Travel and expenses | |

PROCURE TO PAY
Covers sourcing activities:

Vendor sourcing

Purchase requisitioning

Purchase ordering

Purchase contracts

Inbound logistics

Supplier invoicing/matching

Supplier payment/ settlement

Supplier performance

DOCK TO DISPATCH
Covers internal inventory management:

| Warehousing | Forecasting | Physical inventory |
| Distribution planning | Replenishment planning | Material handling |

Source: www.sap.com. © Copyright 2009. SAP AG. All rights reserved.

Advantages and Disadvantages of ERP Systems

We have alluded to some of the pluses and minuses of ERP. Here is a more complete list of both.

Advantages:

1. Provides integration of the supply chain, production, and administrative process.
2. Creates commonality of databases.
3. Can incorporate improved, reengineered, "best processes."
4. Increases communication and collaboration among business units and sites.
5. Has a software database that is off-the-shelf coding.
6. May provide a strategic advantage over competitors.

Disadvantages:

1. Is very expensive to purchase, and even more costly to customize.
2. Implementation may require major changes in the company and its processes.
3. Is so complex that many companies cannot adjust to it.
4. Involves an ongoing process for implementation, which may never be completed.
5. Expertise in ERP is limited, with staffing an ongoing problem.

ERP in the Service Sector

Efficient consumer response (ECR)

Supply chain management systems in the grocery industry that tie sales to buying, to inventory, to logistics, and to production.

ERP vendors have developed a series of service modules for such markets as health care, government, retail stores, and financial services. Springer-Miller Systems, for example, has created an ERP package for the hotel market with software that handles all front- and back-office functions. This system integrates tasks such as maintaining guest histories, booking room and dinner reservations, scheduling golf tee times, and managing multiple properties in a chain. PeopleSoft/Oracle combines ERP with supply chain management to coordinate airline meal preparation. In the grocery industry, these supply chain systems are known as *efficient consumer response* (ECR) systems. As is the case in manufacturing, **efficient consumer response** systems tie sales to buying, to inventory, to logistics, and to production.

CHAPTER SUMMARY

Material requirements planning (MRP) schedules production and inventory when demand is dependent. For MRP to work, management must have a master schedule, precise requirements for all components, accurate inventory and purchasing records, and accurate lead times.

Production should often be lot-for-lot in an MRP system. When properly implemented, MRP can contribute in a major way to reduction in inventory while improving customer service levels. MRP techniques allow the operations manager to schedule and replenish stock on a "need-to-order" basis rather than simply a "time-to-order" basis.

The continuing development of MRP systems has led to its use with lean manufacturing techniques. In addition, MRP can integrate production data with a variety of other activities, including the supply chain and sales. As a result, we now have integrated database-oriented enterprise resource planning (ERP) systems. These expensive and difficult-to-install ERP systems, when successful, support strategies of differentiation, response, and cost leadership.

Key Terms

Material requirements planning (MRP)
Master production schedule (MPS)
Bill of material (BOM)
Modular bills
Planning bills (or kits)
Phantom bills of material
Low-level coding
Lead time
Gross material requirements plan
Net material requirements

Planned order receipt
Planned order release
System nervousness
Time fences
Pegging
Buckets
Bucketless system
Back flush
Supermarket
Lot-sizing decision
Lot-for-lot

Part period balancing (PPB)
Economic part period (EPP)
Wagner-Whitin procedure
Material requirements planning II (MRP II)
Closed-loop MRP system
Load report
Distribution resource planning (DRP)
Enterprise resource planning (ERP)
Efficient consumer response (ECR)

Ethical Dilemma

For many months your prospective ERP customer has been analyzing the hundreds of assumptions built into the $900,000 ERP software you are selling. So far, you have knocked yourself out to try to make this sale. If the sale goes through, you will reach your yearly quota and get a nice bonus. On the other hand, loss of this sale may mean you start looking for other employment.

The accounting, human resource, supply chain, and marketing teams put together by the client have reviewed the specifications and finally recommended purchase of the software. However, as you looked over their shoulders and helped them through the evaluation process, you began to realize that their purchasing procedures—with much of the purchasing being done at hundreds of regional stores—were not a good fit for the software. At the very least, the customizing will add $250,000 to the implementation and training cost. The team is not aware of the issue, and you know that the necessary $250,000 is not in the budget.

What do you do?

Discussion Questions

1. What is the difference between a *gross* requirements plan and a *net* requirements plan?
2. Once a material requirements plan (MRP) has been established, what other managerial applications might be found for the technique?
3. What are the similarities between MRP and DRP?
4. How does MRP II differ from MRP?
5. Which is the best lot-sizing policy for manufacturing organizations?
6. What impact does ignoring carrying cost in the allocation of stock in a DRP system have on lot sizes?
7. MRP is more than an inventory system; what additional capabilities does MRP possess?
8. What are the options for the production planner who has:
   (a) scheduled more than capacity in a work center next week?
   (b) a consistent lack of capacity in that work center?
9. Master schedules are expressed in three different ways depending on whether the process is continuous, a job shop, or repetitive. What are these three ways?
10. What functions of the firm affect an MRP system? How?
11. What is the rationale for (a) a phantom bill of material, (b) a planning bill of material, and (c) a pseudo bill of material?
12. Identify five specific requirements of an effective MRP system.
13. What are the typical benefits of ERP?
14. What are the distinctions between MRP, DRP, and ERP?
15. As an approach to inventory management, how does MRP differ from the approach taken in Chapter 12, dealing with economic order quantities (EOQ)?
16. What are the disadvantages of ERP?
17. Use the Web or other sources to:
   (a) Find stories that highlight the advantages of an ERP system.
   (b) Find stories that highlight the difficulties of purchasing, installing, or failure of an ERP system.
18. Use the Web or other sources to identify what an ERP vendor (SAP, PeopleSoft/Oracle, American Software, etc.) includes in these software modules:
   (a) Customer relationship management.
   (b) Supply-chain management.
   (c) Product life cycle management.
19. The very structure of MRP systems suggests fixed lead times. However, many firms have moved toward JIT and kanban techniques. What are the techniques, issues, and impact of adding JIT inventory and purchasing techniques to an organization that has MRP?

Using Software to Solve MRP Problems

There are many commercial MRP software packages, for companies of all sizes. MRP software for small and medium-size companies includes User Solutions, Inc., a demo of which is available at **www. usersolutions.com,** and MAX, from Exact Software North America, Inc. Software for larger systems is available from SAP, CMS, BEA, Oracle, i2 Technologies, and many others. The Excel OM software that accompanies this text includes an MRP module, as does POM for Windows. The use of both is explained in the following sections.

✗ Using Excel OM

Using Excel OM's MRP module requires the careful entry of several pieces of data. The initial MRP screen is where we enter (1) the total number of occurrences of items in the BOM (including the top item), (2) what we want the BOM items to be called (i.e., Item no., Part), (3) total number of periods to be scheduled, and (4) what we want the periods called (i.e., days, weeks).

Excel OM's second MRP screen provides the data entry for an indented bill of material. Here we enter (1) the name of each item in the BOM, (2) the quantity of that item in the assembly, and (3) the correct indent (i.e., parent/child relationship) for each item. The indentations are critical as they provide the logic for the BOM explosion. The indentations should follow the logic of the product structure tree with indents for each assembly item in that assembly.

Excel OM's third MRP screen repeats the indented BOM and provides the standard MRP tableau for entries. This is shown in Program 14.1 using the data from Examples 1, 2, and 3.

The data in columns A, B, C, D (down to row 15) are entered on the second screen and automatically transferred here.

▶ **PROGRAM 14.1**
Using Excel OM's MRP Module to Solve Examples 1, 2, and 3

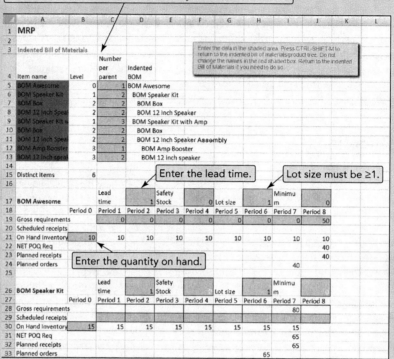

P Using POM for Windows

The POM for Windows MRP module can also solve Examples 1 to 3. Up to 18 periods can be analyzed. Here are the inputs required:

1. *Item names:* The item names are entered in the left column. The same item name will appear in more than one row if the item is used by two parent items. Each item must follow its parents.
2. *Item level:* The level in the indented BOM must be given here. The item *cannot* be placed at a level more than one below the item immediately above.
3. *Lead-time:* The lead time for an item is entered here. The default is 1 week.
4. *Number per parent:* The number of units of this subassembly needed for its parent is entered here. The default is 1.
5. *On hand:* List current inventory on hand once, even if the subassembly is listed twice.
6. *Lot size:* The lot size can be specified here. A 0 or 1 will perform lot-for-lot ordering. If another number is placed here, then all orders for that item will be in integer multiples of that number.
7. *Demands:* The demands are entered in the end item row in the period in which the items are demanded.
8. *Scheduled receipts:* If units are scheduled to be received in the future, they should be listed in the appropriate time period (column) and item (row). (An entry here in level 1 is a demand; all other levels are receipts.)

Further details regarding POM for Windows are seen in Appendix IV.

Solved Problems   Virtual Office Hours help is available at www.pearsonglobaleditions.com/myomlab

▶ **SOLVED PROBLEM 14.1**

Determine the low-level coding and the quantity of each component necessary to produce 10 units of an assembly we will call Alpha. The product structure and quantities of each component needed for each assembly are noted in parentheses.

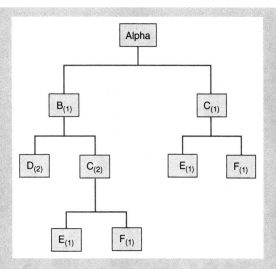

▶ SOLUTION

Redraw the product structure with low-level coding. Then multiply down the structure until the requirements of each branch are determined. Then add across the structure until the total for each is determined.

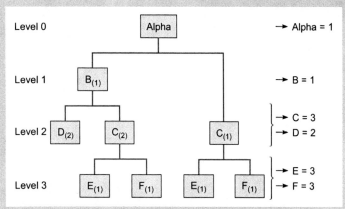

Es required for left branch:

$$(1_{alpha} \times 1_B \times 2_C \times 1_E) = 2 \text{ Es}$$

and Es required for right branch:

$$(1_{alpha} \times 1_C \times 1_E) = \underline{1 \text{ E}}$$
$$3 \text{ Es required in total}$$

Then "explode" the requirement by multiplying each by 10, as shown in the table to the right:

Level	Item	Quantity per Unit	Total Requirements for 10 Alpha
0	Alpha	1	10
1	B	1	10
2	C	3	30
2	D	2	20
3	E	3	30
3	F	3	30

▶ SOLVED PROBLEM 14.2

Using the product structure for Alpha in Solved Problem 14.1, and the following lead times, quantity on hand, and master production schedule, prepare a net MRP table for Alphas.

Item	Lead Time	Quantity on Hand
Alpha	1	10
B	2	20
C	3	0
D	1	100
E	1	10
F	1	50

Master Production Schedule for Alpha

Period	6	7	8	9	10	11	12	13
Gross requirements			50			50		100

▼ SOLUTION

See the chart on following page.

Net Material Requirements Planning Sheet for Alpha

The letter in parentheses (A) is the source of the demand.

Lot Size	Lead Time (# of Periods)	On Hand	Safety Stock	Allocated	Low-Level Code	Item ID		Period (week, day) 1	2	3	4	5	6	7	8	9	10	11	12	13
Lot-for-Lot	1	10	—	—	0	Alpha (A)	Gross Requirements								50			50		100
							Scheduled Receipts													
							Projected On Hand 10								10					
							Net Requirements								40			50		100
							Planned Order Receipts								40			50		100
							Planned Order Releases							40			50		100	
Lot-for-Lot	2	20	—	—	1	B	Gross Requirements							40(A)			50(A)		100(A)	
							Scheduled Receipts													
							Projected On Hand 20							20						
							Net Requirements							20			50		100	
							Planned Order Receipts							20			50		100	
							Planned Order Releases					20			50		100			
Lot-for-Lot	3	0	—	—	2	C	Gross Requirements					40(B)		40(A)	100(B)		200(B) + 50(A)		100(A)	
							Scheduled Receipts													
							Projected On Hand 0													
							Net Requirements					40		40	100		250		100	
							Planned Order Receipts					40		40	100		250		100	
							Planned Order Releases		40		40	100	250		100					
Lot-for-Lot	1	100	—	—	2	D	Gross Requirements					40(B)		40(A)	100(B)		200(B)			
							Scheduled Receipts													
							Projected On Hand 100					100		60						
							Net Requirements				0	0		40						
							Planned Order Receipts				0	0		40		200				
							Planned Order Releases				0			40		200				
Lot-for-Lot	1	10	—	—	3	E	Gross Requirements		40(C)		40(C)	100(C)		250(C)	100(B)	100(C)	200(B)		100(A)	
							Scheduled Receipts													
							Projected On Hand 10		10		10	0			60					
							Net Requirements		30		40	100		250	40	100	200			
							Planned Order Receipts		30		40	100		250	40	100	200			
							Planned Order Releases	30		40	100		250	40	100	200				
Lot-for-Lot	1	50	—	—	3	F	Gross Requirements		40(C)		40(C)	100(C)	250(C)	250(C)		100(C)				
							Scheduled Receipts													
							Projected On Hand 50		50		10									
							Net Requirements		0	30	30	100	250	250		—				
							Planned Order Receipts		0	30	30	100	250	250		100				
							Planned Order Releases	30	30	30	100	250	250		100					

Problems*

• **14.1** You have developed the following simple product structure of items needed for your gift bag for a rush party for prospective pledges in your organization. You forecast 200 attendees. Assume that there is no inventory on hand of any of the items. Explode the bill of material. (Subscripts indicate the number of units required.)

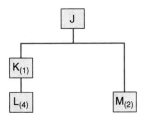

•• **14.2** You are expected to have the gift bags in Problem 14.1 ready at 5 P.M.. However, you need to personalize the items (mono-

*Note: **Px** means the problem may be solved with POM for Windows and/or Excel OM. Many of the exercises in this chapter (14.1 through 14.16 and 14.23 through 14.27) can be done on *Resource Manager for Excel*, a commercial system made available by User Solutions, Inc. Access to a trial version of the software and a set of notes for the user is available at **www. usersolutions.com.**

grammed pens, note pads, literature from the printer, etc.). The lead time is 1 hour to assemble 200 Js once the other items are prepared. The other items will take a while as well. Given the volunteers you have, the other time estimates are item K (2 hours), item L (1 hour), and item M (4 hours). Develop a time-phased assembly plan to prepare the gift bags.

•• **14.3** The demand for subassembly S is 100 units in week 7. Each unit of S requires 1 unit of T and 2 units of U. Each unit of T requires 1 unit of V, 2 units of W, and 1 unit of X. Finally, each unit of U requires 2 units of Y and 3 units of Z. One firm manufactures all items. It takes 2 weeks to make S, 1 week to make T, 2 weeks to make U, 2 weeks to make V, 3 weeks to make W, 1 week to make X, 2 weeks to make Y, and 1 week to make Z.

a) Construct a product structure. Identify all levels, parents, and components.

b) Prepare a time-phased product structure.

•• **14.4** Using the information in Problem 14.3, construct a gross material requirements plan. **Px**

•• **14.5** Using the information in Problem 14.3, construct a net material requirements plan using the following on-hand inventory.

Lot Size	Lead Time (# of periods)	On Hand	Safety Stock	Allo-cated	Low-Level Code	Item ID		Period (week, day)							
								1	2	3	4	5	6	7	8
							Gross Requirements								
							Scheduled Receipts								
							Projected On Hand								
							Net Requirements								
							Planned Order Receipts								
							Planned Order Releases								
							Gross Requirements								
							Scheduled Receipts								
							Projected On Hand								
							Net Requirements								
							Planned Order Receipts								
							Planned Order Releases								
							Gross Requirements								
							Scheduled Receipts								
							Projected On Hand								
							Net Requirements								
							Planned Order Receipts								
							Planned Order Releases								
							Gross Requirements								
							Scheduled Receipts								
							Projected On Hand								
							Net Requirements								
							Planned Order Receipts								
							Planned Order Releases								
							Gross Requirements								
							Scheduled Receipts								
							Projected On Hand								
							Net Requirements								
							Planned Order Receipts								
							Planned Order Releases								

▲ **FIGURE 14.13   MRP Form for Homework Problems in Chapter 14**
For several problems in this chapter, a copy of this form may be helpful.

Item	On-Hand Inventory	Item	On-Hand Inventory
S	20	W	30
T	20	X	25
U	40	Y	240
V	30	Z	40 **Px**

•• **14.6** Refer again to Problems 14.3 and 14.4. In addition to 100 units of S, there is also a demand for 20 units of U, which is a component of S. The 20 units of U are needed for maintenance purposes. These units are needed in week 6. Modify the *gross material requirements plan* to reflect this change. **Px**

•• **14.7** Refer again to Problems 14.3 and 14.5. In addition to 100 units of S, there is also a demand for 20 units of U, which is a component of S. The 20 units of U are needed for maintenance purposes. These units are needed in week 6. Modify the *net material requirements plan* to reflect this change. **Px**

•• **14.8** As the production planner for Gerry Cook Products, Inc., you have been given a bill of material for a bracket that is made up of a base, two springs, and four clamps. The base is assembled from one clamp and two housings. Each clamp has one handle and one casting. Each housing has two bearings and one shaft. There is no inventory on hand.
a) Design a product structure noting the quantities for each item and show the low-level coding.
b) Determine the gross quantities needed of each item if you are to assemble 50 brackets.
c) Compute the net quantities needed if there are 25 of the base and 100 of the clamp in stock. **Px**

•• **14.9** Your boss at Gerry Cook Products, Inc., has just provided you with the schedule and lead times for the bracket in Problem 14.8. The unit is to be prepared in week 10. The lead times for the components are bracket (1 week), base (1 week), spring (1 week), clamp (1 week), housing (2 weeks), handle (1 week), casting (3 weeks), bearing (1 week), and shaft (1 week).
a) Prepare the time-phased product structure for the bracket.
b) In what week do you need to start the castings? **Px**

•• **14.10**
a) Given the product structure and master production schedule (Figure 14.14 below), develop a gross requirements plan for all items.
b) Given the preceding product structure, master production schedule, and inventory status (Figure 14.14), develop a net materials requirements (planned order release) for all items. **Px**

••• **14.11** Given the following product structure, master production schedule, and inventory status (Figure 14.15 on the next page) and assuming the requirements for each BOM item is 1: (a) develop a gross requirements plan for Item C; (b) develop a net requirements plan for Item C. **Px**

•••• **14.12** Based on the data in Figure 14.15, complete a net material requirements schedule for:
a) All items (10 schedules in all), assuming the requirement for each BOM item is 1.
b) All 10 items, assuming the requirement for all items is 1, except B, C, and F, which require *2 each.* **Px**

••• **14.13** Electro Fans has just received an order for one thousand 20-inch fans due week 7. Each fan consists of a housing assembly, two grills, a fan assembly, and an electrical unit. The housing assembly consists of a frame, two supports, and a handle. The fan assembly consists of a hub and five blades. The electrical unit consists of a motor, a switch, and a knob. The following table gives lead times, on-hand inventory, and scheduled receipts.
a) Construct a product structure.
b) Construct a time-phased product structure.
c) Prepare a net material requirements plan. **Px**

Data Table for Problem 14.13

Component	Lead Time	On Hand Inventory	Lot Size*	Scheduled Receipt
20″ Fan	1	100	—	
Housing	1	100	—	
Frame	2	—	—	
Supports (2)	1	50	100	
Handle	1	400	500	
Grills (2)	2	200	500	
Fan Assembly	3	150	—	
Hub	1	—	—	
Blades (5)	2	—	100	
Electrical Unit	1	—	—	
Motor	1	—	—	
Switch	1	20	12	
Knob	1	—	25	200 knobs in week 2

*Lot-for-lot unless otherwise noted

••• **14.14** A part structure, lead time (weeks), and on-hand quantities for product A are shown in Figure 14.16. From the information shown, generate

---

▼ **FIGURE 14.14**   **Information for Problem 14.10**

Master Production Schedule for X1

PERIOD	7	8	9	10	11	12
Gross requirements		50		20		100

ITEM	LEAD TIME	ON HAND		ITEM	LEAD TIME	ON HAND
X1	1	50		C	1	0
B1	2	20		D	1	0
B2	2	20		E	3	10
A1	1	5				

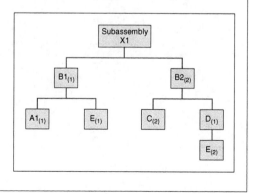

> **FIGURE 14.15**
> **Information for Problems 14.11 and 14.12**

PERIOD	8	9	10	11	12
Gross requirements: A	100		50		150
Gross requirements: H		100		50	

ITEM	ON HAND	LEAD TIME	ITEM	ON HAND	LEAD TIME
A	0	1	F	75	2
B	100	2	G	75	1
C	50	2	H	0	1
D	50	1	J	100	2
E	75	2	K	100	2

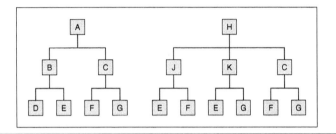

a) An indented bill of material for product A (see Figure 5.9 in Chapter 5 as an example of a BOM).

b) Net requirements for each part to produce 10 As in week 8 using lot-for-lot. **Px**

••• **14.15** You are product planner for product A (in Problem 14.14 and Figure 14.16). The field service manager, Al Trostel, has just called and told you that the requirements for B and F should each be increased by 10 units for his repair requirements in the field.

a) Prepare a list showing the quantity of each part required to produce the requirements for the service manager *and* the production request of 10 Bs and Fs.

b) Prepare a net requirement plan by date for the new requirements (for both production and field service), assuming that the field service manager wants his 10 units of B and F in week 6 and the 10 production units of A in week 8. **Px**

••• **14.16** You have just been notified via fax that the lead time for component G of product A (Problem 14.15 and Figure 14.16) has been increased to 4 weeks.

a) Which items have changed and why?

b) What are the implications for the production plan?

c) As production planner, what can you do? **Px**

Data Table for Problems 14.17 through 14.19*

Period	1	2	3	4	5	6	7	8	9	10	11	12
Gross requirements	30		40		30	70	20		10	80		50

*Holding cost = $2.50/unit/week; setup cost = $150; lead time = 1 week; beginning inventory = 40.

••• **14.17** Develop a lot-for-lot solution and calculate total relevant costs for the data in the preceding table. **Px**

••• **14.18** Develop an EOQ solution and calculate total relevant costs for the data in the preceding table. Stockout costs equal $10 per unit. **Px**

••• **14.19** Develop a PPB solution and calculate total relevant costs for the data in the preceding table. **Px**

••• **14.20** Using the gross requirements schedule in Examples 4, 5, and 6 in the text, prepare an alternative ordering system that always orders 100 units the week prior to a shortage (a fixed order quantity of 100) with the same costs as in the example (setup at $100 each, holding at $1 per unit per period). What is the cost of this ordering system? **Px**

> **FIGURE 14.16**
> **Information for Problems 14.14, 14.15 and 14.16**

PART	INVENTORY ON HAND
A	0
B	2
C	10
D	5
E	4
F	5
G	1
H	10

PART STRUCTURE TREE

A LT = 1
LT = lead time in weeks
(1) = All quantities = 1

B(1) LT = 1   F(1) LT = 1

C(1) LT = 2   D(1) LT = 1   G(1) LT = 3   H(1) LT = 1

E(1) LT = 1   E(1) LT = 1 C(1) LT = 2

••• **14.21** Using the gross requirements schedule in Examples 4, 5, and 6 in the text, prepare an alternative ordering system that orders every 3 weeks for 3 weeks ahead (a periodic order quantity). Use the same costs as in the example (setup at $100 each, holding at $1 per unit per period). What is the cost of this ordering system? **Px**

••• **14.22** Using the gross requirements schedule in Examples 4, 5, and 6 in the text, prepare an alternative ordering system of your own design that uses the same cost as in the example (setup at $100 each, holding at $1 per unit per period). Can you do better than the costs shown in the text? What is the cost of your ordering system? **Px**

••• **14.23** Katharine Hepburn, Inc., has received the following orders:

Period	1	2	3	4	5	6	7	8	9	10
Order size	0	40	30	40	10	70	40	10	30	60

The entire fabrication for these units is scheduled on one machine. There are 2,250 usable minutes in a week, and each unit will take 65 minutes to complete. Develop a capacity plan, using lot splitting, for the 10-week time period.

•• **14.24** David Jurman, Ltd., has received the following orders:

Period	1	2	3	4	5	6	7	8	9	10
Order size	60	30	10	40	70	10	40	30	40	0

The entire fabrication for these units is scheduled on one machine. There are 2,250 usable minutes in a week, and each unit will take 65 minutes to complete. Develop a capacity plan, using lot splitting, for the 10-week time period.

•• **14.25** Heather Adams, production manager for a Colorado exercise equipment manufacturer, needs to schedule an order for 50 UltimaSteppers, which are to be shipped in week 8. Subscripts indicate quantity required for each parent. Assume lot-for-lot ordering. Below is information about the steppers:

Item	Lead time	On-Hand Inventory	Components
Stepper	2	20	$A_{(1)}$, $B_{(3)}$, $C_{(2)}$
A	1	10	$D_{(1)}$, $F_{(2)}$
B	2	30	$E_{(1)}$, $F_{(3)}$
C	3	10	$D_{(2)}$, $E_{(3)}$
D	1	15	
E	2	5	
F	2	20	

a) Develop a product structure for Heather.
b) Develop a time-phased structure.
c) Develop a net material requirements plan for F. **Px**

•••• **14.26** You are scheduling production of your popular Rustic Coffee Table. The table requires a top, four legs, $\frac{1}{8}$ gallon of stain, $\frac{1}{16}$ gallon of glue, 2 short braces between the legs and 2 long braces between the legs, and a brass cap that goes on the bottom of each leg. You have 100 gallons of glue in inventory, but none of the other components. All items except the brass caps, stain, and glue are ordered on a lot-for-lot basis. The caps are purchased in quantities of 1,000, stain and glue by the gallon. Lead time is 1 day for each item. Schedule the order releases necessary to produce 640 coffee tables on days 5 and 6, and 128 on days 7 and 8. **Px**

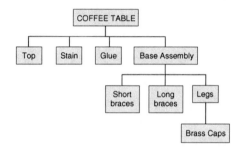

•••• **14.27** Using the data for the coffee table in Problem 14.26, build a labor schedule when the labor standard for each top is 2 labor hours; each leg including brass cap installation requires $\frac{1}{4}$ hour, as does each pair of braces. Base assembly requires 1 labor-hour, and final assembly requires 2 labor-hours. What is the total number of labor-hours required each day, and how many employees are needed each day at 8 hours per day?

▶ Refer to myomlab for these additional homework problems: 14.28–14.32

Case Studies

▶ Hill's Automotive, Inc.

Hill's Automotive, Inc., is an aftermarket producer and distributor of automotive replacement parts. Art Hill has slowly expanded the business, which began as a supplier of hard-to-get auto air-conditioning units for classic cars and hot rods. The firm has limited manufacturing capability, but a state-of-the-art MRP system and extensive inventory and assembly facilities. Components are purchased, assembled, and repackaged. Among its products are private-label air-conditioning, carburetors, and ignition kits. The

downturn in the economy, particularly the company's discretionary segment, has put downward pressure on volume and margins. Profits have fallen considerably. In addition, customer service levels have declined, with late deliveries now exceeding 25% of orders. And to make matters worse, customer returns have been rising at a rate of 3% per month.

Wally Hopp, vice president of sales, claims that most of the problem lies with the assembly department. He says that although the firm has accurate bills of materials, indicating what goes into each product, it is not producing the proper mix of the product. He also believes the firm has poor quality control and low productivity, and as a result its costs are too high.

Melanie Thompson, treasurer, believes that problems are due to investing in the wrong inventories. She thinks that marketing has too many options and products. Melanie also thinks that purchasing department buyers have been hedging their inventories and requirements with excess purchasing commitments.

The assembly manager, Kalinga Jagoda, says, "The symptom is that we have a lot of parts in inventory, but no place to assemble them in the production schedule. When we have the right part, it is not very good, but we use it anyway to meet the schedule."

Marshall Fisher, manager of purchasing, has taken the stance that purchasing has not let Hill's Automotive down. He has stuck by his old suppliers, used historical data to determine requirements, maintained what he views as excellent prices from suppliers, and evaluated new sources of supply with a view toward lowering cost. Where possible, Marshall reacted to the increased pressure for profitability by emphasizing low cost and early delivery.

Discussion Question

1. Prepare a plan for Art Hill that gets the firm back on a course toward improved profitability. Be sure to identify the symptoms, the problems, and the specific changes you would implement.
2. Explain how MRP plays a role in this plan.

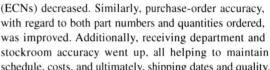

▶ MRP at Wheeled Coach

Video Case

Wheeled Coach, the world's largest manufacturer of ambulances, builds thousands of different and constantly changing configurations of its products. The custom nature of its business means lots of options and special designs—and a potential scheduling and inventory nightmare. Wheeled Coach addressed such problems, and succeeded in solving a lot of them, with an MRP system (described in the *Global Company Profile* that opens this chapter). As with most MRP installations, however, solving one set of problems uncovers a new set.

One of the new issues that had to be addressed by plant manager Lynn Whalen was newly discovered excess inventory. Managers discovered a substantial amount of inventory that was not called for in any finished products. Excess inventory was evident because of the new level of inventory accuracy required by the MRP system. The other reason was a new series of inventory reports generated by the IBM MAPICS MRP system purchased by Wheeled Coach. One of those reports indicates where items are used and is known as the "Where Used" report. Interestingly, many inventory items were not called out on bills-of-material (BOMs) for any current products. In some cases, the reason some parts were in the stockroom remained a mystery.

The discovery of this excess inventory led to renewed efforts to ensure that the BOMs were accurate. With substantial work, BOM accuracy increased and the number of engineering change notices

(ECNs) decreased. Similarly, purchase-order accuracy, with regard to both part numbers and quantities ordered, was improved. Additionally, receiving department and stockroom accuracy went up, all helping to maintain schedule, costs, and ultimately, shipping dates and quality.

Eventually, Lynn Whalen concluded that the residual amounts of excess inventory were the result, at least in part, of rapid changes in ambulance design and technology. Another source was customer changes made after specifications had been determined and materials ordered. This latter excess occurs because, even though Wheeled Coach's own throughput time is only 17 days, many of the items that it purchases require much longer lead times.

Discussion Questions*

1. Why is accurate inventory such an important issue at Wheeled Coach?
2. Why does Wheeled Coach have excess inventory, and what kind of a plan would you suggest for dealing with it?
3. Be specific in your suggestions for reducing inventory and how to implement them.

*You may wish to view the video that accompanies this case before answering the questions.

▶**Additional Case Study:** Visit **www.pearsonglobaleditions.com/myomlab** or **www.pearsonglobaleditions.com/heizer** for this free case study:

Ikon's attempt at ERP: The giant office technology firm faces hurdles with ERP implementation.

Bibliography

Barba-Gutierrez, Y., B. Adenso-Diaz, and S. M. Gupta. "Lot Sizing in Reverse MRP for Scheduling Disassembly." *International Journal of Production Economics* 111, no. 2 (February 2008): 741.

Bell, Steve. "Time Fence Secrets." *APICS* 16, no. 4 (April 2006): 44–48.

Bolander, Steven, and Sam G. Taylor. "Scheduling Techniques: A Comparison of Logic." *Production and Inventory Management Journal* 41, no. 1 (1st Quarter 2000): 1–5.

Crandall, Richard E. "The Epic Life of ERP." *APICS* 16, no. 2 (February 2006): 17–19.

Gattiker, Thomas "Anatomy of an ERP Implementation Gone Awry." *Production and Inventory Management* 43, nos. 3–4 (3rd/4th Quarter 2002): 96–105.

Kanet, J., and V. Sridharan. "The Value of Using Scheduling Information in Planning Material Requirements." *Decision Sciences* 29, no. 2 (Spring 1998): 479–498.

Koh, S. C. L., and S. M. Saad. "Managing Uncertainty in ERP-controlled Manufacturing Environments." *International Journal of Production Economics* 101, no. 1 (May 2006): 109.

Krupp, James A. G. "Integrating Kanban and MRP to Reduce Lead Time." *Production and Inventory Management Journal* 43, no. 3–4 (3rd/4th quarter 2002): 78–82.

Lawrence, Barry F., Daniel F. Jennings, and Brian E. Reynolds. *ERP in Distribution.* Florence, KY: Thomson South-Western, (2005).

Moncrief, Stephen. "Push and Pull." *APICS—The Performance Advantage* (June 2003): 46–51.

Norris, G. *E-Business & ERP.* New York: Wiley (2005).

O' Sullivan, Jill, and Gene Caiola. *Enterprise Resource Planning,* 2nd ed. New York: McGraw-Hill (2008).

Segerstedt, A. "Master Production Scheduling and a Comparison of MRP and Cover-Time Planning." *International Journal of Production Research* 44, no. 18–19 (September 2006): 3585.

Summer, M. *Enterprise Resource Planning.* Upper Saddle River, NJ: Prentice Hall (2005).

Wagner, H. M., and T. M. Whitin. "Dynamic Version of the Economic Lot Size Model." *Management Science* 5, no. 1 (1958): 89–96.

Wu, Jen-Hur, et al. "Using Multiple Variables Decision-Making Analysis for ERP Selection." *International Journal of Manufacturing Technology and Management* 18, no. 2 (2009): 228.

Main Heading	Review Material	PEARSON myomlab
DEPENDENT DEMAND	Demand for items is *dependent* when the relationship between the items can be determined. For any product, all components of that product are dependent demand items. ■ **Material requirements planning (MRP)**—A dependent demand technique that uses a bill-of-material, inventory, expected receipts, and a master production schedule to determine material requirements.	**VIDEO 14.1** MRP at Wheeled Coach Ambulances
DEPENDENT INVENTORY MODEL REQUIREMENTS	Dependent inventory models require that the operations manager know the: (1) Master production schedule; (2) Specifications or bill of material; (3) Inventory availability; (4) Purchase orders outstanding; and (5) Lead times ■ **Master production schedule (MPS)**—A timetable that specifies what is to be made and when. The MPS is a statement of *what is to be produced*, not a forecast of demand. ■ **Bill of material (BOM)**—A listing of the components, their description, and the quantity of each required to make one unit of a product. Items above any level in a BOM are called *parents*; items below any level are called *components*, or *children*. The top level in a BOM is the 0 level. ■ **Modular bills**—Bills of material organized by major subassemblies or by product options. ■ **Planning bills (or kits)**—A material grouping created in order to assign an artificial parent to a bill of material; also called "pseudo" bills. ■ **Phantom bills of material**—Bills of material for components, usually subassemblies, that exist only temporarily; they are never inventoried. ■ **Low-level coding**—A number that identifies items at the lowest level at which they occur. ■ **Lead time**—In purchasing systems, the time between recognition of the need for an order and receiving it; in production systems, it is the order, wait, move, queue, setup, and run times for each component. When a bill of material is turned on its side and modified by adding lead times for each component, it is called a *time-phased product structure*.	Problems: 14.1, 14.3 Virtual Office Hours for Solved Problem: 14.1
MRP STRUCTURE	■ **Gross material requirements plan**—A schedule that shows the total demand for an item (prior to subtraction of on-hand inventory and scheduled receipts) and (1) when it must be ordered from suppliers, or (2) when production must be started to meet its demand by a particular date. ■ **Net material requirements**—The result of adjusting gross requirements for inventory on hand and scheduled receipts. ■ **Planned order receipt**—The quantity planned to be received at a future date. ■ **Planned order release**—The scheduled date for an order to be released. Net requirements = Gross requirements + Allocations − (On hand + Scheduled receipts)	Problems: 14.2, 14.4–14.8 Virtual Office Hours for Solved Problem: 14.2 **ACTIVE MODEL 14.1**
MRP MANAGEMENT	■ **System nervousness**—Frequent changes in an MRP system. ■ **Time fences**—A means for allowing a segment of the master schedule to be designated as "not to be rescheduled." ■ **Pegging**—In material requirements planning systems, tracing upward the bill of material from the component to the parent item. Four approaches for integrating MRP and JIT are (1) finite capacity scheduling, (2) small buckets, (3) balanced flow, and (4) supermarkets. ■ **Buckets**—Time units in a material requirements planning system. Finite capacity scheduling (FCS) considers department and machine capacity. FCS provides the precise scheduling needed for rapid material movement. ■ **Bucketless system**—Time-phased data are referenced using dated records rather than defined time periods, or buckets. ■ **Back flush**—A system to reduce inventory balances by deducting everything in the bill of material on completion of the unit. ■ **Supermarket**—An inventory area that holds common items that are replenished by a kanban system.	
LOT-SIZING TECHNIQUES	■ **Lot-sizing decision**—The process of, or techniques used in, determining lot size. ■ **Lot-for-lot**—A lot-sizing technique that generates exactly what is required to meet the plan. ■ **Part period balancing (PPB)**—An inventory ordering technique that balances setup and holding costs by changing the lot size to reflect requirements of the next lot size in the future.	Problems: 14.17–14.22

Main Heading	Review Material
	■ **Economic part period (EPP)**—A period of time when the ratio of setup cost to holding cost is equal. ■ **Wagner-Whitin procedure**—A technique for lot-size computation that assumes a finite time horizon beyond which there are no additional net requirements to arrive at an ordering strategy. In general, the lot-for-lot approach should be used whenever low-cost deliveries can be achieved.
EXTENSIONS OF MRP	■ **Material requirements planning II (MRP II)**—A system that allows, with MRP in place, inventory data to be augmented by other resource variables; in this case, MRP becomes *material resource planning*. ■ **Closed-loop MRP system**—A system that provides feedback to the capacity plan, master production schedule, and production plan so planning can be kept valid at all times. ■ **Load report**—A report for showing the resource requirements in a work center for all work currently assigned there as well as all planned and expected orders. Tactics for smoothing the load and minimizing the impact of changed lead time include: *Overlapping*, *Operations splitting*, and *Order*, or, *lot splitting*.
MRP IN SERVICES (pp. 596–597)	■ **Distribution resource planning (DRP)**—A time-phased stock-replenishment plan for all levels of a distribution network.
ENTERPRISE RESOURCE PLANNING (ERP)	■ **Enterprise resource planning (ERP)**—An information system for identifying and planning the enterprise-wide resources needed to take, make, ship, and account for customer orders. In an ERP system, data are entered only once into a common, complete, and consistent database shared by all applications. ■ **Efficient consumer response (ECR)**—Supply-chain management systems in the grocery industry that tie sales to buying, to inventory, to logistics, and to production.

Self Test

■ **Before taking the self-test,** refer to the learning objectives listed at the beginning of the chapter and the key terms listed at the end of the chapter.

LO1. In a product structure diagram:
  a) parents are found only at the top level of the diagram.
  b) parents are found at every level in the diagram.
  c) children are found at every level of the diagram except the top level.
  d) all items in the diagrams are both parents and children.
  e) all of the above.

LO2. The difference between a gross material requirements plan (gross MRP) and a net material requirements plan (net MRP) is:
  a) the gross MRP may not be computerized, but the net MRP must be computerized.
  b) the gross MRP includes consideration of the inventory on hand, whereas the net MRP doesn't include the inventory consideration.
  c) the net MRP includes consideration of the inventory on hand, whereas the gross MRP doesn't include the inventory consideration.
  d) the gross MRP doesn't take taxes into account, whereas the net MRP includes the tax considerations.
  e) the net MRP is only an estimate, whereas the gross MRP is used for actual production scheduling.

LO3. Net requirements =
  a) Gross requirements + Allocations − On-hand inventory + Scheduled receipts.
  b) Gross requirements − Allocations − On-hand inventory − Scheduled receipts.

  c) Gross requirements − Allocations − On-hand inventory + Scheduled receipts.
  d) Gross requirements + Allocations − On-hand inventory − Scheduled receipts.

LO4. A lot-sizing procedure that assumes a finite time horizon beyond which there are no additional net requirements is:
  a) Wagner-Whitin algorithm.   **b)** part period balancing.
  c) economic order quantity.   **d)** all of the above.

LO5. MRP II stands for:
  a) material resource planning.
  b) management requirements planning.
  c) management resource planning.
  d) material revenue planning.
  e) material risk planning.

LO6. A(n) _____ MRP system provides information to the capacity plan, to the master production schedule, and ultimately to the production plan.
  a) dynamic   **b)** closed-loop
  c) continuous   **d)** retrospective
  e) introspective

LO7. Which system extends MRP II to tie in customers and suppliers?
  a) MRP III   **b)** JIT
  c) IRP   **d)** ERP
  e) Enhanced MRP II

Answers: LO1. c; LO2. c; LO3. d; LO4. a; LO5. a; LO6. b; LO7. d.

JIT and Lean

16

JIT, Lean Operations and the Toyota Production System

10

OM Strategy Decisions

- ► Design of Goods and Services
- ► Managing Quality
- ► Process Strategy
- ► Location Strategies
- ► Layout Strategies
- ► Human Resources
- ► Supply-Chain Management
- ► Inventory Management
  - ■ Independent Demand
  - ■ Dependent Demand
  - ■ JIT and Lean Operations
- ► Scheduling
- ► Maintenance

GLOBAL COMPANY PROFILE: TOYOTA MOTOR CORPORATION

ACHIEVING COMPETITIVE ADVANTAGE WITH LEAN OPERATIONS AT TOYOTA MOTOR CORPORATION

Toyota Motor Corporation, with annual sales of over 9 million cars and trucks, is the largest vehicle manufacturer in the world. Two techniques, just-in-time (JIT) and the Toyota Production System (TPS), have been instrumental in this post-WWII growth. Toyota, with a wide range of vehicles, competes head-to-head with successful long-established companies in Europe and the U.S. Taiichi Ohno, a former vice president of Toyota, created the basic framework for the world's most discussed systems for improving productivity, JIT and TPS. These two concepts provide much of the foundation for lean operations:

- Central to JIT is a philosophy of continued problem solving. In practice, JIT means making only what is needed, when it is needed. JIT provides an excellent vehicle for finding and eliminating problems because problems are easy to find in a system that has no slack. When excess inventory is eliminated, quality, layout, scheduling, and supplier issues become immediately evident—as does excess production.

- Central to TPS is employee learning and a continuing effort to create and produce products under ideal conditions. Ideal conditions exist only when facilities, machines, and people are brought

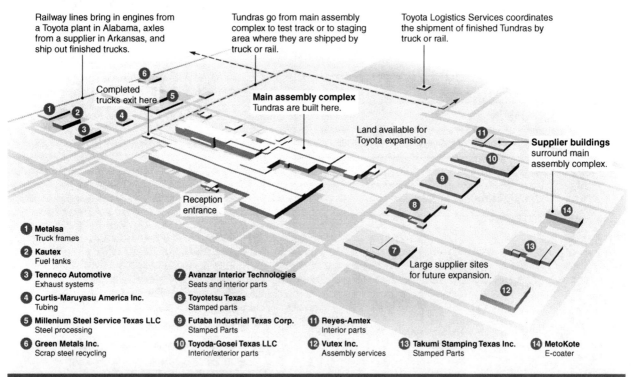

Railway lines bring in engines from a Toyota plant in Alabama, axles from a supplier in Arkansas, and ship out finished trucks.

Tundras go from main assembly complex to test track or to staging area where they are shipped by truck or rail.

Toyota Logistics Services coordinates the shipment of finished Tundras by truck or rail.

Completed trucks exit here

Main assembly complex
Tundras are built here.

Land available for Toyota expansion

Supplier buildings surround main assembly complex.

Reception entrance

Large supplier sites for future expansion.

1 **Metalsa**
Truck frames

2 **Kautex**
Fuel tanks

3 **Tenneco Automotive**
Exhaust systems

4 **Curtis-Maruyasu America Inc.**
Tubing

5 **Millenium Steel Service Texas LLC**
Steel processing

6 **Green Metals Inc.**
Scrap steel recycling

7 **Avanzar Interior Technologies**
Seats and interior parts

8 **Toyotetsu Texas**
Stamped parts

9 **Futaba Industrial Texas Corp.**
Stamped Parts

10 **Toyoda-Gosei Texas LLC**
Interior/exterior parts

11 **Reyes-Amtex**
Interior parts

12 **Vutex Inc.**
Assembly services

13 **Takumi Stamping Texas Inc.**
Stamped Parts

14 **MetoKote**
E-coater

14 Suppliers outside the main plant

Outside: Toyota has a 2,000-acre site with 14 of the 21 onsite suppliers, adjacent rail lines, and near-by interstate highway. The site provides expansion space for both Toyota and for its suppliers — and provides an environment for Just-in-time.

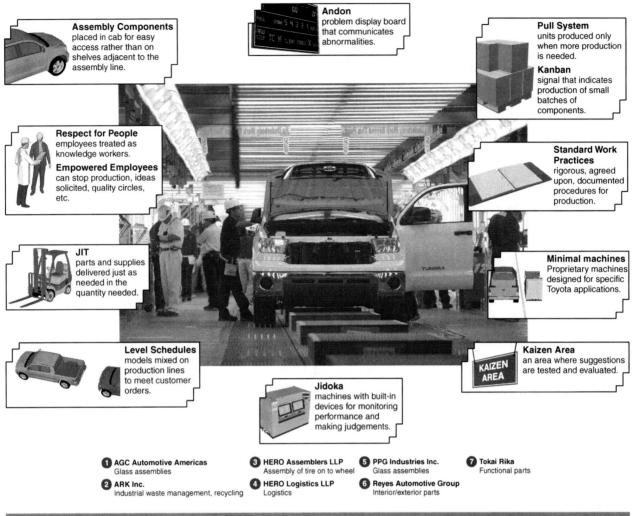

Assembly Components placed in cab for easy access rather than on shelves adjacent to the assembly line.

Andon problem display board that communicates abnormalities.

Pull System units produced only when more production is needed.

Kanban signal that indicates production of small batches of components.

Respect for People employees treated as knowledge workers.

Empowered Employees can stop production, ideas solicited, quality circles, etc.

Standard Work Practices rigorous, agreed upon, documented procedures for production.

JIT parts and supplies delivered just as needed in the quantity needed.

Minimal machines Proprietary machines designed for specific Toyota applications.

Level Schedules models mixed on production lines to meet customer orders.

Kaizen Area an area where suggestions are tested and evaluated.

KAIZEN AREA

Jidoka machines with built-in devices for monitoring performance and making judgements.

1 AGC Automotive Americas
Glass assemblies

2 ARK Inc.
Industrial waste management, recycling

3 HERO Assemblers LLP
Assembly of tire on to wheel

4 HERO Logistics LLP
Logistics

5 PPG Industries Inc.
Glass assemblies

6 Reyes Automotive Group
Interior/exterior parts

7 Tokai Rika
Functional parts

7 Suppliers inside the main plant

Toyota s San Antonio plant has about 2 million interior sq. ft., providing facilities within the final assembly building for 7 of the 21 onsite suppliers, and capacity to build 200,000 pick-up trucks annually. But most importantly, Toyota practices the world-class Toyota Production System and expects its suppliers to do the same thing wherever they are.

together, adding value without waste. Waste undermines productivity by diverting resources to excess inventory, unnecessary processing, and poor quality. Respect for people, extensive training, cross-training, and standard work practices of empowered employees focusing on driving out waste are fundamental to TPS.

Toyota's latest implementation of TPS and JIT is present at its new San Antonio plant, the largest Toyota land site for an automobile assembly plant in the U.S. Interestingly, despite its annual production capability of 200,000 Tundra pick-up trucks, the building itself is one of the smallest in the industry. Modern automobiles have 30,000 parts, but at Toyota, independent suppliers combine many of these parts into sub-assemblies. Twenty-one of these suppliers are on site at the San Antonio facility and transfer components to the assembly line on a JIT basis.

Operations such as these taking place in the new San Antonio plant are why Toyota continues to perform near the top in quality and maintain the lowest labor-hour assembly time in the industry. JIT, TPS, and lean operations work—and they provide a competitive advantage at Toyota Motor Corporation.

Chapter 16 **Learning Objectives**

LO1: Define just-in-time, TPS, and lean operations

LO2: Define the seven wastes and the 5Ss

LO3: Explain JIT partnerships

LO4: Determine optimal setup time

LO5: Define kanban

LO6: Compute the required number of kanbans

LO7: Explain the principles of the Toyota Production System

AUTHOR COMMENT
World-class firms everywhere are using these three techniques.

LO1: Define just-in-time, TPS, and lean operations

Just-in-time (JIT)
Continuous and forced problem solving via a focus on throughput and reduced inventory.

Toyota Production System (TPS)
Focus on continuous improvement, respect for people, and standard work practices.

Lean operations
Eliminates waste through a focus on exactly what the customer wants.

JUST-IN-TIME, THE TOYOTA PRODUCTION SYSTEM, AND LEAN OPERATIONS

As shown in the *Global Company Profile*, the Toyota Production System (TPS) contributes to a world-class operation at Toyota Motor Corporation. In this chapter, we discuss JIT, TPS, and lean operations as approaches to continuing improvement that drive out waste and lead to world-class organizations.

Just-in-time (JIT) is an approach of continuous and forced problem solving via a focus on throughput and reduced inventory. The **Toyota Production System (TPS)**, with its emphasis on continuous improvement, respect for people, and standard work practices, is particularly suited for assembly lines. **Lean operations** supplies the customer with exactly what the customer wants when the customer wants it, without waste, through continuous improvement. Lean operations are driven by workflow initiated by the "pull" of the customer's order. When implemented as a comprehensive manufacturing strategy, JIT, TPS, and lean systems sustain competitive advantage and result in increased overall returns.

If there is any distinction between JIT, TPS, and lean operations, it is that:

- JIT emphasizes forced problem solving.
- TPS emphasizes employee learning and empowerment in an assembly-line environment.
- Lean operations emphasize understanding the customer.

However, in practice, there is little difference, and the terms are often used interchangeably. Leading organizations use the approaches and techniques that make sense for them. In this chapter, we use the term *lean operations* to encompass all of the related approaches and techniques.

Regardless of the label put on operations improvement, good production systems require that managers address three issues that are pervasive and fundamental to operations management: eliminate waste, remove variability, and improve throughput. We first introduce these three issues and then discuss the major attributes of JIT, TPS, and lean operations. Finally, we look at lean operations applied to services.

LO2: Define the seven wastes and the 5Ss

Eliminate Waste

Traditional producers have limited goals—accepting, for instance, the production of some defective parts and some inventory. Lean producers set their sights on perfection; no bad parts, no inventory, only value-added activities, and no waste. Any activity that does not add value in the eyes of the customer is a waste. The customer defines product value. If the customer does not want to pay for it, it is a waste. Taiichi Ohno, noted for his work on the Toyota Production System, identified seven categories of waste. These categories have become popular in lean organizations and cover many of the ways organizations waste or lose money. Ohno's **seven wastes** are:

Seven wastes
Overproduction
Queues
Transportation
Inventory
Motion
Overprocessing
Defective product

- *Overproduction:* Producing more than the customer orders or producing early (before it is demanded) is waste. Inventory of any kind is usually a waste.
- *Queues:* Idle time, storage, and waiting are wastes (they add no value).
- *Transportation:* Moving material between plants or between work centers and handling more than once is waste.
- *Inventory:* Unnecessary raw material, work-in-process (WIP), finished goods, and excess operating supplies add no value and are wastes.

- *Motion:* Movement of equipment or people that adds no value is waste.
- *Overprocessing:* Work performed on the product that adds no value is waste.
- *Defective product:* Returns, warranty claims, rework, and scrap are a waste.

A broader perspective—one that goes beyond immediate production—suggests that other resources, such as energy, water, and air, are often wasted but should not be. Efficient, sustainable production minimizes inputs and maximizes outputs, wasting nothing.

For over a century, managers have pursued "housekeeping" for a neat, orderly, and efficient workplace and as a means of reducing waste. Operations managers have embellished "housekeeping" to include a checklist—now known as the 5Ss.[1] The Japanese developed the initial 5Ss. Not only are the 5Ss a good checklist for lean operations, they also provide an easy vehicle with which to assist the culture change that is often necessary to bring about lean operations. The **5Ss** follow:

- *Sort/segregate:* Keep what is needed and remove everything else from the work area; when in doubt, throw it out. Identify non-value items and remove them. Getting rid of these items makes space available and usually improves work flow.
- *Simplify/straighten:* Arrange and use methods analysis tools (see Chapter 7 and Chapter 10) to improve work flow and reduce wasted motion. Consider long-run and short-run ergonomic issues. Label and display for easy use only what is needed in the immediate work area. For examples of visual displays see Chapter 10, Figure 10.8.
- *Shine/sweep:* Clean daily; eliminate all forms of dirt, contamination, and clutter from the work area.
- *Standardize:* Remove variations from the process by developing standard operating procedures and checklists; good standards make the abnormal obvious. Standardize equipment and tooling so that cross-training time and cost are reduced. Train and retrain the work team so that when deviations occur, they are readily apparent to all.
- *Sustain/self-discipline:* Review periodically to recognize efforts and to motivate to sustain progress. Use visuals wherever possible to communicate and sustain progress.

> **5Ss**
> A lean production checklist:
> Sort
> Simplify
> Shine
> Standardize
> Sustain

U.S. managers often add two additional Ss that contribute to establishing and maintaining a lean workplace:

- *Safety:* Build good safety practices into the above five activities.
- *Support/maintenance:* Reduce variability, unplanned downtime, and costs. Integrate daily shine tasks with preventive maintenance.

The Ss provide a vehicle for continuous improvement with which all employees can identify. Operations managers need think only of the examples set by a well-run hospital emergency room or the spit-and-polish of a fire department for a benchmark. Offices and retail stores, as well as manufacturers, have successfully used the 5Ss in their respective efforts to eliminate waste and move to lean operations. A place for everything and everything in its place does make a difference in a well-run office. And retail stores successfully use the Ss to reduce misplaced merchandise and improve customer service. An orderly workplace reduces waste so that assets are released for other, more productive, purposes.

Remove Variability

Managers seek to remove variability caused by both internal and external factors. **Variability** is any deviation from the optimum process that delivers perfect product on time, every time. Variability is a polite word for problems. The less variability in a system, the less waste in the system. Most variability is caused by tolerating waste or by poor management. Among the many sources of variability are:

> **Variability**
> Any deviation from the optimum process that delivers perfect product on time, every time.

- Poor production processes that allow employees and suppliers to produce improper quantities or late or non-conforming units
- Unknown customer demands
- Incomplete or inaccurate drawings, specifications, and bills of material

---

[1]The term 5S comes from the Japanese words seiri (*sort* and clear out), seiton (*straighten* and configure), seiso (*scrub* and cleanup), seiketsu (maintain *sanitation* and cleanliness of self and workplace), and shitsuke (*self-discipline and standardization* of these practices).

Both JIT and inventory reduction are effective tools for identifying causes of variability. The precise timing of JIT makes variability evident, just as reducing inventory exposes variability. The removal of variability allows managers to move good materials on schedule, add value at each step of the production process, drive down costs, and win orders.

Improve Throughput

Throughput

The time required to move orders through the production process, from receipt to delivery.

Manufacturing cycle time

The time between the arrival of raw materials and the shipping of finished products.

Pull system

A concept that results in material being produced only when requested and moved to where it is needed just as it is needed.

Throughput is a measure (in units or time) that it takes to move an order from receipt to delivery. Each minute products remain on the books, costs accumulate and competitive advantage is lost. The time that an order is in the shop is called **manufacturing cycle time**. This is the time between the arrival of raw materials and the shipping of finished product. For example, phone-system manufacturer Northern Telecom now has materials pulled directly from qualified suppliers to the assembly line. This effort has reduced a segment of Northern's manufacturing cycle time from 3 weeks to just 4 hours, the incoming inspection staff from 47 to 24, and problems on the shop floor caused by defective materials by 97%. Driving down manufacturing cycle time can make a major improvement in throughput.

A technique for increasing throughput is a pull system. A **pull system** *pulls* a unit to where it is needed just as it is needed. Pull systems are a standard tool of JIT systems. Pull systems use signals to request production and delivery from supplying stations to stations that have production capacity available. The pull concept is used both within the immediate production process and with suppliers. By *pulling* material through the system in very small lots—just as it is needed—waste and inventory are removed. As inventory is removed, clutter is reduced, problems become evident, and continuous improvement is emphasized. Removing the cushion of inventory also reduces both investment in inventory and manufacturing cycle time. A push system dumps orders on the next downstream workstation, regardless of timeliness and resource availability. Push systems are the antithesis of JIT. Pulling material through a production process as it is needed rather than in a "push" mode typically lowers cost and improves schedule performance, enhancing customer satisfaction.

> **AUTHOR COMMENT**
> JIT places added demands on performance, but that is why it pays off.

JUST-IN-TIME (JIT)

With its forced problem solving via a focus on rapid throughput and reduced inventory, JIT provides a powerful strategy for improving operations. With JIT, materials arrive *where* they are needed only *when* they are needed. When good units do not arrive just as needed, a "problem" has been identified. By driving out waste and delay in this manner, JIT reduces costs associated with excess inventory, cuts variability and waste, and improves throughput. JIT is a key ingredient of lean operations and is particularly helpful in supporting strategies of rapid response and low cost.

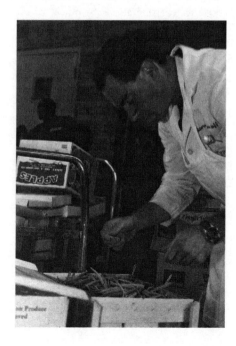

Many services have adopted JIT techniques as a normal part of their business. Restaurants like Olive Garden and Red Lobster expect and receive JIT deliveries. Both buyer and supplier expect fresh, high-quality produce delivered without fail just when it is needed. The system doesn't work any other way.

JIT TECHNIQUES:

Suppliers:	Few vendors; Supportive supplier relationships; Quality deliveries on time, directly to work areas.
Layout:	Work-cells; Group technology; Flexible machinery; Organized workplace; Reduced space for inventory.
Inventory:	Small lot sizes; Low setup time; Specialized parts bins
Scheduling:	Zero deviation from schedules; Level schedules; Suppliers informed of schedules; Kanban techniques
Preventive maintenance:	Scheduled; Daily routine; Operator involvement
Quality production:	Statistical process control; Quality suppliers; Quality within the firm
Employee empowerment:	Empowered and cross-trained employees; Training support; Few job classifications to ensure flexibility of employees
Commitment:	Support of management, employees, and suppliers

WHICH RESULTS IN:

Rapid throughput frees assets

Quality improvement reduces waste

Cost reduction adds pricing flexibility

Variability reduction

Rework reduction

WHICH WINS ORDERS BY:

Faster response to the customer at lower cost and higher quality—

A Competitive Advantage

◀ **FIGURE 16.1**
JIT Contributes to Competitive Advantage

Every moment material is held, an activity that adds value should be occurring. Consequently, as Figure 16.1 suggests, JIT often yields a competitive advantage.

Effective JIT requires a meaningful buyer–supplier partnership.

JIT Partnerships

A **JIT partnership** exists when a supplier and a purchaser work together with open communication and a goal of removing waste and driving down costs. Close relationships and trust are critical to the success of JIT. Figure 16.2 shows the characteristics of JIT partnerships. Some specific goals of JIT partnerships are:

JIT partnerships
Partnerships of suppliers and purchasers that remove waste and drive down costs for mutual benefits.

- *Removal of unnecessary activities*, such as receiving, incoming inspection, and paperwork related to bidding, invoicing, and payment.
- *Removal of in-plant inventory* by delivery in small lots directly to the using department as needed.
- *Removal of in-transit inventory* by encouraging suppliers to locate nearby and provide frequent small shipments. The shorter the flow of material in the resource pipeline, the less inventory. Inventory can also be reduced through a technique known as *consignment*. **Consignment inventory** (see the *OM in Action* box "Lean Production at Cessna Aircraft"), a variation of vendor-managed inventory (Chapter 11), means the supplier maintains the title to the inventory until it is used. For instance, an assembly plant may find a hardware supplier that is willing to locate its warehouse where the user currently has its stockroom. In this manner, when hardware is needed, it is no farther than the stockroom. Schedule and production information must be shared with the consignment supplier, or inventory holding costs will just be transferred from the buyer to the supplier, with no net cost reduction. Another option is to have the supplier ship to other, perhaps smaller, purchasers from the "stockroom."
- *Obtain improved quality and reliability* through long-term commitments, communication, and cooperation.

Consignment inventory
An arrangement in which the supplier maintains title to the inventory until it is used.

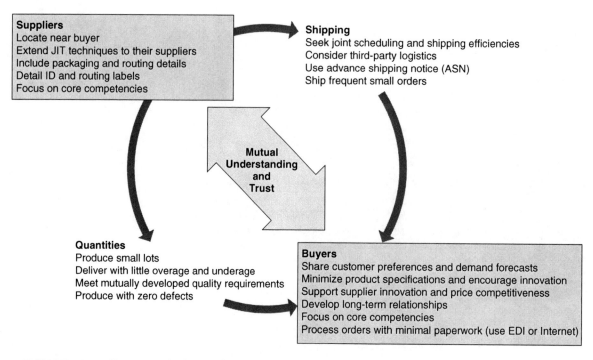

Suppliers
Locate near buyer
Extend JIT techniques to their suppliers
Include packaging and routing details
Detail ID and routing labels
Focus on core competencies

Shipping
Seek joint scheduling and shipping efficiencies
Consider third-party logistics
Use advance shipping notice (ASN)
Ship frequent small orders

Mutual Understanding and Trust

Quantities
Produce small lots
Deliver with little overage and underage
Meet mutually developed quality requirements
Produce with zero defects

Buyers
Share customer preferences and demand forecasts
Minimize product specifications and encourage innovation
Support supplier innovation and price competitiveness
Develop long-term relationships
Focus on core competencies
Process orders with minimal paperwork (use EDI or Internet)

▲ **FIGURE 16.2** **Characteristics of JIT Partnerships**

Leading organizations view suppliers as extensions of their own organizations and expect suppliers to be fully committed to improvement. Such relationships require a high degree of respect by both supplier and purchaser. Supplier concerns can be significant; Harley-Davidson, for example, initially had difficulty implementing JIT because supplier issues outweighed the perceived benefits.

LO3: Explain JIT partnerships

Concerns of Suppliers

Successful JIT partnerships require that supplier concerns be addressed. These concerns include:

1. *Diversification:* Suppliers may not want to tie themselves to long-term contracts with one customer. The suppliers' perception is that they reduce their risk if they have a variety of customers.
2. *Scheduling:* Many suppliers have little faith in the purchaser's ability to produce orders to a smooth, coordinated schedule.

OM in Action ▶ Lean Production at Cessna Aircraft

When Cessna Aircraft opened its new plant in Independence, Kansas, it saw the opportunity to switch from a craftwork mentality producing small single-engine planes to a lean manufacturing system. In doing so, Cessna adopted three lean practices.

First, Cessna set up consignment- and vendor-managed inventories with several of its suppliers. Blanket purchase orders allow Honeywell, for example, to maintain a 30-day supply of avionic parts onsite. Other vendors were encouraged to use a nearby warehouse to keep parts that could then be delivered daily to the production line.

Second, Cessna managers committed to cross-training, in which team members learn the duties of other team members and can shift across assembly lines as needed. To develop these technical skills, Cessna brought in 60 retired assembly-line workers to mentor and teach new employees. Employees were taught to work as a team and to assume responsibility for their team's quality.

Third, the company used group technology and manufacturing cells to move away from a batch process that resulted in large inventories and unsold planes. Now, Cessna pulls product through its plant only when a specific order is placed.

These commitments to manufacturing efficiency are part of the lean operations that has made Cessna the world's largest manufacturer of single-engine aircraft.

Sources: **www.cessna.com** (2007); *Strategic Finance* (November 2002): 32; *Purchasing* (September 4, 2003): 25–30; and *Fortune* (May 1, 2000): 1222B.

3. *Lead time:* Engineering or specification changes can play havoc with JIT because of inadequate lead time for suppliers to implement the necessary changes.
4. *Quality:* Suppliers' capital budgets, processes, or technology may limit ability to respond to changes in product and quality.
5. *Lot sizes:* Suppliers may see frequent delivery in small lots as a way to transfer buyers' holding costs to suppliers.

JIT LAYOUT

JIT layouts reduce another kind of waste—movement. The movement of material on a factory floor (or paper in an office) does not add value. Consequently, managers want flexible layouts that reduce the movement of both people and material. JIT layouts place material directly in the location where needed. For instance, an assembly line should be designed with delivery points next to the line so material need not be delivered first to a receiving department and then moved again. This is what VF Corporation's Wrangler Division in Greensboro, North Carolina, did; denim is now delivered directly to the line. Toyota has gone one step farther and places hardware and components in the chassis of each vehicle moving down the assembly line. This is not only convenient, but it allows Toyota to save space and opens areas adjacent to the assembly line previously occupied by shelves. When a layout reduces distance, firms often save labor and space and may have the added bonus of eliminating potential areas for accumulation of unwanted inventory. Table 16.1 provides a list of JIT layout tactics.

▼ **TABLE 16.1**
JIT Layout Tactics

Build work cells for families of products
Include a large number of operations in a small area
Minimize distance
Design little space for inventory
Improve employee communication
Use poka-yoke devices
Build flexible or movable equipment
Cross-train workers to add flexibility

Distance Reduction

Reducing distance is a major contribution of work cells, work centers, and focused factories (see Chapter 9). The days of long production lines and huge economic lots, with goods passing through monumental, single-operation machines, are gone. Now firms use work cells, often arranged in a U shape, containing several machines performing different operations. These work cells are often based on group technology codes (as discussed in Chapter 5). Group technology codes help identify components with similar characteristics so we can group them into families. Once families are identified, work cells are built for them. The result can be thought of as a small product-oriented facility where the "product" is actually a group of similar products—a family of products. The cells produce one good unit at a time, and ideally they produce the units *only* after a customer orders them.

Increased Flexibility

Modern work cells are designed so they can be easily rearranged to adapt to changes in volume, product improvements, or even new designs. Almost nothing in these new departments is bolted down. This same concept of layout flexibility applies to office environments. Not only is most office furniture and equipment movable, but so are office walls, computer connections, and telecommunications. Equipment is modular. Layout flexibility aids the changes that result from product *and* process improvements that are inevitable with a philosophy of continuous improvement.

Impact on Employees

JIT layouts allow cross-trained employees to bring flexibility and efficiency to the work cell. Employees working together can tell each other about problems and opportunities for improvement. When layouts provide for sequential operations, feedback can be immediate. Defects are waste. When workers produce units one at a time, they test each product or component at each subsequent production stage. Machines in work cells with self-testing poka-yoke functions detect defects and stop automatically when they occur. Before JIT, defective products were replaced from inventory. Because surplus inventory is not kept in JIT facilities, there are no such buffers. Getting it right the first time is critical.

Reduced Space and Inventory

Because JIT layouts reduce travel distance, they also reduce inventory by removing space for inventory. When there is little space, inventory must be moved in very small lots or even single units. Units are always moving because there is no storage. For instance, each month Security

Pacific Corporation's focused facility sorts 7 million checks, processes 5 million statements, and mails 190,000 customer statements. With a JIT layout, mail processing time has been reduced by 33%, salary costs by tens of thousands of dollars per year, floor space by 50%, and in-process waiting lines by 75% to 90%. Storage, including shelves and drawers, has been removed.

AUTHOR COMMENT
Accountants book inventory as an asset, but operations managers know it is costly.

Just-in-time inventory
The minimum inventory necessary to keep a perfect system running.

"Inventory is evil."
S. Shingo

JIT INVENTORY

Inventories in production and distribution systems often exist "just in case" something goes wrong. That is, they are used just in case some variation from the production plan occurs. The "extra" inventory is then used to cover variations or problems. Effective inventory tactics require "just in time," not "just in case." **Just-in-time inventory** is the minimum inventory necessary to keep a perfect system running. With just-in-time inventory, the exact amount of goods arrives at the moment it is needed, not a minute before or a minute after. Some useful JIT inventory tactics are shown in Table 16.2 and discussed in more detail in the following sections.

Reduce Inventory and Variability

Operations managers move toward JIT by first removing inventory. The idea is to eliminate variability in the production system hidden by inventory. Reducing inventory uncovers the "rocks" in Figure 16.3(a) that represent the variability and problems currently being tolerated. With reduced inventory, management chips away at the exposed problems. After the lake is lowered, managers make additional cuts in inventory and continue to chip away at the next level of exposed problems (see Figure 16.3[b,c]). Ultimately, there will be virtually no inventory and no problems (variability).

Dell estimates that the rapid changes in technology costs $\frac{1}{2}$% to 2% of its inventory's value *each week*. Shigeo Shingo, co-developer of the Toyota JIT system, says, "Inventory is evil." He is not far from the truth. If inventory itself is not evil, it hides evil at great cost.

▼ **TABLE 16.2**
JIT Inventory Tactics

Use a pull system to move inventory
Reduce lot size
Develop just-in-time delivery systems with suppliers
Deliver directly to the point of use
Perform to schedule
Reduce setup time
Use group technology

Reduce Lot Sizes

Just-in-time has also come to mean elimination of waste by reducing investment in inventory. The key to JIT is producing good product in small lot sizes. Reducing the size of batches can be a major help in reducing inventory and inventory costs. As we saw in Chapter 12, when inventory usage is constant, the average inventory level is the sum of the maximum inventory plus the minimum inventory divided by 2. Figure 16.4 shows that lowering the order size increases the number of orders but drops inventory levels.

Ideally, in a JIT environment, order size is one and single units are being pulled from one adjacent process to another. More realistically, analysis of the process, transportation time, and containers used for transport are considered when determining lot size. Such analysis typically results in a small lot size but a lot size larger than one. Once a lot size has been determined, the

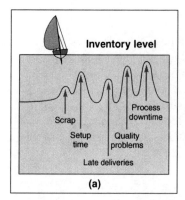
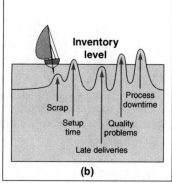
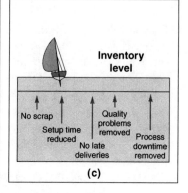

▲ **FIGURE 16.3** High levels of inventory hide problems (a), but as we reduce inventory, problems are exposed (b), and finally after reducing inventory and removing problems we have lower inventory, lower costs, and smooth sailing (c).

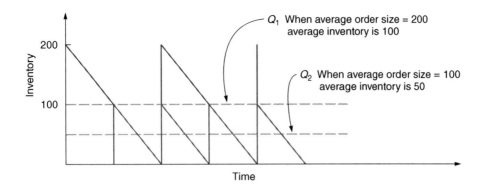

Q_1 When average order size = 200 average inventory is 100

Q_2 When average order size = 100 average inventory is 50

Time

◄ **FIGURE 16.4**
Frequent Orders Reduce Average Inventory
A lower order size increases the number of orders and total ordering cost but reduces average inventory and total holding cost.

EOQ production order quantity model can be modified to determine the desired setup time. We saw in Chapter 12 that the production order quantity model takes the form:

$$Q^* = \sqrt{\frac{2DS}{H[1 - (d/p)]}} \qquad (16\text{-}1)$$

where D = Annual demand d = Daily demand
         S = Setup cost p = Daily production
         H = Holding cost

Example 1 shows how to determine the desired setup time.

Crate Furniture, Inc., a firm that produces rustic furniture, desires to move toward a reduced lot size. Crate Furniture's production analyst, Aleda Roth, determined that a 2-hour production cycle would be acceptable between two departments. Further, she concluded that a setup time that would accommodate the 2-hour cycle time should be achieved.

APPROACH ►   Roth developed the following data and procedure to determine optimum setup time analytically:

D = Annual demand = 400,000 units

d = Daily demand = 400,000 per 250 days = 1,600 units per day

p = Daily production rate = 4,000 units per day

Q = EOQ desired = 400 (which is the 2-hour demand; that is, 1,600 per day per four 2-hour periods)

H = Holding cost = $20 per unit per year

S = Setup cost (to be determined)

SOLUTION ►   Roth determines that the cost, on an hourly basis, of setting up equipment is $30. Further, she computes that the setup cost per setup should be:

$$Q = \sqrt{\frac{2DS}{H(1 - d/p)}}$$

$$Q^2 = \frac{2DS}{H(1 - d/p)}$$

$$S = \frac{(Q^2)(H)(1 - d/p)}{2D} \qquad (16\text{-}2)$$

$$= \frac{(400)^2(20)(1 - 1,600/4,000)}{2(400,000)}$$

$$= \frac{(3,200,000)(0.6)}{800,000} = \$2.40$$

Setup time = $2.40/(hourly labor rate)

= $2.40/($30 per hour)

= 0.08 hour, or 4.8 minutes

◄ **EXAMPLE 1**

Determining optimal setup time

LO4: Determine optimal setup time

Only two changes need to be made for small-lot material flow to work. First, material handling and work flow need to be improved. With short production cycles, there can be very little wait time. Improving material handling is usually easy and straightforward. The second change is more challenging, and that is a radical reduction in setup times. We discuss setup reduction next.

> **AUTHOR COMMENT**
> Reduced lot sizes must be accompanied by reduced setup times.

Reduce Setup Costs

Both inventory and the cost of holding it go down as the inventory-reorder quantity and the maximum inventory level drop. However, because inventory requires incurring an ordering or setup cost that must be applied to the units produced, managers tend to purchase (or produce) large orders. With large orders, each unit purchased or ordered absorbs only a small part of the setup cost. Consequently, the way to drive down lot sizes *and* reduce average inventory is to reduce setup cost, which in turn lowers the optimum order size.

The effect of reduced setup costs on total cost and lot size is shown in Figure 16.5. Moreover, smaller lot sizes hide fewer problems. In many environments, setup cost is highly correlated with setup time. In a manufacturing facility, setups usually require a substantial amount of preparation. Much of the preparation required by a setup can be done prior to shutting down the machine or process. Setup times can be reduced substantially, as shown in Figure 16.6. For instance, in Kodak's Guadalajara, Mexico, plant a team reduced the setup time to change a bearing from 12 hours to 6 minutes! This is the kind of progress that is typical of world-class manufacturers.

Just as setup costs can be reduced at a machine in a factory, setup time can also be reduced during the process of getting the order ready. It does little good to drive down factory setup time from hours to minutes if orders are going to take 2 weeks to process or "set up" in the office. This is exactly what happens in organizations that forget that JIT concepts have applications in offices as well as in the factory. Reducing setup time (and cost) is an excellent way to reduce inventory investment and to improve productivity.

> **AUTHOR COMMENT**
> Effective scheduling is required for effective use of capital and personnel.

JIT SCHEDULING

Effective schedules, communicated both within the organization and to outside suppliers, support JIT. Better scheduling also improves the ability to meet customer orders, drives down inventory by allowing smaller lot sizes, and reduces work-in-process. For instance, Ford

▶ **FIGURE 16.5**
Lower Setup Costs Will Lower Total Cost

More frequent orders require reducing setup costs; otherwise, inventory costs will rise. As the setup costs are lowered (from S_1 to S_2), total inventory costs also fall (from T_1 to T_2).

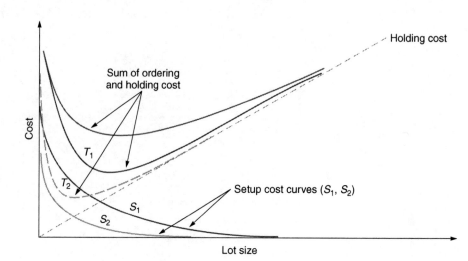

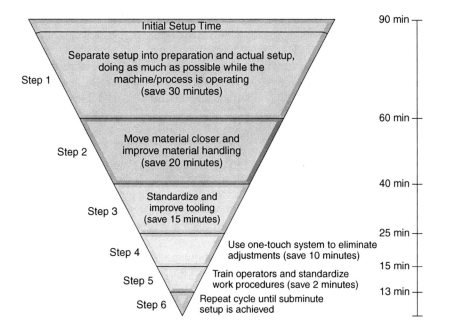

◄ **FIGURE 16.6**
Steps for Reducing Setup Times
Reduced setup times are a major JIT component.

▼ **TABLE 16.3**
JIT Scheduling Tactics

Communicate schedules
  to suppliers
Make level schedules
Freeze part of the
  schedule
Perform to schedule
Seek one-piece-make
  and one-piece-move
Eliminate waste
Produce in small lots
Use kanbans
Make each operation
  produce a perfect part

Motor Company now ties some suppliers to its final assembly schedule. Ford communicates its schedules to bumper manufacturer Polycon Industries from the Ford Oakville production control system. The scheduling system describes the style and color of the bumper needed for each vehicle moving down the final assembly line. The scheduling system transmits the information to portable terminals carried by Polycon warehouse personnel who load the bumpers onto conveyors leading to the loading dock. The bumpers are then trucked 50 miles to the Ford plant. Total time is 4 hours. However, as we saw in our opening *Global Company Profile*, Toyota has moved its seat supplier inside the new Tundra plant; this has driven down delivery time even further.

Table 16.3 suggests several items that can contribute to achieving these goals, but two techniques (in addition to communicating schedules) are paramount. They are *level schedules* and *kanban*.

Level Schedules

Level schedules process frequent small batches rather than a few large batches. Because this technique schedules many small lots that are always changing, it has on occasion been called "jelly bean" scheduling. Figure 16.7 contrasts a traditional large-lot approach using large batches with a JIT level schedule using many small batches. The operations manager's task is to make and move small lots so the level schedule is economical. This requires success with the issues discussed in this chapter that allow small lots. As lots get smaller, the constraints may change and become increasingly challenging. At some point, processing a unit or two may not be

Level schedules
Scheduling products so that each day's production meets the demand for that day.

▼ **FIGURE 16.7**   **Scheduling Small Lots of Parts A, B, and C Increases Flexibility to Meet Customer Demand and Reduces Inventory**

The JIT approach to scheduling produces just as many of each model per time period as the large-lot approach, provided that setup times are lowered.

JIT Level Material-Use Approach

AA BBB C AA BBB C AA BBB C AA BBB C AA BBB C AA BBB C AA BBB C AA BBB C

Large-Lot Approach

AAAAAA BBBBBBBBB CCC AAAAAA BBBBBBBBB CCC AAAAAA BBBBBBBBB CCC

Time

feasible. The constraint may be the way units are sold and shipped (four to a carton), or an expensive paint changeover (on an automobile assembly line), or the proper number of units in a sterilizer (for a food-canning line).

The scheduler may find that *freezing* the portion of the schedule closest to due dates allows the production system to function and the schedule to be met. Freezing means not allowing changes to be part of the schedule. Operations managers expect the schedule to be achieved with no deviations from the schedule.

Kanban

One way to achieve small lot sizes is to move inventory through the shop only as needed rather than *pushing* it on to the next workstation whether or not the personnel there are ready for it. As noted earlier, when inventory is moved only as needed, it is referred to as a *pull* system, and the ideal lot size is one. The Japanese call this system *kanban*. Kanbans allow arrivals at a work center to match (or nearly match) the processing time.

Kanban

The Japanese word for *card*, which has come to mean "signal"; a kanban system moves parts through production via a "pull" from a signal.

Kanban is a Japanese word for *card*. In their effort to reduce inventory, the Japanese use systems that "pull" inventory through work centers. They often use a "card" to signal the need for another container of material—hence the name *kanban*. *The card is the authorization for the next container of material to be produced.* Typically, a kanban signal exists for each container of items to be obtained. An order for the container is then initiated by each kanban and "pulled" from the producing department or supplier. A sequence of kanbans "pulls" the material through the plant.

The system has been modified in many facilities so that even though it is called a *kanban*, the card itself does not exist. In some cases, an empty position on the floor is sufficient indication that the next container is needed. In other cases, some sort of signal, such as a flag or rag (Figure 16.8) alerts that it is time for the next container.

When there is visual contact between producer and user, the process works like this:

1. The user removes a standard-size container of parts from a small storage area, as shown in Figure 16.8.

LO5: Define kanban

2. The signal at the storage area is seen by the producing department as authorization to replenish the using department or storage area. Because there is an optimum lot size, the producing department may make several containers at a time.

Figure 16.9 shows how a kanban works, pulling units as needed from production. This system is similar to the resupply that occurs in your neighborhood supermarket: The customer buys; the stock clerk observes the shelf or receives notice from the end-of-day sales list and restocks. When the limited supply, if any, in the store's storage is depleted, a "pull" signal is sent to the warehouse, distributor, or manufacturer for resupply, usually that night. The complicating factor in a manufacturing firm is the time needed for actual manufacturing (production) to take place.

A kanban need not be as formal as signal lights or empty carts. The cook in a fast-food restaurant knows that when six cars are in line, eight meat patties and six orders of french fries should be cooking.

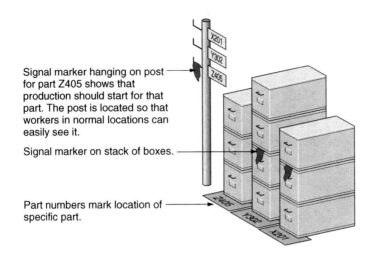

◄ FIGURE 16.8
Diagram of Outbound Stockpoint with Warning-Signal Marker

Signal marker hanging on post for part Z405 shows that production should start for that part. The post is located so that workers in normal locations can easily see it.

Signal marker on stack of boxes.

Part numbers mark location of specific part.

Several additional points regarding kanbans may be helpful:

- When the producer and user are not in visual contact, a card can be used; otherwise, a light or flag or empty spot on the floor may be adequate.
- Because a pull station may require several resupply components, several kanban pull techniques can be used for different products at the same pull station.
- Usually, each card controls a specific quantity of parts, although multiple card systems are used if the producing work cell produces several components or if the lot size is different from the move size.
- In an MRP system (see Chapter 14), the schedule can be thought of as a "build" authorization and the kanban as a type of "pull" system that initiates the actual production.
- The kanban cards provide a direct control (limit) on the amount of work-in-process between cells.
- If there is an immediate storage area, a two-card system may be used—one card circulates between user and storage area, and the other circulates between the storage area and the producing area.

Determining the Number of Kanban Cards or Containers The number of kanban cards, or containers, in a JIT system sets the amount of authorized inventory. To determine the number of containers moving back and forth between the using area and the producing areas, management first sets the size of each container. This is done by computing the lot size, using a

▼ FIGURE 16.9   Kanban Signals "Pull" Material Through the Production Process

As a customer "pulls" an order from finished goods, a signal (kanban card) is sent to the final assembly area. Final assembly produces and resupplies finished goods. When final assembly needs components, it sends a signal to *its* supplier, a work cell. The work cell, in turn, sends a signal to the material/parts supplier.

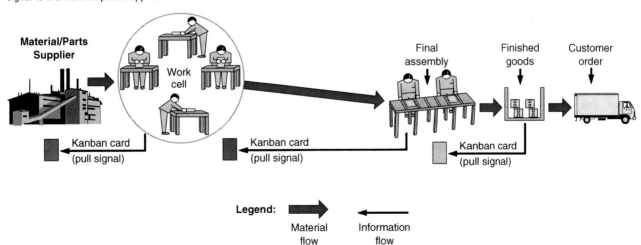

model such as the production order quantity model (discussed in Chapter 12 and shown again on page 661 in Equation [16–1]). Setting the number of containers involves knowing (1) lead time needed to produce a container of parts and (2) the amount of safety stock needed to account for variability or uncertainty in the system. The number of kanban cards is computed as follows:

$$\text{Number of kanbans (containers)} = \frac{\text{Demand during lead time} + \text{Safety stock}}{\text{Size of container}} \quad \text{(16-3)}$$

Example 2 illustrates how to calculate the number of kanbans needed.

EXAMPLE 2 ▶

Determining the number of kanban containers

LO6: Compute the required number of kanbans

Hobbs Bakery produces short runs of cakes that are shipped to grocery stores. The owner, Ken Hobbs, wants to try to reduce inventory by changing to a kanban system. He has developed the following data and asked you to finish the project.

$$\text{Daily demand} = 500 \text{ cakes}$$
$$\text{Production lead time} = \text{Wait time} + \text{Material handling time} + \text{Processing time} = 2 \text{ days}$$
$$\text{Safety stock} = \tfrac{1}{2} \text{ day}$$
$$\text{Container size (determined on a production order size EOQ basis)} = 250 \text{ cakes}$$

APPROACH ▶ Having determined that the EOQ size is 250, we then determine the number of kanbans (containers) needed.

SOLUTION ▶ Demand during lead time =

$$\text{Lead time} \times \text{Daily demand} = 2 \text{ days} \times 500 \text{ cakes} = 1,000$$
$$\text{Safety stock} = 250$$

Number of kanbans (containers) needed =

$$\frac{\text{Demand during lead time} + \text{Safety stock}}{\text{Container size}} = \frac{1,000 + 250}{250} = 5$$

INSIGHT ▶ Once the reorder point is hit, five containers should be released.

LEARNING EXERCISE ▶ If lead time drops to 1 day, how many containers are needed? [Answer: 3.]

RELATED PROBLEMS ▶ 16.1, 16.2, 16.3, 16.4, 16.5, 16.6

Advantages of Kanban Containers are typically very small, usually a matter of a few hours' worth of production. Such a system requires tight schedules. Small quantities must be produced several times a day. The process must run smoothly with little variability in quality of lead time because any shortage has an almost immediate impact on the entire system. Kanban places added emphasis on meeting schedules, reducing the time and cost required by setups, and economical material handling.

Whether it is called kanban or something else, the advantages of small inventory and *pulling* material through the plant only when needed are significant. For instance, small batches allow only a very limited amount of faulty or delayed material. Problems are immediately evident. Numerous aspects of inventory are bad; only one aspect—availability—is good. Among the bad aspects are poor quality, obsolescence, damage, occupied space, committed assets, increased insurance, increased material handling, and increased accidents. Kanban systems put downward pressure on all these negative aspects of inventory.

In-plant kanban systems often use standardized, reusable containers that protect the specific quantities to be moved. Such containers are also desirable in the supply chain. Standardized containers reduce weight and disposal costs, generate less wasted space in trailers, and require less labor to pack, unpack, and prepare items.

AUTHOR COMMENT
Good quality costs less.

JIT QUALITY

The relationship between JIT and quality is a strong one. They are related in three ways. First, JIT cuts the cost of obtaining good quality. This saving occurs because scrap, rework, inventory investment, and damage costs are buried in inventory. JIT forces down inventory; therefore, fewer bad units are produced and fewer units must be reworked. In short, whereas inventory *hides* bad quality, JIT immediately *exposes* it.

This auto plant, like most JIT facilities, empowers employees so they can stop the entire production line by pulling the overhead cord if any quality problems are spotted.

▼ **TABLE 16.4**
JIT Quality Tactics

Use statistical process control
Empower employees
Build fail-safe methods (poka-yoke, checklists, etc.)
Expose poor quality with small lot JIT
Provide immediate feedback

Second, JIT improves quality. As JIT shrinks queues and lead time, it keeps evidence of errors fresh and limits the number of potential sources of error. In effect, JIT creates an early warning system for quality problems so that fewer bad units are produced and feedback is immediate. This advantage can accrue both within the firm and with goods received from outside vendors.

Finally, better quality means fewer buffers are needed and, therefore, a better, easier-to-employ JIT system can exist. Often the purpose of keeping inventory is to protect against unreliable quality. If consistent quality exists, JIT allows firms to reduce all costs associated with inventory. Table 16.4 suggests some requirements for quality in a JIT environment.

TOYOTA PRODUCTION SYSTEM

> **AUTHOR COMMENT**
> TPS brings the entire person to work.

Toyota Motor's Eiji Toyoda and Taiichi Ohno are given credit for the Toyota Production System (TPS) (see the *Global Company Profile* that opens this chapter). Three core components of TPS are continuous improvement, respect for people, and standard work practice.

Continuous Improvement

Continuous improvement under TPS means building an organizational culture and instilling in its people a value system stressing that processes can be improved—indeed, that improvement is an integral part of every employee's job. This process is formalized in TPS by **kaizen**, the Japanese word for change for the good, or what is more generally known as *continuous improvement*. In application, it means making a multitude of small or incremental changes as one seeks ellusive perfection. (See the *OM in Action Box* "Kaizen at Novo Nordisk."). Instilling the mantra of continuous improvement begins at recruiting and continues through extensive and continuing training. One of the reasons continuous improvement works at Toyota, we should note, is because of another core value at Toyota, Toyota's respect for people.

Kaizen
A focus on continuous improvement.

Respect for People

At Toyota, people are recruited, trained, and treated as knowledge workers. Aided by aggressive cross-training and few job classifications, TPS engages the mental as well as physical capacities of employees in the challenging task of improving operations. Employees are empowered. They are empowered to make improvements. They are empowered to stop machines and processes when quality problems exist. Indeed, empowered employees are a necessary part of TPS. This means that those tasks that have traditionally been assigned to staff are moved to employees. Toyota recognizes that employees know more about their jobs than anyone else. TPS respects employees by giving them the opportunity to enrich both their jobs and their lives.

Standard Work Practice

Standard work practice at Toyota includes these underlying principles:

- Work is completely specified as to content, sequence, timing, and outcome.
- Internal and external customer–supplier connections are direct, specifying personnel, methods, timing, and quantity.

LO7: Explain the principles of the Toyota Production System

OM in Action ▶ Kaizen at Novo Nordisk

Novo Nordisk is a health care company and a world leader in diabetes care. With headquarters in Denmark, Novo Nordisk employs more than 29,000 employees in 81 countries, and its markets its products in 179 countries.

The remarkable annual result in 2009 of $9.1 billion was due to a thorough optimization process, especially due to the reengineering of its production processes by using a lean operation called cLEAN. cLEAN allows the same number of workers to produce twice as much of its insulin and growth hormones.

One way Novo Nordisk achieved these results was through kaizen, in which each of the 9,000 employees asks themselves daily whether it would be possible to perform in a smarter way. One employee suggested replacing air-powered cylinders in an engine with server engines, so that the movements could be more; these changes allowed

assembly with greater precision, with less waste and fewer errors. This single suggestion has saved around $143,000 per year at full production.

Everybody at Novo Nordisk is able to see how productivity can be increased and waste can be decreased by applying cLEAN. Every department is expected to hand in a couple ideas every year so that the number of suggestions that lead immediately to significant economic improvements will continue to increase.

cLEAN has positively affected logistics and supply-chain operations at Novo Nordisk, as shown by its 99.9% delivery reliability and quality.

Sources: Mette Buck Jensen, (2009) "Novo fandt gevinsten i de små ting," Ingeniøren, October 2009, 8–14, and **www.novonordisk.com**.

- Product and service flows are to be simple and direct. Goods and services are directed to a specific person or machine.
- Improvements in the system must be made in accordance with the "scientific method," at the lowest possible level in the organization.[2]

TPS requires that activities, connections, and flows include built-in tests to automatically signal problems. Any gap between what is expected and what occurs becomes immediately evident. The education and training of Toyota's employees and the responsiveness of the system to problems make the seemingly rigid system flexible and adaptable to changing circumstances. The result is ongoing improvements in reliability, flexibility, safety, and efficiency.

> **AUTHOR COMMENT**
> Lean drives out non-value-added activities.

LEAN OPERATIONS

Lean production can be thought of as the end result of a well-run OM function. While JIT and TPS tend to have an *internal* focus, lean production begins *externally* with a focus on the customer. Understanding what the customer wants and ensuring customer input and feedback are starting points for lean production. Lean operations means identifying customer value by analyzing all the activities required to produce the product and then optimizing the entire process from the customer's perspective.

Building a Lean Organization

The transition to lean production is difficult. Building an organizational culture where learning, empowerment, and continuous improvement are the norm is a challenge. However, organizations that focus on JIT, quality, and employee empowerment are often lean producers. Such firms drive out activities that do not add value in the eyes of the customer: they include leaders like United Parcel Service, Harley-Davidson, and, of course, Toyota. Even traditionally craft-oriented organizations such as Louis Vuitton (see the *OM in Action* box) find improved productivity with lean operations. Lean operations adopt a philosophy of minimizing waste by striving for perfection through continuous learning, creativity, and teamwork. They tend to share the following attributes:

- *Use JIT techniques* to eliminate virtually all inventory.
- *Build systems that help employees* produce a perfect part every time.
- *Reduce space requirements* by minimizing travel distance.

---

[2]Adopted from Steven J. Spear, "Learning to Lead at Toyota," *Harvard Business Review* 82, no. 5 (May 2004): 78–86; and Steven Spear and H. Kent Bowen, "Decoding the DNA of the Toyota Production System," *Harvard Business Review* 77, no. 5 (September–October 1999): 97–106.

OM in Action ► Going Lean at Louis Vuitton

LVMH Moet Hennessy Louis Vuitton is the world's largest luxury-goods company. Its Louis Vuitton unit, responsible for half of the company's profit, makes very upscale handbags and enjoys a rich markup on sales of about $5 billion. The return-on-investment is excellent, but sales could be even better: the firm often can't match production to the sales pace of a successful new product. In the high fashion business that is all about speed-to-market, this is bad news; a massive overhaul was in order.

Changes on the factory floor were key to the overhaul. The traditional approach to manufacturing at Louis Vuitton was batch production: craftsmen, working on partially completed handbags, performed specialized tasks such as cutting, gluing, sewing, and assembly. Carts moved batches of semi-finished handbags on to the next workstation. It took 20 to 30 workers 8 days to make a handbag. And defects were high. Lean manufacturing looked like the way to go.

Craftsmen were retrained to do multiple tasks in small U-shaped work cells. Each work cell now contains 6 to

12 cross-trained workers and the necessary sewing machines and work tables. Consistent with one-piece flow, the work is passed through the cell from worker to worker. The system reduces inventory and allows workers to detect flaws earlier.

Rework under the old system was sometimes as high as 50% and internal losses as high as 4%. Returns are down by two-thirds. The system has not only improved productivity and quality, it also allows Louis Vuitton to respond to the market faster—with daily scheduling as opposed to weekly scheduling.

Sources: The Wall Street Journal (October 9, 2006): A1, A15 and (January 31, 2006): A1, A13.

- *Develop partnerships with suppliers*, helping them to understand the needs of the ultimate customer.
- *Educate suppliers* to accept responsibility for satisfying end customer needs.
- *Eliminate all but value-added activities*. Material handling, inspection, inventory, and rework are the likely targets because these do not add value to the product.
- *Develop employees* by constantly improving job design, training, employee commitment, teamwork, and empowerment.
- *Make jobs challenging*, pushing responsibility to the lowest level possible.
- *Build worker flexibility* through cross-training and reducing job classifications.

Success requires the full commitment and involvement of managers, employees, and suppliers. The rewards that lean producers reap are spectacular. Lean producers often become benchmark performers.

LEAN OPERATIONS IN SERVICES

AUTHOR COMMENT
JIT, TPS, and lean began in factories but are now also used in services throughout the world.

The features of lean operations apply to services just as they do in other sectors. (See the *OM in Action* box "Toyota University Teaches Lean Thinking.") Here are some examples applied to suppliers, layout, inventory, and scheduling in the service sector.

Suppliers   As we have noted, virtually every restaurant deals with its suppliers on a JIT basis. Those that do not are usually unsuccessful. The waste is too evident—food spoils, and customers complain or get sick.

Layouts   Lean layouts are required in restaurant kitchens, where cold food must be served cold and hot food hot. McDonald's, for example, has reconfigured its kitchen layout at great expense to drive seconds out of the production process, thereby speeding delivery to customers. With the new process, McDonald's can produce made-to-order hamburgers in 45 seconds. Layouts also make a difference in airline baggage claim, where customers expect their bags just-in-time.

Inventory   Stockbrokers drive inventory down to nearly zero every day. Most sell and buy orders occur on an immediate basis because an unexecuted sell or buy order is not acceptable to the client. A broker may be in serious trouble if left holding an unexecuted trade. Similarly, McDonald's reduces inventory waste by maintaining a finished-goods inventory of only 10 minutes; after that, it is thrown away. Hospitals, such as Arnold Palmer (described in this chapter's

VIDEO 16.1
JIT at Arnold Palmer Hospital

Lean operations take on an unusual form in an operating room. McKesson-General, Baxter International, and many other hospital suppliers provide surgical supplies for hospitals on a JIT basis. (1) They deliver prepackaged surgical supplies based on hospital operating schedules, and (2) the surgical packages themselves are prepared so supplies are available in the sequence in which they will be used during surgery.

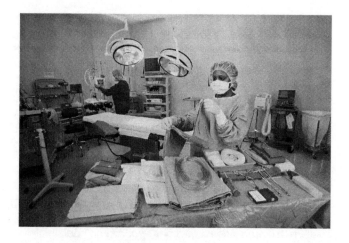

Video Case Study), manage JIT inventory and low safety stocks for many items. Even critical supplies such as pharmaceuticals may be held to low levels by developing community networks as backup systems. In this manner, if one pharmacy runs out of a needed drug, another member of the network can supply it until the next day's shipment arrives.

Scheduling   At airline ticket counters, the focus of the system is on adjusting to customer demand. But rather than being accommodated by inventory availability, demand is satisfied by personnel. Through elaborate scheduling, ticket counter personnel show up just-in-time to cover peaks in customer demand. In other words, rather than "things" inventoried, personnel are scheduled. At a salon, the focus is only slightly different: the *customer* and the staff are scheduled to assure prompt service. At McDonald's and Walmart, scheduling of personnel is down to 15-minute increments, based on precise forecasting of demand. Additionally, at McDonald's, production is done in small lots to ensure that fresh, hot hamburgers are delivered just-in-time. In short, both personnel and production are scheduled to meet specific demand. Notice that in all three of these lean organizations—the airline ticket counter, the salon, and McDonald's— scheduling is a key ingredient. Excellent forecasts drive those schedules. Those forecasts may be very elaborate, with seasonal, daily, and even hourly components in the case of the airline ticket counter (holiday sales, flight time, etc.), seasonal and weekly components at the salon (holidays and Fridays create special problems), and down to a few minutes (to respond to the daily meal cycle) at McDonald's.

To deliver goods and services to customers under continuously changing demand, suppliers need to be reliable, inventories lean, cycle times short, and schedules nimble. A lean focus engages and empowers employees to create and deliver the customer's perception of value, eliminating whatever does not contribute to this goal. Lean operations are currently being developed with great success in many firms, regardless of their products. Lean techniques are widely used in both goods-producing and service-producing firms; they just look different.

OM in Action ▶ Toyota University Teaches Lean Thinking

Based in Gardenia, California, Toyota University teaches its employees the Toyota Production System. But Toyota has also opened its door to others. As a public service, Toyota has been teaching lean thinking classes to the Los Angeles Police Department and the U.S. military. Classes begin, as one might expect, with a car-building exercise. Using model cars and desks as workstations and delivery areas, students begin with a focus on fast throughput and high production goals. This results in a "push" system, with lots of work-in-process piling up, lots of defects to be reworked, and too many of the wrong kind of cars on the "dealer's" lot.

The exercise is then revised, and students are taught to respond to orders and to form *kaizen* (continuous improvement) teams. The revised exercise then uses a "pull" system that responds to orders and fixes even the most minor problems immediately. With a focus only on filling orders and "pulling" demand through the production process with no defects, a faster, more efficient production line is formed.

Instructor Matthew May's observation about adapting lean methods beyond the factory: "If you can do it with LAPD, you can do it anywhere."

Sources: The Wall Street Journal (March 5, 2007): B1, B4; and **www. isosupport.com.**

CHAPTER SUMMARY

JIT, TPS, and lean operations are philosophies of continuous improvement. Lean operations focus on customer desires, TPS focuses on respect for people and standard work practices, and JIT focuses on driving out waste by reducing inventory. But all three approaches reduce waste in the production process. And because waste is found in anything that does not add value, organizations that implement these techniques are adding value more efficiently than other firms. The expectation of these systems is that empowered employees work with committed management to build systems that respond to customers with ever-lower cost and higher quality.

Key Terms

Just-in-time (JIT)	Variability	Consignment inventory
Toyota Production System (TPS)	Throughput	Just-in-time inventory
Lean operations	Manufacturing cycle time	Level schedules
Seven wastes	Pull system	Kanban
5Ss	JIT partnerships	Kaizen

Ethical Dilemma

In this lean operations world, in an effort to lower handling costs, speed delivery, and reduce inventory, retailers are forcing their suppliers to do more and more in the way of preparing their merchandise for their cross-docking warehouses, shipment to specific stores, and shelf presentation. Your company, a small manufacturer of aquarium decorations, is in a tough position. First, Mega-Mart wanted you to develop bar-code technology, then special packaging, then small individual shipments bar coded for each store (this way when the merchandise hits the warehouse it is cross-docked immediately to the correct truck and store and is ready for shelf placement). And now Mega-Mart wants you to develop RFID—immediately. Mega-Mart has made it clear that suppliers that cannot keep up with the technology will be dropped.

Earlier, when you didn't have the expertise for bar codes, you had to borrow money and hire an outside firm to do the development, purchase the technology, and train your shipping clerk. Then, meeting the special packaging requirement drove you into a loss for several months, resulting in a loss for last year. Now it appears that the RFID request is impossible. Your business, under the best of conditions, is marginally profitable, and the bank may not be willing to bail you out again. Over the years, Mega-Mart has slowly become your major customer and without them, you are probably out of business. What are the ethical issues and what do you do?

Discussion Questions

1. What is JIT?
2. What is a lean producer?
3. What is TPS?
4. What is level scheduling?
5. JIT attempts to remove delays, which do not add value. How then does JIT cope with weather and its impact on crop harvest and transportation times?
6. What are three ways in which JIT and quality are related?
7. How does TPS contribute to competitive advantage?
8. What are the characteristics of just-in-time partnerships with respect to suppliers?
9. Discuss how the Japanese word for *card* has application in the study of JIT.
10. Standardized, reusable containers have fairly obvious benefits for shipping. What is the purpose of these devices within the plant?
11. Does lean production work in the service sector? Provide an illustration.
12. Which lean techniques work in both the manufacturing *and* service sectors?

Solved Problems   Virtual Office Hours help is available at www.pearsonglobaleditions.com/myomlab

▼ SOLVED PROBLEM 16.1

Krupp Refrigeration, Inc., is trying to reduce inventory and wants you to install a kanban system for compressors on one of its assembly lines. Determine the size of the kanban and the number of kanbans (containers) needed.

Setup cost = $10

Annual holding cost per compressor = $100

Daily production = 200 compressors

Annual usage = 25,000 (50 weeks × 5 days each × daily usage of 100 compressors)

Lead time = 3 days

Safety stock = $\frac{1}{2}$ day's production of compressors

▼ **SOLUTION**

First, we must determine kanban container size. To do this, we determine the production order quantity (see discussion in Chapter 12 or Equation [16-1]), which determines the kanban size:

$$Q_p^* = \sqrt{\frac{2DS}{H\left(1 - \dfrac{d}{p}\right)}} = \sqrt{\frac{2(25,000)(10)}{H\left(1 - \dfrac{d}{p}\right)}} = \sqrt{\frac{500,000}{100\left(1 - \dfrac{100}{200}\right)}} = \sqrt{\frac{500,000}{50}}$$

$$= \sqrt{10,000} = 100 \text{ compressors. So the production order size and the size of the kanban container} = 100.$$

Then we determine the number of kanbans:

$$\text{Demand during lead time} = 300 \ (= 3 \text{ days} \times \text{daily usage of } 100)$$

$$\text{Safety stock} = 100 \ (= \tfrac{1}{2} \times \text{daily production of } 200)$$

$$\text{Number of kanbans} = \frac{\text{Demand during lead time} + \text{Safety stock}}{\text{Size of container}}$$

$$= \frac{300 + 100}{100} = \frac{400}{100} = 4 \text{ containers}$$

Problems*

•   **16.1**   Leblanc Electronics, Inc., in Nashville, produces short runs of custom airwave scanners for the defense industry. You have been asked by the owner, Larry Leblanc, to reduce inventory by introducing a kanban system. After several hours of analysis, you develop the following data for scanner connectors used in one work cell. How many kanbans do you need for this connector?

Daily demand	1,000 connectors
Lead time	2 days
Safety stock	$\tfrac{1}{2}$ day
Kanban size	500 connectors

•   **16.2**   Chip Gillikin's company wants to establish kanbans to feed a newly established work cell. The following data have been provided. How many kanbans are needed?

Daily demand	250 units
Production lead time	$\tfrac{1}{2}$ day
Safety stock	$\tfrac{1}{4}$ day
Kanban size	50 units

••   **16.3**   Chris Millikan Manufacturing, Inc., is moving to kanbans to support its telephone switching-board assembly lines. Determine the size of the kanban for subassemblies and the number of kanbans needed.

Setup cost = $30
Annual holding
             cost = $120 per subassembly
Daily production = 20 subassemblies
    Annual usage = 2,500 (50 weeks × 5 days each
                    × daily usage of 10 subassemblies)
       Lead time = 16 days
    Safety stock = 4 days' production of subassemblies. **Px**

••   **16.4**   Maggie Moylan Motorcycle Corp. uses kanbans to support its transmission assembly line. Determine the size of the kanban for the mainshaft assembly and the number of kanbans needed.

                    Setup cost = $20
Annual holding cost
of mainshaft assembly = $250 per unit
       Daily production = 300 mainshafts
          Annual usage = 20,000 (= 50 weeks × 5 days each
                          × daily usage of 80 mainshafts)
             Lead time = 3 days
          Safety stock = $\tfrac{1}{2}$ day's production of mainshafts **Px**

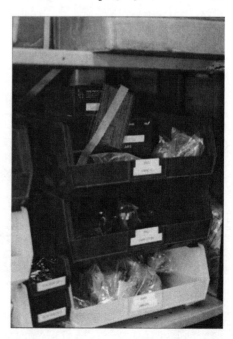

•   **16.5**   Discount-Mart, a major East Coast retailer, wants to determine the economic order quantity (see Chapter 12 for EOQ formulas) for its halogen lamps. It currently buys all halogen lamps from Specialty Lighting Manufacturers, in Atlanta. Annual demand is 2,000 lamps, ordering cost per order is $30, annual carrying cost per lamp is $12.

a) What is the EOQ?

b) What are the total annual costs of holding and ordering (managing) this inventory?

c) How many orders should Discount-Mart place with Specialty Lighting per year? **Px**

••• **16.6** Discount-Mart (see Problem 16.5), as part of its new JIT program, has signed a long-term contract with Specialty Lighting and will place orders electronically for its halogen lamps. Ordering costs will drop to $.50 per order, but Discount-Mart also reassessed its carrying costs and raised them to $20 per lamp.

a) What is the new economic order quantity?

b) How many orders will now be placed?

c) What is the total annual cost of managing the inventory with this policy? **Px**

•• **16.7** How do your answers to Problems 16.5 and 16.6 provide insight into a JIT purchasing strategy?

••• **16.8** Bill Penny has a repetitive manufacturing plant producing trailer hitches in Arlington, Texas. The plant has an average inventory turnover of only 12 times per year. He has therefore determined that he will reduce his component lot sizes. He has developed the following data for one component, the safety chain clip:

$$\text{Annual demand} = 31,200 \text{ units}$$
$$\text{Daily demand} = 120 \text{ units}$$
$$\text{Daily production (in 8 hours)} = 960 \text{ units}$$
$$\text{Desired lot size (1 hour of production)} = 120 \text{ units}$$

$$\text{Holding cost per unit per year} = \$12$$
$$\text{Setup labor cost per hour} = \$20$$

How many minutes of setup time should he have his plant manager aim for regarding this component?

••• **16.9** Given the following information about a product, at Phyllis Simon's firm, what is the appropriate setup time?

$$\text{Annual demand} = 39,000 \text{ units}$$
$$\text{Daily demand} = 150 \text{ units}$$
$$\text{Daily production} = 1,000 \text{ units}$$
$$\text{Desired lot size} = 150 \text{ units}$$
$$\text{Holding cost per unit per year} = \$10$$
$$\text{Setup labor cost per hour} = \$40$$

••• **16.10** Rick Wing has a repetitive manufacturing plant producing automobile steering wheels. Use the following data to prepare for a reduced lot size. The firm uses a work year of 305 days.

Annual demand for steering wheels	30,500
Daily demand	100
Daily production (8 hours)	800
Desired lot size (2 hours of production)	200
Holding cost per unit per year	$10

a) What is the setup cost, based on the desired lot size?

b) What is the setup time, based on $40 per hour setup labor?

▶ **Refer to** myomlab ⊕ **for these additional homework problems: 16.11–16.12**

Case Studies

▶ Mutual Insurance Company of Iowa

Mutual Insurance Company of Iowa (MICI) has a major insurance office facility located in Des Moines, Iowa. The Des Moines office is responsible for processing all of MICI's insurance claims for the entire nation. The company's sales have experienced rapid growth during the last year, and as expected, record levels in claims followed. Over 2,500 forms for claims a day are now flowing into the office for processing. Unfortunately, fewer than 2,500 forms a day are flowing out. The total time to process a claim, from the time it arrives to the time a check is mailed, has increased from 10 days to 10 weeks. As a result, some customers are threatening legal action. Sally Cook, the manager of Claims Processing, is particularly distressed, as she knows that a claim seldom requires more than 3 hours of actual work. Under the current administrative procedures, human resources limitations, and facility constraints, there appear to be no easy fixes for the problem. But clearly, something must be done, as the workload has overwhelmed the existing system.

MICI management wants aggressive, but economical, action taken to fix the problem. Ms. Cook has decided to try a JIT approach to claim processing. With support from her bosses, and as a temporary fix, Cook has brought in part-time personnel from MICI sales divisions across the country to help. They are to work down the claims backlog while a new JIT system is installed.

Meanwhile, Claims Processing managers and employees are to be trained in JIT principles. With JIT principles firmly in mind, managers will redesign jobs to move responsibilities for quality control activities to each employee, holding them responsible for quality work and any necessary corrections. Cook will also initiate worker-training programs that explain the entire claim processing flow, as well as provide comprehensive training on each step in the process. Data-entry skills will also be taught to both employees and managers in an effort to fix responsibility for data accuracy on the processor rather than on data entry clerks. Additionally, cross-training will be emphasized to enable workers within departments to process a variety of customer claim applications in their entirety.

Cook and her supervisors are also reexamining the insurance and claim forms currently in use. They want to see if standardization of forms will cut processing time, reduce data-entry time, and cut work-in-process.

They hope the changes will also save training time. Making changes in work methods and worker skills leads logically to a need for change in the layout of the Claims Processing Department. This potential change represents a major move from the departmental layout of the past, and will be a costly step. To help ensure the successful implementation of this phase of the

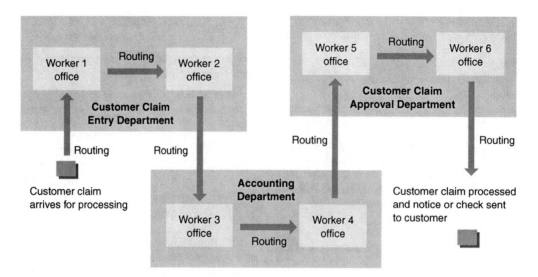

▲ **FIGURE 16.10**   **Claims Processing Department Layout**

changeover, Cook established a team made up of supervisors, employees, and an outside office layout consultant. She also had the team visit the Kawasaki motorcycle plant in Lincoln, Nebraska, to observe their use of work cells to aid JIT.

The team concluded that a change in the office facilities was necessary to successfully implement and integrate JIT concepts at MICI. The team believes it should revise the layout of the operation and work methods to bring them in line with "group technology cell" layouts. An example of the current departmental layout and claim processing flow pattern is presented in Figure 16.10. As can be seen in this figure, customer claims arrive for processing at the facility and flow through a series of offices and departments to eventually complete the claim process. Although the arrangement of the offices and workers in Figure 16.10 is typical, the entire facility actually operates 20 additional flows, each consisting of the same three departments. However, not all of the 20 flows are configured the same. The number of employees, for example, varies depending on the claim form requirements (larger

claims have to be approved by more people). So while all forms must pass through the same three departments (Customer Claim Entry, Accounting, and Customer Claim Approval), the number of workers for each claim may vary from two to four. For this reason, the MICI facility currently maintains a staff of over 180 office workers just to process and route claims. All these people work for Ms. Cook.

Discussion Questions

1. Identify the attributes you would expect the Claims Processing Department at MICI to have once the new JIT system is in place.
2. What will the restructured cell layout for claim processing in Figure 16.10 look like? Draw it.
3. What assumptions are you making about personnel and equipment in the new group technology cell layout?
4. How will the new JIT oriented system benefit the MICI operation? Explain.

Source: Adapted from Marc J. Schniederjans, *Topics in Just-in-Time Management*, pp. 283–285. Reprinted by permission of Pearson Education, Inc., Upper Saddle River, NJ.

▶ JIT after a Catastrophe

You name the catastrophe, and JIT has been through it and survived. Toyota Motor Corporation has had its world-renowned JIT system tested by fire. The massive fire incinerated the main source of crucial brake valves that Toyota buys from the Aisin Seiki plant in Kariya, Japan, and uses in most of its cars. The impact was the loss of 70,000 cars not produced while Toyota got the supply chain repaired. Then an earthquake destroyed Toyota's transmission supplier, Riken, shutting down production in a dozen factories. Chrysler and many others had their JIT systems tested on September 11, 2001, when the terrorists attacks shut down their state-of-the-art air delivery systems. And on February 5, 2008, during the second shift at Caterpillar's high-pressure couplings plant in Oxford, Mississippi, a tornado all but destroyed the facility. Despite these catastrophes, managers at these firms, like other executives all over the world, are still cutting costs by consolidating production, reducing inventory, and implementing JIT.

Consistent with JIT practice, these firms maintain minimal inventory of components and tight supply chains. There are very few components in these closely knit networks that constitute their respective supply chains. Without critical components, production comes to a rapid halt. And in Caterpillar's case, the Oxford plant is the only plant in the world that makes this unique coupling. The couplings link hydraulic hoses on *every* piece of machinery Caterpillar makes. Depending on a single source and holding little inventory is a risk, but it also keeps firms lean and costs low.

The morning after the tornado tore apart the Oxford plant, Greg Folley, who runs Caterpillar's parts division, toured the plant. Much of the roof, including 10-ton heating and air-conditioning units, had fallen onto three critical metal stamping machines. The first piece of equipment was up and running in 2 weeks; getting production back to normal would take 6 months. But the Oxford plant had been making over 1 million of the critical couplings each month; this left a huge hole in Caterpillar's supply line.

Discussion Questions

1. If you are Mr. Folley, looking over the devastation at the Oxford plant, what do you do to keep Caterpillar's worldwide production running?

2. Given the inherent risk in JIT and the trauma that the companies have experienced, why has JIT survived?
3. What do these experiences, and the continuing popularity of JIT, tell you about just-in-time?
4. What actions or changes in policy do you suggest for Caterpillar?

Sources: Case is based on material in: *The Wall Street Journal* (May 19, 2008): B1, B2; (July 20, 2007): B1; **www.USAToday.com/money/world/2007-07-18-toyota-quake**; and *Harvard Business Review* (September–October 1999): 97–106.

▶ JIT at Arnold Palmer Hospital

Video Case

Orlando's Arnold Palmer Hospital, founded in 1989, specializes in treatment of women and children and is renowned for its high-quality rankings (top 10% of 2000 benchmarked hospitals), its labor and delivery volume (more than 16,000 births per year, and growing), and its neonatal intensive care unit (one of the highest survival rates in the nation). But quality medical practices and high patient satisfaction require costly inventory—some $30 million per year and thousands of SKUs.* With pressure on medical care to manage and reduce costs, Arnold Palmer Hospital has turned toward controlling its inventory with just-in-time (JIT) techniques.

Within the hospital, for example, drugs are now distributed at nursing workstations via dispensing machines (almost like vending machines) that electronically track patient usage and post the related charge to each patient. The dispensing stations are refilled each night, based on patient demand and prescriptions written by doctors.

To address JIT issues externally, Arnold Palmer Hospital turned toward a major distribution partner, McKesson General Medical, which as a first-tier supplier provides the hospital with about one quarter of all its medical/surgical inventory. McKesson supplies sponges, basins, towels, mayo stand covers, syringes, and hundreds of other medical/surgical items. To ensure coordinated daily delivery of inventory purchased from McKesson, an account executive has been assigned to the hospital on a full-time basis, as well as two other individuals who address customer service and product issues. The result has been a drop in Central Supply average daily inventory from $400,000 to $114,000 since JIT.

JIT success has also been achieved in the area of *custom surgical packs*. Custom surgical packs are the sterile coverings, disposable plastic trays, gauze, and the like, specialized to each type of surgical procedure. Arnold Palmer Hospital uses 10 different custom packs for various surgical procedures. "Over 50,000 packs are used each year, for a total cost of about $1.5 million," says George DeLong, head of Supply-Chain Management.

The packs are not only delivered in a JIT manner but packed that way as well. That is, they are packed in the reverse order they are used so each item comes out of the pack in the sequence it is needed. The packs are bulky, expensive, and must remain sterile.

Reducing the inventory and handling while maintaining an assured sterile supply for scheduled surgeries presents a challenge to hospitals.

Here is how the supply chain works: Custom packs are *assembled* by a packing company with *components supplied* primarily from manufacturers selected by the hospital, and *delivered* by McKesson from its local warehouse. Arnold Palmer Hospital works with its own surgical staff (through the Medical Economics Outcome Committee) to identify and standardize the custom packs to reduce the number of custom pack SKUs. With this integrated system, pack safety stock inventory has been cut to one day.

The procedure to drive the custom surgical pack JIT system begins with a "pull" from the doctors' daily surgical schedule. Then, Arnold Palmer Hospital initiates an electronic order to McKesson between 1:00 and 2:00 P.M. daily. At 4:00 A.M. the next day, McKesson delivers the packs. Hospital personnel arrive at 7:00 A.M. and stock the shelves for scheduled surgeries. McKesson then reorders from the packing company, which in turn "pulls" necessary inventory for the quantity of packs needed from the manufacturers.

Arnold Palmer Hospital's JIT system reduces inventory investment, expensive traditional ordering, and bulky storage, and supports quality with a sterile delivery.

Discussion Questions**

1. What do you recommend be done when an error is found in a pack as it is opened for an operation?
2. How might the procedure for custom surgical packs described here be improved?
3. When discussing JIT in services, the text notes that suppliers, layout, inventory, and scheduling are all used. Provide an example of each of these at Arnold Palmer Hospital.
4. When a doctor proposes a new surgical procedure, how do you recommend the SKU for a new custom pack be entered into the hospital's supply-chain system?

*SKU = stock keeping unit
**You may wish to view the video that accompanies this case before answering these questions.

Bibliography

Burke, Robert, and Gregg Messel. "From Simulation to Implementation: Cardinal Health's Lean Journey." *Target: Innovation at Work* 19, no. 2 (2nd Quarter 2003): 27–32.

Flinchbauh, Jamie. *The Hitchhiker's Guide to Lean*, Dearborn, MI: Society of Manufacturing Engineers (2006).

Graban, Mark. *Lean Hospitals*. New York: CRC Press (2009).

Hall, Robert W. "'Lean' and the Toyota Production System." *Target* 20, no. 3 (3rd Issue 2004): 22–27.

Keyte, Beau, and Drew Locher. *The Complete Lean Enterprise*. University Park, IL: Productivity Press (2004).

Morgan, James M., and Jeffrey K. Liker. *The Toyota Product Development System*. New York: Productivity Press (2007).

Nelson-Peterson, Dana L., and Carol J. Leppa, "Creating an Environment of Caring Using Lean Principles of the Virginia Mason Production System," *Journal of Nursing Administration* 37 (2007): 289.

Parks, Charles M. "The Bare Necessities of Lean." *Industrial Engineer* 35, no. 8 (August 2003): 39.

Schonberger, Richard J. "Lean Extended." *Industrial Engineer* (December 2005): 26–31.

van Veen-Dirks, Paula. "Management Control and the Production Environment." *International Journal of Production Economics* 93 (January 8, 2005): 263.

Womack, James P., and Daniel T. Jones. "Lean Consumption." *Harvard Business Review* 83 (March 2005): 58–68.

Womack, James P., and Daniel T. Jones. *Lean Solutions: How Companies and Customers Can Create Value and Wealth Together.* New York: The Free Press (2005).

Main Heading	Review Material	PEARSON myomlab
JUST-IN-TIME, THE TOYOTA PRODUCTION SYSTEM, AND LEAN OPERATIONS	■ **Just-in-time (JIT)**—Continuous and forced problem solving via a focus on throughput and reduced inventory. ■ **Toyota Production System (TPS)**—Focus on continuous improvement, respect for people, and standard work practices. ■ **Lean operations**—Eliminates waste through a focus on exactly what the customer wants. *When implemented as a comprehensive manufacturing strategy, JIT, TPS, and lean systems sustain competitive advantage and result in increased overall returns.* ■ **Seven wastes**—Overproduction, queues, transportation, inventory, motion, overprocessing, and defective product. ■ **5Ss**—A lean production checklist: sort, simplify, shine, standardize, and sustain. U.S. managers often add two additional *S*s to the 5 original ones: *safety* and *support/maintenance*. ■ **Variability**—Any deviation from the optimum process that delivers perfect product on time, every time. Both JIT and inventory reduction are effective tools for identifying causes of variability. ■ **Throughput**—The time required to move orders through the production process, from receipt to delivery. ■ **Manufacturing cycle time**—The time between the arrival of raw materials and the shipping of finished products. ■ **Pull system**—A concept that results in material being produced only when requested and moved to where it is needed just as it is needed. Pull systems use signals to request production and delivery from supplying stations to stations that have production capacity available.	
JUST-IN-TIME (JIT)	■ **JIT partnerships**—Partnerships of suppliers and purchasers that remove waste and drive down costs for mutual benefits. Some specific goals of JIT partnerships are: *removal of unnecessary activities*, *removal of in-plant inventory*; *removal of in-transit inventory*; and *obtain improved quality and reliability*. ■ **Consignment inventory**—An arrangement in which the supplier maintains title to the inventory until it is used. Concerns of suppliers in JIT partnerships include: (1) *diversification*; (2) *scheduling*; (3) *lead time*; (4) *quality*; and (5) *lot sizes*.	
JIT LAYOUT	JIT layout tactics include building work cells for families of products, include a large number of operations in a small area, minimizing distance, designing little space for inventory, improving employee communication, using poka-yoke devices, building flexible or movable equipment, and cross-training workers to add flexibility.	
JIT INVENTORY	■ **Just-in-time inventory**—The minimum inventory necessary to keep a perfect system running. The idea behind JIT is to eliminate inventory that hides variability in the production system. JIT inventory tactics include using a pull system to move inventory, reducing lot size, developing just-in-time delivery systems with suppliers, delivering directly to the point of use, performing to schedule, reducing setup time, and using group technology. $$Q^* = \sqrt{\frac{2DS}{H[1 - (d/p)]}} \qquad (16\text{-}1)$$ Using (16–1), for a given desired lot size, *Q*, we can solve for the optimal setup cost, *S*: $$S = \frac{(Q^2)(H)(1 - d/p)}{2D} \qquad (16\text{-}2)$$	Problems: 16.8–16.10

PEARSON
myomlab

Main Heading	Review Material	
JIT SCHEDULING	JIT scheduling tactics include: communicate schedules to suppliers, make level schedules, freeze part of the schedule, perform to schedule, seek one-piece-make and one-piece-move, eliminate waste, produce in small lots, use kanbans, and make each operation produce a perfect part.	Problems: 16.1–16.6
	■ **Level schedules**—Scheduling products so that each day's production meets the demand for that day.	
	■ **Kanban**—The Japanese word for *card*, which has come to mean "signal"; a kanban system moves parts through production via a "pull" from a signal:	
	$$\text{Number of Kanbans (containers)} = \frac{\text{Demand during lead time} + \text{Safety stock}}{\text{Size of container}} \quad (16\text{-}3)$$	Virtual Office Hours for Solved Problem: 16.1
JIT QUALITY	Whereas inventory *hides* bad quality, JIT immediately *exposes* it.	
	JIT quality tactics include using statistical process control, empowering employees, building fail-safe methods (poka-yoke, checklists, etc.), exposing poor quality with small lot JIT, and providing immediate feedback.	
TOYOTA PRODUCTION SYSTEM	■ **Kaizen**—A focus on continuous improvement.	
	At Toyota, people are recruited, trained, and treated as knowledge workers. They are empowered. TPS employs aggressive cross-training and few job classifications.	
LEAN OPERATIONS	Lean operations tend to share the following attributes: *use JIT techniques* to eliminate virtually all inventory; *build systems that help employees* produce a perfect part every time; *reduce space requirements* by minimizing travel distance; *develop partnerships with suppliers*, helping them to understand the needs of the ultimate customer; *educate suppliers* to accept responsibility for satisfying end customer needs; *eliminate all but value-added activities*; *develop employees* by constantly improving job design, training, employee commitment, teamwork, and empowerment; *make jobs challenging*, pushing responsibility to the lowest level possible; and *build worker flexibility* through cross-training and reducing job classifications.	
LEAN OPERATIONS IN SERVICES	The features of lean operations apply to services just as they do in other sectors. Forecasts in services may be very elaborate, with seasonal, daily, hourly, or even shorter components.	**VIDEO 16.1** JIT at Arnold Palmer Hospital

Self Test

■ **Before taking the self-test,** refer to the learning objectives listed at the beginning of the chapter and the key terms listed at the end of the chapter.

LO1. Continuous improvement and forced problem solving via a focus on throughput and reduced inventory is a reasonable definition of:
 a) lean operations.
 b) expedited management.
 c) the 5*S*s of housekeeping.
 d) just-in-time.
 e) Toyota Production System.

LO2. The 5*S*s for lean production are _____, _____, _____, _____, and _____.

LO3. Concerns of suppliers when moving to JIT include:
 a) small lots sometimes seeming economically prohibitive.
 b) realistic quality demands.
 c) changes without adequate lead time.
 d) erratic schedules.
 e) all of the above.

LO4. What is the formula for optimal setup time?
 a) $\sqrt{2DQ/[H(1 - d/p)]}$
 b) $\sqrt{Q^2H(1 - d/p)/(2D)}$
 c) $QH(1 - d/p)/(2D)$
 d) $Q^2H(1 - d/p)/(2D)$
 e) $H(1 - d/p)$

LO5. Kanban is the Japanese word for:
 a) car.   b) pull.
 c) card.   d) continuous improvement.
 e) level schedule.

LO6. The required number of kanbans equals:
 a) 1.   b) Demand during lead time/Q
 c) Size of container.   d) Demand during lead time.
 e) (Demand during lead time + safety stock)/Size of container.

LO7. TPS's standard work practices include:
 a) completely specified work.   b) "pull" systems.
 c) level scheduling.   d) kanbans.
 e) JIT techniques.

Answers: LO1. d; LO2. sort, simplify, shine, standardize, sustain; LO3. e; LO4. d; LO5. c; LO6. e; LO7. a.

Improving Operations

Chapter 20

Organizing for improvement

Key questions

➤ Why does improvement need organizing?

➤ How should the improvement effort be linked to strategy?

➤ What information is needed for improvement?

➤ What should be improvement priorities?

➤ How can organizational culture affect improvement?

➤ What are the key implementation issues?

Introduction

This is the third, and final, chapter devoted to operations improvement. It examines some of the managerial issues associated with improvement can be organized. There are no techniques as such in this chapter. Nor are all the issues dealt with easily defined. Rather it covers the 'soft' side of improvement. But do not dismiss this as in any way less important. In practice it is often the 'soft' stuff that determines the success or failure of improvement efforts. Moreover, the 'soft' stuff can be more difficult to get right than the 'hard', more technique-based, aspects of improvement. The 'hard' stuff is hard, but the 'soft' stuff is harder!

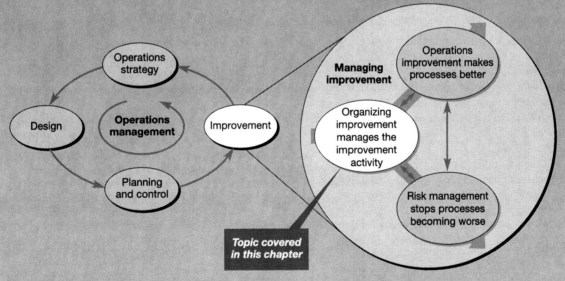

Figure 20.1 This chapter covers organizing of improvement

Check and improve your understanding of this chapter using self assessment questions and a personalised study plan, audio and video downloads, and an eBook – all at www.myomlab.com.

Operations in practice Taxing quality[1]

Operations effectiveness is just as important an issue in public-sector operations as it is for commercial companies. People have the right to expect that their taxes are not wasted on inefficient or inappropriate public processes. This is especially true of the tax collecting system itself. It is never a popular organization in any country, and taxpayers can be especially critical when the tax collection process is not well managed. This was very much on the minds of the Aarhus Region Customs and Tax unit (Aarhus CT) when they developed their award-winning quality initiative. The Aarhus Region is the largest of Denmark's twenty-nine local customs and tax offices. It acts as an agent for central government in collecting taxes in a professional and efficient manner while being able to respond to taxpayers' queries. Aarhus CT must, *'keep the user (customer) in focus'*, they say, *'Users must pay what is due – no more, no less and on time. But users are entitled to fair control and collection, fast and efficient case work, service and guidance, flexible employees, polite behaviour and a professional telephone service.'* The Aarhus CT approach to managing its quality initiative was built around a number of key points.

Source: Rex Features

- A recognition that poor-quality processes cause waste both internally and externally.
- A determination to adopt a practice of regularly surveying the satisfaction of its users. Employees were also surveyed, both to understand their views on quality and to check that their working environment would help to instil the principles of high-quality service.
- Although a not-for-profit organization, quality measures included measuring the organization's adherence to financial targets as well as error reporting.
- Internal processes were redefined and redesigned to emphasize customer needs and internal staff requirements. For example, Aarhus CT was the only tax region in Denmark to develop an independent information process that was used to analyse customers' needs and 'prevent misunderstanding in users' perception of legislation'.

- Internal processes were designed to allow staff the time and opportunity to develop their own skills, exchange ideas with colleagues and take on greater responsibility for management of their own work processes.
- The organization set up what it called its 'Quality Organization' (QO) structure which spanned all divisions and processes. The idea of the QO was to foster staff commitment to continuous improvement and to encourage the development of ideas for improving process performance. Within the QO was the Quality Group (QG). This consisted of four managers and four process staff, and reported directly to senior management. It also set up a number of improvement groups and suggestion groups consisting of managers as well as process staff. The role of the suggestion groups was to collect and process ideas for improvement which the improvement groups would then analyse and if appropriate implement.
- Aarhus CT was keen to stress that their Quality Groups would eventually become redundant if they were to be successful. In the short term they would maintain a stream of improvement ideas, but in the long term they should have fully integrated the idea of quality improvement into the day-to-day activities of all staff.

Why the improvement effort needs organizing

Improvement does not just happen. It needs organizing and it needs implementing. It also needs a purpose that is well thought through and clearly articulated. Although much operations improvement will take place at an operational level, and especially if one is following a continuous improvement philosophy (see previous chapter), it will be small-scale and incremental. Nevertheless, it must be placed in some kind of context. That is, it should be clear *why* improvement is happening as well as what it consists of. This means linking the improvement to the overall strategic objectives of the organization. This is why we start this chapter by thinking about improvement in a strategic context. Improvement must also be based on sound information. If the performance of operations and the processes within them are to be improved, one must first be able to define and measure exactly what we mean by 'performance'. Furthermore, benchmarking one's own activities and performance against other organizations' activities and performance can lead to valuable insights and help to quantify progress. It also helps to answer some basic improvement questions such as who should be in charge of it, when should it take place, and how one should go about ensuring that improvement really does impact the performance of the organization. This is why in this chapter we will deal with such issues as measuring performance, benchmarking, prioritization, learning and culture, and the role of systems of procedures in the implementation process.

Remember also that the issue of how improvement should be organized is not a new concern. It has been a concern of management writers for decades. For example, **W.E. Deming** (considered in Japan to be the father of quality control) asserted that quality starts with top management and is a strategic activity.[2] It is claimed that much of the success in terms of quality in Japanese industry was the result of his lectures to Japanese companies in the 1950s.[3] Deming's basic philosophy is that quality and productivity increase as 'process variability' (the unpredictability of the process) decreases. In his *14 points for quality improvement*, he emphasizes the need for statistical control methods, participation, education, openness and purposeful improvement:

1 Create constancy of purpose.
2 Adopt new philosophy.
3 Cease dependence on inspection.
4 End awarding business on price.
5 Improve constantly the system of production and service.
6 Institute training on the job.
7 Institute leadership.
8 Drive out fear.
9 Break down barriers between departments.
10 Eliminate slogans and exhortations.
11 Eliminate quotas or work standards.
12 Give people pride in their job.
13 Institute education and a self-improvement programme.
14 Put everyone to work to accomplish it.

Linking improvement to strategy

At one level, the objective of any improvement is obvious – it tries to make things better! But, does this mean better in every way or better in some specific manner? And how much better does better mean? This is why we need some more general framework to put any

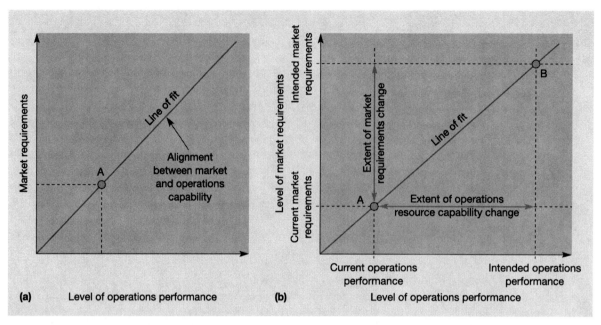

Figure 20.2 In operations improvement should achieve 'fit' between market requirements and operations performance

organization's improvement efforts into a broader context, preferably one that brings together an overall operation's performance with its market objectives. After all, at a strategic level, the whole purpose of operations improvement is to make operations performance better serve its markets. Figure 20.2(a) illustrates this idea by showing diagrammatically the approximate alignment or 'fit' between an operation's performance and the requirements of its markets.

The vertical dimension represents the level of market requirements either because they reflect the intrinsic needs of customers or because their expectations have been shaped by the firm's marketing activity. This includes such factors as the strength of brand and reputation, the degree of market differentiation and the extent of plausible market promises. Moving along this dimension indicates a broadly enhanced level of market performance. The horizontal scale represents the level of the organization's operations performance. This includes such things as its ability to achieve its competitive objectives and the efficiency with which it uses its resources. Again, moving along the dimension indicates a broadly enhanced level of operations performance and therefore operations capabilities. Be careful, however, in using this diagrammatic representation. It is a conceptual model rather than a practical tool. We have deliberately been vague in calibrating or even defining precisely the two axes in the figure. The model is intended merely to illustrate some ideas around the concept of strategic improvement.

In terms of the framework illustrated in Figure 20.2(a), improvement means three things.

1 *Achieving 'alignment'* – This means achieving an approximate balance between 'required market performance' and 'actual operations performance'. So when alignment is achieved a firm's customers do not need, or expect, levels of operations performance which it is unable to supply. Nor does the firm have operations strengths which are either inappropriate for market needs or remain unexploited in the market. The diagonal line in Figure 20.2(a) therefore represents a '**line of fit**' with market and operations in balance.

2 *Achieving 'sustainable' alignment* – It is not enough to achieve some degree of alignment to a single point in time. It also has to be sustained over time. So, asking the question 'how good are our operations at delivering the performance which our market requires?' is necessary but not sufficient over the long term. Equally important questions are 'how

Line of fit

could the market change and make current performance inadequate?' and 'how can we develop our operations processes so that they could adapt to the new market conditions?'

3 *Improving overall performance* – If the requirements placed on the organization by its markets are relatively undemanding, then the corresponding level of operations performance will not need to be particularly high. While the more demanding the level of market requirements, the greater will have to be the level of operations performance. But most firms would see their overall strategic objectives as achieving alignment at a level that implies some degree of long-term competitive success. In Figure 20.2(b) point A represents alignment at a low level, while point B represents alignment at a higher level. The assumption in most firms' operations strategies is that point B is a more desirable position than point A because it is more likely to represent a financially successful position. High levels of market performance, achieved as a result of high levels of operations performance being generally more difficult for competitors to match.

Deviating from the line of fit

During the improvement path from A to B in Figure 20.2 it may not be possible to maintain the balance between market requirements and operations performance. Sometimes the market may expect something that the operation cannot (temporarily) deliver. Sometimes operations may have capabilities that cannot be exploited in the market. At a strategic level, there are risks deriving from any deviation from the 'line of fit'. For example, delays in the improvement to a new web site could mean that customers do not receive the level of service they were promised. This is shown as position X in Figure 20.3. Under these circumstances, the risk to the organization is that its reputation (or brand) will suffer because market expectations exceed the operation's capability to perform at the appropriate level. At other times, the operation may make improvements before they could be fully exploited in the market. For example, the same online retailer may have improved its web site so that it can offer extra services, such as the ability to customize products, before those products have been stocked in its distribution centre. This means that, although an improvement to its ordering processes has been made, problems elsewhere in the company prevent the improvement from giving value to the company. This is represented by point Y on Figure 20.3. In both instances, improvement activity needs to move the operation back to the line of fit.

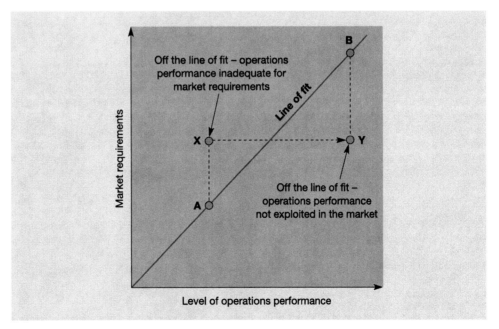

Figure 20.3 Deviation from the 'line of fit' between market requirements and operations performance can expose the operation to risk

Information for improvement

Before operations managers can devise their approach to the improvement of their operations, they need to know how good they are already. The urgency, direction and priorities of improvement will be determined partly by whether the current performance of an operation is judged to be good, bad or indifferent. Therefore all operations need some kind of **performance measurement** as a prerequisite for improvement.

Performance measurement

Performance measurement is the process of *quantifying action*, where measurement means the process of quantification and the performance of the operation is assumed to derive from actions taken by its management.[4] Performance here is defined as the degree to which an operation fulfils the five performance objectives at any point in time, in order to satisfy its customers. Some kind of *performance measurement* is a prerequisite for judging whether an operation is good, bad or indifferent. Without performance measurement, it would be impossible to exert any control over an operation on an ongoing basis. A performance measurement system that gives no help to ongoing improvement is only partially effective. The **polar diagrams** (which we introduced in Chapter 2) in Figure 20.4 illustrate this concept. The five performance objectives which we have used throughout this book can be regarded as the dimensions of overall performance that satisfy customers. The market's needs and expectations of each performance objective will vary. The extent to which an operation meets market requirements will also vary. In addition, market requirements and the operation's performance could change over time. In Figure 20.4 the operation is originally almost meeting the requirements of the market as far as quality and flexibility are concerned, but is under-performing on its speed, dependability and cost. Sometime later the operation has improved its speed and cost to match market requirements but its flexibility no longer matches market requirements, not because it has deteriorated in an absolute sense but because the requirements of the market have changed.

Performance measurement, as we are treating it here, concerns three generic issues.

- What factors to include as performance measures?
- Which are the most important performance measures?
- What detailed measures to use?

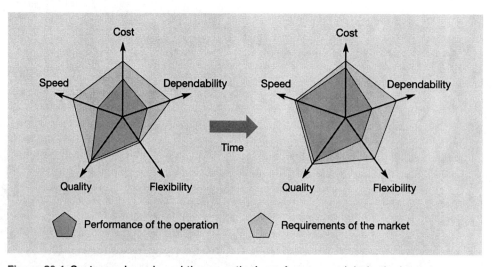

Figure 20.4 Customers' needs and the operation's performance might both change over time

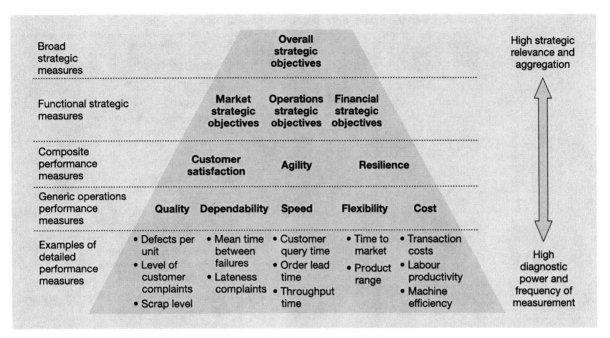

Figure 20.5 Performance measures can involve different levels of aggregation

What factors to include as performance measures?

The five generic performance objectives, quality, speed, dependability, flexibility and cost, can be broken down into more detailed measures, or they can be aggregated into 'composite' measures, such as 'customer satisfaction', 'overall service level', or 'operations agility'. These composite measures may be further aggregated by using measures such as 'achieve market objectives', 'achieve financial objectives', 'achieve operations objectives' or even 'achieve overall strategic objectives'. The more aggregated performance measures have greater strategic relevance insomuch as they help to draw a picture of the overall performance of the business, although by doing so they necessarily include many influences outside those that operations performance improvement would normally address. The more detailed performance measures are usually monitored more closely and more often, and although they provide a limited view of an operation's performance, they do provide a more descriptive and complete picture of what should be and what is happening within the operation. In practice, most organizations will choose to use performance targets from throughout the range. This idea is illustrated in Figure 20.5.

Choosing the important performance measures

One of the problems of devising a useful performance measurement system is trying to achieve some balance between having a few key measures on one hand (straightforward and simple, but may not reflect the full range of organizational objectives), and, on the other hand, having many detailed measures (complex and difficult to manage, but capable of conveying many nuances of performance). Broadly, a compromise is reached by making sure that there is a clear link between the operation's overall strategy, the most important (or '**key**') **performance indicators** (KPIs) that reflect strategic objectives, and the bundle of detailed measures that are used to 'flesh out' each key performance indicator. Obviously, unless strategy is well defined then it is difficult to 'target' a narrow range of key performance indicators.

Key performance indicators

What detailed measures to use?

The five performance objectives – quality, speed, dependability, flexibility and cost – are really composites of many smaller measures. For example, an operation's cost is derived from many factors which could include the purchasing efficiency of the operation, the efficiency

Table 20.1 Some typical partial measures of performance

Performance objective	Some typical measures
Quality	Number of defects per unit Level of customer complaints Scrap level Warranty claims Mean time between failures Customer satisfaction score
Speed	Customer query time Order lead time Frequency of delivery Actual *versus* theoretical throughput time Cycle time
Dependability	Percentage of orders delivered late Average lateness of orders Proportion of products in stock Mean deviation from promised arrival Schedule adherence
Flexibility	Time needed to develop new products/services Range of products/services Machine changeover time Average batch size Time to increase activity rate Average capacity/maximum capacity Time to change schedules
Cost	Minimum delivery time/average delivery time Variance against budget Utilization of resources Labour productivity Added value Efficiency Cost per operation hour

with which it converts materials, the productivity of its staff, the ratio of direct to indirect staff, and so on. All of these measures individually give a partial view of the operation's cost performance, and many of them overlap in terms of the information they include. However, each of them does give a perspective on the cost performance of an operation that could be useful either to identify areas for improvement or to monitor the extent of improvement. If an organization regards its 'cost' performance as unsatisfactory, disaggregating it into 'purchasing efficiency', 'operations efficiency', 'staff productivity', etc. might explain the root cause of the poor performance. Table 20.1 shows some of the partial measures which can be used to judge an operation's performance.

The balanced scorecard approach

Generally operations performance measures have been broadening in their scope. It is now generally accepted that the scope of measurement should, at some level, include external as well as internal, long-term as well as short-term, and 'soft' as well as 'hard' measures. The best-known manifestation of this trend is the **balanced scorecard** approach taken by Kaplan and Norton.

> The balanced scorecard approach brings together the elements that reflect a business's strategic position

'The balanced scorecard retains traditional financial measures. But financial measures tell the story of past events, an adequate story for industrial age companies for which investments in long-term capabilities are customer relationships were not critical for success. These financial measures are inadequate, however, for guiding and evaluating the journey that information age companies must make to create future value through investment in customers, suppliers, employees, processes, technology, and innovation.'[5]

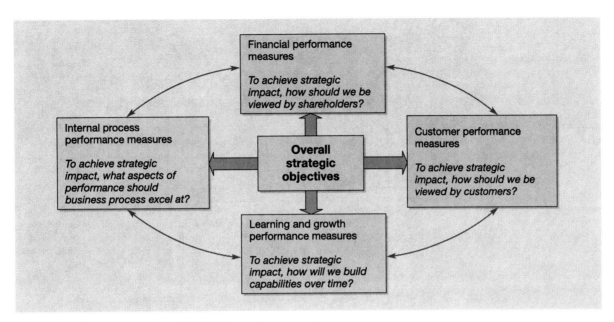

Figure 20.6 **The measures used in the balanced scorecard**

As well as including financial measures of performance, in the same way as traditional performance measurement systems, the balanced scorecard approach, also attempts to provide the important information that is required to allow the overall strategy of an organization to be reflected adequately in specific performance measures. In addition to financial measures of performance, it also includes more operational measures of customer satisfaction, internal processes, innovation and other improvement activities. In doing so it measures the factors behind financial performance which are seen as the key drivers of future financial success. In particular, it is argued that a balanced range of measures enables managers to address the following questions (see Figure 20.6).

- How do we look to our shareholders (financial perspective)?
- What must we excel at (internal process perspective)?
- How do our customers see us (the customer perspective)?
- How can we continue to improve and build capabilities (the learning and growth perspective)?

The balanced scorecard attempts to bring together the elements that reflect a business's strategic position, including product or service quality measures, product and service development times, customer complaints, labour productivity, and so on. At the same time it attempts to avoid performance reporting becoming unwieldy by restricting the number of measures and focusing especially on those seen to be essential. The advantages of the approach are that it presents an overall picture of the organization's performance in a single report, and by being comprehensive in the measures of performance it uses, encourages companies to take decisions in the interests of the whole organization rather than sub-optimizing around narrow measures. Developing a balanced scorecard is a complex process and is now the subject of considerable debate. One of the key questions that have to be considered is how specific measures of performance should be designed. Inadequately designed performance measures can result in dysfunctional behaviour, so teams of managers are often used to develop a scorecard which reflects their organization's specific needs.

Setting target performance

A performance measure means relatively little until it is compared against some kind of target. Knowing that only one document in five hundred is sent out to customers containing an error, tells us relatively little unless we know whether this is better or worse than we were

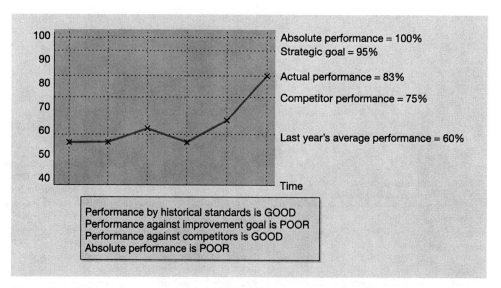

Figure 20.7 Different standards of comparison give different messages

achieving previously, and whether it is better or worse than other similar operations (especially competitors) are achieving. Setting performance targets transforms performance measures into performance 'judgements'. Several approaches to setting targets can be used, including the following.

- *Historically based targets* – targets that compare current against previous performance.
- *Strategic targets* – targets set to reflect the level of performance that is regarded as appropriate to achieve strategic objectives.
- *External performance-based targets* – targets set to reflect the performance that is achieved by similar, or competitor, external operations.
- *Absolute performance targets* – targets based on the theoretical upper limit of performance.

One of the problems in setting targets is that different targets can give very different messages regarding the improvement being achieved. So, for example, in Figure 20.7, one of an operation's performance measures is 'delivery' (in this case defined as the proportion of orders delivered on-time). The performance for one month has been measured at 83 per cent, but any judgement regarding performance will be dependent on the performance targets. Using a *historical* target, when compared to last year's performance of 60 per cent, this month's performance of 83 per cent is good. But, if the operation's *strategy* calls for a 95 per cent delivery performance, the actual performance of 83 per cent looks decidedly poor. The company may also be concerned with how they perform against *competitors'* performance. If competitors are currently averaging delivery performances of around 80 per cent the company's performance looks rather good. Finally, the more ambitious managers within the company may wish to at least try and seek perfection. Why not, they argue, use an *absolute* performance standard of 100 per cent delivery on time? Against this standard the company's actual 83 per cent again looks disappointing.

Performance measurement and performance management

It is worth noting the difference between performance *measurement*, which we describe here, and performance *management*. They are closely related (and sometimes are confused with each other). Performance management is broader than performance measurement. It is the 'process of assessing progress toward achieving predetermined goals. It involves building on that process, adding the relevant communication and action on the progress achieved against these predetermined goals. It helps organizations achieve their strategic goals'.[6] The objectives of performance management are to ensure coordination and coherence between individual, process or team objectives and overall strategic and organizational objectives. But more than that, performance management attempts to influence decisions, behaviours and skills development so that individuals and processes are better equipped to meet strategic objectives.

Benchmarking

Benchmarking, is 'the process of learning from others' and involves comparing one's own performance or methods against other comparable operations. It is a broader issue than setting performance targets, and includes investigating other organizations' operations practice in order to derive ideas that could contribute to performance improvement. Its rationale is based on the idea that (a) problems in managing processes are almost certainly shared by processes elsewhere, and (b) that there is probably another operation somewhere that has developed a better way of doing things. For example, a bank might learn some things from a supermarket about how it could cope with demand fluctuations during the day. **Benchmarking** is essentially about stimulating creativity in improvement practice.

Benchmarking is the process of learning from others

Types of benchmarking

There are many different types of benchmarking (which are not necessarily mutually exclusive), some of which are listed below:

- *Internal benchmarking* is a comparison between operations or parts of operations which are within the same total organization. For example, a large motor vehicle manufacturer with several factories might choose to benchmark each factory against the others.
- *External benchmarking* is a comparison between an operation and other operations which are part of a different organization.
- *Non-competitive benchmarking* is benchmarking against external organizations which do not compete directly in the same markets.
- *Competitive benchmarking* is a comparison directly between competitors in the same, or similar, markets.
- *Performance benchmarking* is a comparison between the levels of achieved performance in different operations. For example, an operation might compare its own performance in terms of some or all of our performance objectives – quality, speed, dependability, flexibility and cost – against other organizations' performance in the same dimensions.
- *Practice benchmarking* is a comparison between an organization's operations practices, or way of doing things, and those adopted by another operation. For example, a large retail store might compare its systems and procedures for controlling stock levels with those used by another department store.

Benchmarking as an improvement tool

Although benchmarking has become popular, some businesses have failed to derive maximum benefit from it. Partly this may be because there are some misunderstandings as to what benchmarking actually entails. First, it is not a 'one-off' project. It is best practised as a continuous process of comparison. Second, it does not provide 'solutions'. Rather, it provides ideas and information that can lead to solutions. Third, it does not involve simply copying or imitating other operations. It is a process of learning and adapting in a pragmatic manner. Fourth, it means devoting resources to the activity. Benchmarking cannot be done without some investment, but this does not necessarily mean allocating exclusive responsibility to a set of highly paid managers. In fact, there can be advantages in organizing staff at all levels to investigate and collate information from benchmarking targets.

Critical commentary

It can be argued that there is a fundamental flaw in the whole concept of benchmarking. Operations that rely on others to stimulate their creativity, especially those that are in search of 'best practice', are always limiting themselves to currently accepted methods of operating or currently accepted limits to performance. In other words, benchmarking leads companies only as far as others have gone. 'Best practice' is not 'best' in the sense that it cannot be bettered, it is only 'best' in the sense that it is the best one can currently find. Indeed accepting what is currently defined as 'best' may prevent operations from ever making the radical breakthrough or improvement that takes the concept of 'best' to a new and fundamentally improved level. This argument is closely related to the concept of breakthrough improvement discussed later in this chapter. Furthermore, methods or performance levels that are appropriate in one operation may not be in another. Because one operation has a set of successful practices in the way it manages its process does not mean that adopting those same practices in another context will prove equally successful. It is possible that subtle differences in the resources within a process (such as staff skills or technical capabilities) or the strategic context of an operation (for example, the relative priorities of performance objectives) will be sufficiently different to make the adoption of seemingly successful practices inappropriate.

Improvement priorities – what to start on?[7]

Improvement priorities

In Chapter 3, when discussing the 'market requirements' perspective, we identified two major influences on the way in which operations decide on their **improvement priorities**:

- the needs and preferences of customers;
- the performance and activities of competitors.

The consideration of customers' needs has particular significance in shaping the objectives of all operations. The fundamental purpose of operations is to create goods and services in such a way as to meet the needs of their customers. What customers find important, therefore, the operation should also regard as important. If customers for a particular product or service prefer low prices to wide range, then the operation should devote more energy to reducing its costs than to increasing the flexibility which enables it to provide a range of products or services. The needs and preferences of customers shape the *importance* of operations objectives within the operation.

The role of competitors is different from that of customers. Competitors are the points of comparison against which the operation can judge its performance. From a competitive viewpoint, as operations improve their performance, the improvement which matters most is that which takes the operation past the performance levels achieved by its competitors. The role of competitors then is in determining achieved *performance*.

Both importance and performance have to be brought together before any judgement can be made as to the relative priorities for improvement. Just because something is particularly important to its customers does not mean that an operation should necessarily give it immediate priority for improvement. It may be that the operation is already considerably better than its competitors at serving customers in this respect. Similarly, just because an operation is not very good at something when compared with its competitors' performance, it does not necessarily mean that it should be immediately improved. Customers may not particularly value this aspect of performance. Both importance and performance need to be viewed together to judge the prioritization of objectives.

(a) Importance scale for competitive factors	
Rating	**Description**
1	Provides a crucial advantage
2	Provides an important advantage
3	Provides a useful advantage
4	Needs to be up to good industry standards
5	Needs to be up to median industry standards
6	Needs to be within close range of rest of industry
7	Not usually important but could become so
8	Very rarely considered by customers
9	Never considered by customers

(b) Performance scale for competitive factors	
Rating	**Description**
1	Considerably better than competitors
2	Clearly better than competitors
3	Marginally better than competitors
4	Sometimes marginally better than competitors
5	About the same as most competitors
6	Slightly worse than the average of most competitors
7	Usually marginally worse than most competitors
8	Generally worse than most competitors
9	Consistently worse than competitors

Figure 20.8 Nine-point scales for judging importance and performance

Judging importance to customers

Order winners
Qualifiers
Less important

In Chapter 3 we introduced the idea of **order-winning, qualifying** and **less important** competitive factors. *Order-winning competitive factors* are those which directly win business for the operation. *Qualifying competitive factors* are those which may not win extra business if the operation improves its performance, but can certainly lose business if performance falls below a particular point, known as the qualifying level. *Less important competitive factors*, as their name implies, are those which are relatively unimportant compared with the others. In fact, to judge the relative importance of its competitive factors, an operation will usually need to use a slightly more discriminating scale. One way to do this is to take our three broad categories of competitive factors – order-winning, qualifying and less important – and to divide each category into three further points representing strong, medium and weak positions. Figure 20.8(a) illustrates such a scale.

Judging performance against competitors

At its simplest, a competitive performance standard would consist merely of judging whether the achieved performance of an operation is better than, the same, or worse than that of its competitors. However, in much the same way as the nine-point importance scale was derived, we can derive a more discriminating nine-point performance scale, as shown in Figure 20.8(b).

The importance–performance matrix

Importance–performance matrix

The priority for improvement which each competitive factor should be given can be assessed from a comparison of their importance and performance. This can be shown on an **importance–performance matrix** which, as its name implies, positions each competitive

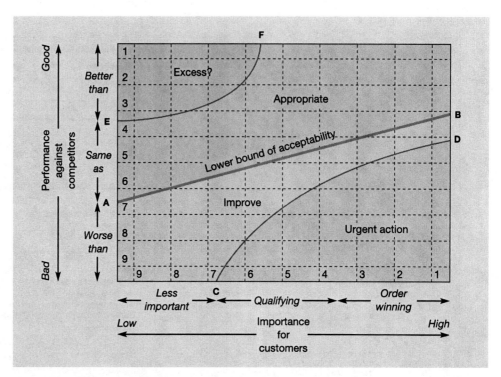

Figure 20.9 Priority zones in the importance–performance matrix

factor according to its scores or ratings on these criteria. Figure 20.9 shows an importance–performance matrix divided into zones of improvement priority. The first zone boundary is the 'lower bound of acceptability' shown as line AB in Figure 20.9. This is the boundary between acceptable and unacceptable performance. When a competitive factor is rated as relatively unimportant (8 or 9 on the importance scale), this boundary will in practice be low. Most operations are prepared to tolerate performance levels which are 'in the same ballpark' as their competitors (even at the bottom end of the rating) for unimportant competitive factors. They only become concerned when performance levels are clearly below those of their competitors. Conversely, when judging competitive factors which are rated highly (1 or 2 on the importance scale) they will be markedly less sanguine at poor or mediocre levels of performance. Minimum levels of acceptability for these competitive factors will usually be at the lower end of the 'better than competitors' class. Below this minimum bound of acceptability (AB) there is clearly a need for improvement; above this line there is no immediate urgency for any improvement. However, not all competitive factors falling below the minimum line will be seen as having the same degree of improvement priority. A boundary approximately represented by line CD represents a distinction between an urgent priority zone and a less urgent improvement zone. Similarly, above the line AB, not all competitive factors are regarded as having the same priority. The line EF can be seen as the approximate boundary between performance levels which are regarded as 'good' or 'appropriate' on one hand and those regarded as 'too good' or 'excess' on the other. Segregating the matrix in this way results in four zones which imply very different priorities:

- *The 'appropriate' zone* – competitive factors in this area lie above the lower bound of acceptability and so should be considered satisfactory.
- *The 'improve' zone* – lying below the lower bound of acceptability, any factors in this zone must be candidates for improvement.
- *The 'urgent-action' zone* – these factors are important to customers but performance is below that of competitors. They must be considered as candidates for immediate improvement.

- *The 'excess?' zone* – factors in this area are 'high-performing', but not important to customers. The question must be asked, therefore, whether the resources devoted to achieving such a performance could be used better elsewhere.

Worked example

EXL Laboratories is a subsidiary of an electronics company. It carries out research and development as well as technical problem-solving work for a wide range of companies, including companies in its own group. It is particularly keen to improve the level of service which it gives to its customers. However, it needs to decide which aspect of its performance to improve first. It has devised a list of the most important aspects of its service:

- *The quality of its technical solutions* – the perceived appropriateness by customers.
- *The quality of its communications with customers* – the frequency and usefulness of information.
- *The quality of post-project documentation* – the usefulness of the documentation which goes with the final report.
- *Delivery speed* – the time between customer request and the delivery of the final report.
- *Delivery dependability* – the ability to deliver on the promised date.
- *Delivery flexibility* – the ability to deliver the report on a revised date.
- *Specification flexibility* – the ability to change the nature of the investigation.
- *Price* – the total charge to the customer.

EXL assigns a score to each of these factors using the 1–9 scale described in Figure 20.8. After this, EXL turned their attention to judging the laboratory's performance against competitor organizations. Although they have benchmarked information for some aspects of performance, they have to make estimates for the others. Both these scores are shown in Figure 20.10.

EXL Laboratories plotted the importance and performance ratings it had given to each of its competitive factors on an importance–performance matrix. This is shown in Figure 20.11. It shows that the most important aspect of competitiveness – the ability to deliver sound technical solutions to its customers – falls comfortably within the appropriate zone. Specification flexibility and delivery flexibility are also in the appropriate zone, although only just. Both delivery speed and delivery dependability seem to be in

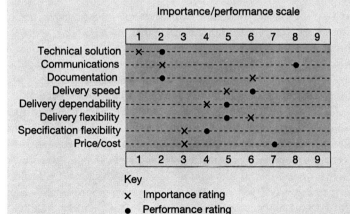

Figure 20.10 Rating 'importance to customers' and 'performance against competitors' on the nine-point scales for EXL Laboratories

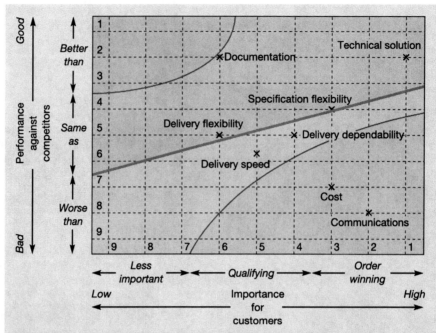

Figure 20.11 The importance–performance matrix for EXL Laboratories

need of improvement as each is below the minimum level of acceptability for their respective importance positions. However, two competitive factors, communications and cost/price, are clearly in need of immediate improvement. These two factors should therefore be assigned the most urgent priority for improvement. The matrix also indicates that the company's documentation could almost be regarded as 'too good'.

The matrix may not reveal any total surprises. The competitive factors in the 'urgent-action' zone may be known to be in need of improvement already. However, the exercise is useful for two reasons:

- It helps to discriminate between many factors which may be in need of improvement.
- The exercise gives purpose and structure to the debate on improvement priorities.

The sandcone theory

As well as approaches that base improvement priority given on an operation's specific circumstances, some authorities believe that there is also a generic 'best' sequence of improvement. The best-known theory is called *the sandcone theory*,[8] so called because the sand is analogous to management effort and resources. Building a stable **sandcone** needs a stable foundation of quality, upon which one can build layers of dependability, speed, flexibility and cost, see Figure 20.12. Building up improvement is thus a cumulative process, not a sequential one. Moving on to the second priority for improvement does not mean dropping the first, and so on. According to the sandcone theory: the first priority should be *quality*, since this is a precondition to all lasting improvement. Only when the operation has reached a minimally acceptable level in quality should it then tackle the next issue, that of internal *dependability*. Importantly though, moving on to include dependability in the improvement process will actually require further improvement in quality. Once a critical level of dependability is reached, enough to provide some stability to the operation, the next stage is to improve the *speed* of internal throughput. But again only while continuing to improve quality and dependability further. Soon it will become evident that the most effective way to improve speed is through improvements in response *flexibility*, that is,

The sandcone theory holds that objectives should be prioritized in a particular order

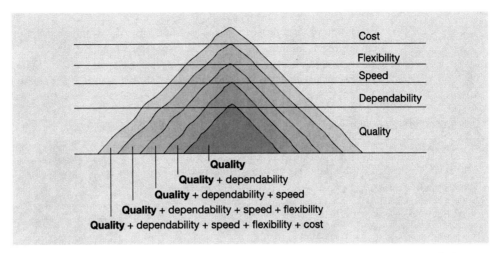

Figure 20.12 The sandcone model of improvement: cost reduction relies on a cumulative foundation of improvement in the other performance objectives

changing things within the operation faster. Again, including flexibility in the improvement process should not divert attention from continuing to work further on quality, dependability and speed. Only now, according to the sandcone theory, should *cost* be tackled head-on.

Improvement culture

Culture is the pattern of shared assumption

It is generally held by most organizational theorists that an organization's ability to improve its operations performance depends to a large extent on its '**culture**'. By 'organizational culture' we here mean '*the pattern of shared basic assumptions . . . that have worked well enough to be considered valid*',[9] or as some put it, '*the way we do things around here*'. Professor Gerry Johnson[10] is more specific, describing the elements of organizational culture as follows.

- The organization's mission and values
- Its control systems
- Its organizational structures, hierarchies, and processes
- Its power structures
- Its symbols, logos and designs including its symbols of power
- Its rituals, meetings and routines
- Its stories and myths that develop about people and events.

So, organizational culture and improvement are clearly related. A receptive organizational culture that encourages a constant search for improved ways to do things nurtures improvement. At the same time the organization's view of improvement is an important indication of its culture. But what is meant by 'an improvement culture'? Here we look at two aspects, first are the various elements that make up an improvement culture, second is the recurring theme of 'learning' as a key element of improvement culture.

Building an improvement capability

The ability to improve, especially on a continuous basis, is not something which always comes naturally to operations managers and staff. There are specific abilities, behaviours and actions which need to be consciously developed if improvement is to be sustained over the long term. Bessant and Caffyn[11] distinguish between what they call 'organizational abilities' (the capacity or aptitude to adopt a particular approach to continuous improvement), 'constituent behaviours' (the routines of behaviour which staff adopt and which reinforce the approach to continuous improvement) and 'enablers' (the procedural devices or techniques used to progress the continuous improvement effort). They identify six generic organizational abilities, each with its own set of constituent behaviours. These are identified

Table 20.2 Continuous improvement (CI) abilities and some associated behaviours

Organizational ability	Constituent behaviours
Getting the CI habit Developing the ability to generate sustained involvement in CI	People use formal problem-finding and solving cycle
	People use simple tools and techniques
	People use simple measurement to shape the improvement process
	Individuals and/or groups initiate and carry through CI activities – they participate in the process
	Ideas are responded to in a timely fashion – either implemented or otherwise dealt with
	Managers support the CI process through allocation of resources
	Managers recognize in formal ways the contribution of employees to CI
	Managers lead by example, becoming actively involved in design and implementation of CI
	Managers support experiment by not punishing mistakes, but instead encouraging learning from them
Focusing on CI Generating and sustaining the ability to link CI activities to the strategic goals of the company	Individuals and groups use the organization's strategic objectives to prioritize improvements
	Everyone is able to explain what the operation's strategy and objectives are
	Individuals and groups assess their proposed changes against the operation's objectives
	Individuals and groups monitor/measure the results of their improvement activity
	CI activities are an integral part of the individual's or group's work, not a parallel activity
Spreading the word Generating the ability to move CI activity across organizational boundaries	People cooperate in cross-functional groups
	People understand and share a holistic view (process understanding and ownership)
	People are oriented towards internal and external customers in their CI activity
	Specific CI projects with outside agencies (customers, suppliers, etc.) take place
	Relevant CI activities involve representatives from different organizational levels
CI on the CI system Generating the ability to manage strategically the development of CI	The CI system is continually monitored and developed
	There is a cyclical planning process whereby the CI system is regularly reviewed and amended
	There is periodic review of the CI system in relation to the organization as a whole
	Senior management make available sufficient resources (time, money, personnel) to support the continuing development of the CI system
	The CI system itself is designed to fit within the current structure and infrastructure
	When a major organizational change is planned, its potential impact on the CI system is assessed
Walking the talk Generating the ability to articulate and demonstrate CI's values	The 'management style' reflects commitment to CI values
	When something goes wrong, people at all levels look for reasons why, rather than blame individuals
	People at all levels demonstrate a shared belief in the value of small steps and that everyone can contribute, by themselves being actively involved in making and recognizing incremental improvements
Building the learning organization Generating the ability to learn through CI activity	Everyone learns from their experiences, both good and bad
	Individuals seeks out opportunities for learning/personal development
	Individuals and groups at all levels share their learning
	The organization captures and shares the learning of individuals and groups
	Managers accept and act on all the learning that takes place
	Organizational mechanisms are used to deploy what has been learned across the organization

in Table 20.2. Examples of enablers are the improvement techniques that were described in Chapter 18.

Improvement as learning

Note that many of the abilities and behaviours describes in Table 20.2 are directly or indirectly related to learning in some way. This is not surprising given that operations improvement implies some kind of intervention or change to the operation, and change will be evaluated in terms of whatever improvement occurs. This evaluation adds to our knowledge of how the operation really works, which in turn increases the chances that future interventions will also result in improvement. This idea of an improvement cycle was discussed in Chapter 18. What is important is to realize that it is a learning process, and it is crucial that improvement is organized so that it encourages, facilitates and exploits the learning that occurs during improvement. This requires us to recognize that there is a distinction between single- and double-loop learning.[12]

Single- and double-loop learning

Single-loop learning
Single-loop learning

Single-loop learning occurs when there is a repetitive and predictable link between cause and effect. Statistical process control (see Chapter 17), for example, measures output characteristics from a process, such as product weight, telephone response time, etc. These can then be used to alter input conditions, such as supplier quality, manufacturing consistency, staff training, with the intention of 'improving' the output. Every time an operational error or problem is detected, it is corrected or solved, and more is learned about the process. However, this happens without questioning or altering the underlying values and objectives of the process, which may, over time, create an unquestioning inertia that prevents it adapting to a changing environment. **Double-loop learning**, by contrast, questions the fundamental objectives or service or even the underlying culture of the operation. This kind of learning implies an ability to challenge existing operating assumptions in a fundamental way. It seeks to re-frame competitive assumptions and remain open to any changes in the competitive environment. But being receptive to new opportunities sometimes requires abandoning existing operating routines which may be difficult to achieve in practice, especially as many operations reward experience and past achievement (rather than potential) at both an individual and a group level. Figure 20.13 illustrates single and double-loop learning.

Double-loop learning

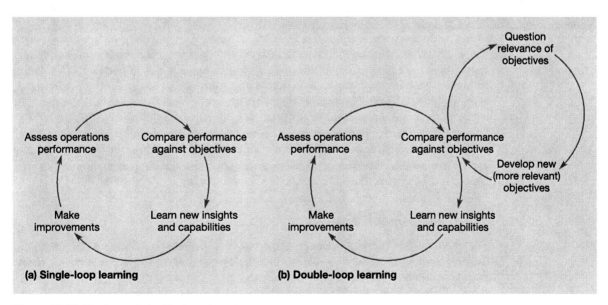

Figure 20.13 Single- and double-loop learning

Short case
Improvement at Heineken – Part II[13]

The improvement approach of Heineken's Zoeterwoude facility was described in Chapter 18. Although this description emphasized issues such as target setting and the use of techniques, of equal or more importance in making a success of the initiative was the way improvement teams were empowered, organized and motivated. In fact, before this improvement initiative, the company had started a 'cultural change' programme. *'Its aim'*, according to Wilbert Raaijmakers, the Brewery Director, *'was to move away from a command-and-control situation and evolve towards a more team-oriented organization.'* Fundamental to this was a programme to improve the skills and knowledge of individual operators through special training programmes. Nevertheless, the improvement initiative exposed a number of challenges. For example, the improvement team discovered that it was easier to motivate people to work on improvements when the demand on the plant clearly exceeded its capacity. What was more difficult was to keep them focused when the pressures of keeping up production levels were lower, such as during the winter season. In an attempt to overcome this, communication was improved so that staff were kept fully informed of future production levels and the upcoming schedule of training and maintenance activities that were planned during

slumps in demand. The lesson that the improvement team learnt was that it is difficult to convince people of the necessity for change if they are not aware of the underlying reason for it. Notwithstanding these efforts it soon became evident that some groups were more ready to make changes than others. Some staff much preferred to stick with their traditional methods rather than explore how these could be improved. Similarly, some team leaders were more skilled at encouraging change than others. Many staff needed coaching and reassurance as well as more formal training on how to take ownership of problems and focus on achieving results in line with targets. Also, it was found that setting improvement targets in a step-by-step series of milestones could help to maintain the momentum of motivation.

During the improvement initiative, Heineken staff worked closely with a group of consultants (Celerant Consulting). Towards the end of the initiative, as is common in such improvement projects, the consultants gradually reduced their involvement to allow Heineken staff to take over control of the initiative. At this point there was a dip in the momentum of the improvement project. It needed the appointment of a special coordinator within the company to 'monitor, secure and audit' the various activities included in the project before it regained its momentum. Yet it did regain its momentum and, looking back over the experience, Heineken see one of the most significant outcomes from the initiative as its success in bringing home to every person in the company the realization that improvement is an ongoing process.

Implementing improvement

Not all of the improvement initiatives which are launched by organizations, often with high expectations, will go on to fulfil their potential of having a major impact on performance. Estimates of failure in improvement efforts range from half to 80 per cent of programmes, resulting in the companies implementing them becoming disillusioned with the results. Yet, although there are many examples of improvement efforts that have failed, there are also examples of successful implementations. So why do some improvement efforts disappoint? Some reasons we have already identified – an organizational culture that discourages any change for example. But there are some more tangible causes of implementation failure. The remainder of this chapter will be devoted to some of these.

Top-management support

Top-management support

The importance of **top-management support** goes far beyond the allocation of resources to the programme; it sets the priorities for the whole organization. If the organization's senior managers do not understand and show commitment to the programme, it is only understandable that others will ask why they should do so. Usually this is taken to mean that top management must:

- understand and believe in the benefits of the improvement approach
- communicate the principles and techniques of improvement
- participate in the improvement process
- formulate and maintain a clear 'improvement strategy'.

This last point is particularly important. Without thinking through the overall purpose and long-term goals of improvement it is difficult for any organization to know where it is going. An improvement strategy is necessary to provide the goals and guidelines which help to keep improvement efforts in line with strategic aims. Specifically, the improvement strategy should have something to say about the competitive priorities of the organization, the roles and improvement responsibilities of all parts of the organization, the resources available for improvement, and its overall improvement philosophy.

Senior managers may not fully understand the improvement approach

In Chapter 18, we described how there were several (related) improvement approaches. Each of these approaches is the subject of several books that describe them in great detail. There is no shortage of advice from consultants and academics as to how they should be used. Yet it is not difficult to find examples of where senior management have used one or more of these approaches without fully understanding them. The details of Six Sigma or lean, for example, are not simply technical matters. They are fundamental to how appropriate the approach could be in different contexts. Not every approach fits every set of circumstances. So understanding in detail what each approach means must be the first step in deciding whether it is appropriate.

Avoid excessive 'hype'

Operations improvement has, to some extent, become a fashion industry with new ideas and concepts continually being introduced as offering a novel way to improve business performance. There is nothing intrinsically wrong with this. Fashion stimulates and refreshes, through introducing novel ideas. Without it, things would stagnate. The problem lies not with new improvement ideas, but rather with some managers becoming victims of the process, where some new idea will entirely displace whatever went before. Most new ideas have something to say, but jumping from one fad to another will not only generate a backlash against any new idea, but also destroy the ability to accumulate the experience that comes from experimenting with each one. Avoiding becoming an improvement fashion victim is not easy. It requires that those directing the strategy process take responsibility for a number of issues.

(a) They must take responsibility for improvement as an ongoing activity, rather than becoming champions for only one specific improvement initiative.
(b) They must take responsibility for understanding the underlying ideas behind each new concept. Improvement is not 'following a recipe' or 'painting by numbers'. Unless one understands *why* improvement ideas are supposed to work, it is difficult to understand *how* they can be made to work properly.
(c) They must take responsibility for understanding the antecedents to a 'new' improvement idea, because it helps to understand it better and to judge how appropriate it may be for one's own operation.
(d) They must be prepared to adapt new ideas so that they make sense within the context of their own operation. 'One size' rarely fits all.
(e) They must take responsibility for the (often significant) education and learning effort that will be needed if new ideas are to be intelligently exploited.
(f) Above all they must avoid the over-exaggeration and hype that many new ideas attract. Although it is sometimes tempting to exploit the motivational 'pull' of new ideas

through slogans, posters and exhortations, carefully thought-out plans will always be superior in the long run, and will help avoid the inevitable backlash that follows 'over-selling' a single approach.

Short case
Work-Out at GE[14]

The idea of including all staff in the process of improvement has formed the core of many improvement approaches. One of the best-known ways of this is the 'Work-Out' approach that originated in the US conglomerate GE. Jack Welch, the then boss of GE, reputedly developed the approach to recognize that employees were an important source of brainpower for new and creative ideas, and as a mechanism for *'creating an environment that pushes towards a relentless, endless companywide search for a better way to do everything we do'*. The Work-Out programme was seen as a way to reduce the bureaucracy often associated with improvement and *'giving every employee, from managers to factory workers, an opportunity to influence and improve GE's day-to-day operations'*. According to Welch, Work-Out was meant to help people stop *'wrestling with the boundaries, the absurdities that grow in large organizations. We're all familiar with those absurdities: too many approvals, duplication, pomposity, waste. Work-Out in essence turned the company upside down, so that the workers told the bosses what to do. That forever changed the way people behaved at the company. Work-Out is also designed to reduce, and ultimately eliminate all of the waste hours and energy that organizations like GE typically expend in performing day-to-day operations.'* GE also used what it called 'town meetings' of employees. And although proponents of Work-Out emphasize the need to modify the specifics of the approach to fit the context in which it is applied, there is a broad sequence of activities implied within the approach:

- Staff, other key stakeholders and their manager hold a meeting away from the operation (a so-called 'off-siter').
- At this meeting the manager gives the group the responsibility to solve a problem or set of problems shared by the group but which are ultimately the manager's responsibility.
- The manager then leaves and the group spend time (maybe two or three days) working on developing

Source: Getty Images

solutions to the problems, sometimes using outside facilitators.
- At the end of the meeting, the responsible manager (and sometimes the manager's boss) rejoins the group to be presented with its recommendations.
- The manager can respond in three ways to each recommendation; 'yes', 'no' or 'I have to consider it more'. If it is the last response the manager must clarify what further issues must be considered and how and when the decision will be made.

Work-Out programmes are expensive; outside facilitators, off-site facilities and the payroll costs of a sizeable group of people meeting away from work can be substantial, even without considering the potential disruption to everyday activities. But arguably the most important implications of adopting Work-Out are cultural. In its purest form Work-Out reinforces an underlying culture of fast (and some would claim, superficial) problem-solving. It also relies on full and near universal employee involvement and empowerment together with direct dialogue between managers and their subordinates. What distinguishes the Work-Out approach from the many other types of group-based problem-solving is fast decision-making and the idea that managers must respond immediately and decisively to team suggestions. But some claim that it is intolerant of staff and managers who are not committed to its values. In fact, it is acknowledged in GE that resistance to the process or outcome is not tolerated and that obstructing the efforts of the Work-Out process is 'a career-limiting move'.

Improvement or quality awards

Deming Prize
Malcolm Baldrige
National Quality Award
European Quality Award

Various bodies have sought to stimulate improvement through establishing improvement (sometimes called 'quality') awards. The three best-known awards are the **Deming Prize**, the **Malcolm Baldrige National Quality Award** and the **European Quality Award**.

The Deming Prize

The Deming Prize was instituted by the Union of Japanese Scientists and Engineers in 1951 and is awarded to those companies, initially in Japan, but more recently opened to overseas companies, which have successfully applied 'company-wide quality control' based upon statistical quality control. There are 10 major assessment categories: policy and objectives, organization and its operation, education and its extension, assembling and disseminating of information, analysis, standardization, control, quality assurance, effects and future plans. The applicants are required to submit a detailed description of quality practices. This is a significant activity in itself and some companies claim a great deal of benefit from having done so.

The Malcolm Baldrige National Quality Award

In the early 1980s the American Productivity and Quality Center recommended that an annual prize, similar to the Deming Prize, should be awarded in America. The purpose of the awards was to stimulate American companies to improve quality and productivity, to recognize achievements, to establish criteria for a wider quality effort and to provide guidance on quality improvement. The main examination categories are: leadership, information and analysis, strategic quality planning, human resource utilization, quality assurance of products and services, quality results and customer satisfaction. The process, like that of the Deming Prize, includes a detailed application and site visits.

The EFQM Excellence Model

The EFQM Excellence Model, or Business Excellence Model

In 1988, 14 leading Western European companies formed the European Foundation for Quality Management (EFQM). An important objective of the EFQM is to recognize quality achievement. Because of this, it launched the European Quality Award (EQA), awarded to the most successful exponent of total quality management in Europe each year. To receive a prize, companies must demonstrate that their approach to total quality management has contributed significantly to satisfying the expectations of customers, employees and others with an interest in the company for the past few years. In 1999, the model on which the European Quality Award was based was modified and renamed **The EFQM Excellence Model or Business Excellence Model**. The changes made were not fundamental but did attempt to reflect some new areas of management and quality thinking (for example, partnerships and innovation) and placed more emphasis on customer and market focus. It is based on the idea that the outcomes of quality management in terms of what it calls 'people results', 'customer results', 'society results' and 'key performance results' are achieved through a number of 'enablers'. These enablers are leadership and constancy of purpose, policy and strategy, how the organization develops its people, partnerships and resources, and the way it organizes its processes. These ideas are incorporated in the EFQM Excellence Model as shown in Figure 20.14. The five enablers are concerned with how results are being achieved, while the four 'results' are concerned with what the company has achieved and is achieving.

Self-assessment

Self-assessment

The European Foundation for Quality Management (EFQM) defines **self-assessment** as '*a comprehensive, systematic, and regular review of an organization's activities and results referenced against a model of business excellence*', in its case the model shown in Figure 20.14. The main advantage of using such models for self-assessment seems to be that companies find it easier to understand some of the more philosophical concepts of TQM when they are translated into specific areas, questions and percentages. Self-assessment also allows organizations to measure their progress in changing their organization and in achieving the benefits of TQM. An important aspect of self-assessment is an organization's ability to judge the relative importance of the assessment categories to its own circumstances. The EFQM Excellence Model originally placed emphasis on a generic set of weighting for each of its nine categories. With the increasing importance of self-assessment, the EFQM moved to encourage organizations using its model to allocate their own weightings in a rational and systematic manner.

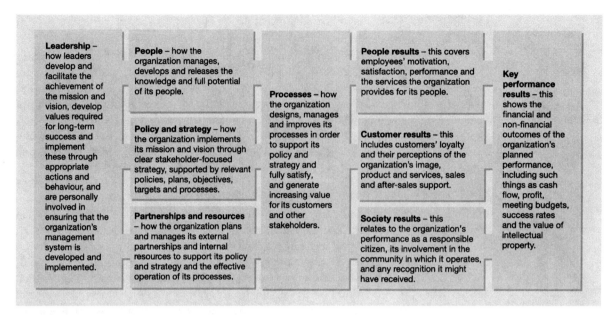

Figure 20.14 The EFQM Excellence Model

Summary answers to key questions

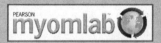

Check and improve your understanding of this chapter using self assessment questions and a personalised study plan, audio and video downloads, and an eBook – all at www.myomlab.com.

➤ Why does improvement need organizing?

▪ Improvement does not just happen by itself. It needs organizing, information must be gathered so that improvement is treating the most appropriate issues, responsibility for looking after the improvement effort must be allocated, and resources must be allocated. It must also be linked to the organization's overall strategy. Without these decisions, it is unlikely that real improvement will take place.

➤ How should the improvement effort be linked to strategy?

▪ At a strategic level, the whole purpose of operations improvement is to make operations performance better serve its markets. Therefore there should be approximate alignment or 'fit' between an operation's performance and the requirements of its markets. In fact, improvement should do three things to achieve this:

   1 It should achieve an approximate balance between 'required market performance' and 'actual operations performance'.

   2 It should make this alignment 'sustainable' over time.

   3 It should 'move up' the line of fit, the assumption being that high levels of market performance, achieved as a result of high levels of operations performance are difficult for competitors to match.

➤ What information is needed for improvement?

- It is unlikely that for any operation a single measure of performance will adequately reflect the whole of a performance objective. Usually operations have to collect a whole bundle of partial measures of performance.

- Each partial measure then has to be compared against some performance standard. There are four types of performance standard commonly used:
    - historical standards, which compare performance now against performance sometime in the past;
    - target performance standards, which compare current performance against some desired level of performance;
    - competitor performance standards, which compare current performance against competitors' performance;
    - absolute performance standards, which compare current performance against its theoretically perfect state.

- The process of benchmarking is often used as a means of obtaining competitor performance standards.

➤ What should be improvement priorities?

- Improvement priorities can be determined by bringing together the relative importance of each performance objective or competitive factor as judged by customers, with the performance which the operation achieves as compared with its competition. This idea can be consolidated on an 'importance–performance matrix'.

- The 'sandcone model' provides an alternative approach to prioritization. It recommends that improvement should cumulatively emphasize quality, dependability, speed, flexibility, and then cost.

➤ How can organizational culture affect improvement?

- An organization's ability to improve its operations performance depends to a large extent on its 'culture', that is '*the pattern of shared basic assumptions . . . that have worked well enough to be considered valid*'. A receptive organizational culture that encourages a constant search for improved ways to do things can encourage improvement.

- According to Bessant and Caffyn there are specific abilities, behaviours and actions which need to be consciously developed if improvement is to sustain over the long term.

- Many of the abilities and behaviours related to an improvement culture relate to learning in some way. The learning process is important because it encourages, facilitates and exploits the learning that occurs during improvement. This involves two types of learning, single- and double-loop learning.
    - Single-loop learning occurs when there is repetitive and predictable link between cause and effect.
    - Double-loop learning questions the fundamental objectives, service or even the underlying culture of the operation.

➤ **What are the key implementation issues?**

▪ Improvement efforts often fail (estimates range from half to 80 per cent of programmes failing). Included in the reasons for this are the following.
  – Top-management support may be lacking
  – Senior managers may not fully understand the improvement approach
  – The improvement may be 'hyped up' excessively, leading to unrealistic (and therefore unrealized) expectations
  – Implementation problems may not be anticipated.

▪ ISO 9000 and its associated family of standards may be used to provide a structure around improvement implementation. They are concerned with the processes and procedures that support quality.

▪ So-called 'quality awards' and models may contribute towards implementation of improvement by providing a focused structure for organizations to assess their improvement efforts. The best known of these is probably the EFQM (Business Excellence Model). This is based on a nine-point model which distinguishes between the 'enablers' of quality and the 'results' of quality. It is often now used as a self-certification model.

Case study
Re-inventing Singapore's libraries[15]

By Professors Robert Johnston, Warwick Business School, Chai Kah Hin and Jochen Wirtz, National University of Singapore, and Christopher Lovelock, Yale University.

The National Library Board (NLB) in Singapore oversees the management of the national, reference, regional, community and children's libraries, as well as over 30 libraries belonging to government agencies, schools and private institutions. Over the last 15 years the NLB has completely changed the nature of libraries in Singapore and its work has been used as a blueprint for many other libraries across the world. Yet it was not always like this. In 1995 libraries in Singapore were traditional, quiet places full of old books where you went to study or borrow books if you could not afford to buy them. There were long queues to have books stamped or returned and the staff seemed unhelpful and unfriendly. But today, things are very different. There are cafés in libraries to encourage people to come in, browse and sit down with a book, and libraries in community centres (putting libraries where the people are). The NLB has developed specialist libraries aimed at children, libraries in shopping malls aimed at attracting busy 18–35-year-olds into the library while they are shopping. There are libraries dedicated to teenagers, one of the most difficult groups to entice into the library. These have

Source: National Library Board Singapore

even been designed by the teenagers themselves so they include drinks machines, cushions and music systems. The library also hosts a wide range of events from mother and baby reading sessions to rock concerts to encourage a wide range of people into the library.

'We started this journey back in 1995 when Dr Christopher Chia was appointed as Chief Executive. Looking back, we were a very traditional public service. Our customers used words like "cold" and "unfriendly", though, in fairness, our staff were working under great *pressure to deal with the long queues for books and to answer enquiries on library materials posed by our customers. Christopher Chia and his team made a study of the problems, undertook surveys and ran focus groups. They then began to address the challenges with vision and imagination through the application of the project management methodology and the innovative use of technology. Staff involvement and contribution was key to the success of the transformation. We knew where we wanted to go, and were committed to the cause.'* (Ms Ngian Lek Choh, the Deputy Chief Executive and Director of the National Library)

Underpinning many of the changes was the NLB's innovative use of technology. It was the first public library in the world to prototype radio-frequency identification (RFID) to create its Electronic Library Management System (ELiMS). RFID is an electronic system for automatically identifying items. It uses RFID tags, or transponders, which are contained in smart labels consisting of a silicon chip and coiled antenna. They receive and respond to radio-frequency queries from an RFID transceiver, which enables the remote and automatic retrieval, storing and sharing of information (see Chapter 8). RFID tags are installed in its 10 million books making it one of the largest users of the technology in the world. Customers spend very little time queuing, with book issuing and returns automated. Indeed books can be returned to any of the NLB's 24-hour book drops (which look a bit like ATM machines) where RFID enables not only fast and easy returns but also fast and easy sorting. The NLB has also launched a mobile service via SMS (text messaging). This allows users to manage their library accounts anytime and anywhere through their mobile phones. They can check their loan records, renew their books, pay library payments, and get reminder alerts to return library items before the due-date.

Improving its services meant fully understanding the Library's customers. Customers were studied using surveys and focus groups to understand how the library added value for customers, how customers could be segmented, the main learning and reading motivators, and people's general reading habits. And feedback from customers, both formal and informal, is an important source of design innovation – as are ideas from staff. Everyone in NLB, from the chief executive to the library assistant is expected to contribute to work improvement and innovations. So much so that innovation has become an integral part of NLB's culture, leading to a steady stream of both large and small innovations. In order to facilitate this, the chief executive holds *'express-o'* sessions discussions with staff. He also has a strategy called 'ask stupid questions' (ASQ) which encourages staff to challenge what is normally accepted. Dr Varaprasad, the chief executive commented, *'In my view there are no stupid questions there are only stupid answers! What we try to do is engage the staff by letting them feel they can ask stupid questions and that they are entitled to an answer.'*

The NLB also makes use of small improvement teams to brainstorm ideas and test them out with colleagues from other libraries across the island. Good ideas attract financial rewards from S$5 to $1,000. One such idea was using a simple system of coloured bands on the spines of books (representing the identification number of each book) which make it much easier to shelve the books in the right places and also spot books that have been misplaced by customers. Staff are also encouraged to travel overseas to visit other libraries to learn about how they use their space, their programmes and collections, attend and speak at conventions and also visit very different organizations to get new ideas. The automatic book return for example was an idea borrowed and modified from the Mass Rapid Transport stations in Hong Kong where, with the flash of a card, the user is identified and given access across the system. NLB applied a similar line of thought for seamless check-in and check-out of books and a return anywhere concept. NLB harvests ideas from many different industries including logistics, manufacturing, IT and supermarkets. However, some elements of NLB's improvement process have changed. In the early days their approach to implementing ideas was informal and intuitive. It is now much more structured. Now, each good idea that comes forward is managed as a project, starting with a 'proof of concept' stage which involves selling the idea to management and checking with a range of people that the idea seems feasible. Then the services or processes are re-engineered, often involving customers or users. The new concepts are then prototyped and piloted allowing managers to gather customer feedback to enable them to assess, refine and, if appropriate, develop them for other sites.

Questions

1 How would the culture of NLB have changed in order for it to make such improvements?

2 Where did the ideas for improvement originate? And how did NLB encourage improvement ideas?

3 Why, do you think, has the improvement process become more systematic over the years?

4 What could be the biggest challenges to NLB's improvement activities in the future?

Problems and applications

These problems and applications will help to improve your analysis of operations. You can find more practice problems as well as worked examples and guided solutions on MyOMLab at www.myomlab.com.

1 Reread the 'Operations in action' piece at the beginning of the chapter on 'Taxing quality' which describes the improvement initiative carried out by the Aarhus region customs and tax unit.

    (a) How does the idea of a customer-focused approach to improvement need to be adapted for a customs and tax unit.

    (b) Generally, how might the ideas of improvement organization outlined in this chapter need to be adapted for public-sector operations such as this one?

2 What are the differences and similarities between the approach taken by the Aarhus customs and tax unit and the example described in the short case on 'Improvement at Heineken'?

3 Compare and contrast the approaches taken by GE in their Work-Out approach described in a short case and that taken by Heineken, also described in a short case.

4 Ruggo Carpets encourages continuous improvement based around the 'drive for customer focus'. The company's total quality process has graduated from 'total customer satisfaction' to 'total customer delight', to its present form – 'bridging the gap', which is effectively a 'where we are' and 'where we should be' yardstick for the company. Developments in the warehouse are typical. The supervisor has been replaced by a group leader who acts as a 'facilitator', working within the team. They are also trained to carry out their own job plus five others. Fixed hours are a thing of the past, as is overtime. At peak times the team works the required hours to dispatch orders, and at off-peak times, when work is completed the team can leave. Dispatch labels and address labels are computer-generated and the carpets are bar-coded to reduce human error. Each process within the warehouse has been analysed and re-engineered.

    (a) What is implied by the progression of the company's three initiatives from 'total customer satisfaction' to 'total customer delight' to 'bridging the gap'?

    (b) Evaluate this example against the criteria included in the Business Excellence Model.

5 Look through the financial or business pages of a (serious) newspaper and find examples of businesses that have 'deviated from the line of fit', as described in the early part of this chapter.

6 Devise a performance measurement scheme for the performance of the course you are following.

Selected further reading

Deming, W.E. (1986) *Out of the Crisis*, MIT Press, Cambridge, Mass. One of the gurus. It had a huge impact in its day. Read it if you want to know what all the fuss was about.

George, M.L., Rowlands, D. and Kastle, B. (2003) *What Is Lean Six Sigma?* McGraw-Hill Publishing Co. Very much a quick introduction on what Lean Six Sigma is and how to use it.

Kaplan, R.S. and Norton, D.P. (2001) *The Strategy Focused Organisation*, Harvard Business School Press, Boston, MA.

Neely, A.D. and Adams, C. (2001) The performance prism perspective, *Journal of Cost Management*, vol. 25, no. 1, 7–15.

Schein, E.H. (2004) *Organizational Culture and Leadership*, 3rd edn, Jossey-Bass. A classic.

Useful web sites

www.quality-foundation.co.uk/ The British Quality Foundation is a not-for-profit organization promoting business excellence.

www.juran.com The Juran Institute's mission statement is to provide clients with the concepts, methods and guidance for attaining leadership in quality.

www.asq.org/ The American Society for Quality site. Good professional insights.

www.quality.nist.gov/ American Quality Assurance Institute. Well-established institution for all types of business quality assurance.

www.gslis.utexas.edu/~rpollock/tqm.html Non-commercial site on total quality management with some good links.

www.iso.org/iso/en/ISOOnline.frontpage Site of the International Standards Organisation that runs the ISO 9000 and ISO 14000 families of standards. ISO 9000 has become an international reference for quality management requirements.

www.opsman.org Lots of useful stuff.

Now that you have finished reading this chapter, why not visit MyOMLab at www.myomlab.com where you'll find more learning resources to help you make the most of your studies and get a better grade?

Introduction to Financial Accounting and The Balance Sheet

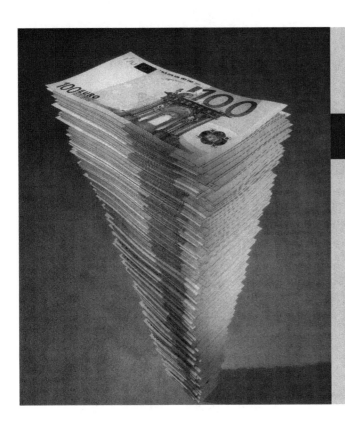

Chapter 2

Measuring and reporting financial position

Introduction

We saw in the previous chapter that accounting has two distinct strands: financial accounting and management accounting. This chapter, and Chapters 3 to 5, examine the three major financial statements that form the core of financial accounting.

We start this chapter by taking an overview of the three statements to show how each contributes towards an assessment of the overall financial position and performance of a business.

Following this overview, we begin a more detailed examination by turning our attention towards one of these financial statements: the balance sheet. We shall see how it is prepared, and examine the principles underpinning this statement. We shall also consider its value for decision-making purposes.

Learning outcomes

When you have completed this chapter, you should be able to

■ explain the nature and purpose of the three major financial statements;

■ prepare a simple balance sheet and interpret the information that it contains;

■ discuss the accounting conventions underpinning the balance sheet;

■ discuss the limitations of the balance sheet in portraying the financial position of a business.

Wealth, cash and profit

We saw in Chapter 1 that most people become involved in business ownership to generate wealth, that is, to make themselves better off economically. This is true whether the people concerned are in business on their own account (as sole proprietors) or jointly with others (as partners or shareholders in a company). This concern for wealth generation raises several important, practical questions, such as:

- How can the amount of wealth generated for a particular period be assessed?
- Is generating wealth the same as making a profit?
- Does generating wealth mean having more cash at the end of the period that at the start?
- Is the wealth of the business the same the wealth of the owners?

These are some of the questions that we shall consider in this chapter.

The major financial statements - an overview

The major financial accounting statements aim to provide a picture of the financial position and performance of a business. To achieve this, a business's accounting system will normally produce three particular statements on a regular, recurring basis. These three are concerned with answering the following questions:

- What cash movements (that is, cash in and cash out) took place over a particular period?
- How much wealth (that is, profit) was generated, or lost, by the business over that period? (Profit (or loss) is defined as the increase (or decrease) in wealth arising from trading activities.)
- What is the accumulated wealth of the business at the end of that period and what form does the wealth take?

To address each of these questions, there is a separate financial statement. The financial statements are:

- the cash flow statement
- the income statement (also known as the profit and loss account)
- the balance sheet (also known as the statement of financial position).

When taken together, they provide a picture of the financial health of the business.

Perhaps the best way to introduce these financial statements is to look at an example of a very simple business. From this we shall be able to see the sort of information that each of the statements can provide. It is, however, worth pointing out that, while a simple business is our starting point, the principles that we consider apply equally to the largest and most complex businesses. This means that we shall meet these same principles again in later chapters.

Example 2.1

Paul was unemployed and unable to find a job. He therefore decided to embark on a business venture. Christmas was approaching, and so he decided to buy gift wrapping paper from a local supplier and to sell it on the corner of his local high street. He felt that the price of wrapping paper in the high street shops was excessive. This provided him with a useful business opportunity.

He began the venture with £40 in cash. On Monday, Paul's first day of trading, he bought wrapping paper for £40 and sold three-quarters of it for £45 cash.

What cash movements took place during Monday?

For Monday, a cash flow statement showing the cash movements for the day can be prepared as follows:

Cash flow statement for Monday

	£
Cash introduced by Paul	40
Cash from sales of wrapping paper	45
Cash paid to buy wrapping paper	(40)
Closing balance of cash	45

The statement shows that Paul placed £40 cash into the business. The business received £45 cash from customers, but paid £40 cash to buy the wrapping paper. This left £45 of cash by Monday evening. Note that we are taking the standard approach found in financial statements of showing figures to be deducted (in this case the £40 paid out) in brackets. We shall take this approach consistently throughout the chapters dealing with financial statements.

How much wealth (that is, profit) was generated by the business during Monday?

An *income statement (profit and loss account)* can be prepared to show the wealth (profit) generated on Monday. The wealth generated will represent the difference between the value of the sales made and the cost of the goods (that is, wrapping paper) sold.

Income statement (profit and loss account) for Monday

	£
Sales revenue	45
Cost of goods sold ($^3/_4$ of £40)	(30)
Profit	15

Note that it is only the cost of the wrapping paper *sold* that is matched against (and deducted from) the sales revenue in order to find the profit. It is not the whole of the cost of wrapping paper acquired. Any unsold inventories (in this case $1/4$ of £40 = £10) will be charged against the future sales revenue that it generates.

What is the accumulated wealth at Monday evening?

To establish the accumulated wealth at the end of Monday's trading, we can draw up a *balance sheet (statement of financial position)*. This will list the resources held at the end of that day.

**Balance sheet (statement of financial position)
as at Monday evening**

	£
Cash (closing balance)	45
Inventories of goods for resale ($1/4$ of £40)	10
Total assets	55
Equity	55

Note the terms 'assets' and 'equity' that appear in the above balance sheet. 'Assets' are business resources (things of value to the business) and include cash and inventories. 'Equity' is the word used in accounting for the investment or stake of the owner(s) (in this case Paul) in the business. Both of these terms will be discussed in some detail a little later in this chapter.

We can see from the financial statements in Example 2.1 that each statement provides part of a picture portraying the financial performance and position of the business. We begin by showing the cash movements. Cash is a vital resource that is necessary for any business to function effectively. Cash is required to meet debts that may become due and to acquire other resources (such as inventories). Cash has been described as the 'lifeblood' of a business, and movements in cash are usually given close scrutiny by users of financial statements.

However, it is clear that reporting cash movements alone would not be enough to portray the financial health of the business. The changes in cash over time do not tell us how much profit was generated. The income statement provides us with information concerning this aspect of performance. For example, we saw that during Monday the cash balance increased by £5, but the profit generated, as shown in the income statement, was £15. The cash balance did not increase by the amount of the profit made because part of the wealth generated (£10) was held in the form of inventories.

A balance sheet can be drawn up as at the end of Monday's trading, which should provide an insight into the total wealth of the business. Cash is only one form in which wealth can be held. In the case of this business, wealth is also held in the form of inventories (also known as stock). Hence, when drawing up the balance sheet, both forms of wealth held will be listed. In the case of a large business, there may be many other forms in which wealth will be held, such as land and buildings, equipment, motor vehicles and so on.

Let us now continue with our example.

Example 2.1 (continued)

On Tuesday, Paul bought more wrapping paper for £20 cash. He managed to sell all of the new inventories and all of the earlier inventories, for a total of £48.

The cash flow statement for Tuesday will be as follows:

Cash flow statement for Tuesday

	£
Opening balance (from Monday evening)	45
Cash from sales of wrapping paper	48
Cash paid to buy wrapping paper	(20)
Closing balance	73

The income statement for Tuesday will be as follows:

Income statement for Tuesday

	£
Sales revenue	48
Cost of goods sold (£20 + £10)	(30)
Profit	18

The balance sheet as at Tuesday evening will be:

Balance sheet as at Tuesday evening

	£
Cash (closing balance)	73
Inventories	–
Total assets	73
Equity	73

We can see that the total business resources (wealth) had increased to £73 by Tuesday evening. This represents an increase of £18 (that is, £73 less £55) over Monday's figure – which, of course, is the amount of profit made during Tuesday as shown on the income statement.

Activity 2.1

On Wednesday, Paul bought more wrapping paper for £46 cash. However, it was raining hard for much of the day and sales were slow. After Paul had sold half of his total inventories for £32, he decided to stop trading until Thursday morning.

Have a go at drawing up the three financial statements for Paul's business for Wednesday.

Cash flow statement for Wednesday

	£
Opening balance (from the Tuesday evening)	73
Cash from sales of wrapping paper	32
Cash paid to buy wrapping paper	(46)
Closing balance	59

Income statement for Wednesday

	£
Sales revenue	32
Cost of goods sold (½ of £46)	(23)
Profit	9

Balance sheet as at Wednesday evening

	£
Cash (closing balance)	59
Inventories (½ of £46)	23
Total assets	82
Equity	82

Note that the total business wealth had increased by £9 (that is, the amount of Wednesday's profit) even though the cash balance had declined. This is because the business is holding more of its wealth in the form of inventories rather than cash, compared with the position on Tuesday evening.

We can see that the income statement and cash flow statement are both concerned with measuring flows (of wealth and cash respectively) during a particular period (for example, a particular day, a particular month or a particular year). The balance sheet, however, is concerned with the financial position at a particular moment in time.

 Figure 2.1 illustrates this point. The financial statements (income statement, cash flow statement and balance sheet) are often referred to as the final accounts of the business.

For external users (that is virtually all except the managers of the business concerned), these statements are normally backward-looking because they are based on information concerning past events and transactions. This can be useful in providing feedback on past performance, and in identifying trends that provide clues to future performance. However, the statements can also be prepared using projected data to help assess likely future profits, cash flows and so on. The financial statements are normally prepared on a projected basis for internal decision-making purposes only, as we shall see in Chapter 9. Managers are usually reluctant to publish these projected statements for external users, as they may reveal valuable information to competitors.

Now that we have an overview of the financial statements, we shall consider each statement in more detail. We shall go straight on to look at the balance sheet. Chapter 3 looks at the income statement; Chapter 5 goes into more detail on the cash flow

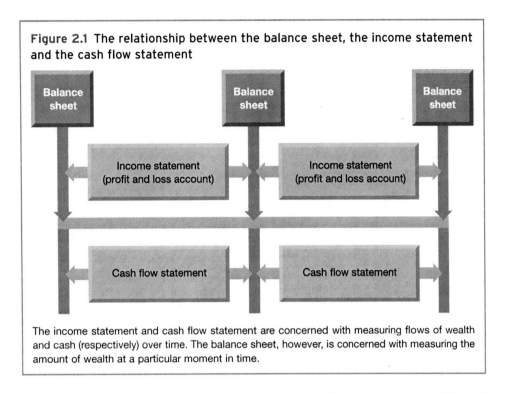

Figure 2.1 The relationship between the balance sheet, the income statement and the cash flow statement

The income statement and cash flow statement are concerned with measuring flows of wealth and cash (respectively) over time. The balance sheet, however, is concerned with measuring the amount of wealth at a particular moment in time.

statement. (Chapter 4 considers the balance sheets and income statements of limited companies.)

The balance sheet

The purpose of the balance sheet is simply to set out the financial position of a business at a particular moment in time (hence its alternative name, *statement of financial position*). We saw above that the balance sheet will reveal the forms in which the wealth of the business is held and how much wealth is held in each form. We can, however, be more specific about the nature of the balance sheet by saying that it sets out the assets of the business on the one hand, and the claims against the business on the other. Before looking at the balance sheet in more detail, we need to be clear about what these terms mean.

Assets

An asset is essentially a resource held by the business. For a particular item to be treated as an asset for accounting purposes it should have the following characteristics:

■ *A probable future benefit must exist.* This simply means that the item must be expected to have some future monetary value. This value can arise through its use within the business or through its hire or sale. Thus, an obsolete piece of equipment that could be sold for scrap would still be considered an asset, whereas an obsolete piece of equipment that could not be sold for scrap would not be regarded as one.

■ *The business must have an exclusive right to control the benefit.* Unless the business has exclusive rights over the resource it cannot be regarded as an asset. Thus, for a business offering holidays on barges, the canal system may be a very valuable resource, but as the business will not be able to control the access of others to the canal system, it cannot be regarded as an asset of the business. (However, the barges owned by the business would be regarded as assets.)

■ *The benefit must arise from some past transaction or event.* This means that the transaction (or other event) giving rise to the business's right to the benefit must have already occurred, and not be going to arise at some future date. Thus an agreement by a business to buy a piece of equipment at some future date would not mean the item is currently an asset of the business.

■ *The asset must be capable of measurement in monetary terms.* Unless the item can be measured in monetary terms, with a reasonable degree of reliability, it will not be regarded as an asset for inclusion on the balance sheet. Thus, the title of a magazine (for example *Hello!* or *Vogue*) that was created by its publisher may be extremely valuable to that publishing business, but this value is usually difficult to quantify. It will not, therefore, be treated as an asset.

Note that all four of these conditions must apply. If one of them does not apply, the item will not be treated as an asset for accounting purposes, and will not appear on the balance sheet.

We can see that these conditions strictly limit the kind of items that may be referred to as 'assets' in the balance sheet. Certainly not all resources exploited by a business will be assets of the business for accounting purposes. Some, like the canal system or the magazine title *Hello!*, may well be assets in a broader sense, but not for accounting purposes. Once an asset has been acquired by a business, it will continue to be considered an asset until the benefits are exhausted or the business disposes of it in some way.

Activity 2.2

Indicate which of the following items could appear as an asset on the balance sheet of a business. Explain your reasoning in each case.

1 £1,000 owing to the business by a customer who is unable to pay.
2 The purchase of a patent from an inventor that gives the business the right to produce a new product. Production of the new product is expected to increase profits over the period during which the patent is held.
3 The business hiring a new marketing director who is confidently expected to increase profits by over 30 per cent during the next three years.
4 The purchase of a machine that will save the business £10,000 each year. It is currently being used by the business but it has been acquired on credit and is not yet paid for.

Your answer should be along the following lines:

1 Under normal circumstances a business would expect a customer to pay the amount owed. Such an amount is therefore typically shown as an asset under the heading 'trade receivables' (or 'debtors'). However, in this particular case the customer is unable to pay, which means that the item is incapable of providing future benefits, and the £1,000 owing would not be regarded as an asset. Debts that are not paid are referred to as 'bad debts'.

2 The purchase of the patent would meet all of the conditions set out above and would therefore be regarded as an asset.

3 The hiring of a new marketing director would not be considered as the acquisition of an asset. One argument against its classification as an asset is that the business does not have exclusive rights of control over the director. (Nevertheless, it may have an exclusive right to the services that the director provides.) Perhaps a stronger argument is that the value of the director cannot be measured in monetary terms with any degree of reliability.

4 The machine would be considered an asset even though it is not yet paid for. Once the business has agreed to buy the machine, and has accepted it, the machine is legally owned by the business (and, therefore, under its control) even though payment is still outstanding. (The amount outstanding would be shown as a claim, as we shall see below.)

The sorts of items that often appear as assets in the balance sheet of a business include:

- property
- plant and equipment
- fixtures and fittings
- patents and trademarks
- trade receivables
- loans made by the business.

Activity 2.3

Can you think of any other items that might appear as assets in the balance sheet of a business?

You may be able to think of a number of other items. Two that we have met so far, because they were the only types of asset that were held by Paul's wrapping-paper business (in Example 2.1), are inventories and cash at bank.

Note that an asset does not have to be a physical item – it may also be a non-physical right to certain benefits. Assets that have a physical substance and can be touched are referred to as tangible assets. Assets that have no physical substance but which, nevertheless, provide expected future benefits (such as patents) are referred to as intangible assets.

Claims

A claim is an obligation on the part of the business to provide cash, or some other form of benefit, to an outside party. A claim will normally arise as a result of the outside party providing funds in the form of assets for use by the business. There are essentially two types of claim against a business:

- Equity. This represents the claim of the owner(s) against the business. This claim is sometimes referred to as the *owner's capital*. Some find it hard to understand how the owner can have a claim against the business, particularly when we consider the example of a sole-proprietor-type business where the owner *is*, in effect, the business. However, for accounting purposes, a clear distinction is made between the business (whatever its size) and the owner(s). The business is viewed as being quite separate from the owner and this is equally true for a sole proprietor like Paul, the wrapping-paper seller in Example 2.1, or a large company like Marks and Spencer plc. It is seen as a separate entity with its own separate existence and when financial statements are prepared, they relate to the business rather than to the owner(s). This means that the balance sheet should reflect the financial position of the business as a separate entity. Viewed from this perspective, any funds contributed by the owner will be seen as coming from outside the business and will appear as a claim against the business in its balance sheet.

  As we have just seen, the business and the owner are separate for accounting purposes, irrespective of the type of business concerned. It is also true that the operation of the equity section of the balance sheet is broadly the same irrespective of the type of business concerned. As we shall see in Chapter 4, with limited companies the owner's claim figure must be analysed according to how each part of it first arose. For example, companies must make a distinction between that part of the owner's claim that arose from retained profits and that part that arose from the owners putting in cash, usually by buying shares in the company.

- Liabilities. Liabilities represent the claims of all individuals and organisations other than the owner(s). Liabilities must have arisen from past transactions or events such as supplying goods or lending money to the business. When a liability is settled it will normally be through an outflow of assets (usually cash).

Once a claim from the owners or outsiders has been incurred by a business, it will remain as an obligation until it is settled.

Now that the meaning of the terms *assets* and *claims* has been established, we can go on and discuss the relationship between the two. This relationship is quite straightforward. If a business wishes to acquire assets, it will have to raise the necessary funds from somewhere. It may raise the funds from the owner(s) or from other outside parties or from both. Example 2.2 illustrates this relationship.

Example 2.2

Jerry and Company start a business by depositing £20,000 in a bank account on 1 March. This amount was raised partly from the owner (£6,000) and partly from borrowing (£14,000). Raising funds in this way will give rise to a claim on the business by both the owner (equity) and the lender (liability). If a balance sheet of Jerry and Company is prepared following the above transactions, it will appear as follows:

Jerry and Company
Balance sheet as at 1 March

	£
Assets	
Cash at bank	20,000
Total assets	20,000
Claims	
Equity (owner's capital)	6,000
Liabilities – borrowing	14,000
Total equity and liabilities	20,000

We can see from the balance sheet that the total claims are the same as the total assets. Thus:

Assets = Equity + Liabilities.

This equation – which is often referred to as the *balance sheet equation* – will always hold true. Whatever changes may occur to the assets of the business or the claims against it, there will be compensating changes elsewhere that will ensure that the balance sheet always 'balances'. By way of illustration, consider the following transactions for Jerry and Company:

2 March	Bought a motor van for £5,000, paying by cheque.
3 March	Bought inventories (that is, goods to be sold) on one month's credit for £3,000. (This means that the inventories were bought on 3 March, but payment will not be made to the supplier until 3 April.)
4 March	Repaid £2,000 of the amount borrowed to the lender, by cheque.
6 March	Owner introduced another £4,000 into the business bank account.

A balance sheet may be drawn up after each day in which transactions have taken place. In this way, the effect can be seen of each transaction on the assets and claims of the business. The balance sheet as at 2 March will be:

→

Jerry and Company
Balance sheet as at 2 March

	£
Assets	
Cash at bank (20,000 – 5,000)	15,000
Motor van	5,000
Total assets	20,000
Claims	
Equity	6,000
Liabilities – borrowing	14,000
Total equity and liabilities	20,000

As can be seen, the effect of buying the motor van is to decrease the balance at the bank by £5,000 and to introduce a new asset – a motor van – to the balance sheet. The total assets remain unchanged. It is only the 'mix' of assets that has changed. The claims against the business remain the same because there has been no change in the way in which the business has been funded.

The balance sheet as at 3 March, following the purchase of inventories, will be:

Jerry and Company
Balance sheet as at 3 March

	£
Assets	
Cash at bank	15,000
Motor van	5,000
Inventories	3,000
Total assets	23,000
Claims	
Equity	6,000
Liabilities – borrowing	14,000
Liabilities – trade payable	3,000
Total equity and liabilities	23,000

The effect of buying inventories has been to introduce another new asset (inventories) to the balance sheet. In addition, the fact that the goods have not yet been paid for means that the claims against the business will be increased by the £3,000 owed to the supplier, who is referred to as a *trade payable* (or trade creditor) on the balance sheet.

Activity 2.4

Try drawing up a balance sheet for Jerry and Company as at 4 March.

The balance sheet as at 4 March, following the repayment of part of the loan, will be:

Jerry and Company
Balance sheet as at 4 March

	£
Assets	
Cash at bank (15,000 – 2,000)	13,000
Motor van	5,000
Inventories	3,000
Total assets	21,000
Claims	
Equity	6,000
Liabilities – borrowing (14,000 – 2,000)	12,000
Liabilities – trade payable	3,000
Total equity and liabilities	21,000

The repayment of £2,000 of the borrowing will result in a decrease in the balance at the bank of £2,000 and a decrease in the lender's claim against the business by the same amount.

Activity 2.5

Try drawing up a balance sheet as at 6 March for Jerry and Company.

The balance sheet as at 6 March, following the introduction of more funds, will be:

Jerry and Company
Balance sheet as at 6 March

	£
Assets	
Cash at bank (13,000 + 4,000)	17,000
Motor van	5,000
Inventories	3,000
Total assets	25,000
Claims	
Equity (6,000 + 4,000)	10,000
Liabilities – borrowing	12,000
Liabilities – trade payable	3,000
Total equity and liabilities	25,000

The introduction of more funds by the owner will result in an increase in the equity of £4,000 and an increase in the cash at bank by the same amount.

Example 2.2 illustrates the point that the balance sheet equation (assets equals equity plus liabilities) will always hold true, because it reflects the fact that, if a business wishes to acquire more assets, it must raise funds equal to the cost of those assets. The funds raised must be provided by the owners (equity), or by others (liabilities), or by a combination of the two. Hence the total cost of assets acquired should always equal the total equity plus liabilities.

It is worth pointing out that in real life, businesses do not normally draw up a balance sheet after each day, as shown in the example above. Such an approach is not likely to be useful, given the relatively small number of transactions each day. We have done this in our examples to see the effect on the balance sheet, transaction by transaction. In real life, a balance sheet for the business is usually prepared at the end of a defined reporting period.

Determining the length of the reporting interval will involve weighing up the costs of producing the information against the perceived benefits of the information for decision-making purposes. In practice, the reporting interval will vary between businesses; it could be monthly, quarterly, half-yearly or annually. For external reporting purposes, an annual reporting cycle is the norm (although certain businesses, typically larger ones, report more frequently than this). However, for internal reporting purposes to managers, many businesses produce monthly financial statements.

The effect of trading operations on the balance sheet

In the example we have just considered (Jerry and Company), we dealt with the effect on the balance sheet of a number of different types of transactions that a business might undertake. These transactions covered the purchase of assets for cash and on credit, the repayment of a loan, and the injection of equity. However, one form of transaction, trading, has not yet been considered. To deal with the effect of trading transactions on the balance sheet, let us return to our example.

Example 2.2 (continued)

The balance sheet that we drew up for Jerry and Company as at 6 March was as follows:

Jerry and Company
Balance sheet as at 6 March

	£
Assets	
Cash at bank (13,000 + 4,000)	17,000
Motor van	5,000
Inventories	3,000
Total assets	25,000

Claims	
Equity (6,000 + 4,000)	10,000
Liabilities – borrowing	12,000
Liabilities – trade payable	3,000
Total equity and liabilities	25,000

On 7 March, the business managed to sell all of the inventories for £5,000 and received a cheque immediately from the customer for this amount. The balance sheet on 7 March, after this transaction has taken place, will be:

Jerry and Company
Balance sheet as at 7 March

	£
Assets	
Cash at bank (17,000 + 5,000)	22,000
Motor van	5,000
Inventories (3,000 – 3,000)	–
Total assets	27,000
Claims	
Equity (10,000 + (5,000 – 3,000))	12,000
Liabilities – borrowing	12,000
Liabilities – trade payable	3,000
Total equity and liabilities	27,000

We can see that the inventories (£3,000) have now disappeared from the balance sheet, but the cash at bank has increased by the selling price of the inventories (£5,000). The net effect has therefore been to increase assets by £2,000 (that is, £5,000 less £3,000). This increase represents the net increase in wealth (the profit) that has arisen from trading. Also note that the equity of the business has increased by £2,000, in line with the increase in assets. This increase in equity reflects the fact that increases in wealth, as a result of trading or other operations, will be to the benefit of the owners and will increase their stake in the business.

Activity 2.6

What would have been the effect on the balance sheet if the inventories had been sold on 7 March for £1,000 rather than £5,000?

The balance sheet on 7 March would then have been:

Jerry and Company
Balance sheet as at 7 March

	£
Assets	
Cash at bank (17,000 + 1,000)	18,000
Motor van	5,000
Inventories (3,000 – 3,000)	–
Total assets	23,000
Claims	
Equity (10,000 + (1,000 – 3,000))	8,000
Liabilities – borrowing	12,000
Liabilities – trade payable	3,000
Total equity and liabilities	23,000

As we can see, the inventories (£3,000) will disappear from the balance sheet, but the cash at bank will rise by only £1,000. This will mean a net reduction in assets of £2,000. This reduction represents a loss arising from trading and will be reflected in a reduction in the equity of the owner.

We can see that any decrease in wealth (that is, a loss) arising from trading or other transactions will lead to a reduction in the owner's stake in the business. If the business wished to maintain the level of assets as at 6 March, it would be necessary to obtain further funds from the owner or from borrowing, or both.

What we have just seen means that the balance sheet equation can be extended as follows:

Assets (at the end = Equity (amount at the start of the period
of the period)   + profit (or – loss) for the period)
**   + Liabilities (at the end of the period)**

(This is assuming that the owner makes no injections or withdrawals of equity during the period.)

As we have seen, the profit (or loss) for the period is shown on the balance sheet as an addition to (or a reduction of) equity. Any funds introduced or withdrawn by the owner for living expenses or other reasons also affect equity, but are shown separately. When this is done, more comprehensive information is provided for users of the financial statements. If Jerry and Company sold the inventories for £5,000, as in Example 2.2, and the owner withdrew £1,500 for his or her own use, the equity of the owner would appear as follows on the balance sheet:

	£
Equity (owner's equity)	
Opening balance	10,000
Profit	2,000
Drawings	(1,500)
Closing balance	10,500

If the drawings were in cash, the balance of cash would decrease by £1,500 in the balance sheet.

Note that, like all balance sheet items, the amount of equity is cumulative. This means that any profit made that is not taken out as drawings by the owner(s) remains in the business. These retained (or 'ploughed-back') profits have the effect of expanding the business.

The classification of assets

If the items on the balance sheet are listed haphazardly, with assets listed on one side and claims on the other, though it may be mathematically correct, it can be confusing. To help users to understand more clearly the information that is presented, assets and claims are usually grouped into categories. Assets may be categorised as being either current or non-current.

Current assets

Current assets are basically assets that are held for the short term. To be more precise, they are assets that meet any of the following conditions:

- they are held for sale or consumption in the normal course of a business's operating cycle;
- they are expected to be sold within the next year;
- they are held primarily for trading;
- they are cash, or near equivalents to cash such as easily marketable, short-term investments.

The most common current assets are inventories, amounts owed by customers for goods or services supplied on credit (known as trade receivables), and cash.

Perhaps it is worth making the point here that most sales made by most businesses are made on credit. This is to say that the goods pass to, or the service is rendered to, the customer at one point but the customer pays later. Retail sales are the only significant exception to this general point.

For businesses that sell goods, rather than render a service, the current assets of inventories, trade receivables and cash are interrelated. They circulate within a business as shown in Figure 2.2. We can see that cash can be used to buy inventories, which are then sold on credit. When the credit customers (trade receivables) pay, the business receives an injection of cash, and so on.

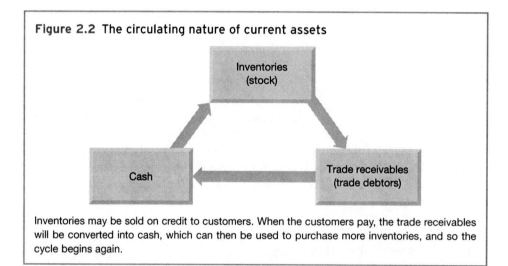

Figure 2.2 The circulating nature of current assets

Inventories may be sold on credit to customers. When the customers pay, the trade receivables will be converted into cash, which can then be used to purchase more inventories, and so the cycle begins again.

For purely service businesses, the situation is similar, except that inventories are not involved.

Non-current assets

Non-current assets (also called fixed assets) are simply assets that do not meet the definition of current assets. Generally speaking, they are held for long-term operations.

This distinction between assets that are continuously circulating within the business and assets used for long-term operations may be helpful when trying to assess the appropriateness of the mix of assets held. Most businesses will need a certain amount of both types of asset to operate effectively.

Activity 2.7

Can you think of two examples of assets that may be classified as non-current assets for an insurance business?

Examples of assets that may be defined as being non-current are:

- property
- motor vehicles
- computers
- computer software
- reference books
- furniture.

This is not an exhaustive list. You may have thought of others.

Classification issues

It is important to appreciate that whether a particular asset is classified as current or non-current may vary according to the nature of the business. This is because the *purpose* for which a particular type of asset is held may differ from business to business. For example, a motor vehicle manufacturer will normally hold inventories of the finished motor vehicles produced for resale, and would therefore classify them as part of the current assets. On the other hand, a business that uses motor vehicles for delivering its goods to customers (that is, as part of its long-term operations) would classify them as non-current assets.

Activity 2.8

The assets of Kunalun and Co., a large advertising agency, are as follows:

- cash at bank
- fixtures and fittings
- office equipment
- motor vehicles
- property
- computer equipment
- work in progress (that is, partly completed work for clients).

Which of these do you think should be classified as non-current assets, and which as current assets?

Your answer should be as follows:

Non-current assets	Current assets
Fixtures and fittings	Cash at bank
Office equipment	Work in progress
Motor vehicles	
Property	
Computer equipment	

The classification of claims

As we have already seen, claims are normally classified into equity or capital (owner's claim) and liabilities (claims of outsiders). Liabilities are further classified as either current or non-current.

Current liabilities

Current liabilities are basically amounts due for settlement in the short term. To be more precise, they are liabilities that meet any of the following conditions:

- they are expected to be settled within the normal course of the business's operating cycle;
- they are due to be settled within twelve months following the date of the balance sheet on which they appear;
- they are held primarily for trading purposes;
- there is no right to defer settlement beyond twelve months following the date of the balance sheet on which they appear.

Non-current liabilities

Non-current liabilities represent amounts due that do not meet the definition of current liabilities.

Classification issues

Note that it is quite common for non-current liabilities to become current liabilities. For example, borrowings that are due to be repaid within eighteen months following the date of a particular balance sheet will appear as a non-current liability, but, if the borrowings have not been paid off in the meantime, they will appear as a current liability in the balance sheet as at one year later.

This classification of liabilities can help the user to gain a clear impression of the ability of the business to meet its maturing obligations (that is, claims that must shortly be met). The value of the current liabilities (that is, the amounts that must be paid within the normal operating cycle) can be compared with the value of the current assets (that is, the assets that either are cash or will turn into cash within the same period).

The classification of liabilities should also help to highlight how the long-term finance of the business is raised. If long-term borrowings are relied on to finance the business, the financial risks associated with the business will increase. This is because these borrowings will bring a commitment to make interest payments and repayments of the amounts borrowed and the business may be forced to stop trading if this commitment is not fulfilled. Thus, when raising long-term finance, a business must strike the right balance between non-current liabilities and owner's equity. We shall consider this issue in more detail in Chapter 6.

Activity 2.9

Can you think of one example of a current liability and one of a non-current liability?

An example of a current liability would be amounts owing to suppliers for goods supplied on credit (known as trade payables or trade creditors) or a bank overdraft (a form of short-term bank borrowing that is repayable on demand). An example of a non-current liability would be a long-term loan.

Balance sheet layouts

Now that we have looked at the classification of assets and liabilities, we shall consider the layout of the balance sheet. Although there is an almost infinite number of ways in which the same balance sheet information could be presented, one particular layout has become clearly the most common, certainly among the larger, better-known businesses. This is the style that we adopted with Jerry and Company earlier (see pages 39–43). A more comprehensive example of this style is shown in Example 2.3.

Example 2.3

Brie Manufacturing
Balance sheet as at 31 December 2008

	£000
Non-current assets	
Property	45
Plant and equipment	30
Motor vans	19
	94
Current assets	
Inventories	23
Trade receivables	18
Cash at bank	12
	53
Total assets	147
Equity (owner's capital)	
Opening balance	50
Profit	14
Drawings	(4)
	60
Non-current liabilities	
Long-term borrowings	50
Current liabilities	
Trade payables	37
Total equity and liabilities	147

The non-current assets have a total of £94,000, which together with the current assets total of £53,000 gives a total of £147,000 for assets. Similarly, the equity totals £60,000, which together with the £50,000 for non-current liabilities and £37,000 for current liabilities gives a total for equity and liabilities of £147,000.

Within each category of asset (non-current and current) shown in Example 2.3, the items are listed in reverse order of liquidity (nearness to cash). This means that the assets that are furthest from cash appear first and the assets that are closest to cash come last. In the case of non-current assets, the property comes first as this asset is usually the most difficult to turn into cash. Motor vans are shown last as there is usually a ready market for them. In the case of current assets, we have already seen that inventories are converted to trade receivables and then trade receivables are converted to cash. This means that, under the heading of current assets, inventories appear first, followed by trade receivables and finally cash itself. This ordering of assets is a normal practice, which is followed irrespective of the layout used.

Note that, in addition to a grand total for assets held, subtotals for non-current assets and current assets are shown. Subtotals are also used for non-current liabilities and current liabilities when more than one item appears within these categories.

A slight variation from the standard layout illustrated in Example 2.3 is as shown in Example 2.4.

Example 2.4

Brie Manufacturing
Balance sheet as at 31 December 2008

	£000
Non-current assets	
Property	45
Plant and equipment	30
Motor vans	19
	94
Current assets	
Inventories	23
Trade receivables	18
Cash at bank	12
	53
Total assets	147
Non-current liabilities	
Long-term borrowings	(50)
Current liabilities	
Trade payables	(37)
Total liabilities	(87)
Net assets	60
Equity (owner's capital)	
Opening balance	50
Profit	14
Drawings	(4)
Total equity	60

We can see that the total liabilities are deducted from the total assets. This derives a figure for net assets – which is equal to total equity. Using this format, the basic accounting equation is rearranged so that

Assets – Liabilities = Equity.

Self-assessment question 2.1

The following information relates to Simonson Engineering as at 30 September 2008:

	£
Plant and equipment	25,000
Trade payables	18,000
Short-term borrowing	26,000
Inventories	45,000
Property	72,000
Long-term borrowing	51,000
Trade receivables	48,000
Equity at 1 October 2007	117,500
Cash	1,500
Motor vehicles	15,000
Fixtures and fittings	9,000
Profit for the year to 30 September 2008	18,000
Drawings for the year to 30 September 2008	15,000

Required:
Prepare a balance sheet as at 30 September 2008 for the business, using the standard layout illustrated in Example 2.3.

The answer to this question can be found at the back of the book in Appendix B.

The balance sheet and time

As we have already seen, the balance sheet is a statement of the financial position of the business at *a specified point in time*. The balance sheet has been compared to a still photograph, in that the balance sheet 'freezes' a particular moment in time and will represent the situation only at that moment. Events may be quite different immediately before and immediately after the particular moment at which the 'snapshot' of the business was taken. When examining a balance sheet, therefore, it is important to establish the date at which it has been drawn up. This information should be prominently displayed in the balance sheet heading, as it is in Example 2.4. When we are using the balance sheet to assess the business's current financial position, the more recent the balance sheet date, the better.

A business will normally prepare a balance sheet as at the close of business on the last day of its accounting year. In the UK, businesses are free to choose their accounting year. When making a decision on which year-end date to choose, commercial convenience can often be a deciding factor. For example, a business operating in the retail trade may choose to have a year-end date early in the calendar year (for example, 31 January) because trade tends to be slack during that period and more staff time is available to help with the tasks involved in the preparation of the annual financial statements (such as checking the amount of inventories held). Since trade is slack, it is also a time when the amount of inventories held by the retail business is likely to be unusually low as compared with other times of the year. Thus the balance sheet, though showing a fair view of what it purports to show, may not show a picture of what is more typically the position of the business over the rest of the year.

Accounting conventions and the balance sheet

Accounting has a number of rules or conventions that have evolved over time. They have evolved as attempts to deal with practical problems experienced by preparers and users of financial statements, rather than to reflect some theoretical ideal. In preparing the balance sheets shown earlier, we have followed various accounting conventions, although they have not been explicitly mentioned. We shall now identify and discuss the major conventions that we have applied.

Business entity convention

For accounting purposes, the business and its owner(s) are treated as being quite separate and distinct. This is why owners are treated as being claimants against their own business in respect of their investment in the business. The business entity convention must be distinguished from the legal position that may exist between businesses and their owners. For sole proprietorships and partnerships, the law does not make any distinction between the business and its owner(s). For limited companies, on the other hand, there is a clear legal distinction between the business and its owners. (As we shall see in Chapter 4, the limited company is regarded as having a separate legal existence.) For accounting purposes these legal distinctions are irrelevant, and the business entity convention applies to all businesses.

Historic cost convention

The historic cost convention holds that the value of assets shown on the balance sheet should be based on their acquisition cost (that is, historic cost). This method of measuring asset value takes preference over other methods based on some form of current value. Many people, however, find the historic cost convention difficult to support, as outdated historic costs are unlikely to help in the assessment of current financial position. It is often argued that recording assets at their current value would provide a more realistic view of financial position and would be relevant for a wide range of decisions. However, a system of measurement based on current values can present a number of problems.

Activity 2.10

Plumber and Company has some motor vans that are used by staff when visiting customers' premises to carry out work. It is now the last day of the business's accounting year.

If it were decided to show the vans on the balance sheet at a current value (rather than a value based on their historic cost), how might the business arrive at a suitable value and how reliable would this figure be?

Two ways of deriving a current value are to find out:

- how much would have to be paid to buy vans of a similar type and condition;
- how much a motor van dealer would pay for the vans, were the company to sell them.

Both options will normally rely on opinion and so a range of possible values could be produced for each. Moreover, the range of values for each option could be significantly different. (The selling prices of the vans are likely to be lower than the amount required to replace them.) Thus, any value finally decided upon could arouse some debate.

Activity 2.10 illustrates that the term 'current value' can be defined in different ways. It can be defined broadly as either the current replacement cost or the current realisable value (selling price) of an asset. These two types of valuation may result in quite different figures being produced to represent the current value of an item. Furthermore, the broad terms 'replacement cost' and 'realisable value' can be defined in different ways. We must therefore be clear about what kind of current value accounting we wish to use.

Activity 2.10 also illustrates the practical problems associated with current value accounting. Current values, however defined, are often difficult to establish with any real degree of objectivity. The figures produced may be heavily dependent on the opinion of managers. Unless current value figures are capable of some form of independent verification, there is a danger that the financial statements will lose their credibility among users.

By reporting assets at their historic cost, it is argued that more reliable information is produced. Reporting in this way reduces the need for judgements, as the amount paid for a particular asset is usually a matter of demonstrable fact. Information based on past costs, however, may not always be relevant to the needs of users.

Later in the chapter, we shall consider the valuation of assets in the balance sheet in more detail. We shall see that the historic cost convention is not always rigidly adhered to. Departures from this convention are becoming more frequent.

Prudence convention

The prudence convention holds that caution should be exercised when making accounting judgements. Uncertainty about the future is dealt with by recording all losses at once and in full; this refers to both actual losses and expected losses. Profits, on the other hand, are recognised only when they actually arise. Greater emphasis is, therefore, placed on expected losses than on expected profits. To illustrate the application of this convention, let us assume that certain inventories held by a business prove unpopular with customers and so a decision is made to sell them below their original cost. The prudence convention requires that the expected loss from future sales be recognised immediately rather than when the goods are eventually sold. If, however, these inventories could have been sold above their original cost, profit would only be recognised at the time of sale.

The prudence convention evolved to counteract the excessive optimism of some managers and owners and is designed to prevent an overstatement of financial position. There is, however, a risk that it will introduce a bias towards understatement of financial position.

Activity 2.11

What problems might arise if an excessively prudent view is taken of the financial position and performance of a business?

Excessive prudence will lead to an overstatement of losses and an understatement of profits and financial position. This will obscure the underlying financial reality and may lead users to make bad decisions. The owners, for example, may sell their stake in the business at a lower price than they would have received if a fairer picture of the financial health of the business had been presented.

In recent years, the prudence convention has weakened its grip on accounting and has become a less dominant force. Nevertheless, it remains an important convention.

Going concern convention

The going concern convention holds that the financial statements should be prepared on the assumption that the business will continue operations for the foreseeable future, unless this is known not to be true. In other words, it is assumed that there is no intention, or need, to sell off the non-current assets of the business. Such a sale may arise where the business is in financial difficulties and needs to pay amounts borrowed that are due for repayment. This convention is important because the market (sale) value of many non-current assets is often low in relation to the values at which they appear in the balance sheet. This means that were a forced sale to occur, there is the likelihood that assets would be sold for less than their balance sheet value. Such anticipated losses should be fully recorded as soon as the business's going concern status is called into question. However, where there is no expectation of a need to sell off the assets, the value of non-current assets can continue to be shown at their recorded values (that is, based on historic cost). This convention therefore provides some support for the historic cost convention under normal circumstances.

Dual aspect convention

The dual aspect convention asserts that each transaction has two aspects, both of which will affect the balance sheet. Thus the purchase of a motor car for cash results in an increase in one asset (motor car) and a decrease in another (cash). The repayment of borrowings results in the decrease in a liability (borrowings) and the decrease in an asset (cash).

Activity 2.12

What are the two aspects of each of the following transactions?

1 Purchase £1,000 inventories on credit.
2 Owner withdraws £2,000 in cash.
3 Repayment of borrowings of £3,000.

Your answer should be as follows:

1 Inventories increase by £1,000, trade payables increase by £1,000.
2 Equity reduces by £2,000, cash reduces by £2,000.
3 Borrowings reduce by £3,000, cash reduces by £3,000.

Recording the dual aspect of each transaction ensures that the balance sheet will continue to balance.

Money measurement

We saw earlier that a resource will only be regarded as an asset and included on the balance sheet if it can be measured in monetary terms, with a reasonable degree of reliability. Some resources of a business, however, do not meet this criterion and so are excluded from the balance sheet. As a result, the scope of the balance sheet is limited.

Activity 2.13

Can you think of resources of a business that cannot usually be measured reliably in monetary terms?

In answering this activity you may have thought of the following:

■ the quality of the human resources of the business
■ the reputation of the business's products
■ the location of the business
■ the relationship a business enjoys with its customers.

There have been occasional attempts to measure and report resources of a business that are normally excluded from the balance sheet so as to provide a more complete picture of its financial position. These attempts, however, invariably fail the reliability test. We saw in Chapter 1 that a lack of reliability affects the quality of financial statements. Unreliable measurement can lead to inconsistency in reporting and can create uncertainty among users, which in turn undermines the credibility of the financial statements.

Some key resources of a business that normally defy reliable measurement are discussed below.

Goodwill and brands

Some intangible non-current assets are similar to tangible non-current assets: they have a clear and separate identity and the cost of acquiring the asset can be reliably measured. Examples normally include patents, trademarks, copyrights and licences. Other intangible non-current assets, however, are quite different. They lack a clear and separate identity and reflect a hotchpotch of attributes, which are part of the essence of the business. Goodwill and product brands can provide examples of assets that lack a clear and separate identity.

The term 'goodwill' is often used to cover attributes such as the skill of the workforce and the relationship with customers. The term 'product brands' is also used to cover various attributes, such as the brand image, the quality of the product, the trademark and so on. Where goodwill and product brands have been generated internally by the business, it is often difficult to determine their cost or to measure their current market value or even to be clear that they really exist. They are, therefore, excluded from the balance sheet.

When they are acquired through an arm's-length transaction, however, the problems of uncertainty about their existence and measurement are resolved. (An 'arm's-length' transaction is one that is undertaken between two unconnected parties.) If goodwill is acquired when taking over another business, or if a business acquires a particular product brand from another business, these items will be separately identified and a price agreed for them. Under these circumstances, they can be regarded as assets by the business that acquired them and included on the balance sheet.

To agree a price for acquiring goodwill or product brands means that some form of valuation must take place and this raises the question as to how it is done. Usually, the valuation will be based on estimates of future earnings from holding the asset, a process that is fraught with difficulties. Nevertheless, a number of specialist businesses now exist that are prepared to take on this challenge. Real World 2.1 reveals how one specialist business ranked and valued the top ten brands in the world.

Real World 2.1

Valuing brands

Millward Brown Optimor, part of WPP marketing services group, recently produced a report which ranked and valued the top ten world brands for 2007 as follows:

Ranking	Brand	Value ($m)
1	Google	66,434
2	GE (General Electric)	61,880
3	Microsoft	54,951
4	Coca-Cola	44,134
5	China Mobile	41,214
6	Marlboro	39,166
7	Wal-Mart	36,880
8	Citi	33,706
9	IBM	33,572
10	Toyota	33,427

We can see that the valuations placed on the brands are remarkable; they show how much of a company's value can be tied up in brand equity.

Source: '2007 Brandz Top 100 Most Powerful Brands' by Millward Brown Optimor, p. 10.

Human resources

Attempts have been made to place a monetary measurement on the human resources of a business, but without any real success. There are, however, certain limited circumstances in which human resources are measured and reported in the balance sheet. These circumstances normally arise with professional football clubs. While football clubs cannot own players, they can own the rights to the players' services. Where these rights are acquired by compensating other clubs for releasing the players from their contracts, an arm's-length transaction arises and the amounts paid provide a reliable basis for measurement. This means that the rights to services can be regarded as an asset of the club for accounting purposes (assuming, of course, that the player will also bring benefits to the club).

Real World 2.2 describes how one leading club reports its investment in players on the balance sheet.

Real World 2.2

Dimitar is on the team sheet and on the balance sheet

Tottenham Hotspur Football Club (Spurs) has acquired several key players as a result of paying transfer fees to other clubs. In common with most UK football clubs, Spurs reports the cost of acquiring the rights to the players' services on its balance sheet. The club's balance sheet for 2007 shows the cost of registering its squad of players as about £109m. The item of players' registrations is shown as an intangible asset in the balance sheet as it is the rights to services, not the players, that are the assets. This figure of £74m includes the cost of bought-in players such as Dimitar Berbatov (for just under £11m from Bayer Leverkusen) and Jermaine Defoe (from West Ham United for £7m). The figure does not include 'home-grown' players such as Ledley King, because Spurs did not pay a transfer fee for them and so no clear-cut value can be placed on their services.

Source: Tottenham Hotspur plc Annual Report 2007.

Monetary stability

When using money as the unit of measurement, we normally fail to recognise the fact that it will change in value over time. In the UK and throughout much of the world, however, inflation has been a persistent problem. This has meant that the value of money has declined in relation to other assets. In past years, high rates of inflation have resulted in balance sheets, which were prepared on a historic cost basis, reflecting figures for assets that were much lower than they would have been if current values had been employed. Rates of inflation have been relatively low in recent years and so the disparity between historic cost values and current values has been less pronounced. Nevertheless, it can still be significant and has added fuel to the debate concerning how to measure asset values on the balance sheet. It is to this issue that we now turn.

Valuing assets on the balance sheet

It was mentioned earlier that, when preparing the balance sheet, the historic cost convention is normally applied for the reporting of assets. However, this point requires further elaboration as, in practice, it is not simply a matter of recording each asset on the balance sheet at its original cost. We shall see that things are a little more complex than this. Before discussing the valuation rules in some detail, however, we should point out that these rules are based on international financial reporting (or accounting) standards, which are rules that are generally accepted throughout much of the world. The nature and role of financial reporting standards will be discussed in Chapter 4.

Tangible non-current assets (property, plant and equipment)

Tangible non-current assets normally consist of property, plant and equipment, and we shall refer to them in this way from now on. This is a rather broad term that covers all items mentioned in its title plus other items such as motor vehicles and fixtures and fittings. All of these items are, in essence, the 'tools' used by the business to generate wealth, that is, they are used to produce or supply goods and services or for administration purposes. They tend to be held for the longer term, which typically means for more than one accounting period.

Initially these items are recorded at their historic cost, which will include any amounts spent on getting them ready for use. However, they will normally be used up over time as a result of wear and tear, obsolescence and so on. The amount used up, which is referred to as *depreciation*, must be measured for each accounting period for which the assets are held. Although we shall leave a detailed examination of depreciation until Chapter 3, we need to know that when an asset has been depreciated, this must be reflected in the balance sheet.

The total depreciation that has accumulated over the period since the asset was acquired must be deducted from its cost. This net figure (that is, the cost of the asset less the total depreciation to date) is referred to as the *carrying amount, net book value,* or *written-down value*. The procedure just described is not really a contravention of the historic cost convention. It is simply recognition of the fact that a proportion of the historic cost of the non-current asset has been consumed in the process of generating benefits for the business.

Although using historic cost (less any depreciation) is the 'benchmark treatment' for recording these assets, an alternative is allowed. Property, plant and equipment can be recorded using fair values provided that these values can be measured reliably. The fair values, in this case, are usually the current market values (that is, the exchange values in an arm's-length transaction). The use of fair values, rather than depreciated cost figures, can provide users with more up-to-date information, which may well be more relevant to their needs. It may also place the business in a better light, since the value of assets such as property may have increased significantly over time. Of course, merely increasing the balance sheet value of an asset does not make that asset more valuable. However, perceptions of the business may be altered by such a move.

One consequence of the upward revaluation of non-current assets is that the depreciation charge will be increased. This is because the depreciation charge is based on the new (increased) value of the asset.

Real World 2.3 shows that one well-known business revalued its land and buildings and, by doing so, greatly improved the look of its balance sheet.

Real World 2.3

Retailer marks up land and buildings

The balance sheet of Marks and Spencer plc, a major high street retailer, as at 1 April 2006 reveals land and buildings at a carrying amount (or net book value) of £2,310.0m. A firm of independent surveyors revalued these land and buildings two years earlier and this has been reflected in subsequent balance sheets. The effect of the revaluation was to give an uplift of £530.9m against the previous carrying amount.

Source: Marks and Spencer plc Annual Report 2006, p. 74, www.marksandspencer.com.

Activity 2.14

Refer to the format balance sheet of Brie Manufacturing, shown earlier in Example 2.3 (page 49). What would be the effect of revaluing the property to a figure of £110,000 on the balance sheet?

The effect on the balance sheet would be to increase the property to £110,000 and the gain on revaluation (that is, £110,000 – £45,000 = £65,000) would be added to the equity of the owner, as it is the owner who will benefit from the gain. The revised balance sheet would therefore be as follows:

Brie Manufacturing
Balance sheet as at 31 December 2008

	£000
Non-current assets (property, plant and equipment)	
Property	110
Plant and equipment	30
Motor vans	19
	159
Current assets	
Inventories	23
Trade receivables	18
Cash at bank	12
	53
Total assets	212
Equity (owner's capital)	
Opening balance	50
Revaluation gain	65
Profit	14
	129
Drawings	(4)
	125
Non-current liabilities	
Long-term borrowings	50
Current liabilities	
Trade payables	37
Total equity and liabilities	212

Once assets are revalued, the frequency of revaluation then becomes an important issue as assets recorded at out-of-date values can mislead users. Using out-of-date revaluations on the balance sheet is the worst of both worlds. It lacks the objectivity and verifiability of historic cost; it also lacks the realism of current values. Revaluations should therefore be frequent enough to ensure that the carrying amount of the revalued asset does not differ materially from its fair value at the balance sheet date.

When an item of property, plant or equipment is revalued on the basis of fair values, all assets within that particular group must be revalued. Thus, it is not acceptable to revalue some property but not others. Although this provides some degree of consistency within a particular group of assets, it does not, of course, prevent the balance sheet from containing a mixture of valuations.

Intangible non-current assets

For these assets, the 'benchmark treatment' is, once again, that they are measured initially at historic cost. What follows, however, will depend on whether the asset has a finite or an infinite useful life. (Purchased goodwill can provide an example of an asset with an infinitely useful life.) Where the asset has a finite life, any depreciation (or *amortisation* as it is usually termed for intangible non-current assets) following acquisition will be deducted from its cost. Where, however, the asset has an infinite life, it will not be amortised. Instead, it will be tested annually to see whether there has been any fall in value. This point is discussed in more detail in the following section.

Once again, the alternative of revaluing intangible assets using fair values is available. However, this can only be used where an active market exists, which allows fair values to be properly determined. In practice, this is a rare occurrence.

The impairment of non-current assets

There is always a risk that both types of non-current asset (tangible and intangible) may suffer a significant fall in value. This may be due to factors such as changes in market conditions, technological obsolescence and so on. In some cases, this fall in value may lead to the carrying amount (or net book value) of the asset being higher than the amount that could be recovered from the asset through its continued use or through its sale. When this occurs, the asset value is said to be impaired and the general rule is to reduce the value of the asset on the balance sheet to its recoverable amount. Unless this is done, the asset will be overstated on the balance sheet.

Activity 2.15

With which one of the accounting conventions that we discussed earlier is this accounting treatment consistent?

The answer is the prudence convention, which states that actual or anticipated losses should be recognised in full.

In many situations, a business may use either historic cost, less any depreciation, or a value-based measure when reporting its non-current assets. However, where the former is greater than the latter, the business has no choice; the use of depreciated historic cost is not an option. Real World 2.4 provides an example of where the application of the 'impairment rule', as it is called, resulted in huge write-downs (that is, reductions in the balance sheet value of the assets) for a well-known mobile phone operator.

Real World 2.4

Talking telephone numbers

Vodafone Group plc (Vodafone), the mobile phone operator, had to incur massive goodwill impairment charges during the year ended 31 March 2007. These totalled £11,600m which, to place it in context, compares with sales revenue for the year of £31,104m. This helped to lead to a loss for the business of £2,383m for the year. This followed similar impairment charges totalling £23,515m for the previous accounting year. These rate as some of the largest impairment charges ever incurred by any business anywhere.

The problem arose from Vodafone's purchase, in 2000, of the German business Mannesmann, which operated mobile phone networks in Germany and Italy. Vodafone paid £101,000m for Mannesmann's business.

Vodafone blamed the large impairment charges on an assessment of the longer-term prospects in the German and Italian markets, which are being hit by tough price competition.

Sources: 'Goodwill charges at record levels', FT.com, 30 May 2006; Vodafone Group plc Annual Report 2007.

We saw earlier that intangible, non-current assets with infinite lives must be tested annually to see whether there has been any impairment. Other non-current assets, however, must be also tested where events suggest that impairment has taken place.

Inventories

It is not only non-current assets that run the risk of a significant fall in value. The inventories of a business could also suffer this fate, which could be caused by factors such as reduced selling prices, obsolescence, deterioration, damage and so on. Where a fall in value means that the amount likely to be recovered from the sale of the inventories will be lower than their cost, this loss must be reflected in the balance sheet. Thus, if the net realisable value (that is, selling price less any selling costs) falls below the historic cost of inventories held, the former should be used as the basis of valuation. This reflects, once again, the influence of the prudence convention on the balance sheet.

Real World 2.5 shows how one well-known business wrote down the inventories of one of its products following a sharp reduction in selling prices.

Real World 2.5

You're fired!

'You're fired!' is what some investors might like to tell Amstrad, run by *Apprentice* star Sir Alan Sugar. . . . Shares in the company fell nearly 10 per cent as it revealed that sales of its much-vaunted videophone have failed to take off.

Amstrad launched the E3, a phone allowing users to hold video calls with each other, in a blaze of publicity last year. But, after cutting the price from £99 to £49, Amstrad sold just 61,000 E3s in the year to June and has taken a £5.7m stock [inventories] write down.

Source: 'Amstrad (AMT)', *Investors Chronicle*, 7 October 2005.

The published financial statements of large businesses will normally show the basis on which inventories are valued. Real World 2.6 shows how one well-known business reports this information.

Real World 2.6

Taking stock

The 2007 financial statements of Greene King plc, the brewer and pub operator, include the following explanation concerning inventories:

> Inventories are valued at the lower of cost and net realisable value. Raw materials are valued at average cost. Finished goods and work in progress comprise materials, labour and attributable production overheads where applicable, and are valued at average cost.

Source: Greene King plc Annual Report 2007, p. 24.

Uses and usefulness of the balance sheet

The balance sheet is the oldest of the three main financial statements and many businesses have consistently prepared one on a regular basis, even where there was no regulation requiring it to be produced. It is clearly, therefore, seen as being capable of providing useful information. The balance sheet can be seen as having several uses, including the following:

- *It provides an insight into how the business is financed and how its funds are deployed.* We can see how much finance is contributed by the owners and how much is contributed by outside lenders. We can also see the different kinds of assets acquired and how much is invested in each kind.
- *It can provide a basis for assessing the value of the business.* Since the balance sheet lists, and places a value on, the various assets and the claims, it can provide a starting point for assessing the value of the business. It is, however, severely limited in the extent to which it can do this. We have seen earlier that accounting rules may result in assets being shown at their historic cost and that the restrictive definition of assets may exclude certain business resources from the balance sheet. Ultimately, the value of a business will be based on its ability to generate wealth in the future. Because of this, assets need to be valued on the basis of their wealth-generating potential. Also, other business resources that do not meet the restrictive definition of assets, such as brand values, need to be similarly valued and included. In Chapter 10 we shall see how assets and other business resources can be valued on the basis of their future wealth-generating ability.
- *Relationships between assets and claims can be assessed.* It can be useful to look at relationships between balance sheet items, for example the relationship between how much wealth is tied up in current assets and how much is owed in the short term (current liabilities). From this relationship, we can see whether the business has

sufficient short-term assets to cover its maturing obligations. We shall look at this and other relationships between balance sheet items in some detail in Chapter 6.

■ *Performance can be assessed.* The effectiveness of a business in generating wealth (making a profit) can usefully be assessed against the amount of investment that was involved. The relationship between profit earned over a particular period and the value of the net assets involved can be very helpful to many of those involved with the business concerned. This is particularly likely to be of interest to the owners and the managers. This and similar relationships will also be explored in detail in Chapter 6.

Summary

The main points of the chapter may be summarised as follows.

The major financial statements

■ There are three major financial statements: the cash flow statement, the income statement (profit and loss account) and the balance sheet (statement of financial position).

■ The cash flow statement shows the cash movements over a particular period.

■ The income statement shows the wealth (profit) generated over a particular period.

■ The balance sheet shows the accumulated wealth at a particular point in time.

The balance sheet

■ This sets out the assets of the business, on the one hand, and the claims against those assets, on the other.

■ Assets are resources of the business that have certain characteristics, such as the ability to provide future benefits.

■ Claims are obligations on the part of the business to provide cash, or some other benefit, to outside parties.

■ Claims are of two types: equity and liabilities.

■ Equity represents the claim(s) of the owner(s) and liabilities represent the claims of others, apart from the owner(s).

Classification of assets and liabilities

■ Assets are normally categorised as being current or non-current.

■ Current assets are cash or near cash or are held for sale or consumption in the normal course of business, or for trading, or for the short term.

■ Non-current assets are assets that are not current assets. They are normally held for the long-term operations of the business.

■ Liabilities are normally categorised as being current or non-current liabilities.

■ Current liabilities represent amounts due in the normal course of the business's operating cycle, or are held for trading, or are to be settled within twelve months of, or cannot be deferred for at least twelve months after, the end of the reporting period.

■ Non-current liabilities represent amounts due that are not current liabilities.

Balance sheet layouts

■ The standard layout begins with the assets at the top of the balance sheet and places equity and liabilities underneath.

■ A variation of the standard layout begins with the assets at the top of the balance sheet. From the total assets figure are deducted the non-current and current liabilities to arrive at a net assets figure. Equity is placed underneath.

Accounting conventions

■ Accounting conventions are the rules of accounting that have evolved to deal with practical problems experienced by those preparing financial statements.

■ The main conventions relating to the balance sheet include business entity, historic cost, prudence, going concern and dual aspect.

Money measurement

■ Using money as the unit of measurement limits the scope of the balance sheet.

■ Certain resources such as goodwill, product brands and human resources are difficult to measure. An 'arm's-length transaction' is normally required before such assets can be reliably measured and reported on the balance sheet.

■ Money is not a stable unit of measurement – it changes in value over time.

Asset valuation

■ The 'benchmark treatment' is to show property, plant and equipment at historic cost less any amounts written off for depreciation. However, fair values may be used rather than depreciated cost.

■ The 'benchmark treatment' for intangible non-current assets is to show the items at historic cost. Only assets with a finite life will be amortised (depreciated) and fair values will rarely be used.

■ Where the recoverable amount from tangible non-current assets is below their carrying amount, this lower amount is reflected in the balance sheet.

■ Inventories are shown at the lower of cost or net realisable value.

Balance sheet uses

■ The balance sheet shows how finance has been raised and how it has been been deployed.

■ It provides a basis for valuing the business, though the conventional balance sheet can only be a starting point.

■ Relationships between various balance sheet items can usefully be explored.

■ Relationships between wealth generated and wealth invested can be helpful indicators of business effectiveness.

> **→ Key terms**
>
> | | |
> |---|---|
> | cash flow statement | non-current (fixed) assets |
> | income statement | current liabilities |
> | balance sheet | non-current liabilities |
> | final accounts | accounting conventions |
> | assets | business entity convention |
> | claims | historic cost convention |
> | tangible assets | prudence convention |
> | intangible assets | going concern convention |
> | equity | dual aspect convention |
> | liabilities | property, plant and equipment |
> | current assets | fair values |

Further reading

If you would like to explore the topics covered in this chapter in more depth, we recommend the following books:

Elliott, B. and Elliott, J., *Financial Accounting and Reporting* (12th edn), Financial Times Prentice Hall, 2008, chapters 16 and 18.

International Accounting Standards Board, International Financial Reporting Standards IAS 16 (revised December 2003), IAS 36 (revised March 2004) and IAS 38 (revised March 2004).

Kirk, R.J., *International Financial Reporting Standards in Depth, Vol. 1. Theory and Practice*, CIMA Publishing, 2005, chapters 2 and 3.

Sutton, T., *Corporate Financial Accounting and Reporting* (2nd edn), Financial Times Prentice Hall, 2004, chapters 2 and 8.

? Review questions

Answers to these questions can be found at the back of the book in Appendix C.

2.1 An accountant prepared a balance sheet for a business. In the balance sheet, the equity of the owner was shown next to the liabilities. This confused the owner, who argued: 'My equity is my major asset and so should be shown as an asset on the balance sheet.' How would you explain this misunderstanding to the owner?

2.2 'The balance sheet shows how much a business is worth.' Do you agree with this statement? Discuss.

2.3 What is meant by the balance sheet equation? How does the form of this equation differ between the two balance sheet layouts mentioned in the chapter?

2.4 In recent years there have been attempts to place a value on the 'human assets' of a business in order to derive a figure that can be included on the balance sheet. Do you think humans should be treated as assets? Would 'human assets' meet the conventional definition of an asset for inclusion on the balance sheet?

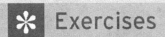 Exercises

Exercise 2.5 is more advanced than Exercises 2.1 to 2.4. Those exercises with coloured numbers have answers at the back of the book in Appendix D.

> If you wish to try more exercises, visit MyAccountingLab/

2.1 On Thursday, the fourth day of his business venture, Paul, the street trader in wrapping paper (see pp. 31–33), bought more inventories for £53 cash. During the day he sold inventories that had cost £33 for a total of £47.

Required:
Draw up the three financial statements for Paul's business venture for Thursday.

2.2 While on holiday in Bridlington, Helen had her credit cards and purse stolen from the beach while she was swimming. She was left with only £40, which she had kept in her hotel room, but she had three days of her holiday remaining. She was determined to continue her holiday and decided to make some money to enable her to do so. She decided to sell orange juice to holidaymakers using the local beach. On day 1 she bought 80 cartons of orange juice at £0.50 each for cash and sold 70 of these at £0.80 each. On the following day she bought 60 cartons at £0.50 each for cash and sold 65 at £0.80 each. On the third and final day she bought another 60 cartons at £0.50 each for cash. However, it rained and, as a result, business was poor. She managed to sell 20 at £0.80 each but sold off the rest of her inventories at £0.40 each.

Required:
Prepare an income statement and cash flow statement for each day's trading and prepare a balance sheet at the end of each day's trading.

2.3 On 1 March, Joe Conday started a new business. During March he carried out the following transactions:

1 March	Deposited £20,000 in a bank account.
2 March	Bought fixtures and fittings for £6,000 cash, and inventories £8,000 on credit.
3 March	Borrowed £5,000 from a relative and deposited it in the bank.
4 March	Bought a motor car for £7,000 cash and withdrew £200 in cash for his own use.
5 March	A further motor car costing £9,000 was bought. The motor car bought on 4 March was given in part exchange at a value of £6,500. The balance of the purchase price for the new car was paid in cash.
6 March	Joe won £2,000 in a lottery and paid the amount into the business bank account. He also repaid £1,000 of the loan.

→

Required:

Draw up a balance sheet for the business at the end of each day.

2.4   The following is a list of the assets and claims of Crafty Engineering Ltd at 30 June last year:

	£000
Trade payables	86
Motor vehicles	38
Long-term borrowings from Industrial Finance Co.	260
Equipment and tools	207
Short-term borrowings	116
Inventories	153
Property	320
Trade receivables	185

Required:

(a) Prepare the balance sheet of the business as at 30 June last year from the above information using the standard layout. (*Hint*: There is a missing item that needs to be deduced and inserted.)

(b) Discuss the significant features revealed by this financial statement.

2.5   The balance sheet of a business at the start of the week is as follows:

	£
Assets	
Property	145,000
Furniture and fittings	63,000
Inventories	28,000
Trade receivables	33,000
Total assets	269,000
Claims	
Equity	203,000
Short-term borrowing (bank overdraft)	43,000
Trade payables	23,000
Total equity and liabilities	269,000

During the week the following transactions take place:

(a) Inventories sold for £11,000 cash; these inventories had cost £8,000.

(b) Sold inventories for £23,000 on credit; these inventories had cost £17,000.

(c) Received cash from trade receivables totalling £18,000.

(d) The owners of the business introduced £100,000 of their own money, which was placed in the business bank account.

(e) The owners brought a motor van, valued at £10,000, into the business.

(f) Bought inventories on credit for £14,000.

(g) Paid trade payables £13,000.

Required:

Show the balance sheet after all of these transactions have been reflected.

THE INCOME STATEMENT

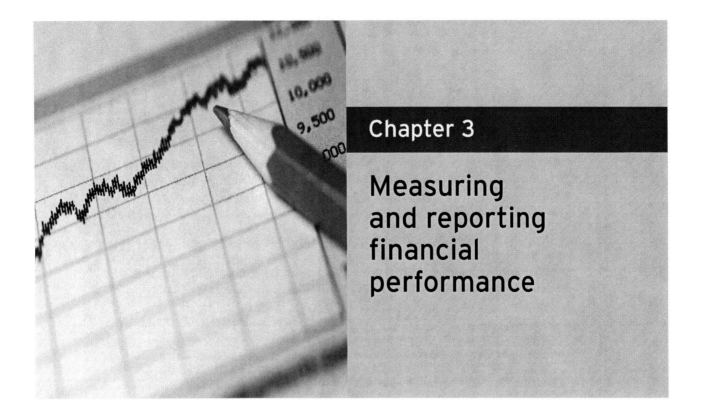

Chapter 3

Measuring and reporting financial performance

Introduction

In this chapter we continue our examination of the major financial statements by looking at the income statement. This statement was briefly considered in Chapter 2 and we shall now examine it in some detail. We shall see how it is prepared and how it links with the balance sheet. We shall also consider some of the key measurement problems to be faced when preparing the income statement.

Learning outcomes

When you have completed this chapter, you should be able to:

■ discuss the nature and purpose of the income statement;

■ prepare an income statement from relevant financial information;

■ discuss the main recognition and measurement issues that must be considered when preparing the income statement;

■ explain the main accounting conventions underpinning the income statement.

What does it mean?

Tate and Lyle plc, whose business is sweeteners, starches and sugar refining, reported sales revenue of £3,814m and a profit of £217m for the year ending on 31 March 2007. To understand fully the significance of these figures, we must be clear about the nature of revenue and profit. This means that we must be able to answer questions such as:

■ Does the sales revenue of £3,814m represent the cash generated from sales for the period?
■ What is the relationship between the sales revenue and the profit for the period?
■ Can the profit for the period of £217m be measured with complete accuracy and certainty?
■ Does the profit figure of £217m mean that the business had £217m *more* in the bank at the end of the year than it had at the beginning?
■ How can the sales revenue and profit figures help in assessing performance?

The answers to these and other questions are covered in the chapter.

The income statement

In Chapter 2 we examined the nature and purpose of the balance sheet. We saw that this statement is concerned with setting out the financial position of a business at a particular moment in time. However, it is not usually enough for users of the financial statements to have information relating only to the amount of wealth held by a business at one moment in time. Businesses exist for the primary purpose of generating wealth, or profit, and it is the profit generated *during a period* that is the main concern of many users of financial statements. Although the amount of profit generated is of particular interest to the owners of a business, other groups such as managers, employees and suppliers will also have an interest in the profit-generating ability of the business. The purpose of the income statement – or profit and loss account, as it is sometimes called – is to measure and report how much profit (wealth) the business has generated over a period. As with the balance sheet, which we examined in Chapter 2, the principles of preparation are the same irrespective of whether the income statement is for a sole proprietorship business or for a limited company.

The measurement of profit requires that the total revenue of the business, generated during a particular period, be identified. Revenue is simply a measure of the inflow of economic benefits arising from the ordinary activities of a business. These benefits, which accrue to the owners, will result in either an increase in assets (such as cash or amounts owed to the business by its customers) or a decrease in liabilities. Different forms of business enterprise will generate different forms of revenue. Some examples of the different forms that revenue can take are as follows:

■ sales of goods (for example, by a manufacturer)
■ fees for services (for example, of a solicitor)

- subscriptions (for example, of a club)
- interest received (for example, on an investment fund).

Real World 3.1 shows the various forms of revenue generated by a leading UK manufacturer.

Generating revenues!

Rolls-Royce plc, the well-known engine and power-generator manufacturer, had total sales turnover for the year ended 31 December 2006 of £7,156m. A breakdown of this amount is shown in Figure 3.1.

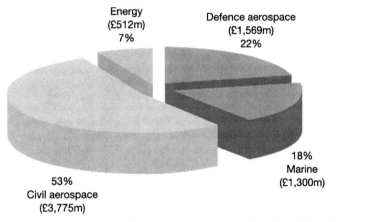

Figure 3.1 Revenues generated by Rolls-Royce plc during the year ended 31 December 2006

The two main sources of revenue are from aerospace (civil and defence). Together, these account for about 75 per cent of the total revenue generated.

Source: Based on information taken from Rolls-Royce plc Annual Report 2006.

The total expenses relating to each period must also be identified. Expense is really the opposite of revenue. It represents the outflow of economic benefits arising from the ordinary activities of a business. This loss of benefits will result in either a decrease in assets (such as cash) or an increase in liabilities (such as amounts owed to suppliers). Expenses are incurred in the process of generating revenue, or attempting to generate it. The nature of the business will again determine the type of expenses that will be incurred. Examples of some of the more common types of expenses are:

- the cost of buying the goods that are sold during the period concerned – known as *cost of sales* or *cost of goods sold*
- salaries and wages
- rent and rates

- motor vehicle running expenses
- insurances
- printing and stationery
- heat and light
- telephone and postage.

→ The income statement simply shows the total revenue generated during a particular period and deducts from this the total expenses incurred in generating that revenue. The difference between the total revenue and total expenses will represent either profit (if revenue exceeds expenses) or loss (if expenses exceed revenue). Thus, we have:

Profit (or loss) for the period = Total revenue for the period *less* Total expenses incurred in generating that revenue

→ The period over which profit or loss is normally measured is usually known as the accounting period, but sometimes known as the 'reporting period' or 'financial period'.

The income statement and the balance sheet

The income statement and the balance sheet should not be viewed in any way as substitutes for one another. Rather they should be seen as performing different functions. The balance sheet is, as stated earlier, a statement of the financial position of a business at a single moment in time – a 'snapshot' of the make-up of the wealth held by the business. The income statement, on the other hand, is concerned with the *flow* of wealth over a period of time. The two statements are, however, closely related.

The income statement links the balance sheets at the beginning and the end of an accounting period. Thus, at the start of a new accounting period, the balance sheet shows the opening financial position. After an appropriate period, an income statement is prepared to show the wealth generated over that period. A balance sheet is then also prepared to reveal the new financial position at the end of the period. This balance sheet will incorporate the changes in wealth that have occurred since the previous balance sheet was drawn up.

We saw in Chapter 2 (page 44) that the effect on the balance sheet of making a profit (or loss) means that the equation can be extended as follows:

Assets (at the end of the period) = Equity (amount at the start of the period
+ profit (or – loss) for the period)
+ Liabilities (at the end of the period).

The amount of profit or loss for the period affects the balance sheet as an adjustment to equity.

The above equation can be extended to:

Assets (at the end of the period) = Equity (amount at the start of the period)
+ (sales revenue – expenses)
+ Liabilities (at the end of the period).

In theory, it would be possible to calculate the profit (or loss) for the period by making all adjustments for revenue and expenses through the equity section of the balance sheet. However, this would be rather cumbersome. A better solution is to have an 'appendix' to the equity section, in the form of an income statement. By deducting expenses from revenue for the period, the income statement derives the profit (or loss) for adjustment to the equity figure in the balance sheet. This profit (or loss) figure represents the net effect of trading for the period. By providing this 'appendix', users are presented with a detailed and more informative view of performance.

Income statement layout

The layout of the income statement will vary according to the type of business to which it relates. To illustrate an income statement, let us consider the case of a retail business (that is, a business that buys goods in their completed state and resells them). This type of business usually has straightforward operations and, as a result, the income statement is relatively easy to understand.

Example 3.1 sets out a typical layout for the income statement of a retail business.

Example 3.1

Better-Price Stores
Income statement for the year ended 31 October 2008

	£
Sales revenue	232,000
Cost of sales	(154,000)
Gross profit	78,000
Salaries and wages	(24,500)
Rent and rates	(14,200)
Heat and light	(7,500)
Telephone and postage	(1,200)
Insurance	(1,000)
Motor vehicle running expenses	(3,400)
Depreciation – fixtures and fittings	(1,000)
Depreciation – motor van	(600)
Operating profit	24,600
Interest received from investments	2,000
Loan interest	(1,100)
Profit for the year	25,500

We can see that revenue, which arises from selling the goods, is the first item to appear. Deducted from this item is the cost of sales (also called the cost of the goods sold) during the period. We saw in Chapter 2 that brackets are used to denote when an item is to be deducted. This convention is used by accountants in preference to + or – signs and will be used throughout the text.

Gross profit

→ The first part of the income statement is concerned with calculating the gross profit for the period. This is simply the difference between the revenue and cost of sales figures and represents the profit from buying and selling goods, without taking into account any other revenues or expenses associated with the business.

Operating profit

From the gross profit, other expenses (overheads) that have been incurred in operating the business (salaries and wages, rent and rates, and so on) are deducted.

→ The resulting figure is known as the operating profit for the accounting period. This represents the wealth generated during the period from the normal activities of the business.

Operating profit does not take account of any income that the business may have from activities that are not included in its normal operations. Better-Price Stores in Example 3.1 is a retailer, so the interest on some spare cash that the business has lent is not part of its operating profit.

Costs of financing the business are also ignored in the calculation of the operating profit.

Profit for the year

Having established the operating profit, we add any non-operating income (such as interest receivable) and deduct any interest payable on borrowings made by the

→ business, to arrive at the profit for the year (or net profit). This is the income that is attributable to the owner(s) of the business and which will be added to the equity figure in the balance sheet. As can be seen, profit for the year is a residual: that is, the amount remaining after deducting all expenses incurred in generating the sales revenue for the period and taking account of non-operating income.

Some further issues

Having set out the main principles involved in preparing an income statement, we need to consider some further points.

Cost of sales

→ The cost of sales (or cost of goods sold) figure for a period can be identified in different ways. In some businesses, the cost of sales amount for each individual sale is identified at the time of the transaction. Each sales revenue is closely matched with the relevant cost of that sale and so identifying the cost of sales figure for inclusion in the income statement is not a problem. Many large retailers (for example, supermarkets) have point-of-sale (checkout) devices that not only record each sale but also simultaneously pick up the cost of the goods that are the subject of the particular sale. Other businesses that sell a relatively small number of high-value items (for example, an engineering business that produces custom-made equipment) also tend to match sales revenue with the cost of the goods sold, at the time of the sale. However, some businesses (for example, small retailers) do not usually find it practical to match each sale to a particular cost of sales figure as the accounting period progresses. They find it easier to identify the cost of sales figure at the end of the accounting period.

Deriving the cost of sales after the end of the accounting period

To understand how this is done, it is important to recognise that the cost of sales figure represents the cost of goods that were *sold* by the business during the period rather than the cost of goods that were *bought* by that business during the period. Part of the goods bought during a particular period may remain in the business, as inventories, and not be sold until a later period. To derive the cost of sales for a period, it is necessary to know the amount of opening and closing inventories for the period and the cost of goods bought during the period. Example 3.2 illustrates how the cost of sales is derived.

Example 3.2

Better-Price Stores, which we considered in Example 3.1 above, began the accounting year with unsold inventories of £40,000 and during that year bought inventories at a cost of £189,000. At the end of the year, unsold inventories of £75,000 were still held by the business.

The opening inventories at the beginning of the year *plus* the goods bought during the year will represent the total goods available for resale. Thus:

	£
Opening inventories	40,000
Goods bought	189,000
Goods available for resale	229,000

The closing inventories will represent that portion of the total goods available for resale that remains unsold at the end of the period. Thus, the cost of goods actually sold during the period must be the total goods available for resale *less* the inventories remaining at the end of the period. That is:

	£
Goods available for resale	229,000
Closing inventories	(75,000)
Cost of sales (or cost of goods sold)	154,000

These calculations are sometimes shown on the face of the income statement as in Example 3.3.

Example 3.3

	£	£
Sales revenue		232,000
Cost of sales:		
Opening inventories	40,000	
Goods bought	189,000	
Closing inventories	(75,000)	(154,000)
Gross profit		78,000

The above is just an expanded version of the first section of the income statement for Better-Price Stores, as set out in Example 3.1. We have simply included the additional information concerning inventories balances and purchases for the year provided in Example 3.2.

Classification of expenses

The classifications for the revenue and expense items, as with the classifications of various assets and claims in the balance sheet, are often a matter of judgement by those who design the accounting system. Thus, the income statement set out in Example 3.1 could have included the insurance expense with the telephone and postage expense under a single heading – say, 'general expenses'. Such decisions are normally based on how useful a particular classification will be to users. This will usually mean, however, that expense items of material size will be shown separately. For businesses that trade as limited companies, there are rules that dictate the classification of various items appearing in the financial statements for external reporting purposes. These rules will be discussed in Chapter 4.

Activity 3.1

The following information relates to the activities of H & S Retailers for the year ended 30 April 2008:

	£
Motor vehicle running expenses	1,200
Closing inventories	3,000
Rent and rates payable	5,000
Motor vans – cost less depreciation	6,300
Annual depreciation – motor vans	1,500
Heat and light	900
Telephone and postage	450
Sales revenue	97,400
Goods purchased	68,350
Insurance	750
Loan interest payable	620
Balance at bank	4,780
Salaries and wages	10,400
Opening inventories	4,000

Prepare an income statement for the year ended 30 April 2008. (*Hint*: Not all items shown above should appear on this statement.)

Your answer to this activity should be as follows:

H & S Retailers
Income statement for the year ended 30 April 2008

	£	£
Sales revenue		97,400
Cost of sales:		
Opening inventories	4,000	
Purchases	68,350	
Closing inventories	(3,000)	(69,350)
Gross profit		28,050
Salaries and wages		(10,400)
Rent and rates		(5,000)
Heat and light		(900)
Telephone and postage		(450)
Insurance		(750)
Motor vehicle running expenses		(1,200)
Depreciation – motor vans		(1,500)
Operating profit		7,850
Loan interest		(620)
Profit for the year		7,230

Note that neither the motor vans nor the bank balance are included in this statement, because they are both assets and so neither revenues nor expenses.

The accounting period

We have seen already that for reporting to those outside the business, a financial reporting cycle of one year is the norm, though some large businesses produce a half-yearly, or interim, financial statement to provide more frequent feedback on progress. For those who manage a business, however, it is probably essential to have much more frequent feedback on performance. Thus it is quite common for income statements to be prepared on a quarterly, monthly, weekly or even daily basis in order to show how things are progressing.

Recognising revenue

A key issue in the measurement of profit concerns the point at which revenue is recognised. Revenue arising from the sale of goods or provision of a service could be recognised at various points. Where, for example, a motor car dealer receives an order for a new car from one of its business clients, the associated revenue could be recognised by the dealer

- at the time that the order is placed by the customer;
- at the time that the car is collected by the customer; or
- at the time that the customer pays the dealer.

These three points could well be quite far apart, particularly where the order relates to a specialist car that is sold to the customer on credit.

The point chosen is not simply a matter of academic interest: it can have a profound impact on the total revenues reported for a particular accounting period. This, in turn, could have a profound effect on profit. If the car transaction straddled the end of an accounting period, the choice made between the three possible times for recognising the revenue could determine whether it is included as revenue of an earlier accounting period or a later one.

When dealing with the sale of goods or the provision of services, the main criteria for recognising revenue are that

- the amount of revenue can be measured reliably, and
- it is probable that the economic benefits will be received.

An additional criterion, however, must be applied where the revenue comes from the sale of goods, which is that

- ownership and control of the items should pass to the buyer.

Activity 3.2 provides an opportunity to apply these criteria to a practical problem.

Activity 3.2

A manufacturing business sells goods on credit (that is, the customer pays for the goods some time after they are received). Below are four points in the production/selling cycle at which revenue might be recognised by the business:

1   when the goods are produced;
2   when an order is received from the customer;
3   when the goods are delivered to, and accepted by, the customer;
4   when the cash is received from the customer.

A significant amount of time may elapse between these different points. At what point do you think the business should recognise revenue?

All of the three criteria mentioned above will usually be fulfilled at point 3: when the goods are passed to, and accepted by, the customer. This is because

- the selling price and the settlement terms will have been agreed and therefore the amount of revenue can be reliably measured;
- delivery and acceptance of the goods leads to ownership and control passing to the buyer;
- transferring ownership gives the seller legally enforceable rights that makes it probable that the buyer will pay.

We can see that the effect of applying these criteria is that a sale on credit is usually recognised *before* the cash is received. Thus, the total sales revenue figure shown in the income statement may include sales transactions for which the cash has yet to be received. The total sales revenue figure in the income statement for a period will often, therefore, be different from the total cash received from sales during that period.

Where goods are sold for cash rather than on credit, the revenue will normally be recognised at the point of sale. It is at this point that all the criteria will usually be met. For cash sales, there will be no difference in timing between reporting sales revenue and cash received.

Real World 3.2 sets out the revenue recognition criteria for one well-known travel business, First Choice Holidays plc. Note that even where clients have already paid for part of their trip (as a deposit), this is not recognised as revenue until the trip takes place.

Real World 3.2

Selling point

(i) Goods sold and services rendered
Revenue from sale of goods is recognised in the income statement when the significant risks and rewards or ownership have been transferred to the buyer.

Revenue in respect of in-house product is recognised on the date of departure. Travel agency commissions and other revenues received from the sale of third-party product are recognised when they are earned on receipt of final payment.

No revenue is recognised if there are significant uncertainties regarding recovery of the consideration due, associated costs or possible return of goods.

(ii) Client monies received in advance (deferred income)
Client monies received at the balance sheet date relating to holidays commencing and flights departing after the year end is deferred and included within trade and other payables.

Source: First Choice Holidays plc Annual Report 2006.

Long-term contracts

Some contracts, both for goods and for services, can last for more than one accounting period. If the business providing the goods or service were to wait until the contract is fulfilled before recognising revenue, the income statement could give a misleading impression of the wealth generated in the various accounting periods covered by the contract. This is a particular problem for businesses that undertake major long-term contracts, where a single contract could represent a large proportion of their total activities.

Construction contracts

Construction contracts often extend over a long period of time. Suppose that a customer enters into a contract with a builder to have a new factory built, that will take three years to complete. In such a situation, it is possible to recognise revenue *before* the factory is completed provided that the building work can be broken down into a number of stages and each stage can be measured reliably. Let us assume that building the factory could be broken down into the following stages:

Stage 1 – clearing and levelling the land and putting in the foundations.
Stage 2 – building the walls.
Stage 3 – putting on the roof.
Stage 4 – putting in the windows and completing all the interior work.

Each stage can be awarded a separate price with the total for all the stages being equal to the total contract price for the factory. This means that, as each stage is completed, the builder can recognise the price for that stage as revenue and bill the customer accordingly.

If the builder were to wait until the factory was completed before recognising revenue, the income statement covering the final year of the contract would recognise all of the revenue on the contract and the income statements for each preceding year would recognise no revenue. This would give a misleading impression, as it would not reflect the work done during each period.

Real World 3.3 sets out the revenue recognition criteria for one large construction business.

Real World 3.3

Tracking revenue

Jarvis plc is a business operating in the areas of road and rail infrastructure renewal, facilities management and plant hire. The point at which revenue on long-term contracts is recognised by the business is as follows:

> When the outcome of a long-term contract can be estimated reliably, contract revenue is recognised by reference to the degree of completion of each contract, based on the amounts certified and to be certified by the customer.

Source: Jarvis plc Annual Report and Accounts 2007, p. 45.

Services

Revenue from contracts for services may also be recognised in stages. Suppose a consultancy business has a contract to install a new computer system for the government, which will take several years to complete. Revenue can be recognised *before* the contract is completed as long as the contract can be broken down into stages and the particular stages of completion can be measured reliably. This is really the same approach as that used in the construction contract mentioned above.

Sometimes a continuous service is provided to a customer; for example, a telecommunications business may provide open access to the Internet to those who subscribe to the service. In this case, revenue is usually recognised as the service is rendered. Benefits from providing the service are usually assumed to flow evenly over time and so revenue is recognised evenly over the subscription period.

Where it is not possible to break down a service into particular stages of completion, or to assume that benefits from providing the service accrue evenly over time, revenue will not usually be recognised until the service is fully completed. A solicitor handling a house purchase for a client would be one such example.

Real World 3.4 provides an example of how one major business recognises revenue from providing services.

Real World 3.4

Sky-high broadcasting revenue

British Sky Broadcasting Group plc is a major satellite broadcaster that generates various forms of revenue. Here are the ways in which some of its revenues are recognised:

- Pay-per-view revenues – when the event (movie or football match) is viewed.
- Direct-to-home subscription services – as the services are provided.
- Cable revenues – as the services are provided.
- Advertising revenues – when the advertising is broadcast.
- Installations and digibox revenues – when the services have been provided.

Source: British Sky Broadcasting Group plc Annual Report and Accounts 2006, p. 84.

When a service is provided, there will normally be a timing difference between the recognition of revenue and the receipt of cash. Revenue for providing services is often recognised *before* the cash is received, as with the sale of goods on credit. However, there are occasions when it is the other way around, usually because the business demands payment before providing the service.

Activity 3.3

Can you think of any examples where cash may be demanded in advance of a service being provided? (*Hint*: Try to think of services that you may use.)

Examples of cash being received in advance of the service being provided may include:

- rent received from letting premises
- telephone line rental charges
- TV licence (BBC) or subscription (for example, Sky) fees
- subscriptions received for the use of health clubs or golf clubs.

You may have thought of others.

Recognising expenses

 Having decided on the point at which revenue is recognised, we can now turn to the issue of the recognition of expenses. The matching convention in accounting is designed to provide guidance concerning the recognition of expenses. This convention states that expenses should be matched to the revenue that they helped to generate. In other words, the expenses that are associated with a particular revenue must be taken into account in the income statement for the same accounting period as that in which that revenue is included in the total sales revenue figure. Applying this convention may mean that a particular expense reported in the income statement for a period may not be the same figure as the cash paid for that item during the period. The expense reported might be either more or less than the cash paid during the period. Let us consider two examples that illustrate this point.

When the expense for the period is more than the cash paid during the period

Example 3.4

Domestic Ltd sells household electrical appliances. It pays its sales staff a commission of 2 per cent of sales revenue generated. Total sales revenue for last year amounted to £300,000. This will mean that the commission to be paid in respect of the sales for the year will be £6,000. However, by the end of the period, the amount of sales commission that had actually been paid to staff was £5,000. If the business reported only the amount paid, it would mean that the income statement would not reflect the full expense for the year. This would contravene the *matching convention* because not all of the expenses associated with the revenue of the year would have been matched in the income statement. This will be remedied as follows:

- Sales commission expense in the income statement will include the amount paid plus the amount outstanding (that is, £6,000 = £5,000 + £1,000).
- The amount outstanding (£1,000) represents an outstanding liability at the balance sheet date and will be included under the heading accrued expenses, or 'accruals', in the balance sheet. As this item will have to be paid within twelve months of the balance sheet date, it will be treated as a current liability.
- The cash will already have been reduced to reflect the commission paid (£5,000) during the period.

These points are illustrated in Figure 3.2.

In principle, all expenses should be matched to the period in which the sales revenue to which they relate is reported. However, it is sometimes difficult to match certain expenses to sales revenue in the same precise way that we have matched sales commission to sales revenue. It is unlikely, for example, that electricity charges incurred can be linked directly to particular sales in this way. As a result, the electricity charges incurred by, say, a retailer would be matched to the *period* to which they relate. Example 3.5 illustrates this.

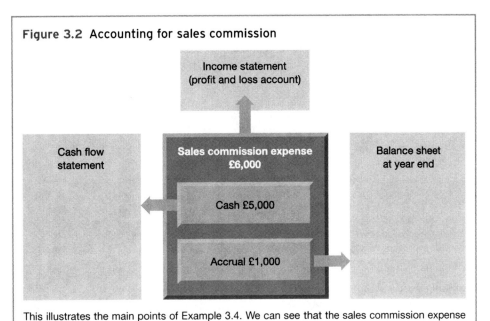

Figure 3.2 Accounting for sales commission

This illustrates the main points of Example 3.4. We can see that the sales commission expense of £6,000 (which appears in the income statement) is made up of a cash element of £5,000 and an accrued element of £1,000. The cash element appears in the cash flow statement and the accrued element will appear as a year-end liability in the balance sheet.

Example 3.5

Domestic Ltd has reached the end of its accounting year and has only paid for electricity for the first three-quarters of the year (amounting to £1,900). This is simply because the electricity company has yet to send out bills for the quarter that ends on the same date as Domestic Ltd's year end. The amount of Domestic Ltd's bill for the last quarter is £500. In this situation, the amount of the electricity expense outstanding is dealt with as follows:

■ Electricity expense in the income statement will include the amount paid, plus the amount of the bill for the last quarter (that is, £1,900 + £500 = £2,400) in order to cover the whole year.
■ The amount of the outstanding bill (£500) represents a liability at the balance sheet date and will be included under the heading 'accruals' or 'accrued expenses' in the balance sheet. This item would normally have to be paid within twelve months of the end of the accounting year and will, therefore, be treated as a current liability.
■ The cash will already have been reduced to reflect the electricity paid (£1,900) during the period.

This treatment will mean that the correct figure for the electricity expense for the year will be included in the income statement. It will also have the effect of showing that, at the end of the accounting year, Domestic Ltd owed the amount of the last quarter's electricity bill. Dealing with the outstanding amount in this way reflects the dual aspect of the item and will ensure that the balance sheet equation is maintained.

Domestic Ltd may wish to draw up its income statement before it is able to discover how much it owes for the last quarter's electricity. In this case it is quite normal to make a reasonable estimate of the amount of the bill and to use this estimated amount as described above.

Activity 3.4

How will the payment of the electricity bill for the last quarter be dealt with in the accounting records of Domestic Ltd?

When the electricity bill is eventually paid, it will be dealt with as follows:

- Reduce cash by the amount of the bill.
- Reduce the amount of the accrued expense as shown on the balance sheet by the same amount.

If an estimated figure is used and there is a slight error in the estimate, a small adjustment (either negative or positive depending on the direction of the error) can be made to the following year's expense. Dealing with the estimation error in this way is not strictly correct, but the amount is likely to be insignificant.

Activity 3.5

Can you think of other expenses for a retailer, apart from electricity charges, that cannot be linked directly to sales revenue and for which matching will therefore be done on a time basis?

You may have thought of the following examples:

- rent and rates
- insurance
- interest payments
- licence fees payable.

This is not an exhaustive list. You may have thought of others.

When the amount paid during the year is more than the full expense for the period

It is not unusual for a business to be in a situation where it has paid more during the year than the full expense for that year. Example 3.6 illustrates how we deal with this.

Example 3.6

Images Ltd, an advertising agency, normally pays rent for its premises quarterly in advance (on 1 January, 1 April, 1 July and 1 October). On the last day of the last accounting year (31 December), it paid the next quarter's rent (£4,000) to the following 31 March, which was a day earlier than required. This would mean that a total of five quarters' rent was paid during the year. If Images Ltd reports all of the cash paid as an expense in the income statement, this would be more than the full expense for the year. This would contravene the matching convention because a higher figure than the expenses associated with the revenue of the year would appear in the income statement.

The problem is overcome by dealing with the rental payment as follows:

- Show the rent for four quarters as the appropriate expense in the income statement (that is, 4 × £4,000 = £16,000).
- The cash (that is, 5 × £4,000 = £20,000) would already have been paid during the year.
- Show the quarter's rent paid in advance (£4,000) as a prepaid expense under assets in the balance sheet. (The rent paid in advance will appear as a current asset in the balance sheet, under the heading prepaid expenses or 'prepayments'.)

In the next accounting period, this prepayment will cease to be an asset and will become an expense in the income statement of that period. This is because the rent prepaid relates to the next period and will be 'used up' during it.

These points are illustrated in Figure 3.3.

In practice, the treatment of accruals and prepayments will be subject to the materiality convention of accounting. This convention states that, where the amounts involved are immaterial, we should consider only what is reasonable. This may mean that an item will be treated as an expense in the period in which it is paid, rather than being strictly matched to the revenue to which it relates. For example, a business may find that, at the end of an accounting period, a bill of £5 has been paid for stationery that has yet to be delivered. For a business of any size, the time and effort involved in recording this as a prepayment would not be justified by the little effect that this would have on the measurement of profit or financial position. The amount would, therefore, be treated as an expense when preparing the income statement for the current period and ignored in the following period.

Profit, cash and accruals accounting

As we have just seen, revenue does not usually represent cash received, and expenses are not the same as cash paid. As a result, the profit figure (that is, total revenue minus total expenses) will not normally represent the net cash generated during a period. It is therefore important to distinguish between profit and liquidity. Profit is a measure of achievement, or productive effort, rather than a measure of cash generated. Although

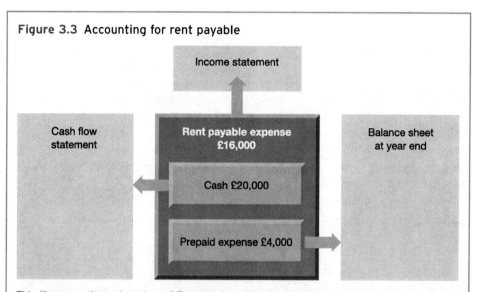

Figure 3.3 Accounting for rent payable

Income statement

Cash flow statement

Rent payable expense £16,000

Cash £20,000

Prepaid expense £4,000

Balance sheet at year end

This illustrates the main points of Example 3.6. We can see that the rent expense of £16,000 (which appears in the income statement) is made up of four quarters' rent at £4,000 per quarter. This is the amount that relates to the period and is 'used up' during the period. The cash paid of £20,000 (which appears in the cash flow statement) is made up of the cash paid during the period, which is five quarters at £4,000 per quarter. Finally, the prepayment of £4,000 (which appears on the balance sheet) represents the payment made on 31 December and relates to the next financial year.

making a profit will increase wealth, as we have already seen in Chapter 2, cash is only one form in which that wealth may be held.

The above points are reflected in the accruals convention of accounting, which asserts that profit is the excess of revenue over expenses for a period, not the excess of cash receipts over cash payments. Leading on from this, the approach to accounting that is based on the accruals convention is frequently referred to as accruals accounting. Thus, the balance sheet and the income statement are both prepared on the basis of accruals accounting. The cash flow statement, on the other hand, is not, as it simply deals with cash receipts and payments.

Depreciation

The expense of depreciation, which appeared in the income statement in Activity 3.1, requires further explanation. Most non-current assets do not have a perpetual existence. They are eventually used up in the process of generating revenue for the business. In essence, depreciation is an attempt to measure that portion of the cost (or fair value) of a non-current asset that has been used up in generating the revenue recognised during a particular period. The depreciation charge is considered to be an expense of the period to which it relates. Depreciation tends to be relevant both to tangible non-current assets (property, plant and equipment) and to intangible non-current assets.

We should be clear that the principle is the same for both types of non-current asset. We shall deal with each of the two in turn.

Tangible non-current assets (property, plant and equipment)

To calculate a depreciation charge for a period, four factors have to be considered:

- the cost (or fair value) of the asset
- the useful life of the asset
- the residual value of the asset
- the depreciation method.

The cost (or fair value) of the asset

The cost of an asset will include all costs incurred by the business to bring the asset to its required location and to make it ready for use. Thus, in addition to the costs of acquiring the asset, any delivery costs, installation costs (for example, setting up a new machine) and legal costs incurred in the transfer of legal title (for example, in purchasing property) will be included as part of the total cost of the asset. Similarly, any costs incurred in improving or altering an asset in order to make it suitable for its intended use within the business will also be included as part of the total cost.

Activity 3.6

Andrew Wu (Engineering) Ltd bought a new motor car for its marketing director. The invoice received from the motor car supplier showed the following:

	£
New BMW 325i	26,350
Delivery charge	80
Alloy wheels	660
Sun roof	200
Petrol	30
Number plates	130
Road fund licence	165
	27,615
Part exchange – Reliant Robin	(1,000)
Amount outstanding	26,615

What is the total cost of the new car that will be treated as part of the business's property, plant and equipment?

The cost of the new car will be as follows:

	£
New BMW 325i	26,350
Delivery charge	80
Alloy wheels	660
Sun roof	200
Number plates	130
	27,420

→

> This cost includes delivery charges, which are necessary to bring the asset into use, and it includes number plates, as they are a necessary and integral part of the asset. Improvements (alloy wheels and sun roof) are also regarded as part of the total cost of the motor car. The petrol and road fund licence, however, represent costs of operating the asset rather than a part of the total cost of acquiring it and making it ready for use: hence these amounts will be charged as an expense in the period incurred (although part of the cost of the licence may be regarded as a prepaid expense in the period incurred).
>
> The part-exchange figure shown is part payment of the total amount outstanding and so is not relevant to a consideration of the total cost.

The fair value of an asset was defined in Chapter 2 as the exchange value that could be obtained in an arm's-length transaction. We have already seen that assets may be revalued to fair value only if this can be measured reliably. When a revaluation is carried out, all items within the same class must be revalued and revaluations must be kept up to date.

The useful life of the asset

A tangible non-current asset has both a *physical life* and an *economic life*. The physical life will be exhausted through the effects of wear and tear and/or the passage of time. It is possible, however, for the physical life to be extended considerably through careful maintenance, improvements and so on. The economic life is decided by the effects of technological progress and by changes in demand. After a while, the benefits of using the asset may be less than the costs involved. This may be because the asset is unable to compete with newer assets, or because it is no longer relevant to the needs of the business. The economic life of a non-current tangible asset may be much shorter than its physical life. For example, a computer may have a physical life of eight years and an economic life of three years.

It is the economic life that will determine the expected useful life for the purpose of calculating depreciation. Forecasting the economic life, however, may be extremely difficult in practice: both the rate at which technology progresses and shifts in consumer tastes can be swift and unpredictable.

Residual value (disposal value)

When a business disposes of a tangible non-current asset that may still be of value to others, some payment may be received. This payment will represent the residual value, or *disposal value*, of the asset. To calculate the total amount to be depreciated, the residual value must be deducted from the cost of the asset. The likely amount to be received on disposal can, once again, be difficult to predict. The best guide is often past experience of similar assets sold.

Depreciation method

Once the amount to be depreciated (that is, the cost, or fair value, of the asset less any residual value) has been estimated, the business must select a method of allocating this depreciable amount between the accounting periods covering the asset's useful life. Although there are various ways in which the total depreciation may be allocated and, from this, a depreciation charge for each period derived, there are really only two methods that are commonly used in practice.

    The first of these is known as the straight-line method. This method simply allocates the amount to be depreciated evenly over the useful life of the asset. In other words, an equal amount of depreciation is charged for each year that the asset is held.

Example 3.7

To illustrate this method, consider the following information:

Cost of machine	£78,124
Estimated residual value at the end of its useful life	£2,000
Estimated useful life	4 years

To calculate the depreciation charge for each year, the total amount to be depreciated must be calculated. This will be the total cost less the estimated residual value: that is, £78,124 − £2,000 = £76,124. Having done this, the annual depreciation charge can be derived by dividing the amount to be depreciated by the estimated useful life of the asset of four years. The calculation is therefore:

$$\frac{£76,124}{4} = £19,031$$

Thus, the annual depreciation charge that appears in the income statement in relation to this asset will be £19,031 for each of the four years of the asset's life.

The amount of depreciation relating to the asset will be accumulated for as long as the asset continues to be owned by the business. This accumulated depreciation figure will increase each year as a result of the annual depreciation amount charged to the income statement. This accumulated amount will be deducted from the cost of the asset on the balance sheet. At the end of the second year, for example, the accumulated depreciation will be £19,031 × 2 = £38,062, and the asset details will appear on the balance sheet as follows:

	£
Machine at cost	78,124
Accumulated depreciation	(38,062)
	40,062

The balance of £40,062 shown above is referred to as the carrying amount (sometimes also known as the written-down value or net book value) of the asset. It represents that portion of the cost (or fair value) of the asset that has still to be charged as an expense (written off) in future years. It must be emphasised that this figure does not represent the current market value, which may be quite different.

The straight-line method derives its name from the fact that the carrying amount of the asset at the end of each year, when plotted against time, will result in a straight line, as shown in Figure 3.4.

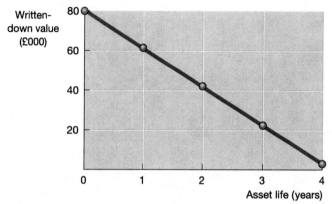

Figure 3.4 Graph of written-down value against time using the straight-line method

The carrying amount of the asset declines by a constant amount each year. This is because the straight-line method provides a constant depreciation charge each year. The result, when plotted on a graph, is a straight line.

The second approach to calculating depreciation for a period, which is found in practice, is referred to as the reducing-balance method. This method applies a fixed percentage rate of depreciation to the carrying amount of an asset each year. The effect of this will be high annual depreciation charges in the early years and lower charges in the later years. To illustrate this method, let us take the same information that was used in Example 3.7. By using a fixed percentage of 60 per cent of the carrying amount to determine the annual depreciation charge, the effect will be to reduce the carrying amount to £2,000 after four years.

The calculations will be as follows:

	£
Cost of machine	78,124
Year 1 Depreciation charge (60%* of cost)	(46,874)
Carrying amount	31,250
Year 2 Depreciation charge (60% of carrying amount)	(18,750)
Carrying amount	12,500
Year 3 Depreciation charge (60% of carrying amount)	(7,500)
Carrying amount	5,000
Year 4 Depreciation charge (60% of carrying amount)	(3,000)
Residual value	2,000

* See Box 3.1 for an explanation of how to derive the fixed percentage.

Box 3.1
Deriving the fixed percentage

Deriving the fixed percentage to be applied requires the use of the following formula:

$$P = (1 - \sqrt[n]{R/C}) \times 100\%$$

where: P = the depreciation percentage
n = the useful life of the asset (in years)
R = the residual value of the asset
C = the cost, or fair value, of the asset.

The fixed percentage rate will, however, be given in all examples used in this text.

We can see that the pattern of depreciation is quite different for the two methods. If we plot the carrying amount of the asset, which has been derived using the reducing-balance method, against time, the result will be as shown in Figure 3.5.

Figure 3.5 Graph of written-down value against time using the reducing-balance method

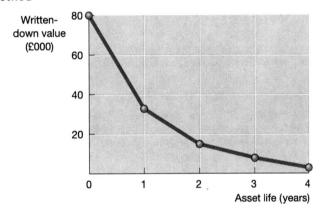

Under the reducing-balance method, the carrying amount of an asset falls by a larger amount in the earlier years than in the later years. This is because the depreciation charge is based on a fixed-rate percentage of the carrying amount.

Activity 3.7

Assume that the machine used in the example above was owned by a business that made a profit before depreciation of £40,000 for each of the four years in which the asset was held.

Calculate the profit for the business for each year under each depreciation method, and comment on your findings.

Your answer should be as follows:

Straight-line method

	(a) Profit before depreciation £	(b) Depreciation £	(a – b) Profit £
Year 1	40,000	19,031	20,969
Year 2	40,000	19,031	20,969
Year 3	40,000	19,031	20,969
Year 4	40,000	19,031	20,969

Reducing-balance method

	(a) Profit before depreciation £	(b) Depreciation £	(a – b) Profit/(loss) £
Year 1	40,000	46,874	(6,874)
Year 2	40,000	18,750	21,250
Year 3	40,000	7,500	32,500
Year 4	40,000	3,000	37,000

The straight-line method of depreciation results in a constant profit figure over the four-year period. This is because both the profit before depreciation and the depreciation charge are constant over the period. The reducing-balance method, however, results in a changing profit figure over time, despite the fact that in this example the pre-depreciation profit is the same each year. In the first year a loss is reported, and thereafter a rising profit is reported.

Although the *pattern* of profit over the four-year period will be quite different, depending on the depreciation method used, the *total* profit for the period (£83,876) will remain the same. This is because both methods of depreciating will allocate the same amount of total depreciation (£76,124) over the four-year period. It is only the amount allocated *between years* that will differ.

In practice, the use of different depreciation methods may not have such a dramatic effect on profits as suggested in Activity 3.7. Where a business replaces some of its assets each year, the total depreciation charge calculated under the reducing-balance method will reflect a range of charges (from high through to low), as assets will be at different points in the replacement cycle. This could mean that each year's total depreciation charge may not be significantly different from the total depreciation charge that would be derived under the straight-line method.

Selecting a depreciation method

How does a business choose which depreciation method to use for a particular asset? The answer is the one that best matches the depreciation expense to the pattern of economic benefits that the asset provides. Where these benefits are provided evenly over time (buildings, for example), the straight-line method is usually appropriate. Where assets lose their efficiency (as with certain types of machinery), the benefits provided will decline over time and so the reducing-balance method may be more appropriate. Where the pattern of economic benefits provided by the asset is uncertain, the straight-line method is normally chosen.

There is an international financial reporting standard (or international accounting standard) to deal with the depreciation of property, plant and equipment. As we shall see in Chapter 4, the purpose of accounting standards is to narrow areas of accounting difference and to try to ensure that information provided to users is transparent and comparable. The relevant standard endorses the view that the depreciation method chosen should reflect the pattern of economic benefits provided but does not specify particular methods to be used. It states that the useful life, depreciation method and residual values of non-current assets should be reviewed at least annually and adjustments made where appropriate.

Real World 3.5 sets out the depreciation policies of Thorntons plc.

Real World 3.5

Sweet talk on depreciation policies

Thorntons plc, the manufacturer and retailer of confectionery, uses the straight-line method to depreciate all its non-current assets. In practice, this appears to be the most widely used method of depreciation. The financial statements for the year ended 30 June 2007 show the period over which different classes of tangible non-current assets are depreciated as follows:

In equal annual instalments	
Freehold premises	50 years
Short leasehold land and buildings	Period of the lease
Retail fixtures and fittings	Up to 5 years
Retail equipment	4 to 5 years
Retail store improvements	Up to 10 years
Other equipment and vehicles	3 to 7 years
Manufacturing plant and machinery	10 to 15 years
Computer licenses and software	3 to 5 years

We can see that there are wide variations in the expected useful lives of the various non-current assets held.

Source: Thorntons plc Annual Report and Accounts 2007, p. 28.

It seems that Thorntons plc is typical of UK businesses in that most use the straight-line approach. The reducing-balance method is not very much used.

The approach taken to calculating depreciation is summarised in Figure 3.6.

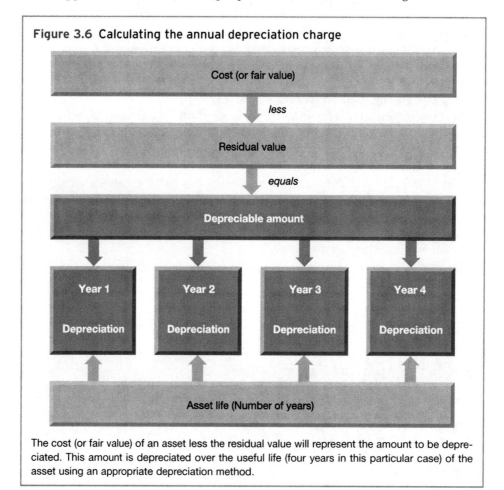

Figure 3.6 Calculating the annual depreciation charge

The cost (or fair value) of an asset less the residual value will represent the amount to be depreciated. This amount is depreciated over the useful life (four years in this particular case) of the asset using an appropriate depreciation method.

Depreciating intangible assets

Where an intangible asset has a finite life, the approach taken for the depreciation (or *amortisation* as it is usually called with intangibles) is broadly the same as that for property, plant and equipment (tangible non-current assets). The asset is amortised (depreciated) over its useful life and the amortisation method used should reflect the pattern of benefits provided. Some differences arise, however, because of the valuation problems surrounding these assets. Intangible assets are normally reported at cost rather than their fair value. They are rarely revalued because there is usually no active market from which to establish fair values. For similar reasons, the residual value of an intangible asset is normally assumed to be zero.

We saw in Chapter 2 that some intangible assets, which may include acquired good-will, have an indefinite useful life. These assets are not amortised but instead are tested for impairment at least annually. While intangible assets with finite lives and property, plant and equipment are also subject to impairment testing, this will only occur when there is some indication that impairment has taken place.

Depreciation and the replacement of non-current assets

There seems to be a misunderstanding in the minds of some people that the purpose of depreciation is to provide the funds for the replacement of an asset when it reaches the end of its useful life. However, this is not the purpose of depreciation as conventionally defined. It was mentioned earlier that depreciation represents an attempt to allocate the cost, or fair value (less any residual value), of an asset over its expected useful life. The resulting depreciation charge in each accounting period represents an expense, which is then used in the calculation of profit for the period. Calculating the depreciation charge for a period is therefore necessary for the proper measurement of financial performance, and must be done whether or not the business intends to replace the asset in the future.

If there is an intention to replace the asset, the depreciation charge in the income statement will not ensure that liquid funds are set aside by the business specifically for this purpose. Although the effect of a depreciation charge is to reduce profit, and therefore to reduce the amount available for withdrawal by the owners, the amounts retained within the business as a result may be invested in ways that are unrelated to the replacement of the specific asset.

Depreciation and judgement

When reading the above sections on depreciation, it may have struck you that accounting is not as precise and objective as is sometimes suggested. There are areas where subjective judgement is required, and depreciation provides a good illustration of this.

Activity 3.8

What kinds of judgements must be made to calculate a depreciation charge for a period?

You may have thought of the following:

■ the expected residual or disposal value of the asset
■ the expected useful life of the asset
■ the choice of depreciation method.

Making different judgements on these matters would result in a different pattern of depreciation charges over the life of the asset, and therefore in a different pattern of reported profits. However, underestimations or overestimations that are made in relation to the above will be adjusted for in the final year of an asset's life, and so the total depreciation charge (and total profit) over the asset's life will not be affected by estimation errors.

Real World 3.6 describes the effect of extending the useful life of property, plant and equipment on the short-term profits of one large business.

Sports massage

JJB Sports plc, a leading retailer, reported interim financial results for the six months ended 30 June 2005 that caused some disquiet among investors and analysts. The business changed the estimates for the useful life of its property, plant and equipment when calculating depreciation. It explained that this was due to new requirements to adopt International Financial Reporting Standards (IFRSs) when preparing financial statements. The article below, however, suggests that not everyone believed this.

JJB massages results to boost profits

High street retailer JJB Sports massaged last week's disappointing interim results by changing its depreciation calculations, in order to boost flagging profits by £4.3m.

Analysts admitted that they were caught on the hop, as the company reported a 35.8% drop in operating profits from £27.4m to £17.6m for six months ended June 2005 on revenues down 6% to £340.4m. Operating profits would have plummeted even further to £14.3m had the company not changed its accounting for depreciation. 'The company explained the change as coming out of its IFRS conversion review, but it was clearly there for other reasons,' said Teather & Greenwood retail analyst Sanjay Vidyarthi.

JJB said that an impairment review ahead of its IFRS transition had forced a rethink on the carrying value of property, plant and equipment.

It concluded that these items had useful economic lives that more closely matched the length of the short-term lease of the property, rather than the 10-year economic life, which had formed the basis of the depreciation charge in previous accounting periods.

Richard Ratner, head of equity research at Seymour Pierce, said: 'They said the way they had depreciated assets previously was not correct but I haven't seen any other companies make this kind of change.'

JJB's share price fell from 168.2p before the results to 164.7p at the end of last week.

Source: 'JJB massages results to boost profits', *Accountancy Age*, 20 October 2005, p. 3.

Costing inventories

The way in which we measure the cost of inventories is important because the cost of inventories sold during a period will affect the calculation of profit and the remaining inventories held at the end of the period will affect the portrayal of financial position in the balance sheet. In Chapter 2, we saw that historic cost is often the basis for reporting assets, and so it is tempting to think that determining the cost of inventories held is very straightforward. However, in a period of changing prices, the costing of inventories can be a problem.

A business must determine the cost of the inventories sold during the period and the cost of the inventories remaining at the end of the period. To do this, some assumption must be made about the way in which the inventories are physically handled. The assumption need have nothing to do with how the inventories are *actually* handled; it is concerned only with providing useful accounting information.

Two common assumptions used are:

- first in, first out (FIFO) – the earliest acquired inventories held are the first to be used;
- last in, first out (LIFO) – the latest acquired inventories held are the first to be used.

Another approach to deriving the cost of inventories is to assume that inventories acquired lose their separate identity and go into a 'pool'. Any issues of inventories then reflect the average cost of the inventories held. This is the weighted average cost (AVCO) method, where the weights used in deriving the average cost figures are the quantities of each batch of inventories acquired.

Example 3.8 provides a simple illustration of the way in which each method is applied.

Example 3.8

A business commenced on 1 May to supply oil to factories. During this month, the following transactions took place:

	Tonnes	Cost per tonne
May 2 Purchased	10,000	£10
10 Purchased	20,000	£13
18 Sold	9,000	

First in, first out (FIFO)

Using the first in, first out approach, 9,000 tonnes of the 10,000 tonnes bought on 2 May are treated as if these are the ones to be sold. The remaining inventories bought on 2 May (1,000 tonnes) and the inventories bought on 3 May (20,000 tonnes) will become the closing inventories. Thus we have:

Cost of sales	(9,000 @ £10 per tonne)	£90,000
Closing inventories		
		£
	(1,000 @ £10 per tonne)	10,000
	(20,000 @ £13 per tonne)	260,000
		270,000

Last in, first out (LIFO)

Using the last in, first out approach, 9,000 tonnes of the inventories bought on 10 May will be treated as if these are the first to be sold. The earlier inventories bought on 2 May (10,000 tonnes) and the remainder of the inventories bought on 10 May (11,000 tonnes) will become the closing inventories. Thus we have:

Cost of sales	(9,000 @ £13 per tonne)	£117,000
Closing inventories		

	£
(11,000 @ £13 per tonne)	143,000
(10,000 @ £10 per tonne)	100,000
	243,000

Weighted average cost (AVCO)

Since newly acquired inventories are treated, for accounting purposes, as if they lose their separate identity, any issues should reflect the weighted average cost of the inventories that are held. The weights used in deriving the average cost figures are the quantities of each batch of inventories bought.

Using this approach, a weighted average cost will be determined that will be used to derive both the cost of goods sold and the cost of the remaining inventories held. This simply means that the cost of the inventories bought on 2 May and 10 May are added together and then divided by the total number of tonnes to obtain the weighted average cost per tonne. That is:

Average cost = $((10,000 \times £10) + (20,000 \times £13))/(10,000 + 20,000)$ = £12 per tonne.

Both the cost of sales and the value of the closing inventories are then based on this average cost per tonne. Thus we have:

Cost of sales	(9,000 @ £12 per tonne)	£108,000
Closing inventories	(21,000 × £12 per tonne)	£252,000

Activity 3.9

Suppose that the 9,000 tonnes of inventories in Example 3.8 were sold for £15 a tonne.

(a) Calculate the gross profit for the period under each of the three costing methods.
(b) What do you note about the different profit and closing inventories valuations when using each method, when prices are rising?

Your answer should be along the following lines:

(a) Gross profit calculation:

	FIFO £000	LIFO £000	AVCO £000
Sales revenue (9,000 @ £15)	135	135	135
Cost of sales	(90)	(117)	(108)
Gross profit	45	18	27
Closing inventories figure	270	243	252

(b) These figures show that FIFO will give the highest gross profit during a period of rising prices. This is because sales revenue is matched with the earlier (and cheaper) purchases. LIFO will give the lowest gross profit because sales revenue is matched against the more recent (and dearer) purchases. The AVCO method will normally give a figure that is between these two extremes.

The closing inventories figure in the balance sheet will be highest with the FIFO method. This is because the cost of oil still held will be based on the more recent (and dearer) purchases. LIFO will give the lowest closing inventories figure as the oil held will be based on the earlier (and cheaper) purchases. Once again, the AVCO method will normally give a figure that is between these two extremes. During a period of falling prices, the position of FIFO and LIFO is reversed.

The different costing methods will only have an effect on the reported profit from one year to the next. The figure derived for closing inventories will be carried forward and matched with sales revenue in a later period. Thus, if the cheaper purchases of inventories are matched to sales revenue in the current period, it will mean that the dearer purchases will be matched to sales revenue in a later period. Over the life of the business, therefore, the total profit will be the same whichever costing method has been used.

Inventories - some further issues

We saw in Chapter 2 that the convention of prudence requires that inventories be valued at the lower of cost and net realisable value. (The net realisable value of inventories is the estimated selling price less any further costs that may be necessary to complete the goods and any costs involved in selling and distributing the goods.) This rule may mean that the valuation method applied to inventories (cost or net realisable value) will switch from one year to the next, depending on which of cost and net realisable value is the lower. In practice, however, the cost of the inventories held is usually below the current net realisable value – particularly during a period of rising prices. It is, therefore, the cost figure that will normally appear in the balance sheet.

Activity 3.10

Can you think of any circumstances where the net realisable value will be lower than the cost of inventories held, even during a period of generally rising prices?

The net realisable value may be lower where:

- goods have deteriorated or become obsolete;
- there has been a fall in the market price of the goods;
- the goods are being used as a 'loss leader';
- bad buying decisions have been made.

There is an international financial reporting standard that deals with inventories. It states that the cost of inventories should normally be determined using either FIFO or AVCO. The LIFO approach is not an acceptable method to use. The standard also requires the 'lower of cost or net realisable value' rule to be used.

Real World 3.7 sets out the costing methods of two large businesses.

Real World 3.7

Costing inventories in practice

Tate and Lyle plc, the sugar and other starch-based food processor, reports inventories on either a 'first in, first out' basis or weighted average costs basis.

Kingfisher plc, the home improvement business (that owns B and Q and other outlets worldwide), uses weighted average cost only.

Sources: Tate and Lyle plc Annual Report 2007, p. 92; Kingfisher plc Annual Report and Accounts 2007, p. 59.

Costing inventories and depreciation provide two examples where the consistency convention must be applied. This convention holds that once a particular method of accounting is selected, it should be applied consistently over time. Thus, it would not be acceptable to switch from, say, FIFO to AVCO between periods (unless exceptional circumstances make it appropriate). The purpose of this convention is to help users make valid comparisons of performance and position from one period to the next.

Activity 3.11

Reporting inventories in the financial statements provides a further example of the need to apply subjective judgement. For the inventories of a retail business, what are the main areas where judgement is required?

The main areas are:

- the choice of cost method (FIFO, LIFO, AVCO);
- deducing the net realisable value figure for inventories held.

Dealing with trade receivables' problems

We have seen that, when businesses sell goods or services on credit, revenue will often be recognised before the customer pays the amounts owing. Recording the dual aspect of a credit sale will involve increasing sales revenue, and increasing trade receivables, by the amount of the revenue from the credit sale.

With this type of sale there is always the risk that the customer will not pay the amount due, however reliable they might have appeared to be at the time of the sale. When it becomes reasonably certain that the customer will never pay, the amount

→ owed is considered to be a bad debt and this must be taken into account when preparing the financial statements.

Activity 3.12

When preparing the financial statements, what would be the effect on the income statement, and on the balance sheet, of not taking into account the fact that a particular debt is bad?

The effect would be to overstate the assets (trade receivables) on the balance sheet, and to overstate profit in the income statement, as the revenue which has been recognised will not result in any future benefit.

To provide a more realistic picture of financial performance and position, the bad debt must be 'written off'. This will involve reducing the trade receivables, and increasing expenses (by creating an expense known as 'bad debts written off'), by the amount of the bad debt.

The matching convention requires that the bad debt is written off in the same period in which the sale that gave rise to the debt is recognised.

Note that, when a debt is bad, the accounting response is not simply to cancel the original sale. If this were done, the income statement would not be so informative. Reporting the bad debts as an expense can be extremely useful in assessing management performance.

Activity 3.13

The treatment of bad debts represents another area where judgement is needed to derive an appropriate expense figure.

What will be the effect of different judgements concerning the appropriate amount of bad debts expense on the profit for a particular period and on the total profit reported over the life of the business?

Judgement is often required in deriving a figure for bad debts incurred during a period. There may be situations where views will differ concerning whether or not a debt is irrecoverable. The decision concerning whether or not to write off a bad debt will have an effect on the expenses for the period and, hence, the reported profit. However, over the life of the business the total reported profit would not be affected, as incorrect judgements in one period will be adjusted for in a later period.

Suppose that a debt of £100 was written off in a period and that, in a later period, the amount owing was actually received. The increase in expenses of £100 in the period in which the bad debt was written off would be compensated for by an increase in revenue of £100 when the amount outstanding was finally received (bad debt recoverable). If, on the other hand, the amount owing of £100 was never written off in the first place, the profit for the two periods would not be affected by the bad debt adjustment and would, therefore, be different – but the total profit for the two periods would be the same.

Real World 3.8 discusses the approach taken by banks trying to avoid bad debts.

Banking on bad debts

Nervousness in the world's financial markets, sparked by sub-prime lending in the US, is causing banks and other financial institutions to take a closer look at their customers.

Banks are tightening their lending policies to shield themselves from the possibility of debtors defaulting. Already, reports are emerging of banks shunning some categories of new borrower and limiting the credit available to existing ones.

But how do they make these decisions?

According to the British Bankers' Association, banks now collect four kinds of data to assess client risk: negative data, such as county-court fines and convictions; 'positive' information on people's financial commitments and loans etc; income data; and reports on spending behaviour.

Apacs, a UK association for the banking industry, says lenders tend to grab these from three sources – the electoral roll, their own systems, which are tied up with other payments organisations such as Visa, and credit-checking agencies.

'People are creatures of habit,' says Eric Leenders, executive director of the BBA. 'You put a salary in your account once a month and may go to the supermarket weekly. From that analysis, you see the ability of someone to repay.

'The software has to achieve the same end and banks all look at the same data.'

While turning some customers away, banks are arguing that lending criteria are unchanged. Mr Leenders says this is true: 'Banks have not recently changed the lending criteria. All they do is raise or lower the threshold score. When you raise the bar, fewer people are accepted for credit. The name of the game is to minimise the risk of whom you lend to.'

Methods used to assess customers, on the other hand, have changed. Lenders now either use their own analytics software, or systems from vendors, such as Fair Isaac. These can calculate a customer's risk based on the available data. HBOS bank, for example, uses Callcredit's software to monitor missed payments in a bid to intervene on bad debts before they mount up.

'The data is held entirely within the bank's own systems,' says Ian Turvill, a senior director at Fair Isaac. 'What may be common across banks is the expertise in developing the analytics that review the data to work out whether delinquency or bankruptcy is likely to take place.

'Most banks have automated links with the credit agencies – now typically using web services – that deliver data automatically into the customer databases. The banks rely on the internal quality processes that the agencies apply to ensure that the data is of an appropriate integrity.'

Martha Bennett, director of research for financial services at analyst Datamonitor, adds: 'There is always an issue around a neural network and predicting the propensity of someone who will fail on a loan. The technology is reasonably sophisticated with that, but the problem is what do you do with the result?'

Today, the same type of CRM systems that allow retailers to monitor spending of customers who carry loyalty cards also run in banks, and these enable them to build more accurate profiles. Combined with predictive software, this can be a powerful alarm system.

'If a business with a fleet of cars has a cash crunch, they will commonly send out the vehicles to fuel up,' says Carl Clump, chief executive of Retail Decisions. 'They'll break through their credit limits all at once.'

> 'You can see similar acts with consumers – if you start to see lots of expenses on payment cards for food shopping, way more than usual, it would seem they are having a cash crunch.'
>
> Mr Turvill adds: 'There is a whole class of applications called credit account management systems, including Fair Isaac's Triad and Probe from Experian, the credit-checking agency. They are sometimes classified as CRM systems, but they are distinct. They are linked to what is called the master data file, a centralised database maintained by the credit card companies.'
>
> Zopa, by contrast, is an online service that allows individuals to lend and borrow money from each other. For its business to operate and to gain the trust of lenders, it bought software from SAS, the data-mining company, to help with credit scoring. It now boasts a 'bad-debt rate' of some 0.05 per cent. This is because the company's IT system performs real-time authentication and credit checks with the Equifax credit rating body. The software then scores the customer into one of four bands: A*, A, B or C.
>
> 'But over the industry in general there is still some difficulty in getting a single view of a client,' says Bart Patrick, head of risk strategy for SAS. 'You basically have various systems linking up the client records.'
>
> 'We do customer experience analytics – looking at what a customer buys and what they could buy. We are getting demand for joining up lending and marketing systems.'
>
> Sources close to the banks, which are reluctant to talk about decision-making processes, say lenders also demand more real-time information.
>
> With increasing sales of financial products over the internet, banks require faster answers on applications for instant mortgage quotes, for example.
>
> But again, this means greater sharing of data, which raises serious security questions over how safe that information is.
>
> Data protection laws are set in many countries to prevent data being shared without consent of the subject. Banks argue this is optional, but in many cases an individual cannot apply for a loan without providing that consent.
>
> 'Lenders are sharing more information and that means a more informed decision,' says Peter Brooker, director of public affairs for Experian. 'The information we hold is by consent. A lender cannot search your credit report without your consent. It must be fully transparent.'
>
> *Source*: 'How the banks assess their customers', Dan Ilett, *Financial Times*, 23 October 2007.

Let us now try to bring together some of the points that we have raised in this chapter through a self-assessment question.

? Self-assessment question 3.1

TT and Co. is a new business that started trading on 1 January 2008. The following is a summary of transactions that occurred during the first year of trading:

1 The owners introduced £50,000 of equity, which was paid into a bank account opened in the name of the business.
2 Premises were rented from 1 January 2008 at an annual rental of £20,000. During the year, rent of £25,000 was paid to the owner of the premises.
3 Rates (a tax on business premises) were paid during the year as follows:

For the period 1 January 2008 to 31 March 2008	£500
For the period 1 April 2008 to 31 March 2009	£1,200

→

4 A delivery van was bought on 1 January 2008 for £12,000. This is expected to be used in the business for four years and then to be sold for £2,000.

5 Wages totalling £33,500 were paid during the year. At the end of the year, the business owed £630 of wages for the last week of the year.

6 Electricity bills for the first three quarters of the year were paid totalling £1,650. After 31 December 2008, but before the financial statements had been finalised for the year, the bill for the last quarter arrived showing a charge of £620.

7 Inventories totalling £143,000 were bought on credit.

8 Inventories totalling £12,000 were bought for cash.

9 Sales revenue on credit totalled £152,000 (cost of sales £74,000).

10 Cash sales revenue totalled £35,000 (cost of sales £16,000).

11 Receipts from trade receivables totalled £132,000.

12 Payments to trade payables totalled £121,000.

13 Van running expenses paid totalled £9,400.

At the end of the year it was clear that a trade receivable who owed £400 would not be able to pay any part of the debt. The business uses the straight-line method for depreciating non-current assets.

Required:
Prepare a balance sheet as at 31 December 2008 and an income statement for the year to that date.

The answer to this question can be found at the back of the book in Appendix B.

Uses and usefulness of the income statement

The income statement, like the balance sheet, has been around for a long time. Most major businesses seem to prepare an income statement on a frequent basis (monthly or even more frequently). This is despite there being no rule requiring an income statement to be produced more frequently than once, or in some cases twice, a year. Income statements are, therefore, seen as being capable of providing useful information. The income statement can be seen as being useful in several ways, including the following:

■ *It provides information on how effective the business has been in generating wealth.* Since wealth generation appears to be a primary reason for most businesses to exist, assessing how much wealth has been created is an important issue. A problem with the profit figure for a particular period, however, is that, had different judgements been made in key areas like depreciation, inventories valuation and bad debts, a different profit figure could have emerged. Whilst these different judgements may be made in good faith, it highlights the fact that there is no single 'correct' profit figure. This can call into question the integrity of the reported profit figure and cause scepticism among users. The problem, however, should not be overstated. For most businesses in most years, making different judgements would probably not affect the profit figure to a significant extent.

■ *It provides information on how the profit was made.* For some users, the only item of concern may be the final profit figure, or *bottom line* as it is sometimes called. Whilst this is a primary measure of performance, and its importance is difficult to overstate, the income statement contains other information that should also be of interest. To evaluate business performance effectively, it is important to find out how the final profit figure was derived. Thus the level of sales revenue, the nature and amount of expenses incurred, and the profit in relation to sales revenue are important factors in understanding the performance of the business over a period. The analysis and interpretation of financial statements is considered in detail in Chapter 6.

Summary

The main points of this chapter may be summarised as follows.

The income statement (profit and loss account)

■ The income statement measures and reports how much profit (or loss) has been generated over a period.

■ Profit (or loss) for the period is the difference between the total revenue and total expenses for the period.

■ The income statement links the balance sheets at the beginning and end of an accounting period.

■ The income statement of a retail business will first calculate gross profit and then deduct any overheads for the period. The final figure derived is the profit (or loss) for the period.

■ Gross profit represents the difference between the sales revenue for the period and the cost of sales.

Expenses and revenue

■ Cost of sales may be identified either by matching the cost of each sale to the particular sale or by adjusting the goods bought during the period to take account of opening and closing inventories.

■ The classification of expenses is often a matter of judgement, although there are rules for businesses that trade as limited companies.

■ Revenue is recognised when the amount of revenue can be measured reliably and it is probable that the economic benefits will be received.

■ Where there is a sale of goods, there is an additional criterion that ownership and control must pass to the buyer before revenue can be recognised.

■ Revenue can be recognised after partial completion provided that a particular stage of completion can be measured reliably.   →

- The matching convention states that expenses should be matched to the revenue that they help generate.
- A particular expense reported in the income statement may not be the same as the cash paid. This will result in some adjustment for accruals or prepayments.
- The materiality convention states that where the amounts are immaterial, we should consider only what is expedient.
- 'Accruals accounting' is preparing the income statement and balance sheet following the accruals convention, which says that profit = revenue less expenses (not cash receipts less cash payments).

Depreciation of non-current assets

- Depreciation requires a consideration of the cost (or fair value), useful life and residual value of an asset. It also requires a consideration of the method of depreciation.
- The straight-line method of depreciation allocates the amount to be depreciated evenly over the useful life of the asset.
- The reducing-balance method applies a fixed percentage rate of depreciation to the carrying amount of an asset each year.
- The depreciation method chosen should reflect the pattern of benefits associated with the asset.
- Depreciation is an attempt to allocate the cost (or fair value), less the residual value, of an asset over its useful life. It does not provide funds for replacement of the asset.

Costing inventories

- The way in which we derive the cost of inventories is important in the calculation of profit and the presentation of financial position.
- The first in, first out (FIFO) method approaches matters as if the earliest inventories held are the first to be used.
- The last in, first out (LIFO) method approaches matters as if the latest inventories are the first to be used.
- The weighted average cost (AVCO) method applies an average cost to all inventories used.
- When prices are rising, FIFO gives the lowest cost of sales figure and highest closing inventories figure and LIFO gives the highest cost of sales figure and the lowest closing inventories figure. AVCO gives figures for cost of sales and closing inventories that lie between FIFO and LIFO.
- When prices are falling, the positions of FIFO and LIFO are reversed.
- Inventories are shown at the lower of cost and net realisable value.
- When a particular method of accounting, such as an inventories costing method, is selected, it should be applied consistently over time.

Bad debts

- Where it is reasonably certain that a credit customer will not pay, the debt is regarded as 'bad' and written off.

Uses of the income statement

- Provides a profit figure.
- Provides information on how the profit was derived.

→ Key terms

profit	accruals accounting
revenue	depreciation
expense	residual value
income statement	straight-line method
accounting period	carrying amount
gross profit	written-down value
operating profit	net book value
profit for the year	reducing-balance method
cost of sales	first in, first out (FIFO)
matching convention	last in, first out (LIFO)
accrued expenses	weighted average cost (AVCO)
prepaid expenses	consistency convention
materiality convention	bad debt
accruals convention	

Further reading

If you would like to explore the topics covered in this chapter in more depth, we recommend the following books:

Elliott, B. and Elliott, J., *Financial Accounting and Reporting* (12th edn), Financial Times Prentice Hall, 2008, chapters 2, 16, 18 and 19.

Kirk, R.J., *International Financial Reporting Standards in Depth*, CIMA Publishing, 2005, chapters 2 and 3.

KPMG, *KPMG's Practical Guide to International Financial Reporting Standards* (3rd edn), Thomson, 2006, sections 3.2, 3.3 and 3.8.

Sutton, T., *Corporate Financial Accounting and Reporting* (2nd edn), Financial Times Prentice Hall, 2004, chapters 2, 8, 9 and 10.

? Review questions

Answers to these questions can be found at the back of the book in Appendix C.

3.1 'Although the income statement is a record of past achievement, the calculations required for certain expenses involve estimates of the future.' What does this statement mean? Can you think of examples where estimates of the future are used?

3.2 'Depreciation is a process of allocation and not valuation.' What do you think is meant by this statement?

3.3 What is the convention of consistency? Does this convention help users in making a more valid comparison between businesses?

3.4 'An asset is similar to an expense.' Do you agree?

✳ Exercises

Exercises 3.4 and 3.5 are more advanced than Exercises 3.1 to 3.3. Those with coloured numbers have answers at the back of the book in Appendix D.

<table><tr><td>If you wish to try more exercises, visit MyAccountingLab/</td></tr></table>

3.1 You have heard the following statements made. Comment critically on them.

(a) 'Equity only increases or decreases as a result of the owners putting more cash into the business or taking some out.'
(b) 'An accrued expense is one that relates to next year.'
(c) 'Unless we depreciate this asset we shall be unable to provide for its replacement.'
(d) 'There is no point in depreciating the factory building. It is appreciating in value each year.'

3.2 Singh Enterprises has an accounting year to 31 December and uses the straight-line method of depreciation. On 1 January 2006 the business bought a machine for £10,000. The machine had an expected useful life of four years and an estimated residual value of £2,000. On 1 January 2007 the business bought another machine for £15,000. This machine had an expected useful life of five years and an estimated residual value of £2,500. On 31 December 2008 the business sold the first machine bought for £3,000.

Required:
Show the relevant income statement extracts and balance sheet extracts for the years 2006, 2007 and 2008.

3.3 The owner of a business is confused, and comes to you for help. The financial statements for the business, prepared by an accountant, for the last accounting period revealed a profit of £50,000. However, during the accounting period the bank balance declined by £30,000. What reasons might explain this apparent discrepancy?

3.4 The following is the balance sheet of TT and Co. at the end of its first year of trading (from Self-assessment question 3.1):

TT and Co. Balance sheet as at 31 December 2008

	£
Non-current assets	
Property, plant and equipment	
Delivery van at cost	12,000
Depreciation	(2,500)
	9,500
Current assets	
Inventories	65,000
Trade receivables	19,600
Prepaid expenses*	5,300
Cash	750
	90,650
Total assets	100,150
Equity	
Original	50,000
Retained profit	26,900
	76,900
Current liabilities	
Trade payables	22,000
Accrued expenses†	1,250
	23,250
Total equity and liabilities	100,150

* The prepaid expenses consisted of rates (£300) and rent (£5,000).
† The accrued expenses consisted of wages (£630) and electricity (£620).

During 2009, the following transactions took place:

1 The owners withdrew equity in the form of cash of £20,000.
2 Premises continued to be rented at an annual rental of £20,000. During the year, rent of £15,000 was paid to the owner of the premises.
3 Rates on the premises were paid during the year as follows: for the period 1 April 2009 to 31 March 2010 £1,300.
4 A second delivery van was bought on 1 January 2009 for £13,000. This is expected to be used in the business for four years and then to be sold for £3,000.
5 Wages totalling £36,700 were paid during the year. At the end of the year, the business owed £860 of wages for the last week of the year.
6 Electricity bills for the first three quarters of the year and £620 for the last quarter of the previous year were paid totalling £1,820. After 31 December 2009, but before the financial statements had been finalised for the year, the bill for the last quarter arrived showing a charge of £690.
7 Inventories totalling £67,000 were bought on credit.
8 Inventories totalling £8,000 were bought for cash.
9 Sales revenue on credit totalled £179,000 (cost £89,000).
10 Cash sales revenue totalled £54,000 (cost £25,000).

11 Receipts from trade receivables totalled £178,000.
12 Payments to trade payables totalled £71,000.
13 Van running expenses paid totalled £16,200.

The business uses the straight-line method for depreciating non-current assets.

Required:
Prepare a balance sheet as at 31 December 2009 and an income statement for the year to that date.

3.5 The following is the balance sheet of WW Associates as at 31 December 2007:

Balance sheet as at 31 December 2007

	£
Non-current assets	
Machinery	25,300
Current assets	
Inventories	12,200
Trade receivables	21,300
Prepaid expenses (rates)	400
Cash	8,300
Total assets	67,500
Equity	
Original	25,000
Retained profit	23,900
	48,900
Current liabilities	
Trade payables	16,900
Accrued expenses (wages)	1,700
	18,600
Total equity and liabilities	67,500

During 2008, the following transactions took place:

1 The owners withdrew equity in the form of cash of £23,000.
2 Premises were rented at an annual rental of £20,000. During the year, rent of £25,000 was paid to the owner of the premises.
3 Rates on the premises were paid during the year for the period 1 April 2008 to 31 March 2009 and amounted to £2,000.
4 Some machinery (a non-current asset), which was bought on 1 January 2007 for £13,000, has proved to be unsatisfactory. It was part-exchanged for some new machinery on 1 January 2008, and WW Associates paid a cash amount of £6,000. The new machinery would have cost £15,000 had the business bought it without the trade-in.
5 Wages totalling £23,800 were paid during the year. At the end of the year, the business owed £860 of wages.
6 Electricity bills for the four quarters of the year were paid totalling £2,700.
7 Inventories totalling £143,000 were bought on credit.
8 Inventories totalling £12,000 were bought for cash.

 9 Sales revenue on credit totalled £211,000 (cost £127,000).
10 Cash sales revenue totalled £42,000 (cost £25,000).
11 Receipts from trade receivables totalled £198,000.
12 Payments to trade payables totalled £156,000.
13 Van running expenses paid totalled £17,500.

The business uses the reducing-balance method of depreciation for non-current assets at the rate of 30 per cent each year.

Required:
Prepare a balance sheet as at 31 December 2008 and an income statement (profit and loss account) for the year to that date.

THE CASH FLOW STATEMENT

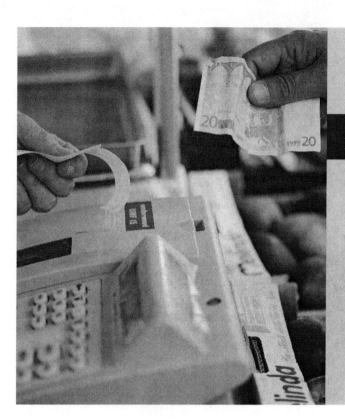

Chapter 5

Measuring and reporting cash flows

Introduction

This chapter is devoted to the third major financial statement identified in Chapter 2: the cash flow statement. This statement reports the movements of cash over a period and the effect of these movements on the cash position of the business. It is an important financial statement because cash is vital to the survival of a business. Without cash, no business can operate.

In this chapter we shall see how the cash flow statement is prepared and how the information that it contains may be interpreted. We shall also see why the deficiencies of the income statement in revealing cash flows over time make a separate cash flow statement necessary.

The cash flow statement is being considered after the chapter on limited companies because the format of the statement requires an understanding of this type of business. Limited companies are required to provide a cash flow statement for shareholders and other interested parties, as well as the more traditional income statement and balance sheet.

Learning outcomes

When you have completed this chapter, you should be able to:

- discuss the crucial importance of cash to a business;
- explain the nature of the cash flow statement and discuss how it can be helpful in identifying cash flow problems;
- prepare a cash flow statement;
- interpret a cash flow statement.

The cash flow statement (or statement of cash flows)

The cash flow statement is a fairly recent addition to the set of financial statements provided to shareholders and to others. There used to be no regulation requiring companies to produce more than an income statement and a balance sheet. The prevailing view seems to have been that any financial information required would be contained within these two statements. This view may have been based partly on the assumption that if a business were profitable, it would also have plenty of cash. Although in the very long run this is likely to be true, it is not necessarily true in the short to medium term.

We have already seen in Chapter 3 that the income statement sets out the revenue and expenses, rather than the cash receipts and cash payments, for the period. This means that profit (or loss), which represents the difference between the revenue and expenses for the period, may have little or no relation to the cash generated for the period. To illustrate this point, let us take the example of a business making a sale (generating a revenue). This may well lead to an increase in wealth and that will be reflected in the income statement. However, if the sale is made on credit, no cash changes hands – at least not at the time of sale. Instead, the increase in wealth is reflected in another asset: an increase in trade receivables. Furthermore, if an item of inventories is the subject of the sale, wealth is lost to the business through the reduction in inventories. This means an expense is incurred in making the sale, which will be shown in the income statement. Once again, however, no cash has changed hands at the time of sale. For such reasons, the profit and the cash generated for a period will rarely go hand in hand.

The following activity should help to underline how profit and cash for a period may be affected differently by particular transactions or events.

Activity 5.1

The following is a list of business/accounting events. In each case, state the effect (increase, decrease or no effect) on both profit and cash:

| | | Effect | |
		on profit	on cash
1	Repayment of borrowings	_____	_____
2	Making a sale on credit	_____	_____
3	Buying a current asset on credit	_____	_____
4	Receiving cash from a credit customer (trade receivable)	_____	_____
5	Depreciating a non-current asset	_____	_____
6	Buying some inventories for cash	_____	_____
7	Making a share issue for cash	_____	_____

You should have come up with the following:

		Effect	
		on profit	*on cash*
1	Repayment of borrowings	none	decrease
2	Making a sale on credit	increase	none
3	Buying a current asset on credit	none	none
4	Receiving cash from a credit customer (trade receivable)	none	increase
5	Depreciating a non-current asset	decrease	none
6	Buying some inventories for cash	none	decrease
7	Making a share issue for cash	none	increase

The reasons for these answers are as follows:

1 Repaying borrowings requires that cash be paid to the lender. This means that two figures in the balance sheet will be affected, but none in the income statement.
2 Making a sale on credit will increase the sales revenue figure (and a profit or a loss, unless the sale was made for a price that precisely equalled the expenses involved). No cash will change hands at this point, however.
3 Buying a current asset on credit affects neither the cash balance nor the profit figure.
4 Receiving cash from a credit customer increases the cash balance and reduces the credit customer's balance. Both of these figures are on the balance sheet. The income statement is unaffected.
5 Depreciating a non-current asset means that an expense is recognised. This causes the carrying amount of the asset, as it is recorded on the balance sheet, to fall by an amount equal to the amount of the expense. No cash is paid or received.
6 Buying some inventories for cash means that the value of the inventories will increase and the cash balance will decrease by a similar amount. Profit is not affected.
7 Making a share issue for cash increases the owners' claim and increases the cash balance; profit is unaffected.

It is clear from the above that if we are to gain an insight into cash movements over time, the income statement is not the place to look. Instead we need a separate financial statement. This fact has become widely recognised in recent years, and in 1991 a UK financial reporting standard, FRS 1, emerged that required all but the smallest companies to produce and publish a cash flow statement. This standard has been superseded for many companies from 2005 by the International Financial Reporting (Accounting) Standard IAS 7. The two standards have broadly similar requirements. This chapter follows the provisions of IAS 7.

Why is cash so important?

It is worth asking why cash is so important. After all, cash is just an asset that the business needs to help it to function. In that sense, it is no different from inventories or non-current assets.

The reason for the importance of cash is that people and organisations will not normally accept other than cash in settlement of their claims against the business. If a business wants to employ people, it must pay them in cash. If it wants to buy a new non-current asset to exploit a business opportunity, the seller of the asset will normally insist on being paid in cash, probably after a short period of credit. When businesses fail, it is their inability to find the cash to pay the amounts owed that really pushes them under.

These factors lead to cash being the pre-eminent business asset. Cash is the thing that analysts tend to watch most carefully when trying to assess the ability of businesses to survive and/or to take advantage of commercial opportunities as they arise. The fact that cash and profits do not always go hand in hand is illustrated in Real World 5.1. This explains how Eurotunnel, the cross-channel business between England and France, continues to struggle to achieve profit, yet generates positive cash flows.

Real World 5.1

Cash flows under the channel

Despite making a loss for the year of £143m for 2006, Eurotunnel managed to increase its bank balance by £71m. This occurred partly because depreciation (of non-current assets) of £115m is an expense in the income statement, but it did not give rise to a cash outflow during 2006.

At the same time the interest expense charged in the income statement amounted to £333m, but the cash outflow was only £237m. This was because the business was authorised by the French Commercial Court to delay these interest payments.

Eurotunnel in 2006 shows a striking example of differences between reported profit and reported cash flow.

Source: Based on information contained in Eurotunnel's 2006 Annual Accounts.

The main features of the cash flow statement

The cash flow statement is a summary of the cash receipts and payments over the period concerned. All payments of a particular type, for example cash payments to acquire additional non-current assets or other investments, are added together to give just one figure that appears in the statement. The net total of the statement is the net increase or decrease of the cash (and cash equivalents) of the business over the period. The statement is basically an analysis of the business's cash (and cash equivalents) movements for the period.

A definition of cash and cash equivalents

IAS 7 defines cash as notes and coins in hand and deposits in banks and similar institutions that are accessible to the business on demand. Cash equivalents are short-term, highly liquid investments that are readily convertible to known amounts of cash and which are subject to an insignificant risk of changes of value. Cash equivalents are held for the purpose of meeting short-term cash commitments rather than for investment or other purposes.

Activity 5.2 should clarify the types of items that fall within the definition of 'cash equivalents'.

Activity 5.2

At the end of its accounting period, Zeneb plc's balance sheet included the following items:

1 *A bank deposit account where one month's notice of withdrawal is required.* This deposit was made because the business has a temporary cash surplus that it will need to use in the short term for operating purposes;

2 *Ordinary shares in Jones plc (a Stock Exchange listed business).* These were acquired because Zeneb plc has a temporary cash surplus and its directors believed that the shares represent a good short-term investment. The funds invested will need to be used in the short term for operating purposes.

3 *A bank deposit account that is withdrawable instantly.* This represents an investment of surplus funds that are not seen as being needed in the short term.

4 *An overdraft on the business's bank current account.*

Which (if any) of these four items would be included in the figure for cash and cash equivalents?

Your response should have been as follows:

1 A cash equivalent because the deposit is part of the business's normal cash management activities and there is little doubt about how much cash will be obtained when the deposit is withdrawn.

2 Not a cash equivalent. Although the investment was made as part of normal cash management, there is a significant risk that the amount expected (hoped for!) when the shares are sold may not actually be forthcoming.

3 Not a cash equivalent because this represents an investment rather than a short-term surplus amount of cash.

4 This is cash itself, though a negative amount of it. The only exception to this classification would be where the business is financed in the longer term by an overdraft, when it would be part of the financing of the business, rather than negative cash.

As can be seen from the responses to Activity 5.2, whether a particular item falls within the definition of cash and cash equivalent depends on two factors:

■ the nature of the item; and
■ why it has arisen.

In practice, it is not usually difficult to decide whether an item is a cash equivalent.

The relationship between the primary financial statements

The cash flow statement is now accepted, along with the income statement and the balance sheet, as a primary financial statement. The relationship between the three statements is shown in Figure 5.1. The balance sheet reflects the combination of assets (including cash) and claims (including the shareholders' equity) of the business *at a particular point in time*. The cash flow statement and the income statement explain the *changes over a period* to two of the items in the balance sheet. The cash flow statement explains the changes to cash. The income statement explains changes to equity, arising from trading.

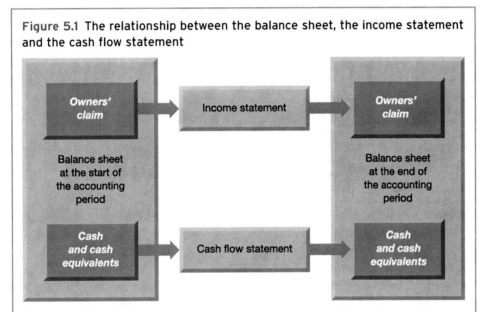

Figure 5.1 The relationship between the balance sheet, the income statement and the cash flow statement

The balance sheet shows the position, at a particular point in time, of the business's assets and claims. The income statement explains how, over a period between two balance sheets, the owners' claim figure in the first balance sheet has altered as a result of trading operations. The cash flow statement also looks at changes over the accounting period, but this statement explains the alteration in the cash (and cash equivalent) balances from the first to the second of the two consecutive balance sheets.

The form of the cash flow statement

The standard layout of the cash flow statement is summarised in Figure 5.2. Explanations of the terms used in the cash flow statement are given below.

Cash flows from operating activities

This is the net inflow or outflow from trading operations, after tax and financing costs. It is equal to the sum of cash receipts from trade receivables, and cash receipts from cash sales where relevant, less the sums paid to buy inventories, to pay rent, to pay

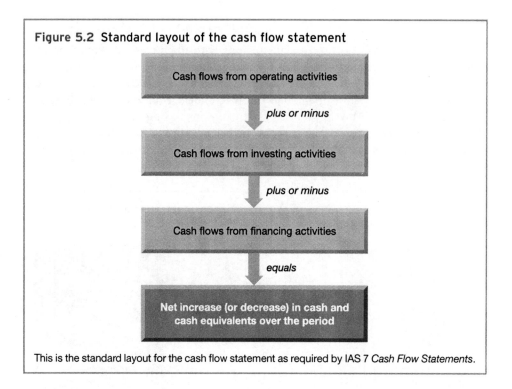

Figure 5.2 Standard layout of the cash flow statement

Cash flows from operating activities

plus or minus

Cash flows from investing activities

plus or minus

Cash flows from financing activities

equals

Net increase (or decrease) in cash and cash equivalents over the period

This is the standard layout for the cash flow statement as required by IAS 7 *Cash Flow Statements*.

wages and so on. From this are also deducted payments for interest on the business's borrowings, corporation tax and dividends paid.

Note that it is the amounts of cash received and paid during the period that feature in the cash flow statement, not the revenue and expenses for that period. It is, of course, the income statement that deals with the revenue and expenses. Similarly the tax and dividend payments that appear in the cash flow statement are those made in the period of the statement. Companies normally pay tax on their profits in four equal instalments. Two of these are during the year concerned, and the other two are during the following year. As a result, by the end of each accounting year, half of the tax will have been paid and the remainder will be a current liability at the end of the year, to be paid off during the following year. During any particular year, therefore, the tax payment would normally equal 50 per cent of the previous year's tax charge and 50 per cent of that of the current year.

The net figure for this section is intended to indicate the net cash flows for the period that arose from normal day-to-day trading activities after taking account of the tax that has to be paid on them and the cost of servicing the finance (equity and borrowings) needed to support them.

Cash flows from investing activities

This section of the statement is concerned with cash payments made to acquire additional non-current assets and with cash receipts from the disposal of non-current assets. These non-current assets will tend to be the usual items such as buildings and machinery. They might also include loans made by the business or shares in another company bought by the business.

The net cash flows from making new investments and/or disposing of existing ones also appear here.

This section also includes cash receipts arising from financial investments (loans and equities) made outside the business. These receipts are interest on loans made by the business and dividends from shares in other companies that are owned by the business.

Cash flows from financing activities

This part of the statement is concerned with the long-term financing of the business. So here we are considering borrowings (other than very short-term) and finance from share issues. This category is concerned with repayment/redemption of finance as well as with the raising of it. It is permissible under IAS 7 to include dividend payments made by the business here, as an alternative to including them in 'Cash flows from operating activities' (above).

This section shows the net cash flows from raising and/or paying back long-term finance.

Net increase or decrease in cash and cash equivalents

The total of the statement must, of course, be the net increase or decrease in cash and cash equivalents over the period concerned.

The effect on a business's cash and cash equivalents of its various activities is shown in Figure 5.3. As explained in the diagram, the arrows show the *normal* direction of cash flow for the typical healthy, profitable business in a typical year.

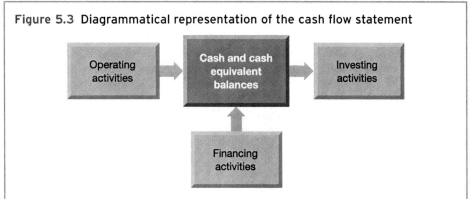

Figure 5.3 Diagrammatical representation of the cash flow statement

Various activities of the business each have their own effect on its cash and cash equivalent balances, either positive (increasing them) or negative (reducing them). The net increase or decrease in the cash and cash equivalent balances over a period will be the sum of these individual effects, taking account of the direction (cash in or cash out) of each activity.

Note that the direction of the arrow shows the *normal* direction of the cash flow in respect of each activity. In certain circumstances, each of these arrows could be reversed in direction.

The normal direction of cash flows

Normally 'operating activities' provide positive cash flows, that is, they help to increase the business's cash resources. In fact, for most UK businesses, in most time periods, cash generated from day-to-day trading, even after deducting tax, interest and dividends, is overwhelmingly the most important source of new finance.

Activity 5.3

Last year's cash flow statement for Angus plc showed a negative cash flow from operating activities. What could be the reason for this, and should the business's management be alarmed by it? (*Hint*: We think that there are two broad possible reasons for a negative cash flow.)

The two reasons are:

- The business is unprofitable. This leads to more cash being paid out to employees, suppliers of goods and services, interest and so on, than is received from trade receivables in respect of sales. This would be particularly alarming, because a major expense for most businesses is depreciation of non-current assets. Since depreciation does not lead to a cash flow, it is not considered in 'net cash inflows from operating activities'. This means that a negative operating cash flow might well indicate a very much larger trading loss – in other words, a significant loss of the business's wealth; something to concern management.

- The other reason might be less alarming. A business that is expanding its activities (level of sales revenue) would tend to spend quite a lot of cash relative to the amount of cash coming in from sales. This is because it will probably be expanding its assets (non-current and current) to accommodate the increased demand. For example, a business may well have to have inventories in place before additional sales can be made. Similarly, staff have to be employed and paid. Even when the additional sales are made, those sales would normally be made on credit, with the cash inflow lagging behind the sale. All of this means that, in the first instance, in cash flow terms, the business would not necessarily benefit from the additional sales revenue. This would be particularly likely to be true of a new business, which would be expanding inventories and other assets from zero. It would also need to employ and pay staff. Expansion typically causes cash flow strains for the reasons just explained. This can be a particular problem because the business's increased profitability might encourage a feeling of optimism, which could lead to lack of attention being paid to the cash flow problem.

Investing activities typically cause net negative cash flows. This is because many types of non-current asset wear out, and many that do not wear out become obsolete. Also, businesses tend to seek to expand their asset base. When a business sells some non-current assets, the sale will give rise to positive cash flows, but in net terms the cash flows are normally negative with cash spent on new assets outweighing that received from disposal of old ones.

Financing can go in either direction, depending on the financing strategy at the time. Since businesses seek to expand, there is a general tendency for this area to lead to cash coming into the business rather than leaving it.

Real World 5.2 shows the summarised cash flow statement of Tesco plc, the UK-based supermarket.

Real World 5.2

Cashing in

An abridged version of the published summarised cash flow statement for Tesco plc for the year ended 24 February 2007 shows the cash flows of the business under each of the headings described above.

Summarised cash flow statement for the year ended 24 February 2007

	£m
Net cash from operating activities	2,611
Net cash used in investing activities	(2,343)
Net cash used in financing activities	(533)
Net (decrease)/increase in cash and cash equivalents	(265)
Cash and cash equivalents at beginning of year	1,325
Effects of foreign exchange rate changes [*]	(18)
Cash and cash equivalents at end of period	1,042

* This adjustment is required because transactions are undertaken by the business in different currencies and movements in exchange rates can lead to gains or losses.

Source: Adapted from Tesco Annual Report 2007.

As we shall see shortly, more detailed information under each of the main headings is provided in the cash flow statement presented to the business's shareholders (and others).

Preparing the cash flow statement

Deducing net cash flows from operating activities

The first section of the cash flow statement is the 'cash flows from operating activities'. There are two approaches that can be taken to deriving this figure: the direct method and the indirect method.

The direct method

The direct method involves an analysis of the cash records of the business for the period, picking out all payments and receipts relating to operating activities. These are summarised to give the total figures for inclusion in the cash flow statement. Done on the computer, this would be a simple matter, but not many businesses adopt this approach.

The indirect method

The indirect method is the more popular method. It relies on the fact that, broadly, sales revenue gives rise to cash inflows, and expenses give rise to outflows. This means that the profit for the year figure will be closely linked to the net cash inflows from operating activities. Since businesses have to produce an income statement in any case, information from it can be used as a starting point to deduce the cash flows from operating activities.

Of course, within a particular accounting period, profit for the year will not normally equal the net cash inflows from operating activities. We saw in Chapter 3 that, when sales are made on credit, the cash receipt occurs some time after the sale. This means that sales revenue made towards the end of an accounting year will be included in that year's income statement, but most of the cash from those sales will flow into the business, and should be included in the cash flow statement, in the following year. Fortunately it is easy to deduce the cash received from sales if we have the relevant income statement and balance sheets, as we shall see in Activity 5.4.

Activity 5.4

How can we deduce the cash inflows from sales using the income statement and balance sheet for the business?

The balance sheet will tell us how much was owed in respect of credit sales at the beginning and end of the year (trade receivables). The income statement tells us the sales revenue figure. If we adjust the sales revenue figure by the increase or decrease in trade receivables over the year, we deduce the cash from sales for the year.

Example 5.1

The sales revenue figure for a business for the year was £34m. The trade receivables totalled £4m at the beginning of the year, but had increased to £5m by the end of the year.

Basically, the trade receivables figure is affected by sales revenue and cash receipts. It is increased when a sale is made and decreased when cash is received from a credit customer. If, over the year, the sales revenue and the cash receipts had been equal, the beginning-of-year and end-of-year trade receivables figures would have been equal. Since the trade receivables figure increased, it must mean that less cash was received than sales revenues were made. This means that the cash receipts from sales must be £33m (that is, $34 - (5 - 4)$).

Put slightly differently, we can say that as a result of sales, assets of £34m flowed into the business during the year. If £1m of this went to increasing the asset of trade receivables, this leaves only £33m that went to increase cash.

The same general point is true in respect of nearly all of the other items that are taken into account in deducing the operating profit figure. The exception is depreciation. This is not necessarily associated with any movement in cash during the accounting period.

All of this means that we can take the profit before taxation (that is, the profit after interest but before taxation) for the year, add back the depreciation and interest expense charged in arriving at that profit, and adjust this total by movements in inventories, trade (and other) receivables and payables. If we then go on to deduct payments made during the accounting period for taxation, interest on borrowings and dividends, we have the net cash from operating activities.

Example 5.2

The relevant information from the financial statements of Dido plc for last year is as follows:

	£m
Profit before taxation (after interest)	122
Depreciation charged in arriving at profit before taxation	34
Interest expense	6
At the beginning of the year:	
Inventories	15
Trade receivables	24
Trade payables	18
At the end of the year:	
Inventories	17
Trade receivables	21
Trade payables	19

The following further information is available about payments during last year:

	£m
Taxation paid	32
Interest paid	5
Dividends paid	9

The cash flow from operating activities is derived as follows:

	£m
Profit before taxation (after interest)	122
Depreciation	34
Interest expense	6
Increase in inventories (17 – 15)	(2)
Decrease in trade receivables (21 – 24)	3
Increase in trade payables (19 – 18)	1
Cash generated from operating activities	164
Less Interest paid	(5)
Taxation paid	(32)
Dividends paid	(9)
Net cash from operating activities	118

As we can see, the net increase in working capital* (that is, current assets less current liabilities), as a result of trading, was £162m. Of this, £2m went into increased inventories. More cash was received from trade receivables than sales revenue was made, and less cash was paid to trade payables than purchases of goods and services on credit. Both of these had a favourable effect on cash, which increased by £164m. When account was taken of the payments for interest, tax and dividends, the net cash flow from operating activities was £118m (inflow).

Note that we needed to adjust the profit before taxation (after interest) by the depreciation and interest expenses to derive the profit before depreciation, interest and taxation.

* Working capital is a term widely used in accounting and finance, not just in the context of cash flow statements. We shall encounter it several times in later chapters.

The indirect method of deducing the net cash flow from operating activities is summarised in Figure 5.4.

Activity 5.5

The relevant information from the financial statements of Pluto plc for last year is as follows:

	£m
Profit before taxation (after interest)	165
Depreciation charged in arriving at operating profit	41
Interest expense	21
At the beginning of the year:	
Inventories	22
Trade receivables	18
Trade payables	15
At the end of the year:	
Inventories	23
Trade receivables	21
Trade payables	17

The following further information is available about payments during last year:

	£m
Taxation paid	49
Interest paid	25
Dividends paid	28

What figure should appear in the cash flow statement for 'Cash flows from operating activities'?

Net cash inflows from operating activities:

	£m
Profit before taxation (after interest)	165
Depreciation	41
Interest expense	21
Increase in inventories (23 – 22)	(1)
Increase in trade receivables (21 – 18)	(3)
Increase in trade payables (17 – 15)	2
Cash generated from operating activities	225
Interest paid	(25)
Taxation paid	(49)
Dividends paid	(28)
Net cash from operating activities	123

Figure 5.4 The indirect method of deducing the net cash flows from operating activities

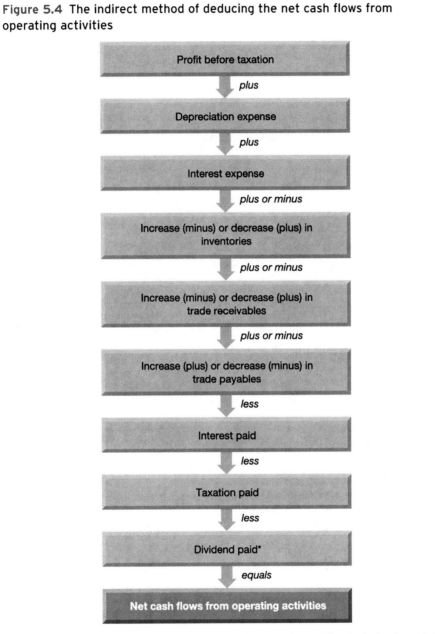

Determining the net cash from operating activities firstly involves adding back the depreciation and the interest expense to the profit before taxation. Next, adjustment is made for increases or decreases in inventories, trade receivables and trade payables. Lastly, cash paid for interest, taxation and dividends is deducted.

* Note that dividends could alternatively be included under the heading 'Cash flows from financing activities'.

Deducing the other areas of the cash flow statement

We can now go on to take a look at the preparation of a complete cash flow statement through Example 5.3.

Example 5.3

Torbryan plc's income statement for the year ended 31 December 2008 and the balance sheets as at 31 December 2007 and 2008 are as follows:

Income statement for the year ended 31 December 2008

	£m
Revenue	576
Cost of sales	(307)
Gross profit	269
Distribution expenses	(65)
Administrative expenses	(26)
	178
Other operating income	21
Operating profit	199
Interest receivable	17
	216
Interest payable	(23)
Profit before taxation	193
Taxation	(46)
Profit for the year	147

Balance sheets as at 31 December 2007 and 2008

	2007 £m	2008 £m
Non-current assets		
Property, plant and equipment		
Land and buildings	241	241
Plant and machinery	309	325
	550	566
Current assets		
Inventories	44	41
Trade receivables	121	139
	165	180
Total assets	715	746
Equity		
Called-up ordinary share capital	150	200
Share premium account	–	40
Retained earnings	26	123
	176	363

Non-current liabilities		
Borrowings – loan notes	400	250
Current liabilities		
Borrowings (all bank overdraft)	68	56
Trade payables	55	54
Taxation	16	23
	139	133
Total equity and liabilities	715	746

During 2008, the business spent £95m on additional plant and machinery. There were no other non-current-asset acquisitions or disposals. A dividend of £50m was paid on ordinary shares during the year. The interest receivable revenue and the interest payable expenses for the year were equal to the cash inflow and outflow respectively.

The cash flow statement would be as follows:

Torbryan plc
Cash flow statement for the year ended 31 December 2008

	£m
Cash flows from operating activities	
Profit before taxation (after interest) (see Note 1 below)	193
Adjustments for:	
Depreciation (Note 2)	79
Interest receivable (Note 3)	(17)
Interest payable (Note 4)	23
Increase in trade receivables (139 – 121)	(18)
Decrease in trade payables (55 – 54)	(1)
Decrease in inventories (44 – 41)	3
Cash generated from operations	262
Interest paid	(23)
Taxation paid (Note 5)	(39)
Dividend paid	(50)
Net cash from operating activities	150
Cash flows from investing activities	
Payments to acquire tangible non-current assets	(95)
Interest received (Note 3)	17
Net cash used in investing activities	(78)
Cash flows from financing activities	
Repayments of loan notes (Note 6)	(150)
Issue of ordinary shares (Note 7)	90
Net cash used in financing activities	(60)
Net increase in cash and cash equivalents	12
Cash and cash equivalents at 1 January 2008 (Note 8)	(68)
Cash and cash equivalents at 31 December 2008	(56)

To see how this relates to the cash of the business at the beginning and end of the year it can be useful to provide a reconciliation as follows:

Analysis of cash and cash equivalents during the year ended 31 December 2008

	£m
Overdraft balance at 1 January 2008	(68)
Net cash inflow	12
Overdraft balance at 31 December 2008	(56)

Notes:

1 This is simply taken from the income statement for the year.
2 Since there were no disposals, the depreciation charges must be the difference between the start and end of the year's plant and machinery (non-current assets) values, adjusted by the cost of any additions.

	£m
Carrying amount at 1 January 2008	309
Additions	95
	404
Depreciation (balancing figure)	(79)
Carrying amount at 31 December 2008	325

3 Interest receivable must be taken away to work towards the profit before crediting it, because it is not part of operations but of investing activities. The cash inflow from this source appears under the 'Cash flows from investing activities' heading.
4 Interest payable expense must be taken out, by adding it back to the profit figure. We subsequently deduct the cash paid for interest payable during the year. In this case the two figures are identical.
5 Taxation is paid by companies 50 per cent during their accounting year and 50 per cent in the following year. As a result the 2008 payment would have been half the tax on the 2007 profit (that is, the figure that would have appeared in the current liabilities at the end of 2007), plus half of the 2008 taxation charge (that is, $16 + (^1/_2 \times 46) = 39$). Probably the easiest way to deduce the amount paid during the year to 31 December 2008 is by following this approach:

	£m
Taxation owed at start of the year (from the balance sheet as at 31 December 2007)	16
Taxation charge for the year (from the income statement)	46
	62
Less Taxation owed at the end of the year (from the balance sheet as at 31 December 2008)	(23)
Taxation paid during the year	39

This follows the logic that if we start with what the business owed at the beginning of the year, add the increase in what was owed as a result of the current year's taxation charge and then deduct what was owed at the end, the resulting figure must be what was paid during the year.
6 It has been assumed that the loan notes were redeemed for their balance sheet value. This is not, however, always the case.
7 The share issue raised £90m, of which £50m went into the share capital total on the balance sheet and £40m into share premium.
8 There were no 'cash equivalents', just cash (though negative).

What does the cash flow statement tell us?

The cash flow statement tells us how the business has generated cash during the period and where that cash has gone. Since cash is properly regarded as the lifeblood of just about any business, this is potentially very useful information.

Tracking the sources and uses of cash over several years could show financing trends that a reader of the statements could use to help to make judgements about the likely future behaviour of the business.

Looking specifically at the cash flow statement for Torbryan plc, in Example 5.3, we can see the following:

- Net cash flow from operations was strong, much larger than the profit for the year figure, after taking account of the dividend paid. This would be expected because depreciation is deducted in arriving at profit. There was a general tendency for working capital to absorb some cash. This would not be surprising had there been an expansion of activity (sales revenue) over the year. From the information supplied, we do not know whether there was an expansion or not. (We have only one year's income statement.)
- There were net outflows of cash for investing activities, but this would not be unusual. Many items of property, plant and equipment have limited lives and need to be replaced with new ones. The expenditure during the year was not out of line with the depreciation expense for the year, which is what we might expect.
- There was a fairly major outflow of cash to redeem some borrowings, partly offset by the proceeds of a share issue. This presumably represents a change of financing strategy. Together with the ploughed-back profit from trading, there has been a significant shift in the equity/borrowings balance.

Real World 5.3 looks at the cash flow statement of an emerging business, LiDCO Group plc, that is experiencing negative cash flows as it seeks to establish a profitable market for its products.

Real World 5.3

Not losing heart

LiDCO Group plc is a smaller business whose shares are listed on the Alternative Investment Market (AIM). AIM is a section of the London Stock Exchange that specialises in providing a market for the shares of smaller up-and-coming businesses. We shall discuss AIM in Chapter 11.

LiDCO makes highly sophisticated equipment for monitoring the hearts of cardiac patients, typically in hospitals and clinics. The business was started by four doctors and scientists. It has spent £6.8m over ten years developing its products, obtaining registration for their use from both the UK and US authorities and creating manufacturing facilities.

LiDCO's cash flow statement for the year to 31 January 2007 was as follows:

	£000
Net cash outflow from operating activities	(1,366)
Returns on invetment and servicing of financing	
Interest received	69
Interest paid	(35)
Net cash inflow from returns on investment	34
Taxation	283
Capital expenditure and financial investment	
Purchase of tangible fixed assets	(137)
Purchase of intangible fixed assets	(410)
Net cash outflow from capital expenditure and financial investment	(547)
Financing activities	
Issue of ordinary share capital	3,245
Convertible loan drawdowns	(1,126)
Net cash inflow from financing	2,119
Increase/(decrease) in cash	523

[Note that this was the statement that appeared in the business's annual report. Some more detail was supplied in the way of notes to the accounts.]

To put these figures into context, the sales revenue for the year was £3,443,000. This means that the net cash outflow from operating activities was equal to nearly 40 per cent of the revenue figure. (This was an improvement, since it was over 50 per cent in 2006.) Such cash flow profiles are fairly typical of 'high-tech' businesses that have enormous start-up costs to bring their products to the market in sufficient quantities to yield a profit. Of course, not all such businesses achieve this, but LiDCO seems confident of success.

Source: Information taken from LiDCO Group plc Annual Report 2007 and AIM company profile, www.londonstockexchange.com.

? Self-assessment question 5.1

Touchstone plc's income statements for the years ended 31 December 2007 and 2008 and the balance sheets as at 31 December 2007 and 2008 are as follows:

Income statements for the years ended 2007 and 2008

	2007 £m	2008 £m
Revenue	173	207
Cost of sales	(96)	(101)
Gross profit	77	106
Distribution expenses	(18)	(20)
Administrative expenses	(24)	(26)
Other operating income	3	4
Operating profit	38	64
Interest payable	(2)	(4)
Profit before taxation	36	60
Taxation	(8)	(16)
Profit for the year	28	44

Balance sheets as at 31 December 2007 and 2008

	2007 £m	2008 £m
Non-current assets		
Property, plant and equipment		
Land and buildings	94	110
Plant and machinery	53	62
	147	172
Current assets		
Inventories	25	24
Treasury bills (short-term investments)	–	15
Trade receivables	16	26
Cash at bank and in hand	4	4
	45	69
Total assets	192	241
Equity		
Called-up ordinary share capital	100	100
Retained earnings	30	56
	130	156
Non-current liabilities		
Borrowings – loan notes (10%)	20	40
Current liabilities		
Trade payables	38	37
Taxation	4	8
	42	45
Total equity and liabilities	192	241

Included in 'cost of sales', 'distribution costs' and 'administration expenses', depreciation was as follows:

	2007 £m	2008 £m
Land and buildings	5	6
Plant and machinery	6	10

There were no non-current asset disposals in either year.

The interest payable expense equalled the cash payment made during the year, in both cases.

The business paid dividends on ordinary shares of £14m during 2007 and £18m during 2008.

The Treasury bills represent a short-term investment of funds that will be used shortly in operations. There is insignificant risk that this investment will lose value.

Required:
Prepare a cash flow statement for the business for 2008.

The answer to this question can be found at the back of the book in Appendix B.

Summary

The main points of this chapter may be summarised as follows.

The need for a cash flow statement

- Cash is important because no business can operate without it.
- The cash flow statement is specifically designed to reveal movements in cash over a period.
- Cash movements cannot be readily detected from the income statement, which focuses on revenue and expenses rather than on cash receipts and cash payments.
- Profit (or loss) and cash generated for the period are rarely equal.
- The cash flow statement is a primary financial statement, along with the income statement and the balance sheet.

Preparing the cash flow statement

- The layout of the statement contains three categories of cash movement:
    - cash flows from operating activities;
    - cash flows from investing activities;
    - cash flows from financing activities.
- The total of the cash movements under these three categories will provide the net increase or decrease in cash and cash equivalents for the period.
- A reconciliation can be undertaken to check that the opening balance of cash and cash equivalents plus the net increase (or decrease) for the period equals the closing balance.

Calculating the cash generated from operations

- The net cash flows from operating activities can be derived by either the direct method or the indirect method.
- The direct method is based on an analysis of the cash records for the period, whereas the indirect method uses information contained within the income statement and balance sheets of the business.
- The indirect method takes the net operating profit for the period, adds back any depreciation charge and then adjusts for changes in inventories, receivables and payables during the period.

Interpreting the cash flow statement

- The cash flow statement shows the main sources and uses of cash.
- Tracking the cash movements over several periods may reveal financing and investing patterns and may help predict future management action.

Key terms

direct method
indirect method
working capital

Further reading

If you would like to explore the topics covered in this chapter in more depth, we recommend the following books:

Elliott, B. and Elliott, J., *Financial Accounting and Reporting* (12th edn), Financial Times Prentice Hall, 2008, chapter 27.

KPMG, *KPMG's Practical Guide to International Financial Reporting Standards* (3rd edn), Thomson, 2006, section 2.4.

Sutton, T., *Corporate Financial Accounting and Reporting* (2nd edn), Financial Times Prentice Hall, 2004, chapters 6 and 18.

? Review questions

Answers to these questions can be found at the back of the book in Appendix C.

5.1 The typical business outside the service sector has about 50 per cent more of its resources tied up in inventories than in cash, yet there is no call for a 'inventories flow statement' to be prepared. Why is cash regarded as more important than inventories?

5.2 What is the difference between the direct and indirect methods of deducing cash generated from operations?

5.3 Taking each of the categories of the cash flow statement in turn, in which direction would you normally expect the cash flow to be? Explain your answer.
(a) Cash flows from operating activities.
(b) Cash flows from investing activities.
(c) Cash flows from financing activities.

5.4 What causes the profit for the year not to equal the net cash inflow?

✳ Exercises

Exercises 5.3 to 5.5 are more advanced than Exercises 5.1 and 5.2. Those with coloured numbers have answers at the back of the book in Appendix D.

> **If you wish to try more exercises, visit MyAccountingLab/**

5.1 How will each of the following events ultimately affect the amount of cash?
(a) An increase in the level of inventories.
(b) A rights issue of ordinary shares.
(c) A bonus issue of ordinary shares.
(d) Writing off part of the value of some inventories.
(e) The disposal of a large number of the business's shares by a major shareholder.
(f) Depreciating a non-current asset.

5.2 The following information has been taken from the financial statements of Juno plc for last year and the year before last:

	Year before last	Last year
	£m	£m
Operating profit	156	187
Depreciation charged in arriving at operating profit	47	55
Inventories held at the end of:	27	31
Trade receivables at the end of:	24	23
Trade payables at the end of:	15	17

Required:
What is the figure for cash generated from operations for Juno plc for last year?

5.3 Torrent plc's income statement for the year ended 31 December 2008 and the balance sheets as at 31 December 2007 and 2008 are as follows:

Income statement

	£m
Revenue	623
Cost of sales	(353)
Gross profit	270
Distribution expenses	(71)
Administrative expenses	(30)
Rental income	27
Operating profit	196
Interest payable	(26)
Profit before taxation	170
Taxation	(36)
Profit for the year	134

Balance sheets as at 31 December 2007 and 2008

	2007 £m	2008 £m
Non-current assets		
Property, plant and equipment		
Land and buildings	310	310
Plant and machinery	325	314
	635	624
Current assets		
Inventories	41	35
Trade receivables	139	145
	180	180
Total assets	815	804
Equity		
Called-up ordinary share capital	200	300
Share premium account	40	–
Revaluation reserve	69	9
Retained earnings	123	197
	432	506
Non-current liabilities		
Borrowings – loan notes	250	150
Current liabilities		
Borrowings (all bank overdraft)	56	89
Trade payables	54	41
Taxation	23	18
	133	148
Total equity and liabilities	815	804

During 2008, the business spent £67m on additional plant and machinery. There were no other non-current asset acquisitions or disposals.

There was no share issue for cash during the year. The interest payable expense was equal in amount to the cash outflow. A dividend of £60m was paid.

Required:
Prepare the cash flow statement for Torrent plc for the year ended 31 December 2008.

5.4 Chen plc's income statements for the years ended 31 December 2007 and 2008 and the balance sheets as at 31 December 2007 and 2008 are as follows:

Income statement

	2007 £m	2008 £m
Revenue	207	153
Cost of sales	(101)	(76)
Gross profit	106	77
Distribution expenses	(22)	(20)
Administrative expenses	(20)	(28)
Operating profit	64	29
Interest payable	(4)	(4)
Profit before taxation	60	25
Taxation	(16)	(6)
Profit for the year	44	19 →

Balance sheets as at 31 December 2007 and 2008

	2007 £m	2008 £m
Non-current assets		
Property, plant and equipment		
Land and buildings	110	130
Plant and machinery	62	56
	172	186
Current assets		
Inventories	24	25
Trade receivables	26	25
Cash at bank and in hand	19	–
	69	50
Total assets	241	236
Equity		
Called-up ordinary share capital	100	100
Retained earnings	56	57
	156	157
Non-current liabilities		
Borrowings – loan notes (10%)	40	40
Current liabilities		
Borrowings (all bank overdraft)	–	2
Trade payables	37	34
Taxation	8	3
	45	39
Total equity and liabilities	241	236

Included in 'cost of sales', 'distribution costs' and 'administrative expenses', depreciation was as follows:

	2007 £m	2008 £m
Land and buildings	6	10
Plant and machinery	10	12

There were no non-current asset disposals in either year. The amount of cash paid for interest equalled the expense in both years. Dividends were paid totalling £18m in each year.

Required:
Prepare a cash flow statement for the business for 2008.

5.5 The following financial statements for Blackstone plc are a slightly simplified set of published accounts. Blackstone plc is an engineering business that developed a new range of products in 2006. These products now account for 60 per cent of its turnover.

Income statement for the years ended 31 March

	Notes	2007 £m	2008 £m
Revenue		7,003	11,205
Cost of sales		(3,748)	(5,809)
Gross profit		3,255	5,396
Operating expenses		(2,205)	(3,087)
Operating profit		1,050	2,309
Interest payable	1	(216)	(456)
Profit before taxation		834	1,853
Taxation		(210)	(390)
Profit for the year		624	1,463

Balance sheets as at 31 March

	Notes	2007 £m	2008 £m
Non-current assets			
Property, plant and equipment	2	4,300	7,535
Intangible assets	3	–	700
		4,300	8,235
Current assets			
Inventories		1,209	2,410
Trade receivables		641	1,173
Cash at bank		123	–
		1,973	3,583
Total assets		6,273	11,818
Equity			
Share capital		1,800	1,800
Share premium		600	600
Capital reserves		352	352
Retained profits		685	1,748
		3,437	4,500
Non-current liabilities			
Borrowings – bank loan (repayable 2012)		1,800	3,800
Current liabilities			
Trade payables		931	1,507
Taxation		105	195
Borrowings (all bank overdraft)		–	1,816
		1,036	3,518
Total equity and liabilities		6,273	11,818

Notes:

1 The expense and the cash outflow for interest payable are equal.

2 The movements in property, plant and equipment during the year are set out below.

	Land and buildings £m	Plant and machinery £m	Fixtures and fittings £m	Total £m
Cost				
At 1 April 2007	4,500	3,850	2,120	10,470
Additions	–	2,970	1,608	4,578
Disposals	–	(365)	(216)	(581)
At 31 March 2008	4,500	6,455	3,512	14,467
Depreciation				
At 1 April 2007	1,275	3,080	1,815	6,170
Charge for year	225	745	281	1,251
Disposals	–	(305)	(184)	(489)
At 31 March 2008	1,500	3,520	1,912	6,932
Carrying amount				
At 31 March 2008	3,000	2,935	1,600	7,535

3 Intangible assets represent the amounts paid for the goodwill of another engineering business acquired during the year.

4 Proceeds from the sale of non-current assets in the year ended 31 March 2008 amounted to £54m.

5 Dividends were paid on ordinary shares of £300m in 2007 and £400m in 2008.

Required:

Prepare a cash flow statement for Blackstone plc for the year ended 31 March 2008. (*Hint*: A loss (deficit) on disposal of non-current assets is simply an additional amount of depreciation and should be dealt with as such in preparing the cash flow statement.)

ANNUAL REPORTS AND RATIOS

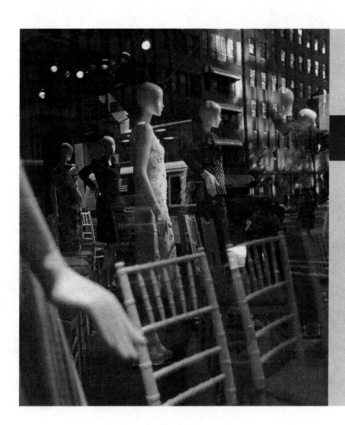

Chapter 4

Accounting for limited companies

Introduction

Most businesses in the UK, except the very smallest, operate in the form of limited companies. More than 2 million limited companies now exist and they account for the majority of UK business activity and employment. The economic significance of this type of business is not confined to the UK; it can be seen in many of the world's developed countries.

In this chapter we consider the nature of limited companies and how they differ from sole proprietorship businesses and partnerships. We examine the ways in which the owners provide finance as well as the rules governing the way in which limited companies must account to their owners and to other interested parties. We shall also see how the financial statements, which were discussed in the previous two chapters, are prepared for this type of business.

Learning outcomes

When you have completed this chapter, you should be able to:

■ discuss the nature of the limited company;

■ describe the main features of the owners' claim in a limited company;

■ discuss the framework of rules that surround accounting for limited companies;

■ explain how the income statement and balance sheet of a limited company differ in detail from those of sole proprietorships and partnerships.

Why limited companies?

Although there are very many businesses in the UK that trade as sole proprietorships, partnerships and other forms, overwhelmingly the most important business form is the limited company. In terms of sales revenue generated, wealth created, number of people employed, exports achieved and virtually any other measure, the limited companies dominate the business scene. We shall be seeing in this chapter that limited companies are subject to a great deal of regulation, particularly in the areas of finance and accounting. This is particularly true of those limited companies whose shares are traded on the London Stock Exchange. All of this regulation can be very tiresome for the companies and, importantly, very expensive.

In this chapter we shall be looking at a number of issues, including:

- What is a limited company?
- Why are limited companies so popular?
- What regulation must limited companies accept?
- Why do some limited companies have their shares traded on the London Stock Exchange, when this leads to even more regulation, at great expense?

We shall be answering these and other questions during this chapter.

The main features of limited companies

Legal nature

Let us begin our examination of limited companies by discussing their legal nature. A limited company has been described as an artificial person that has been created by law. This means that a company has many of the rights and obligations that 'real' people have. It can, for example, sue or be sued by others and can enter into contracts in its own name. This contrasts sharply with other types of businesses, such as sole proprietorships and partnerships (that is, unincorporated businesses), where it is the owner(s) rather than the business that must sue, enter into contracts and so on, because the business has no separate legal identity.

With the rare exceptions of those that are created by Act of Parliament or by Royal Charter, all UK companies are created (or *incorporated*) by registration. To create a company the person or persons wishing to create it (usually known as *promoters*) fill in a few simple forms and pay a modest registration fee. After having ensured that the necessary formalities have been met, the Registrar of Companies, a UK government official, enters the name of the new company on the Registry of Companies. Thus, in the UK, companies can be formed very easily and cheaply (for about £100).

A limited company may be owned by just one person, but most have more than one owner and some have many owners. The owners are usually known as *members* or *shareholders*. The ownership of a company is normally divided into a number, frequently a large number, of shares, each of equal size. Each owner, or shareholder, owns one or more shares in the company. Large companies typically have a very large number of shareholders. For example, at 31 March 2007, BT Group plc, the telecommunications business, had nearly 1.3 million different shareholders.

As a limited company has its own legal identity, it is regarded as being quite separate from those that own and manage it.

It is worth emphasising that this legal separateness of owners and the company has no connection whatsoever with the business entity convention of accounting, which we discussed in Chapter 2. This accounting convention applies equally well to all business types, including sole proprietorships and partnerships where there is certainly no legal distinction between the owner(s) and the business.

The legal separateness of the limited company and its shareholders leads to two important features of the limited company: perpetual life and limited liability. These are now explained.

Perpetual life

A company is normally granted a perpetual existence and so will continue even where an owner of some, or even all, of the shares in the company dies. The shares of the deceased person will simply pass to the beneficiary of his or her estate. The granting of perpetual existence means that the life of a company is quite separate from the lives of those individuals who own or manage it. It is not, therefore, affected by changes in ownership that arise when individuals buy and sell shares in the company.

Though a company may be granted a perpetual existence when it is first formed, it is possible for either the shareholders or the courts to bring this existence to an end. When this is done, the assets of the company are sold off to meet outstanding liabilities. Any surplus arising from the sale will then be used to pay the shareholders. Shareholders may agree to end the life of a company where it has achieved the purpose for which it was formed or where they feel that the company has no real future. The courts may bring the life of a company to an end where creditors have applied to the courts for this to be done because they have not been paid amounts owing.

Where shareholders agree to end the life of a company, it is referred to as a 'voluntary liquidation'. Real World 4.1 describes the demise of one company by this method.

Real World 4.1

Monotub Industries in a spin as founder gets Titan for £1

Monotub Industries, maker of the Titan washing machine, yesterday passed into corporate history with very little ceremony and with only a whimper of protest from minority shareholders.

At an extraordinary meeting held in a basement room of the group's West End headquarters, shareholders voted to put the company into voluntary liquidation and sell its assets and intellectual property to founder Martin Myerscough for £1. [The shares in the company were at one time worth 650p each.]

The only significant opposition came from Giuliano Gnagnatti who, along with other shareholders, has seen his investment shrink faster than a wool twin-set on a boil wash.

The not-so-proud owner of 100,000 Monotub shares, Mr Gnagnatti, the managing director of an online retailer . . . described the sale of Monotub as a 'free gift' to Mr Myerscough. This assessment was denied by Ian Green, the chairman of Monotub, who said the closest the beleaguered company had come to a sale was an offer for £60,000 that gave no guarantees against liabilities, which are thought to amount to £750,000.

The quiet passing of the washing machine, eventually dubbed the Titanic, was in strong contrast to its performance in many kitchens.

Originally touted as the 'great white goods hope' of the washing machine industry with its larger capacity and removable drum, the Titan ran into problems when it kept stopping during the spin cycle, causing it to emit a loud bang and leap into the air.

Summing up the demise of the Titan, Mr Green said: 'Clearly the machine had some revolutionary aspects, but you can't get away from the fact that the machine was faulty and should not have been launched with those defects.'

The usually-vocal Mr Myerscough, who has promised to pump £250,000 into the company and give Monotub shareholders £4 for every machine sold, refused to comment on his plans for the Titan or reveal who his backers were. But . . . he did say that he intended to 'take the Titan forward'.

Source: 'Monotub Industries in a spin as founder gets Titan for £1', Lisa Urquhart, *Financial Times*, 23 January 2003, FT.com.

Limited liability

Since the company is a legal person in its own right, it must take responsibility for its own debts and losses. This means that once the shareholders have paid what they have agreed to pay for the shares, their obligation to the company, and to the company's creditors, is satisfied. Thus shareholders can limit their losses to the amount that they have paid, or agreed to pay, for their shares. This is of great practical importance to potential shareholders since they know that what they can lose, as part owners of the business, is limited.

Contrast this with the position of sole proprietors or partners. They cannot 'ring-fence' assets that they do not want to put into the business. If a sole proprietary or partnership business finds itself in a position where liabilities exceed the business assets, the law gives unsatisfied creditors the right to demand payment out of what the sole proprietor or partner may have regarded as 'non-business' assets. Thus the sole proprietor or partner could lose everything – house, car, the lot. This is because the law sees Jill, the sole proprietor, as being the same as Jill the private individual. The shareholder, by contrast, can lose only the amount committed to that company. Legally, the business operating as a limited company, in which Jack owns shares, is not the same as Jack himself. This is true even if Jack were to own all of the shares in the company.

Real World 4.2 gives an example of a well-known case where the shareholders of a particular company were able to avoid any liability to those that had lost money as a result of dealing with the company.

Carlton and Granada 1 – Nationwide Football League 0

Two television broadcasting companies, Carlton and Granada, each owned 50 per cent of a separate company, ITV Digital (formerly ON Digital). ITV Digital signed a contract to pay the Nationwide Football League (in effect the three divisions of English football below the Premiership) more than £89m on both 1 August 2002 and 1 August 2003 for the rights to broadcast football matches over three seasons. ITV Digital was unable to sell enough subscriptions for the broadcasts and collapsed because it was unable to meet its liabilities. The Nationwide Football League tried to force Carlton and Granada (ITV Digital's only shareholders) to meet the ITV Digital's contractual obligations. It was unable to do so because the shareholders could not be held legally liable for the amounts owing.

Carlton and Granada merged into one business in 2003, but at the time of ITV Digital were two independent companies.

Activity 4.1

The fact that shareholders can limit their losses to that which they have paid, or have agreed to pay, for their shares is of great practical importance to potential shareholders.

Can you think of any practical benefit to a private-sector economy, in general, of this ability of shareholders to limit losses?

Business is a risky venture – in some cases very risky. People with money to invest will usually be happier to do so when they know the limit of their liability. If investors are given limited liability, new businesses are more likely to be formed and existing ones are likely to find it easier to raise more finance. This is good for the private-sector economy and may ultimately lead to the generation of greater wealth for society as a whole.

Although limited liability has this advantage to the providers of equity finance (the shareholders), it is not necessarily to the advantage of all others who have a stake in the business, like the Nationwide Football League clubs (see Real World 4.2). Limited liability is attractive to shareholders because they can, in effect, walk away from the unpaid debts of the company if their contribution has not been sufficient to meet those debts. This is likely to make any individual, or another business, that is considering entering into a contract, wary of dealing with the limited company. This can be a real problem for smaller, less established companies. Suppliers may insist on cash payment before delivery of goods or the rendering of a service. Alternatively, they may require a personal guarantee from a major shareholder that the debt will be paid before allowing trade credit. In the latter case, the supplier circumvents the company's limited liability status by demanding the personal liability of an individual. Larger, more established companies, on the other hand, tend to have built up the confidence of suppliers.

Legal safeguards

Various safeguards exist to protect individuals and businesses contemplating dealing with a limited company. These include the requirement to indicate limited liability status in the name of the company. By doing this, an alert is issued to prospective suppliers and lenders.

A further safeguard is the restrictions placed on the ability of shareholders to withdraw their equity from the company. These restrictions are designed to prevent shareholders from protecting their own investment and, as a result, leaving lenders and suppliers in an exposed position. We shall consider this point in more detail later in the chapter.

Finally, limited companies are required to produce annual financial statements (income statement, balance sheet and cash flow statement), and make them publicly available. This means that anyone interested can gain an impression of the financial performance and position of the company. The form and content of these statements are considered in some detail later in the chapter.

Public and private companies

When a company is registered with the Registrar of Companies, it must be registered either as a public or as a private company. The main practical difference between these is that a public company can offer its shares for sale to the general public, but a private company is restricted from doing so. A public limited company must signal its status to all interested parties by having the words 'public limited company', or its abbreviation 'plc', in its name. For a private limited company, the word 'limited' or 'Ltd' must appear as part of its name.

Private limited companies tend to be smaller businesses where the ownership is divided among relatively few shareholders who are usually fairly close to one another – for example, a family company. Numerically, there are vastly more private limited companies in the UK than there are public ones. Of the 2.1 million UK limited companies now in existence, only 11,500 (representing 0.5 per cent of the total) are public limited companies.

Since individual public companies tend to be larger, they are often economically more important. In some industry sectors, such as banking, insurance, oil refining and grocery retailing, they are completely dominant. Although some large private limited companies exist, many private limited companies are little more than the vehicle through which one-person businesses operate.

Real World 4.3 shows the extent of market dominance of public limited companies in one particular business sector.

Real World 4.3

A big slice of the market

The grocery sector is dominated by four large players: Tesco, Sainsbury, Morrison and Asda. The first three are public limited companies and the fourth, Asda, is owned by a large US public company, Wal-Mart. Figure 4.1 shows the share of the grocery market enjoyed by each.

Figure 4.1 Market share of the four largest grocers: 12 weeks to 15 July 2007

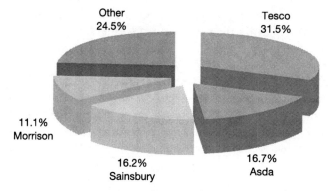

This diagram shows that Tesco had by far the largest market share and that the four largest grocers, when taken together, had more than 75 per cent of the total market during the period.

Source: Compiled from information in 'Tesco share of the UK grocery market is 31.5 per cent', www.investing.reuters.co.uk, 26 July 2007.

Taxation

Another consequence of the legal separation of the limited company from its owners is that companies must be accountable to the tax authorities for tax on their profits and gains. This leads to the reporting of tax in the financial statements of limited companies. The charge for tax is shown in the income statement (profit and loss account). The tax charge for a particular year is based on that year's profit. Since only 50 per cent of a company's tax liability is due for payment during the year concerned, the other 50 per cent will appear on the end-of-year balance sheet as a short-term liability. This will be illustrated a little later in the chapter. The tax position of companies contrasts with that of sole proprietorships and partnerships, where tax is levied not on the business but on the owner(s). Thus tax does not impact on the financial statements of unincorporated businesses, but is an individual matter between the owner(s) and the tax authorities.

Companies are charged corporation tax on their profits and gains. The percentage rates of tax tend to vary from year to year, but have recently been 30 per cent for larger companies and 20 per cent for smaller companies. These rates of tax are levied on the company's taxable profit, which is not necessarily the same as the profit shown on the income statement. This is because tax law does not, in every respect, follow the normal accounting rules. Generally, however, the taxable profit and the company's accounting profit are pretty close to one another.

Transferring share ownership: the role of the Stock Exchange

We have already seen that shares in a company may be transferred from one owner to another. The desire of some shareholders to sell their shares, coupled with the desire of others to buy those shares, has led to the existence of a formal market in which shares can be bought and sold. The London Stock Exchange and similar organisations around the world provide a marketplace in which shares in public companies may be bought and sold. Share prices are determined by the laws of supply and demand, which are, in turn, determined by investors' perceptions of the future economic prospects of the companies concerned. Only the shares of certain companies (*listed* companies) may be traded on the London Stock Exchange. About 1,300 UK companies are listed. This represents only 1 in about 1,600 of all UK companies (public and private) and about 1 in 9 public limited companies. However, many of these 1,300 listed companies are massive. Nearly all of the 'household-name' UK businesses (for example, Tesco, Next, BT, Cadbury Schweppes, Vodafone, BP and so on) are listed companies.

Activity 4.2

If, as has been pointed out earlier, the change in ownership of shares does not directly affect the particular company, why do many public companies actively seek to have their shares traded in a recognised market?

The main reason is that investors are generally very reluctant to pledge their money unless they can see some way in which they can turn their investment back into cash. In theory, the shares of a particular company may be very valuable because the company has bright prospects. However, unless this value is capable of being turned into cash, the benefit to the shareholders is dubious. After all, we cannot spend shares; we generally need cash.

This means that potential shareholders are much more likely to be prepared to buy new shares from the company (thereby providing the company with new finance) where they can see a way of liquidating their investment (turning it into cash) as and when they wish. Stock Exchanges provide the means of liquidation.

Although the buying and selling of 'second-hand' shares does not provide the company with cash, the fact that the buying and selling facility exists will make it easier for the company to raise new share capital when it needs to do so.

Managing a company

A limited company may have legal personality, but it is not a human being capable of making decisions and plans about the business and exercising control over it. People must undertake these management tasks. The most senior level of management of a company is the board of directors.

The shareholders elect directors (by law there must be at least one director for a private limited company and two for a public limited company) to manage the company on a day-to-day basis on behalf of those shareholders. In a small company, the board may be the only level of management and consist of all of the shareholders. In larger companies, the board may consist of ten or so directors out of many thousands of shareholders. Indeed, directors are not even required to be shareholders. Below the board of directors of the typical large company could be several layers of management comprising thousands of people.

In recent years, the issue of corporate governance has generated much debate. The term is used to describe the ways in which companies are directed and controlled. The issue of corporate governance is important because, with larger companies, those who own the company (that is, the shareholders) are usually divorced from the day-to-day control of the business. The shareholders employ the directors to manage the company for them. Given this position, it may seem reasonable to assume that the best interests of shareholders will guide the directors' decisions. However, in practice this does not always occur. The directors may be more concerned with pursuing their own interests, such as increasing their pay and 'perks' (such as expensive motor cars, overseas visits and so on) and improving their job security and status. As a result, a conflict can occur between the interests of shareholders and the interests of directors.

Where directors pursue their own interests at the expense of the shareholders, there is clearly a problem for the shareholders. However, it may also be a problem for society as a whole. If shareholders feel that their funds are likely to be mismanaged, they will be reluctant to invest. A shortage of funds will mean that fewer investments can be made and the costs of funds will increase as businesses compete for what funds are available. Thus, a lack of concern for shareholders can have a profound effect on the performance of individual companies and, with this, the health of the economy. To avoid these problems, most competitive market economies have a framework of rules to help monitor and control the behaviour of directors.

These rules are usually based around three guiding principles:

■ *Disclosure*. This lies at the heart of good corporate governance. An OECD report (*Corporate Governance: Improving Competitiveness and Access to Capital in Global Markets*, report by Business Sector Advisory Group on Corporate Governance, OECD, 1998) summed up the benefits of disclosure as follows:

> Adequate and timely information about corporate performance enables investors to make informed buy-and-sell decisions and thereby helps the market reflect the value of a corporation under present management. If the market determines that present management is not performing, a decrease in stock [share] price will sanction management's failure and open the way to management change. (p. 14)

- *Accountability*. This involves defining the roles and duties of the directors and establishing an adequate monitoring process. In the UK, company law requires that the directors of a business act in the best interests of the shareholders. This means, among other things, that they must not try to use their position and knowledge to make gains at the expense of the shareholders. The law also requires larger companies to have their annual financial statements independently audited. The purpose of an independent audit is to lend credibility to the financial statements prepared by the directors. We shall take a brief look at audit later in this chapter.
- *Fairness*. Directors should not be able to benefit from access to 'inside' information that is not available to shareholders. As a result, both the law and the Stock Exchange place restrictions on the ability of directors to buy and sell the shares of the business. One example of these restrictions is that the directors cannot buy or sell shares immediately before the announcement of the annual trading results of the business or before the announcement of a significant event such as a planned merger or the loss of the chief executive.

Strengthening the framework of rules

The number of rules designed to safeguard shareholders has increased considerably over the years. This has been in response to weaknesses in corporate governance procedures, which have been exposed through well-publicised business failures and frauds, excessive pay increases to directors and evidence that some financial reports were being 'massaged' so as to mislead shareholders. (This last point will be discussed later in the chapter.) Some believe, however, that the shareholders must shoulder some of the blame for any weaknesses. Not all shareholders in large companies are private individuals owning just a few shares each. In fact, ownership, by market value, of the shares listed on the London Stock Exchange is dominated by investing institutions such as insurance businesses, banks and pension funds. These are often massive operations, owning large quantities of the shares of the companies in which they invest. These institutional investors employ specialist staff to manage their portfolios of shares in various companies. It has been argued that the large institutional shareholders, despite their size and relative expertise, have not been very active in corporate governance matters. Thus there has been little monitoring of directors. However, things seem to be changing. There is increasing evidence that institutional investors are becoming more proactive in relation to the companies in which they hold shares.

The Combined Code

During the 1990s there was a real effort by the accountancy profession and the London Stock Exchange to address the problems mentioned above. A Code of Best Practice on Corporate Governance emerged in 1992. This was concerned with accountability and financial reporting. In 1995, a separate code of practice emerged. This dealt with directors' pay and conditions. These two codes were revised, 'finetuned' and amalgamated to produce the Combined Code, which was issued in 1998.

The Combined Code was revised in 2003, following the recommendations of the Higgs Report, and modified slightly in 2006. These recommendations were mainly concerned with the roles of the company chairman (the senior director) and the other directors. The report was particularly concerned with the role of 'non-executive' directors. Non-executive directors do not work full-time in the company, but act solely in the role of director. This contrasts with 'executive' directors who are salaried employees. For example, the finance director of most large companies is a full-time employee. This person is a member of the board of directors and, as such, takes part in the key decision-making at board level. At the same time, he or she is also responsible for managing the departments of the company that act on those board decisions as far as finance is concerned.

The view reflected in the 2003 Combined Code is that executive directors can become too embroiled in the day-to-day management of the company to be able to take a broad view. It also reflects the view that, for executive directors, conflicts can arise between their own interests and those of the shareholders. The advantage of non-executive directors can be that they are much more independent of the company than are their executive colleagues. Non-executive directors are remunerated by the company for their work, but this would normally form only a small proportion of their total income. This gives them an independence that the executive directors may lack. Non-executive directors are often senior managers in other businesses or people who have had good experience of such roles.

The Combined Code has the backing of the London Stock Exchange. This means that companies listed on the London Stock Exchange are expected to comply with the requirements of the Code or must give their shareholders good reason why they do not. Failure to do one or other of these can lead to the company's shares being suspended from listing. This is an important sanction against non-compliant directors.

The Combined Code sets out a number of principles relating to such matters as the role of the directors, their relations with shareholders, and their accountability. Real World 4.4 outlines some of the more important of these.

Real World 4.4

The Combined Code

Some of the key elements of the Combined Code are as follows:

- Every listed company should have a board of directors to lead and control the company.
- There should be a clear division of responsibilities between the chairman and the chief executive officer of the company to ensure that a single person does not have unbridled power.
- There should be a balance between executive and non-executive (who are often part-time and independent) members of the board, to ensure that small groups of individuals cannot dominate proceedings.

- The board should receive timely information that is of sufficient quality to enable them to carry out their duties.
- Appointments to the board should be the subject of rigorous, formal and transparent procedures.
- All directors should submit themselves for re-election at regular intervals, subject to satisfactory performance.
- There should be formal and transparent procedures for developing policy on directors' remuneration.
- The board has a responsibility for ensuring that a satisfactory dialogue with shareholders occurs.
- Boards should use the annual general meeting to communicate with private investors and encourage their participation.
- Institutional shareholders have a responsibility to use their votes.
- The board should publish a balanced and understandable assessment of the company's position and performance.
- Internal controls should be in place to protect the shareholders' wealth.
- Formal and transparent arrangements for applying financial reporting and internal control principles and for maintaining an appropriate relationship with auditors should be in place.

Strengthening the framework of rules has improved the quality of information available to shareholders, resulted in better checks on the powers of directors, and provided greater transparency in corporate affairs. However, rules can only be a partial answer. A balance must be struck between the need to protect shareholders and the need to encourage the entrepreneurial spirit of directors, which could be stifled under a welter of rules. This implies that rules should not be too tight and so unscrupulous directors may still find ways around them.

Financing limited companies

The owners' claim

The owner's claim of a sole proprietorship is normally encompassed in one figure on the balance sheet, usually labelled 'equity' (or 'capital'). With companies, this is usually a little more complicated, although in essence the same broad principles apply. With a company, the owners' claim is divided between shares (for example, the original investment), on the one hand, and reserves (that is, profits and gains subsequently made), on the other. There is also the possibility that there will be more than one type of shares and of reserves. Thus, within the basic divisions of share capital and reserves, there might well be further subdivisions. This might seem quite complicated, but we shall shortly consider the reasons for these subdivisions and all should become clearer. The sum of share capital and reserves is commonly known as equity.

The basic division

When a company is first formed, those who take steps to form it (the promoters) will decide how much needs to be raised by the potential shareholders to set the company up with the necessary assets to operate. Example 4.1 acts as a basis for illustration.

Example 4.1

A group of friends get together and decide to form a company to operate an office cleaning business. They estimate that the company will need £50,000 to obtain the necessary assets to operate. Between them, they raise the cash, which they use to buy shares in the company, on 31 March 2008, with a nominal value (or par value) of £1 each.

At this point the balance sheet of the company would be:

Balance sheet as at 31 March 2008

	£
Net assets (all in cash)	50,000
Equity	
Share capital	
50,000 shares of £1 each	50,000

The company now buys the necessary non-current assets (vacuum cleaners and so on) and inventories (cleaning materials) and starts to trade. During the first year, the company makes a profit of £10,000. This, by definition, means that the equity expands by £10,000. During the year, the shareholders (owners) make no drawings of their claim, so at the end of the year the summarised balance sheet looks like this:

Balance sheet as at 31 March 2009

	£
Net assets (various assets less liabilities*)	60,000
Equity	
Share capital	
50,000 shares of £1 each	50,000
Reserves (revenue reserve)	10,000
Total equity	60,000

* We know from Chapter 2 that Assets = Equity + Liabilities.
This can be rearranged so that Assets – Liabilities = Equity.

The profit is shown in a reserve, known as a revenue reserve, because it arises from generating revenue (making sales). Note that we do not simply merge the profit with the share capital: we must keep the two amounts separate (to satisfy company law). The reason for this is that there is a legal restriction on the maximum drawings of the shareholders' claim (or payment of a dividend) that the owners can make. This is defined by the amount of revenue reserves, and so it is helpful to show these separately. We shall look at why there is this restriction, and how it works, a little later in the chapter.

Share capital

Ordinary shares

Shares represent the basic units of ownership of a business. All companies issue ordinary shares. Ordinary shares are often known as *equities*. The nominal value of such shares is at the discretion of the people that start up the company. For example, if the initial share capital is to be £50,000, this could be two shares of £25,000 each, 5 million shares of one penny each or any other combination that gives a total of £50,000. All shares must have equal value.

Activity 4.3

The initial financial requirement for a new company is £50,000. There are to be two equal shareholders. Would you advise them to issue two shares of £25,000 each? Why?

Such large-denomination shares tend to be unwieldy. Suppose that one of the shareholders wanted to sell her shareholding. She would have to find one buyer. If there were shares of smaller denomination, it would be possible to sell part of the shareholding to various potential buyers. Furthermore, it would be possible to sell just part of the holding and retain a part.

In practice, £1 is the normal maximum nominal value for shares. Shares of 25 pence each and 50 pence each are probably the most common.

Altering the nominal value of shares

We have already seen that the promoters of a new company may make their own choice of the nominal or par value of the shares. This value need not be permanent. At a later date the shareholders can decide to change it.

Suppose that a company has 1 million ordinary shares of £1 each and a decision is made to change the nominal value of the shares from £1 to £0.50, in other words to halve the value. This would lead the company to issue each shareholder with a new share certificate (the shareholders' evidence of ownership of their shareholding) for exactly twice as many shares, each with half the nominal value. The result would be that each shareholder retains a holding of the same total nominal value. This process is known, not surprisingly, as splitting the shares. The opposite, reducing the number of shares and increasing their nominal value per share to compensate, is known as consolidating.

Since each shareholder would be left, after a split or consolidation, with exactly the same proportion of ownership of the company's assets as before, the process should not increase the value of the total shares held.

Splitting is fairly common. The objective is probably to avoid individual shares becoming too valuable and making them a bit unwieldy, in the way discussed in the answer to Activity 4.3. If a company trades successfully, the value of each share is likely to rise, and in time could increase to a level that makes them less marketable. Splitting would solve this problem. Consolidating is relatively rare.

Preference shares

Some companies also issue other classes of shares, preference shares being the most common. Preference shares guarantee that *if a dividend is paid*, the preference shareholders will be entitled to the first part of it up to a maximum value. This maximum is normally defined as a fixed percentage of the nominal value of the preference shares. If, for example, a company issues 10,000 preference shares of £1 each with a dividend rate of 6 per cent, this means that the preference shareholders are entitled to receive the first £600 (that is, 6 per cent of £10,000) of any dividend that is paid by the company for a year. The excess over £600 goes to the ordinary shareholders. Normally, any undistributed profits and gains also accrue to the ordinary shareholders.

The ordinary shareholders are the primary risk-takers as they are entitled to share in the profits of the company only after other claims have been satisfied. There are no upper limits, however, on the amount by which they may benefit. The potential rewards available to ordinary shareholders reflect the risks that they are prepared to take. Since ordinary shareholders take most of the risks, power normally resides in their hands. Usually, only the ordinary shareholders are able to vote on issues that affect the company, such as who the directors should be.

It is open to the company to issue shares of various classes – perhaps with some having unusual and exotic conditions – but in practice it is rare to find other than straightforward ordinary and preference shares. Although a company may have different classes of shares whose holders have different rights, within each class all shares must be treated equally. The rights of the various classes of shareholders, as well as other matters relating to a particular company, are contained in that company's set of rules, known as the 'articles and memorandum of association'. A copy of these rules must be lodged with the Registrar of Companies, who makes it available for inspection by the general public.

Reserves

Reserves are profits and gains that have been made by a company, which still form part of the shareholders' (owners') claim or equity. One reason that past profits and gains may not remain part of equity is that they have been paid out to shareholders (as dividends and so on). Another reason is that reserves will be reduced by the amount of any losses that the company might suffer. In the same way that profits increase equity, losses reduce it.

The shareholders' claim consists of share capital and reserves.

Activity 4.4

Are reserves amounts of cash? Can you think of a reason why this is an odd question?

To deal with the second point first, it is an odd question because reserves are a claim, or part of one, on the assets of the company, whereas cash is an asset. So reserves cannot be cash.

Reserves are classified as either revenue reserves or capital reserves. In Example 4.1 we came across one type of reserve, the revenue reserve. We should recall that this reserve represents the company's retained trading profits and gains on the disposal of non-current assets. It is worth mentioning that retained profits, or earnings, as they are often called, represent overwhelmingly the largest source of new finance for UK companies. For most companies they amount to more than share issues and borrowings combined.

 Capital reserves arise for two main reasons:

- issuing shares at above their nominal value (for example, issuing £1 shares at £1.50);
- revaluing (upwards) non-current assets.

Where a company issues shares at above their nominal value, UK law requires that the excess of the issue price over the nominal value be shown separately.

Activity 4.5

Can you think why shares might be issued at above their nominal value? (*Hint*: This would not usually happen when a company is first formed and the initial shares are being issued.)

Once a company has traded and has been successful, the shares would normally be worth more than the nominal value at which they were issued. If additional shares are to be issued to new shareholders to raise finance for further expansion, unless they are issued at a value higher than the nominal value, the new shareholders will be gaining at the expense of the original ones.

Example 4.2 shows how this works.

Example 4.2

Based on future prospects, the net assets of a company are worth £1.5m. There are currently 1 million ordinary shares in the company, each with a face (nominal) value of £1. The company wishes to raise an additional £0.6m of cash for expansion and has decided to raise it by issuing new shares. If the shares are issued for £1 each (that is 600,000 shares), the total number of shares will be

$$1.0m + 0.6m = 1.6m$$

and their total value will be the value of the existing net assets plus the new injection of cash:

$$£1.5m + £0.6m = £2.1m.$$

This means that the value of each share after the new issue will be

$$£2.1m/1.6m = £1.3125.$$

The current value of each share is

$$£1.5m/1.0m = £1.50$$

so the original shareholders will lose

$$£1.50 - £1.3125 = £0.1875 \text{ a share}$$

and the new shareholders will gain

$$£1.3125 - £1.0 = £0.3125 \text{ a share.}$$

The new shareholders will, no doubt, be delighted with this outcome; the original ones will not.

Things could be made fair between the two sets of shareholders described in Example 4.2 by issuing the new shares at £1.50 each. In this case it would be necessary to issue 400,000 shares to raise the necessary £0.6 million. £1 a share of the £1.50 is the nominal value and will be included with share capital in the balance sheet (£400,000 in total). The remaining £0.50 is a share premium, which will be shown as

a capital reserve known as the share premium account (£200,000 in total).

It is not clear why UK company law insists on the distinction between nominal share values and the premium. In some other countries (for example, the United States) with similar laws governing the corporate sector, there is not the necessity of distinguishing between share capital and share premium. Instead, the total value at which shares are issued is shown as one comprehensive figure on the company balance sheet. Real World 4.5 shows the shareholders' claim of one well-known business.

Real World 4.5

easyFunding

The budget airline easyJet plc had the following share capital and reserves as at 31 March 2007:

	£m
Share capital (25p ordinary shares)	104.7
Share premium account	632.9
Other reserves (capital)	(9.4)
Retained earnings	262.3
Total equity	990.5

Note how the nominal share capital figure is only about one-sixth of the share premium account figure. This implies that easyJet has issued shares at higher prices than the 25p a share nominal value. This reflects its trading success since the company was first formed. Note also how, at balance sheet values, retained earnings (profits) make up only 26 per cent of the total for share capital and reserves. This is probably on the low side of the average for UK companies and reflects the fact that easyJet is a fairly young company.

Source: easyJet plc Interim Report 2007.

Bonus shares

It is always open to a company to take reserves of any kind (irrespective of whether they are capital or revenue) and turn them into share capital. This will involve transferring the desired amount from the reserve concerned to share capital and then distributing the appropriate number of new shares to the existing shareholders. New shares arising from such a conversion are known as bonus shares. Issues of bonus shares are quite frequently encountered in practice. Example 4.3 illustrates this aspect of share issues.

Example 4.3

The summary balance sheet of a company is as follows:

Balance sheet as at 31 March 2008

	£
Net assets (various assets less liabilities)	128,000
Equity	
Share capital	
50,000 shares of £1 each	50,000
Reserves	78,000
Total equity	128,000

The company decides that it will issue existing shareholders with one new share for every share currently owned by each shareholder. The balance sheet immediately following this will appear as follows:

Balance sheet as at 31 March 2008

	£
Net assets (various assets less liabilities)	128,000
Equity	
Share capital	
100,000 shares of £1 each (50,000 + 50,000)	100,000
Reserves (78,000 − 50,000)	28,000
Total equity	128,000

We can see that the reserves have decreased by £50,000 and share capital has increased by the same amount. Share certificates for the 50,000 ordinary shares of £1 each that have been created from reserves will be issued to the existing shareholders to complete the transaction.

Activity 4.6

A shareholder of the company in Example 4.3 owned 100 shares before the bonus issue. How will things change for this shareholder as regards the number of shares owned and the value of the shareholding?

The answer should be that the number of shares will double, from 100 to 200. Now the shareholder owns one five-hundredth of the company (that is, 200/100,000). Before the bonus issue, the shareholder also owned one five-hundredth of the company (that is, 100/50,000). The company's assets and liabilities have not changed as a result of the bonus issue and so, logically, one five-hundredth of the value of the company should be identical to what it was before. Thus, each share is worth half as much.

→ A bonus issue simply takes one part of the owners' claim (a reserve) and puts it into another part (share capital). The transaction has no effect on the company's assets or liabilities, so there is no effect on shareholders' wealth.

Note that a bonus issue is not the same as a share split. A split does not affect the reserves.

Activity 4.7

Can you think of any reasons why a company might want to make a bonus issue if it has no economic consequence?

We think that there are three possible reasons:

■ *Share price*. To lower the value of each share without reducing the shareholders' collective or individual wealth. This has a similar effect to share splitting.
■ *Shareholder confidence*. To provide the shareholders with a 'feel-good factor'. It is believed that shareholders like bonus issues because they seem to make them better off, although in practice they should not affect their wealth.
■ *Lender confidence*. Where reserves arising from operating profits and/or realised gains on the sale of non-current assets are used to make the bonus issue, it has the effect of taking part of that portion of the shareholders' equity that could be drawn by the shareholders, as drawings (or dividends), and locking it up. The amount transferred becomes part of the permanent equity base of the company. (We shall see a little later in this chapter that there are severe restrictions on the extent to which shareholders may make drawings from their claim.) An individual or business contemplating lending money to the company may insist that the dividend payment possibilities are restricted as a condition of making the loan. This point will be explained shortly.

Real World 4.6 provides an example of a bonus share issue.

Real World 4.6

Banking on a bonus

Royal Bank of Scotland Group plc (RBS), the UK banking business, made a 2-for-1 bonus issue of shares on 4 May 2007. The nominal value of a share in the company is 25p and a total of 6,435 million new shares was issued. Following the issue, each RBS shareholder would have had three times as many shares as before the issue. Though RBS was not specific as to why it had made the bonus issue, it seems that the objective was to reduce the market price per share.

Source: Based on information contained in an announcement published by RBS on www.investors.rbs.com.

Share capital jargon

Before leaving our detailed discussion of share capital, it might be helpful to clarify some of the jargon relating to shares that is used in company financial statements.

  Share capital that has been issued to shareholders is known as the issued share capital (or allotted share capital). Sometimes, but not very often, a company may not require shareholders to pay the whole amount that is due to be paid for the shares at the time of issue. This may happen where the company does not need the money all at once. Some money would normally be paid at the time of issue and the company would 'call' for further instalments until the shares were fully paid. That part of the total issue price that has been 'called' is known as the called-up share capital. That part that has been called and paid is known as the paid-up share capital.

Raising share capital

Once the company has made its initial share issue to start business (usually soon after the company is first formed) it may decide to make further issues of new shares. These may be

- *rights issues*, that is, issues made to existing shareholders, in proportion to their existing shareholding
- *public issues*, that is, issues made to the general investing public
- *private placings*, that is, issues made to selected individuals who are usually approached and asked if they would be interested in taking up new shares.

During its lifetime a company may use all three of these approaches to raising funds through issuing new shares (although only public companies can make appeals to the general public). These approaches will be discussed in detail in Chapter 11.

Borrowings

Most companies borrow money to supplement that raised from share issues and ploughed-back profits. Company borrowing is often on a long-term basis, perhaps on a ten-year contract. Lenders may be banks and other professional providers of loan finance. Many companies raise loan finance in such a way that small investors, including private individuals, are able to lend small amounts. This is particularly the case with the larger, Stock Exchange listed, companies and involves their making a loan notes issue, which, though large in total, can be taken up in small slices by individual investors, both private individuals and investing institutions, such as pension funds and insurance companies. In some cases, these slices of loans can be bought and sold through the Stock Exchange. This means that investors do not have to wait the full term of the loan to obtain repayment, but can sell their slice of the loan to another would-be lender at intermediate points in the term of the loan. Loan notes are often known as *loan stock* or *debentures*.

Some of the features of loan notes financing, particularly the possibility that the loan notes may be traded on the Stock Exchange, can lead to a confusion that loan notes are shares by another name. We should be clear that this is not the case. It is the shareholders who own the company and, therefore, who share in its losses and profits. Holders of loan notes lend money to the company under a legally binding contract that normally specifies the rate of interest, the interest payment dates and the date of repayment of the loan itself. Usually, long-term loans are secured on assets of the company. This would give the lender the right to seize the assets concerned, sell them and satisfy the repayment obligation, should the company fail to pay either its interest payments or the repayment of the loan itself, on the dates specified in the contract between the company and the lender. A mortgage granted to a private individual buying a house or a flat is a very common example of a secured loan.

Long-term financing of companies can be depicted as in Figure 4.2.

Figure 4.2 **Sources of long-term finance for a typical limited company**

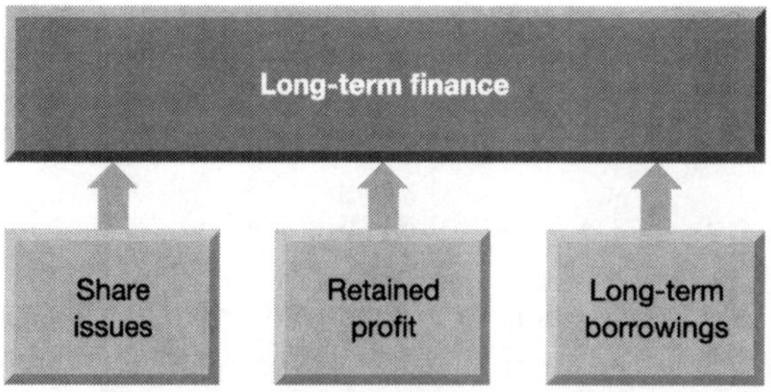

Companies derive their long-term financing needs from three sources: new share issues, retained profit and long-term borrowings. For a typical company, the sum of the first two (jointly known as 'equity finance') exceeds the third. Retained profit usually exceeds either of the other two in terms of the amount of finance raised in most years.

It is important to the prosperity and stability of a company that it strikes a suitable balance between finance provided by the shareholders (equity) and from borrowing. This topic will be explored in Chapter 6. Equity and loan notes are, of course, not the only forms of finance available to a company. In Chapter 11, we consider other sources of finance available to businesses, including companies.

Withdrawing equity

Companies are legally obliged to distinguish, on the balance sheet, between that part of the shareholders' equity that may be withdrawn and that part which may not.

The withdrawable part consists of profits arising from trading and from the disposal of non-current assets. It is represented in the balance sheet by *revenue reserves*.

It is important to appreciate that the total of revenue reserves appearing in the balance sheet is rarely the total of all trading profits and profits on disposals of non-current assets generated by the company. This total will normally have been reduced by at least one of the following three factors:

- corporation tax paid on those profits
- any dividends paid
- any losses from trading and the disposal of non-current assets.

The non-withdrawable part consists of profits arising from shareholders buying shares in the company and from upward revaluations of assets still held. It is represented in the balance sheet by *share capital* and *capital reserves*.

The law does not specify how large the non-withdrawable part of a particular company's shareholders' equity should be. However, when seeking to impress prospective lenders and credit suppliers, the larger this part, the better. Those considering doing business with the company must be able to see from the company's balance sheet how large it is.

Activity 4.8

Why are limited companies required to distinguish different parts of their shareholders' claim whereas sole proprietorship and partnership businesses are not?

The reason stems from the limited liability that company shareholders enjoy but which owners of unincorporated businesses do not. If a sole proprietor or partner withdraws all of the owners' claim, or even an amount in excess of this, the position of the lenders and credit suppliers of the business is not weakened since they can legally enforce their claims against the sole proprietor or partner as an individual. With a limited company, the business and the owners are legally separated and such right to enforce claims against individuals does not exist. To protect the company's lenders and credit suppliers, however, the law insists that the shareholders cannot normally withdraw a specific part of their claim.

Let us now look at another example.

Example 4.4

The summary balance sheet of a company at a particular date is as follows:

Balance sheet

	£
Total assets	43,000
Equity	
Share capital	
20,000 shares of £1 each	20,000
Reserves (revenue)	23,000
Total equity	43,000

A bank has been asked to make a £25,000 long-term loan to the company. If the loan were to be made, the balance sheet immediately following would appear as follows:

Balance sheet (after the loan)

	£
Total assets (£43,000 + £25,000)	68,000
Equity	
Share capital	
20,000 shares of £1 each	20,000
Reserves (revenue)	23,000
	43,000
Non-current liability	
Borrowings – loan	25,000
Total equity and liabilities	68,000

As things stand, there are assets to a total balance sheet value of £68,000 to meet the bank's claim of £25,000. It would be possible and perfectly legal, however, for the company to pay a dividend (withdraw part of their claim) of £23,000. The balance sheet would then appear as follows:

Balance sheet

	£
Total assets (£68,000 – £23,000)	45,000
Equity	
Share capital	
20,000 shares of £1 each	20,000
Reserves [revenue (£23,000 – £23,000)]	–
	20,000
Non-current liabilities	
Borrowings – loan	25,000
Total equity and liabilities	45,000

This leaves the bank in a very much weaker position, in that there are now total assets with a balance sheet value of £45,000 to meet a claim of £25,000. Note that the difference between the amount of the borrowings (bank loan) and the total assets equals the equity (share capital and reserves) total. Thus, the equity represents a margin of safety for lenders and suppliers. The larger the amount of the owners' claim withdrawable by the shareholders, the smaller is the potential margin of safety for lenders and suppliers.

As we have already seen, the law says nothing about how large the margin of safety must be. It is up to each company to decide what is appropriate.

As a practical footnote to Example 4.4, it is worth pointing out that long-term lenders would normally seek to secure a loan against an asset of the company, such as land.

Activity 4.9

Would you expect a company to pay all of its revenue reserves as a dividend? What factors might be involved with a dividend decision?

It would be rare for a company to pay all of its revenue reserves as a dividend: the fact that it is legally possible does not necessarily make it a good idea. Most companies see ploughed-back profits as a major – usually *the* major – source of new finance. The factors that influence the dividend decision are likely to include

- the availability of cash to pay a dividend; it would not be illegal to borrow to pay a dividend, but it would be unusual and, possibly, imprudent;
- the needs of the business for finance for new investment;
- the expectations of shareholders concerning the amount of dividends to be paid.

You may have thought of others.

If we look back at Real World 4.5 (pages 128–9), we can see that at 31 March 2007, easyJet could legally have paid a dividend totalling £262.3m. Of course, the company did not do this, presumably because the funds concerned were tied up in aircraft and other assets, not lying around in the form of cash

The law states, however, that shareholders cannot, under normal circumstances, withdraw that part of their claim that is represented by shares and capital reserves. This means that potential lenders and credit suppliers know the maximum amount of the shareholders' equity that can be withdrawn. Figure 4.3 shows the important division between that part of the shareholders' equity that can be withdrawn as a dividend and that part which cannot.

The main financial statements

As we might expect, the financial statements of a limited company are, in essence, the same as those of a sole proprietor or partnership. There are, however, some differences of detail, and we shall now consider these. Example 4.5 sets out the income statement (profit and loss account) and balance sheet of a limited company.

Figure 4.3 Availability for dividends of various parts of the shareholders' claim

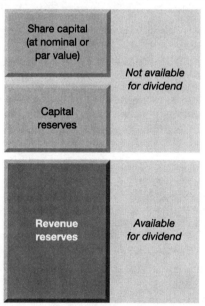

Total equity finance of limited companies consists of share capital, capital reserves and revenue reserves. Only the revenue reserves (which arise from realised profits and gains) can be used to fund a dividend. In other words, the maximum legal dividend is the amount of the revenue reserves.

Example 4.5

Da Silva plc
Income statement for the year ended 31 December 2008

	£m
Revenue	840
Cost of sales	(520)
Gross profit	320
Wages and salaries	(98)
Heat and light	(18)
Rent and rates	(24)
Motor vehicle expenses	(20)
Insurance	(4)
Printing and stationery	(12)
Depreciation	(45)
Audit fee	(4)
Operating profit	95
Interest payable	(10)
Profit before taxation	85
Taxation	(24)
Profit for the year	61

Balance sheet as at 31 December 2008	
	£m
Non-current assets	
Property, plant and equipment	203
Intangible assets	100
	303
Current assets	
Inventories	65
Trade receivables	112
Cash	36
	213
Total assets	516
Equity	
Ordinary shares of £0.50 each	200
Share premium account	30
Other reserves	50
Retained earnings	25
	305
Non-current liabilities	
Borrowings	100
Current liabilities	
Trade payables	99
Taxation	12
	111
Total equity and liabilities	516

Let us now go through these statements and pick up those aspects that are unique to limited companies.

The income statement

There are a few features in the income statement that need consideration.

Profit

We can see that, following the calculation of operating profit, two further measures of profit are shown.

- ■ The first of these is the profit before taxation. Interest charges are deducted from the operating profit to derive this figure. In the case of a sole proprietor or partnership business, the income statement would end here.
- ■ The second measure of profit is the profit for the year. As the company is a separate legal entity, it is liable to pay tax (known as corporation tax) on the profits generated. (This contrasts with the sole proprietor business where it is the owner rather than the business that is liable for the tax on profits, as we saw earlier in the chapter.) This measure of profit represents the amount that is available for the shareholders.

Audit fee

Companies beyond a certain size are required to have their financial statements audited by an independent firm of accountants, for which a fee is charged. As we shall see later in this chapter, the purpose of the audit is to lend credibility to the financial statements. Although it is also open to sole proprietors and partnerships to have their financial statements audited, relatively few do, so this is an expense that is most often seen in the income statement of a company.

The balance sheet

The main points for consideration in the balance sheet are as follows.

Taxation

The amount that appears as part of the current liabilities represents 50 per cent of the tax on the profit for the year 2008. It is, therefore, 50 per cent (£12m) of the charge that appears in the income statement (£24m); the other 50 per cent (£12m) will already have been paid. The unpaid 50 per cent will be paid shortly after the balance sheet date. These payment dates are set down by law.

Other reserves

This will include any reserves that are not separately identified on the face of the balance sheet. It may include a *general reserve*, which normally consists of trading profits that have been transferred to this separate reserve for reinvestment ('ploughing back') into the operations of the company. It is not at all necessary to set up a separate reserve for this purpose. The trading profits could remain unallocated and still swell the retained earnings of the company. It is not entirely clear why directors decide to make transfers to general reserves, since the profits concerned remain part of the revenue reserves, and are, therefore, still available for dividend. The most plausible explanation seems to be that directors feel that placing profits in a separate reserve indicates an intention to invest the funds, represented by the reserve, permanently in the company and, therefore, not to use them to pay a dividend. Of course, the retained earnings appearing on the balance sheet are also a reserve, but that fact is not indicated in its title.

Dividends

We have already seen that dividends represent drawings by the shareholders of the company. Dividends are paid out of the revenue reserves and should be deducted from these reserves (usually retained earnings) when preparing the balance sheet. Shareholders are often paid an annual dividend, perhaps in two parts. An 'interim' dividend may be paid part way through the year and a 'final' dividend shortly after the year end.

Dividends declared by the directors during the year but still unpaid at the year end *may* appear as a liability in the balance sheet. To be recognised as a liability, however, they must be properly authorised before the balance sheet date. This normally means that the shareholders must approve the dividend.

The directors' duty to account

With most large companies, it is not possible for all shareholders to take part in the management of the company, nor do most of them wish to be involved. Instead, they appoint directors to act on their behalf. This separation of ownership from day-to-day control creates the need for directors to be accountable for their stewardship (management) of the company's assets. Thus, the law requires that directors

- maintain appropriate accounting records
- prepare annual financial statements and a directors' report, and make these available to all shareholders and to the public at large.

The financial statements are made available to the public by submitting a copy to the Companies Registry (Department of Trade and Industry), which allows anyone who wishes to do so to inspect them. In addition, listed companies are required to publish their financial statements on their website.

Activity 4.10

Why does the law require directors to account in this way and who benefits from these requirements?

We thought of the following benefits and beneficiaries:

- *To inform and protect shareholders*. If shareholders do not receive information about the performance and position of their investment, they will have problems in appraising their investment. Under these circumstances, they would probably be reluctant to invest and this, in turn, would affect the functioning of the private sector. Any society with a significant private sector needs to encourage equity investment.
- *To inform and protect suppliers of labour, goods, services and finance, particularly those supplying credit (loans) or goods and services on credit*. Individuals and organisations would be reluctant to engage in commercial relationships, such as supplying goods or lending money, where a company does not provide information about its financial health. The fact that a company has limited liability increases the risks involved in dealing with the company. An unwillingness to engage in commercial relationships with limited companies will, once again, affect the functioning of the private sector.
- *To inform and protect society more generally*. Some companies exercise enormous power and influence in society generally, particularly on a geographically local basis. For example, a particular company may be the dominant employer and purchaser of commercial goods and services in a particular town or city. Legislators have tended to take the view that society has the right to information about the company and its activities.

The need for accounting rules

If we accept the need for directors to prepare and publish financial statements, we must also accept the need for a framework of rules concerning how these statements are prepared and presented. Without rules, there is a much greater risk that unscrupulous directors will adopt policies and practices that portray an unrealistic view of financial health. There is also a much greater risk that the financial statements will not be comparable over time or with those of other companies. These risks are likely to undermine the integrity of financial statements in the eyes of users.

Users must, however, be realistic about what can be achieved through regulation. Problems of manipulation and of concealment can still occur even within a highly regulated environment and some examples of both will be considered later in the chapter. The scale of these problems, however, should be reduced. Problems of comparability can also still occur, as accounting is not a precise science. Judgements and estimates must be made when preparing financial statements (for example, relating to depreciation), and these may hinder comparisons. Furthermore, no two companies are identical and the accounting policies adopted may vary between companies for valid reasons.

Sources of accounting rules

In recent years there has been a trend towards the internationalisation of business, which seems set to continue. This trend has led to calls for the international harmonisation of accounting rules to help both users and companies. Harmonisation should help investors and other users of financial statements by making it easier to compare the performance and position of different companies operating in different countries. It should help companies with international operations by reducing the time and cost of producing financial statements: different sets of financial statements would no longer have to be prepared to comply with the rules of different countries.

 The International Accounting Standards Board (IASB) is an independent body, which is at the forefront of the move towards harmonisation. The Board, which is based in the UK, is dedicated to developing a single set of high quality, global accounting rules that provide transparent and comparable information in financial statements. These rules, which are known as International Financial Reporting Standards (IFRSs) or International Accounting Standards, deal with key issues such as:

- what information should be disclosed;
- how information should be presented;
- how assets should be valued;
- how profit should be measured.

In fact we have already met some of the IFRSs when we considered areas including depreciation and inventories valuation in Chapters 2 and 3.

The overriding requirement for financial statements prepared according to IASB standards is to provide a fair representation of the company's financial position, financial performance and cash flows. There is a presumption that this fair representation will be achieved where the financial statements are drawn up in accordance with the various IASB standards that have been issued.

The authority of the IASB was given a huge boost when the European Commission adopted a regulation requiring nearly all Stock Exchange listed companies of EU member states to prepare their financial statements according to IASB standards for accounting periods commencing on or after 1 January 2005. Although non-listed UK companies are not currently required to adopt IASB standards, they have the option to do so. Many informed observers believe, however, that IASB standards will soon become a requirement for all UK companies.

The EU regulation overrides any laws in force in member states that could either hinder or restrict compliance with IASB standards. The ultimate aim is to achieve a single framework of accounting rules for companies from all member states. The EU recognises that this will be achieved only if individual governments do not add to the requirements imposed by the various IASB standards. Thus, it seems that accounting rules developed within individual EU member countries will eventually disappear. For the time being, however, the EU accepts that the governments of member states may need to impose additional disclosures for some corporate governance matters and regulatory requirements. In the UK, company law requires disclosure relating to various corporate governance issues. There is, for example, a requirement to disclose details of directors' remuneration in the published financial statements, which goes beyond anything required by IASB standards. Furthermore, the Financial Services Authority (FSA), in its role as the UK (Stock Exchange) listing authority, imposes rules on Stock Exchange listed companies. These include the requirement to publish a condensed set of interim (half-year) financial statements in addition to the annual financial statements. (These statements are not required by the IASB, although there is a standard providing guidance on their content and structure.)

Figure 4.4 sets out the main sources of accounting rules for Stock Exchange listed companies discussed above. While company law and the FSA still play an important role, in the longer term IASB standards seem set to become the sole source of company accounting rules.

Directors' report

In addition to preparing the financial statements, the law requires the directors to prepare an annual report to shareholders and other interested parties. This report contains information of both a financial and a non-financial nature and goes beyond that which is contained in the financial statements. The information disclosed covers a variety of topics, including details of share ownership, details of directors and their

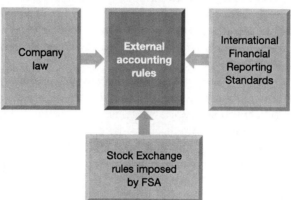

Figure 4.4 Sources of external accounting rules for a UK public limited company listed on the London Stock Exchange

International Financial Reporting Standards provide the basic framework of accounting rules for nearly all Stock Exchange listed companies. These rules are augmented by company law and by the Financial Services Authority (FSA) in its role as the UK listing authority.

financial interests in the company, employment policies, and charitable and political donations. The auditors do not carry out an audit of the directors' report. However, they will check to see that the information in the report is consistent with that contained in the audited financial statements.

The auditors' role

Shareholders are required to elect a qualified and independent person or, more usually, a firm to act as auditors. The auditors' main duty is to report whether, in their opinion, the financial statements do what they are supposed to do, namely to show a true and fair view of the financial performance, position and cash flows of the company by complying with the relevant accounting rules. To be able to form such an opinion, auditors must scrutinise both the annual financial statements and the evidence upon which they are based. The auditors' opinion must be included with the financial statements sent to the shareholders and to the Registrar of Companies.

The relationship between the shareholders, the directors and the auditors is illustrated in Figure 4.5.

The shareholders elect the directors to act on their behalf, in the day-to-day running of the company. The directors are then required to 'account' to the shareholders on the performance, position and cash flows of the company, on an annual basis. The shareholders also elect auditors, whose role it is to give the shareholders an independent view of the truth and fairness of the financial statements prepared by the directors.

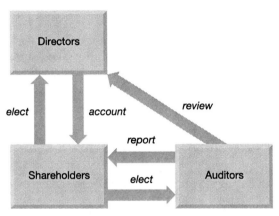

Figure 4.5 The relationship between the shareholders, the directors and the auditors

The directors are appointed by the shareholders to manage the company on the shareholders' behalf. The directors are required to report each year to the shareholders, principally by means of financial statements, on the company's performance, position and cash flows. To give greater confidence in the statements, the shareholders also appoint auditors to investigate the reports and to express an opinion on their reliability.

Creative accounting

Despite the proliferation of accounting rules and the independent checks that are imposed, concerns over the quality of published financial statements surface from time to time. Some directors apply particular accounting policies or structure particular transactions in such a way as to portray a picture of financial health that is in line with what they would like users to see rather than what is a true and fair view of financial position and performance. This practice is referred to as creative accounting and it poses a major problem for accounting rule makers and for society generally.

Activity 4.11

Why might the directors of a company engage in creative accounting?

There are many reasons, and these include:

- to get around restrictions (for example, to report sufficient profit to pay a dividend);
- to avoid government action (for example, the taxation of excessive profits);
- to hide poor management decisions;
- to achieve sales revenue or profit targets, thereby ensuring that performance bonuses are paid to the directors;
- to attract new share capital or loan finance by showing a healthy financial position;
- to satisfy the demands of major investors concerning levels of return.

Creative accounting methods

The ways in which unscrupulous directors can manipulate the financial statements are many and varied. However, they usually involve adopting unorthodox practices for reporting key elements of the financial statements such as revenue, expenses, assets and liabilities. They may also involve the use of complicated or obscure transactions in an attempt to hide the underlying economic reality. The manipulation carried out may be designed to bend the rules or may be designed to break the rules.

Real World 4.7 identifies some of the more popular approaches to creative accounting.

Real World 4.7

Dirty laundry: how companies fudge the numbers

Hollow swaps: telecoms companies sell useless fibre optic capacity to each other in order to generate revenues on their income statements. Example: Global Crossing.

Channel stuffing: a company floods the market with more products than its distributors can sell, artificially boosting its sales. SSL, the condom maker, shifted £60 million in excess inventories on to trade customers. Also known as 'trade loading'.

Round tripping: also known as 'in-and-out trading'. Used to notorious effect by Enron. Two or more traders buy and sell energy among themselves for the same price and at the same time. Inflates trading volumes and makes participants appear to be doing more business than they really are.

Pre-dispatching: goods such as carpets are marked as 'sold' as soon as an order is placed. This inflates sales and profits.

Off-balance sheet activities: companies use special purpose entities and other devices such as leasing to push assets and liabilities off their balance sheets.

Source: 'Dirty laundry: how companies fudge the numbers', *The Times*, Business Section, 22 September 2002.

A few years ago there was a wave of creative accounting scandals, particularly in the US but also in Europe; however, it seems that this wave has now subsided. The quality of financial statements is improving and, it is to be hoped, trust among investors and others is being restored. As a result of the actions taken by various regulatory bodies and by accounting rule makers, creative accounting has become a more risky and difficult process for those who attempt it. However, it will never disappear completely and a further wave of creative accounting scandals may occur in the future.

As Real World 4.8 shows, creative accounting is not a thing of the past. The US computer business Dell was engaged in creative accounting as recently as 2007.

Real World 4.8

Recomputing the numbers

In August 2007, Dell admitted that some unnamed 'senior executives' had been involved in a scheme to overstate sales revenue figures during the period 2003 to 2007. This was done in an attempt to make it appear that quarterly sales targets had been met, when in fact this was not the case. The overstatement of sales revenue was estimated to amount to $92m, about 1 per cent of total profit over the period concerned.

Source: 'Dell reduces profit by $92m', Kevin Allison, *Financial Times*, 30 October 2007.

The recent wave coincided with a period of strong economic growth, and during good economic times, investors and auditors become less vigilant. Thus, the opportunity to manipulate the figures becomes easier. We must not, therefore, become too complacent. Things may change again when we next experience a period of strong growth.

? Self-assessment question 4.1

This question requires you to correct some figures on a set of company financial statements. It should prove useful practice for the material that you covered in Chapters 2 and 3, as well as helping you to become familiar with the financial statements of a company.

Presented below is a draft set of simplified financial statements for Pear Limited for the year ended 30 September 2008.

Income statement for the year ended 30 September 2008

	£000
Revenue	1,456
Cost of sales	(768)
Gross profit	688
Salaries	(220)
Depreciation	(249)
Other operating costs	(131)
Operating profit	88
Interest payable	(15)
Profit before taxation	73
Taxation at 30%	(22)
Profit for the year	51

Balance sheet as at 30 September 2008

	£000
Non-current assets	
Property, plant and equipment	
Cost	1,570
Depreciation	(690)
	880
Current assets	
Inventories	207
Trade receivables	182
Cash at bank	21
	410
Total assets	1,290
Equity	
Share capital	300
Share premium account	300
Retained earnings at beginning of year	104
Profit for year	51
	755

$\rightarrow$

Non-current liabilities	
Borrowings (10% loan notes repayable 2012)	300
Current liabilities	
Trade payables	88
Other payables	20
Taxation	22
Borrowings (bank overdraft)	105
	235
Total equity and liabilities	1,290

The following information is available:

1 Depreciation has not been charged on office equipment with a carrying amount of £100,000. This class of assets is depreciated at 12 per cent a year using the reducing-balance method.

2 A new machine was purchased, on credit, for £30,000 and delivered on 29 September 2008 but has not been included in the financial statements. (Ignore depreciation.)

3 A sales invoice to the value of £18,000 for September 2008 has been omitted from the financial statements. (The cost of sales figure is stated correctly.)

4 A dividend of £25,000 had been approved by the shareholders before 30 September 2006, but was unpaid at that date. This is not reflected in the financial statements.

5 The interest payable on the loan notes for the second half-year was not paid until 1 October 2008 and has not been included in the financial statements.

6 An allowance for receivables is to be made at the level of 2 per cent of receivables.

7 An invoice for electricity to the value of £2,000 for the quarter ended 30 September 2008 arrived on 4 October and has not been included in the financial statements.

8 The charge for taxation will have to be amended to take account of the above information. Make the simplifying assumption that tax is payable shortly after the end of the year, at the rate of 30 per cent of the profit before tax.

Required:
Prepare a revised set of financial statements for the year ended 30 September 2008 incorporating the additional information in 1 to 8 above. (Work to the nearest £1,000.)

The answer to this question can be found at the back of the book in Appendix B.

Summary

The main points of this chapter may be summarised as follows.

Main features of a limited company

- It is an artificial person that has been created by law.

- It has a separate life to its owners and is granted a perpetual existence.

- It must take responsibility for its own debts and losses but its owners are granted limited liability.

- A public company can offer its shares for sale to the public; a private company cannot.
- It is governed by a board of directors, which is elected by the shareholders.
- Corporate governance is a major issue; various scandals have led to the emergence of the Combined Code.

Financing the limited company

- The share capital of a company can be of two main types: ordinary shares and preference shares.
- Holders of ordinary shares (equities) are the main risk-takers and are given voting rights; they form the backbone of the company.
- Holders of preference shares are given a right to a fixed dividend before ordinary shareholders receive a dividend.
- Reserves are profits and gains made by the company and form part of the ordinary shareholders' claim.
- Borrowings provide another major source of finance.

Share issues

- Bonus shares are issued to existing shareholders when part of the reserves of the company is converted into share capital. No funds are raised.
- Rights issues give existing shareholders the right to buy new shares in proportion to their existing holding.
- Public issues are made direct to the general investing public.
- Private placings are share issues to particular investors.
- The shares of public companies may be bought and sold on a recognised Stock Exchange.

Reserves

- Reserves are of two types: revenue reserves and capital reserves.
- Revenue reserves arise from trading profits and from realised profits on the sale of non-current assets.
- Capital reserves arise from the issue of shares above their nominal value or from the upward revaluation of non-current assets.
- Revenue reserves can be withdrawn as dividends by the shareholders whereas capital reserves normally cannot.

Financial statements of limited companies

- The financial statements of limited companies are based on the same principles as those of sole proprietorship and partnership businesses. However, there are some differences in detail.
- The income statement has three measures of profit displayed after the gross profit figure: operating profit, profit before taxation and profit for the year.

- The income statement also shows audit fees and tax on profits for the year.
- Any unpaid tax and unpaid, but authorised, dividends will appear in the balance sheet as current liabilities.
- The share capital plus the reserves make up 'equity'.

Directors' duty

- The directors have a duty to
  - maintain appropriate accounting records;
  - prepare and publish financial statements and a directors' report.

The need for accounting rules

- Accounting rules are necessary to
  - avoid unacceptable accounting practices;
  - improve the comparability of financial statements.

Accounting rules

- The International Accounting Standards Board (IASB) has become an important source of rules.
- Company law and the London Stock Exchange are also sources of rules for UK companies.

Other statutory reports

- The auditors' report provides an opinion by an independent auditor concerning whether the financial statements provide a true and fair view of the financial health of a business.
- The directors' report contains information of a financial and a non-financial nature, which goes beyond that contained in the financial statements.

Creative accounting

- Despite the accounting rules in place there have been examples of creative accounting by directors.
- This involves using accounting practices to show what the directors would like users to see rather than what is a fair representation of reality.

→ Key terms

limited company	corporation tax
shares	director
limited liability	corporate governance
public company	Combined Code
private company	reserves

equity	allotted share capital
nominal value	fully paid shares
par value	called-up share capital
revenue reserve	paid-up share capital
dividend	loan notes
ordinary shares	profit before taxation
splitting	profit for the year
consolidating	International Financial Reporting
preference shares	Standards
capital reserves	International Accounting
share premium account	Standards
bonus shares	directors' report
bonus issue	auditors
issued share capital	creative accounting

Further reading

If you would like to explore the topics covered in this chapter in more depth, we recommend the following books:

Elliott, B. and Elliott, J., *Financial Accounting and Reporting* (12th edn), Financial Times Prentice Hall, 2008, chapters 5, 6, 8 and 21–23.

KPMG, *KPMG's Practical Guide to International Financial Reporting Standards* (3rd edn), Thomson, 2006, section 2.5.

Sutton, T., *Corporate Financial Accounting and Reporting* (2nd edn), Financial Times Prentice Hall, 2004, chapters 6 and 12.

? Review questions

Answers to these questions can be found at the back of the book in Appendix C.

4.1 How does the liability of a limited company differ from the liability of a real person, in respect of amounts owed to others?

4.2 Some people are about to form a company, as a vehicle through which to run a new business. What are the advantages to them of forming a private limited company rather than a public one?

4.3 What is a reserve? Distinguish between a revenue reserve and a capital reserve.

4.4 What is a preference share? Compare the main features of a preference share with those of
(a) an ordinary share, and
(b) loan notes.

✳ Exercises

Exercises 4.4 and 4.5 are more advanced than Exercises 4.1 to 4.3. Those with coloured numbers have answers at the back of the book in Appendix D.

> If you wish to try more exercises, visit MyAccountingLab/

4.1 Comment on the following quote:

> Limited companies can set a limit on the amount of debts that they will meet. They tend to have reserves of cash, as well as share capital and they can use these reserves to pay dividends to the shareholders. Many companies have preference as well as ordinary shares. The preference shares give a guaranteed dividend. The shares of many companies can be bought and sold on the Stock Exchange, and shareholders selling their shares can represent a useful source of new finance to the company.

4.2 Comment on the following quotes:

(a) 'Bonus shares increase the shareholders' wealth because, after the issue, they have more shares, but each one of the same nominal value as they had before.'
(b) 'By law, once shares have been issued at a particular nominal value, they must always be issued at that value in any future share issues.'
(c) 'By law, companies can pay as much as they like by way of dividends on their shares, provided that they have sufficient cash to do so.'
(d) 'Companies do not have to pay tax on their profits because the shareholders have to pay tax on their dividends.'

4.3 Briefly explain each of the following expressions that you have seen in the financial statements of a limited company:

(a) dividend
(b) audit fee
(c) share premium account.

4.4 Presented below is a draft set of financial statements for Chips Limited.

Chips Limited
Income statement for the year ended 30 June 2008

	£000
Revenue	1,850
Cost of sales	(1,040)
Gross profit	810
Depreciation	(220)
Other operating costs	(375)
Operating profit	215
Interest payable	(35)
Profit before taxation	180
Taxation	(60)
Profit for the year	120

Balance sheet as at 30 June 2008

	Cost	Depreciation	
	£000	£000	£000
Non-current assets			
Property, plant and equipment			
Buildings	800	(112)	688
Plant and equipment	650	(367)	283
Motor vehicles	102	(53)	49
	1,552	(532)	1,020
Current assets			
Inventories			950
Trade receivables			420
Cash at bank			16
			1,386
Total assets			2,406
Equity			
Ordinary shares of £1, fully paid			800
Reserves at 1 July 2007			248
Profit for the year			120
			1,168
Non-current liabilities			
Borrowings (secured 10% loan notes)			700
Current liabilities			
Trade payables			361
Other payables			117
Taxation			60
			538
Total equity and liabilities			2,406

The following additional information is available:

1 Purchase invoices for goods received on 29 June 2008 amounting to £23,000 have not been included. This means that the cost of sales figure in the income statement has been understated.

2 A motor vehicle costing £8,000 with depreciation amounting to £5,000 was sold on 30 June 2008 for £2,000, paid by cheque. This transaction has not been included in the company's records.

3 No depreciation on motor vehicles has been charged. The annual rate is 20 per cent of cost at the year end.

4 A sale on credit for £16,000 made on 1 July 2008 has been included in the financial statements in error. The cost of sales figure is correct in respect of this item.

5 A half-yearly payment of interest on the secured loan due on 30 June 2008 has not been paid.

6 The tax charge should be 30 per cent of the reported profit before taxation. Assume that it is payable, in full, shortly after the year end.

Required:

Prepare a revised set of financial statements incorporating the additional information in 1 to 6 above. (Work to the nearest £1,000.)

4.5 Rose Limited operates a small chain of retail shops that sell high quality teas and coffees. Approximately half of sales are on credit. Abbreviated and unaudited financial statements are given below.

Rose Limited
Income statement for the year ended 31 March 2008

	£000
Revenue	12,080
Cost of sales	(6,282)
Gross profit	5,798
Labour costs	(2,658)
Depreciation	(625)
Other operating costs	(1,003)
Operating profit	1,512
Interest payable	(66)
Profit before taxation	1,446
Taxation	(434)
Profit for the year	1,012

Balance sheet as at 31 March 2008

	£000
Non-current assets	2,728
Current assets	
Inventories	1,583
Trade receivables	996
Cash	26
	2,605
Total assets	5,333
Equity	
Share capital (50p shares, fully paid)	750
Share premium	250
Retained earnings	1,468
	2,468
Non-current liabilities	
Borrowings – Secured loan notes (2011)	300
Current liabilities	
Trade payables	1,118
Other payables	417
Tax	434
Borrowings – Overdraft	596
	2,565
Total equity and liabilities	5,333

Since the unaudited financial statements for Rose Limited were prepared, the following information has become available:

1 An additional £74,000 of depreciation should have been charged on fixtures and fittings.
2 Invoices for credit sales on 31 March 2008 amounting to £34,000 have not been included; cost of sales is not affected.

3 Trade receivables totalling £20 are recognised as having gone bad, but they have not yet been written off.

4 Inventories which had been purchased for £2,000 have been damaged and are unsaleable. This is not reflected in the financial statements.

5 Fixtures and fittings to the value of £16,000 were delivered just before 31 March 2008, but these assets were not included in the financial statements and the purchase invoice had not been processed.

6 Wages for Saturday-only staff, amounting to £1,000, have not been paid for the final Saturday of the year. This is not reflected in the financial statements.

7 Tax is payable at 30 per cent of profit after taxation. Assume that it is payable shortly after the year end.

Required:

Prepare revised financial statements for Rose Limited for the year ended 31 March 2008, incorporating the information in 1 to 7 above. (Work to the nearest £1,000.)

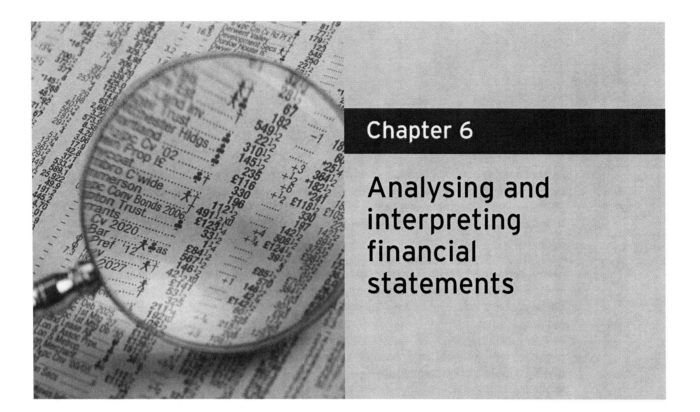

Chapter 6

Analysing and interpreting financial statements

Introduction

In this chapter we shall consider the analysis and interpretation of the financial statements discussed in Chapters 2 and 3. We shall see how financial (or accounting) ratios can help in assessing the financial health of a business. We shall also consider the problems that are encountered when applying this technique.

Financial ratios can be used to examine various aspects of financial position and performance and are widely used for planning and control purposes. As we shall see in later chapters, they can be very helpful to managers in a wide variety of decision areas, such as profit planning, pricing, working capital management, financial structure and dividend policy.

Learning outcomes

When you have completed this chapter, you should be able to:

- identify the major categories of ratios that can be used for analysis purposes;
- calculate important ratios for assessing the financial performance and position of a business;
- explain the significance of the ratios calculated;
- discuss the limitations of ratios as a tool of financial analysis.

Financial ratios

Financial ratios provide a quick and relatively simple means of assessing the financial health of a business. A ratio simply relates one figure appearing in the financial statements to some other figure appearing there (for example, operating profit in relation to capital employed) or, perhaps, to some resource of the business (for example, operating profit per employee, sales revenue per square metre of selling space, and so on).

Ratios can be very helpful when comparing the financial health of different businesses. Differences may exist between businesses in the scale of operations, and so a direct comparison of, say, the operating profit generated by each business may be misleading. By expressing operating profit in relation to some other measure (for example, capital (or funds) employed), the problem of scale is eliminated. A business with an operating profit of, say, £10,000 and capital employed of £100,000 can be compared with a much larger business with an operating profit of, say, £80,000 and sales revenue of £1,000,000 by the use of a simple ratio. The operating profit to capital employed ratio for the smaller business is 10 per cent (that is, (10,000/100,000) × 100%) and the same ratio for the larger business is 8 per cent (that is, (80,000/1,000,000) × 100%). These values (10% and 8%) can be directly compared whereas comparison of the absolute operating profit figures would be less meaningful. The need to eliminate differences in scale through the use of ratios can also apply when comparing the performance of the same business over time.

By calculating a small number of ratios it is often possible to build up a good picture of the position and performance of a business. It is not surprising, therefore, that ratios are widely used by those who have an interest in businesses and business performance. Although ratios are not difficult to calculate, they can be difficult to interpret, and so it is important to appreciate that they are really only the starting point for further analysis.

Ratios help to highlight the financial strengths and weaknesses of a business, but they cannot, by themselves, explain why those strengths or weaknesses exist or why certain changes have occurred. Only a detailed investigation will reveal these underlying reasons. Ratios tend to enable us to know which questions to ask, rather than provide the answers.

Ratios can be expressed in various forms, for example as a percentage or as a proportion. The way that a particular ratio is presented will depend on the needs of those who will use the information. Although it is possible to calculate a large number of ratios, only a few, based on key relationships, tend to be helpful to a particular user. Many ratios that could be calculated from the financial statements (for example, rent payable in relation to current assets) may not be considered because there is no clear or meaningful relationship between the two items.

There is no generally accepted list of ratios that can be applied to the financial statements, nor is there a standard method of calculating many ratios. Variations in both the choice of ratios and their calculation will be found in practice. However, if ratios are to be helpful in drawing comparisons, it is important to be consistent in the way in which ratios are calculated. The ratios that we shall discuss here are those that are widely used. They are popular because many consider them to be among the more important for decision-making purposes.

Financial ratio classifications

Ratios can be grouped into categories, each of which relates to a particular aspect of financial performance or position. The following five broad categories provide a useful basis for explaining the nature of the financial ratios to be dealt with.

- *Profitability*. Businesses generally exist with the primary purpose of creating wealth for their owners. Profitability ratios provide an insight to the degree of success in achieving this purpose. They express the profit made (or figures bearing on profit, such as sales revenue or particular expenses, like labour cost) in relation to other key figures in the financial statements or to some business resource.
- *Efficiency*. The efficiency with which particular resources have been used by the business is a key issue and ratios may be used to assess this. Efficiency ratios are also referred to as *activity* ratios.
- *Liquidity*. It is vital to the survival of a business that there are sufficient liquid resources available to meet maturing obligations (that is, amounts owing that must be paid in the near future). Some liquidity ratios examine the relationship between liquid resources held and amounts due for payment in the near future.
- *Financial gearing*. This is the relationship between the contribution to financing the business made by the owners of the business (typically the shareholders) and the amount contributed by lenders, for example a bank loan. The level of gearing has an important effect on the degree of risk associated with a business, as we shall see. Gearing is, therefore, something that managers must consider when making financing decisions. Gearing ratios tend to highlight the extent to which the business uses borrowings.
- *Investment*. Certain ratios are concerned with assessing the returns and performance of shares in a particular business from the perspective of shareholders who are not involved with the management of the business.

The analyst who is carrying out an assessment of a business's performance must be clear *who* needs the information and *why* they need it. Different users of financial information are likely to have different information needs, which will in turn determine the ratios that they find useful. For example, shareholders are likely to be interested in their returns in relation to the level of risk associated with their investment. Profitability, investment and gearing ratios will, therefore, be of particular interest. Long-term lenders are concerned with the long-term viability of the business and, to help them to assess this, the profitability and gearing ratios of the business are also likely to be of particular interest. Short-term lenders, such as suppliers of goods and services on credit (trade payables), will be interested in the ability of the business to repay the amounts owing in the short term. As a result, the liquidity ratios should be of interest.

We shall consider ratios falling into each of the five categories (profitability, efficiency, liquidity, gearing and investment) a little later in the chapter.

The need for comparison

Merely calculating a ratio will not tell us very much about the position or performance of a business. For example, if a ratio revealed that the business was generating £100 in sales revenue per square metre of counter space, it would not be possible to deduce from this information alone whether this particular level of performance was good, bad or indifferent. It is only when we compare this ratio with some 'benchmark' that the information can be interpreted and evaluated.

Activity 6.1

Can you think of any bases that could be used to compare a ratio you have calculated from the financial statements of a particular period?
We feel that there are three sensible possibilities.

You may have thought of the following bases:

■ past periods for the same business
■ similar businesses for the same or past periods
■ planned performance for the business.

We shall now take a closer look at these three in turn.

Past periods

By comparing the ratio we have calculated with the same ratio, but for a previous period, it is possible to detect whether there has been an improvement or deterioration in performance. Indeed, it is often useful to track particular ratios over time (say, five or ten years) to see whether it is possible to detect trends. The comparison of ratios from different periods brings certain problems, however. In particular, there is always the possibility that trading conditions were quite different in the periods being compared. There is the further problem that, when comparing the performance of a single business over time, operating inefficiencies may not be clearly exposed. For example, the fact that sales revenue per employee has risen by 10 per cent over the previous period may at first sight appear to be satisfactory. This may not be the case, however, if similar businesses have shown an improvement of 50 per cent for the same period.

Finally, there is the problem that inflation may have distorted the figures on which the ratios are based. Inflation can lead to an overstatement of profit and an understatement of asset values, as will be discussed later in the chapter.

Similar businesses

In a competitive environment, a business must consider its performance in relation to that of other businesses operating in the same industry. Survival may depend on the ability to achieve comparable levels of performance. A useful basis for comparing a particular ratio, therefore, is the ratio achieved by similar businesses during the same period. This basis is not, however, without its problems. Competitors may have different year ends and, therefore, trading conditions may not be identical. They may also have different accounting policies, for example, different approaches to calculating depreciation or valuing inventories, which can have a significant effect on reported profits and asset values. Finally, it may be difficult to obtain the financial statements of competitor businesses. Sole proprietorships and partnerships, for example, are not obliged to make their financial statements available to the public. In the case of limited companies, there is a legal obligation to do so. However, a diversified business may not provide a breakdown of activities that is sufficiently detailed to enable analysts to compare the activities with those of other businesses.

Planned performance

Ratios may be compared with the targets that management developed before the start of the period under review. The comparison of planned performance with actual performance may therefore be a useful way of revealing the level of achievement attained. However, the planned levels of performance must be based on realistic assumptions if they are to be useful for comparison purposes.

Planned performance is likely to be the most valuable benchmark for the managers to assess their own business. Businesses tend to develop planned ratios for each aspect of their activities. When formulating its plans, a business may usefully take account of its own past performance and that of other businesses. There is no reason, however, why a particular business should seek to achieve either its own previous performance or that of other businesses. Neither of these may be seen as an appropriate target.

Analysts outside the business do not normally have access to the business's plans. For these people, past performance and the performances of other, similar, businesses may be the only practical benchmarks.

Calculating the ratios

Probably the best way to explain financial ratios is through an example. Example 6.1 provides an income statement and a balance sheet from which we can calculate important ratios.

Example 6.1

The following financial statements relate to Alexis plc, which operates a wholesale carpet business:

Balance sheets as at 31 March

	2007 £m	2008 £m
Non-current assets		
Property, plant and equipment (at cost less depreciation)		
Land and buildings	381	427
Fixtures and fittings	129	160
	510	587
Current assets		
Inventories at cost	300	406
Trade receivables	240	273
Cash at bank	4	–
	544	679
Total assets	1,054	1,266
Equity		
£0.50 ordinary shares (Note 1)	300	300
Retained earnings	263	234
	563	534
Non-current liabilities		
Borrowings – 9% loan notes (secured)	200	300
Current liabilities		
Trade payables	261	354
Taxation	30	2
Short-term borrowings (all bank overdraft)	–	76
	291	432
Total equity and liabilities	1,054	1,266

Income statements for the year ended 31 March

	2007 £m	2008 £m
Revenue (Note 2)	2,240	2,681
Cost of sales (Note 3)	(1,745)	(2,272)
Gross profit	495	409
Operating expenses	(252)	(362)
Operating profit	243	47
Interest payable	(18)	(32)
Profit before taxation	225	15
Taxation	(60)	(4)
Profit for the year	165	11

Notes:

1 The market value of the shares of the business at the end of the year was £2.50 for 2007 and £1.50 for 2008.
2 All sales and purchases are made on credit.
3 The cost of sales figure can be analysed as follows:

	2007 £m	2008 £m
Opening inventories	241	300
Purchases (Note 2)	1,804	2,378
	2,045	2,678
Closing inventories	(300)	(406)
Cost of sales	1,745	2,272

4 At 31 March 2006, the trade receivables stood at £223m and the trade payables at £203m.
5 A dividend of £40m had been paid to the shareholders in respect of each of the years.
6 The business employed 13,995 staff at 31 March 2007 and 18,623 at 31 March 2008.
7 The business expanded its capacity during 2008 by setting up a new warehouse and distribution centre in the north of England.
8 At 1 April 2006, the total of equity stood at £438m and the total of equity and non-current liabilities stood at £638m.

A brief overview

Before we start our detailed look at the ratios for Alexis plc (in Example 6.1), it is helpful to take a quick look at what information is obvious from the financial statements. This will usually pick up some issues that the ratios may not be able to identify. It may also highlight some points that could help us in our interpretation of the ratios. Starting at the top of the balance sheet, the following points can be noted:

- *Expansion of non-current assets.* These have increased by about 15 per cent (from £510m to £587m). Note 7 mentions a new warehouse and distribution centre, which may account for much of the additional investment in non-current assets. We are not told when this new facility was established, but it is quite possible that it was well into the year. This could mean that not much benefit was reflected in terms of additional sales revenue or cost saving during 2008. Sales revenue, in fact, expanded by about 20 per cent (from £2,240m to £2,681m), a greater expansion than that in non-current assets.
- *Major expansion in the elements of working capital.* Inventories increased by about 35 per cent, trade receivables by about 14 per cent and trade payables by about 36 per cent between 2007 and 2008. These are major increases, particularly in inventories and payables (which are linked because the inventories are all bought on credit – see Note 2).
- *Reduction in the cash balance.* The cash balance fell from £4m (in funds) to a £76m overdraft between 2007 and 2008. The bank may be putting the business under pressure to reverse this, which could raise difficulties.

■ *Apparent debt capacity.* Comparing the non-current assets with the long-term borrowings implies that the business may well be able to offer security on further borrowing. This is because potential lenders usually look at the value of assets that can be offered as security when assessing loan requests. Lenders are particularly attracted to land and, to a lesser extent, buildings as security. This is because they tend to hold their market value. For example, at 31 March 2008, non-current assets had a balance sheet value of £587m, but long-term borrowing was only £300m (though there was also an overdraft of £76m). Balance sheet values are not normally, of course, market values. On the other hand, land and buildings tend to have a market value higher than their balance sheet value due to inflation in property values.

■ *Lower operating profit.* Though sales revenue expanded by 20 per cent between 2007 and 2008, both cost of sales and operating expenses rose by a greater percentage, leaving both gross profit and, particularly, operating profit massively reduced. The level of staffing, which increased by about 33 per cent (from 13,995 to 18,623 employees), may have greatly affected the operating expenses. (Without knowing when the additional employees were recruited during 2008, we cannot be sure of the effect on operating expenses.) Increasing staffing by 33 per cent must put an enormous strain on management, at least in the short term. It is not surprising, therefore, that 2008 was not successful for the business.

Having had a quick look at what is fairly obvious without calculating the normal ratios, we shall now go on to calculate and interpret them.

Profitability

The following ratios may be used to evaluate the profitability of the business:

■ return on ordinary shareholders' funds
■ return on capital employed
■ operating profit margin
■ gross profit margin.

We shall now look at each of these in turn.

Return on ordinary shareholders' funds (ROSF)

The return on ordinary shareholders' funds ratio compares the amount of profit for the period available to the owners with the owners' average stake in the business during that same period. The ratio (which is normally expressed in percentage terms) is as follows:

$$ROSF = \frac{\text{Profit for the year (net profit) less any preference dividend}}{\text{Ordinary share capital + Reserves}} \times 100$$

The profit for the year (less preference dividend, if any) is used in calculating the ratio because this figure represents the amount of profit that is left for the owners.

In the case of Alexis plc, the ratio for the year ended 31 March 2007 is

$$\text{ROSF} = \frac{165}{(438 + 563)/2} \times 100 = 33.0\%$$

Note that, when calculating the ROSF, the average of the figures for ordinary shareholders' funds as at the beginning and at the end of the year has been used. It is preferable to use an average figure as this is likely to be more representative. This is because the shareholders' funds did not have the same total throughout the year, yet we want to compare it with the profit earned during the whole period. We know, from Note 8, that the total of the shareholders' funds at 1 April 2006 was £438m. By a year later, however, it had risen to £563m, according to the balance sheet as at 31 March 2007.

The easiest approach to calculating the average amount of shareholders' funds is to take a simple average based on the opening and closing figures for the year. This is often the only information available, as is the case with Example 6.1. Averaging in this way is generally valid for all ratios that combine a figure for a period (such as profit for the year) with one taken at a point in time (such as shareholders' funds).

Where we do not even have the beginning-of-year figure, we are forced to rely on just the year-end figure. This is not ideal, but provided that this approach is consistently adopted it should provide ratios that are useful.

Activity 6.2

Calculate the ROSF for Alexis plc for the year to 31 March 2008.

The ratio for 2008 is

$$\text{ROSF} = \frac{11}{(563 + 534)/2} \times 100 = 2.0\%$$

Broadly, businesses seek to generate as high a value as possible for this ratio, provided that it is not achieved at the expense of potential future returns by, for example, taking on more risky activities. In view of this, the 2008 ratio is very poor by any standards; a very safe bank deposit account will yield a better return than this. We need to try to find out why things went so badly wrong in 2008. As we look at other ratios, we should find some clues.

Return on capital employed (ROCE)

The return on capital employed ratio is a fundamental measure of business performance. This ratio expresses the relationship between the operating profit generated during a period and the average long-term capital invested in the business during that period.

The ratio is expressed in percentage terms and is as follows:

$$\text{ROCE} = \frac{\text{Operating profit}}{\text{Share capital} + \text{Reserves} + \text{Non-current liabilities}} \times 100$$

Note, in this case, that the profit figure used is the operating profit (that is, the net profit *before* interest and taxation), because the ratio attempts to measure the returns to all suppliers of long-term finance before any deductions for interest payable on borrowings, or payments of dividends to shareholders, are made.

For the year to 31 March 2007, the ratio for Alexis plc is

$$\text{ROCE} = \frac{243}{(638 + 763)/2} \times 100 = 34.7\%$$

ROCE is considered by many to be a primary measure of profitability. It compares inputs (capital invested) with outputs (operating profit). This comparison is vital in assessing the effectiveness with which funds have been deployed. Once again, an average figure for capital employed may be used where the information is available.

Activity 6.3

Calculate the ROCE for Alexis plc for the year to 31 March 2008.

For 2008, the ratio is

$$\text{ROCE} = \frac{47}{(763 + 834)/2} \times 100 = 5.9\%$$

This ratio tells much the same story as ROSF, namely, a poor performance, with the return on the assets being less than the rate that the business has to pay for most of its borrowed funds (that is, 9 per cent for the loan notes).

Real World 6.1 shows how financial ratios are used by businesses as a basis for setting profitability targets.

Real World 6.1

Targeting profitability

The ROCE ratio is widely used by businesses when establishing targets for profitability. These targets are sometimes made public and here are some examples:

Tesco plc, the supermarket business, in 2004 set a target to achieve a growth in ROCE of 2 per cent from its 2004 figure of 10.4 per cent. It achieved this with 12.5 per cent in 2006 and increased it further in 2007. Tesco has set a further 2 per cent target growth for ROCE for 2008 and beyond. Tesco uses performance against a target ROCE as a basis of rewarding its senior managers, indicating the importance that the business attaches to this measure of performance.

The satellite broadcaster BSkyB plc has a target ROCE of 15 per cent by 2011 for its broadband operation.

Air France-KLM, the world's largest airline (on the basis of sales revenue), has set itself the target of increasing ROCE from 6.5 per cent in 2006 to 8.5 per cent by 2010.

Sources: Information taken from Tesco plc Annual Report 2007, 'BSkyB/triple play', *Financial Times*, 12 July 2006, and 'Air France-KLM raises targets', K. Done, *Financial Times*, 24 May 2007.

Real World 6.2 provides some insight to the levels of ROCE achieved by UK businesses.

Operating profit margin

The operating profit margin ratio relates the operating profit for the period to the sales revenue during that period. The ratio is expressed as follows:

$$\text{Operating profit margin} = \frac{\text{Operating profit}}{\text{Sales revenue}} \times 100$$

The operating profit (that is, net profit before interest and taxation) is used in this ratio as it represents the profit from trading operations before the interest payable expense is taken into account. This is often regarded as the most appropriate measure of operational performance, when used as a basis of comparison, because differences arising from the way in which the business is financed will not influence the measure.

For the year ended 31 March 2007, Alexis plc's operating profit margin ratio is

$$\text{Operating profit margin} = \frac{243}{2,240} \times 100 = 10.8\%$$

This ratio compares one output of the business (operating profit) with another output (sales revenue). The ratio can vary considerably between types of business. For example, supermarkets tend to operate on low prices and, therefore, low operating profit margins. This is done in an attempt to stimulate sales and thereby increase the total amount of operating profit generated. Jewellers, on the other hand, tend to have high operating profit margins but have much lower levels of sales volume. Factors such as the degree of competition, the type of customer, the economic climate and industry characteristics (such as the level of risk) will influence the operating profit margin of a business. This point is picked up again later in the chapter.

Activity 6.4

Calculate the operating profit margin for Alexis plc for the year to 31 March 2008.

The ratio for 2008 is

$$\text{Operating profit margin} = \frac{47}{2,681} \times 100 = 1.8\%$$

Once again, this shows a very weak performance compared with that of 2007. Whereas in 2007 for every £1 of sales revenue an average of 10.8p (that is, 10.8 per cent) was left as operating profit, after paying the cost of the carpets sold and other expenses of operating the business, for 2008 this had fallen to only 1.8p for every £1. It seems that the reason for the poor ROSF and ROCE ratios was partially, perhaps wholly, a high level of expenses relative to sales revenue. The next ratio should provide us with a clue as to how the sharp decline in this ratio occurred.

Real World 6.3 describes how one well-known business intends to increase its operating profit margin over time.

Real World 6.3

Operating profit margin taking off at BA

British Airways plc, the airline business, more than achieved its 10 per cent operating profit margin target during the three months up to 30 June 2007. The figure was 12 per cent, up from 9.2 per cent for the previous period.

Source: Information taken from 'BA ahead despite Heathrow woes', K. Done, *Financial Times*, 3 August 2007.

Gross profit margin

The gross profit margin ratio relates the gross profit of the business to the sales revenue generated for the same period. Gross profit represents the difference between sales revenue and the cost of sales. The ratio is therefore a measure of profitability in buying (or producing) and selling goods or services before any other expenses are taken into account. As cost of sales represents a major expense for many businesses, a change in this ratio can have a significant effect on the 'bottom line' (that is, the profit for the year). The gross profit margin ratio is calculated as follows:

$$\textbf{Gross profit margin} = \frac{\textbf{Gross profit}}{\textbf{Sales revenue}} \times \textbf{100}$$

For the year to 31 March 2007, the ratio for Alexis plc is

$$\text{Gross profit margin} = \frac{495}{2,240} \times 100 = 22.1\%$$

Activity 6.5

Calculate the gross profit margin for Alexis plc for the year to 31 March 2008.

The ratio for 2008 is

$$\text{Gross profit margin} = \frac{409}{2,681} \times 100 = 15.3\%$$

The decline in this ratio means that gross profit was lower *relative* to sales revenue in 2008 than it had been in 2007. Bearing in mind that

Gross profit = Sales revenue – Cost of sales (or cost of goods sold)

this means that cost of sales was higher *relative* to sales revenue in 2008 than in 2007. This could mean that sales prices were lower and/or that the purchase cost of goods sold had increased. It is possible that both sales prices and prices of goods sold had reduced, but the former at a greater rate than the latter. Similarly they may both have increased, but with sales prices having increased at a lesser rate than the cost of the goods sold.

Clearly, part of the decline in the operating profit margin ratio is linked to the dramatic decline in the gross profit margin ratio. Whereas, after paying for the carpets sold, for each £1 of sales revenue 22.1p was left to cover other operating expenses and leave an operating profit in 2007, this was only 15.3p in 2008.

The profitability ratios for the business over the two years can be set out as follows:

	2007	2008
	%	%
ROSF	33.0	2.0
ROCE	34.7	5.9
Operating profit margin	10.8	1.8
Gross profit margin	22.1	15.3

Activity 6.6

What do you deduce from a comparison of the declines in the operating profit and gross profit margin ratios?

It occurs to us that the decline in the operating profit margin was 9 per cent (that is, 10.8 per cent to 1.8 per cent), whereas that of the gross profit margin was only 6.8 per cent (that is, from 22.1 per cent to 15.3 per cent). This can only mean that operating expenses were greater compared with sales revenue in 2008 than they had been in 2007. The declines in both ROSF and ROCE were caused partly, therefore, by the business incurring higher inventories costs relative to sales revenue and partly through higher operating expenses relative to sales revenue. We should need to compare these ratios with the planned levels for them before we could usefully assess the business's success.

The analyst must now carry out some investigation to discover what caused the increases in both cost of sales and operating expenses, relative to sales revenue, from 2007 to 2008. This will involve checking on what has happened with sales and inventories prices over the two years. Similarly, it will involve looking at each of the individual areas that make up operating expenses to discover which ones were responsible for the increase, relative to sales revenue. Here, further ratios, for example, staff expenses (wages and salaries) to sales revenue, could be calculated in an attempt to isolate the cause of the change from 2007 to 2008. In fact, as we discussed when we took an overview of the financial statements, the increase in staffing may well account for most of the increase in operating expenses.

Real World 6.4 is a *Financial Times* article that discusses the reasons for improving profitability at 'Bollywood'.

Real World 6.4

Investing in Bollywood

Alas for investors, the economics of Bollywood have long been about as predictable as, but rather less uplifting than, the plotline of the average Hindi movie. The world's biggest movie market in terms of number of tickets sold – a massive 3.7bn – has traditionally offered miserable returns to its backers. Instead, revenues were swallowed up by a blend of piracy, taxes and inefficiencies.

Now the script appears to be changing. Big backers – in the shape of international entertainment giants such as Walt Disney and Viacom, and venture capitalists – are starting to enter Bollywood. With a brace of Indian film production companies listed on London's Alternative Investment Market and a third due to follow shortly, smaller investors are also getting in on the act. That is testament to improving industry dynamics. Digital technology and tougher regulation is helping reduce piracy while tax strains are being mitigated either by new rules at home – such as scrapping entertainment tax for multiplexes – or shifting production abroad.

Entertainment companies are also sharpening up their acts and evolving from one-stop shops to specialists in, say, production or distribution. Cleaner corporate structures enable them to access a broader range of financing. The economics of movie-making are improving too. Perhaps 40 per cent of Indian movies are now shot overseas, benefiting from tax breaks, 'captive' actors and producers and – in Europe – longer working days. As a result, a movie may be in the can in perhaps a quarter of the time it would normally take in India.

Evolution in other parts of the media world also plays into the hands of Bollywood moguls; for example, the growth in satellite TV means more channels to bid on movie licensing rights. Industry analysts reckon Bollywood now offers a return on capital employed of about 30–35 per cent, not too dissimilar from Hollywood. Years of tears followed by a happy ending? How Bollywood.

Source: 'Investing in Bollywood', Lex column, *Financial Times*, 26 June 2007.

Efficiency

Efficiency ratios examine the ways in which various resources of the business are managed. The following ratios consider some of the more important aspects of resource management:

- average inventories turnover period
- average settlement period for trade receivables
- average settlement period for trade payables
- sales revenue to capital employed
- sales revenue per employee.

We shall now look at each of these in turn.

Average inventories turnover period

Inventories often represent a significant investment for a business. For some types of business (for example, manufacturers), inventories may account for a substantial proportion of the total assets held (see Real World 12.1, page 443). The average inventories turnover period ratio measures the average period for which inventories are being held. The ratio is calculated as follows:

$$\text{Average inventories turnover period} = \frac{\text{Average inventories held}}{\text{Cost of sales}} \times 365$$

The average inventories for the period can be calculated as a simple average of the opening and closing inventories levels for the year. However, in the case of a highly seasonal business, where inventories levels may vary considerably over the year, a monthly average may be more appropriate.

In the case of Alexis plc, the inventories turnover period for the year ended 31 March 2007 is

$$\text{Average inventories turnover period} = \frac{(241 + 300)/2}{1,745} \times 365 = 56.6 \text{ days}$$

(The opening inventories figure was taken from Note 3 to the financial statements.)

This means that, on average, the inventories held are being 'turned over' every 56.6 days. So, a carpet bought by the business on a particular day would, on average, have been sold about eight weeks later. A business will normally prefer a short inventories turnover period to a long one, because holding inventories has a cost, for example the opportunity cost of the funds tied up. When judging the amount of inventories to carry, the business must consider such things as the likely demand for the inventories, the possibility of supply shortages, the likelihood of price rises, the amount of storage space available, and the perishability/susceptibility to obsolescence of the inventories. The management of inventories will be considered in more detail in Chapter 12.

This ratio is sometimes expressed in terms of months rather than days. Multiplying by 12 rather than 365 will achieve this.

Activity 6.7

Calculate the average inventories turnover period for Alexis plc for the year ended 31 March 2008.

The ratio for 2008 is:

$$\text{Average inventories turnover period} = \frac{(300 + 406)/2}{2,272} \times 365 = 56.7 \text{ days}$$

The inventories turnover period is virtually the same in both years.

Average settlement period for trade receivables

A business will usually be concerned with amount of funds tied up in trade receivables and try to keep this to a minimum. The speed of payment can have a significant effect on the business's cash flow. The average settlement period for trade receivables ratio calculates how long, on average, credit customers take to pay the amounts that they owe to the business. The ratio is as follows:

$$\text{Average settlement period for trade receivables} = \frac{\text{Average trade receivables}}{\text{Credit sales revenue}} \times 365$$

A business will normally prefer a shorter average settlement period to a longer one as, once again, funds are being tied up that may be used for more profitable purposes. Although this ratio can be useful, it is important to remember that it produces an *average* figure for the number of days for which debts are outstanding. This average may be badly distorted by, for example, a few large customers who are very slow or very fast payers.

Since all sales made by Alexis plc are on credit, the average settlement period for trade receivables for the year ended 31 March 2007 is:

$$\text{Average settlement period for trade receivables} = \frac{(223 + 240)/2}{2,240} \times 365 = 37.7 \text{ days}$$

(The opening trade receivables figure was taken from Note 4 to the financial statements.)

Activity 6.8

Calculate the average settlement period for Alexis plc's trade receivables for the year ended 31 March 2008.

The ratio for 2008 is:

$$\text{Average settlement period for trade receivables} = \frac{(240 + 273)/2}{2,681} \times 365 = 34.9 \text{ days}$$

On the face of it, this reduction in the settlement period is welcome. It means that less cash was tied up in trade receivables for each £1 of sales revenue in 2008 than in 2007. Only if the reduction were achieved at the expense of customer goodwill or a high direct financial cost might the desirability of the reduction be questioned. For example, the reduction may have been due to chasing customers too vigorously or as a result of incurring higher expenses, such as discounts allowed to customers who pay quickly.

Average settlement period for trade payables

The average settlement period for trade payables ratio measures how long, on average, the business takes to pay those who have supplied goods and services on credit. The ratio is calculated as follows:

$$\text{Average settlement period for trade payables} = \frac{\text{Average trade payables}}{\text{Credit purchases}} \times 365$$

This ratio provides an average figure, which, like the average settlement period for trade receivables ratio, can be distorted by the payment period for one or two large suppliers.

As trade payables provide a free source of finance for the business, it is perhaps not surprising that some businesses attempt to increase their average settlement period for trade payables. However, such a policy can be taken too far and result in a loss of suppliers, goodwill. We shall return to the issues concerning the management of trade receivables and trade payables in Chapter 12.

For the year ended 31 March 2007, Alexis plc's average settlement period for trade payables is:

$$\text{Average settlement period for trade payables} = \frac{(203 + 261)/2}{1,804} \times 365 = 46.9 \text{ days}$$

(The opening trade payables figure was taken from Note 4 to the financial statements.)

Activity 6.9

Calculate the average settlement period for trade payables for Alexis plc for the year ended 31 March 2008.

The ratio for 2008 is:

$$\text{Average settlement period for trade payables} = \frac{(261 + 354)/2}{2,378} \times 365 = 47.2 \text{ days}$$

There was a very slight increase, between 2007 and 2008, in the average length of time that elapsed between buying inventories and services and paying for them. Had this increase been significant, it would, on the face of it, been beneficial because the business is using free finance provided by suppliers. If, however, this would lead to a loss of supplier goodwill that could have adverse consequences for Alexis plc, it would not necessarily be advantageous.

Sales revenue to capital employed

The sales revenue to capital employed ratio (or asset turnover ratio) examines how effectively the assets of the business are being used to generate sales revenue. It is calculated as follows:

$$\text{Sales revenue to capital employed ratio} = \frac{\text{Sales revenue}}{\text{Share capital} + \text{Reserves} + \text{Non-current liabilities}}$$

Generally speaking, a higher asset turnover ratio is preferred to a lower one. A higher ratio will normally suggest that assets are being used more productively in the generation of revenue. However, a very high ratio may suggest that the business is 'overtrading on its assets', that is, it has insufficient assets to sustain the level of sales revenue achieved. When comparing this ratio for different businesses, factors such as the age and condition of assets held, the valuation bases for assets and whether assets are leased or owned outright can complicate interpretation.

A variation of this formula is to use the total assets less current liabilities (which is equivalent to long-term capital employed) in the denominator (lower part of the fraction). The identical result is obtained.

For the year ended 31 March 2007 this ratio for Alexis plc is:

$$\text{Sales revenue to capital employed} = \frac{2,240}{(638 + 763)/2} = 3.20 \text{ times}$$

(The opening capital employed figure comes from Note 8 to the financial statements)

Activity 6.10

Calculate the sales revenue to capital employed ratio for Alexis plc for the year ended 31 March 2008.

The sales revenue to capital employed ratio for the 2008 is:

$$\text{Sales revenue to capital employed} = \frac{2,681}{(763 + 834)/2} = 3.36 \text{ times}$$

This seems to be an improvement, since in 2008 more sales revenue was being generated for each £1 of capital employed (£3.36) than was the case in 2007 (£3.20). Provided that overtrading is not an issue and that the additional sales are generating an acceptable profit, this is to be welcomed.

Sales revenue per employee

→ The sales revenue per employee ratio relates sales revenue generated to a particular business resource, that is, labour. It provides a measure of the productivity of the workforce. The ratio is:

$$\text{Sales revenue per employee} = \frac{\text{Sales revenue}}{\text{Number of employees}}$$

Generally, businesses would prefer to have a high value for this ratio, implying that they are using their staff efficiently.

For the year ended 31 March 2007, the ratio for Alexis plc is:

$$\text{Sales revenue per employee} = \frac{£2,240m}{13,995} = £160,057$$

Activity 6.11

Calculate the sales revenue per employee for Alexis plc for the year ended 31 March 2008.

The ratio for 2008 is:

$$\text{Sales revenue per employee} = \frac{£2,681m}{18,623} = £143,962$$

This represents a fairly significant decline and probably one that merits further investigation. Labour is a particularly important resource and how well it is managed is a crucial issue for nearly all businesses. As we discussed previously, the number of employees had increased quite notably (by about 33 per cent) during 2008 and the analyst will probably try to discover why this had not generated sufficient additional sales revenue to maintain the ratio at its 2007 level. It could be that the additional employees were not appointed until late in the year ended 31 March 2008.

The efficiency, or activity, ratios may be summarised as follows:

	2007	2008
Average inventories turnover period	56.6 days	56.7 days
Average settlement period for trade receivables	37.7 days	34.9 days
Average settlement period for trade payables	46.9 days	47.2 days
Sales revenue to capital employed (asset turnover)	3.20 times	3.36 times
Sales revenue per employee	£160,057	£143,962

Activity 6.12

What do you deduce from a comparison of the efficiency ratios over the two years?

We feel that maintaining the inventories turnover period at the 2007 level might be reasonable, though whether this represents a satisfactory period can probably only be assessed →

by looking at the business's planned inventories period. The inventories holding period for other businesses operating in carpet retailing, particularly those regarded as the market leaders, may have been helpful in formulating the plans. On the face of things, a shorter receivables collection period and a marginally longer payables payment period are both desirable. On the other hand, these may have been achieved at the cost of a loss of the goodwill of customers and suppliers, respectively. The increased asset turnover ratio seems beneficial, provided that the business can manage this increase. The decline in the sales revenue per employee ratio is undesirable but, as we have already seen, is probably related to the dramatic increase in the level of staffing. As with the inventories turnover period, these other ratios need to be compared with the planned standard of efficiency.

Relationship between profitability and efficiency

In our earlier discussions concerning profitability ratios, we saw that return on capital employed (ROCE) is regarded as a key ratio by many businesses. The ratio is:

$$\text{ROCE} = \frac{\text{Operating profit}}{\text{Long-term capital employed}} \times 100$$

where long-term capital comprises share capital plus reserves plus long-term borrowings. This ratio can be broken down into two elements, as shown in Figure 6.1. The first ratio is the operating profit margin ratio, and the second is the sales revenue to capital employed (asset turnover) ratio, both of which we discussed earlier.

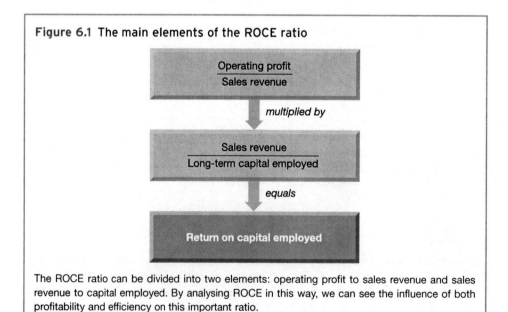

Figure 6.1 The main elements of the ROCE ratio

$$\frac{\text{Operating profit}}{\text{Sales revenue}}$$

multiplied by

$$\frac{\text{Sales revenue}}{\text{Long-term capital employed}}$$

equals

Return on capital employed

The ROCE ratio can be divided into two elements: operating profit to sales revenue and sales revenue to capital employed. By analysing ROCE in this way, we can see the influence of both profitability and efficiency on this important ratio.

By breaking down the ROCE ratio in this manner, we highlight the fact that the overall return on funds employed within the business will be determined both by the profitability of sales and by efficiency in the use of capital.

Example 6.2

Consider the following information, for last year, concerning two different businesses operating in the same industry:

	Antler plc	Baker plc
Operating profit	£20m	£15m
Average long-term capital employed	£100m	£75m
Sales revenue	£200m	£300m

The ROCE for each business is identical (20 per cent). However, the manner in which that return was achieved by each business was quite different. In the case of Antler plc, the operating profit margin is 10 per cent and the sales revenue to capital employed ratio is 2 times (so ROCE = 10% × 2 = 20%). In the case of Baker plc, the operating profit margin is 5 per cent and the sales revenue to capital employed ratio is 4 times (and so ROCE = 5% × 4 = 20%).

Example 6.2 demonstrates that a relatively high sales revenue to capital employed ratio can compensate for a relatively low operating profit margin. Similarly, a relatively low sales revenue to capital employed ratio can be overcome by a relatively high operating profit margin. In many areas of retail and distribution (for example, supermarkets and delivery services), the operating profit margins are quite low but the ROCE can be high, provided that the assets are used productively (that is, low margin, high turnover).

Activity 6.13

Show how the ROCE ratio for Alexis plc can be analysed into the two elements for each of the years 2007 and 2008. What conclusions can you draw from your figures?

	ROCE	=	Operating profit margin	×	Sales revenue to capital employed
2007	34.7%		10.8%		3.20
2008	5.9%		1.8%		3.36

As we can see, the relationship between the three ratios holds for Alexis plc for both years. The small apparent differences arise because the three ratios are stated here only to one or two decimal places.

Although the business was more effective at generating sales revenue (sales revenue to capital employed ratio increased) in 2008 than in 2007, in 2008 it fell well below the level necessary to compensate for the sharp decline in the effectiveness of each sale (operating profit margin). As a result, the 2008 ROCE was well below the 2007 value.

Liquidity

Liquidity ratios are concerned with the ability of the business to meet its short-term financial obligations. The following ratios are widely used:

- current ratio
- acid test ratio.

These two will now be considered.

Current ratio

→ The current ratio compares the 'liquid' assets (that is, cash and those assets held that will soon be turned into cash) of the business with the current liabilities. The ratio is calculated as follows:

$$\text{Current ratio} = \frac{\text{Current assets}}{\text{Current liabilities}}$$

Some people seem to believe that there is an 'ideal' current ratio (usually 2 times or 2:1) for all businesses. However, this fails to take into account the fact that different types of business require different current ratios. For example, a manufacturing business will often have a relatively high current ratio because it is necessary to hold inventories of finished goods, raw materials and work in progress. It will also normally sell goods on credit, thereby giving rise to trade receivables. A supermarket chain, on the other hand, will have a relatively low ratio, as it will hold only fast-moving inventories of finished goods and all of its sales will be made for cash (no credit sales). (See Real World 12.1 on page 443.)

The higher the ratio, the more liquid the business is considered to be. As liquidity is vital to the survival of a business, a higher current ratio might be thought to be preferable to a lower one. If a business has a very high ratio, however, it may be that funds are tied up in cash or other liquid assets and are not, therefore, being used as productively as they might otherwise be.

As at 31 March 2007, the current ratio of Alexis plc is:

$$\text{Current ratio} = \frac{544}{291} = 1.9 \text{ times (or 1.9:1)}$$

Activity 6.14

Calculate the current ratio for Alexis plc as at 31 March 2008.

The ratio as at 31 March 2008 is:

$$\text{Current ratio} = \frac{679}{432} = 1.6 \text{ times (or 1.6:1)}$$

Although this is a decline from 2007 to 2008, it is not necessarily a matter of concern. The next ratio may provide a clue as to whether there seems to be a problem.

Acid test ratio

The acid test ratio is very similar to the current ratio, but it represents a more stringent test of liquidity. It can be argued that, for many businesses, inventories cannot be converted into cash quickly. (Note that, in the case of Alexis plc, the inventories turnover period was about 57 days in both years (see pages 195–196).) As a result, it may be better to exclude this particular asset from any measure of liquidity. The acid test ratio is a variation of the current ratio, but normally excludes inventories.

The minimum level for this ratio is often stated as 1.0 times (or 1:1; that is, current assets (excluding inventories) equals current liabilities). In many highly successful businesses that are regarded as having adequate liquidity, however, it is not unusual for the acid test ratio to be below 1.0 without causing particular liquidity problems. (See Real World 12.1 on page 143.)

The acid test ratio is calculated as follows:

$$\text{Acid test ratio} = \frac{\text{Current assets (excluding inventories)}}{\text{Current liabilities}}$$

The acid test ratio for Alexis plc as at 31 March 2007 is:

$$\text{Acid test ratio} = \frac{544 - 300}{291} = 0.8 \text{ times (or 0.8:1)}$$

We can see that the 'liquid' current assets do not quite cover the current liabilities, so the business may be experiencing some liquidity problems.

Activity 6.15

Calculate the acid test ratio for Alexis plc as at 31 March 2008.

The ratio as at 31 March 2008 is:

$$\text{Acid test ratio} = \frac{679 - 406}{432} = 0.6 \text{ times}$$

The 2008 ratio is significantly below that for 2007. The 2008 level may well be a cause for concern. The rapid decline in this ratio should lead to steps being taken, at least, to stop further decline.

The liquidity ratios for the two-year period may be summarised as follows:

	2007	2008
Current ratio	1.9	1.6
Acid test ratio	0.8	0.6

What do you deduce from the liquidity ratios set out above?

Although it is probably not really possible to make a totally valid judgement without knowing the planned ratios, there appears to have been a worrying decline in liquidity. This is indicated by both of these ratios. The apparent liquidity problem may, however, be planned, short-term and linked to the expansion in non-current assets and staffing. It may be that when the benefits of the expansion come on stream, liquidity will improve. On the other hand, short-term claimants may become anxious when they see signs of weak liquidity. This anxiety could lead to steps being taken to press for payment, and this could cause problems for Alexis plc.

Financial gearing

Financial gearing occurs when a business is financed, at least in part, by borrowing instead of by finance provided by the owners (the shareholders) as equity. A business's level of gearing (that is, the extent to which it is financed from sources that require a fixed return) is an important factor in assessing risk. Where a business borrows, it takes on a commitment to pay interest charges and make capital repayments. Where the borrowing is heavy, this can be a significant financial burden; it can increase the risk of the business becoming insolvent. Nevertheless, most businesses are geared to some extent. (Costain Group plc, the building and construction business, is a rare example of a UK business with no borrowings.)

Given the risks involved, we may wonder why a business would want to take on gearing (that is, to borrow). One reason may be that the owners have insufficient funds, so the only way to finance the business adequately is to borrow from others. Another reason is that gearing can be used to increase the returns to owners. This is possible provided the returns generated from borrowed funds exceed the cost of paying interest. Example 6.3 illustrates this point.

Example 6.3

The long-term capital structures of two new businesses, Lee Ltd and Nova Ltd, are as follows:

	Lee Ltd £	Nova Ltd £
£1 ordinary shares	100,000	200,000
10% loan notes	200,000	100,000
	300,000	300,000

In their first year of operations, they each make an operating profit (that is, profit before interest and taxation) of £50,000. The tax rate is 30 per cent of the profit before taxation after interest.

Lee Ltd would probably be considered relatively highly geared, as it has a high proportion of borrowed funds in its long-term capital structure. Nova Ltd is much lower-geared. The profit available to the shareholders of each business in the first year of operations will be:

	Lee Ltd £	Nova Ltd £
Operating profit	50,000	50,000
Interest payable	(20,000)	(10,000)
Profit before taxation	30,000	40,000
Taxation (30%)	(9,000)	(12,000)
Profit for the year (available to ordinary shareholders)	21,000	28,000

The return on ordinary shareholders' funds (ROSF) for each business will be:

Lee Ltd	Nova Ltd
$\frac{21,000}{100,000} \times 100 = 21\%$	$\frac{28,000}{200,000} \times 100 = 14\%$

We can see that Lee Ltd, the more highly geared business, has generated a better ROSF than Nova Ltd. This is despite the fact that the ROCE (return on capital employed) is identical for both businesses (that is, $(£50,000/£300,000) \times 100 = 16.7\%$).

Note that at the £50,000 level of operating profit, the shareholders of both Lee Ltd and Nova Ltd benefit from gearing. Were the two businesses totally reliant on equity financing, the profit for the year (after taxation) would be £35,000 (that is, £50,000 less 30 per cent taxation), giving an ROSF of 11.7 per cent (that is, £35,000/£300,000). Both businesses generate higher ROSFs than this as a result of financial gearing.

An effect of gearing is that returns to shareholders become more sensitive to changes in operating profit. For a highly geared business, a change in operating profit will lead to a proportionately greater change in the ROSF ratio.

Activity 6.17

Assume that the operating profit was 20 per cent higher for each business than stated above (that is, each had an operating profit of £60,000). What would be the effect of this on ROSF?

The revised profit available to the shareholders of each business in the first year of operations will be:

	Lee Ltd £	Nova Ltd £
Operating profit	60,000	60,000
Interest payable	(20,000)	(10,000)
Profit before taxation	40,000	50,000
Taxation (30%)	(12,000)	(15,000)
Profit for the year (available to ordinary shareholders)	28,000	35,000

The ROSF for each business will now be:

Lee Ltd	Nova Ltd
$\dfrac{28,000}{100,000} \times 100 = 28\%$	$\dfrac{35,000}{200,000} \times 100 = 17.5\%$

We can see that for Lee Ltd, the higher-geared business, the returns to shareholders have increased by one-third (from 21 per cent to 28 per cent), whereas for the lower-geared business, Nova Ltd, the benefits of gearing are less pronounced, increasing ROSF by only one-quarter (from 14 per cent to 17.5 per cent). The effect of gearing can, of course, work in both directions. So, for a highly geared business, a small decline in operating profit will bring about a much greater decline in the returns to shareholders. This makes gearing risky to shareholders.

The reason that gearing tends to be beneficial to shareholders is that interest rates for borrowings are low by comparison with the returns that the typical business can earn. On top of this, interest expenses are tax-deductible, in the way shown in Example 6.3 and Activity 6.17, making the effective cost of borrowing quite cheap. It is debatable whether the apparent low interest rates really are beneficial to the shareholders. Some argue that since borrowing increases the risk to shareholders, there is a hidden cost of borrowing. What are not illusory, however, are the benefits to the shareholders of the tax-deductibility of loan interest.

The effect of gearing is like that of two intermeshing cogwheels of unequal size (see Figure 6.2). The movement in the larger cog (operating profit) causes a more than proportionate movement in the smaller cog (returns to ordinary shareholders). The subject of gearing is discussed further in Chapter 11.

Two ratios are widely used to assess gearing:

- gearing ratio
- interest cover ratio.

Gearing ratio

The gearing ratio measures the contribution of long-term lenders to the long-term capital structure of a business:

$$\text{Gearing ratio} = \frac{\text{Long-term (non-current) liabilities}}{\text{Share capital} + \text{Reserves} + \text{Long-term (non-current) liabilities}} \times 100$$

The gearing ratio for Alexis plc, as at 31 March 2007, is:

$$\text{Gearing ratio} = \frac{200}{(563 + 200)} \times 100 = 26.2\%$$

A gearing ratio of 26.2% would not normally be considered to be very high.

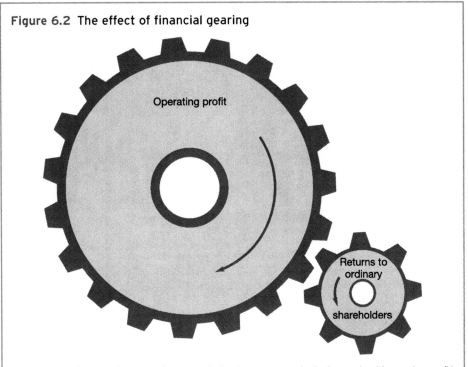

Figure 6.2 The effect of financial gearing

The cogs link the two wheels, so that a small circular movement in the large wheel (operating profit) leads to a relatively large circular movement in the small wheel (returns to ordinary shareholders).

Activity 6.18

Calculate the gearing ratio of Alexis plc as at 31 March 2008.

The ratio as at 31 March 2008 is:

$$\text{Gearing ratio} = \frac{300}{(534 + 300)} \times 100 = 36.0\%$$

This is a substantial increase in the level of gearing over the year.

Interest cover ratio

The interest cover ratio measures the amount of operating profit available to cover interest payable. The ratio may be calculated as follows:

$$\textbf{Interest cover ratio} = \frac{\textbf{Operating profit}}{\textbf{Interest payable}}$$

The ratio for Alexis plc for the year ended 31 March 2007 is:

$$\text{Interest cover ratio} = \frac{243}{18} = 13.5 \text{ times}$$

This ratio shows that the level of operating profit is considerably higher than the level of interest payable. This means that a significant fall in operating profit could occur before operating profit levels failed to cover interest payable. The lower the level of operating profit coverage, the greater the risk to lenders that interest payments will not be met, and the greater the risk to the shareholders that the lenders will take action against the business to recover the interest due.

Activity 6.19

Calculate the interest cover ratio of Alexis plc for the year ended 31 March 2008.

The ratio for the year ended 31 March 2008 is:

$$\text{Interest cover ratio} = \frac{47}{32} = 1.5 \text{ times}$$

Real World 6.5 shows how Tesco plc, the UK and, increasingly, international supermarket chain was able to use financial gearing to boost ROSF in the early 2000s.

Real World 6.5

Changing gear at Tesco

Figure 6.3 plots the ROSF, ROCE and interest cover ratios for Tesco plc over the period 2000 to 2007.

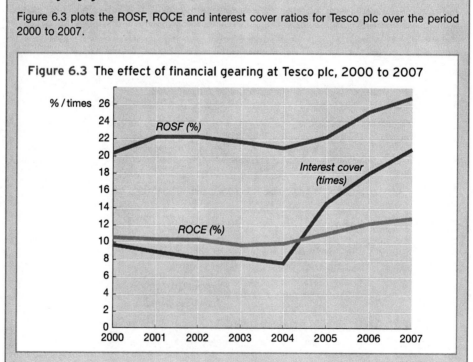

Figure 6.3 The effect of financial gearing at Tesco plc, 2000 to 2007

Tesco was able to boost returns to shareholders (ROSF), despite the business not producing a better ROCE (which reduced slightly between 1999 and 2003). This was achieved as a result of increasing financial gearing (as measured by interest cover) over that period. Since 2004, Tesco has gradually reduced gearing. Now ROSF continued to increase, but as a result of increasing ROCE.

Source: Based on information contained in Tesco plc Annual Reports from 2003 to 2007.

Alexis plc's gearing ratios are:

	2007	2008
Gearing ratio	26.2%	36.0%
Interest cover ratio	13.5 times	1.5 times

Activity 6.20

What do you deduce from a comparison of Alexis plc's gearing ratios over the two years?

The gearing ratio altered significantly. This is mainly due to the substantial increase in long-term lenders to the financing of the business.

The interest cover ratio has declined dramatically from a position where operating profit covered interest 13.5 times in 2007, to one where operating profit covered interest only 1.5 times in 2008. This was partly caused by the increase in borrowings in 2008, but mainly caused by the dramatic decline in profitability in that year. The later situation looks hazardous; only a small decline in future profitability in 2008 would leave the business with insufficient operating profit to cover the interest payments. The gearing ratio at 31 March 2008 would not necessarily be considered to be very high for a business that was trading successfully. It is the low profitability that is the problem.

Without knowing what the business planned these ratios to be, it is not possible to reach a valid conclusion on Alexis plc's gearing.

Real World 6.6 provides some evidence concerning the gearing of listed businesses.

Real World 6.6

The gearing of listed businesses

Larger listed businesses tend to have higher levels of gearing than smaller ones. A Bank of England report on the financing of small businesses found that the average level of gearing among smaller listed businesses was 27 per cent compared with 37 per cent for the top 350 listed businesses. Over recent years the level of borrowing by larger listed businesses has risen steadily (Tesco plc – see Real World 6.5 – provides an example of an exception to this general trend) whereas the level of borrowing for smaller listed businesses has remained fairly stable. This difference in gearing levels between larger and smaller businesses flies in the face of conventional wisdom.

Recent government investigations have found that smaller listed businesses often find it hard to attract investors. Many large institutional investors, who dominate the stock market, are not interested in the shares of smaller listed businesses because the amount of investment required is too small. As a result, shares in smaller businesses are less

→

marketable. In such circumstances, it may be imagined that smaller businesses would become more reliant on borrowing and so would have higher levels of gearing than larger businesses. However, this is clearly not the case.

Although smaller businesses increase the level of shareholder funds by paying relatively low dividends and retaining more profits, they tend to be less profitable than larger businesses. So, higher retained profits do not seem to explain this phenomenon satisfactorily.

The only obvious factors that could explain this difference between smaller and larger businesses are the level of tax relief on interest on borrowings, and borrowing capacity. Broadly, larger businesses pay tax at a higher rate than their smaller counterparts. This means that the tax benefits of borrowing tend to be greater per £ of interest paid for larger businesses than for smaller ones. It may well be that larger businesses can borrow at lower interest rates than smaller ones, if only because they tend to borrow larger sums and so economies of scale may apply. Also, larger businesses tend to be less likely to get into financial difficulties than smaller ones, so they may be able to borrow at lower interest rates.

Source: Adapted from 'Small companies surprise on lending', *Financial Times*, 25 April 2003.

Investment ratios

There are various ratios available that are designed to help investors assess the returns on their investment. The following are widely used:

- dividend payout ratio
- dividend yield ratio
- earnings per share
- price/earnings ratio.

Dividend payout ratio

The dividend payout ratio measures the proportion of earnings (profit for the year) that a business pays out to shareholders in the form of dividends. The ratio is calculated as follows:

$$\text{Dividend payout ratio} = \frac{\text{Dividends announced for the year}}{\text{Profit for the year}} \times 100$$

This ratio is normally expressed as a percentage.

The dividend payout ratio for Alexis plc for the year ended 31 March 2007 is:

$$\text{Dividend payout ratio} = \frac{40}{165} \times 100 = 24.2\%$$

The information provided by this ratio is often expressed slightly differently as the dividend cover ratio. Here the calculation is:

$$\text{Dividend cover ratio} = \frac{\text{Profit for the year}}{\text{Dividend announced for the year}}$$

In the case of Alexis plc (for 2007) it would be 165/40 = 4.1 times. That is to say, the earnings available for dividend cover the actual dividend by just over four times.

Activity 6.21

Calculate the dividend payout ratio of Alexis plc for the year ended 31 March 2008.

The ratio for 2008 is:

$$\text{Dividend payout ratio} = \frac{40}{11} \times 100 = 363.6\%$$

This would normally be considered to be a very alarming increase in the ratio over the two years. Paying a dividend of £40m in 2008 would probably be regarded as very imprudent.

Dividend yield ratio

The dividend yield ratio relates the cash return from a share to its current market value. This can help investors to assess the cash return on their investment in the business. The ratio, expressed as a percentage, is:

$$\text{Dividend yield} = \frac{\text{Dividend per share}/(1-t)}{\text{Market value per share}} \times 100$$

where t is the 'dividend tax credit' rate of income tax. This requires some explanation. In the UK, investors who receive a dividend from a business also receive a tax credit. As this tax credit can be offset against any tax liability arising from the dividends received, the dividends are effectively issued net of income tax, at the dividend tax credit rate.

Investors may wish to compare the returns from shares with the returns from other forms of investment. As these other forms of investment are typically quoted on a 'gross' (that is, pre-tax) basis it is useful to 'gross up' the dividend to make comparison easier. We can achieve this by dividing the dividend per share by $(1-t)$, where t is the 'dividend tax credit' rate of income tax.

Using the 2007/8 dividend tax credit rate of 10 per cent, the dividend yield for Alexis plc for the year ended 31 March 2007 is:

$$\text{Dividend yield} = \frac{0.067^*/(1-0.10)}{2.50} \times 100 = 3.0\%$$

* Dividend proposed/number of shares = 40/(300 × 2) = £0.067 dividend per share (the 300 is multiplied by 2 because they are £0.50 shares).

Activity 6.22

Calculate the dividend yield for Alexis plc for the year ended 31 March 2008.

The ratio for 2008 is:

$$\text{Dividend yield} = \frac{0.067^*/(1-0.10)}{1.50} \times 100 = 4.9\%$$

* 40/(300 × 2) = £0.067.

Earnings per share

→ The earnings per share (EPS) ratio relates the profit for the year to the number of shares in issue. The ratio is calculated as follows:

$$\text{Earnings per share} = \frac{\textbf{Profit for the year}}{\textbf{Number of ordinary shares in issue}}$$

In the case of Alexis plc, the earnings per share for the year ended 31 March 2007 is as follows:

$$\text{EPS} = \frac{£165m}{600m} = 27.5p$$

Many investment analysts regard the EPS ratio as a fundamental measure of share performance. The trend in earnings per share over time is used to help assess the investment potential of a business's shares. Although it is possible to make total profit rise through ordinary shareholders investing more in the business, this will not necessarily mean that the profitability *per share* will rise as a result.

It is not usually very helpful to compare the EPS of one business with that of another. Differences in the constituents of equity (for example, in the nominal value of shares issued or the relative levels of shares and reserves) can render any such comparison meaningless. However, it can be very useful to monitor the changes that occur in this ratio for a particular business over time.

Activity 6.23

Calculate the earnings per share of Alexis plc for the year ended 31 March 2008.

The ratio for 2008 is:

$$\text{EPS} = \frac{£11m}{600m} = 1.8p$$

Price/earnings (P/E) ratio

→ The price/earnings ratio relates the market value of a share to the earnings per share. This ratio can be calculated as follows:

$$\text{P/E ratio} = \frac{\textbf{Market value per share}}{\textbf{Earnings per share}}$$

The P/E ratio for Alexis plc as at 31 March 2007 is:

$$\text{P/E ratio} = \frac{£2.50}{27.5p^*} = 9.1 \text{ times}$$

* The EPS figure (27.5p) was calculated above.

This means that the capital value of the share is 9.1 times higher than the current level of earnings attributable to it. The ratio is a measure of market confidence in the future of the business concerned. The higher the P/E ratio, the greater the confidence in the future earning power of the business and, consequently, the more investors are prepared to pay in relation to the earnings stream of the business.

P/E ratios provide a useful guide to market confidence concerning the future and they can, therefore, be helpful when comparing different businesses. However, differences in accounting policies between businesses can lead to different profit and earnings per share figures, and this can distort comparisons.

Activity 6.24

Calculate the P/E ratio of Alexis plc as at 31 March 2008.

The ratio for 2008 is:

$$\text{P/E ratio} = \frac{£1.50}{1.8p} = 83.3 \text{ times}$$

The investment ratios for Alexis plc over the two-year period are as follows:

	2007	2008
Dividend payout ratio	24.2%	363.6%
Dividend yield ratio	3.0%	4.9%
Earnings per share	27.5p	1.8p
P/E ratio	9.1 times	83.3 times

Activity 6.25

What do you deduce from the investment ratios set out above?

Can you offer an explanation why the share price has not fallen as much as it might have done, bearing in mind the very poor (relative to 2007) trading performance in 2008?

We thought that, although the EPS has fallen dramatically and the dividend payment for 2008 seems very imprudent, the share price seems to have held up remarkably well (fallen from £2.50 to £1.50 – see page 187). This means that dividend yield and P/E value for 2008 look better than those for 2007. This is an anomaly of these two ratios, which stems from using a forward-looking value (the share price) in conjunction with historic data (dividends and earnings). Share prices are based on investors' assessments of the business's future. It seems with Alexis plc that, at the end of 2008, the 'market' was not happy with the business, relative to 2007. This is evidenced by the fact that the share price had fallen by £1 a share. On the other hand, the share price has not fallen as much as the profit for the year. It appears that investors believe that the business will perform better in the future than it did in 2008. This may well be because they believe that the large expansion in assets and employee numbers that occurred in 2008 will yield benefits in the future; benefits that the business was not able to generate during 2008.

Real World 6.7 gives some information about the shares of several large, well-known UK businesses. This type of information is provided on a daily basis by several newspapers, notably the *Financial Times*.

Market statistics for some well-known businesses

The following data were extracted from the *Financial Times* on 6 October 2007, relating to the previous day's trading of the shares of some well-known businesses on the London Stock Exchange.

Share	Price	Chng	2007		Y'ld	P/E	Volume
			High	Low			000s
BP	572.5	+10.5	617	504.5	3.6	12.4	100,518
J D Wetherspoon	571.5	+11	772.5	505	2.1	17.6	289
BSkyB	696	+3	721	521	2.2	24.5	7,463
Marks and Spencer	640	–	759	561	2.9	15.8	11,769
Rolls-Royce	545	+7.5	579	436.65	1.8	14.2	8,642
Vodafone	169.9	+0.80	179.8	133.7	3.6	14.0	207,567

The column headings are as follows:

Price — Mid-market price in pence (that is, the price midway between buying and selling price) of the shares at the end of 5 October 2007.

Chng — Gain or loss in the mid-market price during 5 October 2007.

High/Low — Highest and lowest prices reached by the share during the year 2007 until 5 October 2007.

Y'ld — Gross dividend yield, based on the most recent year's dividend and the current share price.

P/E — Price/earnings ratio, based on the most recent year's (after-tax) profit for the year and the current share price.

Volume — The number of shares (in thousands) that were bought/sold on 5 October 2007.

So, for example, for BP, the oil business,

■ the shares had a mid-market price of £5.725 each at the close of Stock Exchange trading on 5 October 2007;

■ the shares had increased in price by 10.5 pence during trading on 5 October;

■ the shares had highest and lowest prices during 2007 until 5 October of £6.17 and £5.045, respectively;

■ the shares had a dividend yield, based on the 5 October price (and the dividend for the most recent year) of 3.6 per cent;

■ the shares had a P/E ratio, based on the 5 October price (and the after-taxation earnings per share for the most recent year) of 12.4;

■ during trading in the shares on 5 October 2007, 100,518,000 (that is, about 100.5m) of the business's shares had changed hands from one investor to another. To put this into perspective, according to BP's Annual Report for 2006, the total number of shares in the hands of investors was 21,457.3m. This means that the number of BP shares transacted on the London Stock Exchange on that day represented only 0.47 per cent (that is, about 1 in 214) of the total.

Real World 6.8 shows how investment ratios can vary between different industry sectors.

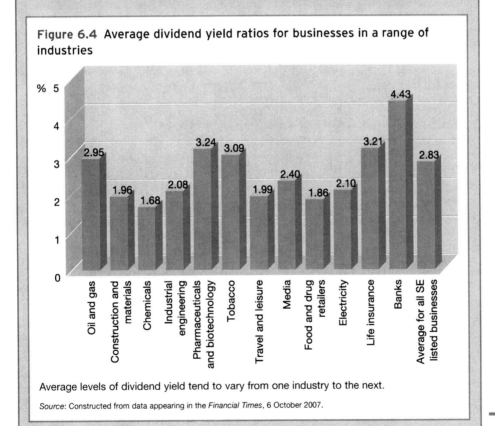

Real World 6.8

How investment ratios vary between industries

Investment ratios can vary significantly between businesses and between industries. To give some indication of the range of variations that occur, the average dividend yield ratios and average P/E ratios for listed businesses in twelve different industries are shown in Figures 6.4 and 6.5, respectively.

The dividend yield ratios are calculated from the current market value of the shares and the most recent year's dividend paid.

Some industries tend to pay out lower dividends than others, leading to lower dividend yield ratios. The average for all Stock Exchange listed businesses was (as is shown in Figure 6.4) 2.83, but there is a wide variation with Chemicals at 1.68 and Banks at 4.43.

Figure 6.4 Average dividend yield ratios for businesses in a range of industries

Average levels of dividend yield tend to vary from one industry to the next.

Source: Constructed from data appearing in the *Financial Times*, 6 October 2007.

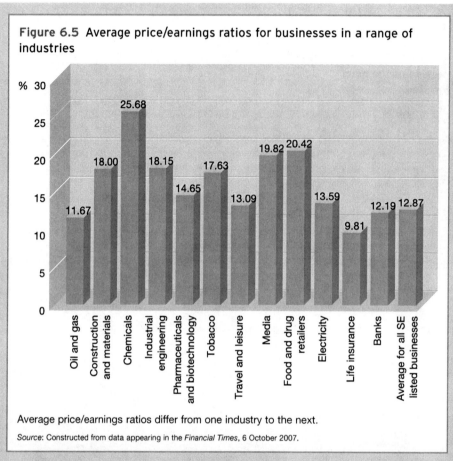

Figure 6.5 Average price/earnings ratios for businesses in a range of industries

Average price/earnings ratios differ from one industry to the next.

Source: Constructed from data appearing in the *Financial Times*, 6 October 2007.

Chemicals businesses tend to invest heavily in developing new products, which possibly explains their tendency to pay low dividends compared with their share prices. Banks, on the other hand, tend not to devote such a large percentage of their profits in new developments.

Some of the differences in the dividend yield ratios from one business to the next can be explained by the nature of the calculation of the ratio. The prices of shares at any given moment are based on expectations of their economic futures; dividends are actual past events. A business that had a good trading year recently may have paid a dividend that, in the light of investors' assessment on the business's economic future, may be high (a high dividend yield).

The P/E ratios are calculated from the current market value of the shares and the most recent year's earnings per share (EPS).

Businesses that have a high share price relative to their recent historic earnings have high P/E ratios. This may be because their future is regarded as economically bright, which may be the result of investing heavily in the future at the expense of recent profits (earnings). On the other hand, high P/Es also arise where businesses have recent low earnings but investors believe that their future is brighter. The average for all Stock Exchange listed businesses was 12.87, but Life Insurance was as low as 9.81 and Chemicals as high as 25.68.

? Self-assessment question 6.1

Both Ali plc and Bhaskar plc operate electrical stores throughout the UK. The financial statements of each business for the year ended 30 June 2008 are as follows:

Balance sheets as at 30 June 2008

	Ali plc £000	Bhaskar plc £000
Non-current assets		
Property, plant and equipment		
(cost less depreciation)		
Land and buildings	360.0	510.0
Fixtures and fittings	87.0	91.2
	447.0	601.2
Current assets		
Inventories	592.0	403.0
Trade receivables	176.4	321.9
Cash at bank	84.6	91.6
	853.0	816.5
Total assets	1,300.0	1,417.7
Equity		
£1 ordinary shares	320.0	250.0
Retained profit	367.6	624.6
	687.6	874.6
Non-current liabilities		
Borrowings – loan notes	190.0	250.0
Current liabilities		
Trade payables	406.4	275.7
Taxation	16.0	17.4
	422.4	293.1
Total equity and liabilities	1,300.0	1,417.7

Income statements for the year ended 30 June 2008

	Ali plc £000	Bhaskar plc £000
Revenue	1,478.1	1,790.4
Cost of sales	(1,018.3)	(1,214.9)
Gross profit	459.8	575.5
Operating expenses	(308.5)	(408.6)
Operating profit	151.3	166.9
Interest payable	(19.4)	(27.5)
Profit before taxation	131.9	139.4
Taxation	(32.0)	(34.8)
Profit for the year	99.9	104.6

All purchases and sales were on credit. Ali plc had announced its intention to pay a dividend of £135,000 and Bhaskar plc £95,000 in respect of the year. The market values of a share in Ali plc and Bhaskar plc at the end of the year were £6.50 and £8.20 respectively.

→

Required:

For each business, calculate two ratios that are concerned with liquidity, gearing and investment (six ratios in total). What can you conclude from the ratios that you have calculated?

The answer to this question can be found at the back of the book in Appendix B.

Trend analysis

It is often helpful to see whether ratios are indicating trends. Key ratios can be plotted on a graph to provide a simple visual display of changes occurring over time. The trends occurring within a business may, for example, be plotted against trends for rival businesses or for the industry as a whole for comparison purposes. An example of trend analysis is shown in Real World 6.9.

Real World 6.9

Trend setting

In Figure 6.6 the current ratio of three of the UK's leading supermarkets is plotted over time. We can see that the current ratio of Tesco plc has risen slightly over the period but it was, nevertheless, consistently lower than that of Sainsbury and Morrison until 2005, when it overtook Morrison.

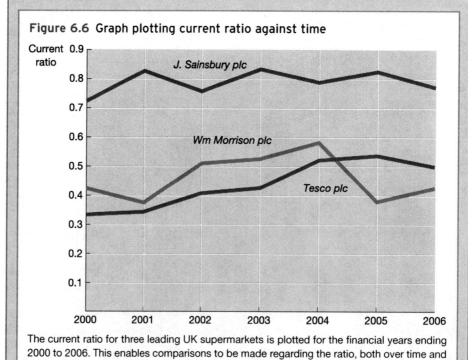

Figure 6.6 Graph plotting current ratio against time

The current ratio for three leading UK supermarkets is plotted for the financial years ending 2000 to 2006. This enables comparisons to be made regarding the ratio, both over time and between the businesses.

Many larger businesses publish certain key financial ratios as part of their annual reports to help users identify significant trends. These ratios typically cover several years' activities. Real World 6.10 shows part of the table of 'key performance measures' of Marks and Spencer plc (M&S), the well-known UK high street store.

Real World 6.10

Key performance measures of Marks and Spencer plc

	2007 52 weeks	2006 52 weeks	2005 52 weeks	2004 53 weeks	2003 52 weeks
Gross margin $\dfrac{\text{Gross profit}}{\text{Revenue}}$	38.9%	38.3%	34.7%	35.4%	34.8%
Net margin $\dfrac{\text{Operating profit}}{\text{Revenue}}$	12.2%	10.9%	8.0%	9.9%	8.6%
Net margin excluding property disposals and exceptional items	12.2%	11.0%	8.7%	10.2%	9.2%
Profitability $\dfrac{\text{Profit before tax}}{\text{Revenue}}$	10.9%	9.6%	6.7%	9.4%	8.4%
Profitability excluding property disposals and exceptional items	11.2%	9.6%	7.4%	9.7%	9.0%
Basic earnings per share $\dfrac{\text{Basic earnings}}{\substack{\text{Weighted average} \\ \text{ordinary shares in issue}}}$	39.1p	31.3p	17.6p	24.2p	21.8p
Earnings per share adjusted for property disposals and exceptional items	40.4p	31.4p	19.2p	24.7p	23.3p
Dividend cover $\dfrac{\substack{\text{Profit attributable} \\ \text{to shareholders}}}{\text{Dividend payable}}$	2.1x	2.2x	2.9x	2.1x	2.1x
Return on equity $\dfrac{\substack{\text{Profit attributable} \\ \text{to shareholders}}}{\substack{\text{Average equity} \\ \text{shareholders' funds}}}$	46.3%	50.0%	35.1%	25.2%	22.4%

Source: Marks and Spencer plc Annual Report 2007. Reproduced by kind permission of Marks and Spencer plc. The 2003 and 2004 results have not been restated following the adoption of the International Financial Reporting Standards in 2005. This means that the results over the five years are not strictly comparable.

After many years of profitable growth, M&S suffered a decline in its fortunes during the late 1990s. This was seen by the directors, and by many independent commentators, as arising from the business allowing itself to be drawn away from its traditional areas of strength. M&S reached its low point in the year ended March 2001 when it incurred a significant overall loss, with an operating profit well below that achieved in 1998. Steps were taken to deal with the problem and the improvements since 2003 are very clear from the table above. The return on equity (return on ordinary shareholders' funds) in 2007 is significantly better than for any other of the five years, except 2006. Although in 2005 both the gross profit and net (operating profit) margins are lower than in 2004, they both recovered strongly in 2006 and continued in 2007.

Using ratios to predict future outcomes

Financial ratios, based on current or past performance, are often used to help predict the future, though both the choice of ratios and the interpretation of results are normally dependent on the judgement of the analyst. Attempts have been made, however, to develop a more rigorous and systematic approach to the use of ratios for prediction purposes. In particular, researchers have shown an interest in the use of ratios to predict financial distress in a business. By financial distress we mean a business getting into financial difficulties or even being made 'bankrupt' and forced out of existence. Several methods and models using ratios have been developed that are claimed to predict future financial distress. Researchers have also developed ratio-based models with which to assess the supposed vulnerability of a business to takeover by another business. These areas, of course, are of interest to all those connected with the business. In the future, it is likely that further ratio-based models will be developed that predict other aspects of future performance.

Limitations of ratio analysis

Although ratios offer a quick and useful method of analysing the position and performance of a business, they are not without their problems and limitations. Some of the more important limitations are described below.

Quality of financial statements

It must always be remembered that ratios are based on financial statements, and the results of ratio analysis are dependent on the quality of these underlying statements. Ratios will inherit the limitations of the financial statements on which they are based. A significant example of this arises from the application of the prudence convention to internally generated intangible non-current assets (as compared with purchased ones). This convention tends to lead to assets of considerable value, such as goodwill and brand names, being excluded from the balance sheet. This can mean that ratios such as ROSF, ROCE and the gearing ratio fail to take account of these assets.

There is also the problem of deliberate attempts to make the financial statements misleading. We discussed this problem of *creative accounting* in Chapter 4.

Inflation

A persistent, though recently less severe, problem, in most western countries is that the financial statements of businesses can be distorted as a result of inflation. One effect of inflation is that the balance sheet values of assets held for any length of time may bear little relation to current values. Generally speaking, the balance sheet value of assets will be understated in current terms during a period of inflation as they are usually recorded at their original cost (less any amounts written off for depreciation).

This means that comparisons, either between businesses or between periods, will be hindered. A difference in, say, ROCE may simply be owing to the fact that assets in one of the balance sheets being compared were acquired more recently (ignoring the effect of depreciation on the asset values). Another effect of inflation is to distort the measurement of profit. Sales revenue for a period is often matched against costs from an earlier period because there is often a time lag between acquiring a particular resource and using it to help generate sales revenue. For example, inventories may be acquired at one point in time and sold perhaps a month or so later. During a period of inflation, this will mean that the expense may not reflect current prices. The cost of sales figure is usually based on the historic cost of the inventories concerned. As a result, expenses will be understated in the income statement and this, in turn, means that profit will be overstated. One effect of this will be to distort the profitability ratios discussed earlier.

The restricted vision of ratios

It is important not to rely exclusively on ratios, thereby losing sight of information contained in the underlying financial statements. As we saw earlier in the chapter, some items reported in these statements can be vital in assessing position and performance. For example, the total sales revenue, capital employed and profit figures may be useful in assessing changes in absolute size that occur over time, or differences in scale between businesses. Ratios do not provide such information. Ratios measure *relative* performance and position, and therefore provide only part of the picture. When comparing two businesses, therefore, it will often be useful to assess the absolute size of profits, as well as the relative profitability of each business. For example, Business A may generate £1m operating profit and have a ROCE of 15 per cent, and Business B may generate £100,000 operating profit and have a ROCE of 20 per cent. Although Business B has a higher level of *profitability*, as measured by ROCE, it generates lower total operating profits.

The basis for comparison

We saw earlier that if ratios are to be useful they require a basis for comparison. Moreover, it is important that the analyst compares like with like. However, no two businesses are identical, and the greater the differences between the businesses being compared, the greater the limitations of ratio analysis. Furthermore, any differences in accounting policies, financing methods (gearing levels) and financial year ends between businesses will add to the problems of comparison.

Balance sheet ratios

Because the balance sheet is only a 'snapshot' of the business at a particular moment in time, any ratios based on balance sheet figures, such as the liquidity ratios, may not be representative of the financial position of the business for the year as a whole. For example, it is common for a seasonal business to have a financial year end that coincides with a low point in business activity. As a result, inventories and trade receivables may be low at the balance sheet date, and so the liquidity ratios may also be low. A more representative picture of liquidity can only really be gained by taking additional measurements at other points in the year.

Real World 6.11 points out another way in which ratios are limited.

Real World 6.11

Remember, it's people that really count . . .

Lord Weinstock (1924–2002) was an influential industrialist whose management style and philosophy helped to shape management practice in many UK businesses. During his long and successful reign at GEC plc, a major engineering business, Lord Weinstock relied heavily on financial ratios to assess performance and to exercise control. In particular, he relied on ratios relating to sales revenue, expenses, trade receivables, profit margins and inventories turnover. However, he was keenly aware of the limitations of ratios and recognised that, ultimately, people produce profits.

In a memo written to GEC managers he pointed out that ratios are an aid to good management rather than a substitute for it. He wrote:

> The operating ratios are of great value as measures of efficiency but they are only the measures and not efficiency itself. Statistics will not design a product better, make it for a lower cost or increase sales. If ill-used, they may so guide action as to diminish resources for the sake of apparent but false signs of improvement.
>
> Management remains a matter of judgement, of knowledge of products and processes and of understanding and skill in dealing with people. The ratios will indicate how well all these things are being done and will show comparison with how they are done elsewhere. But they will tell us nothing about how to do them. That is what you are meant to do.

Source: Extract from *Arnold Weinstock and the Making of GEC*, S. Aris (Aurum Press, 1998), published in *The Sunday Times*, 22 February 1998, p. 3.

Summary

The main points of this chapter may be summarised as follows.

Ratio analysis

- Compares two related figures, usually both from the same set of financial statements.
- Is an aid to understanding what the financial statements really mean.
- Is an inexact science so results must be interpreted cautiously.
- Past periods, the performance of similar businesses and planned performance are often used to provide benchmark ratios.
- A brief overview of the financial statements can often provide insights that may not be revealed by ratios and/or may help in the interpretation of them.

Profitability ratios – concerned with effectiveness at generating profit

- Return on ordinary shareholders' funds (ROSF).
- Return on capital employed (ROCE).
- Operating profit margin.
- Gross profit margin.

Efficiency ratios – concerned with efficiency of using assets/resources

- Average inventories turnover period.
- Average settlement period for trade receivables.
- Average settlement period for trade payables.
- Sales revenue to capital employed.
- Sales revenue per employee.

Liquidity ratios – concerned with the ability to meet short-term obligations

- Current ratio.
- Acid test ratio.

Gearing ratios – concerned with the relationship between equity and debt financing

- Gearing ratio.
- Interest cover ratio.

Investment ratios – concerned with returns to shareholders

- Dividend payout ratio.
- Dividend yield ratio.
- Earnings per share.
- Price/earnings ratio.

Trend analysis

- Individual ratios can be tracked (for example, plotted on a graph) to detect trends.

Ratios as predictors of future outcomes

- Ratios can be used to help predict the future, particularly financial distress.

Limitations of ratio analysis

- Ratios are only as reliable as the financial statements from which they derive.
- Inflation can distort the information.
- Ratios have restricted vision.
- It can be difficult to find a suitable benchmark (for example, another business) as comparator.
- Some ratios could mislead due to the 'snapshot' nature of the balance sheet.

→ **Key terms**

return on ordinary shareholders' funds ratio (ROSF)	sales revenue per employee ratio
return on capital employed ratio (ROCE)	current ratio
operating profit margin ratio	acid test ratio
gross profit margin ratio	financial gearing
average inventories turnover period ratio	gearing ratio
average settlement period for trade receivables ratio	interest cover ratio
average settlement period for trade payables ratio	dividend payout ratio
sales revenue to capital employed ratio	dividend cover ratio
	dividend yield ratio
	dividend per share
	earnings per share (EPS)
	price/earnings ratio

Further reading

If you would like to explore the topics covered in this chapter in more depth, we recommend the following books:

Elliott, B. and Elliott, J., *Financial Accounting and Reporting* (12th edn), Financial Times Prentice Hall, 2008, chapters 28 and 29.

Revsine, L., Collins, D. and Johnson, W.B., *Financial Reporting and Analysis* (3rd edn), Prentice Hall, 2005, chapter 5.

Sutton, T., *Corporate Financial Accounting and Reporting* (2nd edn), Financial Times Prentice Hall, 2004, chapter 19.

Wild, J., Subramanyam, K. and Halsey, R., *Financial Statement Analysis* (9th edn), McGraw-Hill, 2006, chapters 8, 9 and 11.

? ## Review questions

Answers to these questions can be found at the back of the book in Appendix C.

6.1 Some businesses operate on a low operating profit margin (for example, a supermarket chain). Does this mean that the return on capital employed from the business will also be low?

6.2 What potential problems arise for the external analyst from the use of balance sheet figures in the calculation of financial ratios?

6.3 Two businesses operate in the same industry. One has an inventories turnover period that is longer than the industry average. The other has an inventories turnover period that is shorter than the industry average. Give three possible explanations for each business's inventories turnover period ratio.

6.4 Identify and discuss three reasons why the P/E ratio of two businesses operating within the same industry may differ.

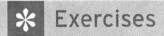 Exercises

Exercises 6.4 and 6.5 are more advanced than Exercises 6.1 to 6.3. Those with coloured numbers have answers at the back of the book in Appendix D.

> **If you wish to try more exercises, visit MyAccountingLab/**

6.1 I. Jiang (Western) Ltd has recently produced its financial statements for the current year. The directors are concerned that the return on capital employed (ROCE) had decreased from 14 per cent last year to 12 per cent for the current year.

The following reasons were suggested as to why this reduction in ROCE had occurred:

1 an increase in the gross profit margin;
2 a reduction in sales revenue;
3 an increase in overhead expenses;
4 an increase in amount of inventories held;
5 the repayment of some borrowings at the year end; and
6 an increase in the time taken for credit customers (trade receivables) to pay.

Required:
Taking each of these six suggested reasons in turn, state, with reasons, whether each of them could lead to a reduction in ROCE.

6.2 Amsterdam Ltd and Berlin Ltd are both engaged in retailing, but they seem to take a different approach to it according to the following information:

Ratio	Amsterdam Ltd	Berlin Ltd
Return on capital employed (ROCE)	20%	17%
Return on ordinary shareholders' funds (ROSF)	30%	18%
Average settlement period for trade receivables	63 days	21 days
Average settlement period for trade payables	50 days	45 days
Gross profit margin	40%	15%
Operating profit margin	10%	10%
Average inventories turnover period	52 days	25 days

Required:
Describe what this information indicates about the differences in approach between the two businesses. If one of them prides itself on personal service and one of them on competitive prices, which do you think is which and why?

6.3 Conday and Co. Ltd has been in operation for three years and produces antique repro-
duction furniture for the export market. The most recent set of financial statements for the
business is set out as follows:

Balance sheet as at 30 November

	£000
Non-current assets	
Property, plant and equipment (cost less depreciation)	
Land and buildings	228
Plant and machinery	762
	990
Current assets	
Inventories	600
Trade receivables	820
	1,420
Total assets	2,410
Equity	
Ordinary shares of £1 each	700
Retained earnings	365
	1,065
Non-current liabilities	
Borrowings – 9% loan notes (Note 1)	200
Current liabilities	
Trade payables	665
Taxation	48
Short-term borrowings (all bank overdraft)	432
	1,145
Total equity and liabilities	2,410

Income statement for the year ended 30 November

	£000
Revenue	2,600
Cost of sales	(1,620)
Gross profit	980
Selling and distribution expenses (Note 2)	(408)
Administration expenses	(194)
Operating profit	378
Finance expenses	(58)
Profit before taxation	320
Taxation	(95)
Profit for the year	225

Notes:
1 The loan notes are secured on the freehold land and buildings.
2 Selling and distribution expenses include £170,000 in respect of bad debts.
3 A dividend of £160,000 was paid on the ordinary shares during the year.
4 The directors have invited an investor to take up a new issue of ordinary shares in the
   business at £6.40 each making a total investment of £200,000. The directors wish to
   use the funds to finance a programme of further expansion.

Required:

(a) Analyse the financial position and performance of the business and comment on any features that you consider to be significant.

(b) State, with reasons, whether or not the investor should invest in the business on the terms outlined.

6.4 Threads Limited manufactures nuts and bolts, which are sold to industrial users. The abbreviated financial statements for 2007 and 2008 are as follows:

Income statements for the year ended 30 June

	2007 £000	2008 £000
Revenue	1,180	1,200
Cost of sales	(680)	(750)
Gross profit	500	450
Operating expenses	(200)	(208)
Depreciation	(66)	(75)
Operating profit	234	167
Interest	(–)	(8)
Profit before taxation	234	159
Taxation	(80)	(48)
Profit for the year	154	111

Balance sheets as at 30 June

	2007 £000	2008 £000
Non-current assets		
Property, plant and equipment	702	687
Current assets		
Inventories	148	236
Trade receivables	102	156
Cash	3	4
	253	396
Total assets	955	1,083
Equity		
Ordinary share capital of £1 (fully paid)	500	500
Retained earnings	256	295
	756	795
Non-current liabilities		
Borrowings – bank loan	–	50
Current liabilities		
Trade payables	60	76
Other payables and accruals	18	16
Taxation	40	24
Short-term borrowings (all bank overdraft)	81	122
	199	238
Total equity and liabilities	955	1,083

→

Dividends were paid on ordinary shares of £70,000 and £72,000 in respect of 2007 and 2008, respectively.

Required:

(a) Calculate the following financial ratios for *both* 2007 and 2008 (using year-end figures for balance sheet items):

1 return on capital employed
2 operating profit margin
3 gross profit margin
4 current ratio
5 acid test ratio
6 settlement period for trade receivables
7 settlement period for trade payables
8 inventories turnover period.

(b) Comment on the performance of Threads Limited from the viewpoint of a business considering supplying a substantial amount of goods to Threads Limited on usual trade credit terms.

6.5 Bradbury Ltd is a family-owned clothes manufacturer based in the southwest of England. For a number of years the chairman and managing director was David Bradbury. During his period of office, sales revenue had grown steadily at a rate of 2 to 3 per cent each year. David Bradbury retired on 30 November 2007 and was succeeded by his son Simon. Soon after taking office, Simon decided to expand the business. Within weeks he had successfully negotiated a five-year contract with a large clothes retailer to make a range of sports and leisurewear items. The contract will result in an additional £2m in sales revenue during each year of the contract. To fulfil the contract, Bradbury Ltd acquired new equipment and premises.

Financial information concerning the business is given below.

Income statements for the year ended 30 November

	2007	2008
	£000	£000
Revenue	9,482	11,365
Operating profit	914	1,042
Interest charges	(22)	(81)
Profit before taxation	892	961
Taxation	(358)	(386)
Profit for the year	534	575

Balance sheets as at 30 November

	2007 £000	2008 £000
Non-current assets		
Property, plant and equipment		
(cost less depreciation)		
Premises	5,240	7,360
Plant and equipment	2,375	4,057
	7,615	11,417
Current assets		
Inventories	2,386	3,420
Trade receivables	2,540	4,280
	4,926	7,700
Total assets	12,541	19,117
Equity		
Share capital	2,000	2,000
Reserves	7,813	8,268
	9,813	10,268
Non-current liabilities		
Borrowing – loans	1,220	3,675
Current liabilities		
Trade payables	1,157	2,245
Taxation	179	193
Short-term borrowings (all bank overdraft)	172	2,736
	1,508	5,174
Total equity and liabilities	12,541	19,117

Dividends of £120,000 were paid on ordinary shares in respect of each of the two years.

Required:

(a) Calculate, for each year (using year-end figures for balance sheet items), the following ratios:

    1 operating profit margin

    2 return on capital employed

    3 current ratio

    4 gearing ratio

    5 days trade receivables (settlement period)

    6 sales revenue to capital employed.

(b) Using the above ratios, and any other ratios or information you consider relevant, comment on the results of the expansion programme.

RISK ASSESSMENT

Chapter 19

Risk management

Key questions

➤ What is risk management?

➤ How can operations assess the potential causes of, and risks from failure?

➤ How can failures be prevented?

➤ How can operations mitigate the effects of failure?

➤ How can operations recover from the effects of failure?

Introduction

No matter how much effort is put into improving operations, there is always a risk that something unexpected or unusual will happen that could reverse much, if not all, of the improvement effort. So, one obvious way of improving operations performance is by reducing the risk of failure (or of failure causing disruption) within the operation. Understanding and managing risk in operations can be seen as an improvement activity, even if it is in an 'avoiding the negative effects of failure' sense. But there is also a more conspicuous reason why risk management is increasingly a concern of operations managers. The sources of risk and the consequences of risk are becoming more difficult to handle. From sudden changes in demand to the bankruptcy of a key supplier, from terrorist attacks to cybercrime, the threats to normal smooth running of operations are not getting fewer. Nor are the consequences of such events becoming less serious. Sharper cost-cutting, lower inventories, higher levels of capacity utilization, increasingly effective regulation, and attentive media, can all serve to make the costs of operational failure greater. So for most operations managing risks is not just desirable, it is essential. But the risks to the smooth running of operations are not confined to major events. Even in less critical situations, having dependable processes can give a competitive advantage. And in this chapter we examine both the dramatic and more routine risks that can prevent operations working as they should. Figure 19.1 shows how this chapter fits into the operation's improvement activities.

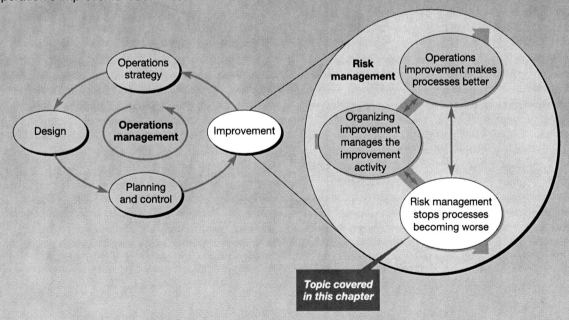

Figure 19.1 This chapter covers risk management

 *Check and improve your understanding of this chapter using self assessment questions and a personalised study plan, audio and video downloads, and an eBook – all at www.myomlab.com.*

Operations in practice Cadbury's salmonella outbreak[1]

In June 2007, Cadbury, founded by a Quaker family in 1824, and now part of Cadbury Schweppes, one of the world's biggest confectionery companies, was fined £1 million plus costs of £152,000 for breaching food safety laws in a national salmonella outbreak that infected 42 people, including children aged under 10, who became ill with a rare strain of Salmonella montevideo. *'I regard this as a serious case of negligence'*, the judge said. *'It therefore needs to be marked as such to emphasise the responsibility and care which the law requires of a company in Cadbury's position.'* One prominant lawyer announced that *'Despite Cadbury's attempts to play down this significant fine, make no mistake it was intended to hurt and is one of the largest of its kind to date. This reflects no doubt the company's high profile and the length of time over which the admitted breach took place, but will also send out a blunt warning to smaller businesses of the government's intentions regarding enforcement of food safety laws.'*

Source: Science Photo Library Ltd

Before the hearing, the company had, in fact, apologized, offering its 'sincere regrets' to those affected, and pleaded guilty to nine food safety offences. But at the beginning of the incident it had not been so open: one of the charges faced by Cadbury, which said it had cooperated fully with the investigation, admitted that it failed to notify the authorities of positive tests for salmonella as soon as they were known within the company. While admitting its mistakes, a spokesman for the confectioner emphasized that the company had acted in good faith, a point that was supported by the judge when he dismissed a prosecution suggestion that Cadbury had introduced the procedural changes that led to the outbreak simply as a cost-cutting measure. Cadbury, through its lawyers, said: *'Negligence we admit, but we certainly do not admit that this was done deliberately to save money and nor is there any evidence to support that conclusion.'* The judge said Cadbury had accepted that a new testing system, originally introduced to improve safety, was a *'distinct departure from previous practice'*, and was *'badly flawed and wrong'*. In a statement Cadbury said: *'Mistakenly, we did not believe that there was a threat to health and thus any requirement to report the incident to the authorities – we accept that this approach was*

incorrect. The processes that led to this failure ceased from June last year and will never be reinstated.'

The company was not only hit by the fine and court costs, it had to bear the costs of recalling one million bars that may have been contaminated, and face private litigation claims brought by its consumers who were affected. Cadbury said it lost around £30 million because of the recall and subsequent safety modifications, not including any private litigation claims. The London *Times* reported on the case of Shaun Garratty, one of the people affected. A senior staff nurse, from Rotherham, he spent seven weeks in hospital critically ill and now he fears that his nursing career might be in jeopardy. *The Times* reported him as being 'pleased that Cadbury's had admitted guilt but now wants to know what the firm is going to do for him'. Before the incident, it said, he was a fitness fanatic and went hiking, cycling, mountain biking or swimming twice a week. He always took two bars of chocolate on the trips, usually a Cadbury's Dairy Milk and a Cadbury's Caramel bar. He also ate one as a snack each day at work. *'My gastroenterologist told me if I had not been so fit I would have died'*, said Mr. Garratty. *'Six weeks after being in hospital they thought my bowel had perforated and I had to have a laparoscopy. I was told my intestines were inflamed and swollen.'* Even after he returned to work he has not fully recovered. According to one medical consultant, the illness had left him with a form of irritable bowel syndrome that could take 18 months to recover.

What is risk management?

Risk management is about things going wrong and what operations can do to stop things going wrong. It is important because there is always a chance that things might go wrong. But recognizing that things will sometimes go wrong is not the same as ignoring, or accepting it as inevitable. Generally operations managers try and prevent things going wrong. The Institute of Risk Management defines risk management as, '*the process which aims to help organisations understand, evaluate and take action on all their risks with a view to increasing the probability of their success and reducing the likelihood of failure*'.[2] They see risk management as being relevant to all organizations whether they are in the public or the private sector, or whether they are large or small, and is something that should form part of the culture of the organization.

From an operations perspective, risk is caused by some type of failure, and there are many different sources of failure in any operation. But dealing with failures, and therefore managing risk, generally involves four sets of activities. The first is concerned with understanding **what failures could potentially occur** in the operation and assessing their seriousness. The second task is to examine ways of **preventing failures** occurring. The third is to minimize the negative consequences of failure (called failure or **risk 'mitigation'**). The final task is to devise plans and procedures that will help the operation **to recover** from failures when they do occur. The remainder of this chapter deals with these four tasks, see Figure 19.2.

Potential risks
Failure prevention
Risk mitigation
Failure recovery

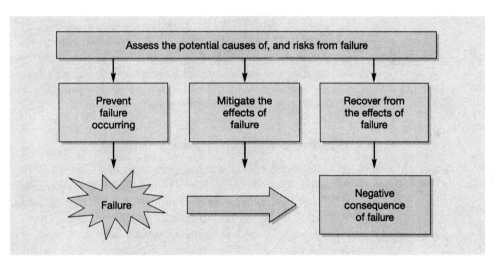

Figure 19.2 Risk management involves failure prevention, mitigating the negative consequences of failure, and failure recovery

Assess the potential causes of and risks from failure

The first aspect of risk management is to understand the potential sources of risk. This means assessing where failure might occur and what the consequences of failure might be. Often it is a 'failure to understand failure' that results in unacceptable risk. Each potential cause of failure needs to be assessed in terms of how likely it is to occur and the impact it may have. Only then can measures be taken to prevent or minimize the effect of the more important potential failures. The classic approach to assessing potential failures is to inspect and audit operations activities. Unfortunately, inspection and audit cannot, on their own, provide complete assurance that undesirable events will be avoided. The content of any audit has to be appropriate, the checking process has to be sufficiently frequent and comprehensive

Table 19.1 The seven management principles essential to effective risk management

Corporate perspective	• Viewing developments within the context of strategic goals • Recognizing both the potential value of opportunity and the potential impact of adverse effects
Forward-looking view	• Thinking toward tomorrow, identifying uncertainties, managing project resources and activities while anticipating uncertainties
Open communication	• Encouraging free-flowing information at and between all levels • Enabling formal, informal and impromptu communication • Using processes that value the individual voice (bringing unique knowledge and insight to identifying and managing risk)
Integrated management	• Making risk management an integral and vital part of operations • Adapting risk management methods and tools to a project's infrastructure and culture
Continuous process	• Sustaining constant vigilance • Identifying and managing risks routinely through all phases of change
Shared vision	• Mutual vision based on common purpose, shared ownership and collective communication • Focusing on results
Teamwork	• Working cooperatively to achieve common goals • Pooling talent, skills and knowledge

and the inspectors have to have sufficient knowledge and experience. But whatever approach to risk is taken, it can only be effective if the organizational culture that it is set in fully supports a 'risk-aware' attitude. This is particularly important where operations are producing new or uncertain outputs, as in software engineering. Carnegie Mellon University Software Engineering Institute has identified seven management principles essential to effective risk management.[3] Table 19.1 is adapted from those principles.

Identify the potential causes of failure

The causes of some failures are purely random, like lightning strikes, and are difficult, if not impossible, to predict. However, the vast majority of failures are caused by something that could have been avoided. So, as a minimum starting point, a simple checklist of failure causes is useful. In fact the root cause of most failure is usually human failure of some type; nevertheless, identifying failure sources usually requires a more evident set, such as that illustrated in Figure 19.3. Here, failure sources are classified as: failures of supply, internal failures such as those deriving from human organizational and technological sources, failures deriving from the design of products and services, failures deriving from customer failures, and general environmental failures.

Supply failure

Supply failure means any failure in the timing or quality of goods and services delivered into an operation. For example, suppliers delivering the wrong or faulty components, outsourced call centres suffering a telecoms failure, disruption to power supplies, and so on. It can be an important source of failure because of increasing dependence on outsourced activities in most industries. Also, global sourcing usually means that parts are shipped around the world on their journey through the supply chain. Microchips manufactured in Taiwan could be assembled to printed circuit boards in Shanghai which are then finally assembled into a computer in Ireland. At the same time, many industries are suffering increased volatility in demand. Perhaps most significantly there tends to be far less inventory in supply chains that could buffer interruptions to supply. According to one authority on supply chain management, 'Potentially the risk of disruption has increased dramatically as the result of a too-narrow focus on supply chain efficiency at the expense of effectiveness.'[4]

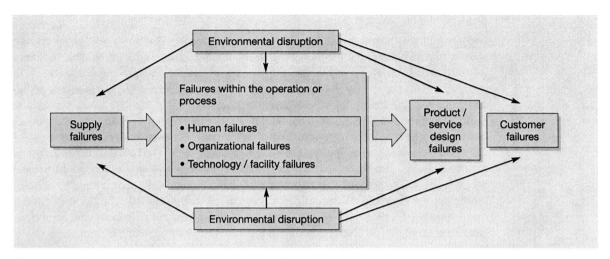

Figure 19.3 The sources of potential failure in operations

Human failures

There are two broad types of human failure. The first is where key personnel leave, become ill, die, or in some way cannot fulfil their role. The second is where people are doing their job but are making mistakes. Understanding risk in the first type of failure involves identifying the key people without whom operations would struggle to operate effectively. These are not always the most senior individuals, but rather those fulfilling crucial roles that require special skills or tacit knowledge. Human failure through 'mistakes' also comes in two types: errors and violations. '**Errors**' are mistakes in judgement, where a person should have done something different. For example, if the manager of a sports stadium fails to anticipate dangerous crowding during a championship event. '**Violations**' are acts which are clearly contrary to defined operating procedure. For example, if a maintenance engineer fails to clean a filter in the prescribed manner, it is eventually likely to cause failure. Catastrophic failures are often caused by a combination of errors and violations. For example, one kind of accident, where an aircraft appears to be under control and yet still flies into the ground, is very rare (once in two million flights). For this type of failure to occur, first, the pilot has to be flying at the wrong altitude (error). Second, the co-pilot would have to fail to cross-check the altitude (violation). Third, air traffic controllers would have to miss the fact that the plane was at the wrong altitude (error). Finally, the pilot would have to ignore the ground proximity warning alarm in the aircraft, which can be prone to give false alarms (violation).

Errors

Violations

Short case
Not what you want to hear[5]

The passengers never knew, and to be fair to the airline the pilot in question was intercepted before he could fly the aircraft, but it is unsettling to think about being flown by a pilot who has been drinking. So, if you are an anxious flyer, or of a nervous disposition, stop reading now.

It was a dramatic example of human failure increasing operational risk. The headline ran – 'Pilot arrested over alcohol fears!' Why? A pilot had been arrested after he had boarded a plane at Heathrow Airport on suspicion of being drunk. After giving a breath test to police, the 44-year-old pilot, who worked for the US carrier United Airlines, was arrested and held on suspicion of 'performing an aviation function whilst exceeding the alcohol limit'. Responding to the incident, United Airlines issued a statement saying that 'Safety is our number one priority' and confirming that the pilot had been 'removed from duty while we are co-operating with the authorities and conducting a full investigation'. A statement released by United Airlines said the company's alcohol policy was 'among the strictest in the industry. We have no tolerance for abuse or violations of this well-established policy', it said.

Organizational failure

Organizational failure is usually taken to mean failures of procedures and processes and failures that derive from a business's organizational structure and culture. This is a huge potential source of failure and includes almost all operations and process management. In particular, failure in the design of processes (such as bottlenecks causing system overloading) and failures in the resourcing of processes (such as insufficient capacity being provided at peak times) need to be investigated. But there are also many other procedures and processes within an organization that can make failure more likely. For example, remuneration policy may motivate staff to work in a way that, although increasing the financial performance of the organization, also increases the risk of failure. Examples of this can range from sales people being so incentivized that they make promises to customers that cannot be fulfilled, through to investment bankers being more concerned with profit than the risks of financial over-exposure. This type of risk can derive from an organizational culture that minimizes consideration of risk, or it may come from a lack of clarity in reporting relationships.

Technology and facilities failures

By 'technology and facilities' we mean all the IT systems, machines, equipment and buildings of an operation. All are liable to failure, or breakdown. The failure may be only partial, for example a machine that has an intermittent fault. Alternatively, it can be what we normally regard as a breakdown – a total and sudden cessation of operation. Either way, its effects could bring a large part of the operation to a halt. For example, a computer failure in a super-market chain could paralyse several large stores until it is fixed.

Product / service design failures

In its design stage, a product or service might look fine on paper; only when it has to cope with real circumstances might inadequacies become evident. Of course, during the design process, potential risk of failure should have been identified and 'designed out'. But one only has to look at the number of 'product recalls' or service failures to understand that design failures are far from uncommon. Sometimes this is the result of a trade-off between fast time-to-market performance and the risk of the product or service failing in operation. And, while no reputable business would deliberately market flawed products or services, equally most businesses cannot delay a product or service launch indefinitely to eliminate every single small risk of failure.

Customer failures

Not all failures are (directly) caused by the operation or its suppliers. Customers may 'fail' in that they misuse products and services. For example, an IT system might have been well designed, yet the user could treat it in a way that causes it to fail. Customers are not 'always right'; they can be inattentive and incompetent. However, merely complaining about customers is unlikely to reduce the chances of this type of failure occurring. Most organizations will accept that they have a responsibility to educate and train customers, and to design their products and services so as to minimize the chances of failure.

Environmental disruption

Environmental disruption includes all the causes of failure that lie outside of an operation's direct influence. This source of potential failure has risen to near the top of many firms' agenda since 11 September 2001 and the global 'credit crunch' of 2008. As operations become increasingly integrated (and increasingly dependent on integrated technologies such as information technologies), businesses are more aware of the critical events and malfunctions that have the potential to interrupt normal business activity and even stop the entire company. Risks in this category include everything from cybercrime to hurricanes, from terrorism to political change.

Short case
Viruses, threats and 30 years of spam[6]

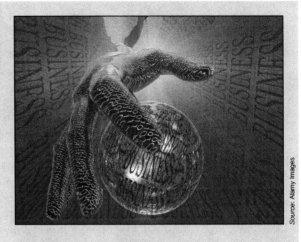

Source: Alamy Images

Happy birthday! 1 May 2008 saw the 30th anniversary of junk electronic mail, or spam as it has become known. It was in 1978 that Gary Thuerk, a Marketing Executive at the Digital Equipment Corporation (DEC), a US mini-computer manufacturer, decided it would be a great sales ploy to let Arpanet (the direct ancestor of the Internet) researchers on the west coast of the USA know that DEC had incorporated the network's protocols directly into one of its operating systems. So Thuerk's secretary typed in all the researchers' addresses and dispatched the message using the e-mail program, which at the time was very primitive. But not all the recipients were happy. Arpanet's rules said that the network could not be used for commercial purposes and not everyone wanted to know about the content of the message; it just seemed intrusive.

Since then unwanted Internet-distributed information has gone on to irritate, infuriate and threaten the whole Internet. For example, on 25 January 2003 the 'SQL Slammer' worm, a rogue program, spread at frightening speed throughout the Internet. It disrupted computers around the world and, at the height of the attack, its effect was such that half the traffic over the Internet was being lost (see Figure 19.4). Thousands of cash dispensers in North America ceased operating and one

police force was driven back to using pencils and paper when its dispatching system crashed. Yet security experts believe that the SQL Slammer did more good than harm because it highlighted weaknesses in Internet security processes. Like most rogue software, it exploited a flaw in a commonly used piece of software. Much commonly used software has security flaws that can be exploited in this way. Software producers issue 'patch' software to fix flaws but this can actually direct Internet terrorists to vulnerable areas in the software, and not all systems managers get around to implementing all patches. Nevertheless, every rogue program that penetrates Internet security systems teaches a valuable lesson to those working to prevent security failures.

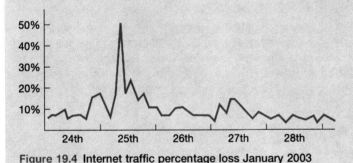

Figure 19.4 Internet traffic percentage loss January 2003

E-security[7]

Any advance in processes or technology creates risks. No real advance comes without threats and even danger. This applies particularly to e-business. In almost all businesses information has become critical. So, information security management has become a particularly high priority. But herein lies the problem. The Internet, which is the primary medium for conducting e-business, is by design an open non-secure medium. Since the original purpose of the Internet was not for commercial purposes, it is not designed to handle secure transactions. There is a trade-off between providing wider access through the Internet, and the security concerns it generates. Three developments have amplified e-security concerns. First, increased connectivity (who does not rely on internet-based systems?) means that everyone has at least the potential to 'see' everyone else. Organizations want to make enterprise systems and information more available to internal employees, business partners and customers (see Chapter 14 on ERP). Second, there has been a loss of 'perimeter' security as more people work from home or through mobile communications. For example, some banks have been targeted by criminals seeking to exploit home working, as a hitherto overlooked flaw in corporate security firewalls. Hackers had hoped to exploit lower levels of security in home computers to burrow into corporate networks. Third, for some new, sometimes unregulated, technologies, such as some mobile networks, it takes time to discover all possible sources of risk. The Internet, after all, is an open system and the rapid rate of development of new software and systems often means that users do not have an adequate knowledge about software and systems architecture. This makes users oblivious to potential vulnerabilities that can lead to serious security breaches.

Yet there is an increasing customer awareness of data security and data confidentiality which means that companies are viewing e-business security as a potential marketing advantage. One specialist in this area, Forrester Research, reported that 74 per cent of online consumers said that online security is an important consideration in choosing a financial service provider.

Post-failure analysis

One of the critical activities of operations and process resilience is to understand why a failure has occurred. This activity is called 'post-failure analysis'. It is used to uncover the root cause of failures. This includes such activities as the following.

- Accident investigation, where large-scale national disasters like oil tanker spillages and aeroplane accidents are investigated using specifically trained staff.
- Failure traceability, where procedures ensure that failures can be traced back to where they originated.
- Complaint analysis, where complaints (and compliments) are used as a valuable source for detecting the root causes of failures of customer service.
- Fault tree analysis, where a logical procedure starts with a failure or a potential failure and works backwards to identify all the possible causes and therefore the origins of that failure. Fault tree analysis is made up of branches connected by two types of nodes: AND nodes and OR nodes. The branches below an AND node all need to occur for the event above the node to occur. Only one of the branches below an OR node needs to occur for the event above the node to occur. Figure 19.5 shows a simple tree identifying the possible reasons for a filter in a heating system not being replaced when it should have been.

Likelihood of failure

The difficulty of estimating the chance of a failure occurring varies greatly. Some failures are well understood through a combination of rational causal analysis and historical performance. For example a mechanical component may fail between 10 and 17 months of its installation in 99 per cent of cases. Other types of failure are far more difficult to predict. The chances of a fire in a supplier's plant are (hopefully) low, but how low? There will be some data concerning fire hazards in this type of plant, but the estimated probability of failure will be subjective.

'Objective' estimates

Estimates of failure based on historical performance can be measured in three main ways: failure rates – how often a failure occurs; reliability – the chances of a failure occurring; and availability – the amount of available useful operating time. 'Failure rate' and 'reliability' are different ways of measuring the same thing – the propensity of an operation, or part of an operation, to fail. Availability is one measure of the consequences of failure in the operation.

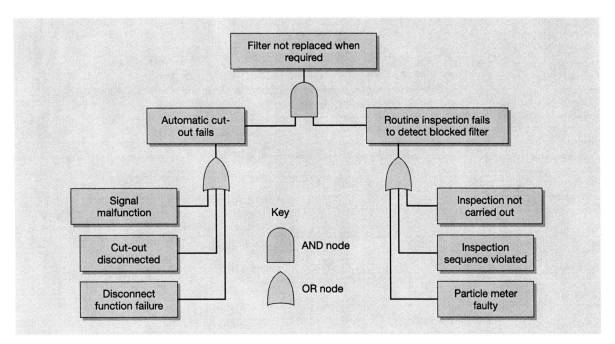

Figure 19.5 **Fault tree analysis for failure to replace filter when required**

Failure rate

Failure rate

Failure rate (FR) is calculated as the number of failures over a period of time. For example, the security of an airport can be measured by the number of security breaches per year, and the failure rate of an engine can be measured in terms of the number of failures divided by its operating time. It can be measured either as a percentage of the total number of products tested or as the number of failures over time:

$$FR = \frac{\text{number of failures}}{\text{total number of products tested}} \times 100$$

or

$$FR = \frac{\text{number of failures}}{\text{operating time}}$$

Worked example

A batch of 50 electronic components is tested for 2,000 hours. Four of the components fail during the test as follows:

Failure 1 occurred at 1,200 hours
Failure 2 occurred at 1,450 hours
Failure 3 occurred at 1,720 hours
Failure 4 occurred at 1,905 hours

$$\text{Failure rate (as a percentage)} = \frac{\text{number of failures}}{\text{number tested}} \times 100 = \frac{4}{50} \times 10 = 8\%$$

The total time of the test = $50 \times 2,000 = 100,000$ component hours

$\rightarrow$

But:

one component was not operating 2,000 − 1,200 = 800 hours
one component was not operating 2,000 − 1,450 = 550 hours
one component was not operating 2,000 − 1,720 = 280 hours
one component was not operating 2,000 − 1,905 = 95 hours

Thus:

$$\text{Total non-operating time} = 1{,}725 \text{ hours}$$

$$\text{Operating time} = \text{total time} - \text{non-operating time}$$

$$= 100{,}000 - 1{,}725 = 98{,}275 \text{ hours}$$

$$\text{Failure rate (in time)} = \frac{\text{number of failures}}{\text{operating time}} = \frac{4}{98{,}275}$$

$$= 0.000041$$

Bath-tub curves

Sometimes failure is a function of time. For example, the probability of an electric lamp failing is relatively high when it is first used, but if it survives this initial stage, it could still fail at any point, and the longer it survives, the more likely its failure becomes. The curve which describes failure probability of this type is called the bath-tub curve. It comprises three distinct stages: the 'infant-mortality' or **'early-life'** stage where early failures occur caused by defective parts or improper use; the **'normal-life'** stage when the failure rate is usually low and reasonably constant, and caused by normal random factors; the **'wear-out'** stage when the failure rate increases as the part approaches the end of its working life and failure is caused by the ageing and deterioration of parts. Figure 19.6 illustrates three bath-tub curves with slightly different characteristics. Curve A shows a part of the operation which has a high initial infant-mortality failure but then a long, low-failure, normal life followed by the gradually increasing likelihood of failure as it approaches wear-out. Curve B is far less predictable. The

Early life failure
Normal life failure
Wear-out failure

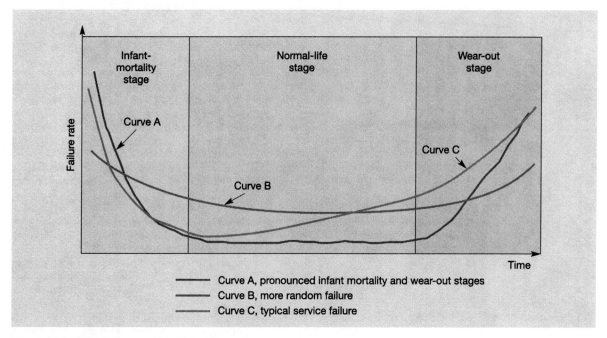

Figure 19.6 Bath-tub curves for three types of process

distinction between the three stages is less clear, with infant-mortality failure subsiding only slowly and a gradually increasing chance of wear-out failure. Failure of the type shown in curve B is far more difficult to manage in a planned manner. The failure of operations which rely more on human resources than on technology, such as some services, can be closer to curve C. They may be less susceptible to component wear-out but more so to staff complacency as the service becomes tedious and repetitive.

Reliability

Reliability measures the ability to perform as expected over time. Usually the importance of any particular failure is determined partly by how interdependent the other parts of the system are. With interdependence, a failure in one component will cause the whole system to fail. So, if an interdependent system has n components each with their own reliability, R_1, R_2, ..., R_n, the reliability of the whole system, R_s, is given by:

$$R_s = R_1 \times R_2 \times R_2 \times \ldots \times R_n$$

where

R_1 = reliability of component 1
R_2 = reliability of component 2

etc.

> ### Worked example
>
> An automated pizza-making machine in a food manufacturer's factory has five major components, with individual reliabilities (the probability of the component not failing) as follows:
>
> | | |
> |---|---|
> | Dough mixer | Reliability = 0.95 |
> | Dough roller and cutter | Reliability = 0.99 |
> | Tomato paste applicator | Reliability = 0.97 |
> | Cheese applicator | Reliability = 0.90 |
> | Oven | Reliability = 0.98 |
>
> If one of these parts of the production system fails, the whole system will stop working. Thus the reliability of the whole system is:
>
> $$R_s = 0.95 \times 0.99 \times 0.97 \times 0.90 \times 0.98$$
> $$= 0.805$$

The number of components

In the example, the reliability of the whole system was only 0.8, even though the reliability of the individual components was significantly higher. If the system had been made up of more components, then its reliability would have been even lower. The more interdependent components an operation or process has, the lower its reliability will be. For one composed of components which each have an individual reliability of 0.99, with 10 components the system reliability will shrink to 0.9, with 50 components it is below 0.8, with 100 components it is below 0.4, and with 400 components it is down below 0.05. In other words, with a process of 400 components (not unusual in a large automated operation), even if the reliability of each individual component is 99 per cent, the whole system will be working for less than 5 per cent of its time.

Mean time between failures

An alternative (and common) measure of failure is the **mean time between failures** (MTBF) of a component or system. MTBF is the reciprocal of failure rate (in time). Thus:

$$\text{MTBF} = \frac{\text{operating hours}}{\text{number of failures}}$$

(margin notes) Reliability

Mean time between failures

Worked example

In the previous worked example which was concerned with electronic components, the failure rate (in time) of the electronic components was 0.000041. For that component:

$$\text{MTBF} = \frac{1}{0.000041} = 24{,}390.24 \text{ hours}$$

That is, a failure can be expected once every 24,390.24 hours on average.

Availability

Availability

Availability is the degree to which the operation is ready to work. An operation is not available if it has either failed or is being repaired following failure. There are several different ways of measuring it depending on how many of the reasons for not operating are included. Lack of availability because of planned maintenance or changeovers could be included, for example. However, when 'availability' is being used to indicate the operating time excluding the consequence of failure, it is calculated as follows:

$$\text{Availability } (A) = \frac{\text{MTBF}}{\text{MTBF} + \text{MTTR}}$$

where

MTBF = the mean time between failures of the operation
MTTR = the mean time to repair, which is the average time taken to repair the operation, from the time it fails to the time it is operational again.

Worked example

A company which designs and produces display posters for exhibitions and sales promotion events competes largely on the basis of its speedy delivery. One particular piece of equipment which the company uses is causing some problems. This is its large platform colour laser printer. Currently, the mean time between failures of the printer is 70 hours and its mean time to repair is 6 hours. Thus:

$$\text{Availability} = \frac{70}{70 + 6} = 0.92$$

The company has discussed its problem with the supplier of the printer who has offered two alternative service deals. One option would be to buy some preventive maintenance (*see* later for a full description of preventive maintenance) which would be carried out each weekend. This would raise the MTBF of the printer to 90 hours. The other option would be to subscribe to a faster repair service which would reduce the MTTR to 4 hours. Both options would cost the same amount. Which would give the company the higher availability?

With MTBF increased to 90 hours:

$$\text{Availability} = \frac{90}{90 + 6} = 0.938$$

With MTTR reduced to 4 hours:

$$\text{Availability} = \frac{70}{70 + 4} = 0.946$$

Availability would be greater if the company took the deal which offered the faster repair time.

'Subjective' estimates

Failure assessment, even for subjective risks, is increasingly a formal exercise that is carried out using standard frameworks, often prompted by health and safety, environmental, or other regulatory reasons. These frameworks are similar to the formal quality inspection methods associated with quality standards like ISO 9000 that often implicitly assume unbiased objectivity. However, individual attitudes to risk are complex and subject to a wide variety of influences. In fact many studies have demonstrated that people are generally very poor at making risk-related judgements. Consider the success of state and national lotteries. The chances of winning, in nearly every case, are so low as to make the financial value of the investment entirely negative. If a player has to drive their car in order to purchase a ticket, they may be more likely to be killed or seriously injured than they are to win the top prize. But, although people do not always make rational decisions concerning the chances of failure, this does not mean abandoning the attempt. But it does mean that one must understand the limits to overly rational approaches to failure estimation, for example, how people tend to pay too much attention to dramatic low-probability events and overlook routine events.

Even when 'objective' evaluations of risks are used, they may still cause negative consequences. For example, when the oil giant Royal-Dutch Shell took the decision to employ deep-water disposal in the North Sea for their Brent Spar oil platform, they felt that they were making a rational operational decision based upon the best available scientific evidence concerning environmental risk. Unfortunately Greenpeace disagreed and put forward an alternative 'objective analysis' showing significant risk from deep-water disposal. Eventually Greenpeace admitted their evidence was flawed but by that time Shell had lost the public relations battle and had altered their plans.

Critical commentary

The idea that failure can be detected through in-process inspection is increasingly seen as only partially true. Although inspecting for failures is an obvious first step in detecting them, it is not even close to being 100 per cent reliable. Accumulated evidence from research and practical examples consistently indicates that people, even when assisted by technology, are not good at detecting failure and errors. This applies even when special attention is being given to inspection. For example, airport security was significantly strengthened after 11 September 2001, yet one in ten lethal weapons that were entered into airports' security systems (in order to test them) were not detected.[8] *'There is no such thing as one hundred per cent security, we are all human beings'*, says Ian Hutcheson, the Director of Security at Airport Operator BAA. No one is advocating abandoning inspection as a failure detection mechanism. Rather it is seen as one of a range of methods of preventing failure.

Failure mode and effect analysis

One of the best-known approaches to assessing the relative significance of failure is failure mode and effect analysis (FMEA). Its objective is to identify the factors that are critical to various types of failure as a means of identifying failures before they happen. It does this by providing a 'checklist' procedure built around three key questions for each possible cause of failure:

- What is the likelihood that failure will occur?
- What would the consequence of the failure be?
- How likely is such a failure to be detected before it affects the customer?

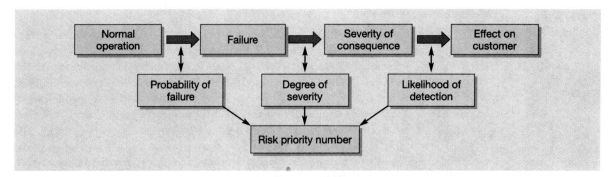

Figure 19.7 Procedure for failure mode and effect analysis (FMEA)

Based on a quantitative evaluation of these three questions, a risk priority number (RPN) is calculated for each potential cause of failure. Corrective actions, aimed at preventing failure, are then applied to those causes whose RPN indicates that they warrant priority, see Figure 19.7.

Worked example

Part of an FMEA exercise at a transportation company has identified three failure modes associated with the failure of 'goods arriving damaged' at the point of delivery:

> Goods not secured (failure mode 1)
> Goods incorrectly secured (failure mode 2)
> Goods incorrectly loaded (failure mode 3).

The improvement group which is investigating the failures allocates scores for the probability of the failure mode occurring, the severity of each failure mode, and the likelihood that they will be detected using the rating scales shown in Table 19.2, as follows:

Probability of occurrence
Failure mode 1   5
Failure mode 2   8
Failure mode 3   7

Severity of failure
Failure mode 1   6
Failure mode 2   4
Failure mode 3   4

Probability of detection
Failure mode 1   2
Failure mode 2   6
Failure mode 3   7

The RPN of each failure mode is calculated:

Failure mode 1 (goods not secured) $5 \times 6 \times 2 = 60$
Failure mode 2 (goods incorrectly secured) $8 \times 4 \times 5 = 160$
Failure mode 3 (goods incorrectly loaded) $7 \times 4 \times 7 = 196$

Priority is therefore given to failure mode 3 (goods incorrectly loaded) when attempting to eliminate the failure.

Table 19.2 Rating scales for FMEA

A. Occurrence of failure

Description	Rating	Possible failure occurrence
Remote probability of occurrence It would be unreasonable to expect failure to occur	1	0
Low probability of occurrence Generally associated with activities similar to previous ones with a relatively low number of failures	2 3	1:20,000 1:10,000
Moderate probability of occurrence Generally associated with activities similar to previous ones which have resulted in occasional failures	4 5 6	1:2,000 1:1,000 1:200
High probability of occurrence Generally associated with activities similar to ones which have traditionally caused problems	7 8	1:100 1:20
Very high probability of occurrence Near certainty that major failures will occur	9 10	1:10 1:2

B. Severity of failure

Description	Rating
Minor severity A very minor failure which would have no noticeable effect on system performance	1
Low severity A minor failure causing only slight customer annoyance	2 3
Moderate severity A failure which would cause some customer dissatisfaction, discomfort or annoyance, or would cause noticeable deterioration in performance	4 5 6
High severity A failure which would engender a high degree of customer dissatisfaction	7 8
Very high severity A failure which would affect safety	9
Catastrophic A failure which may cause damage to property, serious injury or death	10

C. Detection of failure

Description	Rating	Probability of detection
Remote probability that the defect will reach the customer (It is unlikely that such a defect would pass through inspection, test or assembly)	1	0 to 15%
Low probability that the defect will reach the customer	2 3	6 to 15% 16 to 25%
Moderate probability that the defect will reach the customer	4 5 6	26 to 35% 36 to 45% 46 to 55%
High probability that the defect will reach the customer	7 8	56 to 65% 66 to 75%
Very high probability that the defect will reach the customer	9 10	76 to 85% 86 to 100%

Preventing failure occurring

Once a thorough understanding of the causes and effects of failure has been established, the next responsibility of operations managers is to try to prevent the failures occurring in the first place. The obvious way to do this is to systematically examine any processes involved and 'design out' any failure points. Many of the approaches used in Chapters 4 and 5 on process and product/service design and Chapter 17 on quality management can be used to do this. In this section we will look at three further approaches to reducing risk by trying to prevent failure: building redundancy into a process, 'fail-safeing' some of the activities in the process, and maintaining the physical facilities in the process.

Redundancy

Redundancy

Building in **redundancy** to an operation means having back-up systems or components in case of failure. It can be expensive and is generally used when the breakdown could have a critical impact. It means doubling or even tripling some parts of a process or system in case one component fails. Nuclear power stations, spacecraft and hospitals all have auxiliary systems in case of an emergency. Some organizations also have 'back-up' staff held in reserve in case someone does not turn up for work. Rear-brake lighting sets in buses and trucks contain two bulbs to reduce the likelihood of not showing a red light. Human bodies contain two of some organs – kidneys and eyes, for example – both of which are used in 'normal operation' but the body can cope with a failure in one of them. The reliability of a component together with its back-up is given by the sum of the reliability of the original component and the likelihood that the back-up component will both be needed *and* be working.

$$R_{a+b} = R_a + (R_b \times P\,(\text{failure}))$$

where

R_{a+b} = reliability of component a with its back-up component b
R_a = reliability of a alone
R_b = reliability of back-up component b
$P\,(\text{failure})$ = the probability that component a will fail and therefore component b will be needed.

Worked example

The food manufacturer in the earlier worked example has decided that the cheese depositor in the pizza-making machine is so unreliable that it needs a second cheese depositor to be fitted to the machine which will come into action if the first cheese depositor fails.

The two cheese depositors (each with reliability = 0.9) working together will have a reliability of:

$$0.9 + [0.9 \times (1 - 0.9)] = 0.99$$

The reliability of the whole machine is now:

$$0.95 \times 0.99 \times 0.97 \times 0.99 \times 0.98 = 0.885$$

Redundancy is often used for servers, where system availability is particularly important. In this context, the industry used three main types of redundancy.

- *Hot standby* – where both primary and secondary (backup) systems run simultaneously. The data are copied to the secondary server in real time so that both systems contain identical information.
- *Warm standby* – where the secondary system runs in the background to the primary system. Data are copied to the secondary server at regular intervals, so there are times when both servers do not contain exactly the same data.
- *Cold standby* – where the secondary system is only called upon when the primary system fails. The secondary system receives scheduled data backups, but less frequently than in a warm standby, so cold standby is mainly used for non-critical applications.

Fail-safeing

Fail-safeing
Poka-yoke

The concept of **fail-safeing** has emerged since the introduction of Japanese methods of operations improvement. Called **poka-yoke** in Japan (from *yokeru* (to prevent) and *poka* (inadvertent errors)), the idea is based on the principle that human mistakes are to some extent inevitable. What is important is to prevent them becoming defects. Poka-yokes are simple (preferably inexpensive) devices or systems which are incorporated into a process to prevent inadvertent operator mistakes resulting in a defect. Typical poka-yokes are such devices as:

- limit switches on machines which allow the machine to operate only if the part is positioned correctly;
- gauges placed on machines through which a part has to pass in order to be loaded onto, or taken off, the machine – an incorrect size or orientation stops the process;
- digital counters on machines to ensure that the correct number of cuts, passes or holes have been machined;
- checklists which have to be filled in, either in preparation for, or on completion of, an activity;
- light beams which activate an alarm if a part is positioned incorrectly.

More recently, the principle of fail-safeing has been applied to service operations. Service poka-yokes can be classified as those which 'fail-safe the server' (the creator of the service) and those which 'fail-safe the customer' (the receiver of the service). Examples of fail-safeing the server include:

- colour-coding cash register keys to prevent incorrect entry in retail operations;
- the McDonald's french-fry scoop which picks up the right quantity of fries in the right orientation to be placed in the pack;
- trays used in hospitals with indentations shaped to each item needed for a surgical procedure – any item not back in place at the end of the procedure might have been left in the patient;
- the paper strips placed round clean towels in hotels, the removal of which helps house-keepers to tell whether a towel has been used and therefore needs replacing.

Examples of fail-safeing the customer include:

- the locks on aircraft lavatory doors, which must be turned to switch the light on;
- beepers on ATMs to ensure that customers remove their cards;
- height bars on amusement rides to ensure that customers do not exceed size limitations;
- outlines drawn on the walls of a childcare centre to indicate where toys should be replaced at the end of the play period;
- tray stands strategically placed in fast-food restaurants to remind customers to clear their tables.

Much of the previous discussion surrounding the prevention of failure has assumed a 'rational' approach. In other words, it is assumed that operations managers and customers alike will put more effort into preventing failures that are either more likely to occur or more serious in their consequences. Yet this assumption is based on a rational response to risk. In fact, being human, managers often respond to the perception of risk rather than its reality. For example, Table 19.3 shows the cost of each life saved by investment in various road and rail transportation safety (in other words, failure prevention) investments. The table shows that investing in improving road safety is very much more effective than investing in rail safety. And while no one is arguing for abandoning efforts on rail safety, it is noted by some transportation authorities that actual investment reflects more the public perception of rail deaths (low) compared with road deaths (very high).

Table 19.3 The cost per life saved of various safety (failure prevention) investments

Safety investment	Cost per life (€M)
Advanced train protection system	30
Train protection warning systems	7.5
Implementing recommended guidelines on rail safety	4.7
Implementing recommended guidelines on road safety	1.6
Local authority spending on road safety	0.15

Maintenance

Maintenance

Maintenance is how organizations try to avoid failure by taking care of their physical facilities. It is an important part of most operations' activities particularly in operations dominated by their physical facilities such as power stations, hotels, airlines and petrochemical refineries. The benefits of effective maintenance include enhanced safety, increased reliability, higher quality (badly maintained equipment is more likely to cause errors), lower operating costs (because regularly serviced process technology is more efficient), a longer lifespan for process technology, and higher 'end value' (because well-maintained facilities are generally easier to dispose of into the second-hand market).

The three basic approaches to maintenance

In practice an organization's maintenance activities will consist of some combination of the three basic approaches to the care of its physical facilities. These are run to breakdown (RTB), preventive maintenance (PM) and condition-based maintenance (CBM).

Run-to-breakdown maintenance

Run-to-breakdown maintenance – as its name implies involves allowing the facilities to continue operating until they fail. Maintenance work is performed only after failure has taken place. For example, the televisions, bathroom equipment and telephones in a hotel's guest rooms will probably only be repaired when they fail. The hotel will keep some spare parts and the staff available to make any repairs when needed. Failure in these circumstances is neither catastrophic (although perhaps irritating to the guest) nor so frequent as to make regular checking of the facilities appropriate.

Preventive maintenance

Preventive maintenance attempts to eliminate or reduce the chances of failure by servicing (cleaning, lubricating, replacing and checking) the facilities at pre-planned intervals. For example, the engines of passenger aircraft are checked, cleaned and calibrated according to a regular schedule after a set number of flying hours. Taking aircraft away from their regular duties for preventive maintenance is clearly an expensive option for any airline. The consequences of failure while in service are considerably more serious, however. The principle is also applied to facilities with less catastrophic consequences of failure. The regular cleaning and lubricating of machines, even the periodic painting of a building, could be considered preventive maintenance.

Condition-based
maintenance

Condition-based maintenance attempts to perform maintenance only when the facilities require it. For example, continuous process equipment, such as that used in coating photographic paper, is run for long periods in order to achieve the high utilization necessary for cost-effective production. Stopping the machine to change, say, a bearing when it is not strictly necessary to do so would take it out of action for long periods and reduce its utilization. Here condition-based maintenance might involve continuously monitoring the vibrations, for example, or some other characteristic of the line. The results of this monitoring would then be used to decide whether the line should be stopped and the bearings replaced.

Mixed maintenance strategies

Each approach to maintaining facilities is appropriate for different circumstances. RTB is often used where repair is relatively straightforward (so the consequence of failure is small), where regular maintenance is very costly, or where failure is not at all predictable (failure is just as likely to occur after repair as before). PM is used where the cost of unplanned failure is high and where failure is not totally random. CBM is used where the maintenance activity is expensive, either because of the cost of providing the maintenance itself, or because of the disruption which the maintenance activity causes to the operation. Most operations adopt a mixture of these approaches. Even an automobile uses all three approaches (*see* Fig. 19.8). Light bulbs and fuses are normally replaced only when they fail. Engine oil is subject to preventive maintenance at a regular service. Finally, most drivers also monitor the condition of the auto, for example by measuring the amount of tread on the tyre.

Breakdown *versus* preventive maintenance

The balance between preventive and breakdown maintenance is usually set to minimize the total cost of breakdown. Infrequent preventive maintenance will cost little to provide but will result in a high likelihood (and therefore cost) of breakdown maintenance. Conversely, very frequent preventive maintenance will be expensive to provide but will reduce the cost of having to provide breakdown maintenance (*see* Fig. 19.9a). The total cost of maintenance appears to minimize at an 'optimum' level of preventive maintenance. However, the cost of providing preventive maintenance may not increase quite so steeply as indicated in Figure 19.9(a). The curve assumes that it is carried out by a separate set of people (skilled maintenance staff) from the 'operators' of the facilities. Furthermore, every time preventive maintenance takes place, the facilities cannot be used productively. This is why the slope of the curve increases, because the maintenance episodes start to interfere with the normal working of the operation. But in many operations some preventive maintenance can be performed by the operators themselves (which reduces the cost of providing it) and at times

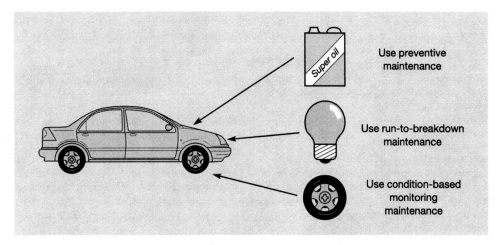

Figure 19.8 A mixture of maintenance approaches is often used – in a car, for example

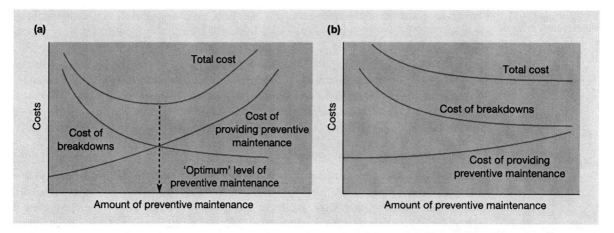

Figure 19.9 Two views of maintenance costs. (a) One model of the costs associated with preventive maintenance shows an optimum level of maintenance effort. (b) If routine preventive maintenance tasks are carried out by operators and if the real cost of breakdowns is considered, the 'optimum' level of preventive maintenance shifts toward higher levels

which are convenient for the operation (which minimizes the disruption to the operation). The cost of breakdowns could also be higher than is indicated in Figure 19.9(a). Unplanned breakdowns may do more than necessitate a repair and stop the operation; they can take away stability from the operation which prevents it being able to improve itself. Put these two ideas together and the minimizing total curve and maintenance cost curve look more like Figure 19.9(b). The emphasis is shifted more towards the use of preventive maintenance than run-to-breakdown maintenance.

Total productive maintenance

Total productive maintenance

Total productive maintenance (TPM) is 'the productive maintenance carried out by all employees through small group activities', where productive maintenance is 'maintenance management which recognizes the importance of reliability, maintenance and economic efficiency in plant design'.[9] In Japan, where TPM originated, it is seen as a natural extension in the evolution from run-to-breakdown to preventive maintenance. TPM adopts some of the team-working and empowerment principles discussed in Chapter 9, as well as a continuous improvement approach to failure prevention as discussed in Chapter 18. It also sees maintenance as an organization-wide issue, to which staff can contribute in some way. It is analogous to the total quality management approach discussed in Chapter 17.

The five goals of TPM

TPM aims to establish good maintenance practice in operations through the pursuit of 'the five goals of TPM':[9]

1 *Improve equipment effectiveness* by examining all the losses which occur.
2 *Achieve autonomous maintenance* by allowing staff to take responsibility for some of the maintenance tasks and for the improvement of maintenance performance.
3 *Plan maintenance* with a fully worked out approach to all maintenance activities.
4 *Train all staff in relevant maintenance skills* so that both maintenance and operating staff have all the skills to carry out their roles.
5 *Achieve early equipment management* by 'maintenance prevention' (MP), which involves considering failure causes and the maintainability of equipment during its design, manufacture, installation and commissioning.

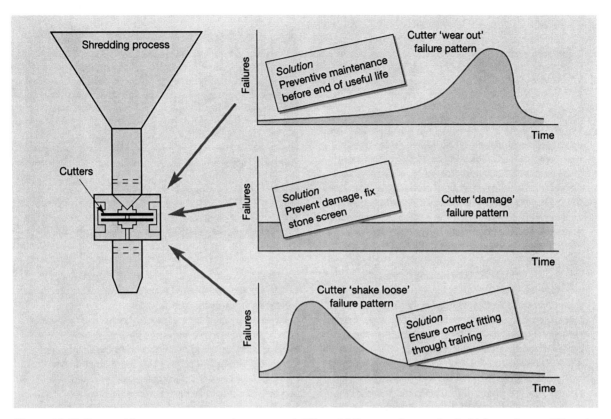

Figure 19.10 One part in one process can have several different failure modes, each of which requires a different approach

Reliability-centred maintenance

Reliability-centred maintenance

Reliability-centred maintenance (RCM) uses the pattern of failure for each type of failure mode of a part of a system to dictate the approach to its maintenance. For example, take the process illustrated in Figure 19.10. This is a simple shredding process which prepares vegetables prior to freezing. The most significant part of the process, which requires the most maintenance attention, is the cutter sub-assembly. However, there are several modes of failure which could lead to the cutters requiring attention. Sometimes they require changing simply because they have worn out through usage, sometimes they have been damaged by small stones entering the process, sometimes they have shaken loose because they were not fitted correctly. The failure patterns for these three failure modes are very different, as illustrated in Figure 19.10. Certainly, 'wear-out' can be managed by timing preventive maintenance intervals just prior to the increased likelihood of failure. But this approach would not help prevent stone damage which could happen at any time with equal likelihood. The approach here would be to prevent stones getting to the cutters in the first place, perhaps through fixing a screen. The failure pattern for the cutters shaking loose is different again. If the cutters have been incorrectly fitted, it would become evident soon after the fitting. Again, preventive maintenance is unlikely to help here; rather effort should be put into ensuring that the cutters are always correctly fitted, perhaps by organizing more appropriate training of staff. The approach of RCM is sometimes summarized as 'If we cannot stop it from happening, we had better stop it from mattering'. In other words, if maintenance cannot either predict or even prevent failure, and the failure has important consequences, then efforts need to be directed at reducing the impact of the failure.

Back in 1853 Elisha Graves Otis introduced the world's first safety elevator in Yonkers, New York. It was to have a remarkable impact on the world's skylines. Without elevators, the skyscraping buildings that dominate most modern cities would probably never have been developed. Given the number of elevators in regular use throughout the world and the Otis Company's position as a leading supplier, Otis is the world's leading people mover. And Otis is very much aware that every time we enter an elevator we are trusting our lives to the people who designed and made it, and, more immediately, the people who maintain it. Without effective maintenance the elevators which are often on duty every minute of every day would literally be death traps. Central to the Otis philosophy of maintenance is its 'Otis Maintenance Management System' (OMMS), a programme that takes into account its clients' elevators' maintenance needs. Using this system Otis can customize inspection and maintenance schedules for up to twelve years of operation or five million trips in advance. Maintenance procedures are determined by each elevator's individual pattern of use. Frequency of trips, the loads carried by the elevator and conditions of use, are all incorporated to determine the frequency and nature of maintenance activities. Because no component part of any equipment is perfect, Otis also monitors the life cycle characteristics of all its elevators' components. This information on wear and failure is made available to its customers via its twenty-four communications centre and web site. This ongoing understanding of component life also is used to update maintenance schedules.

With Otis's call service, when an elevator has a problem, a technician can be on their way to a customer's facility within minutes. Its twenty-four-hours-a-day, seven-days-a-week service which handles over 1.2 million calls a year can get the elevators back in service on average within two and half hours. Also the Otis on-site monitoring equipment system is a sophisticated and interconnected system of sensors, monitors, hardware and software that collects, records, analyses and communicates hundreds of different system functions. If the system detects a problem it automatically makes a service call, calling out a technician who has been provided with the information collected by the system and that will be used to help identify the component causing the problem. *'Around-the-clock response is important'*, says Otis, *'because problems don't keep office hours . . . [the remote sensing] . . . system detects deteriorating components, identifies intermittent anomalies, notes the small nuisances that . . . would have gone undetected. . . . It identifies most potential problems before they occur.'*

Mitigating the effects of failure

Risk, or failure, mitigation means isolating a failure from its negative consequences. It is an admission that not all failures can be avoided. However, in some areas of operations management relying on mitigation, rather than prevention, is unfashionable. For example, 'inspection' practices in quality management were based on the assumption that failures were inevitable and needed to be detected before they could cause harm. Modern total quality management places much more emphasis on prevention. Yet, in operations and process resilience, mitigation can be vital when used in conjunction with prevention in reducing overall risk.

Risk mitigation actions

The nature of the action taken to mitigate failure will obviously depend on the nature of the risk. In most industries technical experts have established a classification of risk mitigation actions that are appropriate for the types of risk likely to be suffered. So, for example, in agriculture, government agencies and industry bodies have published mitigation strategies for such risks as the outbreak of crop disease, contagious animal infections, and so on. Such documents will outline the various mitigation actions that can be taken under different circumstances and detail exactly who are responsible for each action. Although these classifications tend to be industry-specific, the following generic categorization gives a flavour of the types of mitigation actions that may be generally applicable.

Mitigation planning is the activity of ensuring that all possible failure circumstances have been identified and the appropriate mitigation actions identified. It is the overarching activity that encompasses all subsequent mitigation actions, and may be described in the form of a decision tree or guide rules.

Economic mitigation includes actions such as insurance against losses from failure, spreading the financial consequences of failure, and 'hedging' against failure. Insurance is the best known of these actions and is widely adopted, although ensuring appropriate insurance and effective claims management is a specialized skill in itself. Hedging often takes the form of financial instruments, for example, a business may purchase a financial 'hedge' against the price risk of a vital raw material deviating significantly from a set price.

Containment (spatial) means stopping the failure physically spreading to affect other parts of an internal or external supply network. Preventing contaminated food from spreading through the supply chain, for example, will depend on real-time information systems that provide traceability data.

Containment (temporal) means containing the spread of a failure over time. It particularly applies when information about a failure or potential failure needs to be transmitted without undue delay. For example, systems that give advanced warning of hazardous weather such as snow storms must transmit such information to local agencies such as the police and road clearing organizations in time for them to stop the problem causing excessive disruption.

Loss reduction covers any action that reduces the catastrophic consequences of failure by removing the resources that are likely to suffer those consequences. For example, the road signs that indicate evacuation routes in the event of severe weather, or the fire drills that train employees in how to escape in the event of an emergency, may not reduce all the consequences of failure, but can help in reducing loss of life or injury.

Substitution means compensating for failure by providing other resources that can substitute for those rendered less effective by the failure. It is a little like the concept of redundancy that was described earlier, but does not always imply excess resources if a failure has not occurred. For example, in a construction project, the risk of encountering unexpected geological problems may be mitigated by the existence of a separate work plan and that is invoked only if such problems are found.

Recovering from the effects of failure

Failure recovery

In parallel with considering how to prevent failures occurring, operations managers need to decide what they will do when failures do occur. This activity is called **failure recovery**. All types of operation can benefit from well-planned recovery. For example, a construction company whose mechanical digger breaks down can have plans in place to arrange a replacement from a hire company. The breakdown might be disruptive, but not as much as it might have been if the operations manager had not worked out what to do. Recovery procedures will also shape customers' perceptions of failure. Even where the customer sees a failure, it may not necessarily lead to dissatisfaction. Indeed, in many situations, customers may well accept that things do go wrong. If there is a metre of snow on the train lines, or if the restaurant is particularly popular, we may accept that the product or service does not work. It is not necessarily the failure itself that leads to dissatisfaction but often the organization's response to the breakdown. While mistakes may be inevitable, dissatisfied customers are not. A failure may even be turned into a positive experience. A good recovery can turn angry, frustrated customers into loyal ones. One research project used four service scenarios and examined the willingness of customers to use an organization's services again.[11] The four scenarios were:

1 The service is delivered to meet the customers' expectations and there is full satisfaction.
2 There are faults in the service delivery but the customer does not complain about them.
3 There are faults in the service delivery and the customer complains but he/she has been fobbed off or mollified. There is no real satisfaction with the service provider.
4 There are faults in the service delivery and the customer complains and feels fully satisfied with the resulting action taken by the service providers.

Customers who are fully satisfied and do not experience any problems (1) are the most loyal, followed by complaining customers whose complaints are resolved successfully (4). Customers who experience problems but don't complain (2) are in third place and last of all come customers who do complain but are left with their problems unresolved and feelings of dissatisfaction (3).

Recovery in high-visibility services

The idea of failure recovery has been developed particularly in service operations. As one specialist put it, '*If something goes wrong, as it often does, will anybody make special efforts to get it right? Will somebody go out of his or her way to make amends to the customer? Does anyone make an effort to offset the negative impact of a screw-up?*'[12] It has also been suggested that service recovery does not just mean 'return to a normal state' but to a state of enhanced perception. *All breakdowns require the deliverer to jump through a few hoops to get the customer back to neutral. More hoops are required for victims to recover.* Operations managers need to recognize that all customers have recovery expectations that they want organizations to meet. Recovery needs to be a planned process. Organizations therefore need to design appropriate responses to failure, linked to the cost and the inconvenience caused by the failure to the customer, which will meet the needs and expectations of the customer. Such recovery processes need to be carried out either by empowered front-line staff or by trained personnel who are available to deal with recovery in a way which does not interfere with day-to-day service activities.

Failure planning

Failure planning

Identifying how organizations can recover from failure is of particular interest to service operations because they can turn failures around to minimize the effect on customers or even to turn failure into a positive experience. It is also of interest to other industries, however, especially those where the consequences of failure are particularly severe. Bulk chemical manufacturers and nuclear processors, for example, spend considerable resources in deciding how they will cope with failures. The activity of devising the procedures which allow the operation to recover from failure is called **failure planning**. It is often represented by stage models, one of which is represented in Figure 19.11. We shall follow it through from the point where failure is recognized.

Discover. The first thing any manager needs to do when faced with a failure is to discover its exact nature. Three important pieces of information are needed: first of all, what exactly has happened; second, who will be affected by the failure; and, third, why did the failure occur? This last point is not intended to be a detailed inquest into the causes of failure (that comes

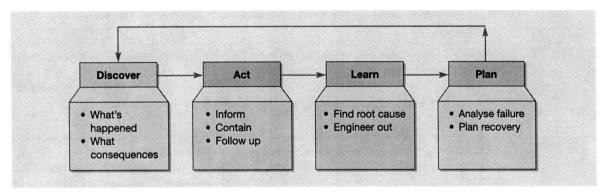

Figure 19.11 **The stages in failure planning**

later) but it is often necessary to know something of the causes of failure in case it is necessary to determine what action to take.

Act. The discover stage could only take minutes or even seconds, depending on the severity of the failure. If the failure is a severe one with important consequences, we need to move on to doing something about it quickly. This means carrying out three actions, the first two of which could be carried out in reverse order, depending on the urgency of the situation. First, tell the significant people involved what you are proposing to do about the failure. In service operations this is especially important where the customers need to be kept informed, both for their peace of mind and to demonstrate that something is being done. In all operations, however, it is important to communicate what action is going to happen so that everyone can set their own recovery plans in motion. Second, the effects of the failure need to be contained in order to stop the consequences spreading and causing further failures. The precise containment actions will depend on the nature of the failure. Third, there needs to be some kind of follow-up to make sure that the containment actions really have contained the failure.

Learn. As discussed earlier in this chapter, the benefits of failure in providing learning opportunities should not be underestimated. In failure planning, learning involves revisiting the failure to find out its root cause and then engineering out the causes of the failure so that it will not happen again. This is the key stage for much failure planning.

Plan. Learning the lessons from a failure is not the end of the procedure. Operations managers need formally to incorporate the lessons into their future reactions to failures. This is often done by working through 'in theory' how they would react to failures in the future. Specifically, this involves first identifying all the possible failures which might occur (in a similar way to the FMEA approach). Second, it means formally defining the procedures which the organization should follow in the case of each type of identified failure.

Business continuity

Business continuity

Many of the ideas behind failure, failure prevention and recovery are incorporated in the growing field of **business continuity**. This aims to help operations avoid and recover from disasters while keeping the business going, an issue that has risen to near the top of many firms' agenda since 11 September 2001. As operations become increasingly integrated (and increasingly dependent on integrated technologies such as information technologies), critical failures can result from a series of related and unrelated events and combine to disrupt totally a company's business. These events are the critical malfunctions which have the potential to interrupt normal business activity and even stop the entire company, such as natural disasters, fire, power or telecommunications failure, corporate crime, theft, fraud, sabotage, computer system failure, bomb blast, scare or other security alert, key personnel leaving, becoming ill or dying, key suppliers ceasing trading, contamination of product or processes, and so on.

The procedures adopted by business continuity experts are very similar to those described in this chapter:

- *Identify and assess risks* to determine how vulnerable the business is to various risks and to take steps to minimize or eliminate them.
- *Identify core business processes* to prioritize those that are particularly important to the business and which, if interrupted, would have to be brought back to full operation quickly.
- *Quantify recovery times* to make sure staff understand priorities (for example, get customer ordering system back into operation before the internal e-mail).
- *Determine resources needed* to make sure that resources will be available when required.
- *Communicate* to make sure that everyone in the operation knows what to do if disaster strikes.

One response to the threat of such large-scale failures has been a rise in the number of companies offering 'replacement office' operations. These are fully equipped offices, often with access to a company's current management information and with normal Internet and telephone communications links. They are fully working offices but with no people. Should a customer's main operation be affected by a disaster, business can continue in the replacement facility within days or even hours. The provision of this type of replacement office is, in effect, a variation of the 'redundancy' approach to reducing the impact of failure that was discussed earlier in this chapter.

Summary answers to key questions

Check and improve your understanding of this chapter using self assessment questions and a personalised study plan, audio and video downloads, and an eBook – all at www.myomlab.com.

➤ What is risk management?

- Risk management is about things going wrong and what operations can do to stop things going wrong. Or, more formally, 'the process which aims to help organizations understand, evaluate and take action on all their risks with a view to increasing the probability of their success and reducing the likelihood of failure'.

- It consists of four broad activities:
  - Understanding what failures could occur.
  - Preventing failures occurring.
  - Minimizing the negative consequences of failure (called risk 'mitigation').
  - Recovering from failures when they do occur.

➤ How can operations assess the potential causes of, and risks from failure?

- There are several causes of operations failure including design failures, facilities failure, staff failure, supplier failure, customer failure and environmental disruption.

- There are three ways of measuring failure. 'Failure rates' indicate how often a failure is likely to occur. 'Reliability' measures the chances of a failure occurring. 'Availability' is the amount of available and useful operating time left after taking account of failures.

- Failure over time is often represented as a failure curve. The most common form of this is the so-called 'bath-tub curve' which shows the chances of failure being greater at the beginning and end of the life of a system or part of a system.
- Failure analysis mechanisms include accident investigation, product liability, complaint analysis, critical incident analysis, and failure mode and effect analysis (FMEA).

➤ How can failures be prevented?

- There are four major methods of improving reliability: designing out the fail points in the operation, building redundancy into the operation, 'fail-safeing' some of the activities of the operation, and maintenance of the physical facilities in the operation.
- Maintenance is the most common way operations attempt to improve their reliability, with three broad approaches. The first is running all facilities until they break down and then repairing them, the second is regularly maintaining the facilities even if they have not broken down, and the third is to monitor facilities closely to try to predict when breakdown might occur.
- Two specific approaches to maintenance have been particularly influential: total productive maintenance (TPM) and reliability-centred maintenance (RCM).

➤ How can operations mitigate the effects of failure?

- Risk, or failure, mitigation means isolating a failure from its negative consequences.
- Risk mitigation actions include:
  - Mitigation planning.
  - Economic mitigation.
  - Containment (spatial and temporal).
  - Loss reduction.
  - Substitution.

➤ How can operations recover from the effects of failure?

- Recovery can be enhanced by a systematic approach to discovering what has happened to cause failure, acting to inform, contain and follow up the consequences of failure, learning to find the root cause of the failure and preventing it taking place again, and planning to avoid the failure occurring in the future.
- The idea of 'business continuity' planning is a common form of recovery planning.

Case study
The Chernobyl failure[13]

At 1.24 in the early hours of Saturday morning on 26 April 1986, the worst accident in the history of commercial nuclear power generation occurred. Two explosions in quick succession blew off the 1,000-tonne concrete sealing cap of the Chernobyl-4 nuclear reactor. Molten core fragments showered down on the immediate area and fission products were released into the atmosphere. The accident cost probably hundreds of lives and contaminated vast areas of land in Ukraine.

Many reasons probably contributed to the disaster. Certainly the design of the reactor was not new – around 30 years old at the time of the accident – and had been

Source: © Vladimir Repik/Reuters/Corbis

conceived before the days of sophisticated computer-controlled safety systems. Because of this, the reactor's emergency-handling procedures relied heavily on the skill of the operators. This type of reactor also had a tendency to run 'out of control' when operated at low power. For this reason, the operating procedures for the reactor strictly prohibited it being operated below 20 per cent of its maximum power. It was mainly a combination of circumstance and human error which caused the failure, however. Ironically, the events which led up to the disaster were designed to make the reactor safer. Tests, devised by a specialist team of engineers, were being carried out to evaluate whether the emergency core cooling system (ECCS) could be operated during the 'free-wheeling' run-down of the turbine generator, should an off-site power failure occur. Although this safety device had been tested before, it had not worked satisfactorily and new tests of the modified device were to be carried out with the reactor operating at reduced power throughout the test period. The tests were scheduled for the afternoon of Friday, 25 April 1986 and the plant power reduction began at 1.00 pm. However, just after 2.00 pm, when the reactor was operating at about half its full power, the Kiev controller requested that the reactor should continue supplying the grid with electricity. In fact it was not released from the grid until 11.10 that night. The reactor was due to be shut down for its annual maintenance on the following Tuesday and the Kiev controller's request had in effect shrunk the 'window of opportunity' available for the tests.

The following is a chronological account of the hours up to the disaster, together with an analysis by James Reason, which was published in the *Bulletin of the British Psychological Society* the following year. Significant operator actions are italicized. These are of two kinds: *errors* (indicated by an '*E*') and *procedural violations* (marked with a '*V*').

25 April 1986

1.00 pm Power reduction started with the intention of achieving 25 per cent power for test conditions.

2.00 pm ECCS disconnected from primary circuit. (This was part of the test plan.)

2.05 pm Kiev controller asked the unit to continue supplying grid. *The ECCS was not reconnected (V)*. (This particular violation is not thought to have contributed materially to the disaster, but it is indicative of a lax attitude on the part of the operators toward the observance of safety procedures.)

11.10 pm The unit was released from the grid and continued power reduction to achieve the 25 per cent power level planned for the test programme.

26 April 1986

12.28 am *Operator seriously undershot the intended power setting (E)*. The power dipped to a dangerous one per cent. (The operator had switched off the 'auto-pilot' and had tried to achieve the desired level by manual control.)

1.00 am After a long struggle, the reactor power was finally stabilized at 7 per cent – well below the intended level and well into the low-power danger zone. *At this point, the experiment should have been abandoned, but it was not (E)*. This was the most serious mistake (as opposed to violation): it meant that all subsequent activity would be conducted within the reactor's zone of maximum instability. This was apparently not appreciated by the operators.

1.03 am *All eight pumps were started (V)*. The safety regulations limited the maximum number of pumps in use at any one time to six. This showed a profound misunderstanding of the physics of the reactor. The consequence was that the increased water flow (and reduced steam fraction) absorbed more neutrons, causing more control rods to be withdrawn to sustain even this low level of power.

1.19 am *The feedwater flow was increased threefold (V)*. The operators appear to have been attempting to cope with a falling steam-drum pressure and water level. The result of their actions, however, was to further reduce the amount of steam passing through the core, causing yet more control rods to be withdrawn. *They also overrode the steam-drum automatic shut-down (V)*. The effect of this was to strip the reactor of one of its automatic safety systems.

1.22 am The shift supervisor requested printout to establish how many control rods were actually in the core. The printout indicated only six to eight rods remaining. It was strictly forbidden to operate the reactor with fewer than twelve rods. *Yet the shift supervisor decided to continue with the tests (V)*. This was a fatal decision: the reactor was thereafter without 'brakes'.

1.23 am *The steam line valves to No 8 turbine generator were closed (V)*. The purpose of this was to establish the conditions necessary for repeated testing, but its consequence was to disconnect the automatic safety trips. This was perhaps the most serious violation of all.

1.24 am An attempt was made to 'scram' the reactor by driving in the emergency shut-off rods, but they jammed within the now-warped tubes.

1.24 am Two explosions occurred in quick succession. The reactor roof was blown off and 30 fires started in the vicinity.

1.30 am Duty firemen were called out. Other units were summoned from Pripyat and Chernobyl.

5.00 am Exterior fires had been extinguished, but the graphite fire in the core continued for several days.

The subsequent investigation into the disaster highlighted a number of significant points which contributed to it:

- The test programme was poorly worked out and the section on safety measures was inadequate. Because the ECCS was shut off during the test period, the safety of the reactor was in effect substantially reduced.
- The test plan was put into effect before being approved by the design group who were responsible for the reactor.
- The operators and the technicians who were running the experiment had different and non-overlapping skills.
- The operators, although highly skilled, had probably been told that getting the test completed before the shut-down would enhance their reputation. They were proud of their ability to handle the reactor even in unusual conditions and were aware of the rapidly reducing window of opportunity within which they had to complete the test. They had also probably 'lost any feeling for the hazards involved' in operating the reactor.
- The technicians who had designed the test were electrical engineers from Moscow. Their objective was to solve a complex technical problem. In spite of having designed the test procedures, they probably would not know much about the operation of the nuclear power station itself.

Again, in the words of James Reason: *'Together, they made a dangerous mixture: a group of single-minded but non-nuclear engineers directing a team of dedicated but over-confident operators. Each group probably assumed that the other knew what it was doing. And both parties had little or no understanding of the dangers they were courting, or of the system they were abusing.'*

Questions

1 What were the root causes which contributed to the ultimate failure?

2 How could failure planning have helped prevent the disaster?

Problems and applications

These problems and applications will help to improve your analysis of operations. You can find more practice problems as well as worked examples and guided solutions on MyOMLab at www.myomlab.com.

1 *'We have a test bank where we test batches of 100 of our products continuously for 7 days and nights. This week only 3 failed, the first after 10 hours, the second after 72 hours, and the third after 1,020 hours.'*

What is the failure rate in percentage terms and in time terms for this product?

2 An automatic testing process takes samples of ore from mining companies and subjects them to four sequential tests. The reliability of the four different test machines that perform the tasks is different. The first test machine has a reliability of 0.99, the second has a reliability of 0.92, the third has a reliability of 0.98, and the fourth a reliability of 0.95. If one of the machines stops working, the total process will stop. What is the reliability of the total process?

3 For the product testing example in Problem 1, what is the mean time between failures (MTBF) for the products?

4 Conduct a survey amongst colleagues, friends and acquaintances of how they cope with the possibility that their computers might 'fail', either in terms of ceasing to operate effectively, or in losing data. Discuss how the concept of redundancy applies in such failure.

5 In terms of its effectiveness at managing the learning process, how does a university detect failures? What could it do to improve its failure detection processes?

Selected further reading

Dhillon, B.S. (2002) *Engineering Maintenance: A Modern Approach*, CRC Press, Boca Raton, Fla. A comprehensive book for the enthusiastic that stresses the 'cradle-to-grave' aspects of maintenance.

Li, Jun | Yu, Kui-Long | Wang, Liang-Xi | Song, Hai-Jun Zhuangjiabing Gongcheng Xueyuan Xuebao (2007) Research on operational risk management for equipment, *Journal of Academy of Armored Force Engineering*, vol. 21, no. 2, 8–11. Not as dull as it sounds. Deals with risks in military operations including complex equipment systems.

Regester, M. and Larkin, J. (2005) *Risk Issues and Crisis Management: A Casebook of Best Practice*, Kogan Page. Aimed at practising managers with lots of advice. Good for getting the flavour of how it is in practice.

Smith, D.J. (2000) *Reliability, Maintainability and Risk*, Butterworth-Heinemann. A comprehensive and excellent guide to all aspects of maintenance and reliability.

Useful web sites

www.smrp.org/ Site of the Society for Maintenance and Reliability Professionals. Gives an insight into practical issues.

www.sre.org/ American Society of Reliability Engineers. The newsletters give insights into reliability practice.

http://csob.berry.edu/faculty/jgrout/pokayoke.shtml The poka-yoke page of John Grout. Some great examples, tutorials, etc.

www.rspa.com/spi/SQA.html Lots of resources, involving reliability and poka-yoke.

http://sra.org/ Site of the Society for Risk Analysis. Very wide scope, but interesting.

www.hse.gov.uk/risk Health and Safety Executive of the UK government.

www.theirm.org The home page of the Institute of Risk Management.

www.opsman.org Lots of useful stuff.

Now that you have finished reading this chapter, why not visit MyOMLab at www.myomlab.com where you'll find more learning resources to help you make the most of your studies and get a better grade?

INDEX